LIBRARY OF NEW TESTAMEN

619

Formerly the Journal for the Study of the New Testament Supplement series

Editor
Chris Keith

Editorial Board
Dale C. Allison, John M.G. Barclay, Lynn H. Cohick, R. Alan Culpepper,
Craig A. Evans, Robert Fowler, Simon J. Gathercole, Juan Hernandez Jr.,
John S. Kloppenborg, Michael Labahn, Love L. Sechrest, Robert Wall,
Catrin H. Williams, Britanny Wilson

By the same author
Retelling Scripture: The Jews and the Scriptural Citations in John 1:19-12:15
(Biblical Interpretation Series, 110; Leiden/Boston: Brill, 2012)
How John Works: Storytelling in the Fourth Gospel (ed. with Douglas Estes;
Atlanta, GA: SBL Press, 2016)
Law and Lawlessness in Early Judaism and Christianity (ed. with David Lincicum
and Charles M. Stang; Tübingen: Mohr Siebeck, 2019)

The Figure of Abraham in John 8

Text and Intertext

Ruth Sheridan

t&tclark
LONDON • NEW YORK • OXFORD • NEW DELHI • SYDNEY

T&T CLARK
Bloomsbury Publishing Plc
50 Bedford Square, London, WC1B 3DP, UK
1385 Broadway, New York, NY 10018, USA
29 Earlsfort Terrace, Dublin 2, Ireland

BLOOMSBURY, T&T CLARK and the T&T Clark logo are trademarks of Bloomsbury Publishing Plc

First published in Great Britain 2020
This paperback edition published in 2021

Copyright © Ruth Sheridan, 2020

Ruth Sheridan has asserted her right under the Copyright, Designs and Patents Act, 1988, to be identified as Author of this work.

For legal purposes the Acknowledgements on p. xi constitute an extension of this copyright page.

All rights reserved. No part of this publication may be reproduced or transmitted in any form or by any means, electronic or mechanical, including photocopying, recording, or any information storage or retrieval system, without prior permission in writing from the publishers.

Bloomsbury Publishing Plc does not have any control over, or responsibility for, any third-party websites referred to or in this book. All internet addresses given in this book were correct at the time of going to press. The author and publisher regret any inconvenience caused if addresses have changed or sites have ceased to exist, but can accept no responsibility for any such changes.

A catalogue record for this book is available from the British Library.

A catalog record for this book is available from the Library of Congress.

ISBN: HB: 978-0-5672-3806-1
PB: 978-0-5677-0211-1
ePDF: 978-0-5674-2402-0
ePUB: 978-0-5676-9285-6

Series: Library of New Testament Studies, 2513-8790, volume 619

Typeset by Deanta Global Publishing Services, Chennai, India

To find out more about our authors and books visit www.bloomsbury.com and sign up for our newsletters.

For my children, James and Sarah

ונאמר
כי פדה יי את־יעקב
וגאלו מיד חזק ממנו
(Maariv Amidah)

Contents

Acknowledgements		xi
Abbreviations		xii

1	Introduction	1
	The range of Abraham's post-biblical 'afterlives'	4
	Abraham in the Gospel of John: A survey of the secondary literature	8
	Full-length studies: Horatio Lona and Tineke de Lange	8
	Shorter studies on Abraham in John 8	15
	Shorter studies: Abraham in the narrative and communal worlds of John 8	15
	Shorter studies: Abraham and intertextuality	20
	Focused studies: The 'seed of Abraham' in John 8.31-34	21
	Focused studies: The 'works of Abraham' (8.39-47)	29
	Focused studies: Abraham saw and rejoiced (John 8.56-58)	33
	Summary and ways forward	40
	The purpose of this book: Outline and argument	41
2	Theoretical foundations: Intertextuality	47
	Introduction	47
	Reflecting on comparative reasoning in textual analysis	51
	Intertextuality	60
	Roland Barthes's theorization of intertextuality	68
	Textual analysis	72
	Writerly and readerly texts	74
	Application to the Gospel of John	78
3	John 8.31-59: Structure, setting, text	89
	Introduction	89
	The problem of the textual addressees: Ch. 8 vv. 30 and 31	90
	A tripartite structure for ch. 8 vv. 31-59	98
	The unity and thematic coherence of John 7.1–8.59	101
	Origins	102
	Knowledge and belief	103

	Judgement	104
	Testimony	106
Scripting the Sukkot intertext		108
	Determining the festival setting of John 7–8	108
	Sukkot as cultural code and intertext	112
	The Torah	112
	The prophets	115
	The writings	117
	Pseudepigrapha	121
	Philo and Josephus	124
	Rabbinic literature	125
4	**Seed of Abraham, slavery and sin (John 8.31-36)**	**131**
	Introduction	131
	Part 1: Scripting the intertextual field	134
	The Hebrew Bible	134
	The Abraham Cycle: Gen. 12.1-9; 13.14-16; 15.1-20; 17.1-27; 21.8-14; 22.15-19	134
	Texts outside the Abraham Cycle: Gen. 26.1-5; 26.23-24b; 28.4-5, 13-15; 35.11-12	139
	Other texts from the Torah	142
	Josh. 24.2-3	145
	Isa. 41.8	146
	Jer. 33.26	149
	Psalm 105.6-12 (MT)/104.6-12 (LXX)	151
	2 Chronicles 20.7	153
	Post-biblical apocrypha and pseudepigrapha	154
	Theme 1: Abraham, Isaac and Jacob help their 'seed'	155
	Theme 2: Abraham as exemplar to his seed	167
	Dead Sea Scrolls	182
	Josephus	184
	Philo	186
	The New Testament	189
	Galatians	189
	Romans 4.13, 16; 9.7-8	197
	2 Cor. 11.22	201
	Luke 1.55	202

	Acts 3.25	204
	Hebrews 2.16; 11.18	205
	Tannaitic rabbinic literature	207
	The seed of Abraham	208
	Abraham's 'children', 'sons' and 'disciples'	214
	Part 2: The Johannine context	215
	Servanthood/slavery	215
	Sin	216
	Part 3: Reading John 8.31-36 intertextually	219
5	The works of Abraham (John 8.39-40 (37-48))	227
	Introduction	227
	Part 1: Scripting the intertextual field	228
	Works as human behaviour in the Hebrew Bible	229
	Apocryphal and pseudepigraphical literature	238
	Josephus and Philo	249
	The Dead Sea Scrolls	252
	The New Testament	256
	'According to works': Judgement	260
	'According to works': Justification	260
	Rom. 4.4-9	262
	Rom. 9.11-12, 30-32	266
	James and Hebrews	269
	Excursus 1: 'Works of the Law'	272
	Excursus 2: Abraham as Torah observant	279
	Tannaitic rabbinic literature	282
	Part 2: The Johannine context	288
	Works as signs and testimony	289
	Works and binary dualism	295
	'Work the works of God'	299
	Part 3: Reading John 8.39-41 intertextually	305
6	Abraham sees and rejoices: John 8.48-59	315
	Introduction	315
	Part 1: Scripting the intertextual field	318
	The Hebrew Bible	319
	Abraham's dream (Gen. 15.12)	319
	Abraham's laughter (Gen. 17.17)	321

Abraham's visitors at the Oaks of Mamre (Gen. 18.1-15)	322
Abraham's intercession (Gen. 18.16-33)	323
Apocryphal and pseudepigraphical literature	325
Abraham as visionary figure	325
Abraham's joy	332
The New Testament	337
Tannaitic rabbinic literature	343
Abraham as seer	343
Abraham's joy	345
Not yet fifty years old?	347
Part 2: The Johannine context	348
'Joy' and 'rejoicing' in the Gospel of John	349
Seeing and sight in the Gospel of John	354
Part 3: Reading John 8.56-58 intertextually	357
Conclusion	365
Bibliography	373
Author index	412
Subject index	420
Reference index	428

Acknowledgements

The research and writing undertaken for this book was made possible by a generous postdoctoral research fellowship at Charles Sturt University, Australia (2012–15). I am particularly thankful to Professor Gerard Moore, who mentored the project and supported me throughout the whole journey, and to Dr Karl Hand for his research assistance in the early years of this book.

Thanks also to Professor Mark Goodacre and Professor Chris Keith for their editorial guidance and enthusiasm for my project from 2011 onwards. Both were supportive and patient as the book required additional time to gestate and come to completion, through many unexpected twists and turns in my personal life. At times, I thought this book would never see the light of day; I thank everyone in my life, my family, friends and colleagues (now at Western Sydney University), who believed I could persevere.

Along the way came my daughter Sarah, born on Rosh Hashanah 5776 (2015), the greatest gift from above. To her, and my beautiful son Jamie, I dedicate this book, with love.

Abbreviations

AB	Anchor Bible
ABR	*Australian Biblical Review*
AEJT	*Australian E-Journal of Theology*
AHR	*American Historical Review*
AJEC	*Ancient Judaism and Early Christianity*
AJSR	*Association of Jewish Studies Review*
ANE	Ancient Near East
ATANT	Abhandlungen zur Theologie des Alten und Neuen Testaments
BAR	*Biblical Archaeology Review*
BBR	*Bulletin for Biblical Research*
BCE	Before the Common Era
BDAG	*A Greek–English Lexicon of the New Testament and Other Early Christian Literature*
BDB	Brown–Drivers–Briggs
BETL	Bibliotheca Ephemeridum Theologicarum Lovaniensium
BHS	*Biblia Hebraica Stuttgartensia*
Bib	*Biblica*
BibInt	*Biblical Interpretation*
BINS	Biblical Interpretation Series
BJRL	*Bulletin of the John Rylands University Library of Manchester*
BN	*Biblische Notizen*
BTB	*Biblical Theology Bulletin*
BSac	*Bibliotheca sacra*
BZ	*Biblische Zeitschrift*
BZAW	Beihefte zur Zeitschrift für die altestamentliche Wissenschaft
BZNW	Beihefte zur Zeitschrift für die neutestamentliche Wissenschaft
CBET	Contributions to Biblical Exegesis and Theology
CBR	*Currents in Biblical Theology*
CBQ	*Catholic Biblical Quarterly*

CD	Damascus Code
CE	Common Era
CI	*Critical Inquiry*
CRINT	*Compendia rerum iudaicarum ad Novum Testamentum*
DJD	Discoveries in the Judean Desert
DSD	*Dead Sea Discoveries*
DSS	Dead Sea Scrolls
EH	Europäische Hochschulschriften
ELH	*English Literary History*
ETL	*Ephemerides Theologicae Lovanienses*
EvQ	*Evangelical Quarterly*
ExpTim	*Expository Times*
FAT	*Forschungen zum Alten Testaments*
HB	Hebrew Bible
HBT	*Horizons in Biblical Theology*
HNT	*Handbuch zum Neun Testament*
HTR	*Harvard Theological Review*
HUCA	*Hebrew Union College Annual*
ICC	International Critical Commentary
Int	*Interpretation*
JAAR	*Journal of the American Academy of Religion*
JBL	*Journal of Biblical Literature*
JECS	*Journal of Early Christian Studies*
JETS	*Journal of the Evangelical Theological Society*
JHS	*Journal of Hebrew Scriptures*
JoSt	Johannine Studies
JPS	Jewish Publication Society
JQR	*Jewish Quarterly Review*
JSNT	*Journal for the Study of the New Testament*
JSNTSup	Journal for the Study of the New Testament – Supplement Series
JSOTSup	Journal for the Study of the Old Testament – Supplement Series
JSJ	*Journal for the Study of Judaism*
JSJS	Journal for the Study of Judaism Supplements
JSP	*Journal for the Study of the Pseudepigrapha*

JSPSup	Journal for the Study of the Pseudepigrapha Supplements
JTS	Journal of Theological Studies
LCL	Loeb Classical Library
LNTS	Library of New Testament Studies
LSTS	Library of Second Temple Studies
LXX	Septuagint
MLN	Modern Language Notes
MLQ	Modern Language Quarterly
MSS	Manuscripts
MT	Masoretic Text
MTZ	Münehner Theologische Zeitschrift
NA^{28}	Nestle-Aland, Novum Testamentum Graece
NBC	New Biblical Commentary
NCBC	New Century Bible Commentary
NICOT	New International Commentary on the Old Testament
NLH	New Literary History
NovT	Novum Testamentum
NovTSup	Novum Testamentum, Supplements
NRSV	New Revised Standard Version
NT	New Testament
NTAbh	Neutestamentliche Abhandlungen
NTL	New Testament Library
NTS	New Testament Studies
OT	Old Testament
OTL	Old Testament Library
ÖTKNT	Ökumenischer Taschenbuchkommentar zum Neuen Testament
OTP	Old Testament Pseudepigrapha
PAAJR	Proceedings of the American Academy for Jewish Research
Pac	Pacifica
PBN	Paternoster Biblical Monographs
PL	Patrologia Latina
PMLA	Proceedings of the Modern Language Association
PNTC	Pillar New Testament Commentary
RevExp	Review and Expositor

RB	*Revue biblique*
RBS	Resources for Biblical Studies
RevQ	*Revue de Qumran*
SANt	Studia Asrhusiana Neotestamentica
SBL	Society of Biblical Literature
SBLDS	Society of Biblical Literature Dissertation Series
SBLMS	Society of Biblical Literature Monograph Series
Sem	*Semeia*
SJT	*Scottish Journal of Theology*
SNTSMS	Society of New Testament Studies Monograph Series
SP	Sacra Pagina
SSEJC	Studies in Scripture in Early Judaism and Christianity
Str-B	*Kommentar zum Neuen Testament aus Talmud und Midrash*. Edited by Herman L. Strack and Paul Billerbeck. 6 vols. Münich, 1922–1961.
StudBibLit	Studies in Biblical Literature
StPhAnnual	*Studia Philonica Annual*
SupJSJ	Supplements to the Journal for the Study of Judaism
T12P	Testaments of the Twelve Patriarchs
TBN	Themes in Biblical Narrative
TrinJ	*Trinity Journal*
TPAPA	*Transactions and Proceedings of the American Philological Association*
TSAJ	Texts and Studies in Ancient Judaism
TVZ	Theologischer Verlag Zürich
TynBull	*Tyndale Bulletin*
VC	*Vigiliae Christianae*
VT	*Vetus Testamentum*
VTSupp	Vetus Testamentum Supplements
WBC	Word Biblical Commentary
WUNT	Wissenschaftliche Untersuchungen zum Neuen Testament
ZBK	Zürcher Bibelkommentare
ZNW	*Zeitschrift für die neuentestamentliche Wissenschaft und die Kunde der älteren Kirche*
ZThK	*Zeitschrift für Theologie und Kirche*

1

Introduction

John 8.31-59 is recognized in the scholarship for two defining features: first, as a distinct literary unit, it is often cited as the *locus classicus* of New Testament (NT) anti-Judaism; and second, it is the only section of John's Gospel to refer to the biblical figure of Abraham.[1] The so-called anti-Jewish dimension of John 8.31-59 appears to be most evident in Jesus' various vituperative statements aimed at a group of characters bluntly designated 'the Jews' – for example, in the heat of the debate, Jesus tells this group that they have the devil as their 'father', and that they do his 'works' (8.44).[2] Jesus also accuses the Jews of being 'slaves of sin', and that they are due to be removed from the 'household' of God (8.34-36). Indeed, the larger literary unit framing the text – narratively speaking, the festival setting of Sukkot (7.1–8.59) – is filled with tense, vituperative dialogue, with no reprieve and with a drastic conclusion.

At the same time, both Jesus and the Jews make repeated reference to the figure of Abraham in John 8.31-59. Outside of this pericope, Abraham does not appear at all in the Johannine corpus; in ch. 8 vv. 31-59, he is referred to twelve times in connection with three contextual traditions: his role as 'father' or progenitor, his exemplary 'works' and his prescient ability to 'see' and 'rejoice' in Jesus' 'day' (8.33, 37, 39 (×3), 40, 52, 53, 56, 57, 58). Each reference to Abraham embroils Jesus and the Jews in deeper polemical disputation: against Jesus' invitation to 'abide' in his 'word' and so to become 'free', the

---

[1] A detailed case for reading John 8.31-59 as a discrete literary unit is made in Chapter 3. Suffice it to note here that the parameters of the unit are disputed in the scholarship based on the fact that the audience(s) addressed by Jesus in ch. 8 vv. 30 and 31 can appear to be either merged or distinct.

[2] Numerous scholars consider this verse to be the nadir of New Testament anti-Jewish diatribe, both of itself and seen from within the remit of its reception history; for example Jürgen Becker, *Das Evangelium nach Johannes* (ÖTKNT 4/1 and 4/2; 2 vols.; Gütersloh-Würzburg: Mohn, 1985), p. 304; Reimund Bieringer, Didier Pollefeyt and Frederique Vandecasteele-Vanneuville, 'Wrestling with Johannine Anti-Judaism: A Hermeneutical Framework for the Current Debate', in Bieringer, Pollefeyt and Vandecasteele-Vanneuville (eds), *Anti-Judaism and the Fourth Gospel: Papers from the Leuven Colloquium* (Louisville: Westminster/John Knox, 2001), pp. 3–37, at p. 14; Adele Reinhartz, *Jesus of Hollywood* (New York: Oxford University Press, 2009), p. 194. Some studies have attempted extended 'contextualization' of this verse, for example Stephen Motyer, *Your Father the Devil? A New Approach to John and the Jews* (Paternoster Biblical Monographs; UK: Paternoster Press, 1997); Urban C. von Wahlde, '"You are of Your Father the Devil" in Its Context: Stereotyped Apocalyptic Polemic in Jn 8:38-47', in Reimund Bieringer, Didier Pollefeyt and Frederique Vandecasteele-Vanneuville (eds), *Anti-Judaism and the Fourth Gospel: Papers from the Leuven Colloqium* (Assen: Van Gorcum, 2001), pp. 437–48; Erich Gräßer, 'Die antijüdische Polemik im Johannesevangelium', *NTS* 11 (1964/5), pp. 74–90. On the reception history of this motif, see the widely cited work by Joshua Trachtenberg, *The Devil and the Jews: The Medieval Conception of the Jew and Its Relation to Modern Anti-Semitism* (Philadelphia: JPS; 2nd edn, 2002).

Jews claim to be 'seed of Abraham' and thus to be inherently un-enslaved (8.31-33). Jesus warns the Jews that although they are Abraham's offspring, they are not children of Abraham, for they are murderous (8.37) and do not do Abraham's 'works' (8.39-40). Ultimately, Jesus provocatively implies superiority to Abraham (8.53) on the basis of pre-existence (8.58), and the fact that Abraham witnessed his 'day' (8.56). The Jews attempt to stone Jesus, but to no avail (8.59). It is worth asking why Abraham is repeatedly invoked in precisely this harsh section of the Gospel. What is the connection between the Gospel's fierce rhetoric at this point and the intertextual evocation of Abraham?

The answer might seem, *prima facie*, rather obvious. After all, early Christian controversies typically invoked Israel's great patriarch as a means of establishing their claims to a richly unique heritage: the one God's covenant with his people.[3] Such claims often indicated issues of central concern. As Samuel Sandmel expressed: 'To see what the writer makes of Abraham is often to see most clearly what the writer has to say'.[4] Tensions between Jesus and the Jews in John's narrative run particularly high in John 8.31-59 when the figure of Abraham enters the fray, and the stakes are suddenly raised to a considerable degree. Recently, Tineke de Lange has claimed that Abraham's 'conspicuous' and 'sudden' appearance in John 8.31-59 suggests that the issues at stake between Jesus and the Jews in this pericope reflected historical instances of Jewish–Christian disputation in the late first century CE.[5] Abraham thus operated as an index to the socio-historical crisis facing the 'Johannine community' as it broke away from its 'opponents' – who are vilified in the text as 'the Jews'.[6] While it is not incorrect to read John 8.31-59 in this manner, the primary purpose of this book is not to uncover the possible historical reality behind the references to Abraham, nor to assess what the figure of Abraham in John 8.31-59 might reveal about the so-called 'parting of the ways' between the constructed 'Johannine community' and emergent Judaism.[7] In particular, the theoretical premises underpinning the more simplistic examples of 'two-level' readings of John – such as an assumed one-on-one correspondence between literature and history – seem to me to be highly problematic.[8]

---

[3] See the primary literature cited in Jeffrey Siker, *Disinheriting the Jews: Abraham in Early Christian Controversy* (Louisville: Westminster/John Knox, 1991).

[4] Samuel Sandmel, *Philo's Place in Judaism: A Study of Conceptions of Abraham in Jewish Literature* (Cincinnati: Hebrew Union College Press, 1956), p. 29.

[5] Tineke de Lange, *Abraham in John 8,31-59: His Significance in the Conflict Between Johannine Christianity and Its Jewish Environment* (Amsterdam: Amphora Books, 2008), p. 28; cf. p. 29. De Lange's scholarly objectives are more diverse than this, of course, and to an extent they overlap with my own. A similar position about John 7.1–8.59 was argued for by Günter Reim, *Studien zum alttestamentlichen Hintergrund des Johannesevangeliums* (SNTSMS 22; Cambridge: Cambridge University Press, 1972).

[6] De Lange, *Abraham in John 8,31-59*, p. 31. De Lange relies on the work of J. Louis Martyn's method of interpreting John's Gospel as a 'two-level drama'; see Martyn, *History and Theology in the Fourth Gospel* (Louisville: Westminster/John Knox, 3rd edn, 2003).

[7] The term 'parting of the ways' to describe a definitive 'split' between early Judaism and Christianity (prior to 400 CE) is now being reconsidered in light of greater historical understanding. Cf. Adam H. Becker and Annette Yoshiko Reed (eds), *The Ways That Never Parted: Jews and Christians in Late Antiquity and the Early Middle Ages* (Philadelphia: Fortress Press, 2007).

[8] Ruth Sheridan, 'Johannine Sectarianism: A Category Now Defunct?' in Hughson Ong and Stanley E. Porter (eds), *The Origins of John's Gospel* (JoSt 2; Leiden: Brill, 2015), forthcoming. Cf. Elizabeth Clark, *History, Theory, Text: Historians and the Linguistic Turn* (Cambridge: Harvard University Press, 2004); Bruce Holsinger, '"Historical Context" in Historical Context: Surface, Depth, and the

While appreciative of such approaches to Abraham's refiguration in the post-biblical literature, this book takes a slightly different angle on the text and the problems it raises. This book critically examines the intertextual function of Abraham in John 8.31-59 both within the context of John 7.1-8.59, and within the wider literary contexts of Second Temple and early rabbinic Judaism where the figure of Abraham featured so significantly in a variety of textual genres. The purpose of this analysis is to situate John's figuration of Abraham within emerging traditions that presented Abraham as a paternal figure of vicarious merit for the sake of his 'seed'. Connected to this idea is the figuration of Abraham as an intercessory (or visionary) figure who rejoices in the future redemption of his 'seed', and whose surplus merits, arising from his faithful 'works', function to attenuate the 'sins' of his descendants. My aim is to provide a holistic, intertextual reading of Abraham in John 8.31-59, from the Jews' perspective and in the context of the Sukkot setting of the wider discourse (John 7–8). These features of Abraham's post-biblical 'afterlife' have not yet been brought to bear upon an analysis of John 8.31-59 or its immediate narrative context.

Before developing this argument through sustained exegetical and intertextual analysis (Chapters 4 through 6), in this chapter I present a review of the literature to date and outline the structure and argument of the rest of the book. First, I provide a cursory overview of the scholarship on Abraham's post-biblical 'afterlives' in the literature of early Judaism in general (including the NT), followed by an in-depth review of the scholarship on Abraham's presence in the Gospel of John. Discussion of Johannine anti-Judaism in John 8 arises in the course of much of this analysis, but I do not engage directly here with issues such as the identity and function of 'the Jews' in John's Gospel, the question of theological supersessionism and the appropriateness of terminology to describe John's view of Jews and Judaism (i.e. 'anti-Semitic', 'anti-Jewish' or 'anti-Judaic') – these have all been covered in my scholarship thus far, and I would direct the reader to my position on those issues.[9] What I present in this chapter instead is evidence from the secondary literature (specifically many Gospel commentaries) that exacerbates the anti-Jewish tenor and substance of John 8.31-59, even while trying to explain it. In light of this evidence, it becomes clear that part of my reason for a detailed intertextual interpretation of Abraham's figuration in John 8.31-59 is to provide a corrective to the overtly 'compliant' readings of the Gospel text found in the commentaries.[10]

Making of the Text', *NLH* 42 (2011), pp. 593–614. This is not to say that de Lange subscribes to such 'simplistic' readings; cf. *Abraham in John 8,31-59*, p. 196.

[9] See especially, Ruth Sheridan, *Retelling Scripture: The Jews and the Scriptural Citations in John 1:19-12:15* (Leiden/Boston: Brill, 2012), pp. 37–45; Ruth Sheridan, 'Issues in the Translation of οἱ Ἰουδαῖοι in the Fourth Gospel', *JBL* 132, no. 3 (2013), pp. 671–96; Ruth Sheridan, 'Identity, Alterity and the Gospel of John', *BibInt* 22, no. 2 (2014), pp. 188–209.

[10] The term 'compliant reading' comes from Adele Reinhartz, *Befriending the Beloved Disciple: A Jewish Reading of the Gospel of John* (New York: Continuum, 2001). My argument about the commentarial trend of interpreting John 8.31-32 with overtly virulent anti-Judaism can be found in Ruth Sheridan, 'Seed of Abraham, Slavery and Sin: Reproducing Johannine Anti-Judaism in the Modern Commentaries on John 8.31-34', in R. Alan Culpepper and Paul N. Anderson (eds), *John and Judaism: A Contested Relationship in Context* (Atlanta: SBL Press, 2017), pp. 313–32.

The range of Abraham's post-biblical 'afterlives'

Biblical figures often assume complex 'afterlives' in various literary traditions. Perceived 'gaps' in the original biblical narratives often necessitate 'retellings' or narrative sequels that extend, modify or subvert the tales found in the Hebrew Bible (HB).[11] Yet, in terms of subsequent religious and cultural importance, not all biblical figures are considered equal. Within the NT, the figure of Moses takes on near-central significance as a leader (cf. Matt. 23.2; John 3.14; 6.32; John 9.28-29; Acts 6.11, 14; 7.35), teacher (cf. Mark 1.44; 7.10; Matt. 19.7-8; 22.24; Luke 2.22; John 1.17; 5.45; 7.19-22; 8.5; Acts 7.22; 13.39; Rom. 9.15; 10.19), prophet (cf. Mark 12.26; Luke 16.29-31; 24.27; John 1.45; Acts 3.22) and typological model for the figure of Jesus (cf. Matt. 7.3; 1 Cor. 10.2; Heb. 3.2); Moses also received extensive, idealized refiguration within early Judaism (cf. *Sir.* 45.1-2; Philo, *Vita* 1.1.158; 4Q347; *Ant.* 3.320).[12] But in Judaism, Christianity and Islam, the biblical figure of Abraham could be said to have become *the* major figure to which adherents of those three religious traditions looked when solidifying their respective claims both to monotheistic vision and praxis, as well as their claims to covenant with the one God.[13]

The biblical figure of Abraham had already attained a status of incomparable importance within the literary landscape of early Judaism, to which the amount and scope of the (ever-increasing) secondary literature on Abraham is testimony. Some studies examine the refiguration of Abraham across the whole spectrum of Second Temple texts and sources.[14] Other studies are more restricted in focus, looking at the use of Abraham in Philo and/or Josephus, or at the use of Abraham in 'Hellenistic Judaism' in general.[15] Other studies again focus on the figure of Abraham in the 'Old

---

[11] A seminal work in this area is James L. Kugel, *The Bible as It Was* (Cambridge: Belknap/Harvard University Press, 1997). A standout study of biblical refiguration across diverse 'secular' literary canons is Yvonne Sherwood, *A Biblical Text and Its Afterlives: The Survival of Jonah in Western Culture* (Cambridge: Cambridge University Press, 2001).

[12] On Moses' presence in John, see especially Wayne A. Meeks, *The Prophet-King: Moses Traditions and the Johannine Christology* (Leiden: Brill, 1967). On Moses idealization within early Judaism, see Kugel, *The Bible*, pp. 311–14.

[13] Cf. Marvin R. Wilson, *Our Father Abraham: Jewish Roots of the Christian Faith* (Grand Rapids: Eerdmans, 1989); Lenn Goodman, *God of Abraham* (Oxford: Oxford University Press, 1996); Jon D. Levenson, 'Abusing Abraham: Traditions, Religious Histories, and Modern Misinterpretations', *Judaism* 47 (1998), pp. 259–77; Jon D. Levenson, 'The Conversion of Abraham to Judaism, Christianity and Islam', in Hindy Najman and Judith H. Newmann (eds), *The Idea of Biblical Interpretation: Essays in Honor of James L. Kugel* (Leiden: Brill, 2004), pp. 3–40; Norman Solomon, Richard Harries and Tim Winter (eds), *Abraham's Children: Jews, Christians and Muslims in Conversation* (London: T&T Clark, 2006). Some studies discuss Abraham as an exemplar of faith (representative is Bernard Och, 'Abraham and Moriah: A Journey to Fulfillment', *Judaism* 38 (1989), pp. 293–309); others question the extent of Abraham's faith in God from the biblical sources (e.g. Lyle M. Eslinger, 'Prehistory in the Call to Abraham', *BibInt* 14, no. 3 (2006), pp. 189–208; Andrew J. Schmutzer, 'Did the Gods Cause Abraham's Wandering? An Examination of אלהים אתי התעו in Genesis 20.13', *JSOT* 35 (2010), pp. 149–66; Howard J. Curzer, 'Abraham, the Faithless Moral Superhero', *Philosophy and Literature* 31 (2007), pp. 344–61).

[14] F. E. Wieser, *Die Abrahamvorstellungen im Neuen Testament* (Bern: Peter Lang, 1987); Siker, *Disinheriting the Jews*; Jon D. Levenson, *Inheriting Abraham: The Legacy of the Patriarch in Judaism, Christianity and Islam* (Princeton: Princeton University Press, 2012).

[15] Sandmel, *Philo's Place in Judaism*; Louis Feldman, 'Abraham the Greek Philosopher in Josephus', *TPAPA* 99 (1968), pp. 143–56; G. Mayer, 'Aspekte des Abrahambildes in der hellenistisch-jüdischen

Testament' (OT) pseudepigraphical and/or apocryphal sources.[16] A smaller number of studies look at the figure of Abraham in the Dead Sea Scrolls (DSS), a body of literature which, on the whole, is surprisingly less interested in refiguring Abraham than might be expected, given its creative concern for rewriting biblical traditions.[17] There have even been studies of the references to Abraham in the pagan writings of the Greco-Roman world.[18] Studies on the figure of Abraham in rabbinic Judaism also have some pedigree. Some of these focus on the haggadic materials, such as the Midrashim, while others focus on the halakhic material in the Mishnah and Talmud.[19] These analyses

Literatur', *ET* 32 (1972), pp. 118–27; Annette Yoshiko Reed, 'The Construction and Subversion of Patriarchal Perfection: Abraham and Exemplarity in Philo, Josephus, and the *Testament of Abraham*', *JSJ* 40 (2009), pp. 185–212; Annette Yoshiko Reed, 'Abraham as Chaldean Scientist and Father of the Jews: Josephus *Ant.* 1.154-168, and the Greco-Roman Discourse about Astronomy/Astrology', *JSJ* 35 (2004), pp. 119–58.

[16] R. Martin-Achard, *Actualité d'Abraham* (Neuchâtel: Delachaux and Niestle, 1969), pp. 111–37; Daniel J. Harrington, 'Abraham Traditions in the *Testament of Abraham* and in the "Rewritten Bible" of the Intertestamental Period', in George Nickelsburg (ed.), *Studies in the Testament of Abraham* (Atlanta: Scholars Press, 1976), pp. 156–71; Louis Finkelstein, 'The Book of Jubilees and the Rabbinic Halaka', *HTR* 16 (1923), pp. 59–61; S. Zeitlin, 'The Book of Jubilees: Its Character and Its Significance', *JQR* 30 (1939/40), pp. 1–31; J. T. A. G. M van Ruiten, 'Abraham, Job and the *Book of Jubilees*: The Intertextual Relationship of Genesis 22.1-19, Job 1.1–2:13, and *Jubilees* 17.15-18:19', in Ed Noort and Eibert Tigchelaar (eds), *The Sacrifice of Isaac: The Aqedah (Gen 22) and Its Interpretations* (TBN 4; Leiden: Brill, 2001), pp. 58–85; J. T. A. G. M van Ruiten, *Abraham in the Book of Jubilees: The Rewriting of Genesis 11.26–25.10 in the Book of Jubilees 11.14–23.8* (JSJS 161; Leiden: Brill, 2012); Adolfo D. Roitman, 'The Traditions about Abraham's Early Life in the Book of Judith (5.6-9)', in Esther G. Chazon et al. (eds), *Things Revealed: Studies in Early Jewish and Christian Literature in Honor of Michael E. Stone* (JSJS 89; Leiden: Brill, 2004), pp. 73–87; Bradley C. Gregory, 'Abraham as the Jewish Ideal: Exegetical Traditions in Sirach 44.19-21', *CBQ* 70 (2008), pp. 66–81.

[17] Craig A. Evans, 'Abraham in the Dead Sea Scrolls: A Man of Faith and Failure', in Peter W. Flint (ed.), *The Bible at Qumran: Text, Shape and Interpretation* (Grand Rapids: Eerdmans, 2001), pp. 149–58; Gary A. Anderson, 'The Status of the Torah before Sinai: The Retelling of the Bible in the Damascus Covenant and the Book of Jubilees', *DSD* 1, no. 1 (1994), pp. 1–29; Mladen Popović, 'Abraham and the Nations in the Dead Sea Scrolls: Exclusivism and Inclusivism in the Texts from Qumran and the Absence of a Reception History for Gen 12.3', in M. Goodman, G. H. van Kooten and J. T. A. G. M. van Ruiten (eds), *Abraham, the Nations, and the Hagarites: Jewish, Christian, and Islamic Perspectives on Kinship with Abraham* (TBN 13; Leiden: Brill, 2010), pp. 77–103.

[18] Cf. Jeffrey Siker, 'Abraham in Graeco-Roman Paganism', *JSJ* 18 (1988), pp. 188–208.

[19] B. Beers, *Leben Abrahams* (Leipzig: Oskar Leiner, 1859); P. Billerbeck, 'Abrahams Leben und Beduetung nach Auffassung der älteren Haggada', *Nathanael* 15 (1899), pp. 43–57, 118–28, 137–57, 161–79; and *Nathanael* 16 (1900), pp. 33–57, 65–80 (later collected in Str-B, vol. 3.186–217: Romans 4; John 8 and Galatians 2-4). Scholars now routinely and rightly approach the results of Str-B cautiously due to their anti-Semitic slant. Otherwise, see the anthology of Louis Ginzberg, *Legends of the Jews* (6 vols.; Philadelphia: Jewish Publication Society, 1909–1928), especially 1.183-308 and 5.207-69. See also Geza Vermes, *Scripture and Tradition in Judaism: Haggadic Studies* (SPB 4; 2nd edn; Leiden: Brill, 1973), pp. 67–126; P. M. Bogaert, *Abraham dans la Bible et dans la tradition juive* (Brussels: Institutum Iudaicum, 1977); Ron Naiweld, 'The Father of Man: Abraham as the Rabbinic Jesus', in Jörg Rüpke and Wolfgang Spikermann (eds), *Reflections on Religious Individuality: Greco-Roman and Judaeo-Christian Texts and Practices* (Berlin: Walter de Gruyter, 2012), pp. 145–71; Rabbi Jeffrey Salkin, *The Gods Are Broken! The Hidden Legacy of Abraham* (Lincoln: University of Nebraska Press/JPS, 2013). For an analysis of the interaction between early Jewish and Christian interpretations of Abraham, see Guenter Stemberger, 'Genesis 15 in Rabbinic and Patristic Interpretation', in Emmanouela Grypeou and Helen Spurling (eds), *The Exegetical Encounter between Jews and Christians in Late Antiquity* (JCP 18; Leiden: Brill, 2009), pp. 143–62; Judith Frishman, '"And Abraham Had Faith": But in What? Ephrem and the Rabbis on Abraham and God's Blessing', in Grypeou and Spurling (eds), *The Exegetical Encounter*, pp. 163–79.

often overlap with a study of Abraham in the prior sources, either the Tanakh or selected texts from the Second Temple Period. Such studies illustrate how later rabbinic traditions developed, altered or reinvented aspects of Abraham's presentation found in those prior sources.

A substantial body of literature exists on the figure of Abraham in the NT and early Christianity. The most comprehensive book to date is Jeffrey Siker's *Disinheriting the Jews*, which covers the NT, the apologists, the apocryphal gospels and proto-heterodox authors of the first and second centuries CE. The purpose of Siker's study is to present a broad argument about Abraham's rhetorical role in the development of early Christian anti-Judaism.[20] Siker detects a diachronic development that initially features Abraham as a means of including Gentiles into the covenant, but that gradually and insistently uses Abraham to exclude Jews from their own covenant.[21] The historical factors that Siker identifies as propelling this rhetorical development included a declining focus on eschatology, an increasing influx of Gentiles into the church, the declining number of 'Jewish Christians', as well as the solidification of Jewish (rabbinic) identity after 70 CE.[22] Siker presents the rhetorical movement to 'disinherit the Jews' as contingent on these historical factors rather than on anything essentially anti-Jewish in Christian doctrine or identity. 'Jewish Christians' such as Paul and John used the figure of Abraham to argue for Gentile inclusion in the Jewish covenant, whereas 'Gentile Christians' in the second century (such as Justin Martyr) used Abraham to justify God's rejection of the Jews in favour of Gentiles.[23] Siker reads Abraham as a rhetorical figure of Christian discursivity, shaping its relationship to its inherited past and its polemical present.

But such a broad-brush thesis has its own weaknesses. Siker does concede that although the author of John's Gospel is a 'Jewish Christian', he nevertheless uses 'Abraham to argue for Jewish exclusion from God's purposes' in contrasting fashion to other early 'Jewish Christians' such as Paul.[24] It is difficult to reconcile this as a point on Siker's continuum, since the polemic in John 8.31-59 does not devolve upon Gentile inclusion as a vital issue. Siker eventually cedes this point, stating that John appears to exclude the Jews quite apart from consideration of Gentiles, and only

---

[20] Siker, *Disinheriting the Jews*, p. 193.
[21] Ibid.
[22] Ibid., pp. 194-5. Siker mentions the *Birkat ha-minim* as constructive in the latter regard, citing work by S. T. Katz, 'Issues in the Separation of Judaism and Christianity After 70 C.E.: A Reconsideration', *JBL* 103 (1984), pp. 43-76 and S. J. D. Cohen, 'The Significance of Yavneh: Pharisees, Rabbis, and the End of Jewish Sectarianism', *HUCA* 55 (1984), pp. 27-53. Research on the relationship between the *Birkat ha-minim* and the NT has moved in uncertain lines since: for example Ruth Langer questions whether the prayer was directed against NT high Christologies (*Cursing the Christians? A History of the Birkat HaMinim* (New York: Oxford University Press, 2011)); but Joel Marcus reasserts the general principles of the original consensus with slight nuancing ('Birkat ha-Minim Revisited', *NTS* 55 (2009), pp. 523-51).
[23] Cf. Siker, *Disinheriting the Jews*, pp. 192-3.
[24] Ibid., p. 193. Siker's reading of Luke/Acts is likewise difficult to fit into this schema. Siker claims that Luke, a Gentile Christian, argues for 'Gentile inclusion' through the use of Abraham, but he overlooks the ways in which Luke deploys Abraham when alluding to Jewish 'exclusion' (see Chapter 6 of this book for an analysis of Luke 16). Siker reaches a compromise by saying that Luke/Acts views Jews and Christians as equal in their heritage of the Abrahamic covenant (*Disinheriting the Jews*, p. 103), but I would consider the anti-Jewish polemics to have greater weight than Siker allows.

upon 'Christological grounds', but that such a presentation of Jewish exclusion would have been nevertheless 'quite amenable to most early Gentile Christians'.[25] This only raises the further question of the original audience and purpose of John's Gospel. Was John 8.31-59 written to appeal to Gentile Christians? Did John 8.31-59 represent a pivot point in the gradual historical development of the Jesus movement from a Jewish sect to a Gentile Christian religion?[26]

Another critique of Siker's methodology can be levelled from the viewpoint of recent scholarship on the history of early Christianity, which has increasingly shied away from meta-narratives of progressive doctrinal developments,[27] for example that the Gentile church came into existence through a persistent, and eventually victorious, doctrinal and rhetorical battle against Jews, pagans and heretics.[28] None of this is meant to fault Siker, whose monograph, published in 1992, cannot be expected to have been conversant with the very recent trends about the variegated and pluriform nature of early Christianity and Judaism; it is only to state *now* that 'diversity' and 'pluralism' are normative for diachronic studies of the period, wide-ranging arguments made about the function of Abraham in early Christianity – or the heuristic function of any character or theme – are going to have to be mapped out with greater theoretical nuance.[29]

Another approach analyses the figure of Abraham in *one* book (or corpus) of the NT.[30] Such studies are often more comparative than diachronic, that is, they examine the use of Abraham in one text against a (pluralistic) 'background' of comparable or parallel texts of the period, rather than interpreting a given text's use of Abraham within a continuum that would reveal something about the historical development of religious thought. Typically, these comparable texts are antecedent to the NT – or are thought to be roughly contemporaneous with it – and they are therefore used in making arguments about the literary indebtedness of the given NT text on prior Abrahamic traditions.[31] Overall, studies on the figure of Abraham in the NT have tended to concentrate on Paul, and the issues distinct to his writings. Often, Paul's writings on the topic are taken

---

[25] Siker, *Disinheriting the Jews*, p. 196.
[26] Most contemporary scholarship would answer 'No' to the latter question. As noted, such a thesis would extrapolate far too much from John 8.31-59, perhaps under the governing influence of Galatians 2–4, since issues of Gentile identity play no role whatsoever in John 7.1–8.59. See further discussion of de Lange's work in the ensuing pages.
[27] Annette Yoshiko Reed, '"Jewish-Christian" Apocrypha and the History of Jewish/Christian Relations', in P. Piovanelli (ed.), *Christian Apocryphal Texts for the New Millennium: Achievements, Prospects, and Challenges*, p. 1 (forthcoming).
[28] Annette Yoshiko Reed, 'Old Testament Pseudepigrapha and Post-70 Judaism', in S. C. Mimouni, B. Pouderon and C. Clivas (eds), *Les Judaïsmes dans tous leurs etats aux Ier-IIIe siecles* (Paris: Cerf, forthcoming).
[29] This is not to say that Siker is unaware of literary pluralism – he does examine the role of Abraham in lesser-known texts from very diverse early Christian sources. But Siker's deployment of totalizing categories ('Jewish-Christian'/'Gentile-Christian' as well as 'Gnostic') tends to squeeze the diversity of the era into two binaries reflecting real social groups in competition.
[30] Nihls Dahl, 'The Story of Abraham in Luke-Acts', in L. Martyn and L. Keck (eds), *Studies in Luke-Acts* (Nashville: Abingdon, 1996), pp. 139–58; Roy Bowen Ward, 'The Works of Abraham: James 2.14-26', *HTR* 61 (1968), pp. 283–90.
[31] Such an approach does of course have its own methodological weaknesses, particularly around issues of 'influence', 'intertextuality' and the question of direct literary dependence on sources. See Chapter 2 for further discussion.

as a centre-point from which to read the significance of 'Abraham in early Christianity' more generally.[32] Given that one can barely discuss Paul's thought, his 'doctrine' of justification – so central to aspects of Protestant theology – without understanding his use of Abraham (cf. Rom. 4.1-25 and Galatians 2–4), the large amount of literature on Paul's figuration of Abraham is not unexpected.

However, one consequence of centralizing Paul has been that certain other NT references to Abraham – particularly those in Jas. 2.24-25 and John 8.31-59 – are unnecessarily forced into the framework of Paul's thought.[33] John's use of Abraham has received comparatively less scholarly attention (or, perhaps more correctly, has been considered less important in view of its implications for Christian theology), but there is still a solid number of exegetical studies, as well as full-length monographs, to be found on the topic, to which I now turn.

Abraham in the Gospel of John: A survey of the secondary literature

Full-length studies: Horatio Lona and Tineke de Lange

Only two full-length monographs on the subject of Abraham in John 8.31-59 have been published so far: one in 1976 by Horatio E. Lona (*Abraham in Johannes 8: Ein Beitrag zur Methodenfrage*), and another in 2008 by Tineke de Lange (*Abraham in John 8,31-59: His Significance in the Conflict between Johannine Christianity and Its Jewish Environment*).[34] I briefly outline and evaluate the main purposes, theses, methods and

---

[32] K. Berger, 'Abraham in den paulischen Hauptbriefen', *MTZ* 17 (1966), pp. 47–89; Nancy Calvert-Koyzis, *Paul, Monotheism and the People of God: The Significance of Abraham Traditions for Early Judaism and Christianity* (JSNTSup 273; London: T&T Clark, 2004); G. Walter Hansen, *Abraham in Galatians: Epistolary and Rhetorical Contexts* (Sheffield: JSOT Press, 1989). The scholarly centralization of Paul's use of Abraham traditions can be ascertained as well in the predominance of smaller studies on Romans and Galatians, many of which attempt to read social crises lying 'behind' the text: cf. Thomas H. Tobin, 'What Shall We Say That Abraham Found? The Controversy behind Romans 4', *HTR* 88, no. 4 (1995), pp. 437–52; but critiquing such a procedure, see, Kelli S. O'Brien, 'The Curse of the Law (Galatians 3.13): Crucifixion, Persecution, and Deuteronomy 21.22-23', *JSNT* 29, no. 1 (2006), pp. 55–76, at p. 62; Nijay Gupta, 'Mirror-Reading Moral Issues in Paul's Letters', *JSNT* 34 (2012), pp. 361–81. The connection between Paul's elucidation of Abraham's significance for theological issues of 'justification', 'righteousness', 'faith' and 'works of the law' has been explored in a large number of articles, many of which are adduced in further chapters in this book (Chapters 4 and 5). It suffices here to note the following: Thomas R. Schreiner, '"Works of Law" in Paul', *NovT* 33 (1991), pp. 217–44; James D. G. Dunn, '4QMMT and Galatians', *NTS* 43 (1997), pp. 147–53; N. T. Wright, 'Paul and the Patriarch: The Role of Abraham in Romans 4', *JSNT* 35 (2013), pp. 207–41; Jan Lambrecht, 'Romans 4: A Critique of N.T. Wright', *JSNT* 36, no. 2 (2013), pp. 189–94. Notably, most of these studies are involved in the larger waxing and waning of ideological trends related to the so-called 'New Perspective' on Paul (NPP); for a solid discussion of this issue, see Pamela Eisenbaum, 'Paul, Polemics, and the Problem of Essentialism', *BibInt* 13 (2005), pp. 224–38; Mark D. Nanos, 'How Inter-Christian Approaches to Paul's Rhetoric Can Perpetuate Negative Valuations of Jewishness: Although Proposing to Avoid That Outcome', *BibInt* 13, no. 3 (2005), pp. 255-69.

[33] I return to this point throughout the book.

[34] Horatio E. Lona, *Abraham in Johannes 8. Ein Beitrag zur Methodenfrage* (EHS 23/65; Frankfurt/M.: Peter Lang, 1976); de Lange, *Abraham in John 8, 31-59*.

conclusions of these two works, before suggesting how my own work differs from, or builds upon, them.

As the subtitle of Lona's work suggests, his examination of Abraham in John 8 is structured around the broader question of methodology, but it focuses on the specific issues involved in reading John 8 against the various literary 'backgrounds' of antiquity. Perhaps ahead of its time, Lona's work argues for the possibility of bringing together two methods typically considered to be diametrically opposed to each other in the field of biblical exegesis: historical criticism and 'literary semiotics'. Lona considers such methodological pluralism to provide the most satisfactory way of interpreting John's use of Abraham traditions in John 8.31-59, as no method realistically exists in isolation from others.[35] Significantly, Lona probes the theoretical foundations of the twin exegetical methodologies that he has postulated as relevant to his study, claiming that the 'place' of the interpreter plays a vital role in understanding the traditional 'conflict' between historical-critical exegesis and contemporary literary semiotics.[36] In many respects, Lona's arguments in this regard are similar to mine (see Chapter 2), but whereas Lona examines the state of exegetical methodologies in Germany up to the early 1970s, my focus is on methodological impasses in the Anglophone world of biblical studies. Additionally, I advocate for a stronger synchronic and poststructuralist interpretive praxis, while also (like Lona) appreciating the possible synergies and integrative possibilities that may exist between semiotics and comparative textual criticism.

Lona argues that the watershed publication of James Barr on the study of 'biblical semantics' (1961) changed the state of play in historical-critical exegesis.[37] According to Barr, semantic meaning was contextual, and Barr especially derided the etymology-based approaches taken in some lexical-theological dictionaries, such as those of Gerhard Kittel.[38] Barr defined the sentence (not the 'word') as the fundamental semantic unit, and this position ran counter to a global, theological understanding of the Bible. Lona shows that Barr's radical critiques initially received little welcome in established German exegetical circles.[39] But other German studies employing 'literary criticism' under the influence of emergent French structuralism gradually began to erode historical-critical dominance.[40]

---

[35] Lona, *Abraham*, p. 66.
[36] Ibid.
[37] James Barr, *The Semantics of Biblical Language* (New York: Oxford, 1961).
[38] Cf. Lona, *Abraham*, pp. 90-1.
[39] Ibid., p. 69. Still, Lona claims that historical-critical exegesis need not forfeit theological understanding, only that it cannot properly become the basis of a systematic 'biblical theology' again (pp. 86-7).
[40] Lona, *Abraham*, pp. 69-70. Lona refers to, and follows, Wolfgang Richter, *Exegese als Literaturwissenschaft: Entwurf einer atl. Literaturtheorie und Methodologie* (Göttingen: Vandenhoeck & Ruprecht, 1971); cf. pp. 92-7. Richter's approach would eventually spawn its own 'school' within OT studies, while also receiving its share of criticism for its specific deployment of structural linguistics. See Helmut Utzschneider, 'Text-Reader-Author. Towards a Theory of Exegesis: Some European Viewpoints', in Ehud Ben Zvi (ed.), *Perspectives on Biblical Hebrew: Comprising the Contents of Journal of Hebrew Scriptures volumes 1-4* (Piscataway: Gorgias Press, 2006), pp. 1-22, at p. 12, n. 24.

In view of this paradigm shift, Lona's objective is to illustrate how three approaches ('classic' philological, historical criticism, structuralist literary criticism and the 'poetics' of literary criticism) can be used together when interpreting Abraham in John 8.[41] Lona does not interpret the Gospel text as a mirror into an historical situation (or *Sitz-im-Leben*, which he thinks 'naïve');[42] and he integrates some of the 'newer' insights derived from linguistics and literary criticism.[43] With regard to literary criticism, Lona follows and adapts Georg Richter's approach, developed for use in OT studies.[44] Richter's 'literary criticism' determines the relationship between a text's form and content on the basis of source criticism. Hence, Lona considers this approach to be a useful fusion between classic historical criticism and 'newer semiotics' *and* to be a helpful method when reading John 8 against a 'background' of antecedent sources. Richter's method understands texts as composite, as containing 'literary' inconsistencies (either linguistic, phraseological or stylistic), which first must be interpreted structurally, pieced together properly and investigated for their prior sources.[45] That means not only establishing the unity/disunity of a text, but also determining the 'original' core of a text.[46] Lona builds on Richter's work inasmuch as he considers an analysis of parallels in the antecedent literature to be a vital part of the 'structuralism' and semantic analysis making up Richter's 'descriptive literary criticism'.[47]

Additionally, Lona engages with various elements of criticism (what he refers to as 'semiotics') derived from the Russian formalists (especially Tzvetzan Todorov).[48] Lona appreciates Todorov's theory of 'reading' a text, which he understands as a concentrated focus upon the text as a 'system'.[49] Todorov's theory of 'reading' emphasizes the autonomy of the text, but it is not averse to situating the text within a 'mutual relationship' of reading with other texts. Lona draws out Todorov's distinction between 'interpretation' and 'description'.[50] 'Interpretation' examines the multilayered nature of a text, focusing on the interrelationship between texts and textual 'influences'. 'Description' basically refers to the application of structural linguistics to the text, looking at the text more or less in its individuality. The grammatical and phonic elements of a text, aspects of literary discourse, are fixed – it is their combination that

---

[41] Lona, *Abraham*, p. 71.
[42] Ibid., p. 91.
[43] Ibid., pp. 90–1.
[44] Ibid.
[45] Cf. John Barton, *Reading the Old Testament: Method in Biblical Studies* (rev. edn; Louisville: Westminster/John Knox, 1996), p. 23.
[46] Cf. John H. Sailhamer, *Introduction to Old Testament Theology: A Canonical Approach* (Grand Rapids: Eerdmans, 1995), p. 88.
[47] Lona, *Abraham*, p. 99; cf. Klaus Koch, *Was ist Formgeschichte? Neue Wege der Bibelexegese* (Neukirchen-Vluyn, 1964), p. 332.
[48] Cf. Tzvetan Todorov, 'Comment Lire?' in *Poétique de la prose* (Paris: Seuil, 1974), pp. 241–53. Todorov's 'descriptive literary criticism' identifies three aspects of reading: 'projection', 'commentary' and 'poetics'; the first of these reads 'through' the text to the author or some other object of historical interest, the second approximates to what critics call the 'close reading', explicating the text on its own terms, and the third seeks to understand the general structural principles defining a work. See Lona, *Abraham*, pp. 113–17.
[49] Lona, *Abraham*, p. 117.
[50] Ibid., pp. 119–20.

is new in each instance.[51] Both elements (interpretation/description) are necessary to the act of reading.[52]

Evaluating the field of structuralism and semiotics, Lona ultimately decides that biblical exegesis can be understood as a 'semiotic' practice.[53] The target of exegesis is, in fact, the 'deciphering' of a broader 'signification system', and a given text should be interpreted as a product of 'other texts'.[54] In this, Lona perceives a convergence between historical criticism – cf. the source criticism of Richter and others – and semiotics, which requires the interpretation of texts as part of a larger 'sign system'.[55] In a 'practical' sense then, the two methods can be used in conjunction, even though they operate on the basis of different theoretical premises.[56] Ultimately, Lona ascribes to a hermeneutical principle of the text as 'communication' – and this on two axes: the 'communication' between the text and its originating historical voice, and the communication between the text and the current reader.[57]

Lona's methodological discussion is detailed and considered primary to his study. His chosen focus (John 8 and Abraham) is basically a case study on the possibility of the methodological convergence that he has outlined. The remaining chapters of Lona's study employ, respectively, the two methods of historical-critical exegesis and the 'semiotic' approach to Abraham's figuration in John 8, with the historical-critical approach 'checked' against the semiotic.[58] In fact, Lona's attention to the methodological divergence – and the possibilities of convergence – in the discipline is similar to the focus of this book. However, there are some areas where this study differs from Lona's: (1) I am not as optimistic about historical-critical exegesis and 'semiotics' functioning as good bedfellows in the field of biblical studies, and in fact my focus on Barthesian intertextuality leads me to conclude that the (poststructuralist) theories of 'intertextuality' are too facilely integrated 'in practice' (Lona) with historicist methods; (2) unlike Lona, I take the text as it is rather than attempting to find its core or to reconstruct its original/originating historical voice (cf. 'Death of the Author' in Chapter 2); (3) while concern with method grounds Lona's study, his exegesis of John 8 is annotative despite its length; (4) historical conclusions are tenuous and based on the literary analysis; and (5) Lona does not consider in any detail the *specific* issue of Jews and Judaism when interrogating the references to Abraham in John 8. Having said that, there are more fundamental issues with the publication of Lona's work that require consideration: Lona's 1976 work is out of print and very difficult to access (I had my copy shipped via interlibrary loan internationally), as well as being in German and untranslated into any other language.

---

[51] Ibid., p. 119.
[52] Lona also considers the 'semiotics' of F. Saussure, A. J. Greimas, Charles S. Pierce and, briefly, Julia Kristeva and Umberto Eco (*Abraham*, pp. 121-6) before evaluating what relevance semiotics has for biblical exegesis.
[53] Lona, *Abraham*, p. 125.
[54] Ibid., p. 126.
[55] Ibid., pp. 127-8. Though Lona does acknowledge that historical criticism and semiotics operate on the basis of different 'questions' posed to the literature: the former asks about the 'sense' of the text in light of social history, or the history of other literary forms, the latter probes the sense of the text on the basis of its structural significance (Lona, *Abraham*, pp. 128-9).
[56] Lona, *Abraham*, p. 129.
[57] Ibid., pp. 130-1.
[58] Ibid., p. 131.

Moreover, literary criticism (and NT scholars' engagement with it) continues to advance. What remains to be asked – at least in my mind – in this regard is what Lona would have argued had he engaged with poststructuralism and intertextuality. Thus, an update on the figure of Abraham in John 8 – especially regarding the anti-Judaism of the text and its commentaries – is urgently required.

The only other scholar who has written a monograph on Abraham in John 8 is Tineke de Lange. De Lange interprets the figure of Abraham in John 8 against the socio-historical context of the Johannine community, although he is well aware of the pitfalls of reading the putative social history of the Johannine community *into* the text of the Gospel.[59] De Lange understands the references to Abraham in John 8 to be a product of the 'conflict' between Johannine Christians and their 'Jewish environment' at the end of the first century CE. De Lange is therefore attuned to the specific significance of Abraham as he pertains to the Jews and Judaism in John 8.

De Lange observes that the depiction of Abraham in John 8 is varied; he questions whether this variety is a result of John's amalgamation of diverse sources or a product of John's creative use of Abraham traditions.[60] De Lange decides upon the latter case, that is that John consciously produced a diverse portrait of Abraham in ch. 8 vv. 31-59 through his indebtedness to a complex tapestry of traditions about Abraham, which de Lange refers to as the 'Abrahamology' of first-century Judaism and Christianity.[61] De Lange makes this determination on the basis of a structural analysis of John 8.31-59, which he finds to be seamless in the sense that it is not a random composite of sources, and on the basis of a comparative analysis of texts. Another issue that occupies de Lange is whether, through such analysis, one can classify parts of John's text as 'echoes' of existing Abraham traditions and other parts as 'essentially Johannine'. These literary questions tie into de Lange's larger historical objective, which is to determine whether the conflict between 'Judaism' and 'Christianity' in Palestine circa 90 CE developed in stages that can be mapped onto the junctures of the text of John 8.31-59.[62]

De Lange finds that the Johannine portrait of Abraham presented in John 8.31-59 relies upon the OT, specifically the Abraham cycle of Genesis, and certain interpretations of the Abraham cycle in early Jewish and early Christian literature. The Johannine innovation, as it were, lies in the fact that the author of the Gospel has turned what is a *positive* self-designation for early Jews (i.e. 'seed of Abraham') into a *negative* factor justifying the exclusion of 'the Jews' of John 8 from the Christological covenant. This innovation is confirmed in the concluding depiction of Abraham as a 'witness' to Jesus above everything else (cf. 8.56-58).[63] De Lange also suggests that

---

[59] De Lange, *Abraham*, p. 94.
[60] Ibid., p. 30. By this dichotomy, de Lange apparently means that either John had control over his composition of ch. 8 vv. 31-59 or he did not. That is, did John, using his own creative agency, intentionally weave together a varied portrait of Abraham in his text, or did later/other authorial and editorial hands mesh together a composite text referencing Abraham in a number of differing contexts?
[61] De Lange, *Abraham*, p. 30.
[62] Ibid., p. 30. My approach is similar, from a literary critical standpoint, although I refrain from drawing historical conclusions about the social conflicts between Jews and Christians at the close of the first century CE.
[63] De Lange, *Abraham*, p. 159.

while the image of Abraham as 'father' of the Jews was prominent in the ancient Jewish sources, the Gospel's distinction between being 'seed' of Abraham and being 'children' of Abraham has no ancient precedent.[64] De Lange concludes that John emphasized the superiority of being a 'child' of Abraham (cf. Lukan and Markan references to being a 'son' or 'daughter' of Abraham) over being the (collective) 'seed' of Abraham.[65] Furthermore, John relied upon traditions of Abraham as a morally upright and 'free' man circulating in early Jewish literature to present the self-conception of 'the Jews' as un-enslaved 'seed' of Abraham (cf. John 8.31-34).[66] While at first sight, the Johannine portrait of Abraham seems fragmentary, and dependent upon a host of unrelated themes present in first-century Abrahamology, de Lange concludes that John has made this amalgamation consistent via his Christology, rendering Abraham, like Moses, 'a focal point in the history of the covenant between God and his people'.[67]

De Lange agrees with the theory originally propounded by J. Louis Martyn that the Gospel of John narratively codes a debate between emerging Christianity and its 'parent' form of Judaism in the late decades of the first century CE (the so-called 'two-level drama' hypothesis).[68] Reflecting some relatively outdated modes of description, de Lange refers to the historical group represented by John's Jews as 'Pharisees', those figures of 'normative Judaism' at the time in which the Gospel was composed.[69] De Lange claims that the debate narrated in John 8.31-59 refers to a real, historical conflict between Johannine Christians and Jews who did not believe in Jesus; the conflict centred upon, and was produced by, a 'radical Christology' and certain other 'tensions' that evolved from the Johannine theology.[70] De Lange concedes the hypothetical nature of his assertions, shying away from stronger language of historical reconstructions of the community.[71] De Lange thus cautiously suggests that John 8.31-59 depicted an historical situation that was not, *pace* Martyn, about a radical choice between Moses/Torah or Jesus (as Christ), but about the choice for Jesus 'as the Son', as distinct from the choice to remain with the 'traditional' marker of Jewish self-definition found in descent from Abraham.[72] Both partners in the debate in John 8 – 'the Jews' and Jesus – represent the alterative self-definitions of the emerging communities of Jews and Christians at the close of the first century, but the views of the former have been subsumed under the weight of the latter.[73] So that, even though John's portrait of

---

[64] Ibid., p. 160.
[65] Ibid.
[66] Ibid., pp. 160–1.
[67] Ibid., p. 162.
[68] Ibid., p. 167. Cf. J. Louis Martyn, *History and Theology in the Fourth Gospel* (New York: Abingdon Press, 1979).
[69] De Lange, *Abraham*, p. 185. The language of 'normativity' with respect to Second Temple Judaism is now generally avoided in the scholarship, and the designation of John's 'Jews' (or any historical real Jews depicted in the Christian literature as Jesus' opponents) as indisputably 'Pharisaic' is also problematic. Still, de Lange observes that the Jews in John 'are principally schematic actors on a theological scene in whom it is difficult to see real life opponents' (ibid., p. 185). If so, then what is de Lange's rationale for assuming an historical conflict behind the representative characters in the text?
[70] De Lange, *Abraham*, p. 192.
[71] Ibid., p. 197; cf. p. 94.
[72] Ibid., p. 197.
[73] Cf. ibid., pp. 202–3.

Abraham can be said to be very 'Jewish' in that it faithfully depicts understandings of the patriarch from early Jewish texts and traditions, the picture of Abraham in John 8 ultimately reflects concerns dear to the Johannine community.[74] To this end, John 8 does not 'echo' first-century Jewish concerns in an unbiased or unfiltered way.[75]

De Lange concludes that John 8 is of limited historical reliability as indicative of first-century conflict between Jews and Christians. While John relied upon traditions present in the 'Abrahamology' of his day and did not alter their original significance, he *did* change their meaning by inserting them into a radically different context in which everything (including Abraham and the first covenant he embodied) is subservient to an understanding of Jesus as Christ.[76] Abraham effectively becomes a 'witness' to Jesus, and a father to those who believe in Jesus. De Lange claims that the context and tone of John 8.31-47 in particular, make it clear that John's intention is to exclude those Jews who refuse to view Jesus (and Abraham) in this way. The text thus produces 'insiders' and 'outsiders' according to the Johannine theology. That 'the Jews who had believed [in Jesus]' in ch. 8 v. 31 continue to be referred to simply as 'the Jews' from ch. 8 v. 32 onward, indicates to de Lange that this character group has now definitively moved from 'insider' to 'outsider' status.[77]

In sum, the two existing monographs on Abraham in John 8 have, when taken together, a combination of strengths and limitations. The extraordinary length and depth of Lona's monograph (over 500 pages) appears to compensate for the brevity of de Lange's slim dissertation. Lona's extensive focus on methodological issues balances de Lange's focus on socio-historical issues. Side by side, these two monographs provide a fulsome picture of Abraham's function in John 8.31-59 from composite scholarly positions. And yet, when taken together, both works reveal certain limitations in the study of Abraham in John's Gospel. De Lange's short monograph is a revision of his doctoral dissertation, written in the year 2000 (although the book itself was published in 2008), containing very few secondary references beyond that year. Thus, significant time has elapsed since the question of Abraham in John 8 was closely and comprehensively examined. Newer methodologies, specifically current literary critical ones, must be incorporated into the question of Abraham's reference in John's Gospel. That is one of the gaps that this study attempts to fill.

A significant portion of de Lange's monograph explores the ancient Abraham traditions of Second Temple Judaism and emerging rabbinic Judaism against the text of John 8 (and this is performed in a thematic fashion similar to this current study); however, de Lange's comparative examinations of these texts are brief, whereas this study attempts to explore the comparative intertexts in considerable depth, looking at the widest possible contextual resonances for understanding Abraham in John 8. Thus, for example, one of de Lange's thematic points of analysis is the concept of the 'seed of Abraham', but his approach to this theme in the entire pseudepigraphical corpus covers only a page and a half of his monograph.[78] One of the unique aspects

---

[74] Ibid.
[75] Cf. ibid.
[76] Ibid., p. 209.
[77] Ibid., p. 212.
[78] Ibid., pp. 98–100.

of this current study is the method of analysis involving the collocation of multiple thematic concepts in the sources that are also combined in John 8 with respect to Abraham (e.g. 'seed', 'slavery' and 'sin'). It is how these concepts interrelate within various narrative contexts that is the important point to consider when reading Abraham 'intertextually'. This approach also avoids an annotative, excerpt-based reading of John 8 against the Jewish and Christian Abraham traditions. My approach of 'scripting' the wide, thematic and narrative-based intertextual field to the Abraham references in John 8, from my social location as a Jewish reader of the text, is outlined in the next chapter.[79]

Another area of difference between de Lange's work and this current study is in the degree of attention to the concept of 'sin' in John 8.32-34. De Lange focuses more attention on select concepts predicated of Abraham in John 8 such as 'seed', 'slavery', 'fatherhood' and 'children', but does not consider how the reference to 'sin' in ch. 8 v. 34 relates to these. This is understandable, inasmuch as it is not 'the Jews' who raise the idea of 'sin' in relation to Abraham (cf. 8.32-33), but in fact, Jesus who raises it in connection with the idea of slavery and freedom (8.34).[80] However, in the dialogue that ensues (8.35-58), the Jews appear to understand, and respond to, Jesus' understanding of 'sin'. One of the key contributions of this study is, therefore, sustained attention to the thematics of sin in relation to Abraham, both in the texts of early Judaism and within early Christianity. I argue that the metaphor of sin as 'debt', present in the key intertexts I adduce plays a vital role in understanding the Jews' references to freedom from slavery and what it means to be Abraham's 'seed' in John 8.31-36.

Shorter studies on Abraham in John 8

Apart from the two monographs already discussed, numerous shorter studies on Abraham's figuration in John 8 merit attention. Because of the diversity and range of these studies, I analyse them here not by formal type (e.g. book, chapter and article), but according to the trends in research that they represent, that is, according to the questions they ask about Abraham in John 8, and the methods they use to answer those questions. These categories are not hermetic and do permit some overlap, but their heuristic convenience governs their deployment in this analysis.

Shorter studies: Abraham in the narrative and communal worlds of John 8

Some relatively recent approaches to the figuration of Abraham in John 8 have come from narrative-critical and sociological perspectives. Scholars adopting these approaches interpret the figure of Abraham in John 8 in the immediate literary context of the Gospel itself, or the constructed narrative world of the Johannine community.

---

[79] See Chapter 2 for more detail.
[80] And in fact, according to some manuscripts, this additional verse (8.34) is not attested.

One insightful example of the narrative-critical approach comes from Paul Miller, in an essay on John's use of OT figures.[81] Miller argues that John's Gospel is distinctive in the way it presents Scripture relating to Christ.[82] In this regard, Miller focuses on three Gospel texts presenting key OT figures: Moses in John 5.46, Abraham in ch. 8 v. 56 and Isaiah in ch. 12 v. 41. All three figures, Miller claims, are connected via their knowledge of Jesus' coming. Moses is said to have had foresight of Jesus' coming; Abraham is said to have 'seen' Jesus' 'day'; and Isaiah is said to have 'seen' Jesus' 'glory'. Miller observes that in each text certain revelatory verbs are prevalent (e.g. 'seeing', 'speaking/writing'). He notices a 'dynamic interaction of seeing and testifying, of vision and witness'.[83] For John, therefore, Scripture is not the 'direct self-disclosure of the Father, but testimony to the Son whom the Father has made known'.[84] Miller finds that John's distinctive scriptural hermeneutic can be defined as the 'enduring record of those who saw the activity of the divine Logos prior to its appearance in Jesus and then testified to what they had seen'.[85]

To support his claim, Miller argues that *vision* is the pre-eminent 'epistemological and theological category' in the Gospel of John.[86] Miller follows G. L. Phillips (1957) in positing a hierarchy of verbs for different levels of 'seeing' in the Gospel, starting with βλέπω which, he claims, connotes mere 'oracular vision' (1.29; 5.19; 9.7, 15, 19, 21, 25, 39, 41; 11.9; 13.22; 20.1, 5; 21.9, 20); then θεωρέω, which refers to thoughtful, but not deep, contemplation (2.23; 4.19; 6.2, 19, 40, 62; 7.3; 8.51; 9.8; 10.12; 12.19, 45; 14.17, 19; 16.10, 16, 17, 19; 17.24; 20.6, 12, 14); and, ultimately, ὁράω, which is a kind of supreme vision that merges with 'belief' (cf. 1.18, 34, 39, 50, 51; 3.11, 32, 36; 4.45; 5.37; 6.36, 46; 8.38, 57; 9.37; 11.40; 14.7, 9; 15.24; 16.16, 17, 19, 22; 19.35, 37; 20.18, 25, 29).[87] Miller uses this hierarchical schema to validate his position that in John's Gospel, Scripture is something that 'originates with those who have "seen" the Logos'. Thus, Moses, Abraham and Isaiah could only have 'seen' Jesus by faith. For John's Gospel, Scripture preserves the 'record of those who have seen the Logos' and borne testimony to that fact.[88] John presents Abraham as one who 'saw the future salvation in Christ'.[89] Abraham's 'faith' in God enabled him to receive visions by which he perceived that in 'perfect obedience', Jesus would glorify God.[90]

Miller's study uniquely recognizes the affinity between Abraham's vision of Jesus' 'day' in ch. 8 v. 56 and Isaiah's vision of Jesus' 'glory' in ch. 12 v. 41. As such, it opens up

---

[81] Paul Miller, '"They Saw His Glory and Spoke of Him": The Gospel of John and the Old Testament', in Stanley E. Porter (ed.), *Hearing the Old Testament in the New Testament* (Grand Rapids: Eerdmans, 2006), 127–51.
[82] Miller, 'They Saw His Glory', p. 133.
[83] Ibid., p. 134.
[84] Ibid.
[85] Ibid.
[86] Ibid.
[87] Ibid., pp. 135–6; cf. G. L. Phillips, 'Faith and Vision in the Fourth Gospel', in F. L. Cross (ed.), *Studies in the Fourth Gospel* (London: Mowbray, 1957), p. 83.
[88] Miller, 'They Saw His Glory', p. 137.
[89] Ibid., p. 141.
[90] Ibid., p. 142, n. 50. Miller adduces certain texts in the 'Jewish tradition' that show Abraham receiving visions of God's future promises being fulfilled (e.g. *Gen. Rab.* 44.22, 28; *4 Ezra* 3.14; *T. Levi* 18.14; *2 Baruch* 4.4; *Apoc. Abr.* 31.1-3).

the fruitful possibility of further synchronic studies on the figure of Abraham in John 8, against the literary texture of the Gospel itself. However, there are some shortcomings with Miller's overall schematic argument. The most obvious is that while 'Scripture' is explicitly spoken of in ch. 5 v. 46 and even *cited* in ch. 12 v. 41, it is not mentioned with respect to Abraham in ch. 8 v. 56. The differences between the three texts are sometimes obscured in view of Miller's larger thesis about how John conceives of Scripture; for example, Isaiah 'sees' and testifies (12.41), while Moses 'testifies' but does not at all 'see' (5.46); Abraham 'sees' but does not testify (8.56). The category of vision does not unite these three texts as neatly as Miller supposes. One could also question Miller's use of a taxonomy of 'vision' verbs in John's Gospel. For example, ὁράω does not always imply 'belief' – as illustrated in texts such as ch. 6 v. 36 and ch. 15 v. 24. One could actually claim that belief *without* seeing is the pre-eminent theological category in the Gospel, at least by its conclusion (cf. 20.29).

A recent sociological approach to the role of Abraham in John 8 has been adopted by Catrin Williams who examines the Gospel against narrative and cultural configurations of memory in the first century.[91] Williams identifies the features of John 8.31-59 that were possibly 'designed for oral delivery' in order to determine the influence of oral techniques on the text's presentation of Abraham, and how this presentation might have shaped the original readers' self-understanding as a group.[92] Williams argues that John 8.31-59 reveals a 'distinctively Johannine collective memory of the patriarch' by drawing on and modifying selected traditions about Abraham – a 'key strategy' for the Johannine community's social demarcation. In short, Williams asks, 'How is Abraham remembered, and what do we learn about those who remember him?'[93] Williams contends that theories based on the role of memory in oral composition provide a suitable lens through which to read the figure of Abraham in the three component parts of John 8.31-59 that she identifies (vv. 31-36; 37-47; 48-59).[94]

One such theory of collective memory, developed by Walter Ong, works on the premise of 'residual orality': that is, certain ancient written texts, designed for the purpose of oral communication, bear traces of their original oral/aural communicative design.[95] Ancient 'oral media' is characterized by vivid, 'agonistic' dialogues or 'visually concrete happenings' in the narrative, or by the frequent use of present tense verbs and the repetition of key words. The canonical Gospels deploy the rhetorical trope of *inclusio*, as well as patterns of repetition that may also indicate oral design.[96] These features show how the text is a product of memory-based oral composition and is designed for aural reception.[97] These assumptions form the basis of William's

---

[91] Catrin Williams, 'First-Century Media Culture and Abraham as a Figure of Memory in John 8.31-59', in Tom Thatcher and Anthony le Donne (eds), *The Fourth Gospel in First-Century Media Culture* (London: T&T Clark, 2011), pp. 205–22.
[92] Ibid., p. 205.
[93] Ibid.
[94] Ibid., p. 206. For my division of the text of ch. 8 vv. 31-59, see Chapter 3.
[95] See Walter Ong, *Orality and Literacy: The Technologizing of the World* (London/New York: Methuen, 1982), p. 43; cited in Williams, 'First-Century Media Culture', p. 206.
[96] Williams, 'First-Century Media Culture', p. 207.
[97] Cf. ibid., p. 206.

18 The Figure of Abraham in John 8

engagement with John 8.31-59, which, she claims, does in fact exhibit a number of the oral/aural features, most notably, repetition. The repetition of themes in John 8, and particularly of the name of Abraham in ch. 8 vv. 31-59 (8.33, 37, 39 (×3), 40, 52, 53, 56, 57, 58), the vitriolic tone of the debate, as well as the text's persuasive appeals to its audience to take sides in the debate, are all mnemonic cues that suggest the Gospel was 'composed for a listening rather than a reading audience'.[98]

Drawing on the work of sociologist Maurice Halbwachs, Williams claims that the Johannine community constituted a social group that was practised in the art of memorialization; their collective memory was malleable and selective, inextricably forming their group identity. Social groups collectively create the memory of a 'shared past' which unites them in the present.[99] Williams also uses the work of Egyptologist Jan Assmann, who famously adapted Halbwach's theory to distinguish between 'communicative memory' and 'cultural memory' – stating that the former is a type of 'everyday', present interaction, whereas the latter is focused on distinct events of the past.[100] 'Cultural' (or 'social') memory 'preserves and communicates a store of knowledge that forms the basis of the group's sense of duration and uniqueness' and relates that knowledge to contemporary situations.[101] Assmann applied these insights to his cultural-historical investigation of Moses as a figure of memory in ancient Egyptian texts, in order to understand the various ways in which Moses was 'remembered' under the pressure of different socio-historical exigencies. Williams finds Assmann's aforesaid investigation particularly relevant for her assessment of Abraham as a 'figure of memory' in John 8.

With this theoretical groundwork laid, Williams then examines the use of Abraham traditions within John 8.31-59. The first subsection (vv. 31-36) centres on the claim of 'the Jews' in v. 32 to be descendants of Abraham – what Williams refers to as the 'living memory' associated with their 'ethnic identity'.[102] The Jews' self-designation as σπέρμα Ἀβραάμ identifies them as 'children of Israel' and identifies Abraham as Israel's great ancestor.[103] The Jews link their descent from Abraham with their claim to have never been enslaved (v. 32). Williams considers the Jews' claim to be in line with the processes of selective commemoration in social groups – that is, that groups will remember one feature (e.g. 'freedom') and project it onto a past 'figure of memory' ('Abraham') in order to serve their own identity configuration. This way of relating to the past 'excludes change' and produces a durable image consistent over time: 'we have *never* been slaves to *anyone*'.[104] In the second subsection (vv. 37-47), Jesus tells the Jews that if they would claim Abraham as their father, they must do as Abraham did (vv. 39, 40). Williams notes the widespread attestation of Abraham as an exemplary figure in early Judaism and Christianity, and then states that the focus in this second subsection is upon 'how retrieving the past should shape present actions, rather than on how

---

[98] Ibid., pp. 208–9.
[99] Ibid., p. 210.
[100] Ibid., p. 211.
[101] Ibid.
[102] Ibid., p. 213.
[103] Ibid. Williams cites Isa. 41.8; Ps. 105.6; *3 Macc.* 6.3; *Pss. Sol.* 9.9; and other NT texts for background.
[104] Williams, 'First-Century Media Culture', p. 213.

present realities can transform the memory of the past'.[105] Williams claims that the phrase τὰ ἔργα τοῦ Ἀβραάμ in ch. 8 v. 39, for which Williams finds 'no precise parallel', is 'a form of metonymic referencing' typical of oral compositions, to recall for listeners a whole network of attributions relating to Abraham's 'works'.[106]

Throughout the first two subsections of John 8.31-59 as Williams reads them (cf. 8.31-36; 37-47), there is a contestation between Jesus and the Jews over paternity and descent, which really touches on the deeper issues of communal belonging and human relation to the divine. The Jews implicitly claim that 'descent from Abraham is synonymous with descent from God' – a claim Jesus rejects on the basis that *only he* is sent from God; to descend from God, in the Gospel's logic, is to accept Jesus' word, which the Jews do not do.[107] Williams likens this to the sociological theory of memorializing group 'origins', that is how social groups locate their beginning in a common ancestry or event in order to solidify their identity in the present.[108] In John's Gospel, group 'origins' can be located on either the 'temporal' plane or the 'horizontal' plane.[109] Williams argues that the Jews' assertion that Abraham is their common ancestor (8.31-47) locates them on the former, temporal plane. The alternative is to be 'of God' (8.47), like Jesus, which comes about through belief in Jesus (cf. 1.12-13), and locates a person on the latter horizontal plane. This alternative 'Johannine memory of origins' solidifies the Gospel audience as a group collectively descended from God if they ascribe to its message.[110]

According to Williams, the memory function of Abraham becomes more marked towards the third subsection of the dialogue (vv. 48-59). In this section, the dispute becomes more hostile, but Jesus again promises his opponents deliverance (this time, from 'death') if they keep his word (8.51). This prompts the re-entry of Abraham into the discussion: '*even* Abraham died', so who does Jesus claim to be? (8.53).[111] Jesus eventually claims that Abraham rejoiced to see his day and adds, 'before Abraham was, I am' (8.58). For Williams, this would have alerted the Gospel audience to how Abraham ought to be remembered, namely, from a 'wealth of Jewish tradition' that associates the patriarch with joy and rejoicing, as well as another body of texts associating Abraham with having had visionary experiences under the influence of God.[112] These traditions are reconfigured in John 8.56-58 to memorialize Abraham as one who 'saw Jesus' day'. The fusion of two disparate traditions attests to the 'mosaic-like character of memory' according to collective memory studies.[113] Abraham is

---

[105] Ibid., p. 215.
[106] Ibid.
[107] Ibid., p. 216.
[108] Ibid.
[109] Ibid., pp. 216–17.
[110] Ibid., p. 217.
[111] Ibid., pp. 218–19.
[112] On Abraham rejoicing, Williams cites Gen. 17.17; *Jub.* 14.21; 15.17; 16.17-19; 17.25-7; *Apoc. Ab.* 10.15; Philo, *Mut.* 154-69. She rightly adds that none of these traditions associates Abraham's 'joy' with his 'seeing', as paired in John 8.56-58. On Abraham's visions, Williams cites Gen. 15.1, 12, 17; *4 Ezra* 3.14; *Apoc. Ab.* 24.2; 9.10; 29.2; 31.1-2; *Gen. R* 44.21, 22. Williams, 'First-Century Media Culture', p. 219.
[113] Williams, 'First-Century Media Culture', p. 220.

remembered as one who rejoiced in Jesus; that is, Abraham had an eschatological vision of the coming 'day' (i.e. 'mission') of Jesus, the Son, and rejoiced over it.[114] Williams concludes that in John 8.31-59, Abraham functions like other 'witnesses' in the Gospel to 'testify' to Jesus, based on the divine disclosure he received.[115] Abraham's joy at seeing Jesus' day thus constitutes part of the 'works of Abraham' (8.39, cf. 40) that the Jews should be emulating – they ought to rejoice at seeing Jesus before them, and so also become witnesses.[116]

Williams' essay is impressive for its reading of John 8.31-59 against theoretical work in the field of social memory studies. Yet, Williams' essay could have been enhanced by a clarification of the relationship between the ancient Jewish textual traditions she identifies and the communal processes of reflection that embodied them in John's text. Were these sources used (in the sense of literary dependency or oral transmission) in the composition of the text, or were they evoked for hearers as the text was performed? If they were performatively evoked, could we assume they were also *used by* the author(s)? In other words, what processes of intertextuality control or cohere with social memory studies when considering the sources of collective memory? Finally, the singular activity of Abraham 'rejoicing' over Jesus' earthly mission (cf. 8.56) does not correspond to the plural form of τὰ ἔργα τοῦ Ἀβραάμ (but it might be reflected in the aorist ἐποιεῖτε in ch. 8 v. 39); thus Abraham's 'rejoicing' is not likely to be equivalent to the 'works' of Abraham.

Shorter studies: Abraham and intertextuality

Another major trend of scholarly analysis explores the intertexts at work in John 8.31-59. The invocation of Abraham automatically calls up for the reader a host of possible texts from the HB relating to Abraham. The first readers of the Gospel would have been additionally attuned to a wider scope of 'Abraham traditions' extraneous to the developing canon of Scripture. These texts and traditions have come down to us in the Targums, the Apocrypha and Pseudepigrapha, the DSS and some writings that postdate the NT, but which codify oral traditions reaching back to before the time of Jesus, such as the Tannaitic rabbinic sources. Scholars concerned with 'intertextuality' in John 8 will pinpoint a text or tradition against which the references to Abraham would make sense. As mentioned at the beginning of this chapter, there are eleven references to Abraham in John 8.31-59 (8.33, 37, 39 (×3), 40, 52, 53, 56, 57, 58). All of these references constitute unmarked allusions – not explicit citations from an identifiable or a stated source – and therefore, scholars have come up with multiple answers to the question of the intertextual background to John's use of Abraham. In other words, the allusive quality of the Abrahamic references in John 8 leaves the scholar with a certain amount of guesswork to do. For the purpose of illustration, we can see that there are about seven qualities or predicates associated with Abraham in ch. 8 vv. 31-59:

---
[114] Ibid.
[115] Ibid.; cf. p. 222.
[116] Ibid., p. 221.

Reference and connotations	Point in text – speaker and audience
'Seed of Abraham'	Claimed by the Jews (8.33, 56) and ceded by Jesus (8.36)
'Our father Abraham'	Claimed by the Jews (8.39a) and ceded by Jesus (8.56)
'Children of Abraham'	Spoken by Jesus to the Jews (8.39b)
'The works of Abraham'	Spoken by Jesus to the Jews (8.39b, cf. v. 40)
'Abraham died ... are you greater than Abraham?'	The Jews' query to Jesus (8.53)
'Abraham "saw" and "rejoiced"'	Jesus' statement to the Jews (8.56)/'Have you seen Abraham?': The Jews' counter-question to Jesus (8.57)
'Before Abraham was, I am'	Jesus' final statement to the Jews (8.58)

These predicates fall into three categories: the relational, the actual and the unforeseen. The first category presupposes a form of relationship with the figure of Abraham: one can belong to Abraham as his 'seed', his 'children' or, alternately, Abraham can be one's 'father'. The second category depends on the qualities Abraham himself possessed, or the actions he performed (his 'works', his 'death', his 'greatness', his 'seeing' and his 'rejoicing'). The third category refers to a feature unknown to the inherited Abraham traditions, added by Jesus himself, which goes beyond what might be expected from the discourse thus far. It is Jesus' 'final say' in the debate, a claim of pre-existence relative to Abraham, which duly reduces the significance of the relational and the actual categories in that same discursive space. Depending on the scholar, any one of these predicates in any of the three categories (as I have defined them) can serve as an entry point for finding an intertext to explain the references to Abraham in the passage as a whole. Perhaps, however, because of the climactic nature of the unforeseen statement in ch. 8 v. 58, the majority of scholars have commonly started with the tail end of the discourse when seeking such intertextual points of reference.

In the next section, I review key studies that have focused specifically on the 'intertextual' background to three thematic components of Abraham's figuration in John 8.31-59. These components centre on the concept of the 'seed of Abraham' (8.31-36), the notion of the 'works of Abraham' (8.37-42) and the references to Abraham 'seeing' and 'rejoicing' in Jesus' 'day' (8.56-58). These three references have the strongest representation in the secondary scholarship.

Focused studies: The 'seed of Abraham' in John 8.31-34

In John 8.31-36, the quasi-technical phrase 'seed of Abraham' (8.32), the notion of 'sin' (8.34) and the metaphor of slavery, are all used in the context of a debate between Jesus and the Jews. These complex themes are intertwined. Jesus offers 'the Jews' freedom, via the truth of his word (8.32), which they question on the basis that they are 'seed of Abraham' and have never been enslaved to anyone (8.33). Jesus replies that slavery to sin constitutes slavery as such (8.34); he then delivers a brief parable on the difference between the 'slave' and the 'son' in a 'household' – the son has a permanent inheritance, whereas the slave does not, and *the* son (i.e. Jesus) is the true liberator (8.36: οὖν ὁ υἱὸς ὑμᾶς ἐλευθερώσῃ). A number of studies examine these concepts but often without probing the coherent intellectual, and intertextual, thought-world underlying them. In any case, three major essays were written on John 8.32-34 between 1968 and 1984.[117] Two of these studies adopt either a *Sitz-im-Leben* or source-critical approach to John 8.31-34, looking mainly at comparative texts within the early Christian traditions. One additional study on John 8.31-34, written in 2001 from a decidedly post-historical-critical perspective, is also considered for the new directions in which it takes the discussion.[118]

The essay written by C. H. Dodd (1968) explores the extent to which John 8.31-58 relates to texts and concepts within the early Christian tradition; relatedly, he posits a *Sitz-im-Leben* for the passage. Dodd situates his study within the wider scholarly endeavour to determine the historical reliability of John's Gospel.[119] He begins by noting an apparent incongruity in John 8.30-31, namely, that Jesus debates with Jews who are described as 'having believed' in him (8.31: πεπιστευκότας αὐτῷ Ἰουδαίους), but who then turn out to be his definite enemies (8.33-47).[120] There is also the issue of the 'many' who are said to have listened to Jesus and so believed in him (8.30: πολλοὶ ἐπίστευσαν εἰς αὐτόν) just prior to the mention of the Jews in ch. 8 v. 31; Dodd understands the audiences in v. 30 and v. 31 as identical.[121]

Dodd's evidence comes from the similar use of the perfect participle of πιστεύω in Acts 21.20 and 25.45; in those texts the subjects of the verb are Jewish converts to the nascent Jesus movement (so-called 'Jewish Christians').[122] Other texts in the book of Acts (e.g. 11.2; 15.5) mention these 'Jewish Christians' in ways that emphasize what Dodd calls their 'Jewish national standpoint', by which he means their faithful adherence to the Torah and *kashrut* (or more specifically, rules of restricted 'table-fellowship', of not eating with Gentiles). In the book of Acts, this group of converts clashes with the apostle Peter, and are spoken of pejoratively by James. Dodd reads Paul's letter to the Galatians in a similar light; he views the group whom Paul calls ἐκ περιτομῆς (Gal. 2.12) as responsible for provoking controversy over Torah observance in the community. These too, according to Dodd, were actual Jewish converts wanting to preserve elements of Judaism among their fellow Gentile believers in Jesus.[123]

---

[117] C. H. Dodd, 'Behind a Johannine Dialogue', in *More New Testament Studies* (Manchester: Manchester University Press, 1968), pp. 41–57; Barnabas Lindars, 'Discourse and Tradition: The Use of the Sayings of Jesus in the Discourses of the Fourth Gospel', *JSNT* 13 (1981), pp. 89–97; cf. idem., 'Slave and Son in John 8.31-36', in W. C. Weinrich (ed.), *The New Testament Age: Essays in Honor of Bo Reicke* (Macon: Mercer University Press, 1984), pp. 270–86; T. B. Dozemann, '*Sperma Abraam* in John 8 and Related Literature: Cosmology and Judgment', *CBQ* 42 (1980), pp. 342–58.
[118] Adele Reinhartz, 'John 8.31-59 from a Jewish Perspective', in John K. Roth and Elisabeth Maxwell (eds), *Remembering for the Future: The Holocaust in an Age of Genocide*, vol. 2: *Ethics and Religion* (Palgrave: Macmillan, 2001), pp. 787–97.
[119] Dodd, 'Behind a Johannine Dialogue', p. 41.
[120] Ibid., p. 42; I attend to this whole issue in greater depth in Chapter 3.
[121] Dodd, 'Behind a Johannine Dialogue', p. 42.
[122] Ibid., p. 43.
[123] Ibid., p. 44.

Dodd writes,

> 'if therefore we enquire for the "*Sitz-im-Leben*", or historical situation within which this (John 8.30-37) dialogue may have taken form, a reasonable hypothesis would be that it goes back to the struggle waged throughout the latter half of the first century in defence of the supra-national character of the Church against those who sought to maintain within it the traditional privilege of the Jew'.[124]

To test this assumption, Dodd explores three thematic parallels between John 8.30-37 and Paul's letter to the Galatians as follows: (i) liberty and servitude; (ii) descent from Abraham; and (iii) sonship to God. Dodd finds it significant that both John and Paul contrast the metaphorical figures of 'son' and 'slave' (cf. Gal. 4.3-7; John 8.35). He suggests that in both authors 'we are overhearing different phases of the same controversy'.[125] Dodd *does* concede that there are critical differences between Galatians and John 8 – for example, John 8.30-37 is not concerned with circumcision and adherence to the Mosaic Law. Dodd thinks that these were not major issues in John's circle, as they were in Paul's; but both Paul and John characterize the view of their 'Judaizers' as follows: 'liberty is the inherent prerogative of the descendants of Abraham'.[126] For Dodd, Paul's Judaizers present this view by stating that the law itself enslaves, but John's Judaizers take a different line. Dodd perceives 'two established axioms of popular Hellenistic philosophy' behind John 8.32: (i) that wisdom/knowledge of truth alone makes one free; and (ii) that the sinner is a slave.[127] For Dodd, the Johannine text develops these axioms to argue that the Jews are not free, since they do not know Jesus, and hence do not know the truth; their 'moral obliquity' towards Jesus (their 'sin') indicates their slavery.[128]

According to Dodd, the context for the dispute between Jesus and the Jews in chapter 8 of the Gospel is 'remote from Paul's rabbinism'.[129] Whereas Paul is concerned that Christians, who like Christ are Abraham's 'seed' (Gal. 3.16-17), reproduce Abraham's faith, John is concerned that the Jews – who call themselves 'seed of Abraham' – reproduce Abraham's 'works' (8.39).[130] The Jews of John 8.30-59 must exhibit a moral likeness to the patriarch, beyond claiming to be physically descended from him.[131] John also deals with the issue of 'sonship' in ch. 8 vv. 34-36 differently than Paul, not along the lines of 'adoption' by faith, but in terms of presenting Jesus as *the* Son who is capable

---

[124] Ibid., p. 47.
[125] Ibid.
[126] Ibid., p. 48.
[127] Ibid., n. 3. To the first axiom, Dodd attributes 'a Stoic commonplace', without specifying a source. To the second axiom, Dodd cites Epictetus, *Diss.* II. 1.23, adding that this idea too is 'another Stoic commonplace' (p. 49, n. 2). In both of these footnotes, Dodd qualifies his comparisons by stating that 'it goes without saying that' John's notion of 'liberty' is not the same as the Stoic notion of liberty, and that John's understanding of 'doing sin' is not the same as Epictetus' concept of 'sin'. Yet, if this goes without saying, it is worth asking why Dodd prefers the Hellenistic metaphors and axioms to the better correspondences in Semitic sources.
[128] Dodd, 'Behind a Johannine Dialogue', p. 49.
[129] Ibid. My analysis in Chapters 3 through 6 contests the assumption behind this idea, viz., that John's presentation of Abraham is more Hellenistic than 'rabbinic'.
[130] Dodd, 'Behind a Johannine Dialogue', p. 49.
[131] Ibid., p. 50, cf. p. 56.

of liberating others.[132] Abraham's fatherhood is also more prominent in John than in Paul. These differences between Galatians and John 8.30-59 suggest to Dodd that other texts from the early Christian tradition that represent the figure of Abraham need to be brought into dialogue with John's presentation.[133] For example, the sayings of John the Baptist in the Synoptic Gospels about the Pharisees' presumption of having Abraham as their 'father' is pertinent (ἐν ἑαυτοῖς·πατέρα ἔχομεν τὸν Ἀβραάμ: cf. Luke 3.8). Dodd understands these sayings to mean that Abrahamic descent pales in comparison to doing what is right (producing 'fruit for repentance'). Dodd finds this to be an apt parallel to John 8.39-40.[134] He further compares Jesus' sayings on those chosen to 'sit down with Abraham' in the eschatological kingdom (Matt. 8.11-12), and the parable of Lazarus and 'Dives' in Luke (16.74-75).[135] Dodd concludes that John's Abraham tradition related to the 'Judaizing' controversy in the early church (such as at Galatia), but that John instead phrased his ideas out of the remnants of the 'earliest strata of the gospel tradition' – specifically from the Synoptic material about 'true' Abrahamic paternity. John thus 'bypasses' Paul's theological agenda, reaching back to the 'primitive testimony' instead.[136]

One can critique Dodd's essay on several grounds. First, Dodd assumes that John depends on the Synoptic tradition. While he does not frame this notion in the language of direct literary dependency, Dodd nevertheless assumes that John's Gospel developed, in some respects, out of the Synoptic tradition. In the 1960s, this assumption was generally held in Johannine scholarship, but today is not widely accepted.[137] Second, there are some contradictions in Dodd's argument. The 'Semitic' flavour of some of the Synoptic sayings about Abraham has been noted in the scholarship, and Dodd himself adduces a *baraitha* as an appropriate background against which to read Matt. 23.9, which he claims might have fed into John 8.31-37. But at the same time, Dodd claims that John 8.31-37 has 'more affinity to Hellenistic models' than to 'rabbinic' thought.[138] This binary requires some more testing and teasing out. Third, the putative Hellenistic background of John 8.32, and the lack of analogy to rabbinic texts in the passage, are overstated. Dodd's posited parallels to Stoicism are not fully explained; while Jesus' assertions about truth and freedom might be considered 'Stoic commonplaces', Dodd adds the qualification that Stoic notions of liberty necessarily differ from John's own. Fourth, Dodd's initial postulate that John 8.30-31 refers to 'Jewish Christians' (or 'Judaizing Christians') is open to question. If John's Jewish converts in ch. 8 v. 31 are historically the same as those in Acts or Galatians, but the discourse of ch. 8 vv. 31-37 is connected more organically with Synoptic disputes with the 'Pharisees' (e.g. the John the Baptist sayings), what does this mean for John's *Sitz-im-Leben*?

---

[132] Ibid., pp. 50–1.
[133] Ibid., p. 52.
[134] Ibid., p. 54.
[135] Ibid., p. 55.
[136] Ibid., pp. 56–7.
[137] Cf. D. Moody Smith, *John among the Gospels* (2nd edn; Columbia: University of South Carolina Press, 2015). However, small shifts back to viewing John as a purposeful redaction of prior Synoptic traditions are appearing: for example Harold W. Attridge, 'Genre', in Douglas Estes and Ruth Sheridan (eds), *How John Works: Storytelling in the Fourth Gospel* (RBS 86; Atlanta: SBL Press, 2016), pp. 7–22.
[138] Dodd, 'Behind a Johannine Dialogue', p. 41.

The second essay to be considered is one written by Thomas Dozeman (1980), titled 'Sperma Abraam in John 8 and Related Literature'. While the title of Dozeman's essay indicates his comparative-critical approach to John 8, Dozeman is also guided by the 'two-level drama' hypothesis of J. Louis Martyn, that is that John's Gospel tells the story of Jesus while also embedding the tale of the Johannine community, the later recipients (and perhaps authors) of the Gospel's tradition towards the end of the first century CE. Players in the historical drama affecting the Johannine community are encoded into the Gospel story of Jesus and his disciples.[139] Dozeman argues that the term σπέρμα Ἀβραάμ in ch. 8 v. 33 'is a technical term ... representing Christian Jews who advocate a law-observing mission'.[140] Dozeman therefore dismisses the reference to believing Jews (τοὺς πεπιστευκότας: 8.31) as a possible editorial mistake.[141] The Johannine community, represented, according to Dozeman, by Jesus' close disciples, 'advocate a Christology which demands freedom' – that is freedom from the Law.[142]

To support his position, Dozeman examines Paul's letter to the Galatians and Justin Martyr's *Dialogue with Trypho*, since he considers that both of these texts exhibit 'parallel controversies' to that represented in John 8.31-59.[143] Another key aspect of Dozeman's argument is that certain apologetic texts from the Second Temple Period presented Abraham as the first believer in monotheism, who was destined to have a role in propagating this belief to the Gentiles as part of his command by God to be a 'blessing to the nations' (cf. Gen. 12.3; Dozeman also cites Eusebius' *Praep. Ev.* 9.17, 102; Josephus' *Ant.* 1.7, 1 §155; and Philo's *Virt.* 39 §217-19, to this effect).[144] In Dozeman's view, the Jews of John 8.32, self-styled as the 'seed of Abraham', see themselves continuing this Abrahamic mission to give the Law to the Gentiles.

Dozeman pays particular attention to Galatians 3 because the term σπέρμα Ἀβραάμ occurs there in connection with the concepts of slavery, law and freedom (cf. 3.9; also Rom. 4; 9.6).[145] The consensus view in the 1970s and 1980s was that a Jewish–Christian dispute could be reconstructed from Galatians, and that Paul was refuting the encroaching law-observant mission of his opponents, who wanted all believers in Christ to be circumcised. This is a view that Dozeman reproduces, stating that Paul's opponents wanted to 'proselytize' Gentile Christians into becoming σπέρμα Ἀβραάμ, a move that Paul tried his best to resist.[146] Paul's opponents, in Dozeman's words, 'elevated the law above faith in Christ'.[147] Dozeman so centralizes his reconstructed context for Paul's letter to the Galatians that even the occurrence of the term σπέρμα Ἀβραάμ in 2 Cor. 11.22, which on Dozeman's own admission has nothing to do with the Law, is interpreted to mean that 'Paul implies a Jewish-Christian mission merely by identifying his opponents as σπέρμα Ἀβραάμ'.[148] Not surprisingly, Dozeman also reads

---

[139] Dozemann, 'Sperma Abraam', pp. 342–3; cf. Martyn, *History and Theology*, pp. 18–21.
[140] Dozemann, 'Sperma Abraam', p. 343.
[141] Ibid.
[142] Ibid.
[143] Ibid.
[144] Ibid., pp. 344–6.
[145] Ibid., p. 346.
[146] Ibid., p. 347.
[147] Ibid., p. 351.
[148] Ibid., p. 349.

Justin's use of the term σπέρμα Ἀβραάμ in *Dialogue with Trypho* 23-24, 44 and 47 in light of the text's polemic against 'Christian Jews' who try to force Gentile Christians to accept the Law. In Dozeman's reading, Justin's designation of σπέρμα Ἀβραάμ includes Jews who believe in Christ, Jews who do not believe in Christ and Jews who oppose and curse Christianity. In *Dialogue with Trypho* 47, some of the Jews coded as σπέρμα Ἀβραάμ try to convert Christians to Judaism, while others try to get Christians to retain belief in Christ but to supplement their belief with Law observance.[149]

This comparative exegesis enables Dozeman to claim that John 8.31-59 deals with the similar historical problem of a Jewish–Christian group (also coded as σπέρμα Ἀβραάμ) who were trying to foist a law-observant mission on the rest of the community (who were presumably Gentile Christians, if we extend the logic of this model to John 8).[150] The Jews of John 8 retort that they have never been enslaved (8.32) which expresses their 'affirmation that the law is not a form of slavery'.[151] This latter statement, according to Dozeman, attractively fits certain early Jewish conceptions of the Law as a liberating agent (cf. *m. Avot* 3.5, Josephus *Ant.* 4.8, 2).[152] But there are some major problems with Dozeman's thesis, the most obvious of which is that *John 8.31-59 nowhere mentions the Law*. The debate across the whole of John 7–8 is not about belief in Christ *versus* observance to the Torah; indeed, on the one occasion that Jesus mentions the Law in this discourse (7.19-21), there is no question of an implied debate with a mission-oriented group of Jews, with Jesus advocating 'freedom from the law' – if anything, Jesus is concerned about *how to interpret the Law rightly*. Dozeman's study allows the letter to the Galatians to overdetermine his interpretation of John 8.31-59. There is also a problem with some of the texts (Eusebius, Josephus and Philo, previously cited) that Dozeman has selected to support his argument about Abraham as a missionary figure in early Judaism. None of these texts uses the term σπέρμα Ἀβραάμ, which Dozeman understands to be a 'technical term' in John 8.32. If the term σπέρμα Ἀβραάμ is Dozeman's concern (as a technical code word) then his study would have been improved by an extended linguistic and philological analysis of the term, starting with the LXX (Septuagint) which we know John utilized in his scriptural citations.[153]

Finally, while there are numerous close linguistic and conceptual parallels between Galatians and John 8, we ought to be aware that Paul's unique concerns (the apparent redundancy of the Law and circumcision; the righteousness of faith) were not shared by John, and that the transparency of Paul's real situation in Galatia, flowing from the genre of his writing as an occasional letter, does not obtain for John's narrative of Jesus. John and Paul conceptualize their similar terms in different ways, a point that should caution us against drawing conclusions about the Johannine Jews on the basis of assumed disputes that affected historical parties in Paul's Galatian church. Dozeman's one-to-one correspondence between Paul's reconstructed situation and all other early

---

[149] Ibid., p. 354.
[150] Ibid., p. 355.
[151] Ibid.
[152] Ibid., n. 42.
[153] Cf. Bruce G. Schuchard, *Scripture within Scripture: The Interrelationship of Form and Function in the Explicit Old Testament Citations in the Gospel of John* (SBLDS 133; Atlanta: Scholars Press, 1992).

Christian and Jewish usages of the term σπέρμα Ἀβραάμ is too simplistic and is not often argued so explicitly today.

The final specific study of John 8.31-34 that is considered here employs a distinctively different theoretical approach. Adele Reinhartz has written on the text of John 8 from a 'Jewish perspective'.[154] This means that Reinhartz has drawn attention to the fact that the 'Jewish voice in John 8.31-59' can be recovered, and its legitimacy reasserted, not only from an ancient perspective but also from a modern one.[155] While John may 'victimize' the Jews in the world of the text, the Jews' response has a legitimacy of its own, and is not simply an intransigent rejection of Jesus' offer of true freedom (8.31-33).[156] The intertextual background that Reinhartz produces focuses on the issue of the Jews' covenant fidelity, indicating that the central issue in John 8.31-59 may be that of monotheism. If the Jews viewed Jesus' claims for himself as an infringement of monotheism, then their own claims in ch. 8 v. 33 reassert their adherence to this fundamental Jewish belief.[157] This 'resistant reading', as Reinhartz calls it, goes against the grain of the text of the Gospel, which generally persuades the reader to side with Jesus' perspective against that of the Jews. And while the contemporary reader-critic need not *be* Jewish in order to successfully perform a resistant reading of the Gospel, it is often Jewish readers of the Gospel who sense the characteristically Johannine anti-Jewishness of the text most acutely. Thus, Reinhartz attempts to critically work through her interest in the Fourth Gospel and what it means for her self-identity as a modern, practising Jewish woman. In short, her social location is a vital, unapologetic aspect of her interpretation.

However, Reinhartz's methodological approach to John 8 is not essentially different to that of the studies previously examined. There is still the engagement with ancient sources as possible influences for John's presentation of the Jews and Abraham. It is only that these antecedent texts from early Judaism and the LXX are examined for how they inform the 'Jewish voice' of the text. In other words, no matter how John rhetorically depicts the Jews' response in ch. 8 v. 32 as inadequate by Johannine standards, the categories that the Jews use to express their position and identity have a textual history. Reinhartz focuses specifically on several post-biblical Jewish texts informing the Jews' response to Jesus that they have never been slaves to anyone (8.32-33).[158] Understanding the Greek verb δουλεύω in ch. 8 v. 33 as 'to serve' rather than 'to be enslaved' (as most commentators take it), Reinhartz claims that the Jews of John 8 express their characteristic monotheism by asserting that they have never 'served' other gods.[159] Reinhartz shows that in the LXX the verb δουλεύω is frequently used with this connotation in mind (1 Sam. 7.3; Jer. 5.19; Ps. 105.36). The Jews' claim in ch. 8 vv. 32-33 might, from this perspective, suggest that they have not been idolaters, but have remained faithful to their covenant with God. Idolatry in this sense is a form

---

[154] Reinhartz, 'John 8.31-59 from a Jewish Perspective'.
[155] Ibid., p. 795.
[156] Ibid., p. 789.
[157] Ibid., p. 798.
[158] Ibid., pp. 787–97.
[159] Ibid., p. 792.

of slavery.[160] Reinhartz supports her reading with attention to post-biblical texts that present Abraham as the first monotheist and as one who emphatically rejected idols (cf. *Apoc. Abr.* 1.1-8.6; *Jub.* 12.12-14; cf. Philo *On Abraham* 69–71; Josephus *Ant.* 1.155). In John 8.33 when the Jews assert their status as 'seed of Abraham', this intertextual understanding of Abraham as one who did not serve other gods is important.[161]

Reinhartz finds another suggestive intertext for John 8.31-59 in *Jub.* 19.29. In that text, Isaac blesses his son Jacob, so that 'the spirit of Mastema' (the evil spirit or the devil) might not 'rule over' him or his 'seed'. The threat that Mastema represents to Jacob's seed is that he might sway them from 'following the Lord God' who is to them a 'father' (v. 29). The primary work of the devil is, in *Jubilees*, to lead the seed of Jacob into idolatry. It is therefore instructive to compare this text with John 8.31-59: the reference to the 'seed' of Jacob (cf. John 8.33, 'seed of Abraham'), the filial aspect of God (cf. 8.38, 47), the role of the devil in his potential to dominate or influence others (cf. 8.44). Reinhartz references the text from *Jubilees* to illustrate its use of filial metaphors in comparison to John 8.31-59, but she remains aware of the connection made between the devil and idolatry, and the importance this connection may have as a background to John 8.31-59.[162] The comparison is not exact: in *Jubilees* 19, Mastema merely has the capacity to influence the children of God and to induce them to betray their covenantal obligations, but in John's more deterministic viewpoint, the Jews are said to have the devil as their 'father', and to assuredly *not* be the 'children of God' (8.44). Nevertheless, Jesus tells the Jews that they *choose* to do their 'father's' desires (καὶ τὰς ἐπιθυμίας τοῦ πατρὸς ὑμῶν θέλετε ποιεῖν), which might imply that their imputed status as the devil's children is not permanent.

In sum, the few specialized studies on John 8.31-36 have predominantly adopted a form-critical or *Sitz-im-Leben* approach to the text. The parallel texts adduced in these instances have been derived from the HB, the post-biblical Pseudepigrapha and early Christian tradition – the Synoptics, Paul's letters and Justin's *Dialogue with Trypho*. The textual difficulty presented by 'the Jews who believed' in Jesus (8.31) has also determined these interpretations, necessitating attempts to identify this group in the context of early church history. The key terms and metaphors that John uses in ch. 8 vv. 31-36 ('seed', 'slavery', 'freedom', 'sin', 'son' and 'the household') are then interpreted in light of the NT and the trajectories it opened up in the early centuries of the Common Era. The studies by Dozeman and Dodd exemplify this approach in order to understand John's metaphors in their contemporary Christian discursive context. But that is the limit of the intertextual engagement – the approach does not allow room for suggesting that John employed the key terms *apart* from that context, in his own unique way and differently to Paul and the early church. For indeed John might have used these metaphors from within the spectrum of a different tradition. This latter point is made by Reinhartz in her investigation of the alternative 'voice' of the Jews in John 8.

This latter point is vitally important, as can be illustrated by a short example (which I develop in more depth at the beginning of Chapter 4). Apart from the small number

---

[160] Ibid., p. 793.
[161] Ibid., p. 791.
[162] Ibid., p. 792.

of studies dedicated to the figure of Abraham in John 8.31-34, the only other form of scholarship examining the text are the Gospel commentaries. In many commentaries, the persuasive tenor of the Gospel's rhetoric influences the commentator's judgement on the Jews and their response, 'We are seed of Abraham, and have been slaves to no one, ever – how do you say, "You shall be set free"?' (8.33). There is a profoundly consistent tendency for commentators to *exacerbate* the anti-Jewish characterization in ch. 8 vv. 32-33, by making statements such as the following: that the Jews' allegedly 'boast in their descent from Abraham'; that they exhibit 'slavery to hollow prestige games'; and even that they 'have no heart for God'.[163] The problem here is twofold: first, the Gospel's 'monologic' rhetoric permits the commentator latitude in evaluating the Jews' negatively, thereby denying their response any legitimacy on its own terms; second, without presenting research on the Jewish backgrounds and contemporaneous traditions that associate Jews with Abraham and his role in alleviating his 'seed' of their sin, the contemporary commentator ends up importing modern, psychological understandings of 'sin' and enslavement into John 8.31-36 to produce an evaluation of 'the Jews' (and sometimes Jews as such) as intransigent and hostile.[164] The importance of continuing Reinhartz's hermeneutic contribution and reading John 8 from my social location as a Jewish reader cannot be overstated in this context.

Focused studies: The 'works of Abraham' (8.39-47)

This section provides an overview of the various proposals for the intertexts shaping the notion of Abraham's 'works' in John 8.39-40 (and the surrounding context of ch. 8 vv. 39-47 more generally). In John 8.39, we find the rare genitive absolute (τὰ ἔργα τοῦ Ἀβραάμ: 'the works of Abraham') expressed idiomatically, typically obscured by its rendering into English as the relative clause 'what Abraham did' (e.g. New Revised Standard Version (NRSV), John 8.39; possibly to match Jesus' statement in v. 40 – viz. that 'this is not what Abraham did': τοῦτο Ἀβραάμ οὐκ ἐποίησεν). When rendered in this manner, John 8.39-40 gives the impression that if the Jews wish to claim Abraham as their father, then they must act the way Abraham acted. In ch. 8 v.40, Jesus charges the Jews with wishing to kill him, a 'man ... from God', adding that this was not what Abraham did (i.e. this is not how Abraham behaved). This translation, of course, obscures the plural τὰ ἔργα (v. 39), connecting it further with Jesus' statement about Abraham's implicit (singular) behaviour or deed in the past (v. 40). Therefore, the rendering 'if you are Abraham's children you must do as Abraham did' (NRSV) effectively presents Abraham as someone who 'did' something quite specific at some point that now needs to be emulated by the Jews of the Johannine narrative.

---

[163] These citations in order are Thomas Brodie, *The Gospel according to John: A Literary and Theological Commentary* (New York: Oxford University Press, 1997), p. 329; Rudolf Schnackenburg, *The Gospel according to St. John* (trans. K. Smyth et al., Volume 2; Herder's Theological Commentary on the New Testament; London: Burns & Oates, 1978), p. 345; Donald A. Carson, *The Gospel According to John* (Grand Rapids: Eerdmans, 1991), p. 352. For more details on this commentarial interpretive trend, see Sheridan, 'Seed of Abraham, Slavery and Sin'.

[164] On the concept of monologic rhetoric in relation to John and 'the Jews' see Ruth Sheridan, 'Issues in the Translation', pp. 671-95.

The interpretive question is, then, 'What did Abraham do?' rather than the more intuitive, 'What were Abraham's works?' (which obtains when the Greek is adhered to more literally). In the scholarship, we therefore tend to find intertextual examples advanced for John 8.39-40 based on the idea of Abraham *doing* something singular and particular; we also find this logic extended to a specific attribute of Abraham detailed in the Scriptures or apocryphal traditions.

One popular view in the secondary literature is the reference to 'what Abraham did' (v. 39) in connection with Abraham's rejoicing at seeing Jesus' 'day' (referred to in v. 58). That is, Abraham's act of rejoicing (v. 58) is understood to be identical to Abraham's exemplary deed (8.39-40), now enjoined by Jesus upon the Jews. In this reading, the Jews fail to do 'what Abraham did': whereas the patriarch *rejoiced* at seeing Jesus, the Jews *wish to kill* him instead.[165] But which specific act of rejoicing on the part of Abraham could possibly correspond to such a reading? The answer requires finding intertextual evidence for Abraham's vision of Jesus – which seems patently absurd in terms of temporal mechanics. The way around this has been for such scholars to latch on to one biblical narrative about Abraham which could *latently* support the interpretation of Jesus appearing to Abraham, and the latter rejoicing at the occasion. That biblical narrative is the story of the patriarch happily welcoming three men – who are later revealed to be angelic figures sent from God – at the Oaks of Mamre on a hot day (Genesis 18). In that text, three visitors approach Abraham to deliver an improbable message: his wife Sarah will have a son. Before they deliver their news, Abraham eagerly welcomes the men, providing for their needs in a superlatively hospitable manner. While there is technically no reference in Genesis 18 to Abraham 'rejoicing' at his visitors' message, his exemplary hospitality towards men sent *from God* is provided as the appropriate intertextual reference for the Jews' lack of hospitality towards Jesus in John 8 – also a man sent 'from God'.[166]

Neither is this interpretation as tendentious as it appears. Indeed, there is support for it in the early reading traditions of the Apostolic Fathers. Justin Martyr was one of the first Christian writers to argue that the pre-existent Logos of whom John speaks (cf. John 1.1-3) appeared in various guises to the patriarchs and holy men of ancient Israel temporally prior to his incarnation in Christ (*Apol.*).[167] The connection between Abraham's visitation by the angelic figures in Genesis 18 and the pre-Nicene Christian exegesis of the work of the Logos in history was explicitly made as early as 1898, in a scholarly treatise by the German scholar W. Baldensperger.[168] In John 8.39-59, the Jews remark the absurdity of Jesus' claim to have 'seen' Abraham – although Jesus in fact claimed that Abraham had 'seen' his day; according to Holtzmann this implied

---

[165] Cf. Jerome H. Neyrey, 'Jesus the Judge: Forensic Processes in John 8.21-59', *Bib* 68 (1987), pp. 509-42, at p. 524; Motyer, *Your Father the Devil*, p. 191.
[166] See Edwyn C. Hoskyns, *The Fourth Gospel* (ed. F. N. Davey; London: Faber & Faber, 1947), p. 342; Andrew Lincoln, *The Gospel according to John* (Black's New Testament Commentary 4; London: Continuum, 2005), p. 271; Steven A. Hunt, 'And the Word Became Flesh – Again? Jesus and Abraham in John 8.31-59', in Steven A. Hunt (ed.), *Perspectives on Our Father Abraham: Essays in Honor of Marvin R. Wilson* (Grand Rapids: Eerdmans, 2010), pp. 81-109, at p. 96.
[167] Cf. M. J. Edwards, 'Justin's Logos and the Word of God', *JECS* 3, no. 3 (1995), pp. 261-80.
[168] W. Baldensperger, *Der Prolog des vierten Evangeliums. Sein polemischapologetischer Zweck* (Tübingen: J.C.B. Mohr, 1898).

that John understood the angelic figures of Genesis 18 to have been the pre-incarnate Logos. At Mamre, Abraham was given a vision of Christ before he appeared.[169]

This interpretation has been adopted and expanded by recent scholars. In his work *The Prophetic Gospel*, Anthony Tyrell-Hanson attempts to 'vindicate' Baldensperger's position by extending the latter's interpretation.[170] Tyrell-Hanson claims that Abraham 'met the pre-existent Word, not in paradise ... but in the course of [his] life'.[171] Tyrell-Hanson reasons that one of the three men at Mamre was 'the pre-existent Word', because Abraham prostrated himself before the men and called one of them 'Lord'.[172] Tyrell-Hanson argues that in the exegetical imagination of the Johannine author, the *son* promised to Abraham and Sarah in Genesis 18 referred to Christ.[173] Accordingly, the pre-incarnate Logos not only appears to Abraham in the guise of the angel(s), but when he appears, he predicts his own incarnation. In Genesis 18, Abraham's response is one of complete joy; in John 8.59, Jesus tells the Jews that Abraham 'rejoiced to see [his] day'. Before the Logos appeared in the flesh of Jesus, he appeared to Abraham in angelic form, hence John can have Jesus say, 'before Abraham was, I am' (8.59).[174]

This same point is advanced by Steven A. Hunt, in an essay studying the pre-existence of Jesus in relation to Abraham. Hunt argues that the Johannine narrator builds on earlier Christological passages in the Gospel to present Jesus as pre-existent in ch. 8 v. 58. Hunt agrees that John 8.31-59 shows familiarity with patristic reading traditions about the pre-existent Logos appearing to Abraham in angelic guise in Genesis 18, and of Abraham showing the Logos due hospitality. Hunt then connects the Jews' rejection of Jesus in John 8.31-59 to the rejection of the pre-existent Word by 'his own' in the Prologue of the Gospel (1.11). But the Prologue identifies some who nevertheless 'received' Jesus and 'believed in his name' (1.12) which Hunt contrasts with the Jews who '*had* believed' in Jesus in ch. 8 v. 31 (adopting the pluperfect reading of πιστεύω to suggest a belief that has not continued). Hunt resolves the discrepancy of positing a specific 'work' of Abraham (i.e. his hospitality at Mamre) for the reference to Abraham's plural 'works' in ch. 8 v. 39 by comparing the text to John 6.28 – there 'the crowd' ask Jesus how they can 'perform the *works* of God', and Jesus responds by turning the plural τὰ ἔργα into the singular: the '*work*' of God (τὸ ἔργον τοῦ θεοῦ) is 'to believe' in the Sent One (6.29). For Hunt, this comparison confirms that *belief* in Jesus is equivalent to 'the works of God', and that therefore the phrase τὰ ἔργα τοῦ Ἀβραάμ in John 8.39 likewise refers to belief in Jesus. Abraham's 'belief' in Jesus was expressed in his hospitality to the angels at Mamre (Genesis 18), which in early Christian interpretation stood for the pre-existent Logos; the same faith was also expressed by Abraham when the 'word' of the Lord (ῥῆμα κυρίου) came to him, and he responded by believing in God (Gen. 15.4, 6, LXX: καὶ ἐπίστευσεν Αβραμ τῷ θεῷ).

---

[169] Whether Jesus was one of the three angelic men or all three of the angelic men is disputed – Holtzmann thinks Jesus was one of the three men; Holtzmann, *Evangelium*.
[170] Anthony Tyrrell-Hanson, *The Prophetic Gospel: A Study of John and the Old Testament* (London: Continuum, 1991), p. 131.
[171] Ibid., p. 126.
[172] Ibid.
[173] Ibid.
[174] Ibid., p. 131.

Hunt writes that 'hospitality for Jesus is simply another way of referring to belief in him, belief that continues in his word, and does not rely on signs alone'.[175]

The commonly espoused thesis of Genesis 18 and its subsequent reading traditions as the appropriate intertext for John 8.58 (and 8.39-40) has the advantage of coherency, but it also has its shortcomings. First, it is problematic in that the reference to Abraham's rejoicing in ch. 8 v. 58 is given *a priori* significance in the schema, such that it forces the idiomatic reference (τὰ ἔργα τοῦ Ἀβραάμ) to be read in its light. Second, Abraham's encounter with the angels in Genesis 18 – which was elaborated on in early Jewish texts and given Christological reference in early Christian texts – is *one event* in the life of the patriarch, but John speaks of Abraham's '*works*' in the plural (v. 39). Third, in the patristic Christophanic exegeses of Genesis 18, Abraham has a vision of the pre-incarnate Logos in the person of the angel(s), but in John 8.58, Jesus specifies that Abraham saw his '*day*' (which need not be equated with Jesus' person). These drawbacks to the 'Mamre hypothesis' (as we might term it) are not insignificant. They prompt us to look for new solutions and for intertextual examples that address what is meant by 'Abraham's *works*' (and more generally, but any figures' 'works' in the context of the divine–human interrelationship). Quite apart from the Mamre hypothesis, it is important to ask why scholars have reduced 'Abraham's works' to his act of 'rejoicing' in ch. 8 v. 58 instead of reading ch. 8 vv. 39-40 in its own context, taking all of ch. 8 vv. 31-38 before it. In other words, why read the pericope 'backwards' as it were? Why not read it 'forwards' (as it is no doubt meant to be read) so that the idiomatic expression 'the works of Abraham' builds and follows on from the earlier discussion of metaphors of 'seed', 'slavery' and 'sin' in ch. 8 vv. 31-34 in particular? That is what this book proposes to do.

Some commentators argue that there is no specific intertextual reference defining Abraham's 'works' in John 8.39-40, especially one that would equate Abraham's 'works' with a singular action in the narratives and traditions pertaining to him; rather, Abraham's general righteousness should be understood as the background to the text.[176] John 8.39-40 is thus taken to be in line with Abraham's exemplary behaviour expressed in many other texts of early Judaism. Catrin Williams states that there is 'no precise parallel' to the phrase τὰ ἔργα τοῦ Ἀβραάμ in ch. 8 v. 39, but that it is 'a verbal signal for a wide range of deeds and attributes for which the patriarch is remembered in late Second Temple Judaism, such as his opposition to idolatry and his role as a model of righteousness, hospitality, faithfulness and receptiveness to God's word'.[177] Williams further contends that to read one narrative episode (such as Genesis 18) behind John 8.39 is reductive and limiting.[178] Also, J. Ramsey Michaels thinks that we miss the point of John 8.39-40 when looking for one example in the tradition of 'what Abraham did' – Michaels considers it better to look at what Abraham did *not* do, that is,

---

[175] Hunt, 'And the Word Became Flesh', pp. 82, 85, 97.
[176] Cf. J. Ramsey Michaels, *The Gospel of John* (Grand Rapids: Eerdmans, 2010). Cf. Rudolf Bultmann, *The Gospel of John: A Commentary* (Louisville: Westminster/John Knox, 1971), p. 442, n. 6; Hunt, 'And the Word Became Flesh', p. 108.
[177] Williams, 'Abraham as a Figure of Memory', p. 215.
[178] Ibid.

according to Jesus' words, seeking to kill a man (8.40).[179] Unlike Michaels, I do not think that it is misguided to find intertextual references for 'Abraham's works' (v. 39) or for what 'Abraham did' (v. 40). However, with Michaels, I would state that it is important to notice how 'Abraham's works' in v. 39 are reiterated by negation in v. 40. By suggesting that Abraham's 'works' do *not* include 'seeking to kill a man', we can infer that some action – or a group of positive, life-preserving actions – is entailed by ch. 8 vv. 39-40.

As I discuss in greater depth in Chapter 5, it will be important to read this suggestion in the context of John 7.19-21, when Jesus debates the overriding priority of the mitzvah of פיקוח נפש ('saving a life') in relation to the Sabbath, the latter of which is said to 'go back to the Patriarchs'. What is more, the *effect* of Abraham's 'works' upon others (notably upon the Jews, cf. 8.32-33, 38) has been overlooked in the scholarship. For while Jesus encourages the Jews to emulate the exemplary 'works of Abraham' (8.39), the understanding of the Jews appears to be that Abrahamic paternity suffices to protect them from the danger of slavery to sin (8.32-34).[180] The connection between Abraham's 'works' (8.39) and the preceding reference to Abraham's 'seed' (vv. 32-33) is entirely neglected. This is the curious effect of reading the possible Abrahamic intertexts 'backward' as it were, seeing the reference in ch. 8 v. 58 as supremely important, and only assigning relative importance to the other references. This is a suitable point to segue to a fuller literature review of the intertexts proposed for John 8.56-59, where Abraham is said to have 'seen' Jesus' day and rejoiced in it.

Focused studies: Abraham saw and rejoiced (John 8.56-58)

After an increasing amount of mutual rancour, the pericope of ch. 8 vv. 31-59 comes to its sonorous conclusion with Jesus claiming to have existed before Abraham ever was (8.58) – a claim that upsets the Jews to such a point that they take up stones to kill Jesus on the spot (8.59a), but Jesus escapes (8.59b). Jesus also tells the Jews that Abraham 'saw' his 'day' and 'rejoiced' in it, after they prod him into explaining how, as a man of less than fifty years of age, he could claim to have 'seen' Abraham (8.56). The unique focus of the last part of the pericope in relation to the rest of it (8.31-47) is the fact of Abraham's 'seeing' and 'rejoicing' – two active qualities that Jesus imputes to Abraham in relation to himself. Secondarily, the Jews' statement about Abraham's mortality, and his connection to the prophets, is also worth noting. I now review the intertextual proposals advanced for John 8.48-59 in the scholarship to date. These proposals have concentrated upon Jesus' ἐγὼ εἰμί statement (8.58: 'Before Abraham was, I am'), the reference to Abraham 'rejoicing' (8.56) and the reference to Abraham 'seeing' Jesus' 'day' (8.56) – keeping in mind that there has already been some reference to these suggestions because of the connections made between Abraham's 'vision' of the preexistent Logos and Abraham's 'works' in the previous section.

Several stand-alone studies have focused on the intertextual background for Jesus' enigmatic statement, 'Before Abraham was, I am' (πρὶν Ἀβραὰμ γενέσθαι ἐγὼ εἰμί: 8.58). Across the span of two separate articles, Edwin Freed has developed the thesis that

---
[179] Ramsey Michaels, *The Gospel of John*.
[180] This is developed in more depth in Chapter 4.

Jesus' ἐγώ εἰμί statement (8.58) refers to Jewish traditions about the hidden messiah.[181] In his first article, Freed examines John 8.24 ('for you will die in your sins unless you believe that I am'; ἐγώ εἰμί) and its surrounding context. Freed claims that John 8.24 evokes three particular messianic themes from early Jewish traditions: (1) that the messiah is expected to reprove sinners (cf. *Pss. Sol.* 17.25; *2 Esd.* 12.32, 13.37); (2) that the messiah will perform the task of judgement (cf. 4QpIsa); and (3) that the servant-messiah will be God's co-witness before the people (cf. LXX Isa. 43.10; 1 Sam. 12.3; *Sir.* 44.19).[182] Freed favours these various intertexts and their conceptualization of the hidden messiah over the more commonly espoused thesis that ἐγώ εἰμί in John 8.24 is an iteration of the divine name (אני יהוה; cf. LXX Isa. 41.4 ἐγώ εἰμί).[183] Freed determines the three 'hidden messiah' themes of Jewish tradition to be present in the immediate context of John 8.24 (reproving sin: 8.21, 24; judging: 7.24, 51; 8.15, 16, 26, 50; and witnessing: 8.17, 18).[184]

In his second article, Freed argues that Jesus' ἐγώ εἰμί statement in John 8.58 refers to these same notions of the 'hidden messiah' putatively present in ch. 8 v. 24.[185] Instead of reading ἐγώ εἰμί (8.58) as a claim to divinity, Freed reads it as a claim to Jesus' messianic status (the larger question of the correlation between pre-existence and divinity is not raised by Freed). To substantiate this reading, Freed states that in the 'hidden messiah' traditions of early Judaism, the messiah (or his Name) was pre-existent (*2 Esd.* 12.32; 13.26, 52; 14.9; Enoch 39.6, 7).[186] Moreover, Enoch 48 (vv. 2, 3, 6) equates the messiah with the 'son of man' who was hidden in God's presence before the creation of the world.[187] Freed posits that John the Evangelist was working with notions of the 'hidden Christ', when, for example, he refers to Jesus 'hiding' or acting 'in secret' (7.1; 8.59; cf. 12.36).[188] Freed adds that on the level of the narrative, Jesus' messianic status is 'hidden from Jewish understanding', as his three ἐγώ εἰμί statements are repeatedly 'misunderstood' by the Jews (8.24, 28, 58).[189]

Four points can be raised against Freed's argument for John 8.58. First, a point on which Freed himself is duly cognisant, is that 'opinions ... vary widely' on the subject of the dating of the Enoch texts, and so it is difficult to determine their influence upon

---

[181] Edwin D. Freed, 'EGŌ EIMI in John VII.24 in the Light of Its Context and Jewish Messianic Belief', *JTS* 33, no. 1 (1982), pp. 163–7; idem. 'Who or What Was Before Abraham in John 8.58?' *JSNT* 17 (1983), pp. 52–9.

[182] Freed, 'EGŌ EIMI in John VII.24', p. 165, pp. 166–7.

[183] The scholars cited by Freed who espouse this alternative are J. P. Charlier, 'L'exégèse johannique d'un precepte legal: Jean VIII 17', *RB* 67 (1960), p. 513; R. E. Brown, *The Gospel according to John, I-XII* (AB 29; Garden City: Doubleday, 1966), pp. 533–8; Phillip B. Harner, *The 'I Am' of the Fourth Gospel: A Study in Johannine Usage and Thought* (Facte Books; Philadelphia: Fortress Press, 1970). See Freed, 'EGŌ EIMI in John VII.24', p. 166, n. 4.

[184] Freed, 'EGŌ EIMI in John VII.24', pp. 165–7.

[185] Freed, 'Who or What Was Before Abraham?', p. 52.

[186] Ibid.; Freed claims there is some scholarly debate over the name or the person – but 'Semitically speaking' these are equivalent.

[187] Freed, 'Who or What Was Before Abraham?', p. 53. Freed adduces further texts in support: LXX Ps. 19.7; Hab. 3.13; Amos 4.13; *Pss. Sol.* 17.32-34; and Enoch 51.3, around the glorification of God provided by the messiah (pp. 56–7), and then Targum to Mic. 5.1, as well as LXX Isa. 45.1-4 on the anointing of the 'name'/the messiah (p. 57).

[188] Freed, 'Who or What Was Before Abraham?', p. 55.

[189] Ibid., p. 57.

John, much less to call upon them as a primary source.[190] Second, Freed never specifies the significance of *Abraham* to Jesus' status as the pre-existent, hidden messiah, and none of the texts cited by Freed incorporates the figure of Abraham into a relationship with the messiah. Third, Freed's equation of 'hiddenness' and misunderstanding is not self-evident; there is no analogous text presenting a connection between cognitive opacity and actual, existential 'hiddenness' in the ancient literature. Fourth, in John 8.58 the Jews intuitively appear to *understand* the import of Jesus' ἐγώ εἰμί claim by virtue of their aggravated response (8.59) – they do not 'misunderstand' Jesus' provocative statement.

A different proposal has been advanced by John Ashton, who attempted to find an allusive background for Jesus' ἐγώ εἰμί statement in ch. 8 v. 58 while integrating more fully the Abrahamic references as well.[191] Ashton considers the *Apocalypse of Abraham* to offer a 'close parallel' to John 8.56-58 and to be 'roughly contemporary' with the Gospel.[192] In *Apocalypse of Abraham* 9–10, Abraham witnesses the destruction of his father's idols but, seeing that Abraham seeks the one true god, he is saved by the Creator God, who calls out to Abraham 'I am he' (8.3).[193] God continues to speak to Abraham in revelatory phrases that begin with 'I am', followed by a predicate (cf. *Apoc. Abr.* 9.2-3). What is more, God promises that Abraham will 'see great things which [he has] not seen' and that God will show him 'the things which were made by the ages and by my word' (9.6). Ashton deduces further evidence for comparison from the semi-divine figure of Yaoel, who appears to Abraham (*Apocalypse of Abraham* 10). According to Ashton, this figure resembles Jesus in John's Gospel, since he claims to be sent from God and to share in the authority of God's name.[194] Additionally, Yaoel charges Abraham to 'be very joyful and rejoice'.[195] Ashton's main point is that the author of the Gospel was 'influenced by the idea of a revealer-figure sent by God and endowed with the authority of his name'.[196] Ashton's analysis is cogent, but he does note one potential drawback affecting his argument – namely the esotericism of *Apocalypse of Abraham* and the broad generic differences between it and the Gospel. However, Ashton does not fully explain the heuristic concepts of parallelism and influence with which he works methodologically, and this detracts from the persuasiveness of his thesis.[197]

---

[190] Ibid., p. 53; Freed demurs that while the 'hidden messiah' traditions of the Enoch writings might not have been widely present and available to John, at least we know that traditions of the messiah, generally speaking, were in high circulation around the time of the Jewish War and the Bar Kochba revolt (p. 54).
[191] John Ashton, *Understanding the Fourth Gospel* (Oxford: Clarendon, 1991), pp. 142–7.
[192] Ibid., p. 142. My own reading of *Apocalypse of Abraham* can be found in Chapter 6 of this book.
[193] Ashton, *Understanding*, p. 142.
[194] Ibid., p. 143.
[195] Ibid., pp. 143–4.
[196] Ibid., p. 144.
[197] Ashton does admit that we cannot be sure if *Apocalypse of Abraham* was written *before* John (i.e. it influenced John) and so he turns to the notion of 'parallels' (which are vaguer and perhaps reader oriented) before switching back to John/the author being 'influenced' by circulating notions of a revealer-figure. See Chapter 2 of this book for a fuller discussion of these theoretical and methodological issues.

Another study, this one by M. J. Edwards, proposes a connection between the Jews' reference to Jesus' relative youth in ch. 8 v. 57, and Jesus' reference to Abraham 'rejoicing' in ch. 8 v. 58, by way of the book of *Jubilees*.[198] Edwards notes the anomalous reference to Jesus' 'fifty years' in ch. 8 v. 57, drawing attention to the fact that ancient commentators emended the text to 'forty years' – as either more historically plausible, or perhaps more numerically symbolic.[199] Edwards argues that the fifty-year period of the Jubilee has a certain symbolic value that has been overlooked; it was important for 'some Jewish authors of the time', and the Jubilee year espoused an ethical idealism in the release of slaves and the expiry of claims on property purchased (cf. Lev. 25.47-55).[200] Calendrical reforms at Qumran, moreover, used the Jubilee year as a unit for measuring the ages and dignity of the patriarchs.[201]

But for Edwards, it is the book of *Jubilees* that displays the closest resonance with the Gospel of John and the reference to Jesus being short of 'fifty years' in ch. 8 v. 57. Edwards cites *Jub.* 23.10-11, the beginning of which reads, 'Abraham was perfect in all his dealings with the Lord, and gained favour by his righteousness throughout his life, yet even he did not complete four jubilees'. The text reflects on the brevity of life in general, and Abraham's life in particular: no matter how exemplary he was, Abraham eventually died. Edwards suggests that this text lies behind the Jews' objection to Jesus in ch. 8 v. 57, which he glosses as follows: 'Since the time of Abraham, many Jubilees have passed, and no-one has lived through more than two of them. How then can you have seen him, who have not completed one?'[202] Edwards detects another allusion in Jesus' reply that Abraham 'saw his day' and rejoiced (8.58). In *Jub.* 16.26, Abraham joyfully receives a prophecy from God that one of his descendants will be a 'holy seed' like the Creator himself. Edwards writes, 'Jesus' claim that Abraham saw his day is therefore no *non sequitur*, for that is the day on which the true descendants of the patriarch will be known'.[203] Edwards thus states that the author of John displays familiarity, if not with the book of *Jubilees* itself, then at least with the significance of the fifty-year cycle as a unit of temporal measurement.[204]

Regrettably, Edwards argues for Johannine familiarity with *Jubilees* partially on the grounds of the 'Pharisaic zeal' he imputes to Jesus' opponents in relation to the Sabbath, and the (assumedly pedantic) 'taste for reckoning the years' in *Jubilees*.[205] This is a questionable assumption, stated wholly in *a priori* fashion; not only is it unproven that *Jubilees* is of Pharisaic origin, but it is problematic because Jesus' opponents in ch. 8 v. 57 are called 'the Jews' and not 'the Pharisees', the latter of whom appear as a different character group in John 7–8. Whether a meticulous attention to calendrical

---

[198] M. J. Edwards, '"Not Yet Fifty Years Old": John 8:57', *NTS* 40 (1994), pp. 449–54. See also the earlier work of P. Grélot, 'Jean 8,56 et Jubilés 16.16-29', *Rev Q* 13 (1988/9), pp. 621–8, who adopts a similar argument.
[199] Edwards, 'Not Yet Fifty Years Old', p. 449.
[200] Ibid., p. 451.
[201] Ibid. Cf. J. Morgenstern, 'The Calendar of the Book of Jubilees', *VT* 5 (1955), pp. 74–6.
[202] Edwards, 'Not Yet Fifty Years Old', p. 453.
[203] Ibid. The 'holy seed' (*Jub.* 16.26) is thus reappropriated as a Christological reference in Edwards' reading.
[204] Edwards, 'Not Yet Fifty Years Old', p. 454.
[205] Ibid., p. 452.

calculations necessarily arises from psychological 'zeal' (not least in an imputably pejorative sense) is also open to question. Edwards' assumption that the Gospel conflates the Jews and the Pharisees – a claim he makes following Malcolm Lowe – needs to be nuanced, and even up to 1994, when Edwards' article was published, there were scholarly suggestions to counter Lowe's own.[206]

Nevertheless, other studies have continued to read John 8.56-58 and its reference to Abraham's rejoicing in light of *Jubilees*. One such example is an article by Mary Coloe, written in 1999.[207] Coloe asks what it was that Abraham 'did' (8.40) and what it is, that in Jesus' understanding, the Jews are purportedly *not* doing. She finds the implicit answer in ch. 8 v. 56, where Abraham is said to have 'rejoiced' in Jesus' day.[208] Coloe finds it curious that, whereas in other early Christian traditions, Abraham was commended for his faithful obedience (cf. Rom. 4.3, 13, 16; Gal. 3.6; Heb. 11.8, 17; Jam. 2.23), in John's Gospel Abraham is remembered for his joy. This observation leads Coloe to search for comparable early Jewish traditions that represented Abraham as a figure who rejoiced – and this she finds in *Jub*. 16.20-27. What is even more striking according to Coloe, is that Abraham's joy in these verses is occasioned by his celebration – and even instigation – of the festival of Sukkot (cf. John 7.1, 11). Abraham perceives the future 'planting' of a 'holy seed' from his loins (16.26) and this causes him joy. Coloe notes this verse as the background against which John 8.56 should be understood, with Jesus stating that Abraham 'saw his day' (the future vision) and 'rejoiced' over it.[209]

The second part of Coloe's argument deals with Jesus' ἐγὼ εἰμί statement; Coloe finds resonances between this text and the Targum to Isa. 43.10-12, connecting both to Abraham's ability to 'see' (John 8.56). Her first observation in this regard is the frequency with which LXX Isaiah translates the Hebrew אני יהוה with ἐγὼ εἰμί, and often in 'juridical'-type scenes where Yhwh asserts his sovereignty over other gods, with the result that his hearers will come to 'know and believe' that ἐγὼ εἰμί ('I am [he]'; see Isa. 41.4; 43.10). Coloe notices the similarly forensic nature of John 8, and the common language of definitive knowledge of divine self-revelation (cf. 8.24, 28). And where Masoretic Text (MT) Isa. 43.10-12, for example, has Yhwh declaring that his 'witnesses' will 'know and believe' אני יהוה, the Targum to this verse inserts a brief passage about how Yhwh revealed 'the things to come' to 'Abraham your father', particularly that he revealed to Abraham the exodus from Egypt.[210] According to Coloe, this aligns with Abraham's ability to see the things that are to come, as suggested by John 8.58. Coloe concludes that 'the Gospel and Targum ... both draw upon a common source of traditional material concerning Abraham available to a

---

[206] Cf. Malcom Lowe, 'Who Were the Ἰουδαῖοι?' *NovT* 18 (1976), pp. 101–30. Edwards writes: 'The term [Ἰουδαῖοι] will always denote the Pharisees of Jerusalem' in the Gospel of John. This is not the case – one simple example is John 6.41, where 'the Jews' emerge from 'the crowd' at Capernaum in Galilee to contend with Jesus. A recent informative discussion on the translation of οἱ Ἰουδαῖοι can be found at http://marginalia.lareviewofbooks.org/jew-judean-forum/.

[207] Mary L. Coloe, 'Like Father, Like Son: The Role of Abraham in Tabernacles (John 8.31-59)', *Pac* 12 (1999), pp. 1–11.

[208] Ibid., p. 6.

[209] Ibid.

[210] Ibid., p. 9.

first century author' as represented in the *Jubilees* tradition.[211] However, it is worth cautioning that the reference to Abraham receiving a divine revelation of the things to come – as it is found both in *Jub.* 16.26 and the Targum to Isa. 43.10-12 – appears to be an inner, cognitive revelation, not one based on the exterior sense of sight, as in John 8.58.

Other scholars have favoured a biblical intertext for John 8.56-59 and its themes of rejoicing and seeing. For example, Andrew Brunson has suggested that Ps. 118.24 (MT; Ps. 117.24 LXX: 'this is the day the Lord has made, let us rejoice and be glad') provides 'a partial background' to the reference of Abraham 'rejoicing' in John 8.56.[212] Brunson's first reason is that LXX Ps. 117.24 uses the rare verb ἀγαλλιάομαι ('to greatly rejoice') in the middle aorist.[213] This verb is also used as a middle aorist in John 8.56. Also, in LXX Ps. 117.24, ἀγαλλιάομαι is combined with ἡ ἡμέρα – also rare in this combination, but found in John 8.56.[214] Brunson's second reason is that both LXX Ps. 117.24 and John 8.56 use ἡ ἡμέρα in a causal sense, meaning that it is the Lord's 'day' (in the psalm) and Jesus' 'day' (in John 8.56) that causes the respective subjects ('us': Ps. 117.24, and 'Abraham': John 8.56) to 'rejoice'.[215] There are, according to Brunson, 'strong and unique verbal ties' that support the possibility that John 8.56 alludes to LXX Ps. 117.24.[216]

Brunson claims that John 8.56 refers to an event that Abraham experienced in his own lifetime, which permitted him to rejoice in 'seeing' Jesus' 'day'.[217] John 8.56 thus conflates the 'day of Jesus' with the 'day of Yhwh' in Ps. 117.24 (LXX), reinforcing John's high Christology.[218] Brunson suggests that the *event* over which Abraham rejoiced, and the 'day' towards which he looked, is encapsulated best in *Jub.* 16.20-30 and its reference to a 'holy seed'.[219] The advantage of Brunson's reading is that it draws attention to the noun ἡ ἡμέρα in John 8.56 in a way that other proposals have not done, but his argument for a connection between Psalms 117/118 and the festival of Sukkot and/or with *Jubilees* is not strong, and is based on the introduction of other liturgical material and metaphors (e.g. the Zecharian 'Messiah-King') to fill in the gaps.[220]

Another position is that Abraham's rejoicing in John 8.56 refers to the birth of his promised son, Isaac, in Gen. 17.17.[221] Abraham's action of falling on his face and

---

[211] Ibid., p. 10.
[212] Andrew Brunson, *Psalm 118 in the Gospel of John: An Intertextual Study on the New Exodus Pattern in the Theology of John* (WUNT 2.158; Tübingen: Mohr Siebeck, 2003), p. 284.
[213] Ibid., p. 285.
[214] Ibid.
[215] Ibid., p. 290.
[216] Ibid.
[217] Ibid., p. 292.
[218] Ibid., p. 302.
[219] Ibid., p. 295. It is nonetheless curious that the connection between *Jubilees*' 'holy seed' of Abraham and John's use of the phrase 'seed of Abraham' in John 8.32-33 is not drawn by Brunson, nor by other scholars. See Chapter 4 for more discussion.
[220] Brunson, *Psalm 118*, 293.
[221] Cf. Herman Ridderbos, *The Gospel of John: A Theological Commentary* (Grand Rapids: Eerdmans, 1997), p. 321; Schnackenburg, *Gospel of John*, Vol. 2, pp. 222-3; Carson, *Gospel*, p. 357; cf. Also Hunt, 'And the Word Became Flesh', p. 99.

laughing when God promises him a son (Gen. 17.17) was interpreted in early Jewish tradition not as faithless incredulity, but as real joy.[222] Steven Hunt, who reads an implicit allusion to Isaac in John 8, adopts a different approach. Hunt reads Jesus' parable about the son and the slave in the household (8.35-36) as an allusion to the conflict between Ishmael and Isaac (Genesis 21).[223] Hunt also claims that an allusive reference to the Akedah surfaces in John 8.56-58. When God provides the lamb of sacrifice in place of Isaac, Abraham 'saw' the animal with his 'eyes'. This brought Abraham a sense of inner joy.[224] Hunt likens the Johannine Jesus to 'the Passover lamb' presumably prefigured in the sacrificial lamb at the Akedah, claiming that John was pointedly using this meaning.[225] John's allusion to the Akedah in ch. 8 vv. 56-58 thus implies that when Abraham 'saw' the lamb for sacrifice, what he really saw was Jesus' day.[226] At this point, Hunt's argument becomes tendentious and speculative: for example, in Genesis 22, Abraham 'saw' that the lamb for sacrifice was 'far away'. Hunt suggests that by this John meant to 'highlight the distance between Abraham and Jesus'. And at a further (and questionable) allusive remove, Hunt reasons that there is a connection between the Akedah and John 2.21 because both texts use the phrase 'on the third day'.[227]

On the subject of Abraham's 'seeing' in John 8.56, Catrin Williams has suggested that Genesis 15 provides the most appropriate intertext, largely because the aorist of ὁράω in ch. 8 v. 56 (ἴδῃ) points to a specific event during the narrated life of Abraham. In Gen. 15.1-17, Abraham receives the covenant promises from God, and has a visionary experience of the future. Later Jewish tradition played upon this to construct Abraham as a figure who was granted visions of the end times (e.g. *4 Ezra* 3.14; *Apoc. Ab.* 24.2; 9.10; 29.2; 31.1-2; *Gen. R.* 44.21, 22).[228] Yet none of these texts associates Abraham's seeing with his rejoicing. Williams resolves this with recourse to her selected method (social memory theory), arguing that John has fused together two disparate traditions (Abraham 'seeing' and 'rejoicing') to create a new 'collective memory' of Abraham in relation to Jesus. This 'fusion' attests to the 'mosaic-like character of memory'.[229] And finally, other scholars think that no specific event is referred to by the reference to Abraham in ch. 8 v. 56; the reference is, instead, a Johannine innovation placing Abraham as a prominent witness to Jesus, akin to Moses (cf. John 5.44) and Isaiah (cf. John 12.42). No intertext is intended, for the reference is Christological, and is not a debt to tradition.[230]

---

[222] Cf. Philo, *Mut.* 131; 154-69; *Jub.* 15.17; cf. Lona, *Abraham*, pp. 305-10.
[223] Hunt, 'And the Word Became Flesh', p. 99.
[224] Ibid., pp. 100-1.
[225] Ibid., p. 100.
[226] Ibid.
[227] Ibid., p. 101.
[228] Williams, 'Abraham as a Figure of Memory', p. 219.
[229] Ibid., p. 220.
[230] Cf. Lona, *Abraham*, 327-32; Margaret Davies, *Rhetoric and Reference in the Fourth Gospel* (JSNTSup 69; Sheffield: Sheffield Academic Press, 1992), p. 136; Leon Morris, *The Gospel according to John* (Grand Rapids: Eerdmans, 1971), pp. 418-19.

Summary and ways forward

It is necessary now to draw together the summary points arising from this presentation of the literature on the figure of Abraham in John 8. A range of short studies have examined the textual backgrounds of the references to Abraham in John 8. I note four pertinent features of the literature:

1. When scholars look for 'background' or 'parallel' texts and intertexts for Abraham in John 8, they have tended to place proportionately greater focus on the last part of the pericope (i.e. 8.56-58), where Jesus claims a unique status relative to Abraham. Other references to Abraham in the pericope (especially 8.32, 39) are not given the same amount or degree of scholarly attention, but they are sometimes integrated into a reading about Jesus' pre-existence and Abraham's vision of Jesus – as we saw with the previously mentioned 'Mamre hypothesis'. This latter example harmonizes 'Abraham's works' in ch. 8 v. 39 with his apparent vision of Jesus in ch. 8 v. 56.
2. Following on from this, insufficient attention is paid to the function of Abraham in John 8 across the *whole* pericope – that is, Abraham's relationship to slavery and sin in ch. 8 vv. 31-36, his paternity and his 'works' in ch. 8 v. 39 and his vision of, and existence relative to, Jesus in ch. 8 vv. 56-58. What is more, the intertexts often found for each reference to Abraham are incredibly diverse. The result is an atomistic intertextual presentation, which reinforces the impression that the references to Abraham in ch. 8 vv. 31-59 are not coherent.
3. Aside from Lona's monograph, there can be a lack of sustained theoretical rigour in the discussion of the comparative use of intertexts suggested for Abraham in John 8. While some scholars take the trouble to use precise terms and to define them (e.g. Brunson's use of 'allusion'), there is often no indication of the scholar's assumptions: did John literarily depend on a given source or did the source influence him in another way? Did the 'author' of the Gospel intend a given allusion to Abraham, or is the task of discerning allusions down to the contemporary reader? When we compare John to roughly contemporaneous texts, can we be sure that they antedate his own? If they do not, on what grounds do we postulate a common source of tradition for both texts? Theoretically, when we compare any texts at all, on what grounds do we do so, and to what end? Do we make analogical comparisons or historical comparisons?
4. When interpreters read John 8, and Abraham's role within it, do they signal their own 'horizon of understanding', locating it as a living 'text' that is part of the intertextual tapestry they are attempting to co-create? Not typically. This may be due to the predominance of source criticism at the time most of these studies were written. The exception is Adele Reinhartz's 'Jewish reading' of John 8 from a perspective of 'resistance'. In this context, I would posit the relevance of my own social location as a Jewish reader of the Gospel as an important factor in the process of interpretation. This is not said from an essentialist, or identity-political standpoint, as though being a Jewish reader provides me with a superior or authentic interpretation of 'the Jews' in John's

Gospel.²³¹ In the next chapter, I discuss in greater detail how the subjective stance of the reader functions in 'scripting' the text, on the basis of my engagement with poststructuralist intertextuality theory.

The purpose of this book: Outline and argument

This book argues that there is a coherent substructure of thought underlying the figuration of Abraham in John 8. It is the contention of this study that the reference to Abraham's 'seed' (8.32-33), the 'works' of Abraham (8.39-40) and Jesus' statement about being 'seen' by Abraham (8.56-58) all have roots in the metaphorical thought-world of early Judaism and in formative rabbinic Judaism, with implications for how early Christianity operated in this context to shape the imperative of concepts such as belief and faith. This study attempts to undertake an integrated reading of John 8.31-59 that, instead of starting at the concluding reference to Abraham in the discourse (Jesus' 'I Am' statement (8.58) and according it pre-eminence on the basis of its theological overtones), starts instead with the reference to the 'seed of Abraham' (8.32) and reads forward from there. Part of the assumption of undertaking an integrated reading is that the text must be read sequentially, as the references to Abraham *can* be interpreted in a consistent light and against a coherent background. The references to Abraham in John 8.31-59 are cumulative, and the dispute between Jesus and the Jews builds on what is predicated at the beginning, that is that the Jews are 'seed of Abraham'. From this point, it is possible to understand what is meant by the 'works' of Abraham, and then finally, what is meant by Jesus telling the Jews that Abraham saw his 'day' and 'rejoiced'. The rest of this book is outlined as follows.

Chapter 2 discusses the theoretical presuppositions of the book. I begin by examining what it means to compare one text to another, and I review the state of the discipline of biblical studies since Samuel Sandmel coined the neologism (that everyone wants to avoid replicating) 'parallelomania'. Source criticism, and the excerpt-based parallels that characterized comparative textual analysis (e.g. reading the HB and other ancient sources as annotative 'background' to the Gospels) in the mid- to late twentieth century was presented as a neutral endeavour. By engaging with scholarship from fields of comparative literature, religion and law, I show that the act of placing texts 'side by side' to explain each other is never neutral but always evaluative from the very beginning. This is not necessarily a bad thing; scholars in a variety of disciplines acknowledge the role of the reader in 'co-creating' the texts he or she interprets. This synchronistic understanding holds much promise in breaking through the stagnation we currently find in methodologies in biblical studies that cannot seem to fully embrace the 'destabilizing' tenets of poststructuralism, and which voice the *language* of theory, but cling to the *practice* of historicism.

---

²³¹ See, for example, Ruth Sheridan, 'Jewish Readings of the Fourth Gospel: Beyond the Pale?' in Jione Havea, David Neville and Elaine Wainwright (eds), *Bible, Borders, Belongings: Engaging Readings from Oceania* (Atlanta: SBL Press, 2014), pp. 93–108.

The second half of Chapter 2 brings the (poststructuralist) literary theories of Roland Barthes into scholarly conversation with the Gospel of John. Barthes asserts that every text exists within a vast echoic web of 'intertextuality'. Every text is 'the text-between' of another text. The hunt for sources, as the hunt for meaning residing in the 'mind' of the 'Author', is a fruitless endeavour. The multiplicity of texts revolves upon *the reader*, who is already a plurality of other texts in the tapestry. The act by which the reader opens the threads of intertextuality (like an organism growing by vital expansion the more the reader is immersed in the network of texts) is what Barthes calls 'textual analysis'. Such analysis can be guided by 'codes' operating on the syntagmatic and paradigmatic dimensions of the text. Barthes elucidates five such codes, two of which pertain to the narrative determinations of the text (its linearity and sequential structure) and three that 'open' the text out, through symbols and cultural references, to the web of *la intertextuelle*, that is that take the text beyond itself. Barthes distinguishes between the 'readerly text' (which is strong in codes that hedge the reader in, either with didacticism, ideology or a totalizing discourse) and the 'writerly text' which gives the reader freedom to create meaning in the process of interpretation, through its fluidity and avenues of plurivocality. I argue in the end that John's Gospel is on the whole a 'readerly text' taken on its own terms but that it has the potential to be a 'writerly text' by probing the ways in which its allusions, symbols and semiotic codes link it to the intertexual. For Barthes, 'intertextuality' can be described as referring to the process of 'scripting' the field of a text, of producing the text's meaning in relation to other texts, of dismantling the monologism of a 'writerly' text in order to open up the plural voices within. In relation to John 8.31-59, the voice of 'the Jews' is delegitimated from the monologic point of view of the Gospel, but their perspective is retrievable through the process of intertextual 'scripting'. This is the very process that I undertake in the analytical chapters that follow.

Chapter 3 has two aims. First, it establishes some preliminary issues about the text of John 8.31-59 itself, such as its internal structure, its narrative setting and the ways in which it relates to the wider context and themes of John 7.1-8.59, at the feast of Sukkot. All of these issues are contentious in the scholarship and therefore require some extended attention. Second, I look at Sukkot as a 'cultural code' (Barthes), 'scripting' an intertextual field for Sukkot from the literature of antiquity. As the analysis shows, the festival of Sukkot provides a fascinating basis upon which to understand the Jews' response to Jesus with respect to the concept of sin (8.31-34), to the role of Abraham as a welcome guest (cf. 8.39-40) under the divine banner of protection (the *sukka*) and to Abraham's joy (cf. 8.56-58) as the founder of Sukkot itself. These intertexts have not yet been brought to bear upon a reading of John 8. Importantly, they reinforce the 'voice' of the Jews in the text through intricate threads of connected motifs such as monotheism, the repudiation of idolatry, the provision and care that God provides through rain and water, and the forgiveness of sin through the merits of the ancestors.

Chapters 4 through 6 analyse the three key concepts reviewed in this chapter: 'seed of Abraham', slavery and sin (Chapter 4), the 'works of Abraham' (Chapter 5) and the vision and joy of Abraham (Chapter 6). Each of these chapters is structured in three parts, beginning with an intertextual analysis of the key metaphors and concepts, followed by an analysis of the same concepts in the Johannine corpus and then a return to the text in light of both the intertextual scripting and the intra textual context. These three chapters form the core of the book, and the intertextual reading that I produce therein is wide-ranging and deep. My method of procedure is to examine the gamut of intertexts from the HB, post-biblical Apocrypha and Pseudepigrapha, the Hellenistic Jewish writings of Philo and Josephus, as well as the DSS, the NT and the Tannaitic literature. As the tapestry of intertexts is so vast, I have concentrated upon the texts within various corpora that collocate concepts (e.g. of 'slavery' and 'sin' *with* the metaphorical appellation 'seed of Abraham') *or* those intertexts that speak of 'the works of [a thing or person]' as either a subjective or attributive genitive, in a similar way in which John uses the phrase 'the works of Abraham'. This is to reign in what would otherwise be an encyclopaedic work. Without pre-empting too much of the ensuing argument (to be found in Chapters 4 through 6), I state the basic contours of it here.

The Jews express their collective identity as 'seed of Abraham' on the premise that they have never been slaves to anyone (8.32). Jesus replies that they are slaves to 'sin' (8.33-34). While many Gospel commentators read this assertion as indicative of stereotypical 'Jewish pride' and 'nationalism', when we open the text to its polysemic intertextual meaning, a different picture emerges. Building on the promises of the land to Abraham's 'seed' in the HB, post-biblical Jewish traditions developed in several key directions: Abraham's 'seed' are unconditionally loved by God and helped in times of need; Abraham's 'seed' are remembered for Abraham's sake because of his merit with God; Abraham himself looks out for the welfare of his 'seed' to prevent them from falling into sin; Abraham's 'seed' inherit not only the land, but the Torah, which protects from sin; and Abraham's 'seed' are purchased as God's slaves, meaning that they do not serve any other master. The NT (especially Paul) develops the motif of Abraham's 'seed' in different directions, to redirect the promises in the Torah to the (singular) 'seed of Abraham', who is Christ. Nevertheless, Paul seems cognisant of the foregoing traditions by virtue of the complexity of his interpretations.

Very few of these intertexts ever make it into the Gospel commentaries on John 8.32. Together they reveal a rich tapestry of traditions that disclose the Jews' perspective in the Gospel text as 'legitimate' in its own right, although it is a perspective that is delegitimated by the voice of the Gospel's implied author and the voice of Jesus himself. This delegitimizing continues in 'compliant' readings of the Gospel that portray the Jews as 'obstinate' and 'privileged' in their reply to Jesus. The purpose of Chapter 4 is to retrieve the voice of the Jews, and to show how the debate between them and Jesus in John 8.31-36 expresses an overarching conversation that was taking place between 200 BCE and 200 CE in early Judaism about the efficacy of the 'merits' of Abraham (and the fathers) to benefit his 'seed' versus the imperative to emulate the deeds that Abraham performed (in order to derive blessing and benefit in life). Or, to put it in other words, is intergenerational merit vicariously efficacious, and does intergenerational sin get imputed to progeny (or in reverse, to deceased ancestors)?

The phrase 'the works of Abraham' (8.39) has no exact parallel in the extant literature. Through 'scripting' the intertextual field for the phrase, I understand it to be an idiomatic expression pointing to different Jewish traditions that portrayed (a) Abraham as an exemplary keeper of the Torah, especially the *mitzvoth* ('works') of צדקה – alternately translated 'righteousness' or 'good works'; and (b) the constellation of Abraham's 'righteous' deeds irrespective of the Torah (his hospitality, his gentleness, his virtue and piety). We also see a diachronic conceptual development across the literature where 'works' function as a precursor to the concept of 'merits', and then where 'works' are the functional equivalent of 'merits'. That is 'works' produce a surplus quantity that takes on a 'thingness' – an accumulation of benefit for others to draw on. The materiality of these 'merits' (especially in the rabbinic literature) is very real; they are considered to be causative of the great redemptive wonders that God has done for Israel. This conceptualization also has roots in the HB, where Abraham, Isaac and Jacob ('the fathers') are 'remembered' by God in times of dire need, so that God's people are saved from destruction.[232]

In early Judaism, we begin to see an intriguing development around the notions of sin and forgiveness, already present in the post-exilic biblical texts, and discernible in a number of apocryphal texts as well. After the exile, sin began to be framed metaphorically as 'debt', and virtue came to be associated with 'credit'. This economic metaphor meant that the performance of *mitzvoth* (concrete expressions of virtue) could be understood as 'merit' that would compensate and alleviate the debt of one's sins. Debt was conceptually understood, moreover, as a form of slavery, predicated on the actual social practice of holding debt-slaves, who needed to work in order to redeem their debt and so become free. Transposed onto the human–divine plane, it was thought that when the children of Israel fell into sin, God gave them a copious Torah filled with *mitzvoth* in order to accumulate a 'treasury' of merits in heaven. One could draw on this treasury as credit – a sign of God's great mercy – and the balance sheets would be corrected, so to speak.

More significantly, the 'fathers' (i.e. Abraham, Isaac and Jacob) had, in their lifetimes, accumulated a great treasury of such merits, and these were collectively referred to as the זכת אבות – the 'merits of the fathers'. Applying this conceptual metaphorical understanding to John 8, I postulate that 'the Jews' reflect on their identity as the 'seed of Abraham' so that *if* they were caught in the 'debt' of sin, they could draw on Abraham's '*works*' and the vicarious merits these works produced. But at the same time there were dissenting voices within early Judaism: e.g. the notion of 'turning' to the 'works of the fathers' did not mean passively relying on their stores of credit, but actively imitating their works (*Mekhilta de-RI*). One had to 'do' the 'works' of one's father, in order to be like one's father (e.g. Josephus and others). This wider debate, I claim, is present in John 8.37-48.

The reference to Abraham 'seeing' Jesus' 'day' and rejoicing in it (8.56-58) is also woven into this coherent conceptual design, with reference to texts in early Judaism and Christianity that depicted Abraham as a righteous 'seer' or prophetic figure, who could watch over his progeny and ensure their well-being. Indeed, some texts speak

---

[232] Gary A. Anderson, *Sin: A History* (New Haven: Yale University Press, 2009). Anderson is highly articulate in refuting the perceptual error that has plagued the scholarship until very recently, that is that such metaphorical schemas were simplistic 'legalism', with God nothing other than a removed accountant. Instead, the metaphorical world views referred to here are rich in nuance, debated even within strands of Jewish literature in antiquity. I engage with Anderson's work in the ensuing chapters; notably he does not look at the Gospel of John in any detail.

of Abraham receiving nocturnal 'visions' from God who reveals himself as the eternal protector of Abraham's 'seed' under a covenant that cannot be revoked. Abraham's capacities for discernment (his inner visions) also tie into the traditions examined in Chapter 5, of Abraham as the exemplary, first monotheist. There are also texts that connect the fathers' 'joy' with their capacity to 'see' the future. Some apocryphal material has Abraham 'seeing' his seed from heaven and interceding for his progeny times a day, or seeing the coming of a messianic figure and rejoicing in the world's redemption. Traditions about Abraham's 'joy' also provide an integrative synthesis of the argument developed here – for example the Targums depict Abraham carrying out the Akedah 'with joy', which has the effect that God will redeem his 'seed' in 'the hour of distress'.

The importance of bringing this richly 'Jewish' world view to bear upon John 8 is evident in light of the propensity of commentators and scholars to read the Jews' claims in this pericope as arising from their obstinacy, blindness or faulty reasoning.[233] At the same time, the *intra*-textual (i.e. Johannine) context is also examined in Chapters 4 through 6, in conjunction with the wide-ranging intertextual interpretation performed. This is because while the intertextual 'Jewish world view' explains much about the Jews' claims in John 8.31-59, the particularly Johannine language and ideas also explain the meaning of the Abraham references in the pericope. This is clearest in the final reference (8.56-58) because collocated instances of 'joy/rejoicing' and 'seeing' are prominent in the Gospel (cf. 16.22-24; 20.20) and cannot be ignored. Therefore, each exegetical chapter concludes with an interpretation of the Johannine contexts (the Gospel and First Epistle) before returning to John 8.31-59 to sum up the findings and arguments.

---

[233] See the following exegetical chapters (4 through 6) for more detail.

2

Theoretical foundations: Intertextuality

Introduction

In his 1857 Oxford Inaugural Lecture, Matthew Arnold famously stated: 'Everywhere there is connection, everywhere there is illustration, no single event, no single literature is adequately comprehended except in relation to other events, to other literatures.'[1] Long before literary theorists developed what came to be termed 'intertextuality', Arnold's conception of the interrelationship between texts and events stood on the record as evidence of a growing concern among the literati of European modernity of the connectedness of life and art.[2] As readers, we grasp the interconnection of texts intuitively; as scholars of comparative literature, we possibly grasp it all the more incisively. The problem involves knowing how to reason through these interconnections, how to responsibly theorize about them and how to explain them persuasively. As we shall see in this chapter, scholars have struggled with each of these aims, and a plethora of nomenclature now exists to describe and define textual interconnections. This plethora of theoretical terms can lead not only to conceptual confusion, but also to clichéd reductions of the original meaning of terms such as 'intertextuality'.[3]

The purpose of this chapter is to advance a theoretical grounding for the comparative analysis of texts, with a particular focus on the ancient Christian and Jewish literatures. While such rigorous theorizing is not wholly absent in the scholarship on the religious

---

[1] Susan Bassnet, 'Influence and Intertextuality: A Reappraisal', *Forum for Modern Language Studies* 43, no. 2 (2007), pp. 134–46, at p. 1. Bassnet cites M. Arnold, On the Modern Element in Literature (Inaugural Lecture delivered at the University of Oxford, 14 November 1857).
[2] The three key figures of *Tel Quel* are Roland Barthes, Julia Kristeva and Jacques Derrida. For an overview of the movement, see Niilo Kauppi, *The Making of an Avant-Garde Tel Quel* (Berlin: de Gruyter, 1994); Patrick Ffrench, *The Time of Theory: A History of Tel Quel* (New York: Oxford: Clarendon Press, 1995); idem, 'Tel Quel 1967: Theory as Excess', *The Comparatist* 38, no. 1 (2014), pp. 97–109; and the very rich work by Johannes Angermuller, *Poststructuralist Discourse Analysis: Subjectivity in Enunciative Pragmatics* (London: Palgrave Macmillan, 2014).
[3] Julia Kristeva eventually lamented the way in which her revolutionary term 'intertextuality' had come to be received and deployed in the scholarship as nothing more than source-hunting; for an excellent assessment of how Kristeva's work has been dismissed by many biblical critics, see Will Kynes, 'Intertextuality: Method and Theory in Job and Psalm 119', in Katharine J. Dell and Paul M. Joyce (eds), *Biblical Interpretation and Method: Essays in Honour of John Barton* (New York: Oxford University Press, 2013), pp. 201–13: 'Critics of diachronic intertextuality in biblical studies often dismiss it as a "banal" study of sources, unfaithful to Kristeva's original intent, and domesticating Theory into method' (p. 201).

literatures of antiquity, historical-critical methodologies (which generally eschew contact with modern – and postmodern – literary theories, either out of an explicit dismissal of their 'faddish' irrelevance or simply because of an implicit assumption about their incompatibility with historicism) still hold hegemonic status in the field of biblical studies.[4] Focusing specifically on John's Gospel, we are beginning to see a diversity of language used to express the connections between texts ('allusion' or 'citation', 'intertextuality', 'textual sources', 'antecedents', 'parallels', 'backgrounds', 'contexts', traditions or 'influences'); other scholars again have gestured towards the concepts of 'scripture', 'Bible' and 'canon'.[5]

However, this range of methodological terminology relating to the Gospel of John and other ancient texts implies a vast divergence in the understandings of readers and authors. For example, in speaking about 'sources', do we assume that 'John' (as 'author') literarily depended on material scrolls in some sense? Or do we assume that we as 'critics' (and other general readers of the Gospel) are detecting possible allusions to these sources? This relates to another fundamental question about literary 'intention' and 'reception': Did the author (or authors) of the Gospel *intend* a given textual allusion, or are perspicacious readers discerning them in the process of textual *reception*? This in turn raises questions about (a) the status – or the entire concept – of 'the author'; (b) the notion of authorial intention versus 'intentionality'; (c) the assumed and varying capacities of real readers – some of whom are invariably going to be more capable of detecting textual connections than others. Additionally, if we directly acknowledge that we are at the helm in constructing our knowledge of John's intertextual fabric, and thus we find ourselves comparing the Gospel to a spate of roughly contemporaneous texts, we are faced with another issue of diachronic priority: does textual comparison require us to look only at antecedent texts? If so, can we be sure that certain texts do indeed antedate the Gospel?

If they do not, on what grounds do we postulate a common source of tradition for both texts? Theoretically, when we compare any texts at all, on what grounds do we do so, and to what end? Do we make analogical comparisons, historical comparisons or evaluative comparisons? These important questions are not often directly addressed in studies dealing with John's Gospel and its use or allusion to early Jewish texts and traditions. When these questions *are* asked, sometimes spurious conclusions have been drawn: for example, that the Fourth Gospel was somehow comparatively 'unique' or special in its difference and divergence from its reputed sources. John's high Christology, woven into his scriptural citations and allusions, has been described as superior to, and elevated well above, the 'Old Testament' texts that shaped the Gospel narrative. These evaluative judgements, which more than betray the interpreter's

---

[4] Cf. Thomas Hatina, 'Intertextuality and Historical Criticism in New Testament Studies: Is There a Relationship?' *BibInt* 7, no. 1 (1999), pp. 28–43; George Aichele and Peter Miscall, 'An Elephant in the Room: Historical-Critical and Postmodern Interpretations of the Bible', *JBL* 128, no. 2 (2009), pp. 383–404; Stephen D. Moore and Yvonne Sherwood, *The Invention of the Biblical Scholar: A Critical Manifesto* (Minneapolis: Fortress Press, 2011). Cf. Hector Avalos, *The End of Biblical Studies* (Amherst: Prometheus, 2007).

[5] Cf. Brunson, *Psalm 118*; M. J. J. Menken, *Old Testament Quotations in the Fourth Gospel: Studies in Textual Form* (CBET 15; Kampen: Kok Pharos, 1996); Schuchard, *Scripture within Scripture*.

bias, are not necessary features of comparative readings, but they unfortunately can make their way into interpretations when prior theoretical questions are not openly addressed.

These questions, and the ambiguity behind them, were famously discussed in a trenchant article by Samuel Sandmel in 1962.[6] Dubbing the excessive scholarly hunt for textual influences and explanatory comparisons as 'parallelomania', Sandmel primarily critiqued 'that extravagance among scholars which first overdoes the supposed similarity in passages and then proceeds to describe source and derivation as if implying literary connection flowing in an inevitable or predetermined direction'.[7] As Sandmel explains, the 'key word' in his essay is 'extravagance' – he does not deny that literary parallels exist, nor does he claim that they ought not to be studied. Sandmel's purpose is to offer a 'word of caution' to scholars about their tendency towards exaggerated conclusions regarding literary parallels. Despite the widespread citation of Sandmel's essay, a cursory glance at a good number of these citations reveals that other scholars summarize Sandmel's article to mean that we ought to be cautious about the conclusions we draw regarding the relationship between ancient Christian and Jewish texts.[8] This has become something of a trend, wherein Sandmel's name is evoked with reference to his article 'Parallelomania' in passing, as an upfront disclaimer on the scholar's limits of engagement with injudicious excesses of interpretation.

But, regrettably, the trend of scholarly deference to Sandmel's criticisms (or often just to the neologism itself) can discourage other scholars from venturing into the choppy waters of adducing 'maximalist' parallels, especially when the literature they read always deploys Sandmel's cautions from the get-go.[9] Wary of appearing to be anachronistic or ignorant about textual chronology, scholars may be less inclined to examine a wide range of antecedent or contemporary texts to the Gospels for fear of appearing to suggest an incorrect relationship between texts. Of course, 'parallels' can be distorting – and not all ancient authors meant the same thing when speaking of similar ideas – which is the chief point of Sandmel's essay, particularly if working 'backwards' as it were, from the rabbis to Paul.[10] Indeed the nadir of excerpt-based comparisons is

---

[6] Samuel Sandmel, 'Parallelomania', *JBL* 81, no. 1 (1962), pp. 1–13. This essay constituted Sandmel's presidential address given at the annual meeting of the Society of Biblical Literature on 27 December 1961 at Missouri (n. 1, p. 1).

[7] Sandmel, 'Parallelomania', p. 1.

[8] Cf. F. L. Cribbs, 'St. Luke and the Johannine Tradition', *JBL* 90, no. 4 (1971), pp. 422–50, at p. 423; Mikeal C. Parsons, 'Son and High Priest: A Study in the Christology of Hebrews', *EvQ* 60 (1988), pp. 198–216, at p. 199; Paul M. Hoskins, 'The Use of Biblical and Extrabiblical Parallels in the Interpretation of First Corinthians 6.2-3', *CBQ* 63, no. 2 (2001), pp. 287–97, at p. 287; H. W. Kuhn, 'The Impact of Selected Qumran Texts on the Understanding of Pauline Theology', in James H. Charlesworth (ed.), *The Bible and the Dead Sea Scrolls: Volume 3: The Scrolls and Christian Origins* (Waco: Baylor University Press, 2006), pp. 153–86, at p. 154, only to cite a few.

[9] Or, as Grant Underwood phrases it, Sandmel's popularization of the concept 'parallelomania' has unwittingly 'given comparative analysis a bad name'. See idem, 'Attempting to Situate Joseph Smith', *Brigham Young University Studies* 44, no. 4 (2005), pp. 41–52.

[10] Sandmel, 'Parallelomania', p. 4. Other scholars have disagreed: see for example, the notable works by Bruce Chilton, *Rabbi Paul: An Intellectual Biography* (Penguin/Random House, 2005); and recently Menahem Kister, 'Romans 5.12-21 against the Background of Torah-Theology and Hebrew Usage', *HTR* 100, no. 4 (2007), pp. 391–424; Michael Benjamin Cover, '*Paulus als Yishmaelit?* The

exemplified in Strack and Billerbeck's *Kommentar zum Neuen Testament aus Talmud und Midrasch* (Str-B). Sandmel considers this five-volume work a 'useful tool' and no more.[11] Yet, these important critiques only go to show why textual comparisons should demonstrate regard for distinctive (textual) contexts. It is the arbitrary *excerption* of parallels texts that Sandmel finds problematic, as well as the theory of textual and/ or authorial relationship upon that exercise of comparative excerption. This is what Sandmel calls 'the question of excerpt versus context'.[12] This is an important point to keep in mind for the topic of this book, as many previous studies on the figure of Abraham in John 8 have tended to shy away from in-depth *contextual* study of comparative texts (what is sometimes called a 'maximalist' approach to allusions) in favour of shorter, annotation-type lists of citations to provide 'background' or 'context'. This is not to accuse previous Johannine scholars of the fallacies that Sandmel laments, but only to say that there is a distinct need for a study such as this, which looks at the widest range of intertextual references in considerable depth as part of my distinctive 'socially located' reading.

With these opening remarks made, I now move on to an extended theoretical discussion that develops as a cumulative argument for my process of interpreting the Gospel text. This chapter is not about advancing a *method* of reading but establishing a philosophical *framework* to validate and support the kind of interpretation in which I am engaging. It is precisely because poststructuralist (or synchronist) interpretations are still contested in New Testament (NT) studies and the term 'intertextuality' is so poorly understood and appropriated, that this discussion is necessary. This chapter proceeds in two parts. I begin with a discussion of comparative reasoning, which forms the basis of methods of interpretation that construct 'parallel' texts as 'background' to the Gospel (or those that find allusions, trace citations or employ any kind of intertextual analysis). Out of this discussion, I argue that the reader/scholar's construction of 'parallels' (or comparisons) can be validly perceived as a synchronic and subjective endeavour, as a procedure of 'articulate choice' (Smith). Next, I discuss poststructuralist intertextuality theory drawn mainly from the theoretical work of Roland Barthes and his notion of the reader's 'scripting' of intertextual fields. Exploring Barthes' concepts of the 'Death of the Author', his method of 'textual analysis' and his binary of the 'readerly'/'writerly' text, I claim that John 8.31-59 is characteristically a 'readerly' text (monologic, guided by a heavy-handed point of view) but that it is potentially 'writerly' ('scriptable') – thus open to the reader's co-creation of meaning – by virtue of its symbolic codes that open it out into the intertextual landscape. Throughout this discussion, I engage with the *status quaestionis* of methodologies in NT criticism, arguing for a renewal of attention to poststructuralism and the radical (even moral) potentialities of theory.

Personification of Scripture as Interpretive Authority in Paul and the School of Rabbi Ishamel', *JBL* 135, no. 3 (2016), pp. 617–37. These latter two articles in particular suggest that the scholarly tide may well be turning in the other direction to once again explore Paul 'in light of' rabbinic parallels.
[11] Sandmel, 'Parallelomania', p. 8.
[12] Ibid., p. 7.

Reflecting on comparative reasoning in textual analysis

Comparison is 'the construction of relations of similarity or dissimilarity between different matters of fact'.[13] Analogical reasoning is but one aspect of comparison, yet it is often deferred to as the primary mode of comparative study for the discernment of similarities.[14] Analogical reasoning is thought to be a helpful means of guiding interpretation and decision-making, shedding light on heretofore undiscovered similarities between things.[15] Every analogy is thus necessarily an act of comparison. Yet, every individual will draw upon different analogues depending not only on their reasoning powers, but also on the contextual limitations of their cognitive contextual knowledge base.[16] Some things are perceived to be similar to other things in terms of a specific feature that they share in common. This feature constitutes the 'third element' in comparison, constructing a triadic relation between two things and the feature that they both share. This 'third element', the *tertium comparationis*, is vital to the discernment of analogies between two things; it signifies that a and b are similar *with regard to* something specific (T).[17] A focus on the difference between two things is also a fruitful way to undertake comparative analysis, as 'difference is essential for constructing identity', meaning that the *tertium comparationis* is used to signify that a and b are unlike in regard to T.[18] We could call this the taxonomic or classificatory model of comparative analysis, whereby T is established as the prior property of similarity/dissimilarity between things, and that which guides comparative reasoning.

Yet, this begs the question of how *tertia comparationis* are selected – is it through an arbitrary act of abstract contemplation? Does one select from certain pre-existing categories and then begin comparing things accordingly? Or should properly comparative reasoning lead us to rethink existing classificatory categories?[19] The whole endeavour of comparative knowledge is more complex than a simple taxonomic model would allow. Certainly, the discernment (or more correctly, construction) of similarities and differences between things relies upon triadic classification; but let us imagine for a moment this triad (a, b and T) as a polygonic triangle – is the triangle equilateral, scalene or isosceles? Suddenly, we introduce the concept of the *angle*, which entails an understanding of *degree*. That is, it is not sufficient to say that a is like or unlike b with respect to T, it is also necessary to ask to what degree a and b are alike or unlike with respect to T. Two professors may be alike in intelligence, but this would not imply that they share the same degree of intelligence – one may be more

---

[13] Nils Jansen, 'Comparative Law and Comparative Knowledge', in Mathias Reimann and Reinhard Zimmermann (eds), *The Oxford Handbook of Comparative Law* (New York: Oxford University Press, 2006), pp. 305–38, at p. 310.
[14] Ibid. p. 310.
[15] Cf. Frederick Schauer, 'Why Precedent in Law (and Elsewhere) Is Not Totally (or Even Substantially) about Analogy', *Perspectives on Psychological Science* 5, no. 6 (1998) pp. 454–60, at p. 456.
[16] Cf. Ken Richardson and David S. Wester, 'Analogical Reasoning and the Nature of Context: A Research Note', *British Journal of Educational Psychology* 66 (1996), pp. 23–32, at p. 31.
[17] Jansen, 'Comparative Law', p. 310.
[18] Ibid., p. 310.
[19] Ibid., p. 311.

intelligent than the other.[20] The concept of degrees of similarity necessarily implies the possibility of difference: where two professors are alike in that they share the property of intelligence, they also necessarily differ in degrees of intelligence. Two cars may share the property of being red, but is their shared colour of the same intensity?

Comparative reasoning is thus, importantly, qualifying by nature. Similarity in kind can yet imply difference by degree, and this is why some analogies (or 'parallels' to gesture Sandmel's arguments once more) can be misleading. Depending upon the context, difference in degree of intelligence between two professors may be more important than the fact that they both have the property of intelligence in common. Likewise, true similarity is determined by both a and b sharing the property of T, and doing so to a reasonably similar degree.[21] Still, an uncomfortable level of arbitrariness is involved in this definition, because it presupposes that we take the very concept of 'similarity' (or 'difference') as granted *a priori*. Is 'similarity' (of property or degree) purely subjective? To an extent, it is; but the fact that we nevertheless make comparisons between objective facts or things to some extent mitigates the outcome of pure arbitrariness. Comparative reasoning therefore proceeds according to the standard of plausibility rather than exact truth.[22]

Comparative reasoning is thus not 'neutral' – as Sandmel's criticisms of 'parallelomania' have made abundantly clear. Comparative judgements necessarily rely upon the epistemological interests of the interpreter, as no empirical criteria truly exist against which to judge similarities and differences. The issue of *a priori* standpoints in the comparative endeavour raises the question of bias. If interpretive interests are unavoidable, are they also deeply problematic? Gayatri Spivak articulates the issue thus: 'Comparison assumes a level playing field, and the field is never level, if only in terms of the interest implicit in the perspective. It is, in other words, never a question of compare and contrast, but rather a matter of judging and choosing.'[23] Neither does evaluation only come in at the end of the comparative endeavour – rather, it starts from the outset, in the selection of the *tertium comparationis*. This selection will be determined by the interpreter's assessment of 'what matters'.[24] According to Niels Jansen, the best way to control for prejudice in comparative reasoning is simply for the interpreter to 'inform others for the reasons or motives for their choice of *tertium comparationis*' from a position of sincerity.[25] Certainly, such disclosures should be normative for any comparative discipline given the tendencies towards Eurocentrism and ethnocentrism in the past. The field of comparative ethnology has been particularly plagued by examples of undisclosed bias – the very concepts of 'culture' and 'society' are Western constructs that skew the perception of comparative social groups under examination.[26]

---

[20] Cf. ibid., p. 312.
[21] Ibid.
[22] Ibid., p. 313.
[23] Gayatri Chakravorty Spivak, 'Rethinking Comparativism', *NLH* 40, no. 3 (2009), pp. 609-26, at p. 609.
[24] Jansen, 'Comparative Law', p. 314.
[25] Ibid., p. 315.
[26] Cf. Laura Nader, 'Comparative Consciousness', in Robert Borofsky (ed.), *Assessing Cultural Anthropology* (4th edn; New York: McGraw Hill, 1993), pp. 84-96, at p. 85.

Many intellectual disciplines have developed comparativist fields of research, and most, if not all of these fields have had to face the nature of bias in comparative reasoning. Notably, these disciplines all emerged in Europe in the nineteenth century: comparative anatomy, comparative philology, comparative religion, comparative literature, comparative ethnology and comparative law (as well as the comparativism distinct to evolutionary biology).[27] Although some disciplines, such as that of comparative literature (or *Weltliteratur*), were formed by 'a cosmopolitan desire to embrace diversity', in practice they often 'became far less global' and more Eurocentric.[28] Likewise, the German *Religionswissenschaft* was motivated, according to its early founding proponent, Friedrich Max Müller, by the desire to break the bounds of 'narrowness' encompassing one's own 'religion's horizon' and to 'enlarge our sympathies'.[29] Yet, almost inescapably, the ideals informing comparative religion and philology settled on the quest for an *Urreligion* that was based on the primal revelation of the One God to the ancient Hebrews, and which filtered down into traces discernible in pagan and Indian religions.[30] The reductive logic behind this move was compelled by Christian missionary bias on the one hand (according to Müller's assessment) and by the need to explain the plurality of modern religions on the basis of a common origin.

Thus, the central assumptions underpinning many of the comparativist disciplines in the human sciences based themselves on a scientistic understanding of typological genesis that was historicized to make sense of progressive differences phrased as differentiation.[31] Saussy calls this model the 'distal tree' logic where an ancestral source is posited as capable of explaining the relation of all subsidiary phenomena – but a model that fails miserably in terms of understanding literature, or indeed anything other than biology, mythology and perhaps linguistics.[32] Instead, Saussy argues that comparative literature – 'lacking a common substance to which the differences among its objects might be reduced' – grows through *ands*, that is, through the 'lateral construction of linking elements'.[33] That is, less like the branches of a tree from a primary root, and more like the International Space Station.[34]

One of the leading theorists of comparative religion over the past several decades has been Jonathan Z Smith, whose work has unrelentingly exposed the various polemical biases behind inter- and intra-religious comparisons.[35] Smith compellingly argues, for example, that the disciplinary study of the NT's relationship to Hellenism, Judaism and the 'mystery religions' of the pagans has been driven by a thinly veiled

---

[27] Cf. Lyle Campbell, 'The History of Linguistics', in Mark Aronoff and Janie Rees-Miller (eds), *The Handbook of Linguistics* (Oxford: Wiley-Blackwell, 2002), pp. 81–104.
[28] Dorothy M. Figueira, 'Comparative Literature versus World Literature', *The Comparatist* 34 (2010), pp. 29–36, at p. 29.
[29] F. Max Müller, *Introduction to the Science of Religion: Four Lectures Delivered at the Royal Institution with Two Essays on False Analogies and the Philosophy of Mythology* (London: Longmans, Green and Co., 1878), p. ix.
[30] Cf. ibid., p. 287.
[31] Cf. Haun Saussy, 'Comparative Literature?' *PMLA* 118, no. 2 (2003), pp. 336–41, at p. 337.
[32] Ibid.
[33] Ibid., pp. 337–8.
[34] Ibid., p. 337.
[35] Cf. Jonathan Z. Smith, *Drudgery Divine: On the Comparison of Early Christianities and the Religions of Late Antiquity* (Chicago: University of Chicago Press, 1990).

apologetic between Protestant and Roman Catholic world views. Smith identifies three polemical trends in the comparative analysis of the NT material: (1) an anti-pagan modulation, which asserted that there were no genuine similarities between ancient mystery religions and true (proto-Pauline) Christianity (and that if Christianities did capitulate to pagan mystery influence, they lost their way in doing so); (2) an ostensibly 'pro-Jewish' modulation that matched any perceived pagan parallel to the NT with a preferable Old Testament or early Jewish parallel (but which refuted the Deutero-Pauline tradition as the degenerate corruption of institutionalized hierarchy); and (3) an anti-Jewish modulation that sought to isolate the NT from Jewish antecedent and contemporaneous traditions.[36] These three approaches commonly emphasized the ideological uniqueness of Christianity, and – according to Smith – they each derived from an anti-Catholic agenda in Protestant scholarship that interpreted ancient mystery cults as embryonic versions of Catholic sacramentalism, and emergent Christian hierarchical formation as early evidence of Catholic papist 'degeneracy'.[37]

Smith establishes a corrective to these covert turf wars and hidden agendas by calling for a renewed rigour in comparative methodology.[38] According to Smith, comparisons should be used to describe degrees of similarity and dissimilarity between two independent objects, regarding a particular question, theory or model. This recalls the triadic function of comparative reasoning that we explored earlier in this chapter, namely, when things are compared with respect to a chosen *tertium comparationis*. In the examples of scholarship probed by Smith, that unstated *tertium* was the assumed uniqueness of Christianity. This tacit bias led scholars to argue that any similarities between early Christianity and pagan religions resulted *either* from coincidental, independent parallels (which therefore did not threaten the uniqueness of Christianity) *or* from the historical fact that Christianity borrowed from paganism and thus corrupted the 'true' faith.[39] To simply state that Christianity displayed similarities to ancient mystery religions, in Smith's view, 'swallowed up the differences that would render such a chain of comparisons interesting', while talk of 'uniqueness' attaches 'ontological meaning to an historical one' and tries to 'make one religion look superior to another'.[40]

Smith draws on the distinction articulated in the biological sciences between 'analogy' and 'genealogy' to explain similarities between things. Smith sees value in the biological concept of 'analogy', where animals belong to different species but share the same function ('convergent' evolution or 'homoplasy'). But he sees no value – indeed much harm – in employing the concept of homology, or what he calls the 'genealogical/diffusion' argument.[41] In Smith's arguments, the conceptual model of genealogy determines relationships of borrowing and dependency (with the aim of privileging one religion over another), but analogy emphasizes the intellectual operations of those

---

[36] Smith, *Drudgery Divine*.
[37] Ibid.
[38] Cf. the similar approach of Sandmel in his essay 'Parallelomania'.
[39] Smith, *Drudgery Divine*, pp. 36–53.
[40] Ibid., pp. 42–3.
[41] Ibid., pp. 36–53. It is also worth noting that Heinrich Frick, *Vergleichende Religionswissenschaft* employed these terms in 1928.

making the comparisons: their nomenclature of similarity and difference, and their choice of what to isolate for comparison. As a synchronic endeavour, comparison will bring objects together solely within the space of the scholar's mind 'imagining their cohabitation'.[42] But that does not mean analogical comparison is an ahistorical operation: one can infer patterns of continuity and discontinuity in the changing development of religious tradition.[43] Finally, Smith advocates for complex analogical comparisons. That is, comparisons ought to be multi-term, although based on a triadic structure (x resembles y more than z with respect to T).[44] And comparison between things is a prior and separate step to making judgements about the historical relationship between things.[45]

Choosing terms of comparison and exempla constitutes an act of 'articulate choice', according to Smith.[46] The scholar is bound neither by the limits of the canon nor by the community, and his or her choice is considered on the grounds of scholarly reasoning. Nancy Levene thinks that Smith's position looks initially like 'a statement of liberation' for the scholar of religion, but something of an equivocal one.[47] Smith's oeuvre generally pushes for more caution to be applied in comparisons; his earlier essays were critical both of the selective reasoning found in inter-religious comparisons, and the style of anthological listing found in the work of his erstwhile favoured mentor, Mircea Eliade.[48] Yet, perhaps the blanket abandonment of homological/diffusion metaphors as applied to comparative historiography is a hasty reaction; as religions use or adapt components of other religions, they transform the other as they simultaneously shape themselves – a phenomenon identified in some of the recent studies on Judeo-Christian formation in the early centuries of the Common Era.[49] As such, it may be the very dichotomy

---

[42] Smith, *Drudgery Divine*; idem, *Relating Religion: Essays in the Study of Religion* (Chicago and London: University of Chicago Press, 2004): 'Comparisons are not given, they are the result of thought' (p. 23).

[43] Yet here caution should also be advocated. Steven Fraade writes: 'The danger with drawing an overly linear schematization of tradition transformation is that it tends to exaggerate and dichotomize the differences between "early" and "late", either within single texts or among clusters of texts, muting the extent of dialectical complexity (even contradiction) within and among those texts, at the redacted textual stage at which they are performatively and dialogically engaged by their readers/auditors'; see Fraade, 'Rabbinic Polysemy and Pluralism Revisited: Between Praxis and Thematization', *AJSR* 31 (2007), pp. 1–40, at p. 39.

[44] Smith, *Drudgery Divine*, pp. 50–1.

[45] Ibid.

[46] Smith, *Imagining Religion*, p. xi.

[47] Nancy Levene, 'Courses and Canons in the Study of Religion (With Continual Reference to Jonathan Z. Smith)', *JAAR* 80, no. 4 (2012), pp. 998–1024, at p. 1008.

[48] Cf. Jonathan Z. Smith, 'Acknowledgements: Morphology and History in Mircea Eliade's "Patterns in Comparative Religion" (1949–1999), Part 2: The Texture of the Work', *History of Religions* 39, no. 4 (2000), pp. 332–51, at p. 333: 'This is surely one's first impression on encountering *Patterns*: the endless comparisons, juxtapositions, enumerations, classifications; the descriptions, but never, as his essay's epigraph suggests, explanations of "thousands … of phenomena"'. Cf. idem, 'When the Bough Breaks', *History of Religions* 12, no. 4 (1973), pp. 342–71, at p. 365: (Comparisons) 'have the common flaw that it compares only one detail [of the complex Balder myth] … or that it cannot adequately account for the transmission of the motif from its presumed point of origin … relying on the vague language of diffusion'.

[49] Cf. Daniel Boyarin, *Borderlines: The Partition of Judaeo-Christianity* (Pennsylvania: University of Pennsylvania Press, 2004); Peter Shäfer, *The Jewish Jesus: How Judaism and Christianity Shaped Each Other* (Princeton: Princeton University Press, 2012).

employed by Smith as a heuristic – the homology/analogy distinction – that should be rethought, for it is 'inspired by an idea of pure borders between natural species. But in the history of religions these are the exceptions, not the rule.'[50]

Recently, more scholars are engaging in literary comparison for its own sake, eschewing the separate methodological move of adducing historical conclusions. Thus, Michal Bar-Asher Siegal, in comparing the anthological literature of the Christian desert fathers with the rabbinic Babylonian Talmud, prefers to present the 'vast array' of examples in 'broad outline' without imposing on them a totalizing theory that would characterize the relationship between the found similarities.[51] Her synchronic, rather than diachronic or genealogical approach, attempts to 'present the texts side by side' in order to obtain a richer understanding of both corpora – what the literary connections suggest, Bar-Asher Siegal claims, is 'shared motifs and ideas', and 'a similar way of looking at the world'.[52]

It is fair to say that Sandmel's article set off a trend for scholars to be more circumspect about comparative methodology, perhaps, even, for them to be unduly or overly cautious about erring in their reasoning. Not only because scholars did not want to unwittingly slip into the triumphalist mindset that interpreted early Christianity as a beacon of light illuminating the dark caverns of 'late Judaism', but also because the task of 'genealogical-historical' comparisons was revealed to be so very convoluted and error-prone: asserting historical literary dependence of one text on an antecedent text meant that the scholar had to be sure about the historical transmission of the antecedent text, which in turn required understanding the 'chronological and geographical specifications of the texts and traditions under consideration'.[53] Anachronism is almost anathema in the discipline of biblical studies.

As a case in point, Lutz Doering implies that anachronism is an abdication of 'critical reasoning' in that later sources cannot be used to validly infer meaning from prior comparative sources – to wit, 'Every *historical* comparison with a later text is a somewhat risky enterprise' (emphasis in the original).[54] The rabbinic texts require the greatest use of caution; even Tannaitic texts are 300 years later than the Dead Sea Scrolls (the primary texts of Doering's concern) and should be used cautiously.[55] Leaving aside for a moment the problem of what might constitute an '*historical* comparison' in Doering's statement, let us probe Doering's solutions in some detail, with reference to the foregoing discussion about comparative knowledge and the comparative method. To be fair, Doering is not dismissing comparative studies, nor is he championing the

---

[50] Hans G. Kippenberg, 'Comparing Ancient Religions: A Discussion of J. Z. Smith's "Drudgery Divine"', *Numen* 39, no. 2 (1992), pp. 220–5, at p. 225.

[51] Michal Bar-Asher Siegal, 'Shared Worlds: Rabbinic and Monastic Literature', *HTR* 105 (2012), pp. 423–56, at p. 430.

[52] Ibid.

[53] H.-J. Klauck, *Herrenmahl und hellenistischer Kult: Eine religionsgeschichtliche Untersuchung zum ersten Korintherbrief* (NTAbh n.s. 15; Münster: Aschendorff, 1982), p. 3.

[54] Lutz Doering, 'Parallels without "Parallelomania": Methodological Reflections on Comparative Analysis of Halakhah in the Dead Sea Scrolls', in Steven D. Fraade, Aharon Shemesh and Ruth A. Clements (eds), *Rabbinic Perspectives: Rabbinic Literature and the Dead Sea Scrolls – Proceedings of the Eighth International Symposium of the Orion Center for the Study of the Dead Sea Scrolls and Associated Literature, 7–9 January 2003* (Leiden: Brill, 2006), pp. 13–42, at p. 31.

[55] Ibid., pp. 31–2.

stolid chauvinism of the biblical 'historical-critical method'; in fact, he finds historicism in biblical studies to be something of a 'pitfall ... with its quasi-objectifying quest for meaning as intended by the author of a text'.[56] But Doering's solutions to this 'pitfall' do not press far enough into the radical potential of synchronism to reshape the way comparisons are explored.

Doering suggests that parallels be explored in the ancient Jewish and Christian literatures by way of reconstructing ancient readers' 'horizons of expectation' rather than guessing the intentions of the historical authors – that way the context of literary parallels is found in the contemporary experience of early readers.[57] But Doering is circumspect: he approves of the alternative theoretical term 'intertextuality' but wants to avoid 'radically subjectivist notions of intertextuality, represented by poststructuralist approaches like deconstruction'.[58] For, according to Doering, poststructuralist approaches allow for 'an infinitude of interplay with all kinds of "texts" within the scholar's mind', whereas more circumscribed approaches to comparative interpretation, such as H. R. Jauß's conception of (historically describable) horizons of expectations 'show much greater affinity with text-analytically informed theories of intertextuality that ask for historically possible and plausible conditions of text reception'.[59]

It is oxymoronic to speak of intertextuality as a type of approach informed by 'historically possible and plausible conditions' of reception (see further in Part II of this chapter). Moreover, 'intertextuality' as a theoretical concept is intrinsically bound up in the development of poststructuralist thought. Doering's middle ground is actually a return to source criticism reframed as reception history, a bid to enlist the sophistication of theory without the destabilizing effects it necessarily brings into play. There is perhaps a subtle judgement in Doering's disavowal of 'radical subjectivism' as an impermissible ideology obscuring 'correct' interpretations of literary texts (nor is Derrida's 'deconstruction' an approach specific to theories of intertextuality). Yet, it is Doering's assumption that poststructuralism permits an 'infinitude of interplay of all kinds of "texts" within the scholars' mind' that requires critique – as though infinitude can reasonably be said to exist within any one mind; and as though the scholar's mind is any more objectionable than seeking to peer into the reconstructed expectations of early readers' minds. But it is the *certitude*, which a finite number of historically plausible texts represents, that informs Doering's preference for reception-historical interpretation. Jauss' notion of the social and literary conditions obtaining for the possibility of a text's reception (i.e. it's understanding on the part of its receiving audience) simply functions to rule out parallels that are implausible (historically), and so to give a more refined body of texts available for comparison.

Doering speaks of the reception-centric approach to 'intertextuality' as a 'paradigm shift' that will assist scholars to avoid the pitfalls of parallelomania. While Doering wants to avoid 'causal' notions of influence, the 'crucial' shift he sees in this new paradigm to 'conditions of reception' seems only to invert the figure of the author (and

---

[56] Ibid., p. 25.
[57] Ibid.
[58] Ibid.
[59] Ibid., pp. 25–6.

his or her causal influences) to the figure of an implied reading community (and the conditions of possibility of their knowledge). Tracing those 'possible and plausible' conditions (in the shape of parallels or intertexts) involves figuring the implied 'expectations' coded within the text, which is an inverse way of tracing the historical influences upon the putative author. Certainly, the paradigm shift takes us away from the psychobiology of the figured author and his repertoire of influences, but the *author* is nevertheless implied in the figure of the reader and the possibilities necessary for the text to be received by a reader. To ask what effect a text might have had on a reader's horizon of expectation is still speculative (and we could say 'subjectivist'). How can we know? And can we control for bias in a more effective way by adopting this approach? Agendas can still creep in: we might assume that early Christian readers expected certain things from texts, and then along comes the Gospel and surprisingly subverts their expectations, their horizons of understanding, in its assumed difference and superiority.

A preferable way forward is to fully embrace the implications of synchronism contained in the comparative method. For Smith, comparison will bring objects together solely within the space of the scholar's mind 'imagining their cohabitation'. The choice of *tertium comparationi* is not necessarily a derisively 'subjectivist' choice, but 'an articulate choice', according to Smith, and the imperative is not to stringently circumscribe which texts historically 'make the cut' as much as it is to declare one's choice of texts upfront. The scholar's choice will necessarily rest upon a determination of 'what matters', on which there is no empirically historicist way to decide. The New Comparativism tells us that comparison is always a matter of perspective, that parallels are not equations but assertions of similarity and difference in degrees of a chosen subject. The function of comparative reasoning (at least in theory) is not to detect *causal influences* but to isolate that which, in Sandmel's words, constitutes an 'area of distinctiveness' amid the 'broad overlapping' areas of similarity. Scholars do not need to continually hedge their bets when making comparisons for fear of falling into anachronism as long as it is clear that the comparisons are made independently of geographic, linguistic or historical contingencies.[60]

Holding two (even two very disparate) things together in the scholars' mind and setting them side by side for comparative purposes is not an affront to critical reasoning. Neither is reading for hidden comparative structures within a literary text an exercise in subjectivist fabrication – witness the stunning vibrancy of Edward Said's 'contrapuntal reading' of *Mansfield Park*.[61] The project of the reader/critic in finding productive connections or disjunctions between different texts (or any work of art or political rhetoric) irrespective of historical limitations (contrapuntal interpretation, poststructuralist intertextuality) is not by any means fantastical or unworthy of the label 'scholarship'.[62] Neither do such readings neglect historical concerns; in fact,

---

[60] Cf. Bar-Asher Siegal, 'Shared Worlds'.
[61] Edward W. Said, *Culture and Imperialism* (London: Vintage (reprint), 1994).
[62] Cf. Darren Cronshaw, 'A Commission "Great" for Whom? Postcolonial Contrapuntal Readings of Matthew 28.18-20 and the Irony of William Carey', *Transformation: An International Journal of Holistic Mission Studies* 33, no. 2 (2016), pp. 110–23.

they often understand the interaction between historiography and narrative in a very sophisticated manner.[63]

I would therefore suggest that we take seriously the statement of Jonathan Smith that comparative analysis is a synchronic endeavour, with texts cohabiting within the scholar's imagination (the latter term is here used in the best, creative sense, rather than in the derogatory sense that would oppose it to factual reality). Indeed, many of the criticisms Samuel Sandmel raises against the excessive piling up of (apparently irrelevant) parallels could today be methodologically justified on such reader-oriented grounds. In like manner, the tacit scholarly taboo against reading the NT in light of later rabbinic literature – which when performed, is always hedged with the disclaimer that the *Tannaitic* material nevertheless gives voice to oral traditions possibly reaching back into the time of Jesus – might be lifting; proceeding by way of synchronic comparative analysis, why can we not view the analogies between the two compilations of texts as part of a broader story, or a wide-ranging conversation on various conceptual themes, instead of viewing them as linear developments with an ordained teleology (tending neither to perfection nor to retrogression)?[64]

According to theorist Hans Saussy, the conjunction '*and*' supplies the *raison d'etre* of comparative literature.[65] The literature under comparison grows laterally, contiguously, by increments and linkages of 'sets of examples whose mutual coherence is not obvious in advance of their combination'.[66] For Saussy, the comparative study of literature is all about the readerly production of semiotics, as if one were to ask 'What do X, Y, and Z have in common?' only to receive the reply, 'Nothing – up to now'.[67] Of course, this construction – what Saussy terms '*and* criticism' – can appear arbitrary, giving rise to the discipline's perceived 'questionable legitimacy'.[68] But 'the willingness to tolerate readings that produce, rather than discover, meanings' is what Saussy considers to be the invariably 'risky' and 'experimental' side of the comparative procedure, which is in fact, also its greatest virtue.[69]

Ultimately, these thoughts take us back to Sandmel's cautions about 'parallelomania' – particularly his awareness of the problem of 'piling up excerpts' in comparisons between texts. But this seems precisely to be what Saussy's '*and* criticism' advocates – the lateral construction of 'ands', the piece-by-piece shaping of a large, comparative texture. It is worth exploring, instead of dismissing, the linkages between chosen texts explained by way of the *tertium comparationis*. This process of shaping a tapestry of linked texts is what I would now like to explore in greater detail by attending to one final aspect of literary theory: poststructuralist intertextuality, specifically the work of Roland

---

[63] Cf. Jihan Mahmoud, 'Dialogic Interaction Between the Historical Background and Events in the Novels of J. M. Coetzee and Jabra Ibrahim Jabra: A Contrapuntal Reading', *International Journal of Arts & Sciences* 7, no. 6 (2014), pp. 561–75.
[64] In a different context, see Steven D. Fraade, *From Tradition to Commentary: Torah and Its Interpretation in the Midrash Sifre to Deuteronomy* (New York: Albany State University of New York Press, 1991).
[65] Saussy, 'Comparative Literature', p. 338.
[66] Ibid., p. 339.
[67] Ibid.
[68] Ibid.
[69] Ibid.

Barthes. I claim that Barthes' concept of 'scripting an intertextual field' corresponds to, and complements, the synchronic construction of comparative analysis explained and discussed in this section of the chapter. The final section of this chapter ties together all of these theoretical insights and sets out my approach to interpreting the Gospel of John in the remainder of the book.

Intertextuality

The theoretical concept of 'intertextuality' has held a somewhat troubled status in the discipline of biblical studies. At the extreme end of polemical resistance to the theories that the concept espouses, we find dismissive remarks such as the following: 'Behind the concept [of intertextuality] hides nothing more than a fashionable upstart version of studies that have already been conducted for centuries', such as form and redaction criticism and the concept of inner-biblical exegesis.[70] Other critics likewise claim that 'there is nothing particularly postmodern about this method' (i.e. intertextuality), and in fact that it has much in common with premodern 'fundamentalist traditions, whether Jewish or Christian'.[71] The idea that intertextuality is both faddish and vacuous is almost cliché in the writings of scholars standing strong on the hegemonic status of historical criticism. Critics lament that 'postmodern' intertextuality is more akin to novel writing than to scholarship – indeed, one such critic considered that practitioners of intertextual theory perhaps unwittingly and secretly aspire to be novelists rather than scholars![72] In fact, the reaction against intertextuality in biblical studies is part of a broader backlash against synchronism and literary theory more generally, whereby those adopting 'newer' theoretical methods of interpretation are simply dismissed as 'ideologically motivated critics' (as though historicism itself is ideologically neutral).[73] Scholarly practitioners of the historical-critical method can tend to speak in defensive terms – for example, John Ashton, one of the premier Johannine scholars of the past century, identifies as 'an unrepentant advocate of the historical critical method'.[74] On the other side, biblical scholars who advocate for the use of literary theory in general,

---

[70] Thomas A. Schmitz, *Moderne Literaturtheorie und antike Texte*, p. 93. The English translation (*Literary Theory and Ancient Texts* (Oxford: Blackwell, 2007) reads, 'no more than a new-fangled catchword to express phenomena that had been analysed long before', p. 76).

[71] John Van Seters, 'A Response to G. Aichelle [sic], P. Miscall and R. Walsh, "An Elephant in the Room: Historical-Critical and the [sic] Postmodern Interpretations of the Bible"', *JHS* 9 (2009), pp. 1–13, at p. 9. Accessed online: http://www.jhsonline.org, at 13 January 2017.

[72] Ibid., p. 10.

[73] The dismissive quote is from Robert Morgan, '*Sachkritik* in Reception History', *JSNT* 32, no. 3 (2010), pp. 175–90, at p. 177. Cf. David Harlan, 'Intellectual History and the Return of Literature', *AHR* 94, no. 3 (1989), pp. 581–609: 'The return of literature has plunged historical studies into an extended epistemological crisis. It has questioned our belief in a fixed and determinable past, compromised the possibility of historical representation, and undermined our ability to locate ourselves in time'. And historians can no longer assume 'the solid foundation of objective method and rational argument' of 'a truly scientific discipline' (all at p. 581).

[74] John Ashton, 'Second Thoughts on the Fourth Gospel', in Thatcher (ed.), *What We Have Heard From the Beginning: The Past, Present and Future of Johannine Studies* (Waco: Baylor University Press, 2007), pp. 1–18, at p. 17.

and intertextuality theory in particular, have been disgruntled by 'the championing of the historical-critical method as the only valid form of interpretation'.[75] There has come to be an unfortunate impasse between 'postmodern' interpretive approaches on the one hand, and established historicist methods on the other.[76]

The charge that intertextuality is merely a superfluous, jargon-dense covering for established source-critical methodologies in biblical studies is certainly incorrect on a conceptual level; but it is precisely this charge that reveals a major problem with the ways in which 'intertextuality' is employed in biblical studies. Because the term itself has been misused and virtually misappropriated by a considerable number of biblical scholars – who use the term without reference to the radical theories behind it and proceed to practice source criticism instead – critics of 'biblical intertextuality' have an easy target: they assume that the concept of 'intertextuality' is itself meaningless, and that the proverbial emperor has been denuded. A range of biblical scholars who have jumped on the bandwagon of 'intertextuality' studies fail to define their key term;[77] and because they proceed to interpret their texts under the rubric of 'influence' (which is a pragmatic descriptor for the use, citation or allusion of one text in relation to another), the concept of intertextuality falls into disrepute among its detractors as an enervating, catch-all, fad-word wielded by would-be sophisticates. If the word is defined, it is often defined so variously that it risks failing to mean anything coherent at all. In another (non-biblical) context, one scholar has captured this problem incisively, that is that the term 'intertextuality' has come 'to have almost as many meanings as users'.[78]

So, what is 'intertextuality'? As the vast majority of scholars note (either in passing or in depth), the term *intertextualité* was coined by Bulgarian-French theorist Julia Kristeva in 1966 upon her reflections on the then little-known writings of Mikhail Bakhtin, particularly the latter's understanding of the dialogic aspect of language.[79]

---

[75] Steve Moyise, 'Intertextuality and Historical Approaches to the Use of Scripture in the New Testament', in Richard B. Hays, Stefan Alkier and Leroy A. Huizenga (eds), *Reading the Bible Intertextually* (Waco: Baylor University Press, 2009), pp. 23–32, at p. 24. Cf. Harlan, 'Intellectual History', p. 584: 'From its origins in Greek mythology through its refinement in nineteenth-century biblical scholarship to its emergence as an academic specialty, the guiding objective of Romantic hermeneutics has remained constant: the recovery of authorial intention.' This sentence – by a non-biblical historian – sums up the approach of the historical-critical method(s) practised in biblical studies up to today: the fundamental excavation of authorial intention as a *Romantic* endeavour, trying to ascertain 'the' unified meaning of the text as it resided in the mind of the lone apostolic (or prophetic) genius, under the influence of other lone apostolic (or prophetic) geniuses.

[76] Cf. Hatina, 'Intertextuality and Historical Criticism', pp. 28–43; George Aichele, Peter Miscall and Richard Walsh, 'An Elephant in the Room: Historical-Critical and Postmodern Interpretations of the Bible', *JBL* 128, no. 2 (2008), pp. 383–404; Steve Motyer, 'Method in Fourth Gospel Studies: A Way Out of the Impasse?' *JSNT* 66 (1997), pp. 27–44.

[77] Cf. Thomas L. Brodie, *The Birthing of the New Testament: The Intertextual Development of the New Testament Writings* (Sheffield: Phoenix Press, 2004); Brunson, *Psalm 118*; K. D. Litwak, *Echoes of Scripture in Luke-Acts: Telling the Story of God's People Intertextually* (JSNTSup 282; London: T&T Clark, 2005); Craig A. Evans and J. D. Zecharias (eds), *Early Christian Literature and Intertextuality* (2 vols.; London: T&T Clark, 2009); B. J. Abasciano, *Paul's Use of the Old Testament in Romans 9.1-9: An Intertextual and Theological Exegesis* (LNTS 317; London: T&T Clark, 2005); Gail R. O'Day, 'Jeremiah 9.22-23 and 1 Corinthians 1.26-31: A Study in Intertextuality', *JBL* 109 (1990), pp. 259–67.

[78] William Irwin, 'Against Intertextuality', *PL* 28, no. 2 (2004), pp. 227–42, at p. 227.

[79] Cf. Julia Kristeva, 'Intertextuality and Literary Interpretation' (interview), in Ross Guberman (ed.), *Julia Kristeva Interviews* (New York: Columbia University Press, 1996), p. 189.

Kristeva understood any text to be 'constructed as a mosaic of quotations; any text is the absorption and transformation of another. The notion of *intertextuality* replaces that of intersubjectivity, and poetic language is read as at least *double*.'[80] The term 'quotation' in the foregoing excerpt is an abstract, not a literal concept; it describes Kristeva's understanding of textual referentiality as distinct from both Romantic and structuralist theories of language. That is, texts refer only to other texts, not to concrete material reality external to the vast network of intertextuality, nor to the ideation of the author(s) of the text. Meaning – *signifiance* – is created in the reading process at the 'intersection of textual surfaces'.[81]

Meaning is not created by the author of a text, for every text evolves out of other texts. This is more than to state that 'no text is an island', for Kristeva conceives of sociocultural fabrics also as 'texts', such that 'a literary text does not live ... closed in on the interior of itself, but borrows always from the discourses of the press, from oral discourse, from political discourses, and from other texts that preceded it, that provide vehicles in turn for these cultural and political texts in history'.[82] Kristeva's vision of intertextuality was not ahistorical, and was certainly political in its radical ramifications. As Graham Allen summarizes, for Kristeva, a text 'is not an isolated object, but rather a compilation of cultural textuality [and] ... texts do not present clear and stable meanings; they embody society's dialogic conflict over the meaning of words'.[83]

Of course, since Kristeva conceived the term 'intertextuality' numerous other literary theorists have developed their own versions of the concept (and in fact, the concept itself was operative in the work of Bakhtin and Barthes prior to Kristeva's neologism). It would be erroneous to suggest that because Kristeva coined the word 'intertextuality', all scholars who use the same term must identify with Kristeva's definition. Other notable theorizations of intertextuality following Kristeva, which have been remarkably influential, include the work of Michael Riffaterre (Kristeva's colleague at Columbia University), and the more circumscribed structuralist approaches of Gérard Genette, the latter of whom considers 'quotation' and 'allusion' as concrete instantiations of transtextuality.[84] More straightforward definitions of intertextuality can be found in the work of scholars disseminating literary theory, such

---

[80] Julia Kristeva, 'Word, Dialogue, Novel', in idem, *Desire in Language: A Semiotic Approach to Literature and Art* (trans. Thomas Gora, Alice Jardine and Leon S. Roudiez; edited by Leon S. Roudiez; New York: Columbia University Press, 1980), p. 66. That is, meaning is not simply conveyed between subjects (the writer's intention and his or her reader's capability to gauge that intention). A text is an intersection of textual surfaces in that meaning is 'conveyed' as it were, between texts – tracing a 'line' (e.g. the author-subject's influences) through time is complicated by the fact that every text or discourse 'is a field of transposition of various signifying systems' (Kristeva, *Revolution in Poetic Language*, p. 60).

[81] Julia Kristeva, 'The Bounded Text', in idem, *Desire in Language*, pp. 35–6.

[82] Julia Kristeva, 'Interview with S. Clark and K. Hulley', in Guberman (ed.), *Julia Kristeva Interviews*, p. 53.

[83] Graham Allen, *Intertextuality* (London/New York: Routledge, 2000), p. 36.

[84] Cf. Michael Riffaterre, *Semiotics of Poetry* (Bloomington: Indiana University Press, 1978); idem, 'Interpretation and Undecidability', *NLH* 12, no. 2 (1980), pp. 227–42; idem, 'Intertextual Representation: On Mimesis as Interpretive Discourse', *CI* 11, no. 1 (1984), pp. 141–62; idem, 'Compulsory Reader-Response: The Intertextual Drive', in Michael Worton and Judith Still (eds), *Intertextuality: Theories and Practices* (Manchester/New York: Manchester University Press, 1990), pp. 56–78. See also Gérard Genette, *Palimpsests: Literature in the Second Degree* (trans. Channa

as John Frow's understanding of intertextuality as 'the elaboration of a text in relation to other texts'.[85] And Graham Allen's description of intertextuality as the process by which we discover meaning 'between a text and all the other texts to which it refers and relates'.[86] While Kristeva's conceptualization of intertextuality is theoretical rather than methodological, Genette's definition includes a programmatic method of discerning and discussing the 'relationship of copresence between two texts or among several texts'.[87] Thus the term 'intertextuality' is not transparent, nor is it monolithic.[88] The term requires careful elucidation when it is invoked, and it must be kept in mind that a 'text' is not restricted to literary or written forms of communication in the works of a considerable number of theorists employing the term.

Although biblical scholars by no means uniformly overlook the critical theory informing the term 'intertextuality', it is fair to say that there is a depressingly common tendency among scholars to perform a perfunctory nod to Kristeva, or to the complexity and variety of intertextuality theories before dispensing with theory altogether and undertaking source-critical exegesis.[89] This tendency is perhaps partially due to the seminal work of Richard B. Hays (*Echoes of Scripture in the Letters of Paul*), which popularized an approach to interpreting the 'use' of the Old Testament in the Pauline corpus based ostensibly on the idea of intertextuality and echoic allusions, but which actually proceeds from a carefully controlled method of adducing valid sources for the NT.[90] Hays referred to his approach as 'metaleptic intertextuality', building on the work of John Hollander, who explored the rhetorical and semantic effects of literary allusions.[91] Hays adapts Hollander's categories of 'overt allusions' and 'allusive echoes' to determine how scriptural 'echoes' function in Paul's letters to recontextualize the existing (original) meaning of a source text. For Hollander, an echo is 'metaleptic', suggesting that the semantic figuration of an echo falls outside the 'frame', residing in what is left unsaid or suppressed ('transumed').[92] When a prior text is 'echoed' in a later text, its entire allusive matrix is potentially carried with it, and is incorporated within the frame of the new text.[93]

Newman and Claude Doubinsky; Lincoln: University of Nebraska Press, 1997); idem, *Paratexts: Thresholds of Interpretation* (trans. Jane E. Lewin; Cambridge: Cambridge University Press, 1997).

[85] See John Frow, *Genre* (London/New York: Routledge, 2005), p. 148.
[86] Allen, *Intertextuality*, p. 1.
[87] Genette, *Palimpsests*, pp. 1–2.
[88] Cf. Mary Orr, *Intertextuality* (Cambridge: Polity Press, 2003).
[89] Cf. the examples cited in David I. Yoon, 'The Ideological Inception of Intertextuality and Its Dissonance in Current Biblical Studies', *CBR* 12, no. 1 (2012), pp. 58–76.
[90] Richard B. Hays, *Echoes of Scripture in the Letters of Paul* (New Haven: Yale University Press, 1989), p. 15.
[91] See John Hollander, *The Figure of an Echo: A Model of Allusion in Milton and After* (Berkeley: University of California Press, 1981). Hollander only employs the term 'intertextuality' once in his work (p. 64).
[92] Cf. Hays, *Echoes*, p. 20.
[93] Ibid., cf. C. H. Dodd, *According to the Scriptures: The Substructure of New Testament Theology* (London: Collins, 1952), who made this assumption credible in later New Testament studies. However, see recently Andrew Elfenbein, 'On the Discrimination of Influences', *MLQ* 69, no. 4 (2008), pp. 481–506. Elfenbein draws on theories articulated in the psychology of memory to demonstrate that allusions do not necessarily work this way (i.e. the allusion, which is the 'tip of the iceberg' necessarily carries with it the whole original context), at p. 486.

Hays relies upon the hermeneutical presupposition of readerly competence to advance his method: in order to successfully extrapolate allusive echoes from a text, the reader in question must be able to recognize them, and, moreover, to situate them within a recognized literary 'canon'.[94] Nevertheless, as we read through Hays' work it is possible to observe that the creative and radical poetics of metaleptic intertextuality initially espoused gives way ever so slightly to an author-centred hermeneutic. We could be excused for thinking that here Hays makes a concession to historically minded critics of the NT who would rather be assured that allusive echoes to the Old Testament are scientifically verifiable. To this end, Hays has famously developed criteria to determine the likelihood that the scriptural echoes perceived by the reader match up with what the original, ancient authors of the NT understood and knew. Hays' list of seven criteria is well known and is frequently rehearsed in scholarly articles.[95] There is no need to discuss his criteria in detail here, only to note that they depend on a sliding scale of probability, and that they aim to measure the degree to which intertextual echoes can be verified or falsified. As such, echoes need to have been 'available' to first audiences, they must display a high 'verbal correspondence' with the precursor text, they must be frequently expressed in contemporaneous ancient literature and they must cohere thematically with the text in which they are apparently transumed.[96]

Hays' approach is emblematic of the caution felt by a large contingent of biblical scholars when addressing the relationship between the NT and other texts of early Judaism. His concession to author-centred (or early-reader-centred) perspectives actually places a great constraint on the contemporary reader's agency to co-create the text from its intertextual field. Hays acknowledges that his seven criteria are only meant to function as a partial corrective to overly subjectivist readings potentially generated by intertextual theory.[97] They are not a hard and fast preliminary constraining device on what constitutes validity in interpretation – but Hays' influential method has often been taken up in a stringent manner by other scholars.[98] Critics of Hays' approach have argued that he ought to have dispensed altogether with the term 'intertextuality', as it has nothing in common with poststructuralism, and is in fact akin to the study of 'influences' or source criticism.[99] Others again have defended Hays for employing an acceptable, albeit 'limited', form of 'intertextuality' that differs from the 'much-maligned author-centred quest for sources'.[100]

Various other examples of biblical and early Christian scholars paying lip service to poststructuralist intertextuality have been found even recently. A case in point

---

[94] Cf. Hays, *Echoes*, pp. 19, 21–2, 24.
[95] See recently the survey in Brittany E. Wilson, 'Pugnacious Precursors and the Bearer of Peace: Jael, Judith and Mary in Luke 1.42', *CBQ* 68 (2006), pp. 436–56.
[96] Hays, *Echoes*, p. 24.
[97] Ibid., pp. 190–1.
[98] Cf. Wilson, 'Pugnacious Precursors'; Timothy Berkley, *From a Broken Covenant to Circumcision of the Heart: Intertextual Exegesis in Romans 2.17-29* (SBLDS 175; Atlanta: SBL Press, 2000).
[99] Cf. Hatina, 'Intertextuality and Historical Criticism', pp. 36–7. Cf. also W. S. Green, 'Doing the Text's Work for It: Richard Hays on Paul's Use of Scripture', in Craig A. Evans and J. A. Sanders (eds), *Paul and the Scriptures of Israel* (JSNTSup 83; Sheffield: Sheffield Academic Press, 1993), pp. 58–63.
[100] Cf. Leroy Huizenga, *The New Isaac: Tradition and Intertextuality in the Gospel of Matthew* (NovTSup 131; Leiden: Brill, 2009), p. 44.

is an article by Candida R. Moss, entitled 'Nailing Down and Tying Up: Lessons in Intertextual Impossibility from the *Martyrdom of Polycarp*'.[101] The title itself is a contradiction in terms, for in poststructuralist intertextuality theory *no* 'text' is an 'impossibility'; there are no 'potential intertexts' – all texts, both anterior and posterior are intertexts in a vast network. The value of intertextuality theory is that it gets beyond the stigma of 'incorrect' readings, of anachronism and of accusations of subjectivism.[102] George Aichele explains this point by suggesting that 'the intertextual context of every text is always *here* and *now*. In other words, reading is always anachronistic'.[103] Even our awareness of how ancient readers may have understood an ancient text 'is itself always conditioned by our present contexts, interests and commitments' so that the act of 'privileging [...] an ancient reading as the text's proper meaning is nothing more than the privileging of the *contemporary* intertext through which that ancient reading is understood'.[104]

In a footnote, Moss nods to Kristeva as follows: 'The term "intertextuality", originally coined by Julia Kristeva, has been adapted and borrowed by many to the point that it does, in many cases, represent a more critically affluent synonym for allusion... but this paper is neither limited to, nor dependent upon Kristeva for its particular perspective.'[105] In the same footnote, Moss proceeds to speak of the 'influence' and 'literary dependence' of sources and cultural ideas within early Christianity.[106] Moss' interest is in showing how previous scholars' reflections on biblical citations or allusions in *Martyrdom of Polycarp* (*M. Pol*) have proceeded from 'untheorized assumptions about how intertexts function'.[107] Her answer is to propose 'a more carefully conceptualized notion of intertextuality, which acknowledges the limits of intertextual analysis'.[108] Moss uses the nominal term 'intertext' (and 'parallel') in her article to denote a prior (usually canonical) written source text.[109] Although Moss does astutely observe that in studies of the canonical influence on *Martyrdom of Polycarp*, source dependency ('intertextuality') has been reduced to mere accurate duplication of source material, and that scholars usually assume (incorrectly) that allusion replicates 'the *meaning* of the intertext', her solution is to mandate intertextual precision: 'one has to make a case for the philological or conceptual similarity of text to intertext'.[110] But equally, one must also make room for the 'hybridity', 'adaptation' and 'subversion' of source material.[111] Moss also rightly notes that 'it is difficult to identify specific literary

---

[101] In *VC* 67, no. 2 (2013), pp. 117–36.
[102] Cf. Kristeva, *Desire in Language*, p. 66: 'To read a text with an eye for its intertextual dimension, therefore, is to recognise an inherent transgression of discreet, self-contained unity, which renders the quest for "correct" interpretation impossible.'
[103] George Aichele, 'Canon as Intertext: Restraint or Liberation?' in Huizenga and Alkier (eds), *Reading the Bible Intertextually*, pp. 139–56, at p. 142.
[104] Ibid., p. 142.
[105] Moss, 'Nailing Down and Tying Up', n. 1, p. 117.
[106] Ibid.
[107] Ibid., p. 119.
[108] Ibid., p. 120.
[109] Cf. ibid., pp. 123, 127, 128, 134.
[110] Ibid., pp. 127 and 128. Emphasis in original.
[111] Ibid., p. 128.

intertexts *to the exclusion of all other* influences'.[112] Both literary and cultural 'texts' have informed *Martyrdom of Polycarp*, Moss writes, and the presumed binary between these 'texts' is false and unhelpful.[113] Even if a source text is satisfactorily identified, Moss argues, its meaning cannot necessarily be confidently asserted, for 'meaning is always unsteady, constantly reproduced, and indeterminate'.[114]

Reading Moss' article, it is evident that she makes some good points about the process of intertextuality and that she accurately states some of the principles about *signifiance* in poststructuralist theory. But it is hard to locate the target of her critique because of the conceptual problems in her piece, which can be obfuscating. Apart from interspersed comments about the indeterminacy of meaning, Moss almost does not need to even use the term 'intertextuality', for she typically uses the nominal term 'intertext' to denote other scholars' attempts at finding a pure source or influence for *Martyrdom of Polycarp*. A considerable number of these scholars (e.g. Lightfoot) likewise do not use the term 'intertext' but use more conventional source-critical terms such as 'quotation', 'allusion', 'source' and 'influence'. To charge previous scholars with failure to consider the processes of intertextuality when they are credibly talking about influence is problematic. This only raises the more pertinent problem that 'intertextuality' and 'influence' are *not the same things*, and that they are in fact diametrically opposed concepts based on very different theories of semiotics. Moss seems to want to circumvent this issue by claiming that Kristeva's concept of 'intertextuality' has taken on a life of its own to the point that it has come to signify 'allusion', and that therefore it is satisfactory to employ the term 'intertextuality' in this manner. This is true to a point – in fact, Kristeva eventually abandoned the term 'intertextuality' altogether, favouring instead the term 'transposition'. This arose out of her eventual realization that most scholars who adopted her original term did so in the 'banal sense of source-criticism', not in keeping with her understanding of psychoanalytic subjectivity.[115] Moss' deployment of intertextuality as a 'more critically affluent' alternative to 'allusion' is ultimately an empty gesture, characteristic of what Irwin has called the simple use of the term as 'a stylish way of talking about influence'.[116]

It has become commonplace in biblical and early Christian studies to 'accommodate' the radical theories of poststructuralism to make them more amenable to the tradition of use within the discipline. This might be in part due to the fact that the destabilizing tenets of poststructuralist intertextuality – the denial of meaning as residing in authorial intention, the plenitude of texts informing intertextual analysis, the threat of anachronism or subjectivism – run against the grain of the authoritative structures in biblical interpretation. If scholars adopted the radical political, subversive implications of poststructuralism, they would necessarily have to negotiate the power dynamics inherent in the cultural texts of the church and the academy: the 'Author-God' (Barthes) inscribing singular theological meaning via purported inspiration,

---

[112] Ibid., p. 135. Emphasis in original.
[113] Ibid., p. 135.
[114] Ibid., p. 136.
[115] Julia Kristeva, *Revolution in Poetic Language* (New York: Columbia University Press, 1984), pp. 59–60.
[116] Irwin, 'Against Intertextuality', p. 228.

the wedded interests of ecclesial politics and academic appointments (e.g. Catholic theology colleges constraining freedom of expression on doctrinal matters deemed *ex cathedra*) and the hegemonic status of historical criticism (once considered a threat to biblical interpretation, and now so thoroughly absorbed as to be normative and 'natural').[117] As such, some scholars countenance as valid a specifically 'New Testament' version of intertextuality – as 'a descriptive category to refer to the relationship between written texts, primarily as the imbedding [*sic*] of fragments of earlier texts within later texts'.[118] The various different 'types' of intertextuality found within the discipline of biblical studies are sometimes contradictory, masquerading as the study of 'influences', other times fully informed by dialogism, poststructuralism and literary theory.[119] No wonder there is frustration on both sides: by historicist scholars in the guild who do not see that the term 'intertextuality' adds to the interpretation undertaken, and by postmodern interpreters of the Bible troubled by the lack of engagement with theory by those purporting to use the concept of intertextuality.

It would be deeply ironic to suggest that all biblical scholars referring to the term 'intertextuality' adhere to Kristeva's original intention, but it is imperative to acknowledge that there is a vital theoretical difference between 'influence' and 'intertextuality'. Literary influence is thought of as something that can be traced and imputed to the author. Influence describes the way in which an author incorporates the work of another (well-known) writer into his or her own work, effectively creating allusions that the astute reader can then further delineate and determine.[120] Discussions of 'influence' in short, have been wed to methodological procedures that analysed texts as products of authorial consciousness. Susan Bassnett has claimed that the once popular exercise of tracking down literary 'influences' was basically a form of 'archive research' based on mistaken theories of direct 'causation' that 'ultimately turned the search for influence into a kind of treasure hunt'.[121] The verification of influences,

---

[117] The potentially infinite plenitude of texts in the intertextual network does not necessarily mean that reading is futile because it is impossible to know infinite reams of textual traces. All interpretations involve delimiting a texts' possible intertexts to arrive at coherent meaning; see Timothy K. Beal, 'Ideology and Intertextuality: Surplus of Meaning and Controlling the Means of Production', in Danna Nolan Fewell (ed.), *Reading Between Texts: Intertextuality and the Hebrew Bible* (Louisville: Westminster/John Knox Press, 1992), pp. 27–40, at pp. 30–1. Cf. Jonathan Smith's notion of 'articulate choice' in comparative criticism.

[118] K. S. Kim, *God Will Judge Each One According to Works: Judgement According to Works and Psalm 62 in Early Judaism and the New Testament* (Berlin: Walter de Gruyter, 2010), p. 27, cited in Yoon, 'The Ideological Inception of Intertextuality', p. 59.

[119] Cf. the works reviewed in Steve Moyise, 'Intertextuality and Biblical Studies: A Review', *Verbum et Ecclesia* 23, no. 2 (2002), pp. 418–31. For examples of full engagement with theory, see Ellen van Wolde, 'Texten lessen we allemaal', *Schrift* 91 (1984), pp. 3–7; idem, *A Semiotic Analysis of Genesis 2-3: A Semiotic Theory and Method of Analysis Applied to the Story of the Garden of Eden* (Assen: Van Gorcum, 1989); Stephen J. Davis, 'Crossed Text, Crossed Sex: Intertextuality and Gender in Early Christian Legends of Holy Women Disguised as Men', *JECS* 10, no. 1 (2002), pp. 1–36; and especially Stephen D. Moore, *Literary Criticism and the Gospels: The Theoretical Challenge* (New Haven and London: Yale University Press, 1989); idem, *Poststructuralism and the New Testament: Derrida and Foucault at the Foot of the Cross* (Minneapolis: Fortress Press, 1994).

[120] Bassnett, 'Influence and Intertextuality', p. 134.

[121] Ibid., pp. 136–7. Cf. Thais E. Morgan, 'Is There an Intertext in This Text?: Literary and Interdisciplinary Approaches to Intertextuality', *American Journal of Semiotics* 3, no. 4 (1985), pp. 1–40, at p. 2: 'The metaphor of influence says that literary history is like the natural flow of water

moreover, had to be determined by other available biographical data about what the author in question was known to have read. Bassnett concludes that 'all that we, as readers, can do is to see parallels, connections, affinities, and this is a more fruitful approach than one which seeks to prove certainty where certainty is a chimera'.[122]

Roland Barthes's theorization of intertextuality

Intertextual analysis begins with 'the creative role of the reader in making connections' between texts on the basis of 'the idea that texts exist in an endlessly interwoven relationship with one another'.[123] We have established the inherent differences between intertextuality as a body of poststructuralist theories, and the practices of 'source criticism' and 'influence' studies as discrete methods of analysis. In this section, I turn in detail to the work of Roland Barthes, who, I believe, provides an exceptionally rich and informative set of theories and insights into language, literature, cultural myth and intertextuality, all of which inform the readings of the Gospel of John and other ancient literature presented in this book.

Roland Barthes's writings have not – to my knowledge – been brought into scholarly conversation with the Gospel of John, nor indeed much of the literature of antiquity. Thomas Schmitz, has this pointed barb to aim at Barthes: '[He] was masterful at letting [a] superficial dilettantism subtly hint at an elitist arrogance.'[124] Indeed? If Schmitz's judgement holds sway in the academy, then we cannot expect to see too many scholars willing to engage with Barthes. In fact, Barthes was deeply anti-elitist, largely self-educated, broad ranging in his intellectual scope and rigour, creative and probing in the questions he asked of the world, and known to be a sympathetic and kind person.[125] Born in Cherbourg on 12 November 1915, Barthes was raised in Bayonne and later Paris, by his war-widowed mother, his aunt and his paternal grandmother.[126] For much of his early adult life, Barthes was a resident of a quarantined sanatorium due to tuberculosis; it was during this period that he taught himself to critically read the French classics (Sade, Fourier, Brecht, Sartre), and began to develop many of his semiological ideas.[127] Barthes did not complete his formal education, instead he 'always wrote from a position outside of established norms and thus outside of positions of power'. His was 'a liminal or borderline voice', questioning

---

and that there is a unidirectional "current" or relationship between an anterior text and a posterior text.' This automatically implies a value judgement – the source text or *Urtext* is superior to the posterior text; 'a river is pure only at its source, and its flow becomes progressively muddier as it travels farther away from the origin' (ibid., p. 3). This insight can be readily applied to the anti-Jewish ideology behind *Spätjudentum* in the study of biblical transmission in the early part of the twentieth century as an imposed narrative of progressive historical degeneration.

[122] Bassnett, 'Influence and Intertextuality', p. 138.
[123] Ibid.
[124] Schmitz, *Modern Literary Theory and Ancient Texts: An Introduction* (Oxford: Blackwell, 2007), p. 52.
[125] Cf. Chantal Thomas, *Pour Roland Barthes* (Paris: Éditions du Seuil, 2015).
[126] Graham Allen, *Barthes* (Routledge Critical Thinkers; Routledge: Abingdon, 2003), pp. 1–2.
[127] Ibid., p. 2.

'commonsensical', 'natural' ideas that in fact inscribed state-sponsored ideologies of power.[128]

A suitable foray into Barthesian intertextuality theory can be found in Barthes' famous essay 'The Death of the Author'.[129] Barthes' discussion of the 'death of the author' is not simply about our inability to circumscribe authorial intention, but is tied inextricably to his articulation of *la intertextuelle*. The psychobiography of the 'author' of a text – so vital to historicist methods of reading the classics – is, in Barthes' theory, merely another text, not an empirical reference by which we deduce correct interpretations.[130] The authority of 'the author' – in the words of Harlan – 'lies in still another text, the authority of that lying in yet another text, and so on, ad infinitum'.[131] The significance of a text lies not in its inscription of authorial intention but 'precisely because it eclipses and transcends its author's intentions'.[132] The meaning of a text does not reside in the authorial consciousness that lies behind the text, neither does meaning reside *only* in the text itself (cf. structuralism). The text's boundaries are undone; there is nothing but the 'intertextual', the plurality of other 'voices', other words and other texts. For Barthes,

> A text is made up of multiple writings, drawn from many cultures and entering into mutual relations of dialogue, parody, contestation, but there is one place where this multiplicity is focused and that place is the reader, not, as was hitherto said, the author.[133]

The idea of the Author and his psychological character imbuing his work with meaning is built upon the metaphor of filiation. The 'Author is thought to *nourish* the book, which is to say that he exists before it, thinks, suffers, lives for it ... [as] a father to his child'.[134] But the 'Author' imposes a limit on the text, furnishing it with 'a single signified', and closing it off.[135] Ever anterior to the text, the Author functions to open the text to linear decipherment (whether in the form of biography, society or history) as a 'context'. However, the 'death of the Author' brings about 'the birth of the reader'.[136] It is the reader who then becomes 'the space on which all the quotations that make up writing are inscribed without any of them being lost; a text's unity lies not in its origin but in its destination'.[137] A text is actually 'a multi-dimensional space in which a variety of writings, none of them original, blend and clash'.[138] Authorial filiation is, according to Barthes, a myth of culture, reducing a text's polyvalence to the psychological domain

---

[128] Ibid., p. 3.
[129] Roland Barthes, 'The Death of the Author', in Stephen Heath (ed. and trans.), *Image-Music-Text* (New York: Hill and Wang, 1977), pp. 142–8.
[130] Cf. also Hans-Georg Gadamer, *Truth and Method* (2nd edn; trans. Joel Weinsheimer and Donald G. Marshall; New York/London: Continuum, 2011), pp. 278–86.
[131] Harlan, 'Intellectual History', p. 585.
[132] Ibid.
[133] Barthes, 'Death of the Author', p. 148.
[134] Ibid., p. 145.
[135] Ibid., p. 147.
[136] Ibid., p. 148.
[137] Ibid.
[138] Ibid., p. 146.

of the 'parent-author'. It is this way of *reading* that Barthes declares to be 'dead'; Barthes knew how easily the interpretive endeavour to legitimate *one true* 'original' meaning could be exploited by hegemonic ideologies, and used by those in power to exclude differences. For Barthes, the 'text' is plural – not merely in the sense that it has many meanings, but in that it accomplishes an irreducible 'plural of meaning'.[139] Barthes writes that the 'text' is,

> woven entirely with citations, references, echoes, cultural languages (what language is not?) antecedent or contemporary, which cut across it through and through in a vast stereophony. The intertextual in which every text is held, it itself being the text-between of another text: to try to find the 'sources', the 'influences' of a work, is to fall in with the myth of filiation: the citations which go to make up a text are anonymous, untraceable, and yet *already read (le déjà)*.[140]

In fact, 'the Author' did not always exist; he or she was a product of the modern *capitalist* society in the West and functioned in that society in the process of literary commodification.[141] Once the name of an author was attached to a work, legislative principles of ownership and copyright came into play. In pre-capitalist societies this was not the case. But in the modern, industrialized market economy, the name of the author turned 'the text' (*le texte*) into 'the work' (*le oeuvre*) and conferred upon it an exchange value.[142] When the author's ownership – or dominance – over the text-as-work is fostered through processes of market exchange, the meaning of the text must be seen to ultimately reside in 'the man or woman who produced it'.[143] The 'work' must read like a 'transparent allegory' of 'the voice of a single person, the *author* "confiding" in us'.[144] The obverse side of this construction presents a view of the reader as 'consumer' of the work.[145]

As in any form of consumption, a product forfeits its ongoing utility once it is consumed; so with the reader-consumer, once a work is read, he or she moves directly to the next work. In line with a capitalist understanding of production and consumption, works are viewed by readers 'as disposable, or at least finite, commodities'.[146] As Michael Moriarty succinctly expresses it, 'a book re-read is one fewer sold'.[147] Rereading is contrary to 'the commercial and ideological habits of our society, which would have us

---

[139] Roland Barthes, 'From Work to Text', in *Image-Music-Text*, p. 159.
[140] Ibid., p. 160. For Barthes, a 'stereophony' is 'a space, it puts thoughts and feelings into place according to different volumes and distances. Obviously if I say, "Come in and close the door", that's not a very stereophonic sentence. But a literary text is truly stereographic'. Roland Barthes, *The Grain of the Voice: Interviews 1962–1980* (trans. Linda Coverdale; Evanston: Northwestern University Press, 1981), p. 104.
[141] Ibid., pp. 160–1.
[142] Ibid., p. 160.
[143] Barthes, 'Death of the Author', p. 143.
[144] Ibid.
[145] Barthes, 'From Work to Text', p. 161.
[146] Allen, *Intertextuality*, p. 71.
[147] Michael Moriarty, *Roland Barthes* (Oxford: Polity Press, 1991), p. 127.

"throw away" the story once it has been consumed'.[148] Barthes' theory of intertextuality therefore, makes a crucial distinction between the 'text' and the 'work'. Whereas *le oeuvre* is a material object, physically bound and sold, *le texte* is unbound – indeed, boundless. While the metaphor of filiation defines 'the work', the 'text' (etymologically, a tissue or woven fabric) is better approximated by the metaphor of 'the organism' growing 'by vital expansion' – or the metaphor of the 'network', as the text extends itself via combination.[149]

Furthermore, Barthes' binary nomenclature of 'the work'/'the text' also stands for two opposite reading processes. A person can read the same piece of literature as either a 'work' *or* a 'text'. For example, reading a love poem as a 'work' involves tracing the author's ideas and feelings, and perhaps his or her biography, from signs in that work. Reading the same poem as a text, however, involves the reader in 'the vast array of codes and conventions, genres and discourses, which make up the modern and traditional notions of love' and romance in our society – these codes and conventions constitute the 'already-read', anonymous traces held in the plural space of intertextuality.[150] Reading a text is performative, an act of production.[151] The reader must open the intertextual threads of the text, providing a limited range for its potentially infinite signifiers. This dynamic is what Barthes calls 'structuration'. The implication of Barthes' understanding of where meaning 'resides' – or better, how meaning arises – is that authorial agency loses its predominance just as readerly agency comes to the fore. It is the reader who detects and makes sense of the interplay of signifiers, which in Barthes' view, is always outside of the control of the author. Barthes' critique shatters our comfortable notion that texts are transparent, that they 'are masks concealing something held in reserve', coding a reality outside the text which acts as its primary reference point.[152] George Aichele summarizes Barthes' understanding of intertextuality well in the following words,

> Meaning does not lie in the text or in the reader. Instead, meaning lies somewhere *between* the text and the reader. Each human being is, among other things, the juxtaposition of all the texts that she has heard, read, written, told, or enacted, a perpetually incomplete totalizing that constantly grows and diminishes as she adds new texts to her reading repertoire and forgets old ones. The individual reader stands at the junctures of an indefinite web or network of texts; the reader is that network.[153]

---

[148] Roland Barthes, *S/Z* (trans. Richard Miller; New York: Hill and Wang, 1970), p. 15. We often speak of 'devouring' a good story.
[149] Barthes, 'From Work to Text', p. 161, cf. p. 159. Compare Hans Saussy's understanding of comparative literature in the first part of this chapter, which grows laterally and incrementally 'like the International Space Station' via a series of 'ands'.
[150] Allen, *Barthes*, p. 83.
[151] Barthes, 'Death of the Author', p. 143; and idem, 'From Work to Text', p. 157.
[152] Cf. Harlan, 'Intellectual History', p. 592.
[153] Aichele, 'Canon as Intertext', p. 141.

Textual analysis

Any form of interpretation that approaches the text from the point of a consumer is based, in Barthes' theory, on the ideology of stable meaning. The concept of intertextuality on the other hand, promotes a form of reading that Barthes calls 'scripting' – this type of reading is *productive of the text*, rather than being bound to interrogate only how the work was produced. It is, in fact, a kind of 'writing' of the text – what Barthes calls 'textual analysis', as opposed to the more traditional styles of 'criticism'.[154] Barthes claims that the structural-linguistic term 'signification' denoted the relationship between signifiers and their referents, (i.e. stable 'signifieds'), but the term *signifiance* connotes the process of readerly meaning-making. Many different types of interpretive practices seek a stable 'signified' as the 'final' or determinative reference behind a text (the signifier). One type of practice, as we have seen, is to look to the figure of the author as the ultimate 'signified'; another might be Marxist criticism, which seeks a socio-historical signifier as the locus of a text's meaning.[155] Such approaches, according to Barthes, treat the text as 'the repository of an objective signification' which supposedly 'appears as embalmed in the work-as-product'.[156] But when we turn from the interpretive practice embodied in 'signification' to the reader-oriented production of *signifiance*, the text becomes 'a polysemic space where the paths of several possible meanings intersect', so that 'it is necessary to cast off the monological, legal status of signification, and to pluralise it'.[157]

Barthes developed a process of 'textual analysis' that reflected his concern with interpretation as *signifiance*. Textual analysis marks a development in Barthes' thinking from structuralism (exploring how a text is constructed) to poststructuralism (exploring a text's 'avenues of meaning' and the manner in which meaning 'explodes and scatters').[158] His most exhaustive application of this mode of reading occurs in his interpretation of Honoré de Balzac's short story *Sarrasine*, which is found in Barthes' work *S/Z*.[159] At this point, I will not run through the plot of *Sarrasine*, as it would make this chapter too unwieldy, even though to do so might assist in better explaining Barthes' process of 'structuration'. Instead, I will abstract the mode of 'textual analysis' that Barthes' uses when 'scripting' Balzac's text as a productive reader. Barthes reads *Sarrasine* by slicing up the text into small units of meaning, called lexias. A lexia is an 'arbitrary' unit of reading, defined by the group of connotations that adhere to the signifier.[160]

The build-up of lexias in Balzac's text allows for the emergence of various 'codes' in the reading process. Barthes uses five codes in his textual analysis to illustrate how meaning is dispersed in the text.[161] Two codes concern the narrative's plot and

---

[154] Roland Barthes, 'Theory of the Text', in Robert Young (ed.), *Untying the Text: A Poststructuralist Reader* (London: Routledge and Kegan Paul, 1981), pp. 31–47, at p. 43.
[155] Ibid., p. 37.
[156] Ibid.
[157] Ibid.
[158] Roland Barthes, *The Semiotic Challenge* (trans. Richard Howard; Oxford: Blackwell, 1988), p. 262.
[159] Barthes, *S/Z*.
[160] Ibid., pp. 13–14.
[161] Ibid., pp. 18–20.

chronological order. The first of these is the *hermeneutic code* (HER), which concerns all those lexias 'whose function it is to articulate in various ways a question, its response, and the variety of chance events which can either formulate the question or delay its answer; or even constitute an enigma and lead to its solution'.[162] The second code is the *proairetic code* (ACT), which concerns the actions performed in the narrative and their effects. These effects produce certain sequences in the narrative that can be titled, such as (for *Sarrasine*) 'Courtship', 'Abduction' and 'Assassination'.[163] In narratives, the discourse – and not only the characters – can determine the action, and thus discursive codes fall under this rubric too.[164] The three remaining codes deal with meaning that takes us outside of the narrative sequence and structure. The *symbolic code* (SYM) refers to symbolic patterns, particularly those of antithesis and opposition, found in the text. The 'symbolic code' of the narrative 'can be entered from any number of points', and thus it is multivalent and 'reversible'.[165] The *code of semes* (SEM) refers to the connotations that build up around each character or character group, and which shape a character's actions, speech and 'personal' qualities.[166] Finally, the *cultural code* (REF) concerns 'the numerous codes of knowledge or wisdom to which the text continually refers'.[167] While all codes are, in a sense, 'cultural', this final code specifies those aspects of a text's discursive structure which point to 'science or a body of knowledge' in an authoritative manner.[168]

It is important to emphasize that Barthes is not saying that these five codes are simply present in the text itself; they are tools that he brings to his active structuration of the text.[169] Barthes' textual analysis reveals the multi-subjectivity of the text. The 'social location' of the reader is of great importance, as each reader (re)-writes the text out of his or her subjectivity: '*I read the text*'.[170] The text is not 'a site' for the reader to 'occupy'; 'this "I" which approaches the text is already itself a plurality of other texts, of codes which are infinite or, more precisely, lost (whose origin is lost)'.[171] The 'I' is never innocent, but is plural and open, just like the text.[172] To say that the origin of codes is

---

[162] Ibid., p. 17.
[163] Ibid., p. 18.
[164] Ibid.
[165] Ibid., pp. 18, 19.
[166] Ibid., p. 17.
[167] Ibid., p. 18.
[168] Ibid., p. 19.
[169] Ibid.
[170] Ibid., p. 10.
[171] Ibid. Barthes also writes, 'Reading involves risks of objectivity or subjectivity (both are imaginary) only insofar as we define the text as an expressive object (presented for our own expression), sublimated under a morality of truth, in one instance laxist; in the other, ascetic. Yet reading is not a parasitical act, the reactive complement of a writing which we endow with all the glamour or creation and anteriority. It is a form of work ... and the method of the work is topological: I am not hidden within the text, I am simply irrecoverable from it ...in operational terms, the meanings I find are established not by "me" or by others, but by their *systematic* mark... To read is to find meanings, and to find meanings is to name them; but these named meanings are swept toward other names; names call to each other, reassemble, and their grouping calls for further naming: I name, I unname, I rename: so the text passes: it is a nomination in the course of becoming, a tireless approximation, a metonymic labor' (Ibid., pp. 10–11).
[172] Cf. Roland Barthes, 'On Reading', in *The Rustle of Language* (trans. Richard Howard; Berkeley and Los Angeles: University of California Press, 1986), p. 42: The subject – no longer the 'thinking

'lost' is not eloquent nihilism – intertextuality alerts us to the fact that 'conventions and presuppositions cannot be traced to their source and thus positively identified'.[173] It is a 'paradox' of the linguistic system that 'utterances or texts are never moments of origin because they depend on the prior existence of codes and conventions ... already in existence'.[174] Barthes' five codes are potential 'formalizations' of the discursive space in which all texts participate.[175]

The five codes enable Barthes to expose the text's 'plurality', the un-foreclosed nature of the text's *signifiance*. The two narrative codes (HER and ACT), however, function to circumscribe and limit the text's polysemy, by means of a chronological, sequential and linear plot development (with the conventional beginning, middle and end), in which an enigma is solved or a drama resolved.[176] The other three codes (SYM, SEM, REF) work against the two narrative codes by opening the text into various intertextual fields outside of the story-world, thereby disrupting the tight narrative flow by producing meaning that is non-sequential. The two narrative codes operate on the text's syntagmatic dimension, and as such, are labelled 'irreversible' by Barthes (that is, not amenable to the reader's deconstruction). The other non-sequential codes permit 'reversibility' by allowing the reader to break the syntagmatic dimension and 'experience the text's explosion and dispersal into the intertextual, into the cultural text'.[177] Barthes concludes his reading of *Sarrasine* by evaluating Balzac's text as partially 'reversible', as permitting the production of a limited plurality. Against this, Barthes posits the modernist, avant-garde text, which he considers completely reversible and plural.[178] This distinction between the reversible and irreversible text receives further sharpening in Barthes' contrast between the 'writerly' (*lisible*) and readerly (*scriptable*) texts.

Writerly and readerly texts[179]

Barthes suggests that no literature prior to the advent of modernism gives us an example of a completely readerly (*scriptible*) text. The so-called 'classic texts' of eighteenth- and nineteenth-century French fiction – particularly realist genres – are for Barthes,

---

subject' of idealist philosophy, but the 'subject' as described by psychoanalytic epistemology – is 'devoid of all meaning ... in the double misreading of his unconscious and his ideology ... every reading proceeds from a subject, and is separated from this subject only by rare and tenuous mediations'. Thus, *I* read the text (Barthes does not deny the social location of the reader), yet my *I* remains ineffable to me in its 'lost origins'.
[173] Jonathan Culler, 'Presupposition and Intertextuality', *MLN* 91, no. 6 (1976), pp. 1380–96, at p. 1382.
[174] Ibid., p. 1382.
[175] Ibid.
[176] Cf. Allen, *Barthes*, p. 87.
[177] Ibid., 88. The paradigmatic/syntagmatic binary is central to classical linguistics as the chief axes of language. See Roland Barthes, *Elements of Semiology* (trans. Annette Lavers and Colin Smith; New York: Hill and Wang, 1964), pp. 58–61.
[178] Cf. Allen, *Barthes*, p. 88.
[179] It is important to note that the terms 'readerly/lisible' and 'writerly/scriptible' are not used by Barthes in a systematic fashion but derive from his oeuvre in a variety of places. Cf. the disseminative work of Annette Lavers (one of the leading commentators on Barthes); cf. Lavers, *Roland Barthes: Structuralism and After* (London: Methuen, 1982), p. 202.

Theoretical Foundations: Intertextuality 75

supreme examples of the 'writerly' (*lisible*) text.[180] Realist literature aims to be mimetic and characteristically presents the reader with a conspicuous narrator who often takes the moral high ground in the rhetorical structure of the narrative. Highly conventional in their presentation, realist genres sometimes reinforce the authority of the narrative voice by aligning it with the voices of other characters (mainly protagonists) in the story. But more often than not, the narrator, the characters and the 'message' of the implied author are clearly delineated.[181] The realist text fosters the illusion of 'reality', persuading the reader to match the novel's representation with reality, and to assent with its perspective. It is characterized by its linear and sequential form, so that the reader is able to 'digest' a plot that has a distinct beginning, middle and an end.[182] All that is required of the reader is a certain consumer-like passivity to follow the plot. The 'realistic' text places reality 'as far back as can be traced, an already written real.'[183] The *lisible* text thereby 'naturalizes' its perspective. A purely 'readerly' text is, in Barthes' words, 'irreversible', meaning that it has no room for the reader to enable it to come undone, that the reader has no 'productive' work to do when reading: 'he [the reader] is left no more than the poor freedom either to accept or to reject the text.'[184]

The 'writerly text' (*scriptible texte*) – the avant-garde or modernist text – disrupts narrative order, breaks up sentences and most often dismantles any sense of a unified, monologic discourse. At times, the writerly text can subvert the notion of 'meaning' altogether with a subtle or more explicit nihilism. For Barthes, the *scriptible*, modernist text, is rich in what he calls 'symbolic codes' but poor in 'narrative codes'.[185] In these ways, it differs from the *lisible* text, which is strong in narrative codes. The writerly (*scriptible*) text aspires to what Barthes perceives to be the proper goal of literature, namely, that the reader becomes a producer of the text; this is, as Barthes styles it, a 'form of work', an active 'writing' of the text out of a consciousness of the 'plurality of entrances' into a text.[186] The writerly text is 'reversible', inasmuch as the reader functions not as a passive consumer but as an active producer of meaning.[187] This means that the 'writerly' texts approximates to Barthes' notion of the 'text' (as opposed to the 'work'-as-product).

Lest this dichotomous view of literary history be taken as a hard and fast rule, Barthes proceeds to offer a disclaimer on the generic distinction articulated in the *lisible* v. *scriptible* opposition. The avant-garde is not *always* a 'text' and the 'classic' is not *always* a 'work'. Indeed, 'there may be a "text" in a very ancient work', as Barthes notes.[188] 'It

---

[180] Roland Barthes, 'From Work to Text', in *The Rustle of Language* (trans. Richard Howard; Berkeley & Los Angeles: California of University Press, 1989), pp. 56–64, at p. 63. Howard's translation of this essay brings out the nuance of 'readerly' and 'writerly' texts more than the translation of Stephen Heath (1977). Barthes notes that if he can 'read' the classic authors (Balzac, Proust, Flaubert, Dumas), then he cannot *rewrite* them.
[181] Cf. Allen, *Barthes*, p. 91.
[182] This (the porairetic code) is what makes it *lisible*, lit., legible, easy to read, readerly. See Barthes, *S/Z*, p. 204.
[183] Barthes, *S/Z*, p. 167.
[184] Barthes, 'From Work to Text' (trans. Howard), p. 57.
[185] Barthes, *S/Z*, p. 134.
[186] Ibid., pp. 5, 10.
[187] Lavers, *Roland Barthes*, p. 202.
[188] Barthes, 'From Work to Text' (trans. Heath), p. 156.

is not a question of drawing up a crude honours list in the name of modernity.'[189] At the same time, 'many products of contemporary literature are not texts at all'.[190] As such, it must be emphasized that *le texte* and *le scriptible texte* are not necessarily solid, determinate objects, nor do they always refer to particular genres over others. They are fluid 'entities' that may *emerge* within any literature; they are, as Annette Lavers writes, '*ourselves writing*', and they are 'created anew in each reader'.[191] Barthes own textual analysis of two 'classic'/realist works (Balzac's *Sarrasine* and Poe's 'The Facts in the Case of M. Valdemar') actually demonstrates how the writerly emerges to undermine their status as readerly texts.[192] When the *scriptible* emerges – the possibility of plurality – so too does the intertextual. Indeed, Barthes claims that the purely writerly does not exist: every writerly text needs its 'shadow', its little '*bit* of ideology' and representation.[193] Along the same line, Balzac's texts are, in Barthes' reading, partly *lisible* and partly *scriptible*, which gives Barthes some latitude in 'rewriting' Balzac's texts.[194]

Perhaps the more important observation we may take away from this is that the readerly text always embodies, to some extent, a totalizing discursive narrative voice. This is the 'monologic' voice of Bakhtin's theorizing, and Barthes styles it as *doxa* (or sometimes, *Endoxa*).[195] According to Barthes, *doxa* is anything presented as if it were 'natural' rather than cultural or ideological. In fact, for Barthes, *doxa* – often an 'unconscious' signified – is 'the essence of ideology'.[196] It is received opinion that is left unquestioned; it is 'myth' that presents its signifieds as inevitable.[197] The readerly text depends upon *doxa* for its readability. The readerly text rehearses and reproduces *doxa* in accordance with bourgeois ideology, and so 'turns culture into nature, appear[s] to establish reality, "Life." "Life" then, in the classic text, becomes a nauseating mixture

---

[189] Ibid., p. 156.
[190] Barthes, 'From Work to Text' (trans. Howard), p. 57.
[191] Lavers, *Roland Barthes*, p. 202, emphasis in original.
[192] Cf. Allen, *Intertextuality*, pp. 78–81.
[193] Roland Barthes, *The Pleasure of the Text* (trans. Richard Miller; New York: Hill and Wang, 1975), p. 32. Cf. also Barthes' reading of Gen. 32.22-32 as an attempt to release the plurality of meaning in the biblical text, to undermine its cultural code; Roland Barthes, 'The Struggle with the Angel: Textual Analysis of Genesis 32.22-32' in *Image-Music-Text*, pp. 125–41. Becoming a 'scriptor' of a text requires pursuing not its 'truth' but 'its dissemination'. And in this case, refraining from reducing the 'Text to a signified, whatever it may be (historical, economic, folkloric or kerygmatic), but to hold its *significance* fully open' (idem, p. 141).
[194] Cf. Allen, *Barthes*, p. 90.
[195] On monologism, see Mikhail Bakhtin, *Problems of Dostoyevsky's Poetics* (trans. and ed. C. Emerson; Minneapolis: University of Minnesota Press, 1984).
[196] Barthes, *Pleasure*, p. 29. Barthes' notes that *doxa* is found across the political spectrum, left, right and everything in between, but that it is often most forceful in the hegemonic discursive structures of society.
[197] Barthes, *S/Z*, p. 206. Earlier in his career, Barthes formulated a similar idea to describe the way 'myth' works in culture. As a second-order semiological system built upon an existing linguistic system, myth operates to 'transform history into nature... what causes mythical speech to be uttered is perfectly explicit, but it is immediately frozen into something natural; it is not read as a motive, but as a reason'. Roland Barthes, *Mythologies* (trans. Annette Lavers; New York: Hill and Wang, 1972), p. 129. The first-order system of language posits a signifier = signified, leading to an associative concept unifying both (= the 'sign'). Myth stratifies a second-order level of meaning on top of this structure, so that the 'sign' becomes a *new* signifier, denoting a new signified, and connoting a third sign (and so on); Barthes, *Mythologies*, pp. 114–15. Barthes' analysis of how myth operates in a racist, pro-imperial French magazine cover in *Mythologies* is superb.

of common opinions, a smothering of received ideas'.[198] Both readerly and writerly texts are characterized by intertextuality. But the frequently banal repetition of tropes, codes and ideas in the readerly text does not lead to the liberating plurality of 'the intertextual' as in the writerly text. On the contrary, the codes rehearsed in the readerly text smother, deaden and produce ennui. The *doxa* of the readerly text reinforces the notion that 'Life' should be unquestioned, and that what is 'natural' cannot be changed.

With this, it is possible to appreciate how Barthes and other members of *Tel Quel* saw intertextuality as not simply a novel neologism for elitist theorists, but as a socially revolutionary concept. Against the saturation of the *doxa* that is produced by the proliferation of readerly works in the current cultural environment, Barthes posits the power of *para-doxa*, that is 'that which would resist and disturb the beliefs and forms and codes' of culture.[199] The writerly text has a plurality of entrance points and exit points, allowing multiple interpretations and denying the dominance of any one code, stereotype or opinion, and as such embodies the *para-doxa*. Each discourse in society (each 'jargon' or 'fiction' as Barthes calls it) 'fights for hegemony: if power is on its side, it spreads everywhere... it becomes *doxa*, nature'.[200] It is important to realize the porousness of these categories, the *doxa* and the *para-doxa*. The *para-doxa* resists and disturbs the *doxa*, and so begins as something of a minority opinion. But if it gains power over time and large-scale societal acceptance, it too may become *doxa*. The task of structuration (becoming a 'scriptor' of the texts we read) is to question *doxa* with *para-doxa*. Barthes himself constantly subjected his own work to critique, concerned that it would be absorbed by mass culture – even the very conflict between *doxa/para-doxa* itself was an element of his own thinking that he wanted to somehow neutralize.[201] To this end, in his later works, Barthes explored more deeply the elements of violence and pleasure in language.

The assertiveness of *doxa* betrays violence in language – what Barthes elsewhere calls *écrivance*, the writing of 'the author'. This is the language of power, an apparently transparent medium that wants to convey a singular or stable meaning.[202] This type of language is self-proclaiming, argumentative, seeking to label and to name.[203] Any explicitly ideological language speaks the *doxa*.[204] It does not matter whether the ideology is dominant or resistant (*para-doxa*), as all ideological language is violent, expressive of *doxa* and seeking to dismantle the Other.[205] It is important to notice that the interpreting subject is never 'innocent': the interpretation 'of any particular text happens only within an intertextual and therefore ideological context'.[206] And *doxa* always seeks to naturalize the text, to make its meaning seem obvious.[207] Aichele states

---

[198] Barthes, *S/Z*, p. 206.
[199] Allen, *Intertextuality*, p. 90.
[200] Barthes, *Pleasure*, p. 28.
[201] Roland Barthes, *Roland Barthes by Roland Barthes* (trans. Richard Howard; London: Macmillan, 1977), p. 68.
[202] Roland Barthes, *The Rustle of Language*, p. 244.
[203] Ibid., p. 291.
[204] Cf. *Roland Barthes*, p. 104.
[205] Cf. *Pleasure of the Text*, pp. 32–3.
[206] Aichele, 'Canon as Intertext', p. 143.
[207] Cf. ibid., p. 143.

that 'ideologies are powerful forces in the human world, for they invariably privilege some groups of human beings' over others; they 'make thought and action possible, and they also make some thoughts and actions *impossible*. Ideologies, therefore, are always contested, and they are always violent'.[208] For Barthes, the 'text of pleasure' reinforces *doxa*, asserting and reasserting cultural stereotypes, thus inducing a sense of comfort in the reader that also masks the violence of ideology.

The 'text of *jouissance*' on the other hand, discomforts the reader, imposing upon him or her 'a state of loss'.[209] The text of *jouissance* does not reinforce any *doxa*, neither does it reply upon stereotypes – *jouissance* does not so much assert a counter ideology as attempt neutrality.[210] Barthes' provocative notion of *jouissance* suggests that the reader is left in limbo with respect of secure questions about identity and naming – texts of *jouissance* confront us with our inability to assert something about ourselves definitively. This is even to the point where the text of *jouissance* leads the reader into 'a crisis with *language* itself'.[211] This is obviously not 'bliss' in the sense of enjoyment, but bliss in the sense of 'pain'. It is the loss of all *doxa* that would give the subject a sense of 'self'.

Application to the Gospel of John

Let us begin to tie these insights together by relating them to the Gospel of John and to the project of textual analysis undertaken in this book. The Fourth Gospel, like many texts from antiquity, bears eponymous attribution. There is no sense in which the 'death of the Author' pertains to the Gospel because the author(s) is unknown already. Neither is there an easily accessible psychobiography of the Apostle John available to us modern interpreters to round out our reading of the Gospel – if indeed this historical 'John' is the same figure as the eponymous one. However, there *is* the influential heuristic of the putative 'Johannine community' behind the Gospel text, which in many ways has functioned in authorial terms for scholars trying to get to the original intention of the Gospel text and its history.[212] The historical situation facing the Johannine community – a stereotypically sectarian social group who both authored and received composite parts of the Gospel text in various stages – is thus deemed an 'original' interpretive context against which to read John's Gospel.[213] The reconstructed social history of the community 'behind' the text can, of course, only be derived from aspects *of* the text, and so there is invariably circular reasoning involved. The assumption is that John's narrative sends the reader 'cues' about the community's trials (the classic example being the 'synagogue-expulsion' passages in 9.22, 12.42 and 16.2). However, this is history practised as narrative – a constructed community *narrative* history is built from the basis of John's *narrative* about Jesus – giving us what J. Louis Martyn has identified as a 'two-level drama'.[214] Even if we do not dispute that

---

[208] Ibid., p. 144.
[209] Ibid., p. 14.
[210] Cf. Allen, *Barthes*, p. 107.
[211] Barthes, *Pleasure of the Text*, p. 14.
[212] For more detail, see Ruth Sheridan, 'Johannine Sectarianism', pp. 142–66.
[213] See literature cited in Sheridan, 'Johannine Sectarianism', pp. 142–66.
[214] J. Louis Martyn, *History and Theology*.

John's story is told on two levels, it does not mean that one level (the community level) is veridically 'historical' while the other (the Jesus level) is simple narrative. Both levels are narratives – or more correctly, as Barthes would phrase it, both are 'texts' and the resulting interpretation is an intertextual one.

Yet, advocates of the Johannine community hypothesis endorse a different reading paradigm, wherein the constructed community history functions as the Author of the text. The mistake that scholars make is to confuse *representation* with *reference*.[215] The Gospel *represents* a story of a community, elusively and obliquely, but it does not *refer* to the history of a community, as though every scene, character and discourse in the Gospel has a one-on-one cryptic correspondence to ecclesial events at the time of the text's composition. The language of the Gospel – indeed no language as such – *refers* to a singular corresponding material thing or person (signified) in the 'real world'. So although the Gospel of John has no identifiable 'Author' in the modern sense found in Barthes' theory, the community hypothesis has very much stood proxy for 'the Author' in critical scholarship. On the extreme end, this has meant that the Johannine community has been virtually reified as properly existent, and that the historical events their members underwent in the 90s CE (such as being subject to the *Birkat Ha-Minim*) were used as quasi-empirical data to force an 'objective' or historically true (and thus definitive) interpretation of the text.

Along with the *de facto* acceptance of the historical-critical method as the legitimated means of interpreting the NT in the better part of the twentieth century, came the gradual establishment of the Gospel community hypotheses as the acceptable way to understand the reception and transmission of the early Christian material. But by the late 1990s, this interpretive paradigm was being put under greater scrutiny; the landmark edited volume titled *The Gospels for All Christians* (1998) began a veritable revolution that shook the foundations of these aforesaid assumptions by proposing that the Gospels were not written for discrete and particular communities, but were written with the view towards broad dissemination.[216]

The point of this discussion is not to prove Gospel community hypotheses wrong as much as it is to indicate that the hegemonic establishment of the historicist method of reading that these hypotheses depend upon has often proceeded out of what John Dupré has called the ideology of 'scientism' – the prevalent but misguided application of methods used in the natural sciences to human society.[217] When historical community situations are framed in such a way that the Gospel text is said not only to have been

---

[215] Clark, *History, Theory, Text*, p. 7.
[216] Richard Bauckham (ed.), *The Gospels for All Christians: Rethinking the Gospel Audiences* (Grand Rapids, MI: Eerdmans, 1998). The essays in this volume have generated debates for decades, with several articles appearing that counter the widespread audience hypothesis: cf. David C. Sim, 'The Gospels for All Christians? A Response to Richard Bauckham', *JSNT* 84 (2001), pp. 3–27, and Margaret Mitchell, 'Patristic Counterevidence to the Claim that the Gospels Were Written for All Christians', *NTS* 51 (2005), pp. 36–79, which in turn garnered a response from Bauckham ('Is There Patristic Counter-Evidence? A Response to Margaret Mitchell', in idem, *The Christian World Around the New Testament: Collected Essays II* (WUNT 2.386; Tübingen: Mohr Siebeck, 2017), pp. 41–80).
[217] John Dupré, 'Materialism, Physicalism, and Scientism', *Philosophical Topics* 16, no. 1 (1998), pp. 31–56.

intended as read by those communities but also to 'reflect' the contingencies leading to the *authorship* of the text itself – and when this is wedded to the historicist endeavour of gauging the 'objective' meaning of the text – we fall into scientistic thinking. Probing the intention of the original author by way of the putative community history behind the Gospel text is thus thought to constitute objective analysis, via the Rankean standard history '*wie es eigentlich gewesen*' – 'as it really happened'.[218] In another context, Barthes explains,

> In 'objective' history, the 'real' is never anything but an unformulated signified, sheltered behind the apparent omnipotence of the referent. This situation defines what we might call the *reality effect*. The extrusion of the signified outside the 'objective' discourse, letting the 'real' and its expression apparently confront each other, does not fail to produce a new meaning, so true is it, once more, that within a system any absence of an element is itself a signification... historical discourse does not follow the real, it merely signifies it, constantly repeating *this happened*, without this assertion being anything but the signified *wrong side* of all historical narration.[219]

The 'Death of the Author' when applied to the Gospel of John might therefore involve questioning the extent to which we allow the 'reality effect' of the representational community history to function as an Author-figure instead as a cultural text or an intertext. Indeed, the *risk* of understanding John's oblique community narrative as empirical data would be to adopt the text's slanted perspective, and to blame 'the Jews' in the narrative (and their 'historical', 'referential' or, it is assumed, 'real' counterpart in the community's history), for the synagogue expulsions of community members. This troubling implication is barely acknowledged – that the Gospel's violent rhetoric against 'the Jews' in the text would appear to be historically justified. Such an implication sanctions the Gospel's inherent anti-Judaism, rather than 'explaining' it so as to 'contextualize' it, as is sometimes purposed.

What Barthes was getting at with his critique of the 'Author' was ultimately the limitations of bourgeois ideology. The text as 'Work' cries out for ownership; as Aichele states, 'one function of ideology is to identify "proper" owners of the text and to serve as a protective fence around the textual property in order to prevent its "theft" by others. Ideology makes this fence seem quite natural and normal'.[220] With respect to the Gospel of John, we can note two pertinent factors: first, the normalization of community-history hypotheses in the scholarship betrays an ideological bid for the collective 'ownership' of a proper interpretation that accords with the status of the text as an *historical* revelation of the divine. This normalization reinforces the boundaries of community identity in the academy as well; where one cannot say that the historical author 'owns' the text (because the historical author is unknown and cannot have his intended meaning defended by copyright laws), one can at least vie for the right way

---

[218] Cf. Clark, *History, Theory, Text*, p. 2.
[219] Barthes, 'The Discourse of History', in idem, *The Rustle of Language*, pp. 127–40, at p. 139.
[220] Aichele, 'Canon as Intertext', p. 144.

to interpret the ancient manuscript culture and transmission history by means of sanctioning a proper historical narrative. Second, again with reference to Aichele, as a *canon*, the Christian bible 'draws property lines, and it excludes outsiders ... Christians are the insiders, the ones who know what the Bible means'.[221] Theological orthodoxy ousted 'heterodox' interpretations, and at the same time implied that 'the imperial church as the true Israel, [is] the only legitimate heir to the divine covenant'.[222] With the Christian canon functioning as a 'Work' in the Barthesian sense, we can see how a certain range of meanings were (and in many believing communities today, remain) admissible and legitimate, while others do not. The 'strong misreading' espoused by some of the early Church Fathers that the Jews failed to grasp the Christocentric meaning of 'their own' Scriptures (the Tanakh) is still in force in much that passes for scholarship even today, due to the legacy of ('proprietary') canonical boundaries. Thus, in employing Barthes' theory of the Death of the Author, we are performing an important interpretive act by reading the Gospel of John as a 'text' rather than a 'work', and looking for the ways in which its meaning 'goes off' rather than the ways in which it is hedged in.

Another means of applying Barthes' thinking to the Gospel of John is by examining how his five codes of textual analysis fit with the text. We recall that Barthes employed this method of reading Balzac's *Sarrasine* by slicing the chronological text up into *lexemes* read contextually, to determine *Qui parlé?* Which code speaks? A cursory overview of John's narrative reveals that the text is strong in hermeneutic (HER) and proairetic (ACT, SYM) codes, which in turn suggests a relatively heavy-handed ideology and thus, a 'readerly' text.

For example, with respect to the hermeneutic code (HER), we notice immediately that John's Gospel is guided by a central 'question': Who is Jesus? What is his identity? Is he a man from heaven, is he the Christ (6.42, 69; 7.26; 10.24)? It is this question that determines the fate of every character in the plot, and those beyond it, even those who read the story, because they have to make an answer or response to Jesus (3.18; 8.24). Jesus is the supreme enigma, and he speaks in riddles, which others may understand correctly or misunderstand (3.9-10). He produces a host of revelatory discourses and signs that function as events to move the plot along. In the end, confronted by Pilate, Jesus is asked to reveal his identity with plain words (18.33-38); yet he is crucified. This, finally, is the full 'resolution' to the story's enigma and the high point of the drama, as it leads to the formation of a community (19.25-27) and to the resurrection and gift of the Spirit (chs 20–21). Barthes' proairetic code (ACT) is similarly pertinent. John's plot is driven by actions and their effects, even if it looks to be made up mainly of long discourses and monologues. If we were to title the sequence of the plot, we could come up with something like this: Descent into the World (1.1-18), Revelation through Signs (1.19–12.1); Trial/Judgement (12.1-50); Farewell of the Christ (13.1–17.26); Departure and Death (18–19); Resurrection and Ascension (20–21). All of these events and sequences are focused very much on the career Jesus, with all other characters effectively filling minor roles insofar as they are relative to him.

---

[221] Ibid., p. 145.
[222] Ibid., p. 146.

Barthes' symbolic code (SYM) is particularly applicable to the Gospel. The Gospel of John is made up of antitheses, oppositions and binaries. These correlate across three levels of the drama identified by Adele Reinhartz – the cosmological, the historical and the ecclesiological – and these antitheses are often abstract nouns (light/darkness, life/death) but also come into focus via contrasting character responses to Jesus (disciples/Jews).[223] Other symbols and patterns are discernible, such as biblical references to wells (cf. 4.1-38) and the symbolic function of the 'Temple' throughout the Gospel.[224] The rich imagery of the discursive sections of the Gospel – bread, water, shepherds and sheep, vines and branches – also goes to make up the SYM code of the text. The intertextual weave of John's symbolic code is thus fine-grained and extensive, and a number of scholars have used the text's imagery to explore allusive resonances, particularly to the Hebrew Bible.

The code of the seme (SEM) is a fascinating one in terms of its replication in John's Gospel. This code refers to the kinds of traits adhering to certain characters in the narrative as they accumulate through the development of the plot. Many studies of Johannine characterization operate on the premise voiced by E. M. Forester, namely, that characters may be either 'round' or 'flat', either richly developed or stereotypically simple.[225] Others prefer to utilize Forester's insight in terms of a character continuum rather than a simple binary.[226] Still other studies approach the Gospel text by applying modern characterization theory (from critical narratology) to the Gospel despite the fact that John's characters exhibit relatively little 'roundedness'. The codes of the seme are highly (stereo)typical in the Gospel of John, given that characterization is basically founded on the existing hermeneutic code (HER) so that each character is portrayed in terms of his or her response to Jesus and to his identity. Few characters exhibit 'individuality' or distinct traits, perhaps with the exception of Peter in John 21, where the reader glimpses his Synoptic-like impetuousness as he jumps into the water from a fishing boat. Yet, on the whole, the SEM operates with respect to a character's response to Jesus – either acceptance, belief and fidelity (1.49; 4.29; 6.68; 8.30; 11.27; 20.8, 16), or rejection, incredulity, suspicion, obstinacy, hostility and homicidal purpose (5.18; 6.41, 66; 7.1, 20; 8.37, 40; 11.53; 18.28-32; 19.7-12). The 'good guys' and the 'bad guys' are clearly drawn in John's narrative; this aspect of the text is highly *lisible*.

The cultural code (REF) is continually present in John's text. This code voices what Barthes calls the 'scientific' or 'moral' authority speaking through the text. It is what Vernon K. Robbins has termed the 'rhetorolect' of early Christian discourse.[227] In John, we glimpse this authority in the very way he presents the journey of the incarnate Word, with Jesus as the pre-existent Wisdom of God (1.1-8). Jesus is situated in the primordial, 'natural' life of God as the agent of all creation (1.1-3). The reader of the

---

[223] Reinhartz, *Befriending the Beloved Disciple*, pp. 32–53.
[224] Cf. Mary L. Coloe, *God Dwells With Us: Temple Symbolism in the Fourth Gospel* (Collegeville: Liturgical Press, 2001).
[225] Cf. literature cited in Sheridan, *Retelling Scripture*, pp. 68–86.
[226] Cf. Cornelis Bennema, *Encountering Jesus: Character Studies in the Gospel of John* (Colorado: Paternoster, 2009).
[227] Vernon K. Robbins, 'Rhetography as a New Way of Seeing the Familiar Text', in C. Clifton Black and Duane F. Watson (eds), *Words Well Spoken: George Kennedy's Rhetoric of the New Testament* (Studies in Rhetoric and Religion 8; Waco, TX: Baylor University Press, 2008), pp. 81–106.

Prologue is privileged with this knowledge before the story has properly begun. This 'privy council' is an example of the supremely *lisible* text, as it gives away the enigma (HER), the answer to the central question dominating the story before the story itself has begun. But it is not just that the reader receives this information early in the piece – the way it is constructed means that the reader is left with the 'poor choice' (Barthes) of either accepting the truth of the story or rejecting the story and its hero. The 'moral' authority of the story also resides within the voice of the narrator and the point of view of the implied author. These authoritative and persuasive voices merge with the voice of Jesus, the protagonist, thus reinforcing the particular perspective of the Gospel that invites a compliant reading in response.[228] Another code of cultural knowledge that carries with it authoritative weight comes in the form of the explicit scriptural citations in the Gospel, many of which have a 'proof-text' type of authority in that they reveal aspects of Jesus' identity (1.23; 2.17; 6.31, 45; 7.37-39; 10.34; 12.13-14), or have a 'fulfilment' theme that demands a specific hermeneutic in which *the* definitive meaning of Scripture is now realized fully in Jesus (12.38; 13.18; 15.25; 19.24, 36).[229] The Scripture citations in John's Gospel thoroughly 'naturalize' the Johannine perspective by backing up Jesus' presentation with supreme authority. Other codes of knowledge function as reference codes, pointing the reader to socially relevant details about relationships (ch. 4), to Jewish festival knowledge and especially to trial knowledge (7-8, 18-19), and knowledge of the ritual of death (13-19).

In light of this presentation of how Barthes' five codes find expression in the Gospel of John, we can conclude that the HER and ACT codes are very strong, limiting polysemy and 'scriptability' on the part of the reader. Barthes calls these two codes (HER and ACT) the narrative codes; they operate on the text's syntagmatic dimension and, as such, are labelled 'irreversible' by Barthes (that is, not amenable to the reader's deconstruction). The other non-sequential codes (SYM, SEM and REF) permit 'reversibility' by allowing the reader to break the syntagmatic dimension and 'experience the text's explosion and dispersal into the intertextual, into the cultural text'.[230] For John, however, we see that even the SEM and REF codes rely heavily on the HER code and its central ideas about Jesus. This integral cycle of semiosis further cements the *lisible*, or readerly, nature of John's Gospel. Akin to Barthes' realist novel (although profoundly different in terms of its genre), the Gospel of John *persuades readers to accept its vision of truth and reality*. To assent to the Gospel's 'case' about Jesus is to 'consume' its message, to 'digest' its plot, in Barthesian language. The Gospel's inherently persuasive design insistently invites what Reinhartz terms a 'compliant reading' (and what I have elsewhere referred to as its monologism).[231]

---

[228] Ruth Sheridan, 'Persuasion', in Estes and Sheridan (eds), *How John Works*, pp. 205-24. This essay contains a fuller discussion of the terms 'implied author' and 'implied reader'.

[229] Andreas Obermann, *Die christologische Erfüllung der Schrift im Johannesevangelium: Eine Untersuchung zur johanneischen Hermeneutik anhand der Schriftzitate* (WUNT 2.83; Tübingen: Mohr Siebeck, 1996), p. 79.

[230] Allen, *Barthes*, p. 88. The paradigmatic/syntagmatic binary is central to classical linguistics as the chief axes of language. See Roland Barthes, *Elements of Semiology* (trans. Annette Lavers and Colin Smith; New York: Hill and Wang, 1964), pp. 58-61.

[231] Sheridan, 'Issues in the Translation'.

That is, John's Gospel would satisfy the criteria of Barthes' 'readerly' (*lisible*) rather than 'writerly' (*scriptible*) text. The Gospel, in other words, speaks the *doxa* of the Johannine kerygma, clearly delineating insiders and outsiders depending upon where they stand with respect to its message. Even if in the wider cultural code, the Gospel's message was at the time of its composition, the voice of *para-doxa* upsetting hegemonic discourses, as available to readers today, bound within the canon (and thus bound as a Work), the Gospel speaks the accepted *doxa* of centuries of ecclesial orthodoxy. But irrespective of its status as 'work', the *text* of John speaks with the exclusionary authority of *écrivance*, the assertive power of *doxa* in its voice. That 'the Jews' are so routinely 'Othered' each time they speak in the text, that there is limited scope for the reader to sympathize with their view but must instead read their words through the judgement of Jesus or the narrator, is evidence of the 'readerly' nature of John's text, and of its *doxa*.

But if we were doomed to digest John's ideological point of view without any thought, it would not be possible to analyse the avenues by which we could perform a resistant reading of the Gospel. In other words, persuasion, no matter how insistent, is never compulsion. Indeed, the irony is that the most heavy-handed of implied authors can prompt suspicion in readers rather than trust, and lead to deconstructive (or 'resistant') readings.[232] It retrieves the legitimacy of 'the Jews' voice in the Gospel by reading against the grain of the text and by filling out the perspective of the Jews through an intertextual reading explaining their position vis-à-vis Jesus. Like Balzac's *Sarrasine*, the Gospel of John is still partially 'reversible'. There are points by which plurality and polysemy can enter to provide a counter-narrative to the story, that is, to provide what Barthes calls *para-doxa*. But it must be kept in mind that *para-doxa*, like *doxa* itself, proceeds from an assertiveness that describes the *écrivance* of language-as-ideology, and that *para-doxa* can also therefore become violent speech.[233]

It is the non-sequential or non-linear codes (SEM, SYM and REF) that provide entry points for intertextuality and plurivocality in the Gospel of John. This is how readers today can find the 'scriptible' in John's readerly text. For example, although John's characters are highly stylized, reduced to the roles of disciples or antagonists in keeping with the Johannine kerygma of the incarnate Word's confrontation with a world in darkness, they nevertheless receive some complexity in terms of their intertextual characterization. Likewise, the symbolic features of the Gospel open the intertextual landscape of the Gospel considerably, making it possible to explore in what ways John's text 'goes off' in unexpected poetic directions. The cultural code of the text also allows readers to question the sources of authoritative knowledge supporting John's narrative to probe fuller dimensions and alternative possibilities in the widest frame of the text; scriptural sources and biblical figures cited or alluded to in the Gospel text invite

---

[232] Sheridan, 'Persuasion', p. 222.
[233] Reinhartz notes this in other words, saying that a resistant reading is not sufficient to counteract the compliant reading of the Gospel, as it proceeds from the same exclusionary basis, just reversing the terms of the debate. A fully integral reading needs neutrality (not 'objectivity'), that is, it needs to accommodate what Reinhartz calls a 'sympathetic' *and* an 'engaged' reading of the Gospel. See idem, *Befriending the Beloved Disciple*.

readers to consider the *deja* of the text, and to weave threads together in different (or *différant*) formations.

This is all of what Barthes described as 'scripting' the intertextual field of a text. It is not merely about tracking down citations to determine John's reconfiguration of the 'original' meaning of the source text (there is no original meaning, neither is there a source as such). Instead, intertextuality is tied up with a sensitive appreciation of, and resistance to, given ideologies. And intertextuality relates intrinsically to what Barthes terms *jouissance*: whereas the 'text of pleasure' does not confront or challenge the reader, but reiterates the established *doxa* or status quo, the text of *jouissance* can undo the subjectivity of the reader, leading her or him into a state of crisis. It is more accurate to describe *plaisir* and *jouissance* as two kinds of reading processes than two types of texts – one can no doubt interpret the Gospel of John along the lines of *plaisir* (e.g. in its familiar status as liturgical work, read and reread in contexts supporting long-established belief systems that produce comfort for its readers) or along the lines of *jouissance* (in ways that upend or even shatter the subjective identity of the reader precisely through its discomforting effects in ways that lead to the text's 'explosion' of meaning). In the latter case, we might recall Kristeva's understanding of intertextuality involving the 'subject-in-process'. As a concrete example, I would posit my own subjective identity as a contemporary Jewish reader of the Gospel of John; it is not that, when encountering the Gospel as a text of *jouissance* my subjective identity is therefore 'shattered' (Barthes), but that the different relationship I have with the polemical language of the Gospel requires a 'resistant' reading of the text. In this case, the non-sequential, intertextual codes of reading are of paramount importance.[234]

In sum, I am not claiming that poststructuralist intertextuality is a perfect approach; however, the preceding discussion of Barthes' theory should indicate that the term 'intertextuality' as he uses it is not just a fashionable code word hiding empty irrelevancies. It raises significant questions about 'ownership' of the canon (as product/'work'), and the voices that are permitted to speak regarding it; it also creates space for readers to 'script' against the grain of John's overdetermined hermeneutic and proairetic codes, and to perform 'resistant' readings that reframe its intertextual field. In that respect, the approach of this book is to 'script' the intertextual field of John 8.31-59, with a focus on the figure of Abraham and 'the Jews'. As Chapter 1 demonstrated, Abraham's characterization in John 8.31-59 is associated with certain nouns, some of them designating his role in relation to other groups (e.g. 'father', 'seed') and some verbs ('saw', 'rejoiced'). Other nouns in the passage are evocative and metaphorical ('seed', 'sin', 'slave', 'son', 'father', 'freedom', 'truth', 'household', 'works') and most of these have direct or indirect connections to the figure of Abraham (SEM, SYM). These metaphors (or 'lexemes' in the Barthesian sense) provide points of entry to 'script' the text intertextually. Thus, the approach adopted in this book is to assess a wide range of texts from antiquity that *collocate* certain of these nouns and metaphors with respect

---

[234] One could also assume that the Gospel text presented ancient readers with a 'crisis' too, but from a different angle – those who came to experience their Judaism in a new light and those who 'converted' to the nascent Christian movement and away from more familiar or established ways of being. This is indeed a part of the Gospel text itself – the 'fear of the Jews' and the references to being 'thrown out of the synagogue'.

to Abraham. Instead of trekking through lexicons to grasp the 'meaning' of words such as 'sin' or 'seed', I trace the intertextual weave of these symbolic codes as they appear together, with respect to the figure of Abraham.

Importantly, the intertextual field that I script in relation to John 8.31-59 relies heavily on literature from within early Judaism, and additionally, the rabbinic corpora (but also includes extensive analysis of the NT). The reason for this selection lies in my interest in performing a 'resistant', or *para-doxical* reading of John 8.31-59 and the voice of the Jews within it. While Adele Reinhartz has written an essay on a 'Jewish Reading of John 8.31-59', the analysis in this book attempts the same procedure but at much greater length and in greater depth. The exegetical chapters of this book (Chapters 4 through 6) discuss the regrettable tendency, particularly in the Johannine commentary tradition, to interpret the Jews' responses to Jesus in ch. 8 vv. 31-59 in egregiously pejorative terms barely warranted by the text itself. Yet, at the same time, these readings, which effectively reproduce the anti-Judaism already present in the text, demonstrate just how persuasively the Gospel invites 'compliant' readings especially towards those who already espouse the tenets of faith expressed by Jesus in the text.[235] By drawing on intertextual aspects of the wider 'Jewish cultural code' (REF) in certain ancient texts, I am able to produce something of a corrective to John's *lisible* vision, and by extension, those modern interpretations of the Gospel that import psycho-theological readings of terms in John 8.31-59 such as 'sin' and 'slavery' which reinforce and reinscribe, to devastating effect, a new legacy of anti-Judaism. Particularly, we include in our analysis the function of Abraham in the early rabbinic material to better showcase how the 'Jewish' perspective decried by John's Jesus in ch. 8 vv. 31-59 spoke on its own terms, in its own voice and for its own legitimate reasons.

The rabbinic intertext offers an 'explosion' (Barthes) into the vast fabric of cultural texts not often brought into conversation with the Fourth Gospel. We explored the reasons for the current scholarly reluctance to engage the NT in conversation with rabbinic material in the first part of this chapter, when we argued that the challenges of anachronism, chronology and the fear of slipping into 'parallelomania', all played their part in limiting interpretations of John's Gospel with the rabbinic texts. The impulse behind this resistance has also been one of trying to perform comparative analysis more rigorously, that is, to compare 'like' with 'like' with respect to something chosen (*tertium comparationis*). While this caution is commendable for restraining absurd comparisons, and for refocusing precision in what a 'parallel' really means, the negative effect has been that John's Gospel is never really brought into conversation with rabbinic material.

I contend that poststructuralist intertextuality theory provides a wholly different angle on this 'problem' – in fact, from a Barthesian perspective, engaging the Gospel of John with chronologically 'later' rabbinic material is not a 'problem' at all. Recall that Jonathan Z. Smith, the doyen of comparative religion, understands that textual comparison is ultimately a synchronistic endeavour, and that two texts will be brought together solely within the imagination of the scholar performing the analysis. From my position as a modern scholar reading ancient texts (which are only ever presented to

---

[235] Sheridan, 'Seed of Abraham, Slavery and Sin'.

me as 'works' in the sense that Barthes phrases it), there is nothing surprising, offensive or irresponsible about my choice to set the texts of the NT into conversation with the rabbinic material of the third to eighth centuries CE, quite apart from the oft-noted caveat that the traditions inscribed in the later rabbinic material express oral discourses circulating in the first century and earlier.

I conclude this chapter then, with the following observations. Poststructuralist intertextuality offers us the *theoretical* resources to think through our relationship to texts, to unoriginated knowledge, to ideology and resistance to ideology. Comparative criticism digs deep into various assumptions and ideas such as how we are always already evaluating texts when comparing them. It should also be clear that the assumptions guiding both approaches are not as disparate as we might fear. Indeed, the 'New Comparativism' and the approach from perspectivism focus on comparative reasoning as – in the last analysis – a subjective and 'articulate choice'. Moving away from the 'distal tree logic' of influence and origins, comparative criticism can proceed through 'and-criticism' (Saussy), co-creative and spontaneous meaning-making in the process of reading. Textual comparisons are an ever-expanding adventure where parallels grow laterally, with connections and associations made by the (naturally subjective) interpreter. Intertextuality theory highlights how the reader is the destination of all the intertextual traces of the text as a vast and vibrant tapestry, and how the reader-as-scriptor shapes and 'writes' the text in the act of interpretation. Barthesian intertextuality theory understands intertextual 'scripting' in much the same light precisely to break through dominant ideologies that would permit some readings but not others. The value of both approaches is that they move us beyond the futile attempt to reify 'objectivity' as an interpretive possibility. As such, these methods and approaches hold great promise for biblical studies to transcend its disciplinary blindness with respect to theory, and its entrenched favouring of historicist paradigms. Together, the ideas and examples discussed in this chapter inform the textual analysis of John 8.31-59 undertaken in the remainder of this book.

3

John 8.31-59: Structure, setting, text

Introduction

Before proceeding to the exegetical analysis that forms the core part of this book's argument (Chapters 4 through 6), it is necessary to address a variety of preliminary issues affecting John 8.31-59 as a discrete unit within its immediate narrative context. In this chapter, I establish the boundaries of ch. 8 vv. 31-59 as a unit of discourse within the narrative setting of John 7.1-8.59. I argue that the festival setting of this broader unit (John 7-8) is the feast of Sukkot (cf. John 7.2). I also demonstrate the thematic coherence of John 7-8 against claims that this section of the Gospel is concerned only with miscellany or material shafted together without concern for narrative coherence.[1] This is not to say that John 7-8 does not therefore exhibit its own complex compositional history; neither is it to equate narrative and thematic coherency with compositional unity. But the text as it stands nevertheless displays a remarkably coherent structure based on overlapping, recurrent themes, much in the manner of the Johannine farewell discourses (13.1-17.26) and their patterns of *relecture*.[2]

Prior to discussing the wider narrative setting of John 7-8, there is a pressing textual issue that first confronts any reader trying to establish John 8.31-59 as a discrete segment – the perplexing identity of the textual addresses in ch. 8 vv. 30, 31. The question could be posed, 'Does the textual segment concerning the Jews and Abraham begin at ch. 8 v. 30 or v. 31?' More specifically, is the group referred to in v. 30 the same as that addressed in v. 31, or are they two different groups? In ch. 8 v. 30, the narrator refers to the 'many' who believed in Jesus as he was speaking to them; then the text abruptly shifts towards 'the Jews who had believed in him' in ch. 8 v. 31. Yet, the tone of conversation between this latter audience and Jesus (cf. 8.32-59) does not resemble a state of 'belief' by any stretch of the imagination. This disparity has given rise to various theories that seek to make sense of the audience(s) and the nature of

---

[1] Cf. Barnabas Lindars, *The Gospel of John* (NCBC; London: Oliphants, 1972), p. 277, with respect to John 7-8: 'dialogue there is in plenty, but it is confused for lack of a single theme... not only does the subject-matter jump from topic to topic, but also the setting is constantly shifting'. Rudolf Schnackenburg, *The Gospel according to St. John. Volume 2 – Commentary on Chapters 5-12* (London: Burns & Oates, 1980), p. 136: Schnackenburg finds ch. 7 to be basically a grouping of individual units centring on the attitude of different audiences to Jesus, collected at the feast of Tabernacles.
[2] Cf. Jean Zumstein, *Kreative Erinnerung: Relecture und Auslegung im Johannesevangelium* (Abhandlungen zur Theologie des Alten und Neuen Testaments 84; Zürich: TVZ, 2004).

their respective level of imputed belief; these theories will be discussed presently. This chapter includes ch. 7 v. 53 to ch. 8 v. 11 (the 'pericope of the adulteress') in the Sukkot context, as integral to the narrative-critical approach taken in this book.[3] This pericope is generally considered to be a later interpolation, is often discounted as an integral part of John 7–8 and is bracketed out of editions of the New Testament (NT), or placed in an appendix in Gospel commentaries.

The problem of the textual addressees: Ch. 8 vv. 30 and 31

John 8.30 appears to conclude a prior segment of discourse already begun in ch. 8 v. 21, for the narrator in v. 21 begins 'So he [Jesus] said to them again...' (πάλιν), while in v. 30 the narrator comments, 'As he [Jesus] was saying these things, many believed in him' (ταῦτα αὐτοῦ λαλοῦντος πολλοὶ ἐπίστευσαν εἰς αὐτόν). Yet, in the very next verse (8.31), the narrator uses the connective (οὖν: 'so') adding: 'Jesus said to the Jews who had believed in him, "If you abide in my word..."' (ἐὰν ὑμεῖς μείνητε ἐν τῷ λόγῳ τῷ ἐμῷ)'. The section of text introduced by Jesus' remark in v. 31 ends in v. 59, with 'the Jews' as the consistent addressees throughout the remainder of this pericope.

The problem for interpreters is in deciding whether the 'many' who believed in Jesus in ch. 8 v. 30 is *the same group* as 'the Jews who had believed in him' in ch. 8 v. 31. Lest this look like an exercise in hair-splitting, it is necessary to point out what is at stake in the discussion. If it is decided, let us say on the basis of the connective οὖν in v. 31a, that 'the Jews' of v. 31 are the same as the 'many' of v. 30, then the nature of the Jews' 'belief' in v. 31 will be interpreted as consistent with their 'belief' in v. 30: this single group believed in Jesus on the basis of his words, even if their belief is expressed in a different grammatical form across the two verses.[4] But this begs another question: how could this group's stated belief in Jesus deteriorate so rapidly across the context of ch. 8 vv. 30-59, to the point where Jesus calls them 'liars' and children of the devil (8.44), and in reply, the Jews attempt to kill Jesus on the spot (8.59)? One scholarly suggestion has been to read the belief of this homogeneous group as superficial, as referring to a group of 'false believers'.[5] As such, the group in vv. 30-31 effectively 'codes' either (a) an historical group of 'Judaizing' Christians trying to infiltrate the Johannine community and proffer a law-based gospel;[6] or (b) a group of nominal 'Christians' who want to

---

[3] The naming of this pericope is critiqued by Frances Taylor Gench, 'John 7.53-8.11', *Interpretation* 63, no. 4 (2009), pp. 398–400: 'The story as it is named (the woman caught in adultery) tends to focus our attention solely on the woman and issues of sexual sin and obscures the significant role that others, too, play in this scene' (p. 398).

[4] The indicative aorist of πιστεύω in v. 30 (followed by the accusative preposition: ἐπίστευσαν εἰς αὐτόν) and the perfect participle of πιστεύω in v. 31 (followed by the dative: πεπιστευκότας αὐτῷ).

[5] Cf. recently, Dale Bruner, *The Gospel of John: A Commentary* (Grand Rapids: Eerdmans, 2012), p. 532. Previous commentators who have held similar views include: Brodie, *Gospel*, p. 328 ('superficial' believers); Ernst Haenchen, *John: A Commentary on the Gospel of John* (2 vols; trans. and ed. Robert W. Funk; Hermeneia; Philadelphia: Fortress Press, 1984), 2.28 (their belief is only 'alleged').

[6] Cf. C. H. Dodd, cited in Moloney, *The Gospel of John* (SP 4; Collegeville: Liturgical Pres, 1998), p. 277, n. 31.

retain adherence to Judaism – the 'Crypto-Christians' of Martyn's 'two-level drama' reading – who are, moreover, afraid to 'come out' and confess Christ (cf. 12.42).[7] This historical explanation then provides the basis for claiming that the 'belief' mentioned in vv. 30-31 is not genuine, but false, and this is why it suddenly breaks down under the pressure of Jesus' subsequent assertions (cf. vv. 33-34).

The problems with this suggestion have already been noted in later scholarship. Donald Carson is astute – and in my view, correct – in his counterargument, claiming that the suggestion 'misconstrues the terms of the debate' in ch. 8 of the Gospel.[8] In other words, the debate in John 8 is not about Judaizers pressing a law-free gospel on 'Christians', comparable to what might have been the case in Paul's Galatia. It might even be accurate to agree with Carson's assessment that this kind of historical explanation is 'a scholarly fad' rather than proper 'exegesis' because it involves manufacturing a group that is not explicitly mentioned in the text.[9] Of course, there are deeper methodological problems here too, such as the assumption about the socio-historical referentiality of narratives in general, and the free and easy use of 'analogical' interpretation – this was discussed in Chapter 2. Raymond Brown rightly notes that there is nothing to indicate that the Jews in v. 31 'hid' their faith (cf. Martyn's suggestive appellation 'Crypto-Christian'), but Brown does claim that the group mentioned in v. 31 represents a segment of the early Christian community in an antagonistic relationship with the Johannine community.[10] Nevertheless, this assertion can only be considered conjectural.

A number of scholars and commentators consider the groups mentioned in vv. 30-31 to be identical, without recourse to historical analogy. These scholars reconcile the group's stated 'belief' with their later hostility (vv. 32-59) by claiming that the belief of 'the many', as well as the belief of 'the Jews', was facile or spurious (v. 30). Their reasoning is as follows: the audience in ch. 8 v. 30 *believe* in Jesus as he speaks, with the verb taking the accusative preposition (εἰς αὐτόν). That 'the many' believe in Jesus while he is talking suggests, in this view, that they simply believe Jesus' words as correct and true assertions – they do not arrive at a deep faith in Jesus.[11] Meanwhile, the group in ch. 8 v. 31 must be the same audience as that mentioned in ch. 8 v. 30, only described in more detail. Thus, 'the Jews who had believed in [Jesus]' (v. 31) are interpreted as exhibiting *failed* faith; they once believed in Jesus, but do so no longer. Scholars espousing this argument merge the audiences of vv. 30-31 on the basis of a presumed inadequate level of belief.

There are two problems with this argument. First, the aorist plus the accusative preposition in the construction ἐπίστευσαν εἰς (8.30) is otherwise used by John to indicate a character's 'personal trust' in Jesus (cf. 2.23-25), and so there is no reason to doubt the genuineness of the audience's belief in v. 30.[12] Second, spurious faith is not a

---

[7] The two-level drama hypothesis was popularized by Martyn, *History and Theology*.
[8] Carson, *The Gospel*, p. 347.
[9] Ibid., p. 347.
[10] Raymond E. Brown, *The Community of the Beloved Disciple* (New York: Paulist Press, 1977), p. 7.
[11] See the discussion of Debbie Hunn, 'Who are "They" in John 8.33?' *CBQ* 66, no. 3 (2004), pp. 387–99, at p. 389.
[12] Ibid., p. 390.

prominent category in the Gospel of John. That is, there are rarely any *degrees* of belief in Jesus – one either believes or does not believe and one either receives life or forfeits life by virtue of the same decision. This is not to discount the category of a 'signs-based' faith which is evidently deemed insufficient by Jesus and the narrator (cf. 2.24), but to emphasize that the stronger focus in John's Gospel is on the dichotomy between belief/unbelief itself. A similar point is made by C. H. Dodd, but from the angle of the Jews in ch. 8 v. 31. Dodd considers the grammatical differences between ch. 8 v. 30 and ch. 8 v. 31 to be nothing more than 'stylistic variation'.[13] He thinks that the reference to 'believing' Jews in v. 31 only makes sense if we posit them as part of the 'many' who believed in Jesus in v. 30. But rather than assuming that the purportedly identical audience in vv. 30-31 exhibits an *insufficient* faith in Jesus, Dodd's line of reasoning requires us to view this integrated audience as exhibiting satisfactory faith, as nothing about v. 30 would of itself suggest otherwise. In that case, however, we are still faced with the problem that 'believers' (of any qualification) become the target of some of Jesus' fiercest reproaches (cf. vv. 44-46).[14]

The alternative, then, is to consider the audiences distinct. That is, the audience addressed in v. 31 – 'the Jews who had believed' in Jesus – are introduced as a *new* group discontinuous with 'the many' of v. 30. This view surmounts the difficulty in imagining that a group of 'many' believers (v. 30) could so quickly become Jesus' adversaries, to the point where Jesus accuses them of refusing to welcome him (8.41) and of actively doing the devil's desires (8.44).[15] 'The Jews' of v. 31 would then constitute Jesus' narrative antagonists, who continue their ongoing antagonism towards him begun in earlier sections of the narrative (cf. 5.16-45 and 7.19-42). The reference to the belief of the 'many' (v. 30) would therefore signal the conclusion of a different discourse. The most immediate problem with this otherwise convincing segmentation of the text is that 'the Jews' in v. 31 are said to have '*believed*' in Jesus – a highly anomalous characterization when compared to the narrative momentum thus far.

One solution, perhaps the least elegant of many, is to consider v. 31 as a gloss.[16] There is no ancient manuscript evidence attesting to this solution; moreover, the supposition of a gloss fails to attenuate the difficulty of squaring the recorded 'belief' of the group in v. 30 with the subsequent demonstrations of 'unbelief' of the group in vv. 32-59.[17] A glossator would in this case have *introduced* a problem into the text, rather than having smoothed one out.[18] But recourse to a glossator who introduced a problem – or an editor who failed to excise a problem – is not too different in essence from other arguments that rationalize the kind of belief imputed to the Jews in v. 31. For example, a strong contingent of Johannine scholars distinguish the Jews of ch. 8 v. 31 from 'the many' of ch. 8 v. 30 by adducing the differences between the grammatical form of πιστεύω in the two verses. The different grammatical forms of the

---

[13] Dodd, 'Behind a Johannine Dialogue', p. 43.
[14] Ibid., p. 43.
[15] Cf. Hunn, 'Who are "They?" in John 8.33?' p. 392.
[16] Brown, *John*, 2.351; Lindars, *The Gospel of John*, p. 323.
[17] Carson, *The Gospel*, p. 346.
[18] Ibid., p. 346.

verb πιστεύω in vv. 30-31, according to this popular view, reflects the different quality of belief demonstrated by 'the many' and 'the Jews'.

James Swetnam claims that in John's Gospel, the phrase πολλοὶ ἐπίστευσαν εἰς αὐτόν is consistently used in contexts that contrast the unreserved belief of the 'many' with the unbelief of the Jews.[19] The case of ch. 8 vv. 30, 31 would therefore be no exception to this rule, with two different (indeed, contrasting) groups mentioned: the 'many' who unreservedly believed in Jesus, and the Jews, who did not. Of course, the problem with this reading is obvious: in ch. 8 v. 31 the Jews *are* described as having believed in Jesus; they are not stigmatized as unbelievers. To make Swetnam's thesis fit the evidence, we would need to posit something comparable about the grammar of πιστεύω in v. 31, and in fact, this is what Swetnam does. Instead of outright unbelief, the Jews in ch. 8 v. 31 would exhibit a comparably negative, insufficient or fickle belief, which provides the so-called Johannine contrast between types of belief. Swetnam argues that the perfect participle πεπιστευκότας (v. 31) carries the sense of a belief once given and now retracted: 'the Jews who (*had*) believed in Jesus' (and, it is implied, did so no longer).[20] This, Swetnam claims, is an instance where the perfect tense can be read with a pluperfect meaning, and it contrasts with the straightforward belief of the 'many' in v. 30, where the aorist of πιστεύω is used (Swetnam also compares this with some Synoptic usages, e.g. Mark 5.15 et al.).[21]

Swetnam is correct to highlight one of the *contrasting patterns* in the Gospel, wherein the characters who believe in Jesus are set against the Gospel's darker story – that of 'the Jews' who opposed Jesus, or who did not believe in him.[22] Given that the group in ch. 8 v. 31 is called 'the Jews' (quite apart from the qualification of their belief), we should seriously consider the possibility that they are an audience distinct from 'the many' in v. 30. For 'the Jews' are regularly in John the enemies of Jesus; it is among the 'many' that some hold a good opinion of him (v. 12), and they are restrained from expressing it for fear of the Jews.[23] The Jews are never elsewhere in the Gospel integrated into the 'many', but act in parallel scenes to plot against Jesus in order to avert further defection from their ranks – or they eventually emerge from the 'crowd' or the multitude to antagonize Jesus (cf. 6.44). What we might have is two parallel and contrasting tales: Jews who 'ran after' Jesus following the Lazarus miracle (11.45; 12.11), and Jews who once believed in Jesus, but did so no longer (8.31). This solution gives credence to the 'sifting' and division of opinion about Jesus that occurs throughout John 7–8.

Some of the drawbacks of Swetnam's otherwise attractive hypothesis are noted by Debbie Hunn.[24] One shortcoming of Swetnam's hypothesis is that 'it is rare for the perfect participle to denote action that no longer continues, at least in its effects, and

---

[19] James Swetnam, 'The Meaning of πεπιστευκότας in John 8.31', *Bib* 61 (1980), pp. 106–9, at p. 106.
[20] Ibid., pp. 106–9.
[21] Ibid.
[22] For an extended discussion of the binaries involving the Jews and the disciples, see Reinhartz, *Befriending the Beloved Disciple*.
[23] C. K. Barrett, *The Gospel According to St John* (2nd edn; London: SPCK, 1978), p. 313.
[24] Hunn, 'Who are "They?" in John 8.33?', pp. 392–3.

that the context makes clear when such meaning is intended'.[25] In the NT, there are seventeen other uses of πιστεύω in the perfect tense (five in John: 3.18; 6.69; 8.31; 11.27; 16.27; 20.29), and none of these carry the implication that the person(s) believing *stopped* believing.[26] Then there is the sense of the passage to consider. Jesus encourages 'the Jews who believed in him' (8.31) to *continue* 'remaining' in his word (8.32a). If the Jews had stopped believing in Jesus, as Swetnam's hypothesis suggests, there would be no need for Jesus to encourage their continuing belief – phrased as 'remaining' in his word.[27] Yet, Swetnam's examples from John's Gospel are compelling. To take only one example: 'Lazarus, who *had died* (implication: but now lives)' (11.39b), provides us with a strong case where the perfect participle is used to describe activity (death) that no longer continues – no matter how counterintuitive that concept may be.

The other main way of distinguishing between the groups in vv. 30, 31 is to differentiate the quality of their belief on the basis of the sentence syntax. We saw that John's use of the verb πιστεύω (8.30) is otherwise used in the Gospel to indicate unconditional belief in Jesus (cf. 2.23-25). Building on this observation, some scholars reiterate the argument that the belief of the 'many' (8.30) is proper and genuine, but that the belief of the Jews in ch. 8 v. 31 is inadequate, this time with attention to the function of the prepositions following the verb. So, in ch. 8 v. 30, we have πιστεύω + accusative, but in ch. 8 v. 31, we have πιστεύω + dat.: τοὺς πεπιστευκότας αὐτῷ – which, these scholars claim, expresses the subject's limited belief.[28] Francis J. Moloney argues that the change in tense as well as syntax makes it necessary to read 'the Jews who believed in Jesus' in v. 31 as a new group, separate and distinct from the 'many' in v. 30. Moloney considers the use of ἐπίστευσαν εἰς in v. 30 to indicate full faith and the use of ἐπίστευσαν εἰς + dat. to indicate partial faith; the perfect participle (v. 31) suggests that 'the Jews' have not advanced in faith.[29] Moloney imagines that the 'many' who believed in Jesus (v. 30) have, by v. 31, left the scene, and the remaining Jews addressed in v. 31 have come to partial faith in Jesus, and remain in that state.[30] Jesus' ensuing dialogue with 'the Jews who believed' is meant to invite their ongoing belief, so that they might move into 'authentic' faith. Yet, there are other instances in the Gospel of John where the difference between *pisteiu* and *pisteie eis* is negligible in terms of semantics.[31] Carson thinks that pinning the distinction between 'genuine' and 'spurious' faith on the presence or lack of a preposition (and its grammatical form) is simply too unreasonable.[32]

Another attempt to solve these thorny issues has been advanced by Debbie Hunn: she posits a change in audience not between v. 30 and v. 31, but between v 32 and v. 33.[33] For Hunn, the context of the wider pericope makes it logical to assume that 'the

---

[25] Ibid., p. 392.
[26] Ibid.
[27] Ibid., p. 393.
[28] Cf. Morris, *The Gospel according to John*, pp. 297-8.
[29] Moloney, *Signs and Shadows: Reading John 5-12* (Minnaepolis: Fortress Press), p. 103; Idem, *John*, p. 275.
[30] Moloney, *John*, p. 275.
[31] E.g. Bultmann, *The Gospel of John*, p. 252, n. 2.
[32] Carson, *The Gospel*, p. 346.
[33] Hunn, 'Who are "They?" in John 8.33?', p. 395.

people in 8.30-32 are not the objectors of 8.33-59'.[34] Rather, these objectors represent, in Hunn's words, 'Jesus' own antagonists'. The only group mentioned in ch. 8 v. 33 is 'they' (i.e. 'they answered him': ἀπεκρίθησαν πρὸς αὐτόν). This is the group that goes on to debate with Jesus for the rest of the pericope, and according to Hunn, 'they' represent a different group, both to 'the Jews who believed' in v. 32, and the 'many' who believed in v. 30. However different, this group is not new: Hunn claims that there is no 'narrative warrant' to manufacture an entirely new group of interlocutors at v. 33, suggesting instead that the group in v. 33 receives its naming further on in the passage. The antecedent of 'they' in v. 33 is not, for Hunn, to be found in the immediately preceding verses, but in the verses *that follow*.[35] To substantiate this claim, Hunn adduces a curious Johannine pattern of specifying 'referents after using a pronoun or the conjugated form of a verb with the pronoun implied' – a pattern Hunn finds 'repeatedly' present 'in this narrative'.[36] Hunn's examples include 'they' in John 2.3; 'we' in ch. 3 v. 11; 'they' in ch. 3 v. 23; 'you' in ch. 4 v. 48; 'you' in ch. 10 v. 1; 'them and they' in ch. 12 v. 37; 'they' in ch. 15 v. 6; 'them' in ch. 19 v. 4; 'them' in ch. 19 v. 16; 'they' in ch. 19 v. 29; 'they' in ch. 20 v. 13' and 'we' in ch. 21 v. 24'.[37]

Hunn also cites multiple other examples of this pattern in John 7–8, apart from ch. 8 v. 33 (viz., 7.12-13, 14-15, 16-19, 26, 32, 35; 8.20). For example, who are 'they' who seek to kill Jesus in ch. 7 v. 25? Writes Hunn, 'the verse following the pronoun names the referent, the rulers, the Jews whom Jesus had just accused (7:26)'.[38] Again, we learn that 'they' were trying to seize him (Jesus) in ch. 7 v. 30: naturally, and in context, we would think the referent is the multitude, as they are the group listening to Jesus' words. But, explains Hunn, the correct referent emerges in ch. 7 v. 32: the officers sent by the Pharisees were those trying to seize Jesus. We could also ask who is addressed by the pronoun 'you' in ch. 7 v. 33? We might think the officers are being spoken to here, but later the Jews identify themselves as those who were addressed by Jesus (7.35). Then, John 8.12-13 has Jesus speaking to 'them' (αὐτοῖς ἐλάλησεν ὁ Ἰησοῦς), but receiving a reply from a subgroup, the Pharisees (8.20). On the basis of this stylistic pattern, Hunn argues that 'in 8.30, "many" believe in Jesus, and in 8.31, Jesus addresses them'. The addressees in vv. 30-31 are therefore one and the same. It is v. 33 that presents a problem: 'Who is it that answers?' Hunn observes another pattern in John 7–8, in addition to that of the delayed naming of referents, and that is that 'only Jesus' opponents speak to him'. What Hunn means is that those groups in John 7–8 who are said to 'believe' or who 'marvel' only end up talking among themselves, but *not directly to Jesus*. Either that, or they say nothing at all. And according to Hunn's reading, only Jesus' enemies in chs 7–8 speak back to him. To quote Hunn once more, 'thus, although Jesus addresses one group in 8.31-32, another answers; and the group that answers is defined not before they answer but afterward'.

Hunn's solution, and those like it, resolves the dilemma of understanding a group of believers (either v. 30 or v. 31) to be later embroiled in a bitter and hostile exchange

---

[34] Ibid., pp. 395–6.
[35] Ibid.
[36] Ibid., p. 396.
[37] Ibid., pp. 396, n. 24.
[38] What follows is summarized from ibid., pp. 396–7.

with Jesus on the basis of what can only be understood as their explicit unbelief. But there are two problems with Hunn's otherwise creative solution: one is that a swift change in dialogue partners between v. 32 and v. 33 seems unlikely even on stylistic grounds. Jesus speaks to 'the Jews who had believed in him' in v. 31, promising them the gift of liberating 'truth' if they continue to abide in his word. The exact subject is echoed by his audience ('they') in v. 32: 'we have been slaves of no one ever, how do you say, "you shall be set free"?'. It seems difficult to imagine that such a specific promise in v. 31 would meet with a rejoinder from a different group in v. 32 who then continue to commandeer the conversation in a hostile direction, and that Jesus' original addressees remain silent. Certainly, this kind of pattern is not found in the rest of the Gospel. More significantly, there are no grounds for thinking that 'the Jews' of vv. 33-59 are but a 'smaller' segment of 'the Jews who believed in him' (v. 31). In fact, it would be more accurate to assume the reverse – that a smaller group of believing Jews (or once-believing Jews) are a subset of the more monolithic category of the hostile Jews in the Gospel.

Towards the conclusion of her article, Hunn is forced to make the qualification: 'The fact that John has changed Jesus' dialogue partners and specified an antecedent after a pronoun in earlier instances in chaps 7–8 does not prove that he does so also in 8.33. It only means that this possibility cannot be ruled out on grammatical or stylistic grounds'.[39] Neither do Hunn's distinctions uniformly hold across John 7–8. It is not the case that only Jesus' opponents speak back to him; other groups who are neutral speak directly to him in response: the crowd in v. 20 (who deny that they are his opponents); the Jews who 'marvel' at Jesus, speaking about him rather than to him (7.15), even though Jesus responds to them (7.16); when the tone becomes more hostile, it is not the Jews who reply to Jesus but 'the crowd' (7.19-20). The Jews do not otherwise consistently speak directly with Jesus, as in ch. 7 v. 35 when they question his claims among themselves (similarly to 'the people' and 'the crowd' in ch. 7 v. 32). Likewise in ch. 8 v. 22, the Jews do not speak directly to Jesus, but turn to each other, as it were, and ponder Jesus' proclamation among themselves. Furthermore, 'the people' talk among themselves about Jesus (7.12-13 – they 'mutter' cf. v. 32). Jesus gives no response, possibly because he is not in hearing range (7.11). But when the Jerusalemites put questions to each other about Jesus (7.25-28), Jesus replies to them in strong terms about his identity. The result is stated succinctly by the narrator: 'So they sought to arrest him' (7.30). The referent 'they' seems misplaced – are the Jerusalemites attempting a 'citizen's arrest'? It is not impossible – in ch. 7 vv. 34-44 it is the *people* (and not the chief priests later specified) who want to arrest Jesus, so the presumably misplaced referent 'they' in ch. 7 v. 30 need not be read as an antecedent referent for a different group.

There is no simple solution to the issue of the textual addressees in ch. 8 vv. 30, 31. But there is something to be said for the hypothesis that 'the Jews who (had) believed in [Jesus]' might have been former believers-turned-enemies. This is not based upon the notion of a semantic difference between the accusative/dative prepositions, but simply based upon the narrative context of the Gospel, and Jesus' words of promise

---

[39] Ibid., p. 397.

in ch. 8 v. 31. What goes unnoticed in discussion on the text is that Jesus does not simply urge this group to 'remain' in his word – that is to believe in him; he expresses a promise in the subjunctive voice – *If* you remain in my word, (*then*) you shall know the truth. This is close to Jesus' conditional statement in John 15.1-6: '*If* you remain in me (*then*) you shall bear fruit.' In both ch. 8 v. 31 and ch. 15 vv. 1-6, there is no guarantee that the hearers will do what is required in the protasis for the apodosis to be realized. This suggests that the fortitude of the respective addressees – whether they are named as 'the Jews' or 'the disciples' – is in question. In fact, what they are called does not seem to matter as much as what they *continue to do* – that is 'to remain' in Jesus or in his 'word'. To the Jews who (had) believed (8.31), the invitation to 'remain' in Jesus' word to ensure knowledge of the truth and freedom is not convincing; they have never been enslaved (8.32). As the debate unfolds, we grasp the irreconcilable nature of the propositions.

Moloney's contextual reading of ch. 8 vv. 30-31 (see n. 30) takes seriously the belief of the group in v. 30, which means that somewhere along the line there must be a change of audience, for the dialogue soon deteriorates into a debate around two mutually opposed perspectives. Moloney concedes that their faith is 'limited' in some sense – specified later by Jesus as the fact that his 'word' finds no 'place' in the Jews (8.42). It is reasonable to posit that the change of audience takes place between v. 30 and v. 31, not later, between v. 31 and v. 32, because reference to 'abiding' in Jesus' 'word' is made in v. 31, and reinforced in ch. 8 v. 42. This could, of course, suggest that the audience in ch. 8 v. 31 – who are differentiated from 'the many' in ch. 8 v. 30, and who remain Jesus' dialogue partners up until ch. 8 v. 59 – are deemed to be apostates by Jesus, which accounts for their narrative hostility. Terry Griffiths has pointed out that of the two occurrences of the perfect participle of πιστεύω in the Apostolic Fathers, both references are in the context of apostasy.[40] Griffiths' interpretation does not postulate that 'the Jews' of John 8.31 begin as solid believers who gradually turn against Jesus in the space of twelve verses to become his mortal enemies (8.59). There is no development in this short plot that would 'signal a change from "sympathetic" Jews who accept Jesus' teaching in some way, to those prepared to stone him. The only development is one from intention to action'.[41] Griffiths finds that the language of diabolization (cf. 8.44) has a parallel in the treatment of Judas as 'a devil' and an apostate (cf. 6.60-71).[42] In both cases, this strong language is reserved for former believers who turn against Jesus in profound ways.

Whether this interpretation reads too much into the character of the Jews in ch. 8 v. 31 is an open question. Of course, there is no prior narrative context in the Gospel to prove that 'the Jews' were once believers in Jesus. But for the purposes of this short section, it supports the idea that the audience of ch. 8 v. 31 differs from that of ch. 8 v. 30, and that therefore the parameters of the text under consideration in this book should be established as beginning at ch. 8 v. 31.

---

[40] Terry Griffiths, '"The Jews Who had Believed in Him" (John 8.31) and the Motif of Apostasy in the Gospel of John', in Richard Bauckham and Carl Mosser (eds), *The Gospel of John and Christian Theology* (Grand Rapids: Eerdmans, 2008), pp. 183–92, at p. 184.
[41] Ibid., p. 191.
[42] Ibid.

The discourse between Jesus and the Jews beginning at ch. 8 v. 31 is generally accepted as concluding at ch. 8 v. 59.[43] This is based on two factors. One is that v. 59 provides closure to the dispute at a climactic point: Jesus has just claimed to exist 'before Abraham was' (v. 58), and in response (οὖν: 'so'), the Jews pick up stones to throw at him (v. 59a). The other factor is that v. 59 introduces a spatial shift, and hence, the beginnings of a change of location: 'but Jesus hid himself and went out of the Temple' (Ἰησοῦς δὲ ἐκρύβη καὶ ἐξῆλθεν ἐκ τοῦ ἱεροῦ: v. 59b). This change in location is continued immediately in ch. 9 v. 1, with a concomitant change of setting and scene. Jesus 'passes by' the exterior of the Temple, and finds a man 'blind from birth' (9.1). A conversation ensues with a new group (Jesus' disciples), who address him with a title not found in chs 7–8: 'rabbi' (9.2). The scene that follows continues right up to ch. 9 v. 41, or, some would argue, well into ch. 10, terminating either at ch. 10 v. 21 or at ch. 10 v. 39.[44] While there are grounds for considering the temporal continuity between ch. 8 v. 59 and ch. 9 v. 1, the change in setting and scene indicates at least that v. 59 closes out the dispute with the Jews begun in v. 31, and introduces a break in spatial continuity.

Having determined the boundaries of our pericope (8.31-59), it is now possible to discern and discuss its internal structure.

A tripartite structure for ch. 8 vv. 31-59

I propose reading a tripartite structure in this pericope. The pericope is internally coherent, held together in part not only by its twelve references to Abraham, but also by the fact that it presents a cumulative dispute between Jesus and the Jews that is carefully crafted and reaches a crescendo at its conclusion.[45] The tripartite structure determined here is based largely on the stages of the argument between Jesus and the Jews. As such, it is a loose structure, but a valuable heuristic guiding the interpretation presented in this book. The first of the three subsections in ch. 8 vv. 31-59 runs from v. 31 to v. 37. In this subsection, Jesus addresses 'the Jews who had believed in him' with the conditional promise, 'If you abide in my word, you are truly my disciples, and you will know the truth that will set you free' (8.31-32).[46] In v. 33 'they' respond with the assertion, 'We are seed of Abraham and have been slaves of no one, ever', and then the question, 'How is it that you say, "You will become free"?' (v. 33). Jesus then replies with the assertion: 'Amen, amen I say to you, everyone who commits sin is a slave to sin' (v. 34) and follows with a small parable about the difference between a 'slave' and 'the son' in the inheritance of a household (v. 35). He couples this with a second promise: 'If the Son sets you free you will be truly free' (v. 36). Jesus continues speaking, and returns to two issues addressed at the start of the subsection, namely, his

---

[43] This is accepted by the vast majority of commentators on the Gospel.
[44] Cf. Moloney, *John*, pp. 233–4; John C. Poirier, 'Hanukkah in the Narrative Chronology of the Fourth Gospel', *NTS* 54, no. 4 (2008), pp. 465–78.
[45] Cf. Dodd, 'Behind a Johannine Dialogue', p. 41.
[46] Reading with an epexegetical καὶ in ch. 8 v. 32b.

interlocutors' status as 'seed of Abraham', and their relationship to Jesus' 'word'.[47] Jesus acknowledges that they are 'seed of Abraham', but asserts that they are trying to kill him because his word 'finds no place' (lit. 'does not advance') in them (v. 37). This statement forms an *inclusio* with v. 31, producing a demarcated subsection. In v. 31, Jesus invited his hearers to 'abide' in his word, and by v. 37 we see that they are not letting his word find a place among them. The main thematic features dominating the dispute in this subsection in relation to the figure of Abraham include the Jews' status as his 'seed', and the connection between this fact and the concepts of slavery and sin.

The second subsection runs from v. 38 to v. 47. In this subsection, the theme of paternity – specifically of belonging to one of two different 'fathers' – gains ascendency. Jesus tells his hearers that he 'speaks' of what he has 'seen' with his 'father', whereas they 'do' what they 'have heard' from their father (v. 38). To this, his audience replies, 'Abraham is our father' (v. 39a) – a further elaboration of the notion of being Abraham's 'seed' raised earlier in v. 33. Jesus seems to take issue with their counterclaim, however, stating a 'contrary-to-fact' condition in the subjunctive: 'if you were Abraham's children, you would do [or "do you"] the works of Abraham' (v. 39).[48] Jesus does not specify what the 'works' of Abraham were, but he implies that his hearers do the opposite, and that their 'work' relates to their attempts to kill him: 'as it is, you seek to kill me, a man who has told you the truth as I heard it from God' (v. 40a). Jesus adds, 'This is not what Abraham did' (v. 40b). Sharpening the contrast between what Abraham did and what his interlocutors are doing, Jesus tells them that they 'do the works' that their 'father did' (v. 41a). This alternative 'father' has not yet been named, but the Jews move on to claim that only God is their father, and that they are therefore not 'born of immorality' (v. 41b).[49] Jesus replies by linking true divine paternity with the expression of love towards God's envoy (v. 42), and he laments that his hearers cannot understand his words (v. 43). Their obduracy (v. 43) is, in Jesus' mind, the product of the fact that the devil is their 'father', and that they want to do their father's desires (v. 44a). Jesus continues to give a relatively lengthy extrapolation of the characteristics of the devil: he was 'a murderer from the start', and 'has nothing to do with the truth because there is no truth in him' (v. 44b). The devil's lying proceeds out of 'his own character' (lit. 'out of his own store'), because he 'is a liar, and the father of lies' (v. 44c). Jesus will later directly call this group 'liars' (v. 55), but here, that accusation is implied. Jesus finishes this speech by telling them that it is *because* he speaks the truth that they do not believe

---

[47] They are not named as (simply) 'the Jews' until v. 48.
[48] The grammar here is complex, and is read either in the imperative or subjunctive mood. A fuller discussion will take place in Chapter 5.
[49] This verse is understood differently in the literature – either as a classic formulation of monotheistic faith, with immorality cast metaphorically as idolatry, or as an insinuation that Jesus is 'born of immorality', Origen, *Contra Celsum* 1.18 (ed. and trans. by Henry Chadwick; Cambridge: Cambridge University Press, 1953), pp. 27–8). Origen, *Contra Celsum*, 1.28; cf. Barrett, *The Gospel*, p. 348; Brown, *John*, p. 357. In context, the latter interpretation seems less likely. The references to Jesus 'leading the people astray' and the Greek verb πλανάω bears strong allusive connotations to the LXX texts describing one who incites others to idolatry. In this case, that could mean the Jews were angered that Jesus was leading others towards high-Christological beliefs that ran counter to monotheism. In v. 41 they would reassert their claims to stand against the new Jesus movement.

him (v. 45), and that this arises from the fact that they are not 'of God' (v. 47a, b). Meanwhile, Jesus presents himself as sinless (v. 46).

The third and final subsection runs from v. 48 to v. 59. The subject of the dispute changes slightly from the theme of contested paternities to conceptions of honour, glory, obedience and Jesus' status in relation to Abraham. In this subsection, the Jews speak first, asking Jesus, 'Are we not right in saying that you are a Samaritan and have a demon?' (v. 48). Jesus then negates the charge of being possessed by a demon, and tells the Jews that he 'honours' his father, whereas they 'dishonour' him (v. 49). Jesus tells them further that he does not seek his own glory – only God seeks it and is the judge of it (v. 50). Jesus proceeds to speak his second 'Amen, amen' saying in this discourse (cf. v. 34), promising that 'if anyone' keeps his word, that person will 'never see death' (v. 51). To the Jews, this statement confirms Jesus' state of demon possession (or possibly, his insanity), and they reply, 'Now we know you have a demon! Abraham died, as did the prophets, yet you say, "If anyone keeps my word he will never taste death"' (v. 52). A minor misquotation in their reported speech – the Jews here emphasize 'tasting' death, whereas Jesus spoke of 'seeing' death – but this is probably not consequential. What the Jews' comment leads into is another question, one rooted in Jesus' presentation of his own status: 'Are you greater than our father Abraham, who died?' (v. 53a). Yet, once again, Jesus replies that he does not seek his own glory (v. 54, cf. v. 50). It is then Jesus' turn to report the speech of the Jews, and he tells them 'It is the Father who glorifies me, of whom you say "He is our God"' (v. 54b). This is only for Jesus to deny that the Jews even know God, and to simultaneously assert that he knows God, because he keeps God's words; on the other hand, Jesus calls the Jews 'liars' (v. 55). Then follows the climactic segment of the whole discourse (i.e. vv. 56-59) with Jesus forthrightly claiming his unique status relative to Abraham: 'Your father Abraham rejoiced that he would see my day; he saw it and was glad' (v. 56). The Jews' probe Jesus' point, responding incredulously, that given his age, Jesus could have 'seen' Abraham (v. 57) – another example of them misquoting in reported speech, but again, inconsequential to the subsequent dialogue. This prompts Jesus to assert his third and final 'Amen, amen' statement in this discourse: 'Before Abraham was, I am' (v. 58). To this, the Jews pick up stones to throw at Jesus, but he hides himself and leaves the Temple (v. 59).

The three subsections in ch. 8 vv. 31-59 (namely, vv. 31-37, 48-47 and 48-59) are not sharply cordoned off from one another, as certain themes and figures resurface throughout to unite the discourse as a whole, such as Abraham (8.33, 37, 39a, 39b, 40, 52, 53, 57, 58), the notion of sin (8.34, cf. 44a, 46), of keeping Jesus' word (8.31, 43, 47, 51, 53) and of truth and lies (8.32, 40, 44d, 45, 46, 55), among others. But the subsections are nevertheless marked by transitions in subject matter: the first subsection centres on the Jews' status in relation to Abraham (and the metaphorical usages of concepts such as 'seed', 'slavery' and 'sin'); the second subsection focuses on the different origins of Jesus and the Jews, a difference metaphorically cast as two contrasting paternal lineages, and the issue of likeness to Abraham ('the works of Abraham') comes to the fore; the third subsection foregrounds Jesus' status relative to Abraham by placing his statements in a climactic, tense conclusion to the discourse, and more enigmatic themes emerge, such as Abraham's 'seeing' and 'rejoicing' in Jesus. As noted previously, these three subsections and their thematic foci form the basis of my own extended engagement with the text of ch. 8 vv. 31-59 relative to its contemporaneous literary environment in Chapters 4 through 6 of this book.

Although ch. 8 vv. 31-59 is internally coherent, it should not be read as disjunctively set off from its surrounding context.[50] It is integral to chs 7–8 as a larger unit, providing the concluding segment of the disputes inside the Temple, begun at Sukkot (cf. 7.1, 10).[51] The ways in which ch. 8 vv. 31-59 interacts with the key themes of chs 7–8 is a topic often overlooked in analysis of John 8 deployment of the figure of Abraham. However, as I shall show, interpreting John 8.31-59 within its Sukkot setting is a vital aspect of coming to terms with its intertexture. Thus, this chapter provides an extensive discussion of these intratextual and intertextual elements to enable a fuller understanding of how Abraham is signified in the pericope. By way of this, I first discuss the interplay of key themes in John 7–8 to illustrate the coherent development of the chapters, showing how these themes are picked and resonate with ch. 8 vv. 31-59. I then examine the question of the festival setting of John 7–8 (although Sukkot is named in ch. 7 v. 1, there have been some recent alternative festival settings advanced for John 7–8 in the scholarly literature). Arguing ultimately, that Sukkot nevertheless remains the most plausible setting for the discourse, I finally undertake an intertextual reading of the significance of Sukkot in the early Jewish texts and traditions to understand the subtle layers of salience present in John's refiguration of Abraham within that context in his narrative.

The unity and thematic coherence of John 7.1–8.59

A steady proportion of Johannine commentators consider John 7–8 a literary unit.[52] Two factors determine this unity: (1) the festival setting of Sukkot, as we have already seen; and (2) the common cast of characters who alternate and resurface in John 7–8.[53] The latter is one factor that lends the discourse internal coherence, which, narratively, produces the impression of unity. Note that this is not the same as suggesting that John 7–8 or the Gospel as a whole is *compositionally* unified, or that it was written in one 'sitting' so to speak. It is important to approach John 7–8 not with the expectation of a seamless read but with an understanding of its present form as a narrative that weaves in cycles of different dialogues between Jesus and other character groups. These

---

[50] Such is the approach, for example, of Dozemann, '*Sperma Abraam*'. Bultmann, *The Gospel of John*, p. 325 considers ch. 8 vv. 31-58 to be a fragment unrelated to the Sukkot context of John 7–8.
[51] Cf. Dodd, 'Behind a Johannine Dialogue', p. 41.
[52] Cf. Barnabas Lindars, *The Gospel of John* (New Century Bible Commentary; Grand Rapids: Eerdmans, 1982), p. 277; Peter F. Ellis, *The Genius of John: A Composition-Critical Commentary on the Fourth Gospel* (Collegevile: Liturgical Press, 1984), p. 135; Bruce Malina and Richard Rohrbaugh, *Social Science Commentary on the Gospel of John* (Minneapolis: Fortress, 1998), p. 139; Craig S. Keener, *The Gospel of John: A Commentary* (Vol. 1; Grand Rapids: Baker, 2003), p. 703.
[53] The festival setting of Sukkot begun in ch. 7 vv. 1-2 could be seen to continue into ch. 9, or even into ch. 10 of the Gospel (cf. Moloney, *John*, p. 233), but the unity of chs 7–8 is determined not only by its festival or temporal setting: the specific location of the Jerusalem Temple is the setting for John 7–8, beginning at ch. 7 v. 1 and ending at ch. 8 v. 59, when Jesus leaves the Temple precincts.

groups resurface throughout chs 7–8, and their interactions with Jesus reveal the close interlocking of various key themes.[54] That is, the overall cast of characters, while in flux, remains consistent: Jesus' brothers are his first interlocutors (7.3, 10); the Jews are present at 'the feast of the Jews' in Judea (7.1-2 (οὐ γὰρ ἤθελεν ἐν τῇ Ἰουδαίᾳ περιπατεῖν, ὅτι ἐζήτουν αὐτὸν οἱ Ἰουδαῖοι ἀποκτεῖναι ... ἑορτὴ τῶν Ἰουδαίων ἡ σκηνοπηγία); 11; 13), and they interact with Jesus as early as ch. 7 v. 15, continuing to do so up to the end of the discourse (8.21, 22, 25, 27, 31, 33, 39, 41, 48, 52, 57).[55] Other character groups specific to Jesus' audience include the Pharisees (7.32, 45, 48 (×2); 8.3, 13, 19), the 'crowd' (7.20, 40-41), the many people (in the crowds; 7.12, 31, 43; 8.12) and the Jerusalemites (7.25, 30). Other groups again make their appearance but do not interact directly with Jesus; these include the 'chief priest' (7.45), the authorities (7.26, 48), the Temple guards (7.32, 45, 46) and Nicodemus (7.50).

John 7–8 exhibits a network of closely interrelated themes which determine it as a coherent literary unit. As is typical of this Gospel, many of these themes are expressed in terms of binary oppositions. Instead of a tangled text, jumping randomly from topic to topic without a connecting thread, John 7–8 displays its own – albeit curious – 'inner logic' because of the way in which its themes overlap. Yet, there is not one 'centring' theme, but rather a plurality of themes present in John 7–8, and none is wholly reducible to another. These themes consist of motifs, figures, tropes, metaphors, keywords and *Stichworten*, which are fluid and associative. In what follows, I present a brief systematization of these major themes to show that the thought and progress of John 7–8 is not disparate but is rather like a kaleidoscope refracting multiple, complex frames that open into each other, such as 'origins', 'knowledge', 'belief', 'judgement' and 'testimony'. The importance of this preliminary overview should be clear: to place ch. 8 vv. 31-59 in the semiotic context of chs 7–8, so that the references to Abraham obtain significance in light of the thematic complex of chs 7–8 as a whole.

Origins

The question of Jesus' origin and destiny, his 'whence and whither', permeates the Gospel of John.[56] It is also a key theme in chs 7–8. In the early stages of the Sukkot discourses, some of Jesus' audience wonder if he is the Messiah (7.21-26). Others object: 'But we know where this man comes from, and when the Messiah appears, no one will know where he comes from' (7.27; cf. 7.41b-42).[57] According to the authorities, Jesus is not the Messiah nor is he the Prophet, for the Law states that 'no prophet is raised in Galilee' (7.52). Jesus' enigmatic response is that he has not come of his own accord, but was sent by one who is true; only Jesus has knowledge of this 'Sender'

---

[54] Cf. Harold W. Attridge, 'Thematic Development and Source Elaboration in John 7.1-36', *CBQ* 42 (1980), pp. 160-70.
[55] Some of these references are to 'them/they' (8.21, 25, 27, 33, 39, 41) rather than 'the Jews': the context determines the referent in most cases.
[56] Cf. Adele Reinhartz, 'And the Word Was Begotten: Divine Epigenesis in the Gospel of John', *Sem* 85 (1999), pp. 83-103.
[57] On the traditions of the 'hidden messiah' in the Gospel of John, see Marinus de Jonge, 'Jewish Expectations about the "Messiah" according to the Fourth Gospel', *NTS* 19, no. 3 (1973), pp. 246-70.

(7.28-29).⁵⁸ Just as the one who 'sent' Jesus is 'true' (7.28), so is Jesus 'true' when he seeks the honour of the one who sent him (7.18; cf. 8.49-50). Jesus has his origins in the one who sent him – otherwise called 'the Father' (8.18-18, 38, 42) or God (8.42).⁵⁹ To the Jews of ch. 8 v. 42, Jesus challenges their relationship to God based on the nature of their relationship to him: since God is Jesus' 'father' and source, the Jews would love Jesus as a brother if they really had God as their father too. Since they do not love Jesus, they do not share Jesus' origins. Though they claim to be 'seed of Abraham' (8.33, cf. v. 37) and 'children of Abraham' (8.39), Jesus denies that God is their father on the basis that they do not love him (8.42, 47, 53). Instead, Jesus tells them that the devil is their father (8.38, 41, 44), and that they are 'from below', whereas Jesus is 'from above' (8.23). Just as Jesus' origins are opaque to them, so too is his destiny: where he goes, they cannot come (7.33-34, 36; 8.21). At the same time, Jesus states that if they do not believe, the destiny of the Jews (8.24) is eventual 'death in sin'.

Knowledge and belief

The themes of knowledge and belief are closely linked to the theme of origins. Other passages suggest that Jesus' knowledge of God is incomparable because of his origins. For example, speaking to the Jews, Jesus says that he does not try to 'glorify' himself; rather, it is the 'Father' who glorifies Jesus – the one of whom the Jews say, 'He is our God' (8.54). But, Jesus tells them, 'you have not known him; I know him' (8.55a; cf. 7.28; 8.19). When Jesus asserts his knowledge of God in John 7–8, it is usually to downplay, at the same time, other characters' claims to knowledge of God. In the Gospel's perspective, when the Jews say that they know God, they lie, and if Jesus were to say that he did not know God, he would lie (8.55b). Jesus knows God not only because he comes from God (cf. 8.14), but also because he 'keeps' God's 'word' (8.55c). If the Jews do not know God, as Jesus claims, it is because they issue from a different 'father' (8.44). The themes of knowledge and belief are also related to the ability to hear and understand. In ch. 8 v. 43a, Jesus questions the Jews, 'Why do you not understand (οὐ γινώσκετε) what I say?' (cf. 8.27). Their incomprehension is then explained by Jesus as a direct consequence of their unwillingness to 'hear' (οὐ δύνασθε ἀκούειν) his 'word' (8.43b). For Jesus, 'Whoever is of God (ὁ ὢν ἐκ τοῦ θεοῦ) hears (ἀκούει) the words of God; the reason why you do not hear (οὐκ ἀκούετε) them is that you are not of God' (8.47). These texts associate Jesus' words (8.43a) with the words of God (8.47). The Jews neither 'understand' Jesus' words nor do they 'hear' the 'words of God'.⁶⁰ Indeed, it is *because* Jesus speaks the truth that the Jews do not 'believe' him

---

⁵⁸ Cf. J. Gerald Janzen, '(Not) of My Own Accord: Listening for Scriptural Echoes in a Johannine Idiom', *Encounter* 67 (2006), pp. 138–60.

⁵⁹ See the excellent study by Turid Karlsen Seim, 'Descent and Divine Paternity in the Gospel of John', in Stephen P. Ahearne-Kroll, Paul A. Holloway and James A. Kelhoffer (eds), *Women and Gender in Ancient Religions: Interdisciplinary Approaches* (WUNT 263; Tübingen: Mohr Siebeck, 2010), pp. 99–123; and recently the fascinating work of Annette Weissenrieder, 'Spirit and Rebirth in the Gospel of John', *Religion and Theology* 21 (2014), pp. 58–85.

⁶⁰ However, as Judith Lieu pointedly remarked, even Jesus' openness and supposedly clear speech 'is not transparent. It does not guarantee understanding and belief'. See Lieu, 'Temple and Synagogue in John', *NTS* 45 (1999), pp. 51–69, at p. 55.

(ἐγὼ δὲ ὅτι τὴν ἀλήθειαν λέγω, οὐ πιστεύετέ μοι; 8.45, 46). Only when Jesus is 'lifted up' will they know 'I am He' (8.28).[61]

Characters in John 7–8 have the chance to 'believe in' Jesus, and so experience his promised salvation (cf. 7.38; cf. 8.32, 52). Yet in John 7–8, the unbelief of Jesus' adversaries is mentioned with greater frequency than the positive belief of other characters (cf. 7.4, 'even Jesus' brothers' did not believe). There are three 'reports' of belief in Jesus (7.31; 8.30, 31), and one reference to discipleship (8.31), articulated as the continuing state of believing in Jesus. There is also a promise made to those who might believe (7.38) and a threat made to those who are intransigent in their unbelief (8.24). The first reported belief occurs in ch. 7 v. 31, with 'many of the people' in the festival crowd believing in Jesus (ἐκ τοῦ ὄχλου δὲ πολλοὶ ἐπίστευσαν εἰς αὐτὸν).[62] Their expression of belief follows, with their question: 'when the Christ appears, will he do more signs than this man has done?' (7.32). Commentators agree that this is a qualitatively poor form of belief – the people do not believe that Jesus is, or could be, the Christ (cf. 4.29; 11.27), but they compare Jesus to the future Christ; furthermore, their belief seems to be based on the number of signs Jesus works. Nevertheless, the Gospel simply refers to their stance as one of belief, without adding a value judgement. Only the subsequent verses give the reader pause, since reference is made to Jesus' 'signs' (cf. 2.24).[63] The promise made to believers in ch. 7 v. 38 is eschatological in nature, speaking of a future time in which believers will drink streams of living water that flow from Jesus' 'heart' – which the narrator adds is symbolic of the coming Spirit (7.37-39).[64] The threat made to the Jews who refuse to believe (8.24) has been noted previously, and refers to their 'death in sin'.

Judgement

The motif of judgement forms an intrinsic part of the texture of John 7–8. The forensic tone and language of John 7–8 are frequently asserted in the scholarship.[65] Jesus is thought to stand trial during his public ministry in John's Gospel (cf. 5, 7–8, 10, 12), rather than – as the Synoptics have it and as would be more historically plausible –

---

[61] A cryptic reference to the crucifixion; cf. Paul M. Hoskins, 'Freedom from Slavery to Sin and the Devil: John 8.31-47 and the Passover Theme of the Gospel of John', *TrinJ* 31 (2010), pp. 47–63, at p. 53. Cf. R. Alan Culpepper, 'The Johannine Hypodeigma: A Reading of John 13', *Sem* 53 (1991), pp. 133–52.

[62] There is also a reference to the 'complaining/marvelling' (γογγυσμὸς) of the crowd in ch. 7 v. 15, which Schnackenburg understands to be a 'sceptical unbelieving' (see *The Gospel* 2.463, n. 45).

[63] Yet, on the other hand, the quality of the crowd's belief must have been substantial enough to motivate the Pharisees to arrest Jesus (7.32b).

[64] There is an enormous body of secondary literature on these obscure verses. See, for example, Cf. Zane C. Hodges, 'Rivers of Living Water – John 7.37-39', *BSac* 136 (1979), pp. 239–48; Juan B. Cortés, 'Yet Another Look at John 7,37-38', *CBQ* 29 (1967), pp. 75–86; M.-E. Boismard, 'De son ventre couleront des fleuves d'eau (Jo. VII, 38)', *RB* 65 (1958), pp. 536–8; Michael Daise, '"If Anyone Thirsts, Let That One Come to Me and Drink": The Literary Texture of John 7.37b-38a', *JBL* 122, no. 4 (2003), pp. 688–9; Menken, *The Old Testament Quotations in the Fourth Gospel*, pp. 190–2.

[65] A. E. Harvey, *Jesus on Trial: A Study in the Fourth Gospel* (Atlanta: John Knox, 1976); Andrew T. Lincoln, *Truth on Trial: The Lawsuit Motif in the Fourth Gospel* (Grand Rapids: Baker Academic, 2000); Neyrey, 'Jesus the Judge', pp. 509–41; George Parsenios, *Rhetoric and Drama in the Johannine Lawsuit Motif* (WUNT 1.258; Tübingen: Mohr Siebeck, 2010).

at the time immediately prior to his execution (although see chs 19–20).[66] On two occasions, Jesus tells his interlocutors that they judge incorrectly – either by inferior standards or by judging unjustly (7.24, 8.15). On both of those occasions, Jesus seeks to defend himself from the allegation that he is a law-breaker. Jesus' admonition in ch. 7 v. 24 ('Do not judge by appearances (μὴ κρίνετε κατ' ὄψιν) but judge with right judgment') concludes a lengthy section in which Jesus proves himself to be operating on a higher moral plane than his opponents, even if Jesus ostensibly breaks the law (7.14-23).[67] If his opponents were judging Jesus according to the higher standard that Jesus perceives himself to be operating by, they would *ipso facto* judge rightly. In ch. 8 v. 15, Jesus asserts that he judges no one, and claims that his interlocutors, the Pharisees, judge 'according to the flesh' (κατὰ τὴν σάρκα).[68] Even though Jesus claims to 'judge no one', he later concedes that *if* he judges, his judgement is 'valid/true' because the Father effectively judges with him (8.16; cf. 5.22, 27). This appears contradictory – Jesus categorically states that he judges no one, but then concedes that if he judges, he judges truly. However, this pattern of 'categorical denial' + 'concession' based on a higher quality is typically Johannine.[69] In the examples given here (7.24; 8.15), we see Jesus initially playing the role of the defendant, but later switching to the role of prosecutor and then to the role of ultimate judge – a technique arising from John's careful use of irony.

Jesus' role as judge continues as the discourse intensifies. Jesus tells the Jews that he has much to say about them and much to condemn (8.26). Jesus' condemnation of them arises from what he hears from the 'father', and the fact that the 'one who sent' him is 'true' (ἀληθής; 8.26). The source of Jesus' judgement is the father who also judges with Jesus; this provides the validation for Jesus' testimony and judgement. His authorization to judge exceeds that of his accusers because only he 'knows where he is from and where he is going' (οἶδα πόθεν ἦλθον καὶ ποῦ ὑπάγω; cf. 8.14, 16). In John 7–8, the emphasis on conviction and judgement, on accusation and counter-accusation is unmistakeable and heavy with irony. Although the law is said to permit a man a fair trial (7.51), the rhetorical thrust of John 7–8 is to present Jesus as misunderstood and unfairly persecuted (cf. 8.56-59). Jesus stands trial and not only gives the requisite testimony (7.14-23; 8.17), but also prosecutes his accusers and

---

[66] Cf. Lieu, 'Temple and Synagogue', p. 52; cf. Catherine Cory, 'Wisdom's Rescue: A New Reading of the Tabernacles Discourse (John 7.1-8.59)', *JBL* 116 (1997), pp. 95–116, at p. 97, cf. p. 104; Barrett, *The Gospel*, pp. 334, 338; Malina and Rohrbaugh, *Social Science Commentary*, p. 161; the notion of Jesus' trial in John 7–8 is disputed by Moloney, *John*, p. 266, and the conceptual function of the 'trial motif' is more broadly questioned by Martin Asiedu-Peprah, *Johannine Sabbath Conflicts as Juridical Controversy: An Exegetical Study of John 5 and 9.1-10.21* (WUNT 2.132; Tübingen: Mohr Siebeck, 2001).

[67] The injunction to 'judge a righteous judgment' (δικαίαν κρίσιν κρίνετε: 7.24) has overtones of 'righteous deeds' or 'works' in the early Jewish literature, which we explore in Chapter 5 in relation to Abraham and his 'works' (8.39-40).

[68] Cf. Deut. 16.18; Barrett, *The Gospel*, p. 334.

[69] Cf. Schnackenburg, *The Gospel* 2.193. His examples include John 1.10-11 followed by ch. 1 v. 12 and ch. 3 v. 32 followed by ch. 3 v. 33. In ordinary legal procedure, evidence is linked to judgement in a determinative manner. But John seems to invert this with his characteristic irony by making Jesus the real judge – not the victim on trial. Jesus' 'evidence', his 'word' becomes the force of judgement against those who fail to believe it, in the here and now as well as at the eschaton.

judges them. Not only does Jesus condemn when necessary (8.26) and refrain from condemnation when necessary (8.15), he turns his own defence into the judgement of the Jews, who will 'die in their sin' (ἀποθανεῖσθε ἐν ταῖς ἁμαρτίαις ὑμῶν) if they do not believe in his revelatory statements (v. 24). Moreover, from the Gospel's perspective, no one can convict Jesus of sin (8.47), as he is a man altogether without dishonesty (7.18); and indeed, the only one fit to judge Jesus is God (8.50).

When Jesus leaves the Temple, he proceeds to heal a blind man (9.1-7), the latter of whom stands trial before 'the Pharisees' and 'the Jews' for being healed on the Sabbath (9.13-34). When the man meets Jesus again, Jesus tells the people that he came into the world 'for judgement' which renders the blind seeing, and those who see, blind (9.39; cf. 12.40). Guilt attaches to those who peremptorily proclaim their ability to 'see' (9.41) – and this is the guilt that 'blinds' them further, effectively functioning as their 'judgement'.[70]

Testimony

Related to the concept of judgement is that of testimony, and its more specific counterpart, self-testimony. The most extensive section dealing with self-testimony occurs in ch. 8 vv. 12-20. In this context, Jesus' claim to testify truly (ἀληθής ἐστιν ἡ μαρτυρία μου) even though he testifies alone (or 'to himself': περὶ ἐμαυτοῦ), corresponds to his claim that his adversaries judge 'according to the flesh'. The Pharisees admit the invalid nature of Jesus' testimony, implying that valid (or true: ἀληθή) testimony requires more than one witness – that is, it cannot proceed solely from the self who is testifying (8.13-14). Jesus provides two responses to their charge: on the one hand, Jesus' testimony is valid because he is aware of his origins and destiny, and this awareness is uniquely his own (8.14); on the other hand, the 'father' is always with Jesus, and so technically Jesus never testifies alone, but the 'father' testifies with him (8.17-18).[71] The concept of Jesus not testifying on his own behalf also relates to other themes, such as Jesus not speaking on his own behalf, but 'of God' (8.26, 28, 38, 40; cf. 5.19-20, 27), and of Jesus not 'coming' of his own accord, but being sent by God (7.28; 8.42). It also relates to Jesus' claim that he does not seek his own glory (8.50, 54). Self-testimony, with no corroborating witness, makes the content of the testimony invalid, as much as seeking one's own glory renders that glory void.

Apart from *self*-testimony there are other references to testifying in John 7–8. Jesus' theophanic pronouncements themselves are a form of testimony inasmuch as they reveal the truth of his identity (ἐγώ εἰμι, 8.24; cf. πρὶν Ἀβραὰμ γενέσθαι ἐγώ εἰμί; 8.58). The theme of testimony is linked to truth and authenticity in Jesus' mission. In John 7.1-7, we read a dispute between Jesus and his brothers over Jesus' decision to stay in Galilee instead of going up immediately to the feast of Sukkot in Jerusalem. Jesus'

---

[70] See Judith Lieu, 'Blindness in the Johannine Tradition', NTS 34 (1988), pp. 83–95; idem, 'What was From the Beginning: Scripture and Tradition in the Johannine Epistles', NTS 39 (1993), pp. 458–77, at p. 472.

[71] Ruth Sheridan, 'The Testimony of Two Witnesses: John 8.17', in Alicia D. Myers and Bruce G. Schuchard (eds), *Abiding Words: The Use of Scripture in the Gospel of John* (RBS 81; Atlanta: SBL Press, 2015), pp. 161–84.

brothers tell him to go to Judea so that others may see the 'works' he is doing (τὰ ἔργα ἃ ποιεῖς: 7.3), and that Jesus may be known 'openly' to the world (7.4; ἐν παρρησίᾳ). The narrator reveals that the brothers' request indicates their lack of belief in Jesus (7.4); Jesus is not one to seek his own glory (cf. 8.50). Jesus replies to his brothers: 'My hour has not yet come, but your hour is always here. The world cannot hate you, but it hates me because I testify about it that its works are evil' (ἐγὼ μαρτυρῶ περὶ αὐτοῦ ὅτι τὰ ἔργα αὐτοῦ πονηρά ἐστιν: 7.6-7). While Jesus' 'works' are not for show before the world, 'the world's works' are evil. Jesus takes up his brothers' neutral reference to 'the world' as a societal structure willing to see wondrous signs, and transforms it into something negative. The 'world' actively 'hates' Jesus because far from seeking glory from it, Jesus testifies about it, that 'its works are evil' (cf. 15.18, 27). An 'evil world' is not only the arena in which Jesus testifies, but the very object against which he testifies.

The theme of testimony is not only linked to notions of divine agency (of Jesus as the 'sent one') and to the Johannine Christology, but it is also wedded to the Gospel's dualism: just as Jesus has a 'father' from whom he testifies, so too do Jesus' enemies, 'the Jews', have a father from whom they testify and to whom they are obedient (8.38). Jesus' father is God, but the Jews' father is the devil (8.41-44). The binary theme of truth/lies plays into the themes of judgement and testimony. The devil is a figure who cannot tell the truth, who cannot help but lie because he 'never stood in the truth' (8.44). The contrast is stark: Jesus' testimony is true (8.17; cf. v. 40), just as his judgement is 'true' (8.16), and as the one who sent him is 'true' (8.26). The only thing the devil is 'true' to, on the other hand, is to his own nature – that is, he tells lies because he is a liar (ψεύστης; 8.44). Because the Jews testify from their father, 'the devil' (8.38), they not only cannot tell the truth (8.55), but they also cannot *hear* the truth when it confronts them in the person of Jesus (8.45, 46). Jesus indicates that apart from his 'word', the Jews cannot even know the truth (8.31-32) and therefore know freedom from slavery to sin (8.34). In fact, death in sin awaits them if they remain as they are (8.24; cf. 7.34), whereas Jesus cannot be 'convicted' of sin (8.46).

The point of this thematic analysis has been to demonstrate that John 7.1-8.59 is structured according to some highly sophisticated narrative and discursive principles. We cannot theoretically determine what those principles were, but we can trace their effect. The four major themes traced were origins/destiny, knowledge/belief, judgement and testimony. Other minor themes were also seen to be woven into these four major ones, such as sin, death/murder and lies/truth. Although it is probably wise to avoid systematizing John's thought, or imposing a thematic grid onto his narrative, it is important to emphasize that John 7–8 exhibits an unconventional kind of structural coherence based on the interplay of themes. It would be incorrect to say that one of these themes acts as a 'governing' or central theme, but it is the case that John 7-8 (as well as 9.1-41; 10.22-39) presents a juridical narrative that nevertheless concludes with Jesus' 'escape' (cf. 8.59; 10.39), and his exoneration in the mind of the reader.

The main pericope under analysis in this book is ch. 8 vv. 31-59, and it deals with themes, figures and motifs explored nowhere else in the Gospel (such as the figure of Abraham and the concept of freedom); but certain other themes present in this pericope resonate with the wider context of John 7.1–8.30, as we have shown here, such as Jesus' 'word' (8.31), his 'truth' (8.32, 45); sin (8.34, 46); paternal origins (8.38);

the performance of 'works' (8.39); Jesus' status as the Sent One (8.42); Jesus' alleged demonic possession (8.52a); death (8.52b); and glory (8.54). These resonances should help us avoid bracketing ch. 8 vv. 31-59 too sharply out from its narrative context.

Scripting the Sukkot intertext

Determining the festival setting of John 7–8

Now that the literary texture of John 7–8 has been outlined by means of thematic analysis, it is necessary to examine the significance of the narrative setting of these same chapters. Commentators generally agree that the festival setting of John 7.1–8.59 is Sukkot, or Tabernacles (ἡ σκηνοπηγία).[72] The approaching feast of Sukkot is mentioned in John 7.2 – a feast that is referred to as being 'of the Jews' (ἡ ἑορτὴ τῶν Ἰουδαίων). Jesus' brothers invite him to go to Judea for this feast (7.3); Jesus declines on the grounds that his 'time had not yet come' (7.8). But then, after Jesus' brothers leave for the feast, Jesus also goes to Jerusalem, 'not openly, but in private' (7.10). The narrator comments that 'the Jews' were 'looking for him [Jesus]' and that there was much 'murmuring' about Jesus among the people (7.10-12a). The 'middle of the feast' is referred to in ch. 7 v. 14 (τῆς ἑορτῆς μεσούσης), and Jesus is described as 'going up into the Temple' to begin his teaching there. Jesus' teaching produces a cacophony of variegated responses among the crowds, and popular division quickly ensues (7.15-36). Finally, the 'last day of the feast, the great day' (τῇ ἐσχάτῃ ἡμέρᾳ τῇ μεγάλῃ τῆς ἑορτῆς) is mentioned in ch. 7 v. 37, as the point at which Jesus offers himself as the source of living water to all who believe (cf. 7.37-39).

The seven – or eight – days of Sukkot are therefore roughly timetabled into John 7.[73] Yet scholars also argue that the Sukkot setting continues to provide the background for the material in ch. 8. No new day is described as having begun after the reference in ch. 7 v. 37 – and as most scholars also exclude John 7.53–8.11 (the *pericopae adultera*) from consideration, the reference to Jesus being the 'light of the world' in ch. 8 v. 12 appears to take up and continue in a symbolic fashion the religious themes, rituals and locations used during the feast of Sukkot, such as the lights present in the Court of Women during the feast. If the 'last great day' in ch. 7 v. 37 was meant to refer to the penultimate, seventh day of the feast of Sukkot, then, some commentators argue, the entirety of ch. 8 must take place on the final day, the eighth day of the feast. If

---

[72] Cf. Bruce Satterfield, 'John 7-9 in Light of the Feast of Tabernacles', in Who (ed.), *The Testimony of John the Beloved: The 1998 Sperry Symposium on the New Testament* (Salt Lake City: Deseret Books, 1998), pp. 249–65. Accessed online: https://emp.byui.edu/SatterfieldB/Papers/John7-9.5.html, 28 September 2018.

[73] There is significant scholarly debate over which day is meant by 'the last day' in John 7.37. It might be the seventh day of Sukkot where water was drawn, or the eighth day of solemn assembly (cf. Lev. 23.36), but neither is attested as the 'great day' in the Jewish literature still available to us. For further discussion, see Brown, *John*, 1.327 (who argues for the seventh day), and Barrett, *The Gospel*, pp. 297–8 (who argues for the eighth day). Scholars favouring a Sukkot setting for John 9 (and thus all of John 8) understand the reference to the Pool of Siloam (9.7) as a nod to the water-drawing celebration of Sukkot that took place at this pool (cf. Isa. 8.6; Neh. 3.15).

the reference in ch. 7 v. 37 was to the eighth day, then the events of ch. 8 refer to that same twenty-four-hour time period. But because the festival days are unmarked in John 8, it is not immediately clear whether the setting of John 7 extends into ch. 8, thus producing the required unity to lend John 7–8 textual and semantic coherence.

A recent article by John Poirier has exposed some of the tensions and problems involved in understanding the festival of Sukkot as the setting for John 8. Against the regnant critical view that interprets Jesus' claim to be the 'light of the world' (John 8.12) in the context of the feast of Sukkot, Poirier argues that Jesus' self-predicated statement evokes, rather, the symbolism of Hanukkah, a feast which receives explicit mention in ch. 10 v. 22, but which, Poirier argues, can be implicitly read backwards into the chronology of John 7.52–10.40.[74] Poirier observes that in John 1.19–12.50, Jesus makes revelatory claims about himself that draw upon the ritual symbolisms of the feasts constituting the narrative occasion for those claims: for example Jesus as the 'Bread of Life' (John 6.35; Passover), and Jesus as the source of Living Water (7.37-39; Sukkoth). Poirier also notes that by the time the next feast occurs in the narrative (10.22, Hanukkah), no declarative statement is made by Jesus that accords with the symbolism of that feast.[75] The first question Poirier puts to this apparent anomaly is 'Why has the pattern from chaps. 6-7 ceased?'.[76] But the actual question – stated by Poirier and guiding his overall argument – is 'Has the pattern *really* ceased?'[77] Poirier's contention is that the pattern has *not* ceased, and that in fact, the symbolism of Hanukkah is associated with the self-revelatory statement made by Jesus in ch. 8 v. 12: 'I am the Light of the World.'

Poirier notes that 'a lack of temporal markers' in the Gospel does not equate to the Evangelist's neglect for marking *time as such*, and correlatively, that the first announcement of an occasion in the Gospel does not always mark the temporal beginning of that occasion (cf. 8.20, and possibly 7.37).[78] Consequently, Poirier claims that the Gospel needs to be 'read backwards, as it were' as well as forwards; only in this way can one appreciate how Hanukkah provides the narrative setting for John 8–10. Because there are no temporal markers between chs 9–10, Poirier contends that the festive setting of Hanukkah can be retrospectively read into ch. 9 also, rather than reading chs 8–9 as a continuation of Sukkoth (7.1-39). Moreover, an 'interweaving' of key phrases takes place in these two chapters (e.g. 8.12; 9.5) which would suggest, according to Poirier, an identical festival setting. The prominence of themes such as 'light' and 'freedom' indicate, for Poirier, that this festival setting is indeed Hanukkah, particularly since freedom (or national liberation) was the major concern of the Maccabees, whose victory over Antiochus Epiphanes IV is celebrated during the festival.

Aspects of Poirier's argument are certainly sound, and he has called attention to a *crux interpretum*: it is otherwise difficult to read a sharp break in the narrative between John 10.21 (and its preceding context) and ch. 10 v. 22 (and what immediately follows).

---

[74] Poirier, 'Hanukkah', pp. 465–78.
[75] Ibid., p. 465.
[76] Ibid.
[77] Ibid.
[78] Ibid., p. 466.

Yet, one major problem with Poirier's thesis is his forced reading of Maccabean allusions into John 10 and John 8. For example, Poirier understands the reference to Hanukkah in ch. 10 v. 22 as a means of contextualizing the otherwise opaque symbolic detail of Solomon's Portico; the detail is usually explained as the most suitable place for Jesus to seek shelter from the 'winter' cold. But Poirier connects this detail with the historiography narrated in *2 Maccabees*, where 'the eight-day dedication ceremony was intended to recall Solomon's consecration of the Temple'.[79] Poirier then uses this one-off reference to Solomon in *2 Maccabees* to argue that Jesus' 'Good Shepherd' discourse in ch. 10 refers to the historical first-century Jewish leadership as collective 'thieves and bandits' (10.1; cf. 10.10), thus likening Jesus' situation to Judas Maccabeus' revolt against the illegitimate non-priestly leadership in Jerusalem in 164 BCE.[80] Poirier also takes it as a given that Jesus' enemies in ch. 9 are the 'thieves and bandits' of ch. 10 v. 10, and that Jesus' confrontation with his opponents in the Temple in ch. 9 alludes to the Maccabees' ousting of 'a cadre of Jewish priests serving God's enemy'.[81]

At some length, Poirier discusses the relevance of the concept of freedom for John 8 (cf. 8.36). This, he states, is the central theme in all of ch. 8, and that it consciously evokes the liberationist ideal espoused by the Maccabees. There is a delicate arbitrariness at work here – much could easily be said about the unifying nature of *other* concepts in John 8 such as 'sin', 'lies', 'truth', 'origins' and 'murder', and how these concepts are intricately interrelated. The concepts of slavery and freedom only gain salience in connection with Jesus' discourse on sin (8.21, 34, 46), death (8.21, 22, 51, 52, 53) and unbelief (8.31, 28, 42-43, 47), which are said to produce slavery (8.34). The type of freedom Jesus mentions is not the kind connected with decolonization (as Poirier aptly concedes), but it cannot be understood apart from the Gospel's dichotomous ideology of predetermined origins (above/below) that either makes one free ('of God', 8.31-32, cf. 1.12) or a slave ('of the devil', 8.44).[82]

Poirier also considers the detail about the blind man washing in the Pool of Siloam (9.7) as a reference to Hannukah. First, he reasons, if the events of ch. 9 took place at Sukkot, they would need to have occurred *either* on the same day as the events of ch. 7 vv. 37-39 (which Poirier takes to be the seventh day of Sukkot) *or* on the succeeding, eighth day.[83] Since ch. 9 is set on Shabbat, it would place the narrative within the eighth day of Sukkot, the culminating day of the festival. Yet, according

---

[79] Ibid., p. 470.
[80] Ibid., p. 471.
[81] Ibid. More probably, the controversy in ch. 9 parallels and builds upon the first Sabbath controversy narrated in ch.5. Martin Asiedu-Peprah has demonstrated that in John 5 and John 9.1-10.21 a 'juridical controversy' is at work between Jesus and his opponents ('the Jews'/the Pharisees), and that the characteristics of this controversy are based on the Hebrew *rib* narratives of the HB, where witnesses are called upon to resolve conflict. See Asiedu-Peprah, *Johannine Sabbath Conflicts*.
[82] Something similar can be said about the evolution of *light* rituals in relation to Hanukkah, which are attested earliest in the rabbinic writings. The lighting of the Hanukkiah menorah was, and remains, a domestic ritual, except of course from public lightings in synagogues on the eve of the first Sabbath of Hanukkah. We do not have historical information about how rituals of light were celebrated at Hanukkah when the Temple stood. When light is used as a metaphor in John it need not denote a religious feast; the symbolism of light infuses the entire Gospel and has vast intertextual points of reference (cf. Gen. 1.3; Isa. 2.5; Ps. 27.1; 36.9; 119.105; Prov. 4.18-19; Qo. 2.13; Job 30.26; Isa. 54.7).
[83] Poirier, 'Hanukkah', p. 471.

to *m. Suk.* 4.9-10, there was no water-drawing ceremony on the eighth day, only on the first seven days.[84] The blind man's washing in Siloam, states Poirier, must have taken place on the first Sabbath of a new seven-day festival cycle – that of Hanukkah. Thus, Jesus' reference to 'working' while it is day (9.5) indicates his desire to work *before* Hanukkah begins (that is at nightfall). Poirier then demonstrates that water-drawing from Siloam feasibly took place at Hanukkah as well as Sukkot.[85] Yet, we could forward the counterclaim that Jesus' mention of nightfall overtaking the day, and of his presence as 'light' for the world (9.4-5) must surely be understood symbolically, rather than as a concrete chronological or seasonal marker.

Neither is Poirier's argument for the transition between Sukkot and Hanukkah convincing. Poirier locates a break in chronology between chs 7 and 8: excluding John 7.53–8.11 from his analysis, Poirier argues that the events beginning in ch. 8 v. 12 define the beginning of the Hanukkah setting, while ch. 7 v. 52 concludes the Sukkot setting. He points to the unusual repetition of the phrase 'his [Jesus'] hour had not come' (7.30; 8.20) as evidence of redundancy *if* we assume the Sukkot setting is continuous.[86] Yet, this claim is somewhat specious given that this key Johannine phrase so frequently peppers the chronology of Jesus' public ministry (2.4; 12.23, 27; 13.1; 17.1; cf. its eschatological use in 4.21, 23; 5.25, 28). Here again it seems Poirier relies on an overly literal reading of the metaphor of Jesus' 'hour' when the repetition may be merely emphatic, suggesting that only Jesus is in charge of his 'hour' and no one can pre-empt its arrival (cf. 2.4).[87] There is no redundancy nor are there grounds for reading a change in setting between ch. 7 and ch. 8.

Besides, even if the events in ch. 8 occur on a different *day* to those narrated in ch. 7, it stands to reason that the events of ch. 8 occur on a different *feast*. If ch. 8 v. 12 introduces a new day, this may be the *next* day than the one recounted in ch. 7 v. 52, that is the eighth day of Sukkot. Moreover, if Poirier is right to claim continuity between ch. 8 and ch. 9, and if ch. 9 occurs on the Sabbath, then we could reasonably contend that ch. 8 may also occur on the final Sabbath of Sukkot. Against this latter possibility, Poirier writes that the Fourth Gospel, 'as a narrative tracing Jesus' ministry through the year long course of the Jewish calendar is not likely to mark the succession of a single day in such a grandiloquent way'.[88] But what are the grounds for assuming that Jesus' public ministry moves fluidly through a *single year* of the festival cycle? There are in fact *three* Passovers mentioned in the Gospel narrative (2.13; 6.4; 12.1). We must also ask whether the feast of Hanukkah – which is not preserved in the Tanakh – was significant enough to warrant placing all of chs 7–9 and half of ch. 10 of the Gospel in its setting, especially in so cryptic a manner.[89]

---

[84] However, the eighth day is a day of convocation independent of Sukkot (Shimini Atzeret). But this is not clear-cut – the same rabbinic texts speak of this day as part of Sukkot, a final 'tarrying' day.
[85] Ibid., p. 471.
[86] Ibid., p. 477.
[87] Other phrases referring to Jesus' not-yet-arrived hour occur in ch. 7, which makes the argument for redundancy not very apt (see for example 7.6, 8).
[88] Poirier, 'Hanukkah', p. 478.
[89] Many studies focus on the fact that John draws extensively on a programme of retelling Scripture through the biblical feasts for their primary significance; cf. Michael Daise, *Feasts in John: Jewish*

It is unlikely, therefore, that Poirier's recent and radically new reading of the festival setting of John 8 will gain wide acceptance. It is thus reasonable to suggest that at least all of chs 7-9 are set at Sukkot. The seasonal indicator 'it was winter' in ch. 10 v. 22 and its proximity to the mention of Hannukah provide a general temporal marker that can be distinguished from the reference to Sukkot in ch. 7 v. 2. There is no strong reason to read a decisive break between ch. 7 and ch. 8 – indeed, thematically, there is much to discredit one. This means that the Sabbath setting of ch. 9 is possibly also the setting for Jesus' discourses in ch. 8. This could be the eighth day of Sukkot, the last great Sabbath, mentioned in ch. 7 v. 37, but the chronology is simply not sufficiently clear-cut to permit definitive claims in this regard.

In the following subsection, I script the festival of Sukkot as a cultural intertext (REF, following Barthes' lexeme theory) informing this interpretation of John 7-9, particularly in terms of its relevance for ch. 8 vv. 31-59 – for the figure of Abraham and the character of 'the Jews'. As I hope to demonstrate, the festival of Sukkot provides a fascinating basis upon which to understand the Jews' response to Jesus with respect to the concept of sin (8.31-34), to the role of Abraham as a welcome guest (cf. 8.39-40) under the divine banner of protection, the *sukka* and to Abraham's joy (cf. 8.56-58) as the founder of Sukkot itself.

Sukkot as cultural code and intertext

In the Hebrew Bible, the feast of Sukkot is mentioned ten times: four times in the Torah (in Exod. 23.16; Lev. 23.33-43; Num. 29.12-38; Deut. 16.13-15), four times in the Prophets (Judg. 21.19; 1 Kgs 8.2; Ezek. 45.25; Zech. 14.16-19) and twice in the Writings (2 Chron 5-7; Neh. 8.14-18). Sukkot is also referred to in the non-canonical book of *Jubilees* (ch. 16), in *1 Macc.* 10.21, *2 Macc.* 10.3-8, as well as in Josephus, Philo and the Dead Sea Scrolls (DSS). The rabbinic texts mention the feast of Sukkot most extensively in *m. Sukk.* (also *m. Yoma* 2.5), and also in the Tosefta (*t. Sukk.* 3.1ff). The Babylonian Talmud (*b. Sukk.* 48b etc.), the Jerusalem Talmud (*y. Sukk.* 48, 54d etc.), and the Amoraic Midrashim (*Gen. R.*) also refer to the feast in some detail. John 7-8 not only refers to the feast of Sukkot explicitly (7.1, 11, 14, 37), but also alludes to it more subtly (e.g. 8.12, 24, 58). The goal of the current section is to examine the differing perspectives taken on Sukkot in Jewish antiquity to provide a basis for reading John 7-8 intertextually within that context, rather than to read that multifaceted context as 'background' to John.

The Torah

The feast of Sukkot is first mentioned in Exod. 23.16, in a section dealing with the religious calendar of ancient Israel and the exclusive worship due to God (23.13b-19).[90]

Festivals and Jesus' Hour in the Fourth Gospel (WUNT 2.229; Tübingen: Mohr Siebeck, 2007); Gail A. Yee, *Jewish Feasts in the Gospel of John* (Eugene: Wipf & Stock; repr. 2007).

[90] I take a canonical-sequential reading of the references to Sukkot in the Tanakh, rather than an historiographical reconstruction of the feast in its theological and social development, as previous scholars have done (cf. Håkan Ulfgard, *The Story of Sukkot: The Setting, Shaping, and Sequel of the*

The Hebrew text of Exod. 23.14 reads, שלש רגלים תחג לי בשנה – 'three times a year you shall hold a festival for me'. In this text, Sukkot is mentioned together with the two other festivals of Pesach and Shavuot as pilgrimage occasions (23.14-17). The three pilgrimage festivals mandated in ch. 23 vv. 14-17 are seasonal festivals rooted in the land and its harvest, a clear feature of the Exodus account.[91] The 'feast of unleavened bread' is to be held in the spring when the barley harvest begins, 'for in it you went forth from Egypt' (23.15). No mention is made of the paschal lamb, even though the connection with God's redemptive activity is maintained. In ch. 23 v. 16, the 'Feast of the Harvest', that is Shavuot, is mentioned as a celebration of the 'first fruits' of the new season. Sukkot is mentioned as the 'feast of Ingathering, at the end of the year, when you gather in the results of your work from the field' (חג האסף; 23.16). Unlike Pesach, the feasts of Shavuot and Sukkot are not historicized with respect to the divine wonders. Sukkot, as it is presented in Exod. 23.16, is an autumn harvest festival when the 'results' of the produce for the whole year are 'ingathered'; nevertheless, all three festivals are sacred in the sense that the men of Israel give God due thanks and mention only God's name on these days (vv. 13-19b).

The feast of Sukkot is mentioned again in Lev. 23.33-43. Like the text from Exodus, Sukkot is mentioned in the context of other major sacred days, but this time Rosh Hashanah and Yom Kippur are included together with Pesach, Shavuot and even Shabbat in a lengthy section dealing with all annual festivals (23.1-44).[92] The text from Leviticus uses the term חג הסכות ('feast of Booths' LXX: ἑορτὴ σκηνῶν, v. 34). The aetiology of Sukkot is only clarified in Lev. 23.42, when the citizens in Israel are commanded to dwell in booths (בסכת תשבו) for seven days. The religious significance of this commandment is provided immediately, with God speaking: 'in order that future generations may know that I made the Israelite people live in booths when I

Biblical Feast of Tabernacles (Tübingen: Mohr Siebeck, 1998)). This is not because in principle I disagree with the existence of documentary sources behind the Torah (or the disparate chronology of the biblical writings for that matter), as per Julius Wellhausen, *Prolegomena to the History of Ancient Israel* (trans. J. Sutherland Black and Allan Menzies; Edinburgh: Adam & Black, 1885), but because of the valuation I place on the literary unity of the Tanakh on the one hand (cf. Umberto Cassuto, *The Documentary Hypothesis and the Composition of the Pentateuch* (Jerusalem: Magnes, 1961)), and because of my agreement with Kaufmann's views that the P source does not necessarily need to be assigned to the post-exilic setting on the evidence provided by Higher Criticism, as well as that the Torah is the basis for and precursor to the prophetic corpus rather than vice versa (cf. Yehezkel Kaufmann, *Toledot Ha-Emunah Ha-yisre'elit* (The History of the Religion of Israel from Antiquity until the End of Second Temple Times), (4 vols.; Tel Aviv: Dvir, 1937–56); in Hebrew). Given the nature of my approach, grounded in poststructuralist intertextuality theory, it is less important for me to demonstrate historical development and influences than it is to lay out the literary evidence in the manner it presents itself to me as a 'Work' (unified, bound canon) so as to read the traces of intertextual codes in the work as 'Text' (cf. the previous chapter on Barthes).

[91] It is probable that the three pilgrimage festivals originated as agricultural rituals. Cf. Lester L. Grabbe, *Judaic Religion in the Second Temple Period: Belief and Practice from the Exile to Yavneh* (London: Routledge, 2000), p. 141. On Sukkot specifically, see George W. MacRae, 'The Meaning and Evolution of the Feast of Tabernacles', *CBQ* 22, no. 3 (1960), pp. 251–76.

[92] Rosh Hashanah is implied rather than named directly. The depth of treatment with which the festival calendar is presented relative to the other Torah texts has led some scholars to posit that Leviticus 23 is the latest of these texts chronologically speaking. See, for example, Karl William Weyde, *The Appointed Festivals of YHWH: The Festival Calendar in Leviticus 23 and the Sukkôt Festival in Other Biblical Texts* (FAT 2/4; Tübingen: Mohr Siebeck, 2004).

brought them out of the land of Egypt' (23.43). The intermediate verses (23.35-41) retain the agricultural and pilgrimage dimensions of the seven-day festival of Sukkot, when the Israelites bring 'gifts to the Lord' (23.36, 37). The 'yield' of the land is to be 'gathered in' (23.39), but on the first day (23.35) and on the *eighth* day (23.37b, 39b) of the festival, there is to be 'complete rest' when no work is performed. On the first day, the so-called 'four species' are to be taken hold of while the people 'rejoice before the Lord' for seven days (23.40a).[93] On the eighth day, a 'solemn assembly' is held (v. 36d), today known as *Shmni Atzeret*.

Compared to the text from Exod. 23.16, the picture given of Sukkot in Lev. 23.33-43 is richer in detail and is more theologically developed. There is a dual focus on human *joy* and divine *care*.[94] The text of Lev. 23.33-43 presents these more refined theological perspectives, historicizing the exodus experience and overlaying it upon the harvest celebrations original to the agricultural feast. The booths constructed in the open fields were suffused with meaning derived from the recollection of tent-dwelling in the desert.[95] In Lev. 23.43, God is depicted as having brought the Hebrews 'out of the land of Egypt', connecting God's care for his people with their obligation to bring forth from *their* good land the bounty provided in the harvest season. God brought his people forth from a land of 'narrow straits' and into a good land (cf. Deut. 8.7), protecting them from the vagaries and harshness of the weather on the way; the reaping of the harvest from that good land that is to occur on Sukkot, as well as the commemorative dwelling in booths, is the correspondingly human expression of thanks and joy to God. As such, Sukkot is considered the most joyful of pilgrimage feasts.

Sukkot is referred to, but not named explicitly, in Num. 29.12-38. The text begins, 'On the fifteenth day of the seventh month, you shall have a holy convocation. You shall not do any ordinary work, and you shall keep a feast to the Lord seven days'. The dating of the feast, as well as its seven-day duration clues the interpreter in to the fact that it is Sukkot. No theological rationale is presented in Num. 29.12-38 for the feast's observation, rather the verses continue to outline in fine detail the kind and number of offerings required for every day of the festival. The eighth day of solemn assembly is also mentioned as a day of rest and offerings (29.35-38). Like the other texts from the Torah, this text also occurs within the context of the festival calendar and the offerings (28.1–29.40).

Finally, Sukkot is mentioned in some detail in Deut. 16.13-15, once more in the context of how to observe the pilgrimage festivals (16.1-17). The section begins not only with a description of how the feast of Pesach is to be celebrated, but also a theological rationale: the month of Avib (Av) was when, at night, 'the Lord your God freed you from Egypt' (16.1); unleavened bread is eaten because it is 'bread of distress' and reminds them that they departed Egypt 'hurriedly' (16.3). Reasons are also provided for the celebration of Shavuot. The feast of Shavuot is mentioned as a feast of 'joy' (16.11) and is to be an inclusive celebration, with male and female children, and male and female slaves, the 'strangers', the Levites, the orphans and the widows all

---

[93] Cf. *m. Sukk.* 3.5-8.
[94] Ulfgard, *The Story of Sukkot*, p. 86.
[95] Cf. MacRae, 'Meaning and Evolution', p. 255.

taking part, for the Israelites were once slaves in Egypt (16.11-12). The feast of Sukkot is likewise to be a festival of rejoicing (16.14a) that includes the same reach of social relations detailed for Shavuot (16.14b). The festival is to be held for seven days, and there is no mention of an eighth day of solemn assembly and rest, as there was in Leviticus (16.15a). Unlike Pesach and Shavuot, no extraneous reasons are given for why Sukkot should be celebrated, but Sukkot is, like the other feast, to be held at the 'place the Lord will choose' (i.e. the Jerusalem Temple; 16.2, 7, 15) – a characteristically Deuteronomic innovation.

The feast of Sukkot is also linked to its agricultural origins in Deut. 16.13-15: 'after the ingathering from your threshing floor and your vat, you shall hold the Feast of Booths for seven days' (16.13). Sukkot is a time of rejoicing (שמח; 16.14), when God will bless the crops of the Israelites, and they 'will have nothing but joy' (16.15b). There is no reference to the theological significance of the booths, or even to their usage. The three pilgrimage festivals are connected by the occasion they give for 'all the males' to appear before the Lord in the Temple with a 'gift' – an offering for God based on the 'blessing' bestowed on each of them by God (16.16-17). Sukkot is the last of these pilgrimage festivals, taking place at the end of the summer when the harvest of grain and wine is stored for the coming year.

The prophets

The feast of Sukkot is alluded to three times in the *Nevi'im* (Judg. 21.19; 1 Kgs 8.2; Eze. 45.25), and explicitly named once (Zech. 14.16-19). In Judges 21, Sukkot is simply mentioned as 'the yearly feast of the Lord at Shiloh' (v. 19) in the context of a war narrative where the elders plan to capture wives for the men of the tribe of Benjamin. The reference to Sukkot in Ezekiel is likewise made in passing, as follows: 'In the seventh month, on the fifteenth day of the month and for the seven days of the feast, he [the prince, see v. 22] shall make the same provision for sin offerings, burnt offerings, and grain offerings, and for the oil'. This reference to Sukkot has no bearing on the direction that the text continues to take. On the other hand, the reference in the first book of Kings is slightly more substantial, with Sukkot providing the narrative occasion for the dedication of Solomon's Temple. Sukkot is not named as such, but is referred to as 'the Feast' taking place in 'the seventh month' (1 Kgs 8.2). On the second day of Sukkot, the people assemble to hear a reading from the scroll of Deuteronomy. The 'Presence of the Lord' is said to have filled the Temple to such a degree that the priests were unable to remain inside (8.11). Solomon concludes his prayer for the consecration of the Temple with the supplication that 'all the peoples of the earth may know that the Lord alone is God, there is no other' (8.60).

Solomon's prayer that the oneness of the Lord will be recognized by the entire world resonates with the final text in the prophetic corpus that refers to Sukkot – Zech. 14.16-19.[96] Of all the references to Sukkot in this genre, the post-exilic text of Zechariah 14 is

---

[96] This passage is read as the haftarah text on the first day of Sukkot in the synagogue liturgy (cf. Gemarah on *Megillah* 3.5; in Charles W. F. Smith, 'No Time for Figs', *JBL* 79, no. 4 (1960), pp. 315–27, at p. 320.

the most detailed and theologically intuitive.[97] It is set within a concluding oracle of the prophet announcing an apocalyptic war waged by the Lord, a war in which all the 'nations' will take part in Jerusalem (14.1-2). The Lord, the oracle continues, will then make war on 'those nations' (14.3) in a cataclysmic upheaval of the natural order (14.4-5).[98] This war will herald the coming of the Lord to his people (14.5b) and the result will be a situation of 'continuous day', with light produced by neither the sun nor the moon (14.6). On that day 'fresh water will flow from Jerusalem, part of it to the Eastern Sea, and part of it to the Western Sea, throughout the summer and winter' (14.8). The apex of the climactic battle between God and the nations is that on 'that day' the Lord will reign sovereign over the earth, and 'the Lord shall be one, and his name shall be one' (14.9) – that is, the Lord alone shall be worshipped (cf. Deut. 6.4). But a different fate awaits those peoples who fought against Jerusalem: they shall suffer the plague (14.12, 15), and a general panic will befall everyone in the land (14.13). In the process of fighting, 'the wealth of all the nations roundabouts – vast quantities of gold, silver and clothing – shall be gathered in' (14.14).

The survivors of the surrounding nations will then find themselves making annual pilgrimages to that city, to 'bow low to the Lord of hosts, and to observe the feast of Booths' (14.16). Those nations that exclude themselves from coming to Jerusalem to observe the feast of Booths – whether or not they took part in the apocalyptic battle scene just described – will not receive any rain from God (14.17). This apocalyptic 'day', the time in which the Lord will reign over Jerusalem and in which it will be perpetual day, with all the nations coming to annually observe Sukkot, will also be a time in which everything mundane will be made holy to the Lord. 'Even the bells on the horses shall be inscribed, "Holy to the Lord" (14.20), and base metal pots will be like holy vessels used before the altar' (14.21). The book of Zechariah then closes with the final promise that on that day there will be no more traders in 'the House of the Lord of Hosts', that is, in the holy Temple (14.21).

The agricultural practice of 'ingathering' the harvest from the fields, which served as the basis of the primitive festival, is eschatalogically reconfigured in this post-exilic text. The return to Judah from exile was only the beginning of a worldwide 'ingathering' of the nations to worship the One God of Israel. When the final divine – human war is waged in Jerusalem, the 'booty' of the nations will first be 'gathered in' – quantities of clothing, gold and silver (14.14). To follow will be the ingathering of the nations themselves, who will come to worship God in the sovereignty of his rule. The most appropriate feast to be celebrated in this context, according to the prophet, is Sukkot,

---

[97] Scholars generally consider Zechariah 14 to be of late dating, as late as the second century BCE – see the discussion in Jeffrey Rubenstein, *The History of Sukkot in the Second Temple and Rabbinic Periods* (Atlanta: Scholars Press, 1995), p. 45. An earlier date of around 475–425 BCE is suggested by Carol L. Meyers and Eric M. Meyers, *Zechariah 9–14* (AB 25C; New York: Doubleday, 1998), pp. 26–8.

[98] Reisenfeld claims that the festival of Sukkot always had a pronounced eschatological connotation, which Zechariah 14 only pronounces most clearly; see H. Riesenfeld, *Jésus Transfiguré* (Uppsala, 1947), p. 240; cf. pp. 29–54. However, Rubenstein disputes this contention, claiming that the Zecharian text possesses an eschatological character on its own terms, which it transfers to Sukkot in the context of a restored Temple and city due to 'a radical upheaval through divine intervention'. Thus, Rubenstein, *The History of Sukkot*, p. 49.

for it signifies an ingathering of the *peoples* to Jerusalem – the great and final 'harvest' of the end times. Whereas the Torah commands the people of Israel to dwell in booths to commemorate and give thanks for the divine care lavished upon their ancestors in the wilderness years, the Zecharian text envisages all of the nations taking part in this practice in submission to the 'oneness' of God. But any reference to the joy we find in the Torah texts is absent – rather the sense is that the nations observe Sukkot out of a serious obligation and on pain of death (through the forcible withdrawal of rain). Failure to observe Sukkot as the most significant of Temple festivals 'is tantamount to rebellion against God and receives due punishment'.[99]

However, the fresh water flowing from Jerusalem, to east and west, continually throughout summer and winter (14.8) more than satisfies for the punitive lack of rain – and the nations, it is presumed, can partake of its benefits if they make the pilgrimage to Jerusalem to honour Sukkot. Jerusalem appears in this text to be the 'navel of the earth', the centre from which flows fresh ('living') water. Moreover, Jerusalem shall be 'raised high' while the surrounding geographical expanse is depressed ('like the *arabah*' – i.e. like the desert, cf. 14.11-12). The fresh water flowing from Jerusalem is thus depicted as flowing *down* to the east and the west, saturating the rest of the world much like natural rainfall. God's care and protection of Israel in the wilderness years – the reason for the observance of Sukkot in Leviticus 23 – becomes in Zechariah, God's care for all of the nations (through the provision of fresh water) who honour the name of the Lord.[100] We will later illustrate the significance of divinely bestowed rainfall in its connection to Abraham's merits in the context of Sukkot.

The writings

Sukkot receives attention in three key texts of the *Kethuvi'im*: 2 Chronicles 5–7, Nech. 8.14-18 and Ezra 3.1-6. The episode recounted in 2 Chron. 5.2-14 retells the narrative of 1 Kgs 8.1-13, when Solomon dedicated the Temple at the feast of Sukkot. The twin historiographies are fascinating to compare side by side. The entire Kings narrative runs from 1 Kgs 8.2-66, and in 2 Chronicles, it runs from ch 5 v. 1 to ch. 7 v. 10. Both texts open with a reference to the placement of the Ark in the Temple upon its consecration, as well as to the 'feast of the seventh month' (1 Kgs 8.1-2; cf. 2 Chron. 5.1-3). The consecration itself results in the cloud of the Lord's glory filling the Temple to the point where the ministers cannot do their duties (1 Kgs 8.10; 2 Chron. 5.14 – and the chronicler adds his characteristic 'Levitical singers' into the ministerial mix, cf. 5.12; 7.6). After the ceremony, Solomon then cites a relevant psalm; in the Kings

---

[99] Rubenstein, *The History of Sukkot*, p. 46.
[100] The intertextuality of this passage with respect to John 7.37-39, in which the Evangelist prohesizes 'rivers of living water' to all who would come to Jesus is quite striking. Joel Marcus proposes that the text of Isa. 12.3 ('With joy you will draw water from the wells of salvation') forms the most relevant scriptural source for John 7.38, a biblical text which was associated with Sukkot in a critical rabbinic text (*y. Sukk.* 5.1). The Yerushalmi glosses Isa. 12.3 as follows (and Marcus reads the final noun (ישוע) not as 'Joshua' but as 'Jesus', or Yeshua): 'Do not read, "From the wells of salvation" (ממעיני הישועה) but "from the belly of Jesus" (ממעי ישוע), for rivers of living water shall flow from his belly'. See Marcus, 'Rivers of Living Water from Jesus' Belly (John 7.38)', *JBL* 117, no. 2 (1998), pp. 328–30, at p. 330. The theme of flowing water in the Zecharian text accords with the Isaian motif in ch. 12 v. 3.

account, this is a combination of two so-called 'enthronement psalms' (Pss. 18.11 (cf. 97.2) and 132.13-14), which together depict the Lord taking his abode in the residence built for him by Solomon's hands (1 Kgs 8.13). The chronicler makes two adaptations to this: first, it is not Solomon but the people who cite a psalm, and second, the psalm is not a regal enthronement psalm, but a thanksgiving psalm, viz. Psalm 118, which then functions as a refrain for the people in the narrative (7.3, 6c). Only later does Solomon cite the complex of psalms in the Kings narrative (2 Chron. 6.1-2). This is of interest because in the early rabbinic writings, we see that this same refrain from Psalm 118 was codified as part of the Hoshanah Rabbah celebrations at Sukkot.

In both narratives, Solomon gives a disquisition about his father David, and how he was given the task of building the Lord's Temple (1 Kgs 8.14-21; 2 Chron. 6.1-11). This is followed by Solomon's prayer for himself (1 Kgs 8.22-29; 2 Chron. 6.12-20) and then his lengthy prayer to God on behalf of the people (1 Kgs 8.30-51; 2 Chron. 6.22-42). In his supplicatory prayer, Solomon presents the Lord with multiple possibilities of the people's future sins, asking that in the event of their sinning, God might forgive them if they entreat him appropriately in the Temple via repentance. In fact, the repeated references to 'sin' in these texts (חטאת/ἁμαρτία) is a striking element, often overlooked in commentaries for its significance in the Sukkot setting. References to 'sin' occur nine times in the Kings narrative (1 Kgs 8.33, 34, 35 (×2), 36, 46 (×2), 47, 50) and ten times in the Chronicles text (6.22, 24, 25, 26 (×2), 27, 36 (×2), 37, 39). The consequence of the people's sin would be alienation from their land. Thus, Solomon prays that, upon their repentance, the Lord will bring them back to their land, which is the 'inheritance promised to their ancestors' (1 Kgs 8.34, 36, 40, 48; 2 Chron. 6.25, 27) – a distinct allusion to the divine promises made to Abraham in the Torah (cf. Gen. 12.1-3, etc.).

References to the covenant that God made with Israel after taking them out of Egypt also permeate both narratives (1 Kgs 8.9, 16, 21, 51, 53; 2 Chron. 5.10; 6.5). In 1 Kgs 8.59-61, moreover, Solomon concludes his speech by reminding the people that the Lord was always with their ancestors, and then he urges them to find the Lord by following his 'ways' (דרכיו), 'commandments' (מצותיו), 'laws' (חקיו) and 'ordinances' (משפטיו).[101] Both narratives end with the people returning home at the end of the feast. In 1 Kgs 8.66, Solomon sends the people home on the 'eighth day', himself full of joy and gladness (שמח/χαίρω). In 2 Chron. 7.10, Sukkot is celebrated for seven days, with an additional eighth day of assembly, and it is the *people* who return home full of joy and gladness – but on the twenty-third day!

Sukkot is referred to extensively in a narrative section of Neh. 8.14-18. After the exile, the returnees from exile gather at the Water Gate in Jerusalem to hear Ezra read the Torah, on 'the first day of the seventh month' (Neh. 8.1-2). Ezra's fellow scribes interpret the Torah so that the assembly understand it (8.8). The people respond by weeping and grieving at the words of the Torah (8.9d, 11).[102] Ezra then counsels them

---

[101] This verse is absent from the Chronicles account. Importantly, this verse is very close to Gen. 26.5, where Abraham teaches his children how to follow God's 'ways' and 'commandments', 'laws' and 'ordinances' (see Chapter 5 for further discussion).

[102] Some scholars interpret the weeping of the people to mean that they are engaged in a kind of atonement ceremony, like a precursor to Yom Kippur; see Rubenstein, *The History of Sukkot*, p. 35, n. 11.

not to weep, but rather to *rejoice*, for the occasion of discovering the words of the Torah is an occasion of joy, and the day is therefore 'holy to the Lord' (8.9). On the second day of the seventh month, the male heads of households, together with the priests and Levites, continue to study the words of the Torah with Ezra (8.13). They make, what appears to them, to be a remarkable discovery: 'the Lord had commanded by Moses that the people of Israel should dwell in booths during the feast of the seventh month' (8.14). The Torah also commanded them to proclaim the feast in their towns and to go out into the hills to find branches from which to construct the booths (8.15).[103] This happy coincidence spurs the people – who are hearing the words of the Torah in the seventh month – to go and make booths for themselves, in the Temple precincts (e.g. at the Water Gate) and in their towns (8.16). The narrator explains that 'from the days of Joshua the son of Nun' until that time, the people of Israel had not observed Sukkot and, consequently, there was 'very great rejoicing' (שמחה גדלה; 8.17). The people kept the feast of Sukkot for seven days, with an additional eighth day of solemn assembly, 'according to the rule' (8.18). Throughout the entire feast, Ezra read from the 'book of the Torah of God' (8.18).

Sukkot is also mentioned in Ezra 3.1-6, with a focus not so much on the specificities of the festival as on the returnees' strict observance of it.[104] The version in Ezra 3.1-6 describes how the people assembled in Jerusalem at the beginning of the seventh month, as in Nehemiah (Ezra 3.1). Yeshua the high priest, and Zerrubavel, the surviving descendant of the last king, offer sacrifices at an altar they have built (3.3-6). They celebrate the festival of Booth, 'as it is written' (3.3-4). It is these Sukkot sacrifices that reinstate the cultic worship that was lost when the First Temple was destroyed. This is an important point: although the text from Ezra contains far less detail about Sukkot than the texts in Nehemiah and Chronicles, the singularity of Sukkot as the festival that renews the Temple cult attests to its crucial valuation in the post-exilic period at the dawn of 'early Judaism'. The observance of Sukkot mediates the divine presence for the assembled returnees from exile – in Ezra 3, via the Temple and in Nehemiah 8, via the Torah.[105] Both foci illustrate the concern felt over making sure that 'the renewed sacrificial order conformed to the commandments of God'.[106] The picture given by Ezra 3 of the renewal of sacrifices at the Second Temple at Sukkot also demonstrates the legitimation of the Second Temple as connected to, and continuous with, the operations of the First Temple.[107] However, at the same time, the passage from Ezra 3 seems to imply that Sukkot, as it functioned in the Second Temple Period, arose out of a 'vacuum'.[108] The restoration of the cult was not immediate, but historically quite

---

[103] Note that the Torah only refers to the duty to collect the four species in a ritual of rejoicing before God, not that the *sukkot* themselves should be constructed out of the material of the species, the palms and branches (cf. Lev. 23.39-43).
[104] Cf. Ulfgard, *The Story of Sukkot*, p. 123.
[105] Cf. ibid., p. 124.
[106] Rubenstein, *History of Sukkot*, p. 34.
[107] Mary Spaulding, *Commemorative Identities: Jewish Social Memory and the Johannine Feast of Booths* (LNTS 396; London: T&T Clark, 2009), p. 57.
[108] Rubenstein, *History of Sukkot*, p. 34.

protracted. And generally, Sukkot was not uniquely associated with inaugurations or dedications – Pesach also bore such associations.[109]

K. F. Pohlman has proposed that Josephus (*Ant.* 11.154-158) follows 1 Esdras (the Septuagintal Greek version of MT Ezra), reproducing a more faithful version of that text, which was eventually cut off in its final part.[110] As Josephus recounts it, the people 'mourn the sins of the previous generations, which resulted in the exile, but having been comforted by Ezra that there is nothing to fear for those who remain obedient to the *Torah*, the whole people joins in a joyful celebration of *sukkot*'.[111] The people are grateful to God, and to Ezra, for it was through the latter that the sins of the previous generations were corrected (cf. Chronicles and 1 Kings). Josephus' reconstructed ending hones in on these issues of vicarious, intergenerational sin/forgiveness. It is worth noting also that obedience to the Torah is presented as a remedy for any lapses into future sin, or more specifically, that such obedience functions to protect and prevent the people from coming under the divine judgement – and that these collective themes are framed at the celebration of Sukkot.

To sum up, what can we say about the intertextual resonances of the biblical material on Sukkot when brought into conversation with John 8.31-59? The sample of studies with which we have engaged has primarily focused upon the development of Sukkot from an historical perspective, which of course, is not unimportant. The comparatively condensed overview of the biblical material presented here has not aimed to reiterate those historical elements, largely dealing with issues of dating, of the Pentateuchal source material, the exile and the chronistic editing of the historiographic biblical texts. The purpose here, rather, has been to draw out certain overlooked thematic elements of the textual representation of Sukkot that, in terms of scripting the Johannine text, have a particular salience to the figuration of Abraham found therein.

One intertextual feature to note is the motif of sin (cf. John 8.34). Besides the extensive reworking of Esdras preserved in Josephus' *Antiquities*, we find the motif of sin expressed in some depth in 1 Kings 8 and in 2 Chronicles 6. As Solomon dedicates the Temple during the celebration of Sukkot, he intercedes for the people so that their future sins might be forgiven upon their proper repentance. The connection between Israel's sin and the *land* is also important, for their sin would effect the punishment of alienation from the land promised to their ancestors – an implicit connection to the inheritance of Abraham (cf. John 8.32-33). The text of Leviticus makes explicit the fact that Sukkot should be celebrated as a culmination of the freedom of the exodus experience, when God liberated his chosen people from Egypt and led them into the land. The centrality of observing the commandments of God in the Torah is also a strong motif, expressed in 1 Kings, and as a remedy against sin in the text from Esdras (cf. John 8.38-40). In Nehemiah, we find a strong association between the observance of Sukkot and the occasion of learning about the Law of God. The recurrent motif of joy and of rejoicing at Sukkot is common to many of the texts analysed in this chapter

---

[109] See Jeffrey L. Rubenstein, 'Sukkot, Eschatology and Zechariah 14', *RB* 103 (1996), pp. 161–95.
[110] K. F. Pohlmann, '3. Esra-Buch', in *Historische und legendarische Erzählungen* (Gütersloh, 1980), pp. 375–425. Cited in Ulfgard, *Story of Sukkot*, p. 179.
[111] Ulfgard, *Story of Sukkot*, p. 179.

(cf. John 8.56-58). In the eschatological flavour of Sukkot's celebration in Zechariah, we also find the motif of worshipping the one God – that God is one and there is no other. Later rabbinic texts will draw this idea out in terms of Sukkot being the occasion for repudiating idolatry (cf. John 8.32-33). All of these connections are drawn out in greater detail in the following chapters; it suffices here to note that the festival setting of Sukkot operates as an intertextual 'cultural code' in which all of these motifs bear a particular resonance.

Pseudepigrapha

Outside of the Tanakh, references to Sukkot continue in the apocryphal literature, in the Hellenistic Jewish writings and in the rabbinic corpora. The book of *Jubilees*, which is usually dated to the early or mid-second century BCE, provides us with the most developed set of references to Sukkot outside of the canonical literature, and before the rabbinic era.[112] *Jubilees* is an extended retelling of the biblical book of Genesis; as such, it retrojects many later festivals and rituals into the lives of Israel's patriarchs. In particular, *Jubilees* associates Sukkot with Abraham, Isaac and Jacob. In *Jub.* 16.20-31, Abraham is presented as the first person on earth to observe Sukkot, and to do so with great joy (this motif of joy is emphasized repeatedly: 16.20, 25, 27, 28, 29, 31; cf. Deut. 16.15; Lev. 23.40).[113] As Abraham celebrates Sukkot, an angel appears in order to promise that a 'holy seed' will descend from his son Isaac. Abraham's practical observance of Sukkot (for example, building the *sukka*, using the *lulav* and rejoicing) is in line with the Torah's stipulations regarding the feast (cf. Deut. 16.14). But unlike some of the Torah texts, the book of *Jubilees* does not historicize Sukkot with respect to the Exodus (cf. Leviticus 23). Instead, the feast is connected to future events that are revealed to Abraham, and which are as yet unrealized. That Abraham circumambulates the altar he has built with 'praise' and 'thanks' might suggest that the depiction of Sukkot in *Jubilees* 16 signifies a liturgical recitation of some kind.[114]

Sukkot is also referred to in *Jub.* 32.1-9, this time with reference to the figure of Jacob. During Sukkot (which is obliquely referred to by its dating: 'on the fifteenth of the seventh month and for the following seven days'; 32.4-6), Jacob appoints his son Levi and his descendants as priests of the Lord. Jacob then attempts to build a Temple for the Lord at Bethel, but an angel appears to him with seven stone tablets upon which Jacob learns that Bethel is the wrong location for the Temple (32.16-22). This is an implicit intertextual connection with the narrative of Solomon dedicating the Temple at Sukkot (cf. 1 Kings 8).[115] These texts are important for what they present about the 'seed' (descendants) of two of the patriarchs (Abraham and Jacob), and the revelations that both patriarchs receive during Sukkot. Scholars have not yet noticed or discussed this presentation in connection with John 8.32, and the Jews' claim to be

---

[112] *OTP II*, pp. 35–142.
[113] There is no need to suppose, as per Rubenstein, *History of Sukkot*, p. 52, that this 'striking repetition' of the theme of 'joy' indicates that the author of *Jubilees* personally experienced emotions of joy when celebrating Sukkot – cf. Barthes' critique of psycho-autobiographical readings of texts.
[114] Cf. Rubenstein, *History of Sukkot*, p. 55.
[115] Cf. ibid., p. 56.

'seed of Abraham' at the feast of Sukkot. As we will note in Chapter 4, in the book of Genesis, Bethel is frequently the site of divine disclosures made about Abraham's 'seed'.

The text of Pseudo-Philo (*LAB*) connects the feast of Sukkot with the divine gift of rain.[116] Following the text of Lev. 23.40, the author of *LAB* improvises considerably in his interpretation of the rewards that God will send to the Israelites for their observance of the four species at Sukkot: 'And I will remember the whole earth with rain ... and I will fix the stars and command the clouds, and the winds will resound, and lighting bolts will scurry, and there will be a thunderstorm, and this will be an everlasting sign; and the nights will yield dew, as I said after the flooding of the earth'. The Sukkot rituals act like a kind of 'rain charm' in this text.[117] The connection between rain and Sukkot found in Zechariah 14 is made explicit. The intertextual links between *LAB* and Gen. 5.9-9.17 should also be evident, as the text from Pseudo-Philo recalls the flooding of the whole earth with rain, and the enduring covenant that follows. That covenant was bound on God's promise never to destroy the earth again by water; in Pseudo-Philo's interpretation of the blessings of Sukkot, a covenantal sign follows the hyperbolic 'flooding' of the earth with rain as a reward for the observance of Sukkot. We return to this important motif in the discussion of the rabbinic and medieval liturgical material, where Abraham figures as a means of inducing God to provide rain at Sukkot.

There is a brief reference to the feast of Sukkot in *1 Macc.* 10.21.[118] In that text, the high priesthood is handed over to the Hasmonean family in 152 BCE, when Jonathan assumes office, which takes place at 'the feast of Shelters'.[119] Jonathan takes on the role of high priest by donning the sacred vestments, and immediately sets about raising troops for the coming war, and manufacturing arms (10.21b). The text of *Macc.* 1.10 gives no indication of the symbolic significance of the feast of Sukkot as the backdrop for Jonathan's assumption of office; it appears to be a calendrical reference more than anything else, as if to merely specify that the Hasmonean dynasty came into effect in October of that year. Spaulding states that Sukkot was 'a publically officious occasion' and that for Jonathan to assume office during that feast 'reveals the power of the Hasmoneans as well as their desire to continue ancient ritual observances and associations'.[120] But this seems conjectural given the lack of reference in *1 Macc.* 10.21 to the family's ritual observance of the feast (cf. to the contrary, Ezra, 2 Chronicles, 1 Kings). In fact, somewhat jarringly, we simply read of Jonathan's immediate war efforts during the feast and his preparation to fight (v. 21b), which run counter to the joy mandated for this feast in other biblical and apocryphal texts.

Another reference to Sukkot is found in *2 Macc.* 10.6, this time, showing greater harmony with the biblical traditions. In this text, Judas Maccabaeus and his followers, 'under the Lord's guidance', restore the Second Temple in Jerusalem after the desecration imposed upon it by Antiochus Epiphanes IV (*2 Macc.* 10.1). They set up a new altar and offer sacrifices upon it to God (10.3). After this, they fall prostrate and implore God that if they should ever sin, he deal with them moderately and not hand them

---

[116] *OTP II*, pp. 297–378.
[117] Cf. Rubenstein, *History of Sukkot*, p. 74.
[118] The translation followed is from the NRSV (*Apocrypha*).
[119] Cf. Spaulding, *Commemorative Identities*, p. 62. Cf. Rubenstein, *History of Sukkot*, p. 64.
[120] Ibid., p. 62.

over to the power of other 'barbarous' nations again (10.4). The day on which this is said to have occurred is then stated – the 25th of Chislev (10.5), which became the feast of Hannukah (cf. *1 Macc.* 4.59).[121] The text goes on to say that the feast of Hannukah was kept over eight days 'with rejoicing, in the manner of the feast of Shelters' (10.6a). The recent experience of the guerrillas is stated as a commemorative factor overlaid upon the feast of Hannukah, which makes it comparable to the feast of Sukkot: 'not long before, at the time of the feast of Shelters, they had been living in the mountains and caverns like wild beasts' (10.6b). Although their hideout rendered them like wild animals, their caverns nevertheless recalled – indeed, effectively fulfilled – the mandate to dwell in booths during Sukkot. Now, at the time of their victory over foreign, tyrannical rule, Maccabaeus and his group establish Hannukah as a feast 'in the manner of Sukkot'. Together they carry leafy boughs and palms and sing songs (10.7). Sukkot is depicted as 'the Temple festival *par excellence*'.[122]

An intriguing overlap between this text and the biblical historiographies is also evident: in 2 Chronicles 5–7 and 1 Kings 8, we noted that Solomon interceded on behalf of the nation, that if they fall into sin, they might be forgiven by God after repenting; this would obviate the punishment of exile and the destruction of the Temple. A similar plea is voiced by Judas Maccabaeus in *2 Maccabees* 10, but the punishment to be avoided is the reinvasion of Judea by foreign powers, and the divestment or profanation of the Temple. While the biblical texts place Solomon's plea in the context of the celebration of Sukkot and the dedication of the First Temple, the apocryphal *2 Macc.* 10.1-8 situates Judas' plea in the context of the rededication of the Second Temple during the feast of Hannukah. This certainly indicates not only that the textual connections between Sukkot and the Temple/inauguration ceremonies was strong, but it also draws attention to an overlooked aspect, namely, the association between this festival and God's forgiveness of his people's sin in time of need.[123]

Sukkot is mentioned four times in the Qumran documents, all in the Temple Scroll (11QT).[124] The first two references (cols. 11.13 and 27.10–29.6) are worded almost identically to the Torah texts. Regarding the first reference, as much as can be gleaned from the damaged state of the parchment, Sukkot is mentioned in the context of instructions for the ritual offerings.[125] The second reference concludes the list of sacrificial legislation for the festivals, and closely parallels Num. 29.12-39.[126] Sukkot is mentioned again in col. 29, once more in the context of stipulating festival offerings. Yet this time, the document adds some detail about the future worship to take place

---

[121] See previous section (and cf. 1 Macc. 4.59).
[122] Rubenstein, *History of Sukkot*, p. 63.
[123] This text does indicate that Poirier is correct to claim that liberation themes run through the celebration of Hanukkah in the context of the Maccabean revolt. However, in relation to John 8–10, Poirier did not draw attention to the connection between sin and slavery (cast in Maccabees, implicitly as being under foreign rule).
[124] Ulfgard, *The Story of Sukkot*, p. 175.
[125] Ibid. Cf. Yigal Yadin, *The Temple Scroll* (Vol. 1; Jerusalem: Israel Exploration Society and Shrine of the Book, 1983), pp. 135; 143. Rubenstein, *History of Sukkot*, p. 66, states that the fragmentary nature of the scrolls makes it difficult to arrive at strong conclusions about the mandates to celebrate Sukkot in the Scrolls.
[126] Ulfgard, *The Story of Sukkot*, p. 176.

at Sukkot in an eternal Temple (v. 8), with God speaking: 'And I will consecrate my [t]emple by my glory. [...] on which I will settle my glory until the day of blessing on which I will create my Temple and establish it for myself for all times, according to the covenant which I have made with Jacob at Bethel'.[127] The future, eschatological Temple envisioned here resonates with some of the prophetic literature in the Bible, and the mention of the covenant made with Jacob at Bethel – in the context of Sukkot – parallels the text from *Jubilee* 32, discussed earlier in this chapter. The third reference to Sukkot in 11QT occurs in col. 42.10-17.[128] Instructions are given to build *sukkot* (booths), according to certain measurements, on the roof that runs along the inside of the Temple wall – an injunction not found inside the Bible or in extant apocryphal and deutero-canonical texts. The fourth text (col. 44.6) continues this line of instruction, adding that these booths shall be given to the twelve tribes of Israel and to Aaron's sons.

Philo and Josephus

Philo discusses Sukkot in his exegetical treatise on biblical laws, *De Spec. Leg.* 2.204-214.[129] Philo refers to the festival of Sukkot as σκηναί, an unusual reference that means 'booths' or 'tents'.[130] The LXX (cf. *2 Maccabees*) uses σκηνοπηγία ('pitching tents/booths'), which is also the term preferred by Josephus (and, incidentally, John 7.2). Philo draws out the thanksgiving themes of the festival by playing on the Greek word μετωπορινη (autumnal), which he considers to be the appropriate season for Sukkot, as it follows the 'ripening' (μετα την οποραν) of fruits. The ripening of the harvest is a time to give thanks to God (2.204-206). Sukkot is also the time for (men) to rest from their labours – Philo argues that the reason for dwelling in σκηναί is that weary labourers should come into the protection of shelter to rest with their harvests, which must also be protected from the coming harsh weather (2.207). There is no shelter outside in the autumn – all the trees are losing their shade, and it makes eminent sense, in Philo's interpretation, that the σκηναί are available for both men and the fruits that they have harvested (2.207). Men, in this special instance, are to become like a domiciled woman, who usually 'shuts [herself] up' and 'never stirs outside her quarters' (2.207). Philo's understanding of the practical, seasonal functionality of the 'booths' differs from other biblical and post-biblical narratives that see the booths as temporary, providing somewhat flimsy and provisional shelter. Philo regards the booths as a more solid and enduring type of construction.[131] Beyond the pragmatic interpretation, Philo naturally offers his readers a moralistic and historicized explanation of the necessity to dwell in 'booths'. It is because, as per Lev. 23.43, God required the Israelites to dwell in tents as they journeyed through the desert – a journey that is recalled during the celebration of Sukkot (2.208-10). The moral lesson that Philo derives from this

---

[127] Yadin, *The Temple Scroll*, 1.136, notes that the building of sukkot within the precincts of the Temple recalls Neh. 8.16.
[128] Yadin, *The Temple Scroll*, 2.179–80.
[129] F. H. Colson (ed. and trans.), Philo, *On the Special Laws II* (LCL 320; Cambridge: Harvard University Press, 1937).
[130] Cf. Rubenstein, *History of Sukkot*, p. 69.
[131] Ibid., p. 70.

commemorative practice is that one should recall the misfortunes of old during times of present prosperity so as to always remain aware of, and grateful to, God (2.211).

Josephus similarly interprets the commandment to dwell in booths as a necessity against the adverse weather of the season (*Ant.* 3.244).[132] Unlike Philo, however, Josephus refers to the connection between the dwelling in booths and the Temple, drawing on the law outlined in Leviticus 23: 'On the fifteenth of the same month, when the cycle of year turns and approaches the wintry season, he [Moses] bids each family to fix up booths, apprehensive of the cold... they were to repair to that city which they would in honour of the Temple regard as their metropolis, and there for eight days keep festival' (*Ant.* 3.244-247). The inclement weather is not the only rationale Josephus cites for the mandate to dwell in booths. In *BJ* 1.73, he refers in passing to the 'national custom' of the Jews to make 'booths for God'.[133] The contemporary observance of Sukkot therefore rests upon the ritual of thanksgiving to God.[134] Other passages in Josephus' work that retell key biblical narratives suggest that 'Sukkot was the paramount festival in Josephus's day', observed with special care and devotion.[135] Moreover, Josephus' historical account of the War (66–70 CE) suggests that everyone took very seriously the pilgrimage aspect of Sukkot: when Antipatris Cestius marched into Lydda during Sukkot, he found the city virtually deserted because the vast majority of the inhabitants had journeyed to the Temple in Jerusalem (*BJ* 2.515).

Rabbinic literature

Historically speaking, the destruction of the Second Temple by the Romans in 70 CE profoundly affected the celebration of Sukkot. The practices bound up with the celebration of Sukkot in the Temple, such as the sacrificial cult, were destroyed. As such, Sukkot was modified and adapted after the loss of the Temple so that it could continue to be celebrated in the diaspora.[136] Yet, these modifications also reflected the gradual evolutions affecting Sukkot that were already underway prior to the Temple's destruction and practised in the synagogue.[137] The early rabbinic literature attests to the changes in Sukkot – both in functional ritual activities and in symbolic figuration – and it is mainly the latter point that concerns us here.

Rabbinic tradition held that on the end of the first day of Sukkot while the Temple still stood, a special water-drawing ceremony was held in Jerusalem (*b. Suk.* 51a-b; cf. 4.9-10) – a ceremony not mentioned in the biblical material or elsewhere. This ceremony was called *Simchat Beit ha-Sho'evah* ('rejoicing of the house of water-drawing').[138] The rabbinic name of the ceremony was possibly derived from the references in the Torah

---

[132] Ralph Marcus, *Josephus, Jewish Antiquities Volume III: Books 7-8* (LCL 281; Cambridge: Harvard University Press, 1934).

[133] H. St. J. Thackeray, *Josephus: The Jewish War, Volume I: Books 1-2* (LCL 203; Cambridge: Harvard University Press, 1927).

[134] Rubenstein, *History of Sukkot*, p. 77.

[135] Ibid., p. 79.

[136] Marianne Dacy, *The Separation of Early Christianity from Judaism* (Amherst: Cambria Press, 2010), p. 125.

[137] Ibid.

[138] This is not to say that the Mishnah preserves the more accurate record of this cultic ritual; indeed, the Mishnah, redacted around 200 CE, should not be used as an historical source for information

to Sukkot being a festival of joy, and to a verse from the prophet Isaiah, which reads, 'Joyfully will you draw water from the fountains of salvation' (Isa. 12.3). This water-drawing ceremony was considered to be the pinnacle of joy for the human spirit (*b. Suk.* 51b). The ceremony included the bringing of water in a golden flask from the Pool of Siloam to the Temple, where it was used in the libations at the altar, while prayers for abundant rain were recited (cf. *m. Suk.* 4.10). The Talmud describes 'four youths' convening in the 'Court of Women' in the Temple, where three large, golden candlesticks 'with four golden bowls on top of each'. They poured oil into the bowls, made wicks and kindled the large lamps. All of Jerusalem was thereby illuminated by this light. The Kohanim (priests) would then finally declare their unswerving devotion to the true God and their rejection of idolatry (*b. Suk.* 51a-b). Johannine commentators have frequently noted these rabbinic references to the water from Siloam, and to the light in the Court of Women and placed them against John 9.7 and 8.12, respectively. What is not often noted is the connection between the celebration of Sukkot and the priests' complete rejection of idolatry, and their commitment to monotheism. As we have occasion to note in Chapter 4, this forms a pertinent parallel with the debate between Jesus and the Jews in John 7–8.

Another feature of the rabbinic description of Sukkot's ritual has important intertextual connections with John 7–8. The 'willow procession' is required to be performed on the Sabbath falling within Sukkot (*m. Suk.* 4.3). On the seventh day of Sukkot, a distinct willow procession was also observed (*m. Suk.* 4.5). The seventh day of Sukkot is called 'Hoshana Rabbah' ('the great praise'). Seven circuits (*hakafot*) were thought to have been made around the Temple altar while celebrants held the 'four species'. On every other day of Sukkot, the procession with the four species was only made once. This last and greatest day (cf. possibly John 7.37) was also the day in which liturgical recitations were said to have taken centre stage (*m. Suk.* 4.5). The first of these recitations ('O Lord, deliver us!') is derived from Ps. 118.25, one of the Hallel Psalms.[139] The psalm continues, 'Bind the festal procession with branches, up to the horns of the altar', a verse which appears to indicate a *Sitz-im-Leben* within the very festival of Sukkot itself.[140] What is of interest here, however, is that R. Yehuda preserves a different recitation on Hoshanah Rabbah from the *piyyutim*: 'אני והוא deliver us!'.[141] The signifier אני והוא replaces the Name ('O Lord') in the alternative recitation, and is usually translated 'I and He' – a distinct, substitutive appellation for God that prevented the worshipper from having to vocalize the Name of God explicitly.[142] Why this matters in the Johannine context is that numerous scholars have drawn attention to John's idiosyncratic formulation 'I and He' spoken by Jesus at the festival of Sukkot as a possible Christological pronouncement of divine oneness with God.

Another theme is the theurgic ritual for rain. The palm branches were apparently gathered together and struck upon the side of the altar (*m. Suk.* 4.6; cf. *b. Suk.* 45b).

about how Sukkot was practised while the second Temple stood (cf. Rubenstein, *History of Sukkot*, p. 103).
[139] Rubenstein, *History of Sukkot*, p. 111 indicates that this derivation is debated in the scholarship, however. See his bibliography, fn. 25, p. 111.
[140] Thus, Rubenstein, *History of Sukkot*, pp. 111–12.
[141] Ibid., p. 112.
[142] Ibid.

The willow itself, more than the other three 'species', 'require copious amounts of water, and rapidly wither in times of drought'.[143] As such, it is an apt symbol of the dependence upon rain for survival.[144] We have already seen the intrinsic connections between Sukkot and water/rain in Zechariah 14, the Mishnah and the Babylonian Talmud's tractate Sukkot (as well as John 7.37-39). The Tosefta adds the detail that water libations were necessary at Sukkot because it is the season for rains, and that God would thus bless the coming rains (*t. Suk.* 3.18).[145] In the rabbinic mythic world view, the foundations of the earth were laid beneath the Temple – the source (or 'the Deep') from which water sprang to flood the earth when rain fell.[146] The rain prayed for at Sukkot thus has fundamental connections with God's blessing the earth with fertility and fecundity. But there are other crucial associations with the symbolism of rain and Sukkot that were worked out in the rabbinic material – the most significant of these in terms of its intertextual connection with John 8.31-59 and the figure of Abraham is the connotations of sin and divine judgement.

According to the Mishnah and Tosefta, God rendered judgement upon the inhabitants of the earth four times a year – once for each season. In *m. RoshHa* 1.2, God is said to judge the world at Pesach with respect to grain, at Shavuot with respect to tree-fruits, at Rosh Hashana with respect to the inner workings of human hearts and at Sukkot with respect to water.[147] That is, the harvest of the earth and the rain due to fall depends upon the behaviour of the people of the world – if there is sin, the bounty is withheld. The Tosefta concurs, but frames the ideas in a different sense, so that at each seasonal festival the people are to perform certain rituals (at Sukkot, the water libation) so that God will bless them with grain, fruits and rain (*t. RoshHa* 1.12). Divine judgement occurs across the board on Rosh Hashana, and it is 'sealed' at Yom Kippur, but specific judgements still occur at seasonal times: at Pesach, on grain; on Shavuot, on the fruit of the tree; on Sukkot, on water (*t. RoshHa* 1.13). The Mishnah is more explicit than the Tosefta in stressing that divine judgement alone determines the amount of rainfall at Sukkot, rather than the proper observance of the water libation cult, meaning that for the traditions preserved in the Mishnah, Sukkot rituals are not strictly theurgic. In another early rabbinic text, Mishnah Ta'anit, there is a discussion between E. Eliezer and R. Joshua about the prayer for the rains. They basically agree that the phrase '[God] who makes the wind blow and the rain descend' refers to 'the powers of rain' and that it begins to take shape in the *tefilah* (the Amida, or Eighteen Benedictions) at some point in Sukkot (*m. Tan.* 1.1; cf. variations in *b. Tan.* 2b and *y. Tan.* 1.1).[148] While Sukkot continues today as a festival of joy rather than of solemn repentance, in the kabbalistic traditions we also see that Hoshanah Rabbah was viewed as 'the close of the judgment of the world' (*Tsav* 31b), perhaps because it closes the High Holy Days, central to which is Yom Kippur.[149]

---

[143] Rubenstein, *History of Sukkot*, p. 117.
[144] Cf. R. Patai, 'The Control of Rain in Ancient Palestine', *HUCA* 14 (1930), p. 275.
[145] www.Sefaria.org.
[146] Rubenstein, *History of Sukkot*, p. 130.
[147] Michael Danby (ed. and trans.), *The Mishnah* (New York: Oxford University Press, 1933).
[148] Cf. Dacy, *The Separation*, p. 135.
[149] Ronald L. Eisenberg, *Jewish Traditions: A JPS Guide* (Philadelphia: Jewish Publication Society, 2008), p. 238. Yom Kippur – the Day of Atonement – is the holiest day of the Jewish calendar, when

The patriarch Abraham features explicitly in a liturgical prayer composed by Eleazar ben Kalir (c. 750 CE) that is still recited today during the Amida on Shemini Atzeret following Sukkot.[150] Kalir's prayer is an alphabetic acrostic poem that sings the connections between the three 'fathers' (Abraham, Isaac and Jacob) and water, as well as the leaders of the Israelites in the exodus (Moses, Aaron and the whole people of Israel). The prayer is inserted in the first blessing of the Amidah (*avot*), which celebrates God as the 'shield of Abraham'; it reads:

> Af-bri is the name of the angel of rain
> Who overcasts (the sky),
> Forms clouds and precipitates them, making them rain
> Water to crown the valley with green
> May rain not be withheld from us because of our unpaid debts
> May the merit of the faithful patriarchs
> Protect their offspring who pray for rain.[151]

אַף־בְּרִי אִתַּת שֵׁם שַׂר מָטָר
לְהַעֲבִיב וּלְהַעֲנִין לְהָרִיק וּלְהַמְטֵר
מַיִם אֵבִים בָּם גֵיא לַעֲטֵר
לְבַל יֵעָצְרוּ בְּנִשְׁיוֹן שְׁטָר
אֱמוּנִים גְּנוֹן בָּם, שׁוֹאֲלֵי מָטָר

The same prayer is recited in a slightly different way in the Land of Israel; it reads: 'Remember the father [Abraham] who followed you like water. You blessed him like a tree planted beside streams of water. You shielded him and rescued him from fire and water. You sought him because he sowed [righteousness] by all waters. For his sake, do not withhold water.'[152] Jonathan Sacks comments on this prayer, noting that rabbinic tradition preserved a story of Abraham cast into a fiery furnace by Nimrod, and was later saved by God. Likewise, rabbinic *aggadah* told the tale of how Satan made a river to block Abraham on his way to sacrifice his son Isaac, but that Abraham walked through the water without fear – when the water was up to Abraham's neck, God rebukes Satan and the water dispelled.[153]

---

the deeds of individuals are said to be inscribed in the Book of Life or the Book of Judgment, and when *selichot* (penitential prayers) are recited throughout a 25-hour period, while fasting from food and water.

[150] Cf. A. Feldman, 'The Bible in Neo-Hebraic Poetry', *JQR* 11, no. 4 (1899), pp. 569–84; Israel Davidson, 'The Study of Mediaeval Hebrew Poetry in the XIX Century', *PAAJR* 1 (1928–1930), pp. 33–48, at p. 36. Kalir's biographical chronology is difficult to establish, with various scholars placing his life anywhere between the seventh and tenth centuries: cf. Alexander Marx, 'A Survey of the Literature of Judaism', *JQR* 14, no. 2 (1923), pp. 275–80, at p. 276.

[151] *The Koren Siddur, with Introduction, Translation and Commentary by Rabbi Sir Jonathan Sacks* (Jerusalem: Koren Publishers, 2009), pp. 846–7.

[152] *The Koren Siddur*, p. 848. Kalir's *piyyutim* are preserved in the Ashkenazic *machzorim*; it has been proposed that the laboured style of Kalir's poetry and its violation of grammatical rule s explains why these *piyyutim* were not preserved in the Sephardic siddurim – thus, William Chomsky, 'The Growth of Hebrew During the Middle Ages', *JQR* 57 (1967), pp. 121–36, at pp. 134–5.

[153] *The Koren Siddur*, pp. 849; 848 – these traditions will be discussed in the following chapters.

The fascinating aspects of these *piyyutim* preserved in the Siddur for recitation after Sukkot lie in the fact that they extend the notion of divine judgement via rain to the realm of the 'merits of the fathers'. While the quasi-doctrinal term זכות אבות ('merits of the fathers') is not used in Kalir's poem, the concept is the same. The congregation pray to God to receive the blessings of rain *for the sake of Abraham* (and Isaac and Jacob) in the (assumed) event that their own righteousness or merits might not suffice to avert the divine judgement. Moreover, Abraham's 'merits' shield his descendants from requisition upon their 'unpaid debts' – a clear economic metaphorization of sin and forgiveness, which we discuss at great length in Chapters 4 and 5 of this book. In the early Jewish and rabbinic understanding, sin was conceived of as 'debt' and the vicarious 'merits' of the fathers were conceived of as a counteracting store of 'credit' that balanced the 'books' so to speak. Of course, Kalir's poem does not predate the rabbinic material, but builds upon it. However, the theoretical approach to the literature undertaken in this study does not draw upon historicist presuppositions, but a broad-ranging intertextuality in which we 'script' the field of literary codes (see Chapter 2). In the Israeli version of Kalir's prayer, we see that Abraham was active in 'sowing righteousness' – a shorthand expression (as we argue in Chapter 5) for Abraham's 'works' that result in his store of efficacious merits that his children (or 'seed') can reply upon. That these codes occupy a central place in the Sukkot liturgy is highly significant for our study of Abraham, Jesus and the Jews in John 8.31-59 at Sukkot, where the notions of the Jews as Abraham's 'seed', their relationship to 'sin' and to Abraham's 'works' (8.32, 33-34, 39-40) all coalesce. Remarkably, no other study to date has foregrounded these critical issues.

Finally, there is one more late rabbinic theologizing of Sukkot that deserves mention. Amoraic traditions reflected and expanded upon the texts from the Torah that depicted the *sukkah* as a symbol of divine care. *Gen. R.* (48.10 on Gen. 18.2-5) states that God protected the Israelites in booths during their journey through the wilderness for the sake of their 'father Abraham', who provided shelter to the three angelic strangers under the Oaks of Mamre (cf. Genesis 18). In contemporary Jewish religious practice, seven *ushpizin* (Aramaic for 'honoured guests') are 'entertained' at Sukkot, a ritual practice deriving from medieval Kabbalah. According to the Zohar (*Emor* 103a), seven biblical 'guests' should be welcomed into the family *sukkah* every year – and the first of them is Abraham (the other guests are Isaac, Jacob, Moses, Aaron, Joseph and King David).[154] Because of Abraham's own hospitality, he is to be invited first into the *sukkah* at Sukkot.[155] The custom of welcoming the *ushpizin* relates inextricably to the mitzvah of *tzedakah* (the Hebrew term for 'righteousness' which may be better translated as 'justice' or loving-kindness towards others). The portion of food set aside for the *ushpizin* is used in the service of *tzedakah* towards the poor. Abraham himself is said to represent these qualities of love and kindness (*Emor* 103a).[156]

---

[154] Cf. Eisenberg, *Jewish Traditions*, p. 235.
[155] Abraham represents the lower order of the sephirot (emanations of the Divine), that of *chesed* (loving-kindness); cf. Morris M. Faierstein, 'Kabbalistic Customs and Rituals: An Introduction', *Conservative Judaism* 60, no. 3 (2008), pp. 90–8, at p. 96.
[156] Eisenberg, *Jewish Traditions*, p. 235.

In sum, the rabbinic material, as well as the other pseudepigraphical post-biblical literature, provides significant thematic expansions upon the associations found in the biblical sources with respect to Sukkot. The motif of joy at Sukkot (already present in Lev. 23.33-43; Deut. 16.13-17; Neh. 8.14-18) is reworked in *Jubilees* with a focus on Abraham as the one who first celebrated Sukkot with profound joy. In 1 Esdras, the motif of joy is reconfigured around Ezra's speech to the gathered exiles to the effect that they no longer mourn for the sins of their ancestors but rejoice in the fact that observance of the Torah can mitigate the divine punishment due to sin. Philo's focus on joy at Sukkot draws attention to the gratitude owed to God for his provision and care, and Josephus' historiographic accounts also refer to the importance of Sukkot as the most joyful of festival celebrations. In John 8.31-59, Jesus alludes to Abraham's 'rejoicing' against the backdrop of Sukkot's celebration in the Temple (8.56-68) – a theme that we explore in detail in Chapter 6 of this book.

Other motifs that, in my view, are not as frequently explicated in studies on Sukkot are important for the attention they draw to key features in the debate between Jesus and the Jews in John 8.31-40. First of all, is the significance of monotheism: in 1 Kgs 8.60 and in Zech. 14.16-19, we saw the reiteration of God's sovereignty and oneness in the context of Sukkot: 'the Lord alone is God'. This is drawn out in the rabbinic texts (e.g. *b. Sukk.* 51) that describe the celebration of the water libations, as the priests turn towards Jerusalem and repudiate idolatry. As we see in Chapter 4, the concept of 'slavery' was often connoted with the worship of foreign gods in the Hebrew Bible, such that the Jews' assertion that they have never been slaves (John 8.32-33) can be read as their legitimate insistence upon fidelity to the Abrahamic covenant. The other motif is that of sin, and its corollary, divine judgement. The biblical texts allude to this already in the context of Sukkot (e.g. Zechariah 14 and the withholding of rain for disobedience), but the theme gains momentum as the rabbinic period evolves. In 1 Chron. 6.22-39 (cf. 1 Kgs 8.33-50), the sin of the people eventuates in divine judgement in the form of being alienated from the land of their inheritance. But in *m. RoshHa* 1.2; 1.13, and in *t. Sukk.* 3.18, the rain is apportioned to the land to the degree in which the people have not strayed into sin – either that, or rain is provided as a blessing for the appropriate celebration of the Sukkot rituals. The medieval poetry of Eleazar ben Kalir develops this even further: rain is prayed for at Sukkot on the basis of the vicarious merits of Abraham, Isaac and Jacob, which rabbinic traditions described as being so powerful that they covered over the sins of Israel and drew down the divine favour (see Chapter 4 for more detail).

This chapter has demarcated the boundaries of the Abraham pericope (8.31-59), delineating its immediate narrative audience, establishing its internal structure and setting it within a complex thematic intertext spanning the larger Sukkot discourse (7.1-8.59). It has also shown that key themes give the Sukkot discourse its coherence, establishing a symbolic world in which the connotations of Sukkot (sin, merit and mercy; repudiation of idolatry; joy; the gift of water/rain; the pre-eminence of Abraham as both exemplar and guest; God's unconditional care for his people; and the learning of Torah) can be appreciated. Several of these key themes overlap and interweave with the figuration of Abraham in early Jewish tradition – as the following chapters demonstrate.

4

Seed of Abraham, slavery and sin (John 8.31-36)

Introduction

In this chapter, I 'script' an intertextual field for particular terms relating to the figure of Abraham as they are expressed in John 8.31-36. 'The Jews' describe themselves as the 'seed of Abraham'; they assert that they have never been 'slaves' to anyone because of this status (8.32-33). But Jesus counters with an assertion about the connection between 'sin' and 'slavery': 'whoever commits sin is a slave' (8.34). He follows with a parabolic point about the intrinsic difference between 'sons' and 'slaves' in the household (8.35-36). Thus, we have a metaphorical complex of terms associated with, and introduced by, the figure of Abraham in ch. 8 vv. 31-36: 'seed', 'slavery', 'sin' and 'sonship' (an alliterative play purely coincidental in English translation). It is important to point out that the idiomatic expression 'seed of Abraham' in ch. 8 v. 32 functions as the determining metaphor in this short passage, out of which the other metaphors flow 'organically'. As such, it would be unduly simplistic to trace an intertextual background for the term 'seed of Abraham' without reference to the associated metaphors of 'sin', 'slavery' and 'sonship'. This is because we are dealing with an intertextuality of collocated concepts.

I am suggesting that the debate between Jesus and 'the Jews' in ch. 8 vv. 31-36 alludes to more than one demonstrable 'intertext'. I examine texts that position Abraham in relation to themes of slavery and sin, focusing upon what it means to derive one's lineage from Abraham, to be 'seed of Abraham'. This textual analysis differs from the singular 'word study' or the scoping of a 'semantic domain' for each noticeable term.[1] Not every use of the noun 'seed' (of Abraham) in the ancient biblical literature will be of relevance to John 8.31-36; the same can be said for every instance of the nouns 'slavery' and 'sin' that bear no direct relation to the figure of Abraham. When scripting an intertextual field such as for ch. 8 vv. 31-36, a combination of semantic factors such as context, connotation and conceptual metaphorical usage are more crucial than a narrow lexical examination.

---

[1] For the most relevant, trenchant critique of the 'word study' method in biblical studies, see James Barr, *The Semantics of Biblical Language*.

This analysis will reveal that within the Jews' speech lies a subtle register frequently undetected in the secondary literature: they express a sense of identity based on Abraham that is 'legitimate' on its own terms but obscured by the rhetorical discourse of John 8 more broadly – a discourse I have previously described as 'monologic' following the theories of Mikhail Bakhtin.[2] Detecting this grain of resistance in the speech of 'the Jews' is a means of 'resisting' the caricatures imputed to the Jews in the scholarly commentaries. The Jews' speech in John 8.33 ought not to be interpreted as 'proud' assertions of their 'aristocratic' genealogy – as many commentators presume – but a multivalent way of emphasizing their unbreakable covenant with God, and their trust in God's faithful help.

This caricatured interpretation of the Jews in John 8.33 is, unfortunately, still prevalent in the Gospel commentary tradition.[3] Since the late nineteenth century, commentators have been interpreting the Jews' words in ch. 8 v. 33 ('We are seed of Abraham, and have never been slaves of anyone') as indicative of their inordinate 'religious privilege', their 'national boast' and even their 'close affinity with the powers of evil'.[4] The Jews' self-asserted freedom was interpreted by commentators as 'empty pretensions' and unadulterated 'arrogance'.[5] Moreover, their 'boasting' in Abraham was inferred as evidence of their 'self-delusion' because they were not, in reality, free.[6] For example, Rudolf Bultmann concluded that the Jews of John 8 'commit themselves to their lost condition' for they are 'blind men who think that they see'.[7] Even the moderate Raymond Brown veered towards pejorative language, writing that the Jews' boast was 'ill-founded' and based on a 'privileged' world view.[8] Brown's contemporary, Rudolf Schnackenburg, concurred, as he commented upon the Jews' 'pride and complacency'.[9] Ernst Haenchen wrote that the Jews 'appear to be free, but they will really be free only as Christians'.[10] Another influential commentator wrote that the Jews' unfounded assertion was 'the boast of the rabbis' and 'a typical statement ... of Jewish propaganda calculated to destroy faith in Jesus'.[11] Still later, other commentators have described the Jews' response as 'fickle', with 'an ugly, challenging tone' based on an overweening sense of 'inherited privilege'. Or worse: as indicative of 'a vicious slavery to moral failure' and 'an evil and enslaving devotion to created things'.[12]

---

[2] Sheridan, 'Issues in the Translation', pp. 671–96.
[3] Sheridan, 'Seed of Abraham, Slavery and Sin', pp. 313–32.
[4] Cf. Brooke Foss Westcott, *The Gospel according to St. John* (London: John Murray, 1892), p. 133.
[5] Ernst Hengstenberg, *Über den Eingang des Evangeliums St. Johannis* (Berlin: Schlawitz, 1859), pp. 453, 450.
[6] John Henry Bernard, *A Critical and Exegetical Commentary on the Gospel according to St. John* (2 vols; ICC; Edinburgh: T&T Clark, 1928), p. 306.
[7] Rudolf Bultmann, *Das Evangelium des Johannes* (KEK; Göttingen: Vandenhoeck & Ruprecht, 1941; English edition: *The Gospel of John: A Commentary*; trans. George Beasley-Murray et al.; Philadelphia: Westminster, 1971), p. 433.
[8] Brown, *The Gospel according to John, I–XXII*, p. 355.
[9] Schnackenburg, *The Gospel*, 2.207.
[10] Ernst Haenchen, *John* (trans. Robert W. Funk; Hermeneia 2 vols; Philadelphia: Fortress, 1984), p. 28.
[11] George Beasley-Murray, *John* (WBC 36; Waco: Word Books, 2nd edn, 1999), p. 133.
[12] Carson, *The Gospel*, pp. 348, 350.

Such interpretive embellishments import concerns more relevant to secularist modernity than to religious antiquity. The latitude that Gospel commentators have taken with the Jews' presumed psychological state in ch. 8 vv. 32-33 is stunning. Carson called the Jews 'self-centred' and without 'heart for God'.[13] Other commentators prescribed a limited self-awareness to the Jews – an inability to see outside 'the framework of their Jewishness'.[14] Worst of all, one recent commentator pontificated that the Jews of John 8.32-33 were hypocrites 'following the enslaved tradition of Judaism', symbolically representing 'all those who abuse religion, and all who, in place of genuine believing, substitute some form of triviality, superstition, idol or lie'.[15] As recently as 2012, Frederick Bruner continued this interpretive trend, remarking that the Jews have assumed they are without 'problems', and that they 'bring pedigree and privileges of the highest sort' into their relationship with Jesus; sardonically, Bruner added, 'these converts ['the Jews who had believed'] don't *need* Jesus' promised freedom; they already have it in Abraham'.[16] What solution does Bruner posit? That the Jews be 'converted from their righteousness to a confession of their ties to sin' – and this is surely an unwarranted evangelical extrapolation.[17]

Although this pejorative characterization of the Jews in John 8.32-33 is highly prevalent, there are – thankfully – many commentarial exceptions. Indeed, several recent German commentaries on the Gospel appear to be self-consciously correcting this anti-Jewish trend. For example, Christian Dietzfelbinger wrote that the Jews' reference to their freedom in Abraham 'does not mean an external, political freedom, but expresses the dignity [*die Würde*] of Israel as God's "first-born son" (Exod 4.22; cf. Hos 11.1), their covenant which, throughout each age, cannot be forfeited'.[18] Similarly, Hartwig Thyen wrote that the Jews 'speak of their sense of religious freedom which redounds to them as the chosen, covenant people of God, something that almost goes without saying'.[19] Michael Theobald explicitly disputes the older commentarial tradition that interpreted the Jews' response as evidence of their 'self-delusion'. Theobold insists that the debate between Jesus and the Jews should be read as the intersection of 'two *theological* convictions that are brought together: being children of Abraham – participating in the freedom afforded by their covenant with God – and faith in Jesus as the Messiah'.[20]

This brief tour of the polemically charged tone of the Gospel commentaries provides sufficient reason as to why a responsible, 'resistant' intertextual reading of the passage

[13] Ibid., p. 352.
[14] Herman Ridderbos, *The Gospel of John: A Theological Commentary* (Grand Rapids: Eerdmans, 1997), p. 309.
[15] Thomas Brodie, *The Gospel according to John: A Literary and Theological Commentary* (New York: Oxford University Press, 1993), pp. 328-9. Brodie infers, further, that the Jews were 'corrupt' and apt to let 'evil flourish' (idem, p. 329).
[16] Bruner, *The Gospel of John*, p. 532. Emphasis in the original.
[17] Ibid., p. 532.
[18] Christian Dietzfelbinger, *Das Evangelium nach Johannes* (2 vols.; ZBK; Zürich: Theologischer Verlag, 2001), 1.251. My translation.
[19] Hartwig Thyen, *Das Johannesevangelium* (HNT 6; Tübingen: Mohr Siebeck, 2005), p. 437. My translation.
[20] Michael Theobald, *Das Evangelium nach Johannes: Kapitel 1-12* (RNT; Regensburg: Friedrich Pustet, 2009), pp. 592-3. My translation.

is so important. In what follows, therefore, I interrogate the use of the concept 'seed' of Abraham in the ancient and early Jewish literature, to assess what connotations accrete around the idiomatic expression. This extensive section of textual analysis proceeds according to literary chronology *and* thematic categories accepted in the scholarship. That is, the textual data are analysed beginning with the biblical material, then the post-biblical, which includes Apocrypha and Pseudepigrapha, the New Testament (NT), other Second Temple literature (Philo, Josephus) and early rabbinic literature. Within each of these categories, certain subcategories are classed according to the density of the relevant material – for example within the Torah, there is the 'Abraham Cycle' which contains a solid amount of allusions, and the particular components of the prophetic texts that build on aspects of associations between Abraham and slavery.

Part 1: Scripting the intertextual field

The Hebrew Bible

The Abraham Cycle: Gen. 12.1-9; 13.14-16; 15.1-20; 17.1-27; 21.8-14; 22.15-19

The first reference to the 'seed' of Abraham occurs in Gen. 12.7 in the context of a short narrative about God's call to Abram (12.1-9).[21] Up to this point in Genesis, Abraham has only been known to the reader as the son of Terah (11.31), but here he erupts into the story (Gen. 12.1) as a figure uniquely called by God to become a 'great nation' (12.2a) and to be a 'blessing' (12.2b) – in fact, to become a figure in whom 'all the families of the earth will be blessed' (12.3). The condition for these blessings is Abraham's obedience to God's injunction that he leave his country and his 'father's house' and go to an unnamed land that God will show him (12.1).[22] Abraham's response is prompt: he 'went, as the Lord had told him, together with his wife Sarai and his nephew Lot' (12.4-5).[23] On the way, Abraham is met by 'the Lord', who tells him, 'To your seed I will give this land' (MT: הזאת הארץ את אתן לזרעך; LXX: Τῷ σπέρματί σου δώσω τὴν γῆν ταύτην 12.7).[24] That is, the Lord intends the land of Canaan *not* for Abraham – nor indeed,

---

[21] For the sake of consistency, I will use the name 'Abraham' throughout my analysis, rather than 'Abram' and 'Abraham' separately.

[22] There are acknowledged syntactical and morphological ambiguities in the 'call of Abraham' in Gen. 12.1-3, especially around the sequences of the verbs involved (the imperative + cohortative structures). For further discussion, see Keith N. Grüneberg, *Abraham, Blessing, and the Nations: A Philological and Exegetical Study of Genesis 12.3 in Its Narrative Context* (BZAW 332; Berlin/New York: de Gruyter, 2003), pp. 143–5. Recently, Joel Baden has eschewed the 'successive' interpretation of the string of verbs, arguing rather that they be read as temporally simultaneous (idem, 'The Morpho-Syntax of Genesis 12.1-3: Translation and Interpretation', *CBQ* 72, no. 2 (2010), pp. 223–37). However, the resulting connotative changes of Baden's alternative are, in my view, not significant enough to warrant abandoning the status quo in this area (p. 237).

[23] The fact that Lot came with him has been taken to mean that Abraham was not fully obedient: cf. Eslinger, 'Prehistory in the Call to Abraham', pp. 189–208, at p. 197. Cf. Curzer, 'Abraham, the Faithless', pp. 344–61.

[24] In Septuagint Greek, the noun σπέρμα while grammatically singular, has the connotative force of the plural. That is, it is used to refer to the multiple offspring of one father. The noun σπέρμα can

it appears, for the Canaanites who were 'then in the land' (12.6) – but for Abraham's 'seed', his posterity.[25] Abraham himself does not dwell, but only sojourns in the land, receiving revelations from the Lord within it (12.7b).

The next mention of Abraham's 'seed' occurs in Gen. 13.14-16, when Abraham returns north after a dramatic stay in Egypt (12.10-20), and a sojourn via Bethel and Ai, to the place where he first erected an altar to the Lord (13.1-4). What follows is a tense dispute between the shepherds of Abraham and Lot due to their competition for scant resources (13.5-7); Abraham deals courteously with Lot and they part ways,[26] dividing the land between them (13.8-9), as Abraham moves on to Canaan (13.12a).[27] Then, the Lord speaks to Abraham for a third time, with a more fully developed expression of the promise:

> Lift up your eyes and look from the place where you are, northward and southward and eastward and westward, for all the land that you see I will give to you and to your seed (MT: לְזַרְעֲךָ/LXX: τῷ σπέρματί σου) forever. I will make your seed (זַרְעֲךָ/τὸ σπέρμα σου) as the dust of the earth, so that if one can count the dust of the earth, your seed (זַרְעֲךָ/τὸ σπέρμα σου) can also be counted. (Gen. 13.14-16)[28]

While residing in Canaan, Abraham has a 'vision', in which the Lord counsels him to 'fear not', for his reward will be great (Gen. 15.1).[29] But Abraham objects, arguing that there is no greater reward than having 'seed' of his own – and this, he claims, has so far been denied him (15.1-2a). Abraham laments that 'Eliezar of Damascus', a hired member of the household, is his only heir (15.2b-3). The Lord replies that 'none but [Abraham's] very own' (MT: כִּי־אִם אֲשֶׁר יֵצֵא מִמֵּעֶיךָ/LXX: ὃς ἐξελεύσεται ἐκ σοῦ) will be his heir (15.4). Abraham is then told to: 'Look toward heaven and number the stars,

---

literally refer to plant-seed (cf. Gen. 1.11; 47.19) but it is also used in a metaphorical sense for the 'male seed', that is, semen (cf. Lev. 18.21), which was thought in the Ancient Near East to be the primary reproductive agent. By extension, the nouns σπέρμα/σπέρματος came to be used of human beings themselves, when their status as descendants, children or posterity was emphasized (cf. 4 Macc. 18.1). The Hebrew root זרע likewise expresses the concept of 'seed' in both an agricultural and human biological (albeit metaphorical) sense (Lust, Eynikel and Hauspin (eds), *Greek-English Lexicon of Septuagint Greek* (rev. edn; Peabody: Hendriksen, 2008; σπέρμα sv.)).

[25] As also noted by Joel Baden, *The Promise to the Patriarchs* (New York/Oxford: Oxford University Press, 2013), p. 66.

[26] Lot's choice to reside outside of Canaan, 'eliminates him as Abram's heir'; cf. Victor P. Hamilton, *Genesis 1–17* (NICOT; Grand Rapids: Eerdmans, 2001), p. 393. Lot's removal from the plot could also be seen as a technique to focus more on Abraham's occupation of the land, the chief motif of ch. 12 v. 1; thus, Dan Rickett, 'Rethinking the Place and Purpose of Genesis 13', *JSOT* 36, no. 1 (2011), pp. 31–53, at p. 51.

[27] There may be an allusion here to the Cain–Abel narrative (Abel, the shepherd of Genesis 4), where strife over the scarcity of agricultural resources led to fratricide rather than, as here, amicable resolution and equal division.

[28] The promise is more explicit than that found in Gen. 12.7. The promise is of 'all the land' (13.14a), it is given both to Abraham and his seed, not merely the latter (13.14b), and it is given in perpetuity ('...forever', 13.16). See Gordon J. Wenham, *Genesis 1–15* (Waco: WBC, 1986), p. 298.

[29] The divine reassurance may be necessary if Abraham is in a state of 'present trauma' during his vision, where the introductory אל־תירא (15.1) implies trauma (Gen. 21.17; 26.24; 35.17; 43.23; [46.3]; 50.19, 21; see, Paul R. Williamson, *Abraham, Israel and the Nations: The Patriarchal Promise and Its Covenantal Development in Genesis* (JSOTSup 315; Sheffield: Sheffield Academic Press, 2000), p. 96.

if you are able to number them... so shall be your seed' (MT: זרעך/LXX: τὸ σπέρμα σου; 15.5). The narrator provides Abraham's response: 'and he believed the Lord, and he counted it to him as righteousness' (15.6; MT: והאמן ביהוה ויחשבה לו צדקה/LXX: καὶ ἐπίστευσεν Αβραμ τῷ θεῷ, καὶ ἐλογίσθη αὐτῷ εἰς δικαιοσύνην).[30]

The promise expressed in Gen. 15.1-6 plays on the grammatically singular form of the noun 'seed', even as it implies a plurality: Abraham speaks of his desired biological son and heir (15.1-2), but the Lord's promise reveals that Abraham's 'seed' will be multitudinous like the stars in the sky (15.5). However, Abraham is uncertain – or at the very least, curious – about this aspect of the promise: 'O, Lord, how am I to know that I shall possess it [the land]?' (15.8). By way of reply, the Lord commands Abraham to cut five species of animals in half (15.9), with which the latter duly complies (15.10-11).[31] What follows next in the narrative is mysterious and unexpected (see 15.12-20). Abraham falls into a 'deep sleep' and a 'dreadful and great darkness' falls upon him (15.12). In this state, the 'word of the Lord' comes to Abraham, saying, 'Know for certain that your seed (MT: זרעך/LXX: σπέρματί) will be sojourners in a land that is not theirs and will be slaves (MT: ועבדום/LXX: δουλώσουσιν αὐτοὺς) there, and they will be afflicted for four hundred years' (15.13). But eventually the Lord will bring judgement upon that 'nation' and, in the 'fourth generation', Abraham's seed will 'come out with great possessions' (15.15). The only explanation given for the duration of servitude is that 'the sin of the Amorites is not yet complete' (MT: כי לא־שלם עון האמרי עד־הנה/ LXX: οὔπω γὰρ ἀναπεπλήρωνται αἱ ἁμαρτίαι τῶν Αμορραίων ἕως τοῦ νῦν; 15.16b).[32] Once the 'measure' of the Amorites' iniquity is 'full', possession of Canaan will revert to Abraham's 'seed', and the latter's slavery will end. This explanation ties important metaphors together: 'sin' as something calculable, and which reaches its 'full measure' when punishment arrives; slavery as something attenuated by the release of divine punishment upon sinners; and the 'seed of Abraham' as mysteriously enslaved for a time, but due to return to their land of promise.[33]

---

[30] The literature on this verse is extensive, much of it caught up in the Pauline doctrine of 'justification by faith' – see Hermann Gunkel, *Genesis* (trans. Mark E. Biddle; 3rd edn; Macon: Mercer University Press, 1997 (orig. 1910)); H. Seebas, 'Gen 15,2b', *ZAW* 75 (1963), pp. 317–19; N. Lohfink, *Die Landverheissung als Eid* (Stuttgart: Katholisches Bibelwerk, 1967), p. 32; Claus Westermann, *Genesis 37–50* (Neukirchener, 1981), p. 263. The Hebrew text does not make it clear who reckons righteousness to whom – does Abraham 'count' it (i.e. the promise) to God as 'righteousness'? (cf. Manfred Oeming, 'Ist Genesis 15,6 ein Beleg für die Anrechnung des Glaubens zur Gerechtigkeit?' *ZAW* 95, no. 2 (1983), pp. 182–97, at p. 185). If, in the MT, we take לו as a reflexive connector to the subject of the verb חשב Abraham could be reckoning to himself his own faith as an act of righteousness. Or is Abraham the subject of both verses: he believes in God, and is therefore 'reckoned' as 'righteous' *by* God? (the consensus view, more in line with the LXX translation). Chapter 5 will discuss the use of צדק in the HB as a '(righteous) work', which accrues merits for the doer.

[31] There is also much debate in the ancient literature about the tone of Abraham's question, and whether it signified Abraham's doubt in God; the suffering of Abraham's 'seed' in Egypt would thus have been divine punishment for doubt.

[32] Canaan is the land of the Amorites at this point (cf. Josh. 24.5-7), who are elsewhere in the Torah depicted as being removed from their land as a punishment for their iniquity (Deut. 9.5).

[33] We begin to see the conceptualization of sin (ἁμαρτία/עון) as generationally expansive, accumulative and due to be 'repaid' or 'requited' through punishment (cf. Jer. 27.7; 29.10; Isa. 40.1-15); sin deeply affects the land and has profound consequences for the fate of its inhabitants (cf. 2 Chron. 36.20-21). This argument will be brought to the fore as this chapter progresses.

The Genesis 15 narrative concludes at night: when it is completely dark, the Lord makes a 'smoking fire pot and a flaming torch' pass between the halved animals laid out by Abraham, vividly illustrating the 'cutting' of the covenant between God and Abraham.[34] Then, the Lord restates the promise to Abraham about his 'seed' inheriting 'this land' – although now the geographical terrain is considerably expanded (15.18b-20). What is striking about the covenant made with Abraham in Gen. 15.1-20 is its promissory nature: no conditions are laid down for Abraham to follow, which possibly led early Christians to use this proof text as evidence of Abraham's faith warranting God's unconditional regard.[35] The relationship between Abraham's 'seed' and the land in Genesis 15 is very marked, and elements of the language are Deuteronomistic in formulation.[36] Abraham's call out from Ur is established as the pattern for God's eventual deliverance of Abraham's 'seed' out of Egyptian exile.[37]

The next reference to Abraham's 'seed' draws upon the language of mutual obligation in the covenant of circumcision – which is a new addition to the theme of Abraham's 'seed' (Gen. 17.1-27).[38] God, who is revealed now as 'El Shaddai', also promises Abraham that Sarah will conceive and give birth to a son within the year (17.15-21).[39] Abraham promptly responds by having all the men in his household circumcised (17.22-27). Even the men 'not of [Abraham's] "seed"' should be circumcised, according to the divine command (17.12b).[40] In this text, both the cessation of Sarah's infertility and the promises made to Abraham are intricately connected to the covenant of circumcision of which Abraham is the original bearer. The text is also replete with references to Abraham's eventual 'fruitfulness': he will be made 'exceedingly numerous' (17.2b), become the 'father of a multitude of nations' (17.4, 5), be made 'exceedingly fruitful' (17.6a); he will be 'made nations' of (17.6b) and 'kings' will proceed from him (17.6c; and, note, from Sarah too: 17.16); Abraham's 'seed' shall possess the land in perpetuity, and be in covenant with the God of Abraham for all time through the sign of 'the flesh' (17.7, 8, 9, 14). Despite Abraham's incredulous response (17.17), God insists that his

---

[34] The ceremony in Genesis 15 has been viewed less a ritual (animal) sacrifice and more a rite of contract between the two parties, God and Abraham: W. Robertson Smith, *The Religion of the Semites* (3rd edn; London: A&C Black, 1927), pp. 48–81; E. Bikerman, 'Couper une alliance', *Archies d'Histoire du droit Oriental* 5 (1950/51), pp. 133–56. More likely, it is a covenant ratification rite, where Yhwh binds himself to his promise to Abraham in promissory nature: Gerhard F. Hasel, 'The Meaning of the Animal Rite in Genesis 15', *JSOT* 19 (1981), pp. 61–78.

[35] Cf. Levenson, *Inheriting Abraham*, p. 44.

[36] Cf. Diana Lipton, *Revisions of the Night: Politics and Promises in the Patriarchal Dreams of Genesis* (Sheffield: Sheffield Academic Press, 1999), p. 209.

[37] Moshe Anbar, 'Genesis 15: A Conflation of Two Deuteronomic Narratives', *JBL* 101, no. 1 (1982), pp. 39–55, at p. 55.

[38] Desmond Alexander, 'Genesis 22 and the Covenant of Circumcision', *JSOT* 25 (1983), pp. 17–22, at p. 18.

[39] Van Seters argues that 'covenant' and 'oath' (promise) are equated here, which stresses the promissory nature of the covenant; this is an important conceptual development because it shows how the promise of 'seed' and 'land' to Abraham is covenantal in its expression; see J. van Seeters, *Abraham in History and Tradition* (New Haven/London: Yale University Press, 1975), p. 283.

[40] The antiquity of circumcision in Israel and in Canaan prior to the conquest is well documented: Erich Isaac, 'Circumcision as a Covenant Rite', *Anthropos* 59, nos. 3 and 4 (1964), pp. 444–56, at p. 451.

covenant will be with Isaac, the son of Sarah (17.19, 21) and Isaac's *seed*, although Ishmael will not be forgotten (17.20).

Reference to Abraham's 'seed' occurs seven times in this lengthy passage (17.7a, b, c, 8a; 9, 10a, 19), mostly predicated of Abraham directly (except ch. 17 v. 19 which refers to the covenant made with Isaac and his 'seed'). Each reference is made in connection with the everlasting nature of the covenant. The covenant endures *through* Abraham's seed, continuing throughout the generations. The rich texture of concepts connected to Abraham's 'seed' thus far include: the promise of the land, perpetual fecundity, the covenant of circumcision and the promise of a specific son and heir. Abraham's status as 'father' is about to be realized, but the tension between this and the prospects of his existing, slave-born son are also only beginning (cf. the later narrative of 20.1–21.16). The necessity of Ishmael's expulsion from the household with his mother, the 'slave-woman' Hagar, is made bearable for Abraham because of God's promise: 'I will make a nation of the son of the slave woman also, because he is your seed' (MT: זרעך/LXX: σπέρματί; 20.13). Abraham therefore sends Hagar and Ishmael on their way early the next morning, into the wilderness, with minimal alimentary provisions (20.14a).[41] The focus of this narrative is the *naming* of Abraham's seed through Isaac rather than Ishmael.[42]

The next reference to Abraham's 'seed' occurs in the narrative traditionally called the *Akedah*, the story of Abraham's near-sacrifice of his son, Isaac, on Mount Moriah (Gen. 22.1-19).[43] At the conclusion of the event, an angel speaks to Abraham 'from heaven', for the 'second time', relating the words of the Lord in direct discourse:

> By myself I have sworn, declares the Lord, because you have done this and have not withheld your son, your only son, I will surely bless you and I will surely multiply your seed as the stars of heaven and as the sand that is on the seashore. And your seed shall possess the gate of their enemies, and in your seed, shall all the nations of the earth be blessed, because you have obeyed my voice. (22.16-18)

The promised multiplication of Abraham's seed in these verses is reminiscent of Genesis 15 and 17 with the same metaphors of 'sand' and 'stars' employed. Finally, we re-encounter the notion of all the families or nations of the earth being blessed in

---

[41] Thomas B. Dozeman, 'The Wilderness and Salvation History in the Hagar Story', *JBL* 177, no. 1 (1998), pp. 23–43, views the expulsion as the narrator's way of casting Hagar as a Moses-type figure of heroic qualities.

[42] G. W. Ramsey, 'Is Name-Giving an Act of Domination in Genesis 2.23 and Elsewhere?' *CBQ* 50, no. 1 (1988), pp. 24–35.

[43] There is an extensive body of secondary literature on the *Akedah*. An exemplary text is Jon D. Levenson, *The Death and Resurrection of the Beloved Son: The Transformation of Child Sacrifice in Judaism and Christianity* (New Haven: Yale University Press, 1995), and the bibliography therein. Cf. Ed Noort and Eibert Tigchelaar (eds), *The Sacrifice of Isaac: The Aqedah (Genesis 22) and its Interpretations* (TBN 4; Leiden/Boston: Brill, 2002); Bradley Beach and Matthew Powell (eds), *Interpreting Abraham: Journeys to Moriah* (Minneapolis: Fortress Press, 2014). Because of the influence of the *Akedah* myth on Western intellectual history, the scholarship is prohibitively profuse, spiralling into debates within German idealism, Freudian psychoanalysis and other forms of biblical reception; cf. David Baumgardt, 'Man's Morals and God's Will: The Meaning of Abraham's Sacrifice', *Commentary* 10 (1950), pp. 244–51.

Abraham's seed. In the *Akedah*, the Lord's promises are expressed on the condition that Abraham willingly sacrifices the son of the covenant, Isaac himself; but this is a condition that is revealed only 'after the fact'. God does not imply that blessings will come to Abraham's seed *if* he offers Isaac (22.1) – he only commands Abraham to do so, so that the reader is aware of some kind of 'test'.[44] After Abraham has almost accomplished the sacrifice, his hand is stayed, and he is rewarded with numerous blessings promised to his 'seed'. The *Akedah* was one of the most commented upon texts of antiquity.[45] Worth noting for the purposes of this chapter is the rereading presented in *Targum Pseudo-Jonathan (Tg. Ps.-Jon.)* (on Genesis 22), which although late (dated c. 850 CE), provides continuity of perspective on the role of Isaac in the *Akedah* from the Tannaitic midrashim.[46] For example, the Targumist adds, in v. 18, a reference to Isaac's 'merit' (זכת): all the peoples of the earth will be blessed, God tells Abraham, 'because of the merit of your son, because you have obeyed my voice'.[47]

Texts outside the Abraham Cycle: Gen. 26.1-5; 26.23-24b; 28.4-5, 13-15; 35.11-12

There are five final texts in Genesis outside of the narrated life of Abraham that refer to the 'seed' of Abraham. These final texts occur, therefore, as promises made to the subsequent patriarchs, Isaac and Jacob, but the *name* of Abraham is still invoked in the context of the original promise of the land to his 'seed'. Moreover, in these texts, we begin to see the emergence of new motifs regarding Abraham's 'seed': the rendering of blessings to Abraham's 'seed' *for Abraham's sake*, and the notion of Abraham 'keeping' the laws and commandments of God for the benefit of his 'seed'.

The text of Gen. 26.1-33 deals with the narrative encounter between the grown Isaac and King Abimelech of the Philistines. A famine in the land precipitates Isaac's move southward, into Gerar, where he settles and resides – but the Lord appears to Isaac and warns him not to go further into the land of Egypt:

> Reside in this land, and I will be with you and will bless you, because to you and to your seed I will give all these lands (כי־לך ולזרעך אתן את־ כל־הארצת/τῷ σπέρματί σου δώσω πᾶσαν τὴν γῆν ταύτην), and I will establish the oath that I swore to Abraham your father. I will multiply your seed as the stars of heaven and will give to your

---

[44] Also confirmed lexicographically; cf. R. W. L. Moberly, 'The Earliest Commentary on the Akedah', *VT* 38, no. 3 (1988), pp. 302–23, at p. 304.

[45] Thus, the following articles in Noort and Tigchelaar (eds), *The Sacrifice of Isaac*: F. Garcia Marrtinez, 'The Sacrifice of Isaac in 4Q225', pp. 44–57 and van Ruiten, 'Abraham, Job and the Book of *Jubilees*', pp. 58–85.

[46] Ernest G. Clarke (ed.), *Targum Pseudo-Jonathan of the Pentateuch: Text and Concordance* (Hoboken: Ktav Publishing, 1984). On the *Akedah* in *Tg. Ps.-Jonathan*, see J. Bowker, *The Targums and Rabbinic Literature* (Cambridge: Cambridge University Press, 1969), pp. 224–34.

[47] In some editions, the word for 'merit' is translated as 'righteousness' – this will be an important point to keep in mind for the analysis of the rabbinic concept of the זכת אבות (the 'merits of the fathers') later in this chapter, and in the argument presented in Chapter 5, which deals with the evolution of the concepts 'works' – 'righteousness' – 'merits' in the Second Temple and early rabbinic periods. Note also that in *Tg. Ps.-Jonathan* to Gen. 22.14, Abraham prays that when 'the children of Isaac' call on God in 'their hour of need' the 'binding of Isaac' shall serve to 'remit and forgive their sins'.

seed all these lands. And in your seed, all the nations of the earth shall be blessed because Abraham obeyed my voice and kept my charge, my commandments, my statutes, and my laws. (Gen. 26.2b-5)[48]

The language here mirrors the covenant blessings bestowed on Abraham in the prior texts of Genesis.[49] But in the current text, it is not *Abraham's* seed that receive the promise, but Isaac's *own* seed. As Abraham's son and heir, Isaac inherits the promises from God: he is himself the 'seed' of Abraham, but he and his own 'seed' will be likewise blessed (26.4). Notably, this blessing accrues to Isaac *for the sake of* Abraham – the phrase 'your father Abraham' (לאברהם אביך/Ἀβρααμ τῷ πατρί σου) enters the specific form of the patriarchal promises at this juncture.[50] The land was sworn to 'your father Abraham' by oath; that same land will be given to Isaac and to Isaac's 'seed' (26.3).

Indeed, the function of Abraham in this version of the promise is perhaps its most remarkable element. The realization of the promise is not nearly as contingent upon Isaac's present obedience as it is upon Abraham's past exemplarity. To be sure, the blessing Isaac will receive appears to be conditioned upon his willingness to sojourn in Gerar and to avoid Egypt (cf. 26.2a), but the original covenant has been established before Isaac's birth (26.3b). Isaac's 'seed' will be multiplied, and in them all nations of the earth will be blessed, *because* Abraham was superlative in obedience: Abraham obeyed God's voice, kept God's charge (/משמרת/πρόσταγμα), commandments (/מצוה/ ἐντολή), statutes (/חקה/δικαίωμα) and laws (/תורה/νόμιμος; 26.5). This text reveals that Abraham's exemplarity has a vicariously beneficial effect beyond Abraham's lifetime, and that Abraham's 'seed' continue to receive the promises for the sake of their 'father Abraham' and his observance of God's laws.

The detailed description of Abraham observing the Law of God (not just God's 'charge', but also his 'commandments', his 'statutes' and his 'laws') hints at how the 'legacy' of Abraham was being formulated in the biblical period. Did not Abraham merely observe *one* commandment – circumcision (Genesis 17)? God's statutes, laws and commandments were not relayed until Sinai, so does this text propose that Abraham somehow kept the whole of the Torah before it was given?[51] Indeed, in Genesis 18, we see that in Abraham's lifetime, he was depicted as instructing his posterity to obey the laws of God: Abraham will 'command his *children* (בניו/τοῖς υἱοῖς αὐτοῦ) and his *household*' (ביתו/ᾧ οἴκῳ αὐτοῦ) by *doing righteousness and justice* (לאשות צדקה ושפט/ ποιεῖν δικαιοσύνην καὶ κρίσιν) so that the Lord may bring to Abraham 'what he has

---

[48] Cf. Levenson, 'The Conversion of Abraham, pp. 3–40. Levenson notes near exact the parallels between this text ('charge', 'laws', 'commandments') and Deut. 11.1, arguing that Gen. 26.5 presents Abraham as a meticulous observer of the Sinaitic revelation before it was given.
[49] Boase argues that 'Isaac has no actions in the chapter [26] that do not mirror or echo Abraham's' and that this is clearly intentional; Elizabeth Boase, 'Life in the Shadows: The Role and Function of Isaac in Genesis: Synchronic and Diachronic Readings', *VT* 51, no. 3 (2001), pp. 312–35, at p. 319.
[50] Boase, 'Life in the Shadows', p. 320: 'The promises extended to Jacob do not contain this conditional element. For Isaac alone, the promises are extended on account of his parentage, reinforcing his position as a link between two strong generations'.
[51] Levenson, *Inheriting Abraham*, pp. 141–8, provides an extensive discussion. We will return to this point towards the end of Chapter 5, when viewing 'the works of Abraham' (cf. John 8.39-41) as his observance of the Torah in the post-biblical period.

promised him' (Gen. 18.19).⁵² Yet, Gen. 26.1-5 reveals that outside the 'Abraham Cycle' there is a rhetorical elevation of Abraham and his legacy, and more importantly, I suggest, the emergence of a perspective about the real efficacy of Abraham's 'works' (conceived in terms of his law observance) to produce vicarious blessings for his 'seed', in line with the covenant promises. Abraham begins to be remembered both as a figure of 'merit' *and* as one who kept God's laws – and what holds these strands together in these texts is the concept of Abraham's 'seed' (Gen. 26.4), or his 'household' and 'children' (Gen. 18.18).

The motif of the divine blessings imparted 'for the sake of Abraham' continues in Gen. 26.23-24b. Isaac sojourns in Gerar (26.6-22), moves north to Beersheba (26.23), and then encounters the Lord in a night-time vision (26.24), who tells him, 'I am the God of Abraham your father; fear not, for I am with you and will bless you and multiply your seed for my servant Abraham's sake' (MT: והרביתי את־זרעך בעבור אברהם עבדי/ LXX: πληθυνῶ τὸ σπέρμα σου διὰ Αβρααμ τὸν πατέρα σου; 26.24b).⁵³ Isaac, in response, builds an altar, calls upon the 'name of the Lord' and his 'servants' dig a well there (26.25b). This version of the promise to the patriarchs reinforces what was established in Gen. 26.1-5, namely, that Isaac's seed will be blessed *because of Abraham*, not because of anything Isaac has done. In ch. 26 v. 24b, Abraham is referred to as the Lord's 'servant' – a rare but not uncommon appellation for Abraham in the Tanakh. The general sense of the promise seems to be that Isaac's 'seed' will be multiplied 'for Abraham's sake', because Abraham was God's servant.⁵⁴

In Genesis 28, Isaac blesses his son Jacob with 'the blessing of Abraham' (28.4); this blessing is later confirmed for Jacob in a vivid dream (28.13). The prior narrative context prepares the ground for Jacob's reception of the promise to his 'seed'. In Gen. 27.1-40, Jacob and his mother Rebekah successfully plot to steal the 'birthright' from Jacob's twin brother Esau, by taking advantage of Esau's ravenous hunger and Isaac's failing eyesight. When Esau's retaliatory anger catches up with Jacob, Rebekah advises him to flee to Haran – the territory of Abraham's remaining kin (27.41-45). Rebekah fears that her son might take a Hittite wife along the way, so Isaac intervenes, instructing Jacob to marry one of his uncle's daughters at Paddan-aram (27.46–28.2). Out of this word of caution arises Isaac's blessing to Jacob:

> God Almighty bless you and make you fruitful and multiply you, that you may become a company of peoples. May he give to you and to your seed with you the

---

52 The expression 'to do righteousness' [לעשת צדקה] in the HB is often glossed as 'doing good works', or 'doing what is right' in connection with the laws of God, and as a means of atoning for sins (cf. Ps. 106.3; Isa. 56.1; 58.2; Ezek. 18.22; BDB, צדק s.v.). In the words of Nathan MacDonald, the phrase 'doing justice and righteousness' in Gen. 18.19 signifies 'an active attempt to negate the forces of injustice' through the delivery of the oppressed from forces of violence (Ps. 103.6; Jer. 22.3, 15-16; Ezek. 45.9)'; thus, the 'bargaining' between Abraham and God over Sodom in Genesis 18; idem, 'Listening to Abraham – Listening to Yhwh: Divine Justice and Mercy in Genesis 18.16-33', *CBQ* 66, no. 1 (2004), pp. 25–43, at p. 37.

53 The LXX differs from the MT; while the latter emphasizes the blessing 'for my servant Abraham's sake', the LXX only mentions the blessing 'through your father Abraham'.

54 This emphasis may well be a means of legitimating Isaac's position; thus, Boase, 'Life in the Shadows', p. 326.

blessing of Abraham that you may take possession of the land of your sojourning that God gave to Abraham. (28.3-4)

Isaac relays the promise he had received with respect to his own 'seed'. It is now Jacob's 'seed' that will be blessed, but this blessing is still tied inextricably with the figure of Abraham, who was the recipient of the original blessing, and whose 'seed' both Isaac and Jacob continue to represent and embody. The covenantal overtones of the promises made to Abraham's 'seed' are emphasized in this text, with the references to future 'peoplehood' and to the possession of the land. Jacob's possession of the land is thus positioned as the ongoing fulfilment of the original promise made to Abraham. As Jacob travels to Haran, he stops to sleep and he dreams of angels upon a ladder joining heaven and earth (28.10-11). At the top of the ladder stands the Lord (28.12-23), who reveals himself as 'the Lord, the God of Abraham your father', reinforcing the promise of the land to Jacob's 'seed' – indeed, the land on which he lies (28.14).[55] When Jacob returns from Paddan-aram (35.9), he receives the promise again in language that mirrors the creation account: 'I am God Almighty: be fruitful and multiply. A nation and a company of nations shall come from you and kings shall come from your own body. The land that I gave to Abraham and Isaac I will give to you and I will give the land to your seed after you' (35.11-12).[56]

Other texts from the Torah

There are five other references to Abraham's 'seed' in the Torah outside of Genesis (Exod. 32.13; (par. 33.1); Deut. 1.8; 34.4). One of those texts concerns the incident of the 'golden calf' at Mount Sinai (Exod. 32.1-6). The dramatic force of this scene is intensified when set against the previous revelation of the covenant between the Lord and his newly redeemed people, and the first of the 'ten commandments' which proscribed idolatry. Feeling desperate at Moses' delay atop the mountain, the people – with Aaron as their substitute leader – fashion a god to function in the stead of the absent Moses (32.1).[57] In anger, the Lord informs Moses of his will to consume the people in his 'hot wrath' and to 'make a great nation' out of Moses instead (32.9-10). Moses is thus a 'new Abraham', as one out of whom a 'great nation' will be produced at the Lord's instigation. Furthermore, (in a response reminiscent of Abraham in Genesis 18) Moses intercedes with the Lord to avert the destruction of his people.[58] Moses proffers the interrogative rejoinder to the Lord, 'Why does your wrath burn hot against your people whom you have brought out of the land of Egypt?' (32.11). Moses

---

[55] Yitzhak Peleg posits that following Jacob's dream, the patriarch resolves to return to the Land, seeing that the promise of 'seed' is realized in Rachel's labour and birth; cf. Peleg, *Going Up and Going Down: A Key to Interpreting Jacob's Dream (Gen 28.10-22)* (trans. Betty Rozen; London: Bloomsbury T&T Clark, 2015), p. 181, n. 91.

[56] Jacob's seed will also 'spread out' beyond the Land, so that other families of the earth will be blessed through him – a narrative point realized in Gen. 30.27. See, Lipton, *Revisions of the Night*, pp. 71–2.

[57] John van Seeters, *The Life of Moses: The Yahwist as Historian in Exodus-Numbers* (CBET 10; Kampen: Kok Pharos, 1994), p. 311.

[58] The parallels between Moses' intercession in Exod. 32, and Abraham's in Gen. 18.23-32 have been acknowledged, but only in terms of the context of sin: Cf. Patrick D. Miller, *They Cried to the Lord: The Form and Theology of Biblical Prayer* (Minneapolis: Fortress Press, 1994), pp. 266–71.

does not accept ownership of the people he has led; they belong to the Lord. Moses presses his case, stating,

> Remember Abraham, Isaac and Israel, your servants/slaves (MT: וְלִיִשְׂרָאֵל עֲבָדֶיךָ זְכֹר לְאַבְרָהָם לְיִצְחָק/LXX: μνησθεὶς Ἀβρααμ καὶ Ισαακ καὶ Ιακωβ τῶν σῶν οἰκετῶν), to whom you swore by your own self, and said to them, 'I will multiply your seed (זַרְעֲךָ/τὸ σπέρμα σου) as the stars of heaven and all this land that I have promised I will give to your seed, and they shall inherit it forever.' (Exod. 32.13)

At this, the Lord relents, without comment, from his planned destruction of the people (32.14). Two notable elements are added that were absent in the Genesis formulae. First, Abraham, Isaac and Israel (Jacob) are joined together in Moses' speech as the collective referent of the noun זַרְעֲךָ/τὸ σπέρμα σου. Second, Moses pleads with the Lord to avert his anger *in remembrance* of the three key patriarchal figures. This is more than simply Moses' request that the Lord act for the sake of the patriarchs: Moses asks the Lord to actively remember them as recipients of his own promise. The Hebrew root of the imperative 'remember' in v. 13 is זכר, and it primarily denotes the act of calling something or someone to mind in a way that will affect the present.[59] In Exod. 32.13, it is in remembrance of the three patriarchs in the past that Moses implores the Lord to act appropriately towards his people, who are their 'seed', in the present – and who must inherit the land. The patriarch's status as 'servants' of the Lord suggests a fidelity deserving of remembrance, but in Moses' speech it is meant in a vicarious sense.[60] This text draws out the important motif of God 'remembering' Abraham in order to act mercifully towards his descendants.[61]

While the motifs around Abraham's 'seed' found in Genesis continue in Exodus 32, a key difference in the Exodus text is that of the liberation from slavery in Egypt. The exodus is the rationale upon which the promise must finds its imminent realization – it is not the original gift of the land as such, but the liberation from slavery achieved in order to *return* to the land of the promise. The reference to the 'seed' of Abraham in Exod. 32.13-14 therefore expresses a collocation of themes: liberation from slavery, the idolatry at the incident of the 'golden calf' and the need for the Lord to 'remember' the three patriarchs for the sake of their 'seed' in the present time of the narrative. The positive 'servitude' of the patriarchs is also keyed in this text – and their exemplarity offsets the failings of their descendants. These failings are explicitly mentioned as 'sins' in Deut. 9.27, the earliest 'retelling' of the golden calf narrative. There, Moses pleads with God, saying 'Remember your servants, Abraham, Isaac, and Jacob; pay no attention to the stubbornness of this people their wickedness (רֶשַׁע/ἀσέβημα) and their sin (חַטָּאת/ἁμάρτημα; NRSV)'. Moses' plea in Deut. 9.27 banks on God protecting his awesome reputation as the deliverer of his people from Egypt (v. 29) so that

---

[59] BDB sv זכר.
[60] Cf. Michael Widmer, *Moses, God, and the Dynamics of Intercessory Prayer: A Study of Exodus 32-34 and Numbers 13-14* (FAT 2/8; Tübingen: Mohr Siebeck, 2004), pp. 113–18.
[61] Another text in the book of Exodus mentions the 'seed' of Abraham (33.1), but since it basically repeats Exod. 32.13-14 as a parallel structure, it does not require close analysis here.

the promise to inhabit the Land could be fulfilled (v. 28). However, the controlling metaphor of Abraham's 'seed' is absent in Deut. 9.27.[62]

Other texts in Deuteronomy mention Abraham's 'seed'. Two of these texts refer to the covenant and the land of Canaan, and are strategically placed at the beginning and the end of the book (1.8; 34.4).[63] Deuteronomy opens with Moses standing in the desert beyond the Jordan, prepared to expound the Torah to all the people (1.1-5). The time is ripe to enter and take possession of the land that God promised 'on oath' to give to their 'fathers, Abraham, Isaac and Jacob, and to their seed after them' (1.8).[64] The people have *already* become 'as numerous as the stars of heaven', and they will be increased 'a thousand times more' and blessed as God promised (1.10-11). Indeed, their numerousness is the very reason that Moses cannot assume sole responsibility for them, and why the task of leading them seems to him too difficult (1.9). The final reference to Abraham's 'seed' occurs in Deut. 34.4, when Moses climbs atop Mount Nebo so that the Lord can show him 'the whole country' to its greatest extent (34.1-3). The Lord then says to Moses, 'This is the country which I promised on oath to give to Abraham, Isaac and Jacob, saying: "I shall give it to your seed"' (34.4a). Moses is not allowed to enter this land himself (34.4b).

Two final texts that mention the 'seed' of Abraham also add a nuance particular to the Deuteronomist within the Torah. In Deut. 4.37, for example, we encounter an explanation for God's promise of the land of Canaan to Abraham's 'seed'. God elected his people Israel because of the love he had for Abraham, Isaac and Jacob:

> Because he [God] loved your fathers, and after them, chose their seed (MT: ויבחר בזרעו/LXX: ἐξελέξατο τὸ σπέρμα αὐτῶν), he has brought you out of Egypt, displaying his presence and mighty power, dispossessing for you nations who were larger and stronger than you to make way for you and to give you their country as your inheritance, as it still is today. (Deut. 4.37)

God's love for the 'fathers' and God's choice of their seed are related to each other and both have to do with the exodus from Egypt and the inheritance of the land.[65] It is not just for the sake of the fathers that God acted on behalf of Abraham's 'seed' to liberate them (cf. Exod. 32.13), but also because God chose Abraham's seed for *their own sake*.[66] Similarly, we read in Deut. 10.15, that although heaven and earth belong to the Lord as God, 'yet it was on your fathers, for love of them, that the Lord set his heart to love them, and he "chose their seed after them", you yourselves, out of all the nations, up to

---

[62] The Moses of Deut. 9.18-29 is, moreover, more tolerant towards the people, and considerably more desperate in his care and intercession on their behalf.
[63] Terence E. Fretheim, *Abraham: Trials of Family and Faith* (Columbia: University of South Carolina Press, 2007), p. 147.
[64] The geographical terrain is mentioned first, followed by the significance of divine oath and promise so as to motivate Israel to take possession of the Land; Peter C. Craigie, *The Book of Deuteronomy* (NICOT; Grand Rapids: Eerdmans, 1976), p. 96.
[65] Cf. Fretheim, *Abraham*, p. 148.
[66] Notice also that while God made the promise of the land's inheritance to Abraham *for his seed*, God made the covenant at Sinai neither with Abraham, nor with the 'fathers', 'but with us', with their 'seed' (Deut. 5.3).

the present day' (10.10-15).⁶⁷ The dual mention of God's love for the fathers provides rhetorical intensity to the verse, as God's choice of their 'seed' is connected to his prior love of their fathers, and is an ongoing expression of it. They are to 'walk' in God's 'ways' (10.12) and to keep all of the commandments in love (10.13). They are to 'circumcise their hearts' and 'be obstinate no longer' (10.16-17). God's love for the fathers, and his choice of their seed, is uncompelled and free of favouritism, but it requires love in its turn, particularly towards those who have little or no protection in society (10.18-20).

These texts add an intriguing dimension to the promises to Abraham and his 'seed'. The original covenant with the fathers (Abraham, Isaac and Jacob) is separated from the present covenant with their 'seed' at Sinai (cf. 5.3), even as one is predicated on the other. This enables the expression of two lines of thought: on the one hand, that being Abraham's 'seed' entails a certain responsibility – to follow the commandments and to protect the helpless (10.15-20); and on the other hand, the implication follows that the three 'fathers' – chosen by God out of love – must have embodied the observance of these very same commandments. Finally, the motif of God's love of the 'fathers' and his free choice of their 'seed' is taken up with more attention in some of the texts from the Prophets and the Writings, and it is to these texts that I now turn.

Josh. 24.2-3

In Josh. 24.2-3 we find reference to the 'seed' of Abraham, in the narrative of the covenant renewal at Shechem (24.1-28). Israel declares fidelity to the Lord by renouncing their foreign gods (24.14-24), and the statutes of the covenant are once more written down (24.25-28).⁶⁸ Joshua's narrative audience are part of the non-Canaanite northern tribes who had experienced neither the exodus from Egypt nor the revelation at Sinai; by adopting the covenant with Joshua on the terms given at Sinai, they become part authentic of the Lord's people,⁶⁹ even though they already call Abraham their 'father'. Joshua voices the Lord's narrative of this ancestral continuity across the generations:

> Long ago, your fathers lived beyond the Euphrates, Terah, the father of Abraham and of Nahor; and they served other gods. Then I took your father Abraham (MT: אֲבִיכֶם אֶת־אַבְרָהָם/LXX: τὸν πατέρα ὑμῶν τὸν Ἀβρααμ) from beyond the River and led him through all the land of Canaan, and made his seed many (MT: וָאַרְבֶּה אֶת־זַרְעוֹ/ LXX: ἐπλήθυνα αὐτοῦ σπέρμα) ... I then sent Moses and Aaron and plagued Egypt

---

⁶⁷ This 'future perspective' is important, as it displays the Deuteronomist's emphasis on the unconditional nature of the promise, which in the post-exilic writings will expand to become a fully fledged eschatological hope – for want of a better expression. For a similar point, see Ronald Hendel, *Remembering Abraham: Culture, Memory, and History in the Hebrew Bible* (New York/Oxford: Oxford University Press, 2005), p. 37.

⁶⁸ Scholars typically see ch. 24 as the strongest evidence of the final Deuteronomistic redaction for the book of Joshua. Cf. Gordon J. Wenham, 'The Deuteronomic Theology of the Book of Joshua', *JBL* 90, no. 2 (1971), pp. 140–8, at p. 148. Scholars now agree on the post-exilic composition, or final redaction, of the book. See, Thomas B. Dozeman, 'The Book of Joshua in Recent Research', *CBR* 15, no. 3 (2017), pp. 270–88, at p. 272.

⁶⁹ Contra E. Kutsch, 'Der Begriff *bryt* in vordeuteronomidcher Zeit', in F. Maass (ed.), *Das Ferne und Nahe Wort* (FS L. Ost; BZAW; Berlin: De Gruyter 1967), at p. 133.

with the wonder that I worked there; finally, I brought you out. I brought your fathers out of Egypt. (Josh. 24.2-6)[70]

What stands out in this passage is the presence of Abraham's 'back-story'. Terah, Abraham's father, is included in the plural 'your fathers' – a phrase usually reserved for the three key patriarchal figures: Abraham, Isaac and Jacob. This reference to the idolatrous past of Abraham, Nahor and Terah has the rhetorical function of foregrounding his audience's current worship of idols.[71] As their fathers once worshipped idols, but came to worship only the Lord after experiencing his interventions, so also must Joshua's audience disband from idolatrous practices and follow the Lord alone. Joshua's speech thus groups *all* of the 'fathers' together with his audience – they are all construed as leaving idolatry behind when God called forth 'your father Abraham', who is singled out as one whose 'seed' was multiplied.

But it is the experience of Jacob's direct descendants in the land of Egypt that serves as the lynchpin of this speech and heralds its redemptive moment. Jacob's audience ('you') are aligned with Jacob's sons and their travail in Egypt. In one verse, Joshua mediates the divine voice, with sweeping narrative collusion: 'finally I brought *you* out; I brought *your fathers* out of Egypt' (24.5). What the 'seed' of Abraham experienced in the historical narrative that Joshua recounts is caught up in the present moment of its retelling and applied to the distant 'seed' of Abraham now inhabiting the northern part of the land of Canaan.[72] This text therefore associates the 'seed' of Abraham with obedience to the Sinaitic covenant (long after it was given) and the abandonment of idolatry by the 'fathers'.

Isa. 41.8

The term 'seed of Abraham' occurs in Isa. 41.8, a text that forms part of the series of oracles introducing Deutero-Isaiah (Isa. 40–55). Consolation is the dominant theme of these chapters, in contrast to the more ominous tones of chs 1–39.[73] Isaiah 40 opens, for example, with strong words of comfort in the face of the Babylonian exile:

> 'Console my people, console them', says your God. Speak to the heart of Jerusalem and cry to her that her term of service is reached completion (MT: מלאה צבאה/LXX: ἐπλήσθη ἡ ταπείνωσις αὐτῆς) that her guilt has been satisfied (MT: נרצה עונה,/ LXX: λέλυται αὐτῆς ἡ ἁμαρτία) that, from the hand of the Lord, she has received double punishment for all her sins. (Isa. 40.1-2)[74]

---

[70] This citation follows the MT more closely than the LXX, which displays several slight alterations.
[71] William T. Koopmans, *Joshua 24 as Poetic Narrative* (JSOT 93; Sheffield: Sheffield Academic Press, 1990), p. 315.
[72] Cf. Bernard Gosse, 'Abraham père des exiles en Josué', in Ed Noort (ed.), *The Book of Joshua* (BETL 250; Leuven/Paris: Peeters, 2012), pp. 295–300.
[73] The two segments are also dated some 200 years apart, reflecting different historical events and theological outlooks. *Isaiah 40–55* concerns Judah/Israel/Zion's hope in Yhwh as their redeemer from the oppressive servitude they experience in Babylon. Walter Brueggemann, *Isaiah 40–66* (Louisville: Westminster/John Knox, 1998), pp. 10–11.
[74] See Shalom M. Paul, *Isaiah 40–66: A Commentary* (Grand Rapids: Eerdmans, 2012), p. 129.

These verses set the scene for the oracular cycles that follow (40.6-31; 41.1-20; 21-29) and the series of 'Servant songs' that later emerge (e.g. 42.1-9). In a perceptive analysis of this passage, Gary Anderson has argued that Isa. 40.1-2 represents the earliest stages of a lexical transformation concerning the notion of *sin*: the most ancient biblical sources conceived of sin, metaphorically, in terms of a burden to be borne, a weight carried by the individual or carried away by a scapegoat.[75] But in the Second Temple Period, the Jewish (and early Christian) literature reflects a remarkable shift in the metaphorization of sin as a *debt to be repaid* or remitted. This metaphorical shift is detectable even within the later strata of the Hebrew Bible, particularly, suggests Anderson, in texts such as Isa. 40.1-2, 50.1, Leviticus 26 and Daniel 9.[76]

Indeed, Anderson's translation of Isa. 40.1-2 brings to the fore the text's conceptualization of sin as debt-slavery: 'Speak tenderly to Jerusalem, and declare to her that her term of service is over, that [the debt owed for] her iniquity has been satisfied'.[77] Isa. 40.1-2 envisages the captivity of the debt-slave, obligated to fulfil (מלא)[78] his 'term of service' (צבא cf. Job 7.1), that is to labour until his debt is repaid and he can be released from slavery. The punishment of captivity generated the 'currency' necessary to pay down the debt of iniquity, but in this case, Jerusalem paid more than was owed in suffering – 'double for all her sins'.[79] Anderson demonstrates that the niphil נרצה accords with Second Isaiah's usage of רצה to indicate that Jerusalem's sin has been 'satisfied' – that is, Jerusalem has 'payed' in the manner of a vow or sacrifice to God (cf. Ps. 22.26-27) such that their 'payment' was redeemed or 'accepted', that is Lev. 26.41.[80] God was 'satisfied' in the way a seller might be satisfied with a successful monetary transaction, and declare the buyer 'quitted' of further payment.[81] Anderson contends that in Isa. 40.1-2, we begin to see a shift from the use of נרצה describing 'an individual quit of his obligation to pay a vow' to its use describing 'someone who is quit of his obligation to repay a debt that has accrued through sin'.[82] In ch. 40 vv. 1-2, on that reading, the Babylonian exile is configured as a form of 'debt-bondage', a kind of indentured servitude befitting a slave, from which God releases Israel out of love. Notice also that the LXX translates the Hebrew מלאה צבאה as ἐπλήσθη ἡ ταπείνωσις αὐτῆς: literally, Jerusalem has 'fulfilled her humiliation'. When translating the MT נרצה עונה (sins/guilt have been satisfied), the LXX opts for λέλυται αὐτῆς ἡ ἁμαρτία: Jerusalem has been 'loosed of her sins'. The idea is similar: Jerusalem has been released from debt-bondage (i.e. 'sin') – she is no longer tied.

This context is important because it frames the reference to the 'seed of Abraham' in Isa. 41.8. The futile idolatry of the 'nations' cannot compare to God's majesty. Similarly,

---

[75] Cf. also Blaženka Scheuer, *The Return of YHWH: The Tension Between Deliverance and Repentance in Isaiah 40–55* (Berlin: De Gruyter, 2008), pp. 126–7. Scheuer sees the noun עון as a form of iniquity that is deeply personal.
[76] Anderson, *Sin*, p. 46.
[77] Ibid.
[78] The verb means 'to reach completion': cf. Gen. 25.24; Lam. 4.18.
[79] Anderson, *Sin*, p. 47.
[80] Paul, *Isaiah 40–66*, p. 129.
[81] Anderson, *Sin*, pp. 50–2.
[82] Ibid., p. 53. Additionally, עון can mean 'sin' or 'punishment'. The construction נצאה עון means to bear the weight of a sin. The Aramaic moves to קעבל חובה = 'to assume a debt'.

the idols of the 'nations' cannot compare to God's love for Israel, his chosen servant (41.1-8a), to whom he speaks:

ואתה ישראל עבדי
יעקב אשר בחרתיך
זרע אברהם אהבי
אשר החזקתיך מקצות הארץ
ומאציליה קראתיך
ואמר לך עבדדי־אתה (MT Isa. 41.8-9c)

Σὺ δέ, Ισραηλ, <u>παῖς μου</u>
Ιακωβ, <u>ὃν ἐξελεξάμην</u>,
σπέρμα Ἀβρααμ, <u>ὃν ἠγάπησα</u>,
οὗ ἀντελαβόμην ἀπ' ἄκρων τῆς γῆς
καὶ ἐκ τῶν σκοπιῶν αὐτῆς ἐκάλεσά σε
καὶ εἶπά σοι <u>Παῖς μου εἶ</u> (LXX Isa. 41.8-9c)

But you, Israel, my servant
Jacob, whom I have chosen
The seed of Abraham, my love
You whom I took from the ends of the earth
And called from its farthest corners
Saying to you, 'you are my servant'. (41.8-9c)

The point of this extended invocation is to reassure the exilic community that God has chosen them – the 'seed of Abraham' – in love, and that he has not 'cast' them 'off' (41.9d; 41.10; cf. 40.31; 41.1).[83] To that end, 'the entire memory of Israel is mobilized ... to assure the exiles that this guaranteed relationship still operates and is decisive for the present and for the future'.[84] The invocation is developed through a series of appositions.[85] In Isa. 41.8-9c, the 'seed of Abraham' parallels the figure of 'Jacob' (who is 'chosen') and 'Israel' (who is God's servant). Three parallel appellations are found in this one verse (Isa. 41.8): Israel/Jacob/seed of Abraham. Their respective characteristics also function as synthetic parallelisms: servant/chosen/beloved.[86] The qal participle construct (singular) אברהם אהבי conveys the senses: 'Abraham (whom) I am loving',

---

[83] Claus Westermann, *Isaiah 40–66* (trans. David M. G. Stalker; OTL 19; Philadelphia: Westminster Press, 1969), p. 69.
[84] Walter Brueggeman, *Isaiah 40–66*, p. 33.
[85] Westermann, *Isaiah 40–66*, p. 69.
[86] For Israel to be God's 'servant' means 'that she has a master with whom she feels secure, whom she can trust, and who cares for her': Westermann, *Isaiah 40–66*, p. 70. Contrast this with the servitude/slavery of Israel in Babylon (Isa. 40.1-2). God, the true Master, has redeemed his people for his service. Cf. Gen. 24.14; 26.24; Exod. 14.31; Nu. 12.7, 8; Deut. 34.5 – all of these contexts refer to the person as serving God through worship – the dedicated servant of God. Indeed, the Targums interpreted the Isaian 'Servant' figure as Abraham himself (41.2, 25), a view with which one early critical commentator fully concurred; see Charles C. Torrey, 'Isaiah 41', *HTR* 44, no. 3 (1951), pp. 121–36, at pp. 122, 126, 129.

'Abraham (who) loves me'.[87] The participle reinforces the ongoing 'element of activity in the relationship' between God and Abraham – rather than expressing a static status ('loved one' or 'friend').[88] The *seed* of Abraham are the indirect objects of the participle, and thus are to be interpreted as loved for Abraham's sake. The LXX translates the Hebrew as 'the seed of Abraham whom I loved' (ὂν ἠγάπησα, aorist). One should note that 'the appearance of Israel before Jacob in the parallel stich here is a deviation from the prophet's norm' (40.27, 44.1, 5).[89] However, because of the synthetic parallelisms in Isa. 41.8-9c, anything predicated of 'Israel' or 'Jacob' is also predicated of 'Abraham'. And those qualities also flow on to characterize the 'seed of Abraham', which form the collective plural (as per the associated nouns 'Israel' and 'Jacob').

There may also be a subtle poetic play on the twin notions of Abraham as 'beloved' and as 'servant' in this passage. Sara Japhet claims that the root א-ה-ב describing Abraham as 'friend of God' (Isa. 41.8) is used as a synonym for ע-ב-ד (to 'serve/worship'). Japhet argues that this is a technical meaning that 'appears in contracts and treaties and is the result of the Assyrian-Babylonian influence on Israelite usage'.[90] Also, a significant theme in the broader context of this passage is the oneness and incomparability of God over against futile idols (43.10-13; 45.4-6).[91] The Isaian references to Israel/Jacob as God's 'slave', as well as the prominent themes of exclusive worship of the Lord, recall the slavery of the Hebrews in Egypt and the commandment at Sinai to worship only the Lord.[92] Being the 'slave' or 'servant' of God is a powerful way of expressing Israel's commitment to monotheism (cf. John 8.32-33). God's people were redeemed from slavery in Egypt in order to be 'slaves of God' (cf. Lev. 25.42; cf. Lev. 25.55; 26.13), brought out of Egypt, the house of slavery, in order to obey God's commandments (cf. Exod. 13.3; Deut. 5.6-10; 6.12-15a; 7.8-10a, 14; Josh. 24.16-18).

Jer. 33.26

The phrase 'seed of Abraham' also occurs in Jer. 33.26 – a text that is absent from the LXX, although present in the MT as it has come down to us.[93] This might indicate that

---

[87] Westermann, *Isaiah 40–66*, p. 70. The question of 'who loves whom' is a debated one: see Peter Höffken, 'Abraham und Gott, oder: wer liebt wen? Anmerkungen zu Jes 41.8', *BN* 103 (2000), pp. 17–22.
[88] Westermann, *Isaiah 40–66*, p. 70.
[89] Paul, *Isaiah 40–66*, p. 164. For the figure of Abraham used with the substantive 'servant' and the verb בחר in conjunction, see Ps. 105/106.42 (LXX).
[90] Sara Japhet, *The Ideology of the Book of Chronicles and Its Place in Biblical Thought* (Leuven: Peeter Lang, 1997), p. 95, n. 276.
[91] Hywel Clifford, 'Deutero-Isaiah and Monotheism', in John Day (ed.), *Prophecy and Prophets in Ancient Israel: Proceedings of the Oxford Old Testament Seminar* (New York: T&T Clark, 2010), pp. 267–89; Martin Leuenberger, *Ich bin Jwhw und Keiner Sonst: Der Exklusive Monotheismus des Kyros-Orakels Jes 45, 1–7* (Stuttgart: KBW Bibelwerk, 2010).
[92] The Exodus allusions in Deutero-Isaiah are well noted: see the literature cited in Paul, *Isaiah 40–66*, for example Bernard W. Anderson, 'Exodus Typology in Second Isaiah', in B. Anderson and W. Harrelson (eds), *Israel's Prophetic Heritage: Essays in Honor of James Muilenberg* (New York: Harper & Brothers, 1962), pp. 177–95. See also the excellent work by Hans M. Barstad, *A Way in the Wilderness: The 'Second Exodus' in the Message of Second Isaiah* (JJS 12; Manchester: University of Manchester Press, 1989).
[93] Cf. John Bright, *Jeremiah* (AB 21; New York: Doubleday, 1964), pp. 297–8. The segment of text absent from the LXX is Jer. 33.14-26. However, the poetic cohesiveness of Jer. 30.1–33.26 in the MT

the text is a late addition to the book, composed and inserted after the translation of the Hebrew Bible into Septuagint Greek.[94] Jeremiah's reference to the 'seed of Abraham' occurs in the context of the Lord's promise to realize his eternal covenant with David following the exile (33.14-26), which will also involve restoring the Levitical priesthood (33.17-18). Remarkably, David is spoken of in terms reminiscent of the patriarchal promises in the Torah: 'As the hosts of heaven cannot be numbered, and the sands of the sea cannot be measured, so will I multiply the seed of David, my servant (כן ארבה את־זרע דוד עבדי) and the Levitical priests who minister to me' (33.22). But the promise made to David will not supplant the original divine covenant made with Abraham. A final 'word of the Lord' comes to Jeremiah on this subject, framed as a rhetorical question: 'Have you not observed that these people are saying, "The Lord has rejected the two clans that he chose?"' (33.23). To repudiate this pernicious rumour, the Lord reasserts an oath:

> If I have not established my covenant with day and night and the fixed order of heaven and earth then I will reject the seed of Jacob, and David my servant will not choose one of his seed to rule over the seed of Abraham, Isaac and Jacob (זרע אברהם ישחק ויעקב). For I will restore their fortunes and have mercy on them. (33.25-26)

This final promise concludes the longer oracle of ch. 33 vv. 1-26, as well as the particular segment concerning the Lord's promises to David and his line (vv. 14-26), found in the MT. The last two verses (vv. 25-26) make a distinction between 'David my servant and ... his seed' (v. 25), and the 'seed of Abraham, Isaac and Jacob' (v. 26). This is the only canonical text (of the 'Old Testament') that collocates the 'seed' of David with the 'seed' of Abraham. David is referred to as the Lord's 'servant', but Abraham is grouped together with the other patriarchal figures in v. 26; notably, unlike Isa 41.8 analysed earlier in this chapter, it is not Abraham as such but his 'seed' that is in view in this passage. The 'seed' of David will rule over the 'seed of Abraham Isaac and Jacob'.[95] This is a 'fixed order' comparable to the 'covenant' that the Lord upholds with nature, with the 'night and the day'. This is all part of the Lord's desire to be merciful by restoring the fortunes of the 'two clans' he appears to have rejected through the exile (v. 24).[96] Jeremiah's reference to the 'seed of David' and the 'seed of Abraham, Isaac and Jacob' (v. 26) is most interesting when read against John 7–8, where some festivalgoers identify Jesus as the messianic 'seed of David'. By comparison, in ch. 8 vv. 31-33, the Jews' assertion that they are 'seed

---

has long been recognized. Thus, Mark Biddle, 'The Literary Frame Surrounding Jeremiah 30.1–33.26', *ZAW* 100, no. 2 (1988), p. 409.

[94] Ibid., p. 298. Another explanation, of course, is that the translator omitted ch. 33 vv. 14-26.

[95] Despite the problematic Christocentric interpretations voiced by Tiberius Rata in his monograph on Jeremiah 33, his point is nonetheless correct that the Abrahamic covenant is not nullified but reaffirmed in the Davidic covenant at ch. 33 v. 26. See idem, *The Covenant Motif in Jeremiah's Book of Comfort: Textual and Intertextual Studies of Jeremiah 30-33* (StudBibLit 105; New York: Peter Lang, 2007), p. 88.

[96] The two clans being the north and south of divided Israel; thus, Walter Bruggemann, *A Commentary on Jeremiah: Exile and Homecoming* (Grand Rapids: Eerdmans, 1998), p. 321.

of Abraham' holds little currency in the Evangelist's theological world view when faced with the apparent supremacy of 'abiding' in Jesus' 'word'.

We now turn to the final section of the Tanakh, the Writings, to examine the intertextual connotations of the 'seed of Abraham', particularly in light of the concepts of slavery and sin.

Psalm 105.6-12 (MT)/104.6-12 (LXX)

In sweeping fashion, Psalm 105 retells the narrative arc of the entire Torah, beginning with the patriarchs (105.8-15) and culminating in the possession of the land of Canaan by their multitudinous offspring (105.44-45).[97] The psalm begins with a series of calls to give thanks to God (105.1), to sing to God (105.2), to glory in God (105.3), to seek God (105.4) and to remember God (105.5). Then, both the 'seed of Abraham' and the 'children of Jacob' are named in parallel fashion as the psalm's addressees:

זרע אברהם עבדו
בני יעקב בחיריו
(MT 105.6)

ᵃO, Seed of Abraham, ᵇhis servant/slave,
ᶜSons of Jacob, ᵈhis chosen one!
(MT 105.6)

σπέρμα Αβρααμ δοῦλοι αὐτοῦ,
υἱοὶ Ιακωβ ἐκλεκτοὶ αὐτοῦ
(LXX 104.6)

ᵃO, Seed of Abraham, ᵇhis slaves,
ᶜSons of Jacob, ᵈhis chosen ones!
(LXX 104.6)

The 'seed of Abraham' and 'sons of Jacob' are reassured that the Lord is 'our God' who remembers his covenant forever (105.7b-8) – one 'concluded with Abraham' (105.9), sworn on oath to Isaac and ordained for Jacob (105.10).[98] The Abrahamic covenant is also for their posterity in the 'land [of] Canaan, your allotted inheritance' (חבל נחלה/σχοίνισμα κληρονομίας; 105.11). The word 'anointed' (במשיחי/τῶν χριστῶν) is also pluralized, 'moving it away from its normal Davidic connotation and applying it instead to the descendants of Abraham as a community of "anointed ones"'.[99]

---

[97] The poetic style is, however, not much more than 'a simple versification of known events': Robert Alter, *The Book of Psalms: A Translation with Commentary* (New York: W. W. Norton & Company, 2007), p. 369.

[98] This triple formula (Abraham/Isaac/Jacob) frequently emerges in the post-biblical literature and in the rabbinic writings. Note also that the phrase זכר ברית is used only in the characteristically priestly (P) material of the Torah (Gen. 9.15-16; Exod. 2.24; 6, 5); see George J. Brooke, 'Psalms 105-106 at Qumran', *RevQ* 14, no. 2 (1989), pp. 267–92, at p. 275.

[99] Ted Hildebrandt, 'A Song of Our Father Abraham: Psalm 105', in Hunt (ed.), *Perspectives on Our Father Abraham*, pp. 44–67, at p. 66.

The most obvious difference between the MT and the LXX versions of this psalm is that the Hebrew uses the singular suffix for its construct nouns, but the Greek translates these into plural nominatives, with the genitive pronoun. This difference occasions a considerable change in the meaning of the texts. The Hebrew text favours a reading where Abraham is 'God's servant', but the 'seed of Abraham' (his descendants and the addressees of the psalm) are implied by the common (i.e. plural sense) form of the noun זרע. The verses showcase a neat parallelism:

Seed = Son
Abraham = Jacob
Servant = chosen one

To be the 'seed' of Abraham is equivalent to being the 'sons' of Jacob. Where Abraham was God's 'servant', Jacob was 'chosen' by God. The audience is not addressed simply as the 'seed of Abraham' in this regard; they are addressed as the 'seed of Abraham *who is* the "servant" of God'; they are addressed as the 'sons of Jacob; *who is* the "elect of God"'. The poetic structure of Ps. 105.6 implies that to be the 'seed of Abraham' is, *ipso facto*, to be a servant (or 'slave') of God. In the LXX, the nouns 'slaves', 'sons' and 'chosen ones' are pluralized. This makes them read as pendant nominatives, referring back to the head nouns 'seed' (of Abraham) and 'Jacob'. The addressees of the psalm are therefore denoted as 'Abraham's seed' and 'Jacob's sons' (cola *a/c*), respectively. Unlike the MT version, therefore, the LXX reads the collective 'seed of Abraham' as God's 'slave' (not Abraham himself), and it reads the collective 'sons of Jacob' as God's chosen ones (rather than Jacob himself).[100]

The conclusion of the psalm (vv. 44-45) is worth examining. The psalm gains its momentum after mentioning the gift of the land to the patriarchs (v. 11), and it begins to soar into a triumphant retelling of the power of the Lord in the lives of his people. The story of Joseph is recounted (vv. 16-23), followed by the mission of Moses (vv. 24-27), the plagues in Egypt (vv. 28-36), the exodus and wilderness wanderings (vv. 37-43) and the entry into the land as promised to Abraham (vv. 42-45):

He [God] gave them the territories of nations,
They reaped the fruit of other people's labours,
On the condition that they kept his statutes,
And remained obedient to his laws. (vv. 44-45)

The gift of Canaan is presented as the fulfilment of God's promises.[101] But the psalmist adds an unexpected twist, a future condition expressed as past tense: the possession of Canaan occurred *only to the extent that* the people 'kept' God's 'statutes'

---

[100] The LXX uses the plural δοῦλοι to describe Abraham's 'seed' as 'slaves of God', which in the LXX denotes a state of being subject or subservient to God's dominion (cf. Ps. 188/199.91), rather than the more benign state of servanthood. See LEH dictionary, sv. δοῦλος.
[101] Cf. Hildebrandt, 'A Song of Our Father Abraham', p. 61.

(שְׁמְרוּ חֻקָּיו/ὅπως ἂν φυλάξωσιν τὰ δικαιώματα αὐτοῦ) and remained obedient to (Gk. lit: 'searched earnestly for') God's laws (וְתוֹרֹתָיו יִנְצֹרוּ/καὶ τὸν νόμον αὐτοῦ ἐκζητήσωσιν).[102] This kind of language (keeping/observing God's statutes and laws) is redolent of the post-exilic psalmody (cf. Psalm 119) and the increased reverence for the Torah as a means of encountering God.[103] But because in Psalm 105 these themes are contextualized with reference to *Abraham* as God's 'servant' (v. 42), it is worth recalling Gen. 26.5 as an intertext. In Gen. 26.5, Abraham was said to faithfully keep God's 'laws, decrees, ordinances and statutes', enabling Isaac to merit the promise of 'seed' as well as the eventual gift of the land (Gen. 26.3-5). In Ps. 105.44-45, the 'seed of Abraham' will *keep* the land inasmuch as they – like their father Abraham – also keep God's laws. This intertextual link suggests that inasmuch as Abraham's 'seed' behave as Abraham did, they will keep the blessings won by Abraham. However, in Ps. 105.42-45 the condition of inheriting the promise is not predicated on Abraham's past obedience – rather, Abraham's status as 'servant' is simply asserted – but upon his descendants' observance of the law. Psalm 105 reveals a cumulative portrait of Abraham's exemplary 'servanthood', his Torah obedience and the inheritance of the land promised to his 'seed'.

2 Chronicles 20.7

The text of 2 Chron. 20.7 refers to Abraham's 'seed' in language similar to that of Isa. 41.8. As the chronicler retells the Judahite monarchic history, he includes a moderately long segment about King Jehosaphat's reforms (2 Chron. 19.1–20.37; cf. 1 Kgs 16.1).[104] When neighbouring tribes wage war on Jehosaphat (20.1), the king 'set(s) his face to seek the Lord' (20.4), reciting a public prayer in the manner of a national lament:

> O, Lord, God of our fathers, are you not God in heaven? You rule over all the kingdoms of the nations. In your hand are power and might, so that none is able to withstand you. Did you not, our God, drive out the inhabitants of this land before your people Israel, and give it forever to the seed of Abraham your beloved? (לְזֶרַע אַבְרָהָם אֹהַבְךָ/σπέρματι Αβρααμ τῷ ἠγαπημένῳ σου; 20.6-7)

As it turns out, the Judahites do not even fight, but rise early in the morning to praise the Lord together, while the invading armies end up destroying each other (20.20-23). The chronicler creatively weaves the promise to the patriarchs found in the Torah into

---

[102] Note that there is little directly said in Psalm 105 about the covenant at Sinai as a narrative retold: Brooke, 'Psalms 105 and 106 at Qumran', p. 277.

[103] K. A. Reynolds, *Torah as Teacher: The Exemplary Torah Student in Psalm 119* (Leiden: Brill, 2010); Benjamin G. Wright, 'Torah and Sapiential Pedagogy in the Book of Ben Sira', in Bernd U. Schipper and D. Andrew Teeter (eds), *Wisdom and Torah: The Reception of 'Torah' in the Wisdom Literature of the Second Temple Period* (Leiden: Brill, 2013), pp. 157–86, esp. pp. 167–8; Marc Zvi Brettler, 'The Riddle of Psalm 111', in Deborah A. Green and Laura S. Lieber (eds), *Scriptural Exegesis: The Shapes of Culture and the Religious Imagination: Essays in Honour of Michael Fishbane* (New York/Oxford: Oxford University Press, 2009), pp. 62–73.

[104] The chronicler has thus made Jehoshaphat 'one of the major kings of his book': Pancratius C. Beentjes, 'Tradition and Transformation Aspects of Innerbiblical Interpretation in 2 Chronicles 20', *Bib* 74, no. 2 (1993), pp. 258–68, at p. 258.

his narrative of Jehosaphat's victory. In the chronicler's presentation of this episode, the Lord is proclaimed as the one who brought the 'seed of Abraham' into the land of the promise (20.7) – a feat which is now under threat of coming undone because of the impending invasion of non-Israelite armies. But, so efficacious is the invocation of Abraham as God's 'beloved', that all threat dissipates under the might of God's deliverance.[105] The 'people Israel', in the view of the chronicler, are the very 'seed of Abraham' to whom the ancient promises are presently speaking.[106]

Although the passage in 2 Chron. 20.6-7 actively reshapes theologies present in the Torah, they are also shaped by Isa. 41.8 ('Israel, my servant, Jacob, whom I have chosen, the seed of Abraham whom I love'). God chose Israel not because of his love for Abraham, but because of Abraham's love for him.[107] In LXX Isa. 41.8, we read: σπέρμα Αβρααμ, ὃν ἠγάπησα ('the seed of Abraham whom I loved') and in LXX 2 Chron 20.7, we read: σπέρματι Αβρααμ τῷ ἠγαπημένῳ σου ('the seed of your beloved Abraham').[108] In the chronicler's version of events, it is the plural object 'the seed of Abraham' who are loved and helped by God. Yet, in other passages from the Septuagint, those who love God take the subject position, with the Hebrew translated verbatim (Deut. 5.10; 7.9; Judg. 5.31; Ps. 97.10; Neh. 1.5).[109] In 2 Chron. 20.7, 'the seed of Abraham' are God's 'beloved', and for their *own* sake. However, Abraham himself is also signified by the term 'beloved'. When read in light of other references to Abraham as 'friend of God', Reinhard Kratz argues that 2 Chron. 20.7 presents Abraham as law-observant, and as separated – or chosen out from – other peoples.[110]

This picture accords with an emergent strain of thought in the post-exilic biblical writings about the 'seed of Abraham', that is that God helps and loves Abraham's 'seed', especially demonstrating this love in times of distress.

Post-biblical apocrypha and pseudepigrapha

The apocryphal and pseudepigraphical writings postdate most of the canonical biblical material, and predate the writings collected in the NT. For this reason, the material was once referred to as the 'intertestamental' literature, but this designation has rightly fallen out of favour for its implicit presumption that canonicity determines the relevant standing of all extant literary material in early Judaism, and for the fact that it reinforces the value-laden dichotomy of the 'Old' and 'New' Testaments.[111] Furthermore, the

---

[105] H. G. M. Williamson, *1 and 2 Chronicles* (NCBC; Eugene: Wipf & Stock, 2010), p. 296.

[106] Cf. Scott W. Hahn, *The Kingdom of God as Liturgical Empire: A Theological Commentary on 1-2 Chronicles* (Grand Rapids: Baker Academic, 2012), p. 28.

[107] The English translation 'my friend' obscures the distinction between active and passive in the Hebrew. In the Hebrew 'loved' (אוהב) and 'beloved' (אהוב) look similar, as Sara Japhet has demonstrated (*The Ideology*, p. 96, n. 277).

[108] The difference is between the aorist and the perfect passive participle, so that Chronicles gives a sense of God's ongoing care and love: 'whom I have been loving'.

[109] Japhet, *The Ideology*, p. 96, n. 277.

[110] R. G. Kratz, 'Friend of God, Brother of Sarah, and Father of Isaac: Abraham in the Hebrew Bible and in Qumran', in D. Diamont and R. G. Kratz (eds), *The Dynamics of Language and Exegesis at Qumran* (Tübingen: Mohr Siebeck, 2009), pp. 80–7.

[111] John F. A. Sawyer, 'Combating Prejudices about the Bible and Judaism', *Theology* 94, no. 760 (1991), pp. 269–78.

'Christianization' and very late dating of some of the pseudepigraphical material has made the designation 'intertestamental' temporally problematic too. I will refer to the diverse collection of texts – preserved in languages as varied as Syriac, Coptic, Ethiopic, Greek and Hebrew, sometimes as third-degree translations from the Aramaic or Hebrew – as the 'Apocrypha' and 'Pseudepigrapha', without making any judgement on whether these writings were 'Jewish' or 'Christian'; like the NT itself, these writings emerged from a period (mostly c. 200 BCE to 200 CE) when such referents were fluid and contested.[112]

The purpose of this section is to trace the literary and thematic contours of the metaphor 'seed of Abraham' in the apocryphal and pseudepigraphical writings, with attention to how the concepts of 'sin' and 'slavery' are collocated. To that end, historical-critical issues will remain in the background, as in the foregoing analysis of the biblical material. This is not to discount historicism's evident value, but only to draw out some neglected features commonly uniting this body of disparate literature as a whole. We can identify two main trajectories in relation to how Abraham's 'seed' is configured herein: (1) Abraham, Isaac and Jacob attain an exalted status in the afterlife, from whence they effectively intercede for their 'seed' on earth. This theme is evident in prayers, laments, testaments and biblical retellings, when God is called upon to have 'mercy' upon Abraham's 'seed' because they have fallen into sin, or they are oppressed by foreign dominions. (2) Abraham's 'seed' are blessed or chosen because of Abraham's exemplarity; the biblical stories of God's election of Abraham is explained by virtue of Abraham possessing one or more outstanding characteristics: his law observance, his aniconism, his fidelity or piety and so on. These two themes are related by way of the emerging debate within early Judaism about whether the fathers' virtues could vicariously benefit their posterity, or whether such virtues required imitation for the promises to the patriarchs to be fully realized.

Theme 1: Abraham, Isaac and Jacob help their 'seed'

As we saw in the previous analysis of the biblical material, late Hebrew texts (such as 2 Chron. 20.7 and Isa. 41.8) were beginning to manifest a concern with God's deliverance of 'Abraham's seed' in times of acute political distress. This motif was expressed in communal prayers or national laments; the theme found its resolution and rationale in God's choice of, and love for, Abraham (cf. Isa. 41.7-8), or indeed, in God's unconditioned love for 'Abraham's seed' (2 Chron. 20.7). In the apocryphal literature of early Judaism, this motif was developed and expanded in various directions.

Let us first examine the *Prayer of Azariah* (PrA). This twenty-two verse lamentation was embedded into the Old Greek (OG) version of the book of Daniel, between

---

[112] This is not to say that the categories could be utterly merged without consequent historiographical errors either; cf. Daniel Boyarin, 'Rethinking Jewish Christianity: An Argument for Dismantling a Dubious Category', *JQR* 99, no. 1 (2007), pp. 7–36. Also, uncommonly late preservations, such as the second half of the *Apocalypse of Abraham* (Slovakian manuscript preservation, early Middle Ages) will not be considered in this analysis.

ch. 3 v. 23 and ch. 3 v. 24, and is not preserved in the MT.[113] Whether the *Prayer of Azariah* was independently composed and circulated, or was structurally integral to the OG version is still debated.[114] The Semitisms – or more correctly, linguistic Aramaic inflexions – of the *Prayer of Azariah* are sometimes posited as a basis for presuming a Semitic *Vorlage*.[115] The book of Daniel is generically considered to be an 'historical apocalypse'.[116] This is evident in the narrative setting in the Greek version of Daniel 3, which depicts Azariah and his two young Jewish companions in the court of King Nebuchadnezzar of Babylon (c. 500 BCE), cast inside a burning furnace to meet a gruesome death (chs 1–3). Yet, Daniel is dated to c. 164–168 BCE and is thus acknowledged as responding to the circumstances within Seleucid Judea at that time, and the brutal reign of Antiochus IV Epiphanes.[117] Indeed, Portier-Young has classified Daniel as a form of apocalyptic 'resistance literature', actively embodying 'discursive resistance to imperial domination and hegemony, offering an alternative mythology, cosmology, language, and vision'.[118] Azariah and his companions refuse the food and drink of the king – amounting to resistance to his patrimony – which precipitates the royal decision to have the men executed (vv. 1-2).[119] But while inside the furnace, the men begin to pray, calling upon God to show his mercy in the absence of their ability to offer sacrifices to atone for their sins, and to miraculously rescue them (vv. 3-20).

Azariah begins his prayer by blessing God's glorious name (1.3), conceding that God's judgement is true (1.4). A confession follows: due to the sins of their ancestors in breaking God's law, Azariah and all Jews are suffering the fate of exile (1.4-9). The text expresses a collective sense of guilt 'accumulated from generation to generation'.[120] This is despite the fact that the three men are depicted as absolutely meticulous in their own

---

[113] Yet the OG 'did not stand the test of time', only the Revised Greek (RG) version of Daniel 'became the authoritative Scripture for Catholics and Christians within the Orthodox communion' and appears to have influenced the NT writers; see Anathea Portier-Young, 'Three Books of Daniel: Plurality and Fluidity among the Ancient Versions', *Int* 71, no. 2 (2017), pp. 143–53, at p. 144. The RG also contains the Prayer of Azariah as an addition in chapter 3.

[114] Although the Prayer of Azariah (and other 'additions' to the book of Daniel) are printed in modern Bibles this way today, that is as separate and separable compositions under the label 'Apocrypha' or 'Deutero-Canonical' writings, the Prayer of Azariah was only ever preserved integrally in the Greek versions. See Portier-Young, 'Three Books', p. 149.

[115] Thomas Heike, 'Atonement in the Prayer of Azariah (Dan 3.40)', in Géza G. Xeravits and Jósef Zsengellér (eds), *Deuterocanonical Additions of the Old Testament Books: Selected Studies* (Berlin: de Gruyter, 2010), pp. 43–59, at p. 44.

[116] That is, on the distinction made by Collins between the 'heavenly journey' type of apocalypse, and the 'historical apocalypse'. See John J. Collins, *The Apocalyptic Imagination: An Introduction to Jewish Apocalyptic Literature* (Grand Rapids: Eerdmans, 1988), pp. 23–9.

[117] Daniel J. Harrington, *Invitation to the Apocrypha* (Grand Rapids: Eerdmans, 1999), p. 110.

[118] Anathea Portier-Young, 'Jewish Apocalyptic Literature as Resistance Literature', in John J. Collins (ed.), *The Oxford Handbook of Apocalyptic Literature* (New York/Oxford: Oxford University Press, 2014), pp. 145–62, at p. 162.

[119] Anathea Portier-Young, *Apocalypse Against Empire: Theologies of Resistance in Early Judaism* (Grand Rapids: Eerdmans, 2011), p. 211.

[120] Hieke, 'Atonement', p. 46.

Torah observance (Dan. 3.28). The next segment, Azariah's petition (vv. 10-22), is the core of the *Prayer of Azariah*. Azariah pleads:

> For your name's sake do not give us up forever,
> and do not annul your covenant (τὴν διαθήκην)
> Do not withdraw your mercy (τὸ ἔλεός σου) from us,
> for the sake of Abraham your beloved (διὰ Αβρααμ τὸν ἠγαπημένον ὑπὸ σοῦ)
> and for the sake of your servant Isaac (τὸν δοῦλόν σου)
> and Israel your holy one, to whom you promised
> to multiply their seed (πληθῦναι τὸ σπέρμα αὐτῶν) like the stars of
> heaven, and like the sand on the shore of the sea. (1.11-13)[121]

Azariah's petition draws on the language of Genesis 12–22 and the promises to the patriarchs ('covenant', 'multiply their seed', 'like the stars of heaven' and 'sand on the shore of the sea'). But it also weaves in language familiar to us from Isa. 41.8 and 2 Chron. 20.7, referring to Abraham as God's 'beloved'. What is novel here is the collective petition that God rescue Azariah and his friends from death – who according to the narrative are blameless in their observance of the Torah, but are suffering the effects of their fathers' neglect of the Torah – and this *for the sake of* Abraham, Isaac and Israel (Jacob). Azariah does not call upon his own righteousness as a mitigating factor, but accepts that God is just in making him suffer for the sins of past generations. And just as guilt can be imputed across the generations, so also can righteousness: thus Azariah asks God to be merciful to him *because* of Abraham, Isaac and Jacob, who were loved by God. Otherwise, how can God's promise to the fathers' 'seed' be realized? (v. 13). And does God want the shame of being seen as less than magnificent? (cf. vv. 12-20). The divine promise to Abraham's 'seed' endures, despite the ostensible sins of Israel that have landed Azariah in his predicament. Abraham, Isaac and Jacob together (1.12) hold the powerful potential to literally save Azariah and his friends from death due to sin.

The *Prayer of Azariah* thus fits within a theological strain within post-exilic Judaism emphasizing the role of intergenerational sin – the vicarious punishment of ancestral sins, now imputed to later generations of their descendants. It is a post-exilic penitential prayer like Ezra 9.1–10.6; Neh. 1.1-11; 9.1–10.40; then Dan. 9.1-27.[122] And it is also one of the earliest Jewish (non-rabbinic) texts that alludes to the intercessory power of the 'the fathers', in connection with the biblical promise that God would multiply Abraham's 'seed'. The context of the prayer adds another dimension: Jews suffering under a form of foreign dominion akin to 'slavery', requiring either accommodation or resistance in response.

The *Prayer of Azariah* was taken as an example of proto-martyrology literature in its earliest reception – the LXX version of Dan. 3.28 has the three men 'offering up their bodies' for death so as not to worship idols; early Jewish tradition likewise

---

[121] Michael D. Coogan (ed.), *The New Oxford Annotated Apocrypha: New Revised Standard Version* (4th rev. edn; New York: Oxford University Press, 2010), pp. 185–9.
[122] Hieke, 'Atonement', p. 46.

saw Isaac as offering his body in 'martyrdom' at the *Akedah* even though his slaughter was not carried out (*y. Taan.* 2.1; *b. Zev.* 62a goes a step further to say Isaac actually dies). Azariah and the men in the furnace also became prototypes of martyrs in their *willingness* to die, although they lived.[123] Other scholars perceive a different paradigm: the three men in the furnace are examples of 'the wise and righteous Jew who remains steadfastly loyal to God' and are thus 'protected and saved' even to the point of escaping death (Wisdom 2–5).[124] This sapiential paradigm positions Daniel and his companions as the ideal sage/wise prophet witnessing to God, and being rescued from death.

Similar themes are to be found in *3 Maccabees*, where we find reference to the 'seed of Abraham' in the main narrative section recounting Ptolemy's persecution of the Jews in Alexandria (*3 Macc.* 2.25–7.23).[125] After two aborted attempts at exterminating all of Alexandria's Jews (3.11-30; 4.1-21), Ptolemy almost succeeds the third time by unleashing intoxicated elephants upon the Jews, who are crammed inside the hippodrome (5.1-51). The elderly and revered priest Eleazar then stands up in the midst of the people, ordering them to 'stop calling upon the holy God', and to pray according to his lead (6.1-15):

> King of great power, Almighty God Most High, governing all creation with mercy, look upon the descendants of Abraham (ἔπιδε ἐπὶ Ἀβρααμ σπέρμα), O Father, upon the children of the sainted Jacob, a people of your consecrated portion who are perishing as foreigners in a foreign land. (*3 Macc.* 6.1-3)

Eleazar's prayer works most effectively: Ptolemy has a miraculous change of heart; he decides to halt the charge of drunken elephants, and release the Jewish prisoners (6.16-29).[126] So complete is the immediacy of divine deliverance that angels emerge from the sky and rescue *all the Jews* of Alexandria from Ptolemy's armies (*3 Macc.* 9.16-29).

---

[123] Ibid. (and texts cited therein), p. 50. Justin Martyr also read the text as the three men offering a substitute sacrifice through their contrition and confession (*Apology* 1.46).

[124] Lawrence M. Wills, 'Prayer of Azariah and the Song of the Three Young Men', in Gale A. Yee, Hugh R. Page Jr. and Matthew J. M. Coomber (eds), *The Apocrypha: Fortress Commentary on the Bible Study Edition* (Minneapolis: Fortress Press, 2016), pp. 1043–6, at p. 1043.

[125] N. Clayton Croy, *3 Maccabees* (SCS; Boston: Brill, 2006), p. ix structures the book into three sections, which I follow here. Croy explains that *3 Maccabees* is an 'oddity' among the writings bearing that name, as it does not deal with the Maccabean family, the revolt (167–64 BCE) or the dynasty. Rather, the narrative dealing with Ptolemy IV Philopator predates the Maccabean revolt by about half a century; Croy, *3 Maccabees*, p. x. The text is attested in Alexandrius (A), dated to the mid-fifth century CE, with versions in the Syriac Peshitta and an Armenian translation. Different dates have been proposed for the book's composition but no consensus has been reached. H. Anderson (*OTP II*, p. 512) favours the early first century BCE; M. Hadas, *The Third and Fourth Books of Maccabees* (New York: Harper & Row, 1953), pp. 20–1, favours the late first century BCE; while Collins, *Between Athens and Jerusalem: Jewish Identity in the Hellenistic Diaspora* (2nd edn; Grand Rapids: Eerdmans, 2000), pp. 124–5, suggests the early first century CE as the *terminus post quem*.

[126] This may be a feature of the author's comedic bent, cf. Erich Gruen, *Heritage and Hellenism: The Reinvention of Jewish Tradition* (Los Angeles: University of California Press, 1998), p. 234. But it also reflects a dual theological agenda: the 'reversal' motif, wherein God cuts down the haughty, and the effectiveness of prayer. Cf. J. H. Newman, 'God Condemns the Arrogance of Power: The Prayer in 3 Maccabees 6.2-15', in M. Kiley et al. (eds), *The Prayer from Alexander to Constantine* (London: Routledge, 1997), pp. 48–52, and J. R. C. Cousland, 'Reversal, Recidivism, and Reward

The prayer of Eleazar in *3 Macc.* 6.1-3 moves one step further than the *Prayer of Azariah*, previously analysed. Recall that, in the fiery pit, Azariah called upon God to rescue him 'for the sake of Abraham' whom God loved, mindful of the covenant promise that Abraham's 'seed' would be multiplied. Here, in *3 Macc.* 6.1-3, the high priest Eleazar calls upon God to deliver 'the seed of Abraham' *directly*. It is the 'seed of Abraham' (Αβρααμ σπέρμα), the 'children of the sainted Jacob' (ἡγιασμένου τέκνα Ιακωβ) who are God's 'consecrated portion' perishing under foreign dominion. 'Seed' and 'sons' are one and the same: the 'descendants of Abraham' are the 'children of Jacob'. In fact, the text of *3 Macc.* 6.1-3 is unique in its presentation of 'the seed of Abraham' petitioning God for mercy for their own sake, as it were; in other words, there is a tacit assumption that God shows mercy to the 'seed of Abraham' as the sovereign master of all creation, and that his love for his consecrated people is embedded in the order of creation. Sarah Pearce notes that the message of *3 Maccabees* is that God, as King, has ultimate dominion over the fate of the Jews that no oppressive human king can thwart. The consequent purpose of the text is to encourage Jewish readers to have confidence in God's providence and his responsiveness to prayer. Loyalty to Judaism will be rewarded with life, but apostasy with death (cf. *3 Maccabees* 7). There is thus a Deuteronomistic overlay to the narrative of reversals in *3 Maccabees*.[127] But essentially, there is a focus on the efficaciousness of being the 'seed of Abraham' with regard to calling down God's provident mercy in the context of powerlessness and foreign oppression.

The late Second Temple testamentary work, the *Testament of Asher* (*T. Ash.*), expresses this motif according to the structures of its genre.[128] As he lies on his deathbed, Asher is depicted as drawing his sons near, to warn them about the future. He tells them: 'For I know that you will sin and be delivered into the hands of your enemies ... you will be thoroughly disobedient ... not heeding God's Law but human commandments, being corrupted by evil. For this reason, you will be scattered ... but he [God] will gather you in faith through his compassion and on account of Abraham, Isaac, and Jacob' (*T. Ash* 7.2; 5; 6a; 7). Although this text does not refer to the 'seed' of Abraham, Asher's sons are considered the descendants of the twelve patriarchs of Israel, and thus come under the mercy of God. Indeed, although they *sin* – which, it should be noted, is construed specifically as disobedience to the Law – they will be rescued from the consequences of their own corruption solely through God's great compassion, which he holds 'on account of Abraham, Isaac, and Jacob'.[129] This

---

in 3 Maccabees: Structure and Purpose', *JSJ* 34, no. 1 (2003), pp. 39–51. Note also the theme of dramatic reversals in the book of Esther following prayer, which strongly parallels *3 Macc.* 6.1-24. Thus, Noah Hacham, '3 Maccabees and Esther: Parallels, Intertextuality, and Diaspora Identity', *JBL* 126, no. 4 (2007), pp. 765–85, at p. 768.

[127] Sarah Pearce, '3 Maccabees', in Martin Goodman, John Barton and John Muddiman (eds), *Apocrypha* (Oxford: Oxford University Press, 2012), pp. 328–31. I would add that the language of the Jews as God's 'consecrated portion' confirms this tone; cf. Deut. 26.28.

[128] *OTP I*, pp. 816–18. The debate about the 'Jewish' or 'Christian', or 'Jewish and Christian' status of the T12P is, to my mind, satisfactorily resolved in a recent work by Joel Marcus, 'The *Testaments of the Twelve Patriarchs* and the *Didascalia Apostolorum*: A Common Jewish Christian Milieu?' *JTS* 61, no. 2 (2010), pp. 596–626.

[129] The *Testament of Asher* displays a concern with the 'two ways' available to humans, common to the sapiential genres of the period. In the *Testament of Asher* the paranaetic discourse is more individualized compared to the other testaments in the T12P. For fuller discussion, see M. Jack Suggs,

'Sin-Exile-Return' motif is an acknowledged part of the T12P as a whole, deriving from Deuteronomistic theologies.[130] Here, however, it draws particularly upon the role of the three patriarchs in 'returning' their sinful and wayward descendants back to God.

A similar scene is set out in the *Testament of Levi*.[131] As Levi reaches the end of his testamentary speech, he warns his kin that he can foresee their awful fate (*T. Levi* 14.1). Because Levi's sons will choose to do 'every evil deed', they will be 'humiliated among the nations' (14.1). The hatred that will fall upon Levi's sons is so great that 'unless [they] had received mercy through Abraham, Isaac, and Jacob, our fathers, not a single one of [their] *seed* would be left on the earth' (15.4). This text attests to the notion that the three fathers (Abraham, Isaac and Jacob) have power in the afterlife to influence their descendants for their benefit, and through their mercy – a perceptible precursor to the more developed concept of the זכות אבות in the rabbinic literature. What stands out in *T. Levi* 15.4 is the notion of Abraham bringing mercy to his sinful 'seed' as a 'last resort', as a measure that prevents their ultimate destruction for their 'deeds'.

Another apocryphal text, the *Prayer of Manasseh* (*Pr. Man.*) takes a similar stance, but weaves in poetic originalities of its own. The prayer was probably composed around the turn of the Common Era, originally in Greek rather than Hebrew (although it is only preserved in Syriac).[132] It purports to represent the prayer of the idolatrous seventh-century (BCE) Judean King Manasseh, who according to 2 Chronicles 33, was taken captive to Babylon and shackled in chains. In that text, Manasseh subsequently repents, beseeching God to forgive him and restore his life.[133] The genre of the *Prayer of Manasseh* has traditionally been understood as an extension of the 'corporate penitential prayer' common in Second Temple literature, but expressed in the first-person singular.[134] However, scholars now question the thematic and structural commonalities between

---

'The Christian Two Ways Tradition: Its Antiquity, Form and Function', in David E. Aune (ed.), *Studies in New Testament and Early Christian Literature: Essays in Honor of Allen P. Wikgren* (Leiden: Brill, 1972), pp. 60–74, at p. 68.

[130] M. De Jonge, 'The Two Great Commandments in the Testaments of the Twelve Patriarchs', *NovT* 44, no. 4 (2002), pp. 371–92, at p. 380.

[131] *OTP I*, pp. 788–95. Part of the T12P, the text of the *Testament of Levi* is considered unique for its focus upon sacerdotal themes (cf. Simon Mimouni, *Comptes rendus de l'Académie des inscriptions & belles lettres*, 2015 (Janvier–Mars, 2015), pp. 114–47), or for its perceived 'Jewish' flavour such as God's commitment to Levi's sons for the sake of the patriarchs (Marcus, 'A Common Jewish Christian Milieu', p. 603).

[132] David Lambert, 'The Prayer of Manasseh', in Marc Brettler, Carol Newsome, and Pheme Perkins (eds), *The New Oxford Annotated Bible with Apocrypha* (New York: Oxford University Press, 2018), pp. 1656–8, at p. 1656.

[133] The *Prayer of Manasseh* is preserved in two Syriac variants, between chapters 6 and 7 of the *Didascalia Apostolorum* (early third century CE), and some Peshitta variants appended to 2 Chronicles. Other Greek versions (appendices to LXX Psalter) and Latin versions (Jerome) also exist, transmitted later. See Ariel Gutman and Wido van Peursen, *The Two Syriac Versions of The Prayer of Manasseh* (Piscataway: Gorgias Press, 2011). The prayer's abrupt introduction in the *Didascalia* suggests that it was inserted between chapters 6 and 7, rather than being an organic part of the text. Thus, Judith H. Newman, 'Three Contexts of Manasseh's Prayer in the *Didascalia*', *JCSSyrSt* 7 (2007), pp. 3–15, at p. 7. The Hebrew 'Prayer of Manasseh' fragment at Qumran (4Q381, 33.1-11) represents an unrelated extra-biblical tradition. See, William M. Schniedewind, 'A Qumran Fragment of the Ancient "Prayer of Manasseh"?' *ZAW* 108, no. 1 (1996), pp. 105–7.

[134] Cf. J. H. Charlesworth, *OTP II*, pp. 629–30, noting the thematic and structural similarities between the *Prayer of Manasseh* and Psalm 51. Other late-biblical prayers expressed as corporate pleas for forgiveness are: Ezra 9.1-5; Neh. 1.4-11; 9.6-37; Dan. 9.4-19; and the apocryphal *Bar.* 1.15-3.8;

the corporate penitential prayers and the *Prayer of Manasseh*.[135] David Lambert has recently argued that the *Prayer of Manasseh* showcases a novel use of the emergent doctrine of repentance, which was not a thematic feature of the penitential prayer genre in the late Second Temple Period. The idea in the *Prayer of Manasseh* is that God has appointed repentance *for sinners*, as part of the order of creation itself, indeed as a feature of the world created at the very beginning of time.[136] Newman also recognizes the novelty of this idea in relation to the extant Second Temple Jewish literature – as nowhere else do we find a distinction between the righteous and the sinners, whereby repentance is created for the latter, and not for the former.[137]

The figure of Abraham also features in the prayer in an idiosyncratic manner. The *Prayer of Manasseh* begins with Manasseh calling out to God: 'O Lord Almighty, God of our ancestors, of Abraham,[138] Isaac and Jacob and of their *righteous seed*; you who made heaven and earth with all their order' (vv. 1-2).[139] The 'seed of Abraham' in this text are connoted as righteous in their own right, going further along in the continuum than texts such as Deut. 4.37; Isa. 41.8-9, that spoke of God honouring Abraham's seed for their own sake, or of God's direct love for the seed of Abraham' (Jer. 33.23-25; Ps. 105.6-12; 2 Chron. 20.7). There is no hint that the offspring of Abraham, Isaac and Jacob are deemed righteous for the sake of their fathers, but simply that they are righteous by virtue of *being* the 'seed of Abraham'.[140] Indeed, this text uniquely describes God as 'God of Abraham' *and* as 'God of [the] righteous seed' (of Abraham). A further innovation is found in Manasseh's perception of Israel's ancestors, and how it relates to the appreciation of his own sinfulness, as just noted:

> O Lord, according to your great goodness, you have promised repentance and forgiveness to those who have sinned against you, and in the multitude of your mercies you have appointed repentance for sinners so that they may be saved. Therefore you, O lord, God of the righteous, have not appointed repentance for the righteous, for Abraham, Isaac and Jacob, who did not sin against you, but you have appointed repentance for me, who am a sinner. (vv. 7c-8)[141]

Tob. 3.2-6. The language of *the Prayer of Manasseh* is consistently personal rather than national; cf. George W. E. Nickelsburg, 'Prayer of Manasseh', in *Apocrypha*, pp. 322–6.

[135] Cf. Judith H. Newman, 'The Form and Settings of the Prayer of Manasseh', in Mark J. Boda, Daniel K. Falk and Rodney A. Werline (eds), *Seeking the Favor of God, Volume 2: The Development of Penitential Prayer in Second Temple Judaism* (Atlanta: SBL Press, 2007), pp. 105–25, at p. 109.

[136] David Lambert, *How Repentance Became Biblical: Judaism, Christianity, and the Interpretation of Interpretation of Scripture* (New York: Oxford University Press, 2016), p. 170.

[137] Newman, 'The Form and Settings', p. 111.

[138] Cod. Borgia inserts the phrase 'for our father' before the name of Abraham; George Wilkins, 'The Prayer of Manasseh', *Hermathena* 16, no. 36 (1910), pp. 167–78, at p. 174.

[139] The phrase 'their righteous seed' is unusual in the extant literature. Lambert suggests that it may indicate that the prayer was meant to be uttered by a convert, but it is hard to see how this explanation follows (Lambert, 'The Prayer', p. 1656, n. to vv. 1-8).

[140] The need to express this connection has apparently receded in the author's view; if the three fathers were righteous, then the implication is that their 'seed' are also righteous.

[141] NRSV.

This extraordinary text moves in the opposite direction to the *Prayer of Azariah*, for example, which made a long introductory point about how the ancestors had all sinned, and how Azariah and his companions were now suffering the eventual punishment due to those sins. And while many other early Jewish and rabbinic texts would praise the virtues and righteousness of Abraham and the fathers, markedly few would entertain the idea that they were altogether sinless. The implication is that Manasseh does not see himself as part of the 'righteous seed' of Abraham, Isaac and Jacob (v. 1). For the sinful Manasseh, repentance has been appointed by God as a means of deliverance (1.8). In a marvellously poetic passage, Manasseh confesses:

> For the sins I have committed are more in number than the sand of the sea; my transgressions are multiplied, O Lord, they are multiplied! I am not worthy to look up and see the height of heaven because of the multitude of my iniquities. (1.9)

Notice how this text plays upon the biblical language of the promises to the patriarchs (Abraham, Isaac and Jacob) about their descendants being more numerous than the sand of the sea or the stars of heaven; this motif is turned into a lament about how *Manasseh's sins* are more numerous than the sand on the seashore, and how his sins are 'multiplied'. This scriptural allusion serves to reinforce Manasseh's position that through repentance, he might become one of the multitudinous, righteous 'seed of Abraham' as promised at the dawn of Israel's election. At the same time, the allusion neatly conveys the theological notion expressed in the prayer that repentance has an established existence as part of the order of creation, as Manasseh's reference to 'the sand of the sea' connects to Manasseh's introductory passage praising the power of God as creator of the world, 'who shackled the sea by [his] word of command' (v. 3). In sum, like the *Prayer of Azariah* and *3 Maccabees*, the text of the *Prayer of Manasseh* is contextualized by the circumstances of distress and captivity in a foreign land because of sin, but the reference to the 'seed of Abraham' turns upon the individual Manasseh in his difference and marginalized state, rather than upon the corporate connectedness of Israel as the 'seed of Abraham' who are rescued by God out of love.

Themes of personal and communal sin, intergenerational intercession and the status of Abraham's descendants receive extensive attention in the apocalypse known as *4 Ezra* (chs 3–14 of *2 Esdras* of the Apocrypha, and *4 Esdras* of the Vulgate).[142] Composed around the turn of the first century CE, in the aftermath of the Temple's destruction (c. 70 CE), the apocalypse *4 Ezra* represents *one* Jewish response to the calamity. It is commonly acknowledged as a work of theodicy that tries to grasp the continued reality of God's justice and election in the face of desperation in the wake of the destruction wrought by Rome.[143] Although the structural unity and narrative coherence of the text

---

[142] *OTP I*, pp. 525–59. The supposed Semitic *Vorlage* is not preserved, nor is its ancient Greek translation. There are eight 'daughter' translations surviving, all of which were made from the Greek (Latin, Syriac, Ethiopic, Georgian, Armenian and two Arabic versions). See Michael E. Stone and Matthias Henze (eds), *4 Ezra and 2 Baruch: Translations, Introductions, and Notes* (Minneapolis: Fortress Press, 2013), pp. 8, 12.

[143] Bruce W. Longenecker, *Two Esdras* (Sheffield: Sheffield Academic Press, 1995), p. 12; Dereck Daschke, *City of Ruins: Mourning the Destruction of Jerusalem Through Jewish Apocalypse* (Leiden: Brill, 2010), p. 105.

have been disputed, the form of the text – as, alternately, a dialogic debate or a 'test' of Ezra's resolve – has come up for renewed discussion in recent scholarship.[144] The text presents the biblical Ezra engaging in a series of conversations with God/the angel Uriel via revelatory visions revolving around God's covenant with Israel.

In the early stage of the eponymous visionary's discussion with God, the primordial biblical story and the call of Abraham is contextualized in light of human sin; thus, Abraham emerges as one who virtually corrects the human degeneration into accumulated iniquity, rescuing God's creation from its inexorable roll down the path of destruction. As Ezra explains,

> When those who lived on earth began to multiply, they produced children and peoples and many nations, and again they began to be more ungodly than were their ancestors. And when they were committing iniquity in your sight, you chose for yourself one of them, whose name was Abraham; you loved him, and to him alone you revealed the end of the times, secretly by night. You made an everlasting covenant with him, and promised him that you would never forsake his *seed*; and you gave him Isaac, and to Isaac you gave Jacob and Esau. (3.12-15)

According to this text, God's unique choice of Abraham leads him to disclose secret nocturnal revelations to Abraham alone, so that Abraham is privy to the divine plans about the end times.[145] Second, the covenant and promise made to Abraham mean that God will *never forsake* Abraham's 'seed' – for the simple fact, it seems to be implied here, that they *are* Abraham's seed. Although the biblical allusions are present – visions given to Abraham (cf. Gen. 15.1-26), God's choice of Abraham (Gen. 12.1-3), his love for Abraham (cf. Isa. 41.8; 2 Chron. 20.7) and the covenant with Abraham (cf. Gen. 17.1-30) – there is no associated mention of the Promised Land of Canaan. The 'promise' in *4 Ezra* 3.15 is, strikingly, simply that God will forever 'be there' for his people, never forsaking them. Third, in this context, the notion of sin (or 'iniquity') is foregrounded: just as people were sinning, God chose Abraham, and God chose him 'for himself'.[146]

The angel Uriel continues to mediate the divine revelations to Ezra, and the discussion moves into more complicated territory. Granted that Abraham's 'seed' continue to have a particular standing with God, Ezra wants to know more about the role of individual merit and vicarious merit, about individual punishment and vicarious punishment, and about the possibility of intercession in the end times. Ezra

---

[144] Cf. Karina Hogan, *Theologies in Conflict in 4 Ezra: Wisdom, Debate, and Apocalyptic Solution* (JSJSupp 130; Leiden: Brill, 2008), p. 4; Tzvi Novick, 'Test and Temptation in *4 Ezra*', *JSP* 22, no. 3 (2013), pp. 238–44.

[145] Much like the seer Ezra himself, who has privileged access to the divine secrets because of his piety and wisdom; thus Michael E. Stone, *Fourth Ezra: A Commentary on the Book of Fourth Ezra* (Hermeneia; Minneapolis: Fortress Press, 1990), pp. 174–5. Others see Ezra as a 'second Moses' in his relationship to the divine; Michael A. Knibb, 'Apocalyptic and Wisdom in 4 Ezra', *JSJ* 13, nos. 1–2 (1982), pp. 56–74, at p. 62.

[146] It is unclear whether God chose Abraham because he was *unlike* the other sinners, or whether he was also a sinner ('one of them') and that God chose him nevertheless. Because *4 Ezra* imagines the 'evil heart' planted in Adam as, essentially, a prototypical יצר הרע that flowed down through the generations (3.4-21), possibly the latter view of Abraham is the correct one.

asks God whether on the 'day of judgement', the righteous will be able to intercede 'for the ungodly' – 'fathers for sons or sons for parents, brothers for brothers, relatives for their kindred, or friends for those who are dearest' (*4 Ezra* 7.102). God's reply is pessimistic. Just as a father does not send his son (or vice versa) 'to be ill or sleep or eat or be healed in his place', so neither can one pray for the other, but 'all shall bear their own righteousness and unrighteousness' (7.102ff). However, Ezra finds this response unsatisfactory. He replies to God, 'How then do we find that first Abraham prayed for the people of Sodom, and Moses for our ancestors who sinned in the desert...?' And, Ezra wonders, why would it not be this way at the day of judgement, when sin and corruption have become far worse? (cf. 7.102).

God explains the difference as follows: in the times of Abraham and the great men of Israel, 'those who were strong prayed for the weak'. But the end times herald a new 'immortal age' when sin has ended and truth has appeared. In that time, no one will be able to stand proxy for another, 'to have mercy on someone who has been condemned in the judgment, or to harm someone who is victorious' (*4 Ezra* 7.102-115 (36-45)).[147] The strong merits of Abraham may have covered over the weakness of his seed's sin in the present world, but in the age to come, such merits – and the capacity for intercession that they bring – will be of no avail to his descendants if they do not themselves 'bear their own righteousness'. The 'inheritance' of the promise to Abraham will be revealed in the world to come, not in this world.[148] Although these ideas have unfortunately become embroiled – if not entrenched – in the scholarship within the apparent interpretive divide between 'grace' and 'legalism' in early Judaism and Christianity, they are profoundly important for how the figure of Abraham was beginning to be understood as a protector of his 'seed', and an exemplar of the 'righteous works' that shape a person in this life.[149] If any 'resolution' of the many dilemmas posed in *4 Ezra* can be said to be evident in the text, it may be the notion of 'rededication and commitment to the law'.[150]

All of the texts analysed here have displayed an insistence upon God's election of, and love for Abraham and his 'seed'. In times of peril and anguish, both seer and penitent alike called upon God to be merciful for the sake of Abraham and the

---

[147] 'In 7.112-13 the angel points out to [Ezra] that it is precisely because this world is imperfect that there is no intercession in it, but the day of judgment is the end of this imperfect world': Michael E. Stone, 'Coherence and Inconsistency in the Apocalypses: The Case of "The End" in 4 Ezra', *JBL* 102, no. 2 (1983), pp. 229–43, at p. 239.

[148] Jason M. Zurawski, 'The Two Worlds and Adam's Sin: The Problem of *4 Ezra* 7.10-14', in Gabriele Boccaccini and Jason M. Zurawski (eds), *Interpreting 4 Ezra and 2 Baruch: International Studies* (LSTS 87; London: T&T Clark, 2014), pp. 97–106, at p. 100.

[149] Bruce W. Longenecker, *Eschatology and the Covenant: A Comparison of 4 Ezra and Romans 1–11* (JSNTSup 57; Sheffield: Sheffield Academic Press, 1991). Other heuristic lenses that have coloured (and obscured) an adequate reading of *4 Ezra* include the facile dichotomy of 'universalism' v. 'particularism' – which is often aligned with the 'Jewish' v. 'Christian' binary – as though Ezra's theodicy can satisfactorily be resolved according to whichever world view gets the upper hand in the text. The 'universalism/particularism' lens is evident in the work of Alden Thompson, *Responsibility for Evil in the Theodicy of IV Ezra: A Study Illustrating the Significance of Form and Structure for the Meaning of the Book* (SBLDS 29; Missoula: Scholars Press, 1977), and is critiqued in Hogan, *Theologies in Conflict*, pp. 25–6.

[150] Alexander E. Stewart, 'Narrative World, Rhetorical Logic, and the Voice of the Author in 4 Ezra', *JBL* 132, no. 2 (2013), pp. 373–91, at p. 382, n. 31.

covenant. However, in the *Apocalypse of Zephaniah*, this motif shifts ever so subtly towards the idea of the patriarchs *themselves* coming to the aid of their own 'seed' from their vantage point in heaven. That is, Abraham, Isaac and Jacob are given agency – divine-like prerogatives – to intercede for their suffering descendants upon earth. In the text, the pseudonymous seer has a vision of souls in torment, those suffering in the afterlife because of their unjust practices (e.g. taking bribes and usury).[151] The seer Zephaniah wonders if repentance is available to the said souls but God tells him that they must wait until the final judgement (10.1-14). The seer then turns his attention to three men who are praying and interceding for the souls in torment (11.1-3). An angel informs him that these men are the three fathers Abraham, Isaac and Jacob (11.4) who come forth daily at an appointed hour to pray for sinners (11.5). At the same time, all the righteous in heaven and earth join their prayers to those of the fathers, on behalf of sinners awaiting judgement (11.5-6).

One final text from the Apocrypha will conclude this section. The text of *4 Maccabees* is a philosophical reflection on the supremacy of piety and religion over 'the passions', based on the martyrology found in *2 Maccabees*, especially the stories of Eleazar and the mother with her seven martyred sons.[152] By this, the author means that living by the dictates of the Torah will produce virtue, which in turn will curb the instinct to be led astray into vice by excessive emotions and desires.[153] For the author of *4 Maccabees*, the trials of the martyrs best exemplify this philosophy.[154] *4 Maccabees* places comparatively more emphasis on the phrase 'children of Abraham' (οἱ Αβρααμ παῖδες) than the other Greek apocryphal literatures, only using the phrase 'seed of Abraham' once at ch. 18 v. 1 (and somewhat idiosyncratically). In the text of *4 Maccabees*, the phrase 'children of Abraham' (οἱ Αβρααμ παῖδες) occurs in contexts emphasizing the necessity of enduring under severe and brutal trials, when the collective identity of the Jewish people is placed under most pressure.

For example, in the narrative of Eleazar's martyrdom, which is precipitated by his refusal to eat pork, the hero cries out with aplomb, 'Never may we, the children of Abraham (οἱ Αβρααμ παῖδες), think so basely that out of cowardice we feign a role unbecoming to us' (*4 Macc.* 6.17).[155] As Eleazar is subsequently burnt alive 'for the sake

---

[151] *OTP I*, pp. 497–516. *Apocalypse of Zephaniah* (preserved in Sahidic and Akhmimic fragments) was deemed by Richard Bauckham – as early as 1986 – to be the only extant apocalypse almost certainly of 'pre-Christian Jewish' origin. Baukham also lamented that *Apocalypse of Zephaniah* had been 'extraordinarily neglected by scholars' prior to its inclusion in Charlesworth's *OTP*. See Bauckham, 'The Apocalypses in the New Pseudepigrapha', *JSNT* 26 (1986), pp. 97–117, at pp. 100–1. Unfortunately, *Apocalypse of Zephaniah* is relatively under-investigated in the scholarship even today.

[152] David A. deSilva, 'The Sinaiticus Text of 4 Maccabees', *CBQ* 68, no. 1 (2006), pp. 47–62, at pp. 48–9.

[153] Cf. Ibid., p. 49.

[154] It is well known that *4 Maccabees* is an eclectic text, preserved in a variety of Greek manuscripts appended to the LXX. It is usually dated between the first century BCE and the first century CE, composed by a diaspora Jew using Greco-Roman rhetorical conventions. See Walter T. Wilson, '4 Maccabees', in Michael D. Coogan (ed.), *The New Oxford Annotated Apocrypha: Augmented Third Edition* (New York/Oxford: Oxford University Press, 2007), pp. 362–3, at p. 362; Anna-Lüsa Tolonen and Elisa Uusimäki, 'Managing the Ancestral Way of Lide in the Roman Diaspora: The Mélange of Philosophical and Scriptural Practice in 4 Maccabees', *JSJ* 48 (2017), pp. 113–41.

[155] The NRSV obscures the phrase κακῶς φρονήσαιμεν ('think evilly'), rendering it 'think so basely'. To contravene the Torah is, in Eleazar's view, deeply vicious and opposed to 'the good'. See the analysis

of the law', he offers his martyrdom to God as a vicarious atonement for the sins of his people, interceding that his death might function as sufficient 'punishment' for their sins (*4 Macc.* 6.27b-29). The didactic narrator later reflects upon Eleazar to the effect that he is now 'alive to God', like 'our patriarchs Abraham and Isaac and Jacob' (7.18-20; cf. 16.24-25), for Eleazar attended wholeheartedly to religion; he and those like him, will be welcomed into the heavenly realm by the three fathers (cf. *4 Macc.* 13.14-17).[156]

Another theme found in *4 Maccabees* is that of the patriarch Abraham himself being the prototypical, faithful martyr. One tortured youth is described as being 'courageous' and 'worthy of Abraham' (*4 Macc.* 9.21 NRSV) as he died in defence of his religion (9.22-24). The Sinaiticus version of ch. 9 v. 21 reads ὁ Αβρααμ υἱὸς ('son of Abraham') to describe the young man, but the Rahlfs reading prefers 'Ἀβραμιαῖος' ('Abraham-like-one'), which is followed by the New Revised Standard Version (NRSV). This curious title accords with the tendency of *4 Maccabees* to use terms evoking imitation of an archetype, rather than terms of biological descent.[157] The mother of the seven martyred sons was not swayed by 'sympathy for her children', and thus 'she was of the same mind (lit. "soul") as Abraham' (τὴν Αβρααμ ὁμόψυχον; 14.20).[158] As the 'daughter of God-fearing Abraham', this mother 'remembered his fortitude' (15.27-28) as she watched her sons being killed. The narrator therefore extols her as the 'daughter of Abraham' (18.20) and her sons as 'the sons of Abraham' (18.23).[159] Speaking to the mother of the murdered sons, the narrator claims, 'Your children were truly of father Abraham' (γὰρ ἡ παιδοποιία σου ἀπὸ Αβρααμ τοῦ πατρός; 17.5-6; cf. 9.21; 15.28; 18.20, 23). In a most

---

in Hans Moscicke, 'The Concept of Evil in 4 Maccabees: Stoic Absorption and Adaptation', *JJTP* 25 (2017), pp. 163–95, at p. 183. Eleazar's composed and courageous assertion of Jewish group identity ('we, the children of Abraham') recalls John 8.32-33.

[156] The idea that the patriarchs are alive in the presence of God, although dead, gets stronger in *4 Maccabees*; note that this notion of Abraham, Isaac and Jacob as active agents in ensuring the welfare of their 'seed' from their place in the afterlife took on other forms in the *Testament of Levi*, *Testament of Asher* and *Apocalypse of Zephaniah* analysed formerly.

[157] deSilva, 'The Sinaiticus Text of 4 Maccabees', p. 60; and Turid Karlsen Seim, 'Abraham, Ancestor or Archetype? A Comparison of Abraham-Language in 4 Maccabees and Luke-Acts', in Adela Yarbro Collins and Margaret M. Mitchell (eds), *Antiquity and Humanity: Essays on Ancient Religions and Philosophy Presented to Hans Dieter Betz on His 70th Birthday* (Tübingen: Mohr Siebeck, 2001), pp. 27–42, at p. 30.

[158] Scholars see this text as a clear reference to the *Akedah*; see also *4 Macc.* 16.20 for a direct comparison between the mother and Abraham at the *Akedah*. See L. Kundert, *Die Opferung/Bindung Isaaks, Vol. 1* (WMANT 78/79; Neukirchen-Vluyn: Neukirchener, 1998), pp. 169–72; Sandmel, *Philo's Place in Judaism*, pp. 56–9; Seim, 'Abraham, Ancestor or Archetype?' pp. 30–6; Fretheim, *Abraham*, pp. 154–5; cf. David deSilva, *4 Maccabees: Introduction and Commentary on the Greek Text in Codex Sinaiticus* (Leiden: Brill, 2006), pp. 219–30. On the mother as 'like-souled' to Abraham, see the excellent analysis of David deSilva, 'The Perfection of "Love for Offspring": Greek Representations of Maternal Affection and the Achievement of the Heroine of 4 Maccabees', *NTS* 52 (2006), pp. 251–68, at p. 256.

[159] The mother's love for her sons revolves around two concepts: the moral likeness between the mother and her sons, which is expressive of the maternal bond, and the biological basis of that bond, which the author locates in the implantation of the 'seed' within her womb (15.6). Thus, deSilva, 'Love for Offspring', p. 258.

curious use of the phrase 'seed of Abraham', the narrator concludes his disquisition on the supremacy of piety with the words:

> O Israelite children, offspring of the seed of Abraham (ὦ τῶν Ἀβραμιαίων σπερμάτων ἀπόγονοι, παῖδες Ἰσραηλῖται), obey this law and exercise piety in every way, knowing that devout reason is master of all emotions, not only of sufferings from within, but also of those from without. (18.1-2)[160]

The phrase is the culmination of the narrative, an exhortation 'to find honour and advantage' in 'their Jewish identity' and in their praxis.[161] But the phraseology is most unusual: 'the offspring *of* the offspring *of* Abraham'. It is as though 'the seed of Abraham' is the head noun phrase – signifying a subgroup, perhaps Abraham's direct descendant/s, Isaac (and Jacob) – with the dependent noun phrase 'offspring of [the seed]' perhaps designating the author's rhetorical audience – the Jews in the Roman diaspora. That two different Greek nouns used (σπέρμα (gen.) and ἀπόγονος (adj.), respectively) suggest that the author is making a slight distinction – and the latter noun is rare in the LXX (2 Sam. 21; 1 Chron. 20.6; Jud. 5.6).

A final point to make about *4 Maccabees* is that there is less of a discussion about whether or not the fathers can intercede for their descendants on earth (compared to *4 Ezra, Testament of Levi and Testament of Asher* for example) and more of an assumed focus on the active role that Abraham, Isaac and Jacob perform in the afterlife, in welcoming those like them into the place of God. But like other apocryphal text, *4 Maccabees* situates its exhortations to Abraham's 'seed'/'offspring' within the context of foreign persecution and the deprivation of political liberty (cf. *Prayer of Azariah, Prayer of Manasseh, 3 Maccabees, 4 Ezra*). The motif of imitation in *4 Maccabees* – so common in martyrdom literature – merges with other Abraham tropes, such as the exemplarity of the patriarch in his righteous 'works' and the necessity of imitating him. To these texts we now turn.

Theme 2: Abraham as exemplar to his seed

The apocryphal book of Tobit is a rich and engaging narrative that presents its eponymous hero as a morally upright diaspora Jew who is concerned with social justice and the observance of the Torah.[162] Amy-Jill Levine comments that the book's 'rollicking plot and vivid characters' make it a 'splendid example of the Jewish novella or short historical fiction'.[163] The tones of whimsy and comedy resonating throughout

---

[160] *OTP II*, pp. 531-64.
[161] David A. deSilva, *4 Maccabees* (Sheffield: Sheffield Academic Press, 1998), p. 49.
[162] The Greek texts of Tobit have been transmitted in three text forms, the first of which is attested by Codex Vaticanus (B), Codex Alexandrinus (A) and Codex Venetus (minuscule derivative), all between the fourth and fifth centuries CE; the long version is the uncial Codex Sinaiticus (S) from the fourth century CE. Of the S family is the important MS 319 from Mt Athos, which contains the lacuna *Tob.* 4.7-19. Two Hebrew fragments of *Tobit* were also uncovered at Qumran. For a full discussion of S, see Robert J. Littman, *Tobit: The Book of Tobit in Codex Sinaiticus* (Leiden/Boston: Brill, 2008).
[163] Amy-Jill Levine, 'Tobit', in Michael D. Coogan, Mark Zvi Brettler, Carol Ann Newsome and Pheme Perkins (eds), *The New Oxford Annotated Bible with Apocrypha: New Revised Standard Version* (3rd ed; New York: Oxford University Press, 2001), p. 11.

the story have also been discussed at length.[164] Yet, the historical-narrative context is serious enough: the Assyrian conquest of the kingdom of Israel in 722 BCE. The book of Tobit was likely composed in the third century BCE, probably in an Aramaic original that was later translated (and finally preserved) in Greek.[165]

Tobit's upright behaviour includes refraining from idolatrous practices (1.5-7), walking 'in the ways of truth and righteousness' (1.3), giving alms regularly (1.8-9) and refusing to eat with Gentiles (1.10-12). Tobit buries the dead – despite the risks involved (1.16; 2.7-9) – gives his food to the hungry and his clothing to the naked (1.17). When an unfortunate accident renders him blind, Tobit's wife Anna is forced to earn a livelihood (2.11-12). Anna excels in her work, so that her employer gives her a goat over and above her usual wages (2.13). Tobit does not believe his wife when she protests that the goat was a gift; he assumes, instead, that Anna had stolen it. Anna retorts that she, like Tobit, has righteous deeds of her own (2.14).[166] But, unconvinced and inconsolable, Tobit turns to prayer, imploring that God not punish his sins (ταῖς ἁμαρτίαις μου), his unwitting offenses (τοῖς ἀγνοήμασίν μου) or the sin and disobedience of his 'fathers' (3.3). At the same time, Tobit determines that Anna's presumably impious behaviour is God's just penalty for Tobit's sins (3.5a). Meanwhile, God hears Tobit's prayer and sends the angel Raphael to heal Tobit of his blindness (3.16), but Tobit is busy preparing himself for death, believing that God has answered his request to die.

Tobit therefore calls his son Tobias to his bedside to provide him with final instructions (4.1-19).[167] It is in this context that Tobit refers to 'Abraham ... and [his] seed' (4.12).[168] Tobit associates Abraham's righteous behaviour with the reward given to Abraham's 'seed', buttressed by Tobit's particular conceptualizations of 'righteousness' and 'sin'. Tobit instructs Tobias as follows:

> First of all, marry a woman from among the seed of your fathers (ἀπὸ τοῦ σπέρματος τῶν πατέρων σου) ... Remember, my son, that Noah, Abraham, Isaac, and Jacob, our ancestors of old, all took wives from among their kindred (ἐκ τῶν ἀδελφῶν αὐτῶν). They were blessed in their children, and their 'seed' will inherit the land (καὶ τὸ σπέρμα αὐτῶν κληρονομήσει γῆν). (4.12)

---

[164] Anathea Portier-Young, 'Alleviation of Suffering in the Book of Tobit: Comedy, Community, and Happy Endings', *CBQ* 63 (2001), pp. 35–54; Lawrence M. Wills, *The Jewish Novel in the Ancient World* (Ithaca/London: Cornell University Press, 1995), p. 69.

[165] Levine, 'Tobit', in Coogan (ed.), *The New Oxford Apocrypha*, p. 11.

[166] Jonathan R. Trotter sees a correspondence with the book of Job in this narrative of marital altercation; see idem, 'The Developing Narrative of the Life of Job: The Implications of Some Shared Elements of the Book of Tobit and the *Testament of Job*', *CBQ* 77, no. 3 (2015), pp. 449–66, at p. 450.

[167] The genre is disputed. *Tobit* 4 has been read as a didactic narrative or a wisdom book. Thus, Hans-Peter Müller, 'Die weisheitliche Lehrerzählung im Alten Testament und in seiner Umwelt', *Die Welt des Orients* 9, no. 1 (1977), pp. 77–98, at pp. 80–1; it has also been read as a farewell testament: Francis M. Macatangay, *The Wisdom Instructions in the Book of Tobit* (Deuterocanonical and Cognate Literature Studies 12; Berlin: de Gruyter, 2011), chapter 2.

[168] As noted in n. 166, the text of *Tob.* 4.7-19 is found only in MS 319, and skipped over in S. The lacuna is, however, most likely to have been part of the original. Macatangay, *The Wisdom Instructions*, p. 46.

The exemplarity of the patriarchs is called upon to enhance Tobit's instruction: Abraham, Isaac, Jacob (and curiously, Noah) all entered into endogamous unions;[169] Tobias must do the same.[170] Tobit's insistence on endogamous marriage draws its seriousness from the assumption that the exile and diaspora were the consequences of exogamy.[171] The precedent for such thinking was established in texts such as Exod. 34.16 and Deut. 7.3-4, where the Israelites were warned, upon entering Canaan, not to intermarry lest they give way to idolatry (cf. also Josh. 23.12-13; Ezra 10.10-12).[172] The theme of endogamy was generally prominent in the post-exilic period, notably in Ezra's concern that 'the holy seed' of Israel not pollute itself through mixed marriages (Ezra 9.2). This 'seed' of Israel is, according to Michael Satlow, literally the male semen that must not be mixed with other peoples.[173] It is possible that *Tob.* 4.12 uses the noun σπέρμα in a double sense to mean both the holy male semen and the holy people of Israel. But, as Geoffrey Miller points out, the term ἀδελφός in ch. 4 v. 12 means not only 'tribe' but also 'close relative'.[174] Abraham, Isaac, Jacob and Noah all entered into marriages of this more restricted kind. The book of Tobit is the only post-exilic Jewish text to use the examples of the patriarchs to promote such circumscribed endogamy.[175] Notice in particular how Tobit reconfigures the Torah's trope of Abraham's 'seed' inheriting the land – the Genesis texts connected the covenant with the gift of the land (Gen. 12.1-9, 13.14-15, 15.1-20, 17.1-27, 21.8-14, 22.15-19) while Tobit believes that Abraham's 'seed' will inherit the land as a reward for marrying exclusively within their kinship circles. At the conclusion of the book, Tobit prophesizes that the survivors of exile will return forever to Jerusalem, the 'land of Abraham' (τῇ γῇ Ἀβρααμ; (Codex S; 14.7).

The verses bracketing Tobit's injunction in ch. 4 v. 12 deal with the subject of almsgiving (4.6-11; 14, 16–17). Tobit counsels Tobias to avoid sinning against the commandments (4.5-6), to practise 'righteousness' and to give alms (4.7-8) in order to 'store up a good treasure' in times of necessity that will 'deliver' Tobias from 'death' (4.9-11). Tobit further advises his son to always pay the workers' wages immediately (4.14a), which is akin to 'serving God'; such service will lead Tobias to 'receive payment' (4.14b) in return. All of Tobias' surplus wealth should be given as alms (4.16) – and God will recompense Tobias accordingly (cf. 4.19). In Tobit's vision, almsgiving not only saves from death but also 'purges away' all sin (ἀποκαθαίρει πᾶσαν ἁμαρτίαν; 12.9).[176] What

---

[169] *Jub.* 4.33 highlights Noah as one who marries a close relative, while his immediate descendants largely practise exogamy.

[170] Lawrence Wills notes with some wit that, given the story's context and set of characters, 'it seems unlikely that Tobias could ever meet anyone who was not a relative' (*The Jewish Novel*, p. 78).

[171] Cf. Amy-Jill Levine, 'Diaspora as Metaphor: Bodies and Boundaries in the Book of Tobit', in J. Andrew Overman and Robert S. MacLennan (eds), *Diaspora Jews and Judaism* (Atlanta: Scholars Press, 1992), pp. 105–18, at p. 105.

[172] C. Carmichael, 'Forbidden Mixtures', *VT* 32 (1982), pp. 394–415.

[173] Michael L. Satlow, *Jewish Marriage in Antiquity* (Oxford and Princeton: Princeton University Press, 2001), p. 137.

[174] Geoffrey David Miller, *Marriage in the Book of Tobit* (Berlin: Walter de Gruyter, 2011), p. 72.

[175] Miller, *Marriage in the Book of Tobit*, p. 73.

[176] The term 'purge' (ἀποκαθαίρω) in ch. 12 v. 9 'comes from a Semitic original that meant "to cleanse"', or perhaps better, 'clear' an account of any outstanding obligation – in other words, to pay off a debt. Almsgiving is uniquely able to do this because it funds a treasury in heaven, something that neither prayer nor fasting can accomplish on its own'. See Gary A. Anderson, *Charity: The Place of the Poor in the Biblical Tradition* (New Haven: Yale University Press, 2013), p. 138.

is the rhetorical purpose of sandwiching the reference to Abraham's endogamy – and the reward that his 'seed' will inherit the land – between detailed exordiums about almsgiving producing a storehouse of credit with God?

Abraham's exemplary endogamy functions as a mirror image of almsgiving – leading not only to Tobias' personal 'reward' in his heavenly 'account', which can be redrawn upon in times of need, but also to the good of the whole tribe: endogamy leads to the ongoing reward enjoyed (or yet to be enjoyed again after the exile) by the seed of Abraham – the gift of the land in perpetuity. Endogamous union constitutes both 'love' for Tobias' kin and avoidance of 'sin'. On a quotidian level, the giving of alms is an expression of kinship love which accumulates in Tobias' 'treasury' (4.14-17). Almsgiving is a charitable work operating as a 'storable commodity' – a vital practice if the promises made to Abraham's seed are to be realized (cf. 14.10).[177]

In the post-biblical period, the concept of Abraham's exemplarity became a full-blown literary motif, almost to the point of assuming pietistic expression. Yet, the reasons for which Abraham was held in high esteem varied between authors. In the book of *Sirach*, written originally in Hebrew (c. 180 CE) and later translated into Greek (c. 117 CE), Abraham is praised as being incomparable in 'glory'.[178] While *Sirach* is considered a sapiential text, the encomium of Israel's fathers and heroes in chs 44–50 conclude the book on a note of sustained reverence. Abraham is third in line, following brief praises[179] of Enoch and Noah (44.16-18):

> Abraham was the great father (μέγας πατὴρ) of a multitude of nations, and no one
>   has been found like him in glory (δόξῃ).
> He preserved the law (συνετήρησεν νόμον) of the Most High,
> and entered into a covenant (ἐν διαθήκῃ) with him;
> he certified the covenant in his flesh,
> and when he was tested he proved faithful (πιστός).
> Therefore, the Lord assured him with an oath
> that the nations would be blessed in his seed (ἐνευλογηθῆναι ἔθνη ἐν
>   σπέρματι αὐτοῦ);
> that he would make him as numerous as the dust of the earth,
> and lift up his seed (ἀνυψῶσαι τὸ σπέρμα αὐτοῦ) like the stars,
> and give them an inheritance from sea to sea
> and from the Euphrates to the ends of the earth. (*Sir.* 44.19-21)

This text captures certain themes expressed in Genesis, such as 'the multitude of nations' proceeding from Abraham, the covenants made with Abraham and the blessing of

---

[177] The descriptive term is Anderson; see idem, *Charity*, p. 111.
[178] On this dating of *Sirach*, see Gregory, 'Abraham as the Jewish Ideal, pp. 66–81, at p. 66. Fragments of the Hebrew were found in the Cairo Genizah in 1896, and other chapters were discovered during excavations at Masada in 1963–1964. See, Harrington, *Invitation to the Apocrypha*, p. 79.
[179] Yet, as Benjamin G. Wright notes, Noah and Abraham are linked; Noah is a 'remnant' saved from the flood and his legacy continues in the figure of Abraham: 'Biblical Interpretation in the Book of Ben Sira', in Matthias Henze (ed.), *A Companion to Biblical Interpretation in Early Judaism* (Grand Rapids: Eerdmans, 2011), pp. 361–86, at p. 382.

the 'nations' through his 'seed'. However, Sirach considers these promises as already realized – Abraham *was* the 'great father' of 'a multitude of nations' (44.19). Sirach also develops the notion of Abraham as Torah observant, a tradition that was to spring forth in the post-biblical period with considerable alacrity.[180] There is, furthermore, an oblique reference to the *Akedah*; Abraham is described as having been 'tested' by God and found faithful.[181] Ben Sira's reference to the divine 'blessing' as a consequence of Abraham's fidelity (44.20) echoes the second angelic address to Abraham after the near-sacrifice of his son (Gen. 22.15-18).[182] But Abraham's fidelity – as well as the reference to the uniqueness of his 'glory' – also refers to his observance of the Law of God.[183] Abraham's faith when 'tested' structurally corresponds to his faithfulness in keeping 'the Law of the Most High'.[184] The fragment of ch. 44 v. 19 reads מצות (pl. 'commandments'), but the LXX (uncharacteristically) translated this to the singular νόμος ('law'), rather than the plural ἐντολή. The LXX almost uniformly renders the singular תורה as νόμος, and this suggests that the translator understood the sense of מצות as the whole Torah – thus, Abraham was completely Torah observant.[185] Abraham's 'seed' share in Abraham's blessing: they are 'exalted' like the 'stars of heaven' – a unique elaboration of the Genesis texts referring to the numerous nature of Abraham's seed.[186]

When extolling the praises of Isaac, Ben Sira asserts that the 'same assurance' given to Abraham was also given to Isaac *'for the sake of his father Abraham'* (Sir. 44.22). This important theme – that of vicarious blessing – is echoed in the later strata of the biblical texts dealing with Abraham's 'seed'. The truly innovative aspect of Sirach's text, however, is its focus on Abraham's observance of the Law, his fidelity when tested and the enduring 'glory' accruing to Abraham (Sir. 44.19-20). The wider context of Sirach's hymn to the ancestors illustrates that 'eternal glory' is found only by those who live in piety, wisdom and obedience to God's commandments – while the contrasting, temporary 'glory' based on power (political and interpersonal) is not something that endures in memory.[187] Sir. 44.19-21 thus celebrates the inheritance coming to Abraham's 'seed' in connection with themes such as 'glory', fatherhood, Torah observance, the covenant and Abraham's personal fidelity to God. It is *because of these features* that Abraham's 'seed' are said to be exalted in the future and are to receive the whole earth as their inheritance.

We will examine three more Pseudepigrapha that deal with Abraham's exemplarity in relation to his 'seed' – Pseudo-Philo's *Biblical Antiquities* (hereafter, *LAB*),[188] the book of *Jubilees* and the *Testament of Abraham* (*T. Abr.*). But first, a word of caution: the first

---

[180] I will give more examples of this motif in Chapter 5 on 'Abraham's works'.
[181] Sir. 44.20d. Cf. Gregory, 'Abraham as the Jewish Ideal', p. 73.
[182] Levenson, *The Death and Resurrection of the Beloved Son*, p. 175.
[183] Gregory, 'Abraham as the Jewish Ideal', p. 77.
[184] Ibid.
[185] Ibid., p. 69. The plural מצות in ch. 44 v. 19 also recalls Gen. 26.5, where Abraham was said to have kept individual 'commandments' given by God, as well as his 'statutes', 'charge' and 'laws'.
[186] The Greek text adds 'to make him as numerous as the dust of the earth and exalt his seed like the stars' (44.21a). The sentence is absented from the Hebrew version.
[187] Eric D. Reymond, 'Prelude to the Praise of the Ancestors, Sirach 44.1-15', *HUCA* 72 (2001), pp. 1–14.
[188] From the Latin title for the book, *Liber Antiquitatum Biblicarum*, as traditionally accepted in the scholarship, and based on the critical edition preserved in Latin (C. Perrot and O.-M. Bogaert,

two of these texts have, in scholarly discourse, been classified generically as 'biblical retellings', or 'rewritten bible'. As Hindy Najman argues, however, such taxonomies presume untenable facts about the (Hebrew) biblical canon in the second century, such as that the canon was closed (and able to be supplemented by 'rewritings'), *or* that the canon was superior to later derivative interpretations ('retellings' such as *Jubilees*).[189] I suggest that we could use a descriptive (rather than classificatory) concept, such as Gérard Gennette's 'paratexts', to refer to this literature in view of the well-known developmental status of both the canonical – and 'pseudepigraphical' – literatures in the third to first centuries CE.[190] The *Testament of Abraham* also requires preliminary remarks. Although it is titled a 'testament', it has little in common with the testamentary genre. It is a sophisticated narrative with regard to plotting, (humorous) characterization and simultaneity in its temporal perspective. It also contains many apocalyptic features. In short, it mixes a variety of genres, as did many Jewish and Christian works of antiquity.

In several key places, Pseudo-Philo's *LAB* weaves together notions of slavery and freedom, while referencing the biblical promises made by God to Abraham's 'seed'. The text is also deeply concerned with idolatry – with both its proscription and its detrimental effects upon humanity (cf. 6.1-18; 25.9-13; 36.3; 44.1-5).[191] And like several other early Jewish texts, *LAB* contributes to the discussion about vicarious merit, the efficacy of intercession and proxy punishments for ancestral sins. We also begin to see more clearly, as in *4 Ezra*, the crystallization of a debate about the propriety (or even the possibility) of relying on the merits of Abraham and the fathers to counteract the effects of personal sin – Can the dead intercede for the living? Can the living intercede for the dead?[192]

Pseudo-Philo first refers to Abraham when narrating the tower of Babel (cf. Genesis 11), expanding the story by characterizing the Chaldean builders of the tower as keen idolaters. By inscribing their names upon the bricks, the men hubristically promote themselves through their handiwork (*LAB* 6.2-3). But a minority refuse

---

Pseudo-Philon: Les Antiquités Bibliques (SC, 229/30; Paris: Les Éditions du Cerf, 1976) upon which the English translation of Daniel Harrington is based; cf. *OTP II*, pp. 304–77).

[189] Hindy Najman, 'Reconsidering Jubilees: Prophecy and Exemplarity', in Gabriele Boccaccini and Giovanni Ibba (eds), *Enoch and the Mosaic Torah: The Evidence of Jubilees* (Grand Rapids: Eerdmans, 2009), pp. 229–43.

[190] Gérard Genette, *Paratexts: Thresholds of Interpretation* (Cambridge: Cambridge University Press, 1997); idem, *Palimpsestes: Literature in the Second Degree* (trans. Channa Newman and Claude Doubinsky; Lincoln: Indiana University Press, 1997). Other scholars have previously used Genette's theories as a heuristic in this regard; see A. Lange, 'In the Second Degree: Ancient Jewish Paratextual Literature in the Context of Graeco-Roman and Ancient Near Eastern Literature', in P. Alexander, A. Lange and R. Pillinger (eds), *In the Second Degree: Paratextual Literature in Ancient Near Eastern and Ancient Mediterranean Culture and Its Reflections in Medieval Literature* (Leiden: Brill, 2010), pp. 3–40.

[191] 'Pseudo-Philo is preoccupied with idolatry' throughout the composition: see Frederick J. Murphy, *Pseudo-Philo: Rewriting the Bible* (New York: Oxford University Press, 1993), p. 39. Indeed, the emphasis is aetiological and fundamental: 'Israel begins with Abraham's rejection of idolatry and choice to serve God': Frederick J. Murphy, 'Retelling the Bible: Idolatry in Pseudo-Philo', *JBL* 107, no. 2 (1988), pp. 275–87, at p. 276; cf. 284.

[192] The Latin edition of *LAB* is thought to be a translation from a Greek text, which in turn is based on an initial Hebrew. See Daniel J. Harrington, 'The Original Language of Pseudo-Philo's "Liber Antiquitatum Biblicarum"', *HTR* 63, no. 4 (1970), pp. 503–14.

to join in, chief among them Abraham (6.3); he interprets the men's scheme as self-worship and therefore also as a betrayal of 'the one Lord' (6.4). Abraham and his faithful comrades declare that they would prefer to be thrown into the kiln with the bricks, rather than defect from monotheism.[193] And indeed, Abraham is about to be thrown into the furnace, but God stages a cataclysmic rescue. God rewards Abraham by electing him and making a covenant with him (6.13-18).[194] Abraham and his comrades return to Chaldea 'rejoicing in the name of the Lord' (6.18-19). At this point, Pseudo-Philo recounts the promise made to Abraham and his 'seed' in Genesis: because of Abraham's trust, God will bless his 'seed' in perpetuity (7.5).[195]

Abraham's 'seed' are mentioned in Pseudo-Philo's narration of the 'prophet' Balaam and Balak (cf. Num. 21–22; *LAB* 18.1-14). Speaking at night to a confused Balaam, God gradually persuades him to refrain from cursing the wandering Hebrews, who are the 'seed' of Abraham; the Hebrews in the desert are those who will be 'like the stars of heaven', as God had originally promised (18.5a). God explains that at the *Akedah*, Abraham's 'offering was acceptable' (18.5b), and that it was 'on account of [Isaac's] blood' that God chose his people (18.5b).[196] So how could Balaam even consider going out to curse the people whom God has chosen? (18.6b). Since God's people are blessed, and consequently are of themselves a source of blessing to others, who will be left to bless Balaam if he curses them? (18.6b). Convinced by this reasoning, Balaam resolves not to follow Balak's order to curse God's people (18.7a).[197] In his creative paratextual narration, Pseudo-Philo suggests that the 'seed of Abraham' are blessed *because* of Abraham's obedience at the *Akedah*. Abraham merited the divine blessing there, and so did his 'seed', therefore it is impossible for Balaam to curse Abraham's distant progeny.[198]

---

[193] Other apocryphal and rabbinic traditions about Abraham delivered out of a fiery furnace exist (*ûr* is both a place name, and a noun meaning 'fire'): see Vermes, *Scripture and Tradition in Judaism*.

[194] The Genesis texts do not provide a 'reason' for God's call of Abraham, a lacuna that later haggadic traditions were keen to fill. Here, Pseudo-Philo claims that God chose Abraham because he was not an idolater like everyone else around him. This is the central conclusion reached by Bogaert in his study of Abraham in *LAB*. See Pierre-Maurice Bogaert, 'La figure d'Abraham dans les Antiquités Bibliques du Pseudo-Philon', in Bogaert (ed.), *Abraham dans la Bible et dans la tradition juive*, pp. 40–55.

[195] The Greek uses παῖς to refer to Abraham as God's 'servant' (7.5); cf. Isa. 41.8. Earlier in *LAB*, Abraham and Noah are described as 'blameless' and 'perfect' (3.4).

[196] This idea was gaining traction in early Judaism, and it grew also within rabbinic Judaism: see b. *Yoma* 5a and *Mekhilta de R. Simon bar Yochai* 4 – but there could be a reverse influence here chronologically speaking. Isaac did not shed his blood, but the *Akedah* had an atoning value of some sort – an alternative 'paschal mystery' as it were. The tradition of Isaac's blood having atoning value may be a reply to Christian polemicists, but this remains hypothetical. See Robert Hayward, *Targums and the Transmission of Scripture into Judaism and Christianity* (Leiden: Brill, 2009), pp. 74–86.

[197] Pseudo-Philo implies that Balaam's obedience to God parallels Abraham's own obedience at the *Akedah*, departing significantly from other ancient retellings of the Numbers 22–24 story that excoriated Balaam as a false prophet. See Bruce N. Fisk, 'Offering Isaac Again and Again: Pseudo-Philo's Use of the Aqedah as Intertext', *CBQ* 62, no. 3 (2000), pp. 481–507, at pp. 485, 489.

[198] Also note that the wider context reveals that the blessings themselves stand, even if Abraham's seed are rebellious (in their complaints in the desert) and thus unworthy of the blessings; Bruce N. Fisk, *Do You Not Remember? Scripture, Story and Exegesis in the Rewritten Bible of Pseudo-Philo* (JSPSupp 37; Sheffield: Sheffield Academic Press, 2001), p. 162.

In recounting Joshua's 'covenant' speech at Shechem, Abraham is mentioned as one who believed in the Lord, and was therefore rescued by God (*LAB* 23.5; cf. 6–7 and echoing Gen. 15.6), Pseudo-Philo then channels the voice of the Lord:

> I did not let my people be scattered, but I gave them my law and enlightened them in order that by doing these things they would live ...And I brought you into this land ... And I fulfilled my covenant that I promised your fathers. And now, if you listen to your fathers, I will set my heart among you forever and overshadow you; And your ... seed (*semini tuo*) will be special among all the peoples, who will say, 'See, a faithful people! Because they believe in the Lord, therefore the Lord freed them and planted them'. And ... they will know through you that I have not chosen you in vain. (*LAB* 23.10-13)[199]

The people, who are the children of Abraham, are *like* Abraham in that they also believe in the Lord – they are a 'faithful people' who were rescued by the Lord because of their faith.[200] Pseudo-Philo's narration of Joshua's speech brings to the fore the fact that God has *already realized* the covenant promises to Abraham.[201] The metaphorical reference to Abraham's progeny as his 'seed' is extended in the language of God actively 'planting' his people in the land that he chose for them (23.13). God is the vivifying principle of their life in the land, as his presence will 'overshadow' them forever (23.12). The relationship between God and his covenant people is organic and defined by natural care: God tends his people 'like a desirable vine' and 'like a lovable flock'; God will provide the 'rain' and 'dew' for them to dwell abundantly in the land (23.14). But even though the relationship obeys the natural order of things, there is still a *condition* for all of this to occur: they must *listen to their fathers* if they are to become the blessed 'seed' in the sight of other peoples.

God's unconditional love for Abraham's 'seed' is drawn out in more 'theological' terms in the context of *LAB* 13.10. Although there are conditions for God's blessing ('walking in his ways'), and although sin will produce the consequences of divine abandonment, God's mercy and love ultimately triumph:

> If they will walk in my ways, I will not abandon them but will have mercy on them always and bless their seed; and the earth will quickly yield its fruit ... but I know for sure that they will make their ways corrupt and I will abandon them, and they will forget the covenants that I have established with their fathers; but nevertheless, I will not forget them forever. For they will know that ... on account of their own sins their seed has been abandoned, because I am faithful in my ways.

These twin examples of how the covenant obligations function as conditions for the covenant blessings clash somewhat with the subtle reference in the Balaam narrative to Abraham's vicarious merits benefitting his 'seed' (*LAB* 18). But these examples of

---

[199] *OTP II*, pp. 297–378.
[200] Cf. Fisk, *Do You Not Remember?*, p. 300.
[201] Ibid., p. 302.

conditionality should also be read together with the more sceptical ideas of sin and merit found later in *LAB*. In Pseudo-Philo's narration of Deborah's last testament, for example (*LAB* 33; cf. Judges 4–5), Deborah instructs her listeners about the finality of life and its opportunity to collect merit before God.[202] Thus, the importance of following the Law while alive is paramount (*LAB* 33.1-3). Deborah explains that after death there is no chance to repent of sins (33.2). Employing a distinctly economic metaphor, Pseudo-Philo has Deborah opine that 'Death is sealed up and brought to an end, and the measure and the time of the years have returned their deposit' (33.3a). Just as no one can repent after death, so no one can intercede for another after death (33.5a). Intercession works while one is alive, but after death one cannot be 'mindful' of anyone (33.5a). Therefore, Deborah counsels them:

> Do not hope in your fathers. For they will not profit you at all unless you be found like them. But then you will be like the stars of the heaven, which now have been revealed among you. (33.5b)

The allusions to the Genesis texts that mention the 'seed of Abraham' are evident in the language of being 'like the stars of heaven' – but *not* by virtue of being descendants of 'your fathers'; rather, by virtue of imitating them in their righteousness.[203] In this way will the promises made to Abraham be realized. Deborah claims that it is not fruitful to rely upon the merits of the fathers, but only to emulate the fathers' worthy deeds, here construed as obeying the Law while they live (cf. 33.3). There are a number of layers to this text: the assumption that the fathers observed the Law; the judgement that their observance of the Law was meritorious and good; and the view that emulating such meritorious observance leads to the same rewards enjoyed by the fathers. In this context, the Lord's previous injunction that the people 'listen to their fathers' for their 'seed' to be blessed in the land (*LAB* 13.10) gains added salience.[204]

But even this is not the entire picture. Pseudo-Philo immediately retells the narrative of the Israelites becoming enslaved to the Midianites after Deborah's death (cf. Judg. 6.1-10; *LAB* 35.1-5). The story centres upon Gideon's encounter with an angel. Gideon laments that 'Israel has fallen into distress' (35.2), to which the angel replies that Israel's slavery is the result of their abandonment of the divine commandments (35.3). Nevertheless, the angel promises Gideon that God will have incomparable

---

[202] Note that in the biblical text, Deborah does not speak to the people directly; cf. Murphy, 'Idolatry in Pseudo-Philo', p. 281. Note also that Deborah compares her victory with Abraham's rescue by God from the fire in Chaldea (*LAB* 32, referencing chs 6–7). There is an inner-textual connection between Abraham and Deborah on multiple levels.

[203] The notion of the just becoming 'like' the immortal astral bodies after their death receives mention in some apocalyptic texts (cf. Dan. 12.2; 1 *En.* 104.2, 6; *Asc. Moses* 109). Here, however, there is a distinct biblical allusion also to the 'seed of Abraham'.

[204] Deborah's exalted role in *LAB* has been previously studied, and her position as a 'Mother in Israel' on par with the patriarchs has been convincingly advanced (Pieter W. van der Horst, 'Portraits of Women in Pseudo-Philo's *Liber Antiquitatum Biblicarum*', *JSP* 5 (1989), pp. 29–46; Donald C. Polanski, 'On Taming Tamar: Amram's Rhetoric and Women's Roles in Pseudo-Philo's *Liber Antiquitatum Biblicarum* 9', *JSP* 13 (1995), pp. 79–99, at p. 83; Murphy, *Pseudo-Philo*, pp. 136–53). Yet, Deborah's discussion about intercession and sin, and the 'hope in the fathers' has not received critical attention beyond remarks in *OTP II*, p. 348.

mercy upon Israel – but only on account of those who have died (35.3). The angel then commissions Gideon to free the Israelites from the Midianites (35.4). This text counterbalances the ideas in Deborah's testament, emphasizing instead the powerful effect that the merits of the fathers (or 'those who have died') have upon captive Israel. Punished for not keeping the commandments and therefore 'falling into distress' and slavery, Israel will nonetheless be rescued by God for the sake of their worthy fathers. God's mercy covers over even the sin of idolatry, because the good works of those who have died still hold power in God's eyes – a remarkable concession given Pseudo-Philo's polemic against idolatry. The discrepancy between this text and the Deborah narrative (33.1-6) is not irreconcilable; in both texts God judges humanity according to deeds (cf. also *LAB* 44.10), but in the Gideon narrative, the deeds of the worthy dead retain efficacy on behalf of those who are suffering the consequences of their sins.

Other shorter references to Abraham's 'seed' and the divine promises made to the fathers reinforce the strength of Pseudo-Philo's convictions about the eternal nature of God's covenant. Thus, Abraham's 'covenant' cannot be broken, and his 'seed' shall be 'multiplied forever' (*LAB* 4.5); Abraham and Sarah's 'seed' will be 'everlasting' as will be the divine covenant made with Abraham (8.3); and this extends to the covenant at Sinai, where God established 'the Law of his eternal covenant' with the 'sons of Israel' (alternate for 'seed', 11.5). Thus, while *LAB* certainly articulates the Deuteronomistic perspective in places, its larger contribution is the 'hope based on the irrevocability of God's commitment to Israel, a commitment that has been constant since the time of Abraham'.[205]

The book of *Jubilees*, and Abraham's role within it, has been extensively studied.[206] *Jubilees* mentions the figure of Abraham for the first time when recounting his birth in 'the thirty-ninth jubilee' (11.14-17).[207] The text depicts Abraham as one who, even from a young age, begins to understand the impiety of the idolatrous culture that surrounds him in Chaldea (11.16). When he is older, Abraham confronts his father Terah about the futility of idols, saying:

> What help or advantage do we have from these idols before which you worship and bow down? Because there is not any spirit in them, for they are mute, and they are misleading of the heart; do not worship them; worship the God of heaven, who sends down rain and dew upon the earth ... all life is in his presence. (12.1-4)[208]

---

[205] Frederick J. Murphy, 'The Eternal Covenant in Pseudo-Philo', *JSP* 3 (1988), pp. 43–57, at p. 54.

[206] Cf. van Ruiten, *Abraham in the Book of Jubilees*, pp. 8–12, and the notes for just a sample of the vast, recent scholarship on the book. For a foundational study, see James C. VanderKam, *Textual and Historical Studies in the Book of Jubilees* (Missoula: Scholars Press, 1977).

[207] Scholars date *Jubilees* to the second century BCE. Fourteen copies of *Jubilees* were discovered at Qumran, and carbon dating of 4Q216 (the oldest fragment) reveals a date of 125–110 BCE. Following *OTP II*, pp. 35–142.

[208] Abraham addresses Terah in the second-person singular (at 12.2), but the remaining pronouns ('you') are all in the second-person plural in vv. 3-5. This, combined with the repeated imperative refrain ('Do not worship them', v. 3b, 5b), indicates that Abram's speech may be an adaptation of a prior liturgical hymn proscribing idolatry. If so, the author of *Jubilees* is presenting Abram as a mouthpiece and exemplar for the repudiation of idolatry (Charlesworth, *OTP II*, p. 80, note *a*).

While Terah concurs with Abraham's view, he worries that speaking out against idolatry would mean courting death at the hands of the authorities. Abraham is duly silent on the matter for some twenty years as he settles into marriage (12.9-11), but when he turns sixty, he rises in the night and burns down 'the house of idols' (12.12). Haran, Abram's brother, frantically tries to save his own idols, but he is consumed by the fire and dies (12.13-14). The text notes that Haran dies and is buried 'in Ur of the Chaldees' (12.14), playing on the word Ur (Heb. 'fire'; cf. *LAB* 6–7). Consequently, Terah and his remaining sons leave Ur and dwell in Lebanon (12.15). This characterization of Abraham as an aniconic, zealous devotee of the One God serves as a 'back story' to the retelling of the biblical Abraham as it unfolds across the rest of *Jubilees*.[209]

References to Abraham's 'seed' occur with some frequency in the narrative of *Jubilees* from this point forward (cf. 12.20, 24; 13.4, 20 (×3), 21; 14.2, 5, 7, 13, 21, 22; 15.9 (×2), 10, 12, 20; 16.9 (×2), 16, 17 (×2), 18, 22, 26, 28; 17.3, 7 (×2); 18.15, 16, 19), yet for the most part, they follow the text of Genesis quite closely, with little variation in the retelling. One exception is the retelling of Gen. 15.15, where Abraham receives God's promise to his 'seed', before the constellation of stars at night. In *Jub.* 12.16, Abraham is represented as an experienced agriculturalist, who wakes in the night to discern the weather patterns for the coming year by the arrangement of the stars. In the course of this activity, God makes Abraham aware that all weather phenomena are not to be divined but are delivered only by the will of God (12.17-18).

God's gentle chastisement causes Abraham to pray that he might be saved 'from the power of evil spirits who rule the thoughts of peoples' minds', and lead people astray into the way of idolatry (12.20a). Abraham prays, 'Establish me and my seed forever; may we not go astray from now until eternity' (20.20b). This text narrates a brisk and complete 'conversion' for Abraham: early in his life, Abraham rejected manufactured idols, and now he rejects astrology and divination – both inheritances from Chaldea – but both implicated in the same idolatrous mentality. Abraham acknowledges that his inclination towards divination constitutes 'the error of [his] heart', and he refers to himself as God's 'servant', willing henceforth to 'serve' God alone (12.21). The 'evil spirits' who rule human thoughts in this passage – like Prince Mastema – seem to determine the human inclination towards sin.[210] But Abraham's prayer on behalf of his 'seed' is efficacious, indicating that the influence of the evil spirits can be conquered.[211]

This text positions Abraham's 'seed' as distinctive for their divine servitude, specifically articulated as the repudiation of all forms of idolatry. Abraham himself is the exemplar of such servitude; he wants his 'seed' to continue this servitude indefinitely and eternally. God responds by inviting Abraham to leave his land and his kin and to move into the land which God will show him (12.22); there God will bless Abraham

---

[209] Prior to this episode, Abraham battles ravens sent by 'Prince Mastema' – the chief evil spirit, and leader of all evil spirits, who entices people towards idolatry – but Abraham prevails (*Jub.* 11.11-13; on Mastema, see also 10.1-13; 18.18-19; 12.22b; 19.28; 49.2 (where Mastema inspires the murder of innocents in Egypt); and compare 4Q225).

[210] Cf. Michael Segal, *The Book of Jubilees: Rewritten Bible, Redaction, Ideology and Theology* (SupJSJ 117; Leiden: Brill, 2007), p. 261. Perhaps for this reason 'unintentional sins' are viewed by the author of *Jubilees* as forgivable whereas 'intentional sins' are not – thus, Anderson, 'The Status of the Torah before Sinai', pp. 1–29, at p. 5.

[211] Ibid., p. 261.

(12.23) and become the God of Abraham's 'seed' (12.24). The original Genesis text that depicted *God* promising to establish Abraham's 'seed' in the land (Gen. 12.1-7) is in *Jubilees* 12 reimagined to show *Abraham* imploring God to establish his 'seed' in the path of monotheistic worship and away from idolatry.[212]

One of the most unique texts to feature Abraham is found in *Jub*. 16.20-31. God has just appeared to Abraham and Sarah on the occasion of Sarah's pregnancy with Isaac (16.15-16). God promises more sons to the pair, telling them that they will have a 'holy seed' from one of the 'sons of Isaac' – he will become a 'portion of the Most High', a 'kingdom of priests' and give rise to a 'holy people' (16.17-19a-c).[213] This news makes Sarah and Abraham 'rejoice greatly' (16.19d). Abraham immediately builds an altar to God and celebrates the festival of Sukkot (16.20). Abraham is described as full of joy (16.20) and as the first person on earth to celebrate Sukkot (16.21). This innovative retelling of Gen. 20.1–21.7 includes a substantial, interpolated narrative about Abraham's festival observance; indeed, the text presents Sukkot resulting from Abraham's spontaneous, joyful celebration of the divine news about his future offspring. Subsequent celebrations of the feast on earth, it is implied, result from the fact that Abraham initiated the festival, and his 'seed' simply followed his example.[214] No mention is made of the booths constructed in the wilderness (cf. Lev. 23.40-42), or of Abraham observing the feast because God mandated it.[215]

But Abraham's joy is not the sole reason he comes to observe the seven-day festival of Sukkot. Abraham continues to make 'offering every day, day by day' as an intercessor: he offers the animals to God 'on behalf of sins so that he [Abraham] might atone thereby on behalf of himself and his seed' (16.22). Abraham is not presented as sinless; he needs to offer atonement sacrifices for his own sins. However, this is one of the first texts in early Judaism that so clearly associates Abraham's behaviour with the fate of his 'seed' – in other words, Abraham's behaviour can affect the well-being of his own posterity. Abraham is narratively presented as, in his own lifetime, looking out for his future 'seed' to ensure their well-being. *Jub*. 16.24-27 goes on to detail how Abraham was 'rejoicing with all his heart and all his soul' because God the Creator made it known to Abraham

---

[212] Van Ruiten observes in this passage a continuation from the story of the ravens in *Jubilees* 11; idem, *Abraham in the Book of Jubilees*, p. 29.

[213] Shozo Fujita, 'The Metaphor of Plant in Jewish Literature of the Intertestamental Period', *JSJ* 7, no. 1 (1976), pp. 30–45. Fujita shows that the metaphors of 'shoot', 'seed', 'branch' or 'plant' were typically messianic in focus.

[214] Cf. *Jub*. 22.1; Beate Ego, 'Heilige Zeit – heiliger Raum – heiliger Mensch', in Matthias Albani, Jörg Frey and Armin Lange (eds), *Studies in the Book of Jubilees* (TSzAJ 65; Tübingen: Mohr Siebeck, 1997), pp. 207–20, at p. 208. Sukkot is otherwise associated with Abraham's own travel itinerary (*Jub*. 18.18) in terms of its seven-day duration, which is 'most unusual': Betsy Halpern-Amaru, *The Perspective from Mt Sinai: The Book of Jubilees and Exodus* (Göttingen: Vandenhoeck and Ruprecht, 2015), pp. 85–6.

[215] Cf. James L. Kugel, *A Walk Through Jubilees: Studies in the Book of Jubilees and the World of Its Creation* (SupJSJ 156; Leiden: Brill, 2012), p. 8.

that from him would come a 'righteous planting' and a 'holy seed'[216] so that 'he might be like the one who made everything' (v. 26).[217]

In *Jub.* 20.2, Abraham instructs his children by way of a last testament, 'demanding his male offspring [seed] to guard the way of the Lord'. David Lambert reads this text as an application of Gen. 18.19, where Abraham is described as teaching his children what is 'right' and 'just'.[218] 'Doing what is right' is defined by an intertextual interpolation (Lev. 19.18), namely, love of one's neighbour.[219] And 'doing what is just' is described as loving God and holding fast to his commandments and avoiding idolatry.[220] Abraham teaches his 'seed' to obey the commandments – additionally, specific regulations, such as to stay away from 'fornication' and to keep the covenant of circumcision. Intermarriage is also expressly proscribed, since the consequences are annihilation – a retrospective punishment gleaned from the fate of the Canaanites in the Torah (20.4).[221] Abraham's final testament is given to Jacob (*Jubilees* 22). All of 'the blessings of Adam and Noah' will rest upon 'Jacob's seed'. The core stipulation that Abraham gives to Jacob is to avoid eating with the nations, for their ways are 'impure' and 'defiled' (22.16). Such assimilation would only lead to idolatry.[222] Endogamy is also strongly mandated (*Jub.* 25.5; 30).[223] Obeying these laws will keep Jacob from inadvertent sins. The 'pre-Mosaic authority' of Abraham's 'laws' in these testaments suggest that the author of *Jubilees* viewed pre-Sinaitic legal traditions as on par with those revealed following the Exodus.[224] Abraham's 'seed' are – like their father – law-observant, and thus, blessed.[225]

Finally, we will consider the *Testament of Abraham*. The text exists in two different Greek recensions. The 'long recension' is usually labelled 'Recension A' and the 'short

---

[216] Given *Jubilees*' excessive concern with endogamy, this reference to the 'holy seed' might be a priestly-type echo of Ezra 9.2, where the people of Israel are collectively positioned as a 'holy seed' that is not to be 'mixed' with the גרים. See Betsy Halpern-Amaru, *The Empowerment of Women in the Book of Jubilees* (Leiden/Boston: Brill, 1999), pp. 150–1.

[217] This phrase is enigmatic, as the pronoun is not clear: Who becomes like 'the one who made everything' – the 'holy seed', or Abraham? A parallel text is *1 En.* 10.16, 93.5, 10, where 'a man shall be elected as a plant of righteous judgment, and his offspring shall become the plant of righteousness forever' (93.5). Fujita, 'The Metaphor of Plant', pp. 33–4, argues that the context of *1 En.* 93.5 reveals Abraham to be the man (a 'chosen seed') and the people Israel to be the 'righteous plant' that will grow from him in the future. Fujita reads *Jub.* 16.26 in this light; thus, the 'holy seed' who sprout forth from Abraham in the future, will become god-like – a completely unique feature within the non-Christian literature of antiquity.

[218] The two words צדק and משפט are, in Gen. 18.19 hendiadyses, but in *Jubilees* 20, they are separated out: cf. David Lambert, 'Last Testaments in the Book of Jubilees', *DSD* 11, no. 1 (2004), pp. 82–107, at p. 88.

[219] Ibid., p. 91.

[220] Ibid.

[221] Cf. Anderson, 'The Status of the Torah', p. 29.

[222] Christian Frevel, '"Separate Yourself from the Gentiles" (*Jubilees* 22.16): Intermarriage in the Book of *Jubilees*', in C. Frevel (ed.), *Mixed Marriages: Intermarriage and Group Identity in the Second Temple Period* (New York: T&T Clark, 2011), pp. 220–49, at p. 227.

[223] Cf. *Tob.* 4.12.

[224] Hindy Najman, 'Interpretation as Primordial Writing: Jubilees and Its Authority Conferring Strategies', *JSJ* 30, no. 4 (1999), pp. 379–410.

[225] Note also that *Jubilees* does not excessively elevate the figure of Abraham as one beyond compare. He is often paralleled with Noah, Gideon and Moses; cf. D. Andrew Teeter, 'On "Exegetical Function" in Rewritten Scripture: Inner-Biblical Exegesis and Abram/Ravens Narrative in *Jubilees*', *HTR* 106, no. 4 (2013), pp. 373–402.

recension' is labelled 'Recension B' in the scholarship. Recension A boasts a relatively larger number of manuscript witnesses, and in its critical edition, it is often the version that is more studied for its evidently superior plot and command of narrative style.[226] Here, in discussing the text of the *Testament of Abraham*, I follow the *Testament of Abraham* (Rec. A), published in the *Old Testament Pseudepigrapha* (volume 2).[227] As previously noted, the genre of the *Testament of Abraham* is disputed.[228] The work contains no testament, no speech, no instruction from Abraham to his sons. Rather, the *Testament of Abraham* is apocalyptic in flavour, containing tours of the heavens, judgement of souls and divine visitations.[229] But new scholarly attention to the humour of the text suggests that the title is ironic, perhaps a parody.[230] In the following brief discussion, I will focus on how the *Testament of Abraham* blends together themes of sin, servanthood, the promises to Abraham's 'seed' and Abraham's intercessory capacities.

After the narrator introduces Abraham as outstanding in hospitality and kindness, in righteousness and holiness (*T. Abr.* 1.1-2), the story shifts to the heavenly real, where God speaks about Abraham to the archangel Michael, saying 'For I have blessed him as the stars of heaven, and as the sand by the shore of the sea' (1.5).[231] The blessings of multitudinous 'seed' to Abraham have already been realized in the patriarch's lifetime, and now it is time for Abraham to die. God therefore commands Michael to warn Abraham about his impending death (1.4), but also to reassure him of his place with 'the good' in the world to come (1.7). But when Michael begins his mission, Abraham resists, prevaricating by taking Michael for a long walk, and then into his house to stay (2.5-12). Abraham's hospitality to the archangel becomes more extravagant as time goes by (4.1-5). Michael grows fond of Abraham, and increasingly reluctant to bring about his imminent death (4.6).[232]

God thus encourages Michael to try a different tactic, namely, to have Isaac dream of his father's death so that Michael can gently interpret it (4.6). Isaac narrates his dream, full of symbolism, in detail to his father (7.2-7); Michael explicates the dream to Abraham, telling him that his soul is about to be taken from the earth (7.8-9). Abraham responds with wonderment, asking Michael if he is to be the agent of his death (7.10). Michael assents, and again, Abraham refuses to 'follow' him (7.11). In the face of Abraham's resistance to his divinely appointed death, Michael returns to heaven to speak with God about what to do next (8.1-4). Michael must remind Abraham that God blessed him beyond measure in his lifetime, and that even now, God promises to

---

[226] See the discussion in Dale C. Allison, *The Testament of Abraham* (Berlin: de Gruyter, 2003), pp. 4–7; 13; and challenged by Françoise Mirguet, 'Attachment to the Body in the Greek *Testament of Abraham*: A Reappraisal of the Short Recension', *JSP* 19, no. 4 (2010), pp. 251–75.

[227] *OTP II*, pp. 871–902.

[228] Anitra Bingham Kolenkow, 'What is the Role of Testament in the Testament of Abraham?' *HTR* 67, no. 2 (1974), pp. 182–4.

[229] Cf. John J. Collins, 'The Jewish Apocalypses', *Sem* 14 (1979), pp. 21–59, at p. 23.

[230] George W. E. Nickelsburg, 'Stories of Biblical and Early Post-Biblical Times', in Michael E. Stone (ed.), *Jewish Writings of the Second Temple Period* (Philadelphia: Fortress Press, 1984), pp. 33–81, at pp. 61–3; Jared W. Ludlow, *Abraham Meets Death: Narrative Humor in the Testament of Abraham* (JSPSup 41; Sheffield: Sheffield Academic Press, 2002), pp. 21–2.

[231] Following Allison's translation.

[232] Reed, 'The Construction and Subversion', p. 207: Abraham is a 'paragon of virtue' but uses that virtuous record to effectively disobey God's decree.

'multiply' and 'bless' Abraham's 'seed' and to give him anything he asks (8.7).[233] Michael queries Abraham about his resistance to death, when every living creature must die, even the prophets and kings (8.9). Does not Abraham realize that he is not above the will of God, and that if God gives 'permission to Death' then it is up to God whether 'Death' comes or not? (8.12b).

Abraham – now described as 'pious and righteous' (9.2a) – proceeds to cry profusely, begging Michael for one final request: that he be permitted to 'see all the inhabited world' before he dies (9.3-6) so that he does not die in sorrow (9.6). Abraham prostrates himself before Michael, referring to himself as a 'sinner' (9.4), and the 'servant/slave' (δουλός) of God. Then Abraham, mindful of his mortality, will cede to God's might (9.5). Michael immediately begins a soaring tour over the inhabited world (10.1). Accordingly, Abraham sees the whole host of humanity and the various activities with which they are occupied. Abraham sees everything, both 'good and evil' (10.3b). When Abraham witnesses thievery and assault (10.4-5), he asks that God kill the men via wild beasts (10.6); his request is granted (10.7). Carnage continues in this pattern as Abraham witnesses more and more sin on earth (10.8-11). God fears that Abraham might destroy the whole world in this manner (cf. 11.12), and so orders that Michael halt the tour immediately (10.12-13a). 'For behold', God explains, '*Abraham has not sinned and he has no mercy on sinners*' (10.13b), whereas the Creator God 'delay[s] the death of the sinner so that he should convert and live' (10.14).

The irony is thick: the story's opening frame lauds Abraham for his superlative exemplarity – he was quiet, gentle, righteous, 'very hospitable' (1.1), 'entirely holy' and pious (1.3), 'loving' and 'above all others' in goodness (1.5), traits of which God seems to be well aware (1.6-7). However, Abraham's zealous desire to mercilessly destroy 'sinners' reveals a lack of empathy arising, God concludes, from a lack of experience in actually sinning. Abraham has been too perfect and as a result, is lacking in compassion for sinners. His pious exemplarity is not such a desirable thing after all.[234] But Abraham is about to learn an important lesson that will change the nature of his perception.

While with Michael, Abraham has a vision about the last judgement, where innumerable souls pass through into the throne room (12.1-2). Abraham sees a 'wondrous man, bright as the sun' sitting on a 'terrifying throne' (12.3-4) with a book lying open before him (12.7); this man is 'the righteous Abel whom Cain the wicked killed' (13.3). Two angels flank Abel's side, with a third in front holding a 'balance in his hand' (12.8-9). The flanking angels record each soul's deeds, both 'righteous deeds' and 'sins' (12.12), while Abel sentences souls (12.11). Each soul is 'weighed' and 'tested' (12.13-14). Then Abel asks the angels to open the book and find the sins of a particular soul (12.17); the angels find that his 'sins' and 'righteous deeds' are 'equally balanced' (12.18). Therefore, this soul is 'set in the middle' rather than turned over to destruction or to salvation. Abraham asks Michael (who presumably shares the vision) about the soul whose good deeds and sins were evenly balanced: why was this soul put in the

---

[233] Reference to Abraham's 'seed' is absent from Rec. B. See Ludlow, *Abraham Meets Death*, p. 161.
[234] Here, we have an inversion of the Sodom and Gomorrah narrative in Genesis 18–19: there, Abraham interceded with God to save the city for the sake of even one righteous man, and to not destroy it for the sake of the many sinners. In the *Testament of Abraham*, we see Abraham striking sinners dead on the spot, even as he stalls and resists his own death.

middle? (14.1). Michael replies that the soul was placed 'in the middle' provisionally, until 'the judge of all should come' (14.2c). When Abraham enquires about what this soul lacks in order for it to be saved, Michael responds, 'If it could acquire one righteous deed more than (its) sins, it would enter in to be saved' (14.3-4).[235] Significantly, 'sins' and 'righteous deeds' are mutually opposed; one makes up for the other, one reduces the weight of the other. One's salvation is within one's own hands while on earth, but God's mercy is still at play.

Abraham is moved to assist the middling soul that needs only one more righteous deed to its name. He declares his solution: 'Let us offer a prayer on behalf of this soul and see if God will heed us' (14.5).[236] Abraham then asks the angel about the fate of this soul – and he replies, 'it was saved through your righteous prayer' (14.7-8). This news stimulates Abraham towards further prayer: he glorifies God's mercy (14.9), and then persuades Michael to continue 'beseeching' the Lord for his compassion (14.10). Abraham wants to intercede for all the sinners whom he had previously 'cursed and destroyed' through his wanton 'evil-mindedness' (14.11; cf. ch. 10). His eyes opened, Abraham 'beseech[es] God with tears' that he may be forgiven his 'sinful act' and that the sinners he destroyed might be brought back (4.12). In God's 'great goodness' (14.14), all the sinners are returned to life.[237] In satirical fashion, the *Testament of Abraham* might well have been an attempt to discourage the burgeoning patriarch-piety of the post-biblical era and to send the message that great figures like Abraham were not always such great and perfect exemplars after all.[238]

Dead Sea Scrolls

Abraham appears in some of the fragmentary manuscripts from Qumran, but 'he does not feature prominently'.[239] The manuscript of 4Q252 (the *Commentary on Genesis A*) is the best preserved example on the figuration of Abraham. But even in this large text, some sections are not well-preserved.[240] The exception is 4Q252 II (5-8), where Abraham surprisingly arises in the context of a retelling of Genesis 9. There, Noah curses his youngest son, Canaan, but spares Ham; the narrator then explains: 'For God had blessed the sons of Noah. And in the tents of Shem may he dwell. He gave the land to Abraham, his beloved'.[241] This text draws upon the motif of Abraham as loved by God (cf. Isa. 41.8; 2 Chron. 20.7), and (for that reason) as the recipient of the land

---

[235] Cf. *y. Kidd* 1.10 (61d); *b. Rosh Hashanah* 17a. If a soul's sins and good deeds are evenly balanced, God removes an iniquity so that the good deeds outweigh the sins.

[236] Other texts in the Pseudepigrapha deny the efficacy of intercessory prayer after death (cf. *LAB* 33.5; *2 En.* 53.1; *4 Ezra* 7.102-15).

[237] The editors of Rec. B (Greek) omit the final resuscitation of the sinners whom Abraham destroyed. The earliest critical translator of Rec. B, M. R. James posited that this was because the theological implication was too radical: sinners would come to think that they could get away with murder as long as they could call upon Abraham's intercession. See the discussion in Ludlow, *Abraham Meets Death*, pp. 177–8.

[238] Reed, 'The Construction and Subversion', p. 209.

[239] Popovic, 'Abraham and the Nations', p. 77; Evans, 'Abraham in the Dead Sea Scrolls', pp. 149–58.

[240] Popovic, 'Abraham and the Nations', p. 82.

[241] Cf. 4Q176, 1-2; George J. Brooke, 'Commentary on Genesis C', in G. J. Brooke et al. (eds), *Qumran Cave 4.XVII: Parabiblical Texts, Part 3* (DJD 22; Oxford: Oxford University Press, 1996), pp. 220–1.

that God chose for him and his descendants. Brooke reads the text as polemical: that the author integrates the motif of Abraham's election in the land, with the exclusion of Canaan's descendants, indicates the sectarians' rejection of foreigners from the land in the first century CE.[242]

The term 'seed of Abraham' is found once in the fragment known as *Aramaic Levi* (16-17), which some scholars think has influenced the Qumran community rule (CD 4).[243] *Aramaic Levi* was discovered in the Cairo Genizah and also at Qumran.[244] The fragment is innovative in ascribing to the character Levi a priestly role – one that he does not hold in the canonical biblical literature.[245] In fact, Levi is centralized in the re-narration of biblical history: at Shechem, Levi plays a role in the covenant-making act; his priesthood is connected to eschatological peace and renewed imperial reign.[246] In vv. 16-17 of the text, Isaac instructs his grandson Levi about the appropriate sexual relations for priests[247]:

> And you, take a wife from my family to yourself and do not defile your seed with fornication. For you are a holy seed, and holy is your seed, like the holy [Temple]. For you are a holy priest called for all the seed of Abraham (לכל זרע אברהם).[248]

We have already heard resonances of this idea in a few texts analysed earlier, for example *Jub.* 16.21, where Abraham was promised a 'holy seed'. In *Tob.* 4.12, the 'seed of Abraham' were said to receive the inheritance of the land on the proviso that Tobias continue the fathers' tradition of endogamous marriage. In Ezra 9.2, the concept of the 'holy seed' – overlaid with priestly overtones – is possibly the precedent for these developments. But *Aramaic Levi* blends these nuances together: the pure semen/seed of Levi is to remain without foreign admixture; taking a 'wife' (from among close 'family' relatives) is the preferable way to ascertain this outcome; and then – the novel element – Levi will become a 'holy priest' over all of the 'seed of Abraham'.[249]

The other shade of meaning in *Aramaic Levi* deserving of attention is the subtle distinction made between members of Abraham's 'seed'. The modifier כל ('all')

---

[242] Brooke, 'Commentary on Genesis C', pp. 300-1.
[243] MS A (Cambridge b; pl. VII). Jonas Greenfield, 'The Words of Levi Son of Jacob in Damascus Document IV,15-19', *RevQ* 13 (1998), pp. 319-22.
[244] Ian C. Werrett, *Ritual Purity and the Dead Sea Scrolls* (STDJ 72; Leiden: Brill, 2007), p. 78. For a full explication of the manuscripts of *Aramaic Levi*, as well as a review of the *status quaestionis* (which still revolves mostly around the relationship between the *Testament of Levi* and *Aramaic Levi*), see Henryk Drawnel, *An Aramaic Wisdom Text from Qumran: A New Interpretation of the Levi Document* (JSJSup 86; Leiden: Brill, 2004). The text is attested in seven Aramaic fragments, one Greek manuscript and a Syriac fragment.
[245] Cana Werman, 'Levi and Levites in the Second Temple Period', *DSD* 4, no. 2 (1997), pp. 211-25, at p. 211.
[246] Marinus de Jonge, 'The Testament of Levi and "Aramaic Levi"', *RevQ* 13, no. 1 (1988), pp. 367-85, at pp. 379-80.
[247] Annette Y. Reed considers *Aramaic Levi* as part of 'the prehistory of the parabiblical testament'. Idem, 'Textuality between Death and Memory: The Prehistory and Formation of the Parabiblical Testament', *JQR* 104, no. 3 (2014), pp. 381-412, at p. 391.
[248] Werrett, *Ritual Purity*, pp. 78-9.
[249] In the text of Jeremiah 33, analysed in the first section of this chapter, recall that it was the royal 'seed of David' who was to have sovereignty over the 'seed of Abraham' for all time.

immediately strikes the reader: prior examples of the 'seed of Abraham' motif never needed to imply categories of 'some' and 'all', because Abraham's 'seed' was thought of as a totality.[250] The author of *Aramaic Levi* 16–17 possibly had a different view. He appears to have thought of Abraham's 'seed' as a plurality, a variegated collective only to be brought together as one under the banner of Levi's sacerdotal calling. As shown in the following section, the Apostle Paul likewise exploited the grammatical idiosyncrasy of the noun σπέρμα to distinguish between the 'true' and 'false' members of Abraham's 'seed' – an interpretive agenda that also occupied the rabbis of the Amoraic period.

Josephus

Josephus (ca. 37–100 CE) evidently held the patriarch Abraham in high esteem, as his well-preserved writings to non-Jewish Hellenistic audiences amply attest. Louis Feldman summarizes the evidence well when he writes, 'in his portrayal of Abraham, Josephus stresses those qualities, notably the four cardinal virtues – wisdom ... courage, temperance, and justice (with emphasis on the qualities of honesty, hospitality, and gratefulness), together with the spiritual quality of piety – that would ... have appealed to' Hellenized readers.[251] According to Josephus, Abraham was 'a typical national hero such as was popular in Hellenistic times' – defined by his capacities as a 'philosopher, scientist, and general'.[252] In his concern to present Abraham also as 'the model Jew', Josephus interprets the biblical stories of the patriarch in such a way as to skirt over any perceived negative elements, and highlight the positive, virtuous elements of his life instead.[253]

But this interpretive strategy had the consequence of erasing certain 'Jewish' aspects of the biblical material that might have been too unpalatable for Josephus' audience. Thus, Josephus' rendition of the patriarchal narratives in the *Antiquities* avoids covenantal language associated with Abraham's 'seed' in Genesis. The Torah texts consistently associated three key concepts with Abraham's 'seed': the covenant, the land and the multitudinous nature of their existence. In the *Antiquities*, the 'land' motif is, according to Betsy Halpern-Amaru, 'dramatically altered' in relation to the Abrahamic promises.[254] Josephus reads Abraham's departure from Chaldea not as a response to God's command (cf. Gen. 12.1-3), but as the result of Abraham's own growth in understanding about, and subsequent repudiation of, his environs (*Ant.* 1.157).[255] In retelling the narrative of Genesis 15, Josephus again omits reference to the covenant and the inheritance of the land of Canaan for the 'seed of Abraham'. Instead, he downplays

---

[250] The singular noun, with its plural connotations, makes it open to polysemy, but *Aramaic Levi* is the first to exploit that grammatical feature.

[251] Louis H. Feldman, *Josephus' Interpretation of the Bible* (Berkeley: University of California Press, 1998), p. 224.

[252] Ibid., p. 223. Cf. Reed, 'Abraham as Chaldean Scientist', pp. 119–58.

[253] Reed, 'The Construction and Subversion', p. 196; the quote is from Paul Spilsbury, *The Image of the Jew in Flavius Josephus' Paraphrase of the Bible* (TSzAJ 69; Tübingen: Mohr Siebeck, 1998) p. 62, cited in Reed.

[254] Betsy Halpern-Amaru, 'Land Theology in Josephus' "Jewish Antiquities"', *JQR* 71, no. 4 (1981), pp. 201–29, at p. 205.

[255] Ibid.

the 'promise' by turning it into a simple 'prediction': Abraham's 'seed' will be afflicted in Egypt, but will eventually triumph over their oppressors and take possession of their land and cities (*Ant.* 1.185).[256] Josephus not only omits aspects of the biblical text, but sometimes also adds new elements in his retelling. The covenant of circumcision made with Abraham (Genesis 17) provides Josephus with a chance to explain the logic of the practice, which the Roman elite frequently satirized.[257] Circumcision, for Josephus, was not so much covenantal as practical, as it would prevent Abraham's 'seed' from 'mixing' with foreign peoples (*Ant.* 1.191). Abraham's circumcision thus initiated an exclusivist custom, which Josephus explains, preserves endogamy among Jews (who are Abraham's 'seed') to the current day. The last promise made to Abraham in the Torah, following the *Akedah* (Genesis 22), is also slightly altered by Josephus. Abraham's 'seed' will grow into a 'multitude of nations', possess great wealth and overtake Canaan by military force (*Ant.* 1.235). The language of inheritance and reward for Abraham's faithfulness is not explicit.[258]

Samuel Sandmel is critical of Josephus' omissions and expansions in relation to Abraham. He summarizes his reading of the evidence thus: 'Josephus says not one thing about Abraham's relationship to the Law of Moses or to the Greek notions of law'.[259] Abraham is 'not a crucial figure' to Josephus, but 'just one of many biblical figures'; Josephus does not mention 'Abraham as a source of merit to his descendants', not does he refer to the covenant.[260] Abraham is 'simply the philosopher who left the land of Canaan to his descendants'. Of course, 'Abraham is the first to declare the unity of God... he teaches the Egyptians mathematics and astronomy' which filters through to the Greeks. But ultimately the Abraham of *Jubilees* and of the rabbinic literature does not match Josephus' vision.[261]

Scholars have since nuanced Sandmel's assertions.[262] Relevant to this chapter is the notion of Abraham as a source of merit to his descendants. Feldman draws attention to *Ant.* II.169, where Josephus expands upon Nehemiah's words of reassurance (cf. Neh. 2.17) to declare that 'God cherishes the memory of our fathers, Abraham, Isaac, and Jacob, and because of their righteousness (δικαιοσύνης) he does not give up his providential care for us.'[263] It is worth unpacking this statement. That God 'remembers' the fathers is familiar to us from biblical texts such as Exod. 32.12-14, where, for example, Moses pleads with God to be merciful to the idolatrous Hebrews for the sake of his remembrance of Abraham, Isaac and Jacob. I suggested that this biblical

---

[256] Ibid., p. 207.
[257] See the sources in John G. Gager, *The Origins of Anti-Semitism: Attitudes Toward Judaism in Pagan and Christian Antiquity* (New York: Oxford University Press, 1985), p. 56.
[258] Thus, Halpern-Amaru, 'Land Theology', p. 208.
[259] Samuel Sandmel, 'Philo's Place in Judaism: A Study of Conceptions of Abraham in Jewish Literature, Part II', *HUCA* 26 (1955), pp. 151-332, at p. 196.
[260] Ibid., p. 197.
[261] Ibid.
[262] Cf. Feldman, *Josephus' Interpretation*, p. 224. However, one should not overstate the importance of Abraham to Josephus' *Antiquities*, as Martin Goodman aptly notes: 'It is hard not to feel that Josephus' account of Abraham in the *Antiquities* was an opportunity missed'. See M. Goodman, 'Josephus on Abraham and the Nations', in *Abraham, the Nations, and the Hagarites*, pp. 177-84, at p. 183.
[263] Ibid., p. 224.

concept of זכר אבות (remembering the fathers) is an allusive precedent for the rabbinic concept of זכות אבות (the merits of the fathers). Josephus' addition to Nehemiah's prayer goes even further: God *cherishes* the memory of Abraham, Isaac and Jacob, calling to mind the many passages previously examined where Abraham figures as one who is singularly loved by God as his faithful servant (cf. Isa. 41.8; 2 Chron. 20.7). But this divine love also has a reason: the fathers were *righteous* in their behaviour, which motivates God to continuously care, in his providence, for the 'seed' of Abraham – for all the descendants of the fathers. Several previously examined nuances here converge – God's love for Abraham's seed because of Abraham's own righteousness; God's unconditional, providential love for Abraham's seed that rescues them in times of distress; God's faithfulness in never abandoning his people; and God's remembrance of the fathers.

So, while Josephus' substitution of the biblical language of 'covenant' for the more general rationale of divine providence and care is accepted in the scholarship, this factor does not necessarily denude the *Antiquities* of its 'Jewishness' but may, in fact, enhance it.[264] By condensing so many traditions that were present in the literatures of early Judaism into his reading of Nehemiah's prayer, Josephus demonstrated how aware he was of the 'merits of Abraham' – and how, and why, these applied to Abraham's 'seed' – even if he did not express this awareness in retelling the texts of Genesis directly. Even this is not quite accurate: Josephus hints at Abraham's exemplary virtues in the narrative of his separation from Lot (cf. Genesis 13),[265] and in Josephus' expansion of the war of Sodom, where Abraham is said to have refused to partake of the spoils of war (*JW* 4.483). According to Josephus' text, Abraham's behaviour pleased God, who assured Abraham that he 'would not lose the rewards' of his 'glorious actions' (*Ant.* 1.183). After this, God promises Abraham the reward: a son of his own, and numerous posterity who would triumph over their captors (cf. Genesis 15; *Ant.* 1.184-85).[266]

Philo

Abraham takes a more significant role in the works of Philo of Alexandria (ca. 20 BCE–50 CE) compared to the works of Josephus. Yet, like Josephus, Philo draws on common traditions about Abraham as the first man to discover monotheism. In Philo's writings, Abraham abandons futile astrological divinations, and learns about the one God through reason and analogy, which were intellectual capacities bestowed upon him by God (*Abr.* 71). Abraham conquers his passions through reason, he is an avid philosopher and reader, a mystic and prophet (*Abr.* 99).[267] While Abraham's ancestors were men of guilt, his own life was virtuous and worthy of emulation. Abraham was

---

[264] Contra Halpern-Amaru; cf. Harold Attridge, *The Interpretation of Biblical History in the Antiquitates Judaicae of Flavius Josephus* (Missoula: Scholars Press, 1976), pp. 71–107.

[265] Michael Avioz, 'Josephus' Portrayal of Lot and His Family', *JSP* 16, no. 1 (2006), pp. 3–13, at p. 6.

[266] Levenson, *Inheriting Abraham*, p. 133, writes of Josephus' focus upon Abraham as a philosopher-teacher, and how this status corresponds with his righteous behaviour. We will address this aspect more closely in Chapter 5.

[267] Cf. Sandmel, 'Philo's Place in Judaism, Part II', p. 263, for more sources.

perfect (*QG* 4.60), although Sarah was also praised by Philo as equally stoic as her husband (*Abr.* 62-65), and as supreme in loving-kindness towards him (*Abr.* 248-50).[268]

In Philo's writings, Abraham displays such great faith in God that he is named as God's friend (*Abr.* 273-75). Abraham achieves perfection and wisdom (*Abr.* 262). Yet, Abraham is not, like Moses in Philo's works, so utterly perfect as to be beyond human imitation. Michael Satlow argues that Philo presents the fathers Abraham, Isaac and Jacob as models of three different paths to perfection. Abraham exemplifies a life of contemplation, teaching and philosophical study (*Abr.* 52-4; *Cher.* 10; *Leg.* 3.244).[269] In the words of Samuel Sandmel, 'Abraham is an exemplar of the religious mystic who rises above the sense [*sic*] and body into communion with God'.[270] Isaac is an example of 'natural perfection' since his name means 'perfect joy' and because he was the reward of Abraham and Sarah's virtues (*Cher.* 1-10). Isaac needs no teacher: he listens to, and learns from, only himself (*Somn.* 1.160).[271] And finally, Jacob is the man of action, exemplifying a practical life of virtue (*Congr.* 69; *Mut.* 84).[272] Isaac was naturally perfect and so his 'path' is not actually imitable, but Abraham (and Jacob) were perfected in their lifetimes so that they became 'equal to the angels' (*Sac.* 1-10).[273] Thus, the paths of philosophy and practice remained the twin avenues by which, according to Philo, others may emulate the fathers and so attain their virtue.[274]

None of this tells us much about Philo's perspective on Abraham's 'seed', although it does indicate – if only indirectly – that Philo viewed Abraham as almost 'sinless' (i.e. perfected in virtue through learning). Abraham's fatherhood and foundational status for the Jewish people are emphasized (*Abr.* 88-89), but this is rather a truism than an innovation. Philo does not focus upon the identity of Abraham's 'offspring', and who may be considered the 'true heirs' to Abraham. Philo instead allegorizes Gen. 12.2-3 to insist that the 'offspring' of the soul's labours are inferior to the graces that God bestows (*Migr.* 34-35).[275] In fact, Philo writes of Abraham's exit from Chaldea not as a physical migration but as a journey of Abraham's soul (*Migr.* 28), a spiritual homecoming (*Abr.* 66). Abraham does 'see' the land of Canaan, but this vision is interior, and is given to him as a reward from God for transitioning to a higher spiritual realm than before.[276]

---

[268] Maren Niehoff, 'Mother and Maiden, Sister and Spouse: Sarah in Philonic Midrash', *HTR* 97, no. 4 (2004), pp. 413–44.
[269] Michael L. Satlow, 'Philo on Human Perfection', *JTS* 59, no. 2 (2008), pp. 500–19, at pp. 509–10.
[270] Sandmel, 'Philo's Place in Judaism, Part II', p. 224.
[271] Satlow, 'Philo on Human Perfection', p. 510.
[272] Ibid.
[273] Cf. Colleen M. Conway, 'Gender and Divine Relativity in Philo of Alexandria', *JSJ* 34, no. 4 (2003), pp. 471–91, at p. 483. Conway convincingly shows that Philo coordinates real divinity with 'perfect masculinity', leading to a deification of Moses in particular. The implications for Johannine Christology arising from Philonic and Greco-Roman conceptions of masculinity are fascinatingly drawn out in Conway's monograph, *Behold the Man: Jesus and Greco-Roman Masculinity* (New York: Oxford University Press, 2008), pp. 143–58.
[274] Satlow, 'Philo on Human Perfection', p. 515: of these two examples, 'Philo is clearly partial to philosophy as a path to virtue' because he considers philosophy as a means of effecting permanent changes in a person's character, whereas he views virtuous practice as less consistent on a quotidian level.
[275] Phoebe Makiello, 'Abraham and the Nations in the Works of Philo of Alexandria', in *Abraham, the Nations, and the Hagarites*, pp. 139–62, at pp. 142–3.
[276] Sandmel, 'Philo's Place in Judaism, Part II', p. 237.

Towards the end of his life, Abraham is completely able to renounce materiality through the higher states that his mind has attained, and here we see Philo linking Abraham's capacities in speculative philosophy to his perfection via asceticism.[277] One can attain virtue like Abraham's by following the example of Abraham – but does that virtue hold any merit for Abraham's 'seed'? That question does not appear to be addressed by Philo. Still, for Philo, the 'God of Abraham, Isaac, and Jacob' is also the God of the people of Israel, who are the offshoot of Abraham (*Her.* 277-79); they are the ethnos 'beloved of God' (*Migr.*113-14).[278]

Philo's portrait convinces Sandmel that 'the rabbinic Abraham' – or indeed the Abraham of early Jewish texts – has little in common with the Philonic Abraham.[279] The status of 'the Law' in Philo's writings is contested in the scholarship.[280] Philo refers to the Mosaic Law as a copy of the unwritten law of nature (*Mos.* 2.12-14). He may also consider the Mosaic Law to be a lower form of religiosity by his preference for Abraham's contemplative virtue, over Jacob's life of active virtue.[281] But it is clear in Philo's mind that the commandments of the Mosaic Law assisted people in attaining the best virtues through the encouragement of self-restraint (*Det.* 16).[282] Furthermore, Abraham's deeds *became* recorded Law, but Abraham was the first to observe this Law in the unwritten law of nature – as it was divinely laid out. Philo's 'revolution' in this instance, was to show how the Mosaic Law had universal application, while still applying it particularly to the Jewish people: take any universal norm, Philo appears to be saying, and you may find a perfect copy of it in the written Law.[283]

Like the Apocrypha and Pseudepigrapha, we find in the fragments from Qumran and the Hellenistic Jewish writings of Philo and Josephus, a focus on Abraham as an exemplar for posterity. Either that, or we find a focus on his status as chosen/beloved by God, as well as the injunctions to avoid exogamous marriage so as to keep the holy 'seed' of Abraham pure and sinless. While there is less of an outright debate on matters of imputed sin and the role that Abraham may play in attenuating the effects of sin on behalf of his 'seed' (when compared to the preceding corpora), the theme of God cherishing the *memory* of the fathers because of their righteousness – and as a result, never failing to care for their seed – comes through in the work of Josephus as he builds upon the post-exilic narratives of the biblical text. In Philo's writings, Abraham's exemplarity is supremely idealized, but Philo appears convinced that Abraham is not therefore beyond imitability.

---

[277] Ibid., p. 139.
[278] Karl-Gustav Sandelin, 'Philo as a Jew', in Torrey Seland (ed.), *Reading Philo: A Handbook to Philo of Alexandria* (Grand Rapids: Eerdmans, 2014), pp. 19–46, at p. 24.
[279] Sandmel, 'Philo's Place in Judaism, Part II', p. 225.
[280] Cf. Satlow, 'Philo on Human Perfection', p. 517. This contestation reflects the ambivalence about the Mosaic Law expressed in Philo's own writings, which no doubt had its origin in a political context where Philo needed to 'authorize Mosaic Law against competing non-Jewish traditions'. See Hindy Naijman, 'The Law of Nature and the Authority of the Mosaic Law', *StPhAnnual* 11 (1999), pp. 55–73, at p. 56.
[281] Thus, Sandmel, 'Philo's Place in Judaism, Part II', p. 315.
[282] Satlow, 'Philo on Human Perfection', p. 517.
[283] Cf. Naijman, 'The Law of Nature', p. 60.

The New Testament

Whereas a substantial number of the biblical and early Jewish references to Abraham's 'seed' revealed a subtle connection to the concepts of sin and slavery, some key texts of the NT make that connection explicit (cf. Gal. 3.16, 29). The NT evidence is therefore vital for a fuller understanding of how the earliest Jesus followers – themselves Jewish – inherited the language of 'Abraham's seed', and towards which new vistas (and valleys) they extended the intertextual connotations. I begin this section by looking at the term 'seed of Abraham' in the writings of Paul. The letters to the Galatians and Romans remain the most researched 'intertexts' for the Johannine expression 'seed of Abraham' (8.31, 36) to date.[284] As noted in Chapter 1, Paul's influence on John's use of the term 'seed of Abraham' has perhaps been overstated. The following analysis will begin with Paul's letter to the Galatians, since that Epistle shares a condensed mass of metaphors ('slavery', 'seed', 'sin') akin to John 8.31-37.

However, it is worth stating upfront some crucial differences between the texts. Unlike Galatians, John 8 has no conception of slavery or sin *in relation to the law*. If anything, there is intense focus in the Sukkot narrative on what it means to keep the Law (cf. 7.19-20) or to keep it rightly. Also, Paul constructs the 'doing' of the works of the Law as against 'righteousness'; for John 8.39-40, the 'works of Abraham' *are* his righteous works (an argument I draw out more in Chapter 5). In Second Temple Judaism, as we have seen in the previous texts, Abraham was the doer of the 'works of the law' (the Law) – Paul overrides this prominent tradition, whereas it seems that John's Jews give voice to it. Having mentioned these caveats, let us return to Paul's discussion of Abraham's 'seed'.

Galatians

In his letter to the Galatians, Paul refers to Abraham's 'seed' four times (3.16 (×3), 29). Although all these references occur in ch. 3 of the letter, it will be necessary here to consider the whole of chs 3–4, and much of ch. 2, in order to grasp the flow and richness of Paul's thought on the topic of Abraham.[285] Paul introduces the context of his letter by referring to certain 'false brothers' (ψευδαδέλφους) who secretly slipped into his midst to 'spy' on him when he went to Jerusalem to see the 'pillars' of the church. These spies, suspicious of Paul proclaiming 'freedom' (ἐλευθερία) in Christ, tried to bring Paul and his group 'into slavery', but were unsuccessful (2.4-5a). This

---

[284] Dozeman, '*Sperma Abraam*', pp. 342–58; Lindars, 'Discourse and Tradition', pp. 89–97.

[285] The literature on the supposed social context of Paul's 'opponents' is too vast to cite in great depth here. All of the standard commentaries include some acknowledgement that Paul's audience was made up (predominantly, if not exclusively) of Gentile believers: Hans Dieter Betz, *Galatians* (Hermeneia; Minneapolis: Fortress Press, 1989); Martinus C. de Boer, *Galatians* (Louisville: Westminster John Knox, 2011); J. Louis Martyn, *Galatians* (New York: Yale University Press, 2004). Traditionally, commentators and scholars have considered Paul's 'opponents' in the letter to be 'Judaizers' – proponents of the full observance of the law, especially of circumcision, for Gentiles adopting the Christian faith; cf. Ronald Y. K. Fung, *The Epistle to the Galatians* (Grand Rapids: Eerdmans, 1988), p. 137, 194; Richard Longenecker, *Galatians* (WBC 41; Texas: Zondervan, 2015), p. 6, 15–16, 290–3; while Betz (*Galatians*, pp. 8–9) expressed the consensus view that Paul's opponents (1.6-7; 2.6; 3.1-2) were Torah-observant 'Jewish Christians' who advocated full integration of Christian existence into the terms of the Mosaic covenant.

metaphorical 'slavery' is not explicated by Paul, only associated with the teachings of the influential spies (cf. 2.6) and, apparently, with their perspective that Paul's Greek companion Titus be circumcised (2.3). Alluding to his clash in Jerusalem with Peter for 'compelling' Gentiles to live like Jews, Paul asks whether one could feasibly request a similar task of Jews: does preaching the Gospel mean forcing Jews to live without the Law, like the Gentiles? (2.11-14).[286]

After this 'autobiographical' opening, Paul abruptly switches key – he addresses his readers directly, in the first-person plural: 'We ourselves are natural Jews (φύσει Ἰουδαῖοι) and not Gentile sinners (ἐθνῶν ἁμαρτωλοί); yet we know that a person is not accounted righteous (οὐ δικαιοῦται) by the works of the law, but through faith in Jesus Christ' (2.15-16a).[287] Paul then poses a rhetorical question, 'But if in our attempt to be accounted righteous in Christ we also were found to be sinners, is Christ then a slave of sin?' (ἁμαρτίας διάκονος; 2.17a). Paul answers his own question with his characteristic rhetorical rejoinder, 'certainly not!' (μὴ γένοιτο; 2.17b). But Paul's explanation is so laconic as to be obscure: 'through the law I died to the law, so that I might live to God; I have been crucified with Christ' (2.19-20a). Christ's own death is presented as the singular means of righteousness: 'if righteousness were through the law, then Christ died in vain' (2.21). The repeated use of the verb δικαιόω (three times in the passive form, 2.16) and the cognate noun δικαιοσύνη (2.21) signals the core of Paul's message, which he will continue to develop as the letter unfolds.[288]

Paul then laments that the 'foolish Galatians' have been 'bewitched' by a rival Gospel (3.1), returning to the issue that motivated the letter – viz. that his community

---

[286] The historicity of Paul's 'autobiographical' account ought not to be taken at face value; thus Jack T. Sanders, 'Paul's "Autobiographical" Statements in Galatians 1–2', *JBL* 85, no. 3 (1966), pp. 335–43, at p. 336. Brigitte Kahl has argued that, by persistently attempting to harmonize Galatians 2 with the five Jerusalem visits in Acts, scholars risk losing sight of who Paul's audience actually were in Galatia. Brigitte Kahl, *Galatians Re-Imagined: Reading with the Eyes of the Vanquished* (Minneapolis: Fortress Press, 2010), pp. 25–30. For Kahl, the ancient history of the Gaul's violent defeat by Rome provides the vital contextual clue to the ethnic specificity of Paul's church in Galatia.

[287] Paul's first-person plural address has been adduced as evidence that his audience is a mix of Jews and 'Gentile' Jesus-believers. Alternatively, Paul could be referring to himself, Peter and Barnabas (cf. 1–2) in an exclusive 'we'-voice. See Bas Van Os, 'The Jewish Recipients of Galatians', in Stanley E. Porter (ed.), *Paul: Jew, Greek, and Roman* (PSP 5; Leiden: Brill, 2008), pp. 51–64, at pp. 60–1; cf. Gal. 4.3 (p. 56). Cf. also Mark D. Nanos, *The Irony of Galatians: Paul's Letter in First-Century Context* (Minneapolis: Fortress Press, 2002); and idem, 'How Inter-Christian Approaches to Paul's Rhetoric Can Perpetuate Negative Valuations of Jewishness', pp. 254–69. Nanos argues that the Galatians debate is intra-Jewish (i.e. neither 'intra-Christian' as per the 'New Perspective on Paul', nor Jewish-Christian, as per the so-called 'Old' perspective). Paul's 'opponents' are, in Nanos's reading, Jews (most likely proselytes – thus, neither Gentile 'God-fearers' nor fully fledged 'Christians') who argue that integration into the people of Israel must come (for men) by way of circumcision.

[288] The meaning of Paul's 'righteousness' language can, by no means, be resolved in a footnote; suffice it to say at this point, that scholars (invariably) disagree on what Paul means by the verbal, nominal and adjectival forms. The 'New Perspective on Paul' (NPP) position, sanctioned by N. T. Wright, understands δικαιοσύνη to mean the state of being 'acquitted' by God in a forensic sense (e.g. if the subject is a human sinner), but predicated of God, the noun means 'faithfulness', the correct actions of a judge. Cf. Wright, *Justification: God's Plan and Paul's Vision* (Downer's Grove: IVP Academic, 2009), pp. 86–108. If a person is 'justified' (or 'made righteous'), he is therefore vindicated, quit of all charges, released. The NPP reacts to the so-called 'Old Perspective' that was thought to have viewed 'justification/righteousness' as a (Jewish legalism striving to win God's good graces ('salvation') through Torah observance. Chapter 5 problematizes this dichotomous heuristic.

was turning to 'a gospel other than' the one Paul preached (1.6, 7).[289] Paul 'portrayed' his teaching of 'Christ crucified' before the Galatians, who heard his words in 'faith' and 'received the spirit' (3.2b); now they want to 'end with the flesh' (3.3). The 'flesh', for Paul, in this context connotes the 'works of the law' that the community appear to have newly adopted, or to have readopted (3.2a).[290] Paul tells them they did not receive the spirit through 'works of the law'. If they think so, then they have 'suffered in vain' (3.4a; cf. 2.21).

At this point, Paul invokes the biblical Abraham as a point of comparison: 'just as Abraham believed in God (καθὼς Ἀβραὰμ ἐπίστευσεν τῷ θεῷ), and it was accounted to him as righteousness' (ἐλογίσθη αὐτῷ εἰς δικαιοσύνην; 3.6; directly citing LXX Gen. 15.6). Abraham is mentioned for the first time in Paul's letter to the Galatians as a model of the kind of faith that 'makes' one 'righteous' apart from 'works of the law' (cf. 2.15-16).[291] Expanding on this, Paul considers 'those of faith' (3.7a, cf. v. 9) to be 'the sons of Abraham' (υἱοί Ἀβραάμ; 3.7b). Their status as 'sons' rests on the identical quality of faith they share with Abraham, a 'faith' that – if the reader fills in the gap – is the same as the ex-pagan Gentile's faith in Christ.[292] Indeed, 'the Scripture' foreknew God would plan to 'make righteous' the Gentiles 'by faith', and thus preached the Gospel to Abraham before the event (3.8b). The substance of that preaching – and Paul's 'Gospel' in a nutshell – is a loose citation from LXX Gen. 12.3: 'in you all the nations shall be blessed' (3.8c). God's promise of blessing to Abraham, which includes a blessing of 'all the nations' is realized, on Paul's reading, in the Gentiles' faith in Christ.[293]

---

[289] Jae Won Lee, *Paul and the Politics of Difference: A Contextual Study of the Jewish-Gentile Difference in Galatians and Romans* (James Clarke & Co, 2015), p. 112. NB. John M. G. Barclay: 'In answering the Galatians Paul is in fact countering the opponents themselves and their message', but not in a way that is a 'direct response' (Barclay, 'Mirror-Reading a Polemical Letter: Galatians as a Test Case', *JSNT* 31 (1987), pp. 73-93, at p. 75).

[290] The meaning of 'works of the law' in Galatians and Romans is addressed in Chapter 5 on the 'works' of Abraham. However, it is worth foreshadowing my perspective on the topic here, as one that diverges from the 'New Perspective on Paul' paradigm; I find the categories explicated by Dunn ('kashrut, Shabbat and circumcision' being the referents for 'works of the law') too limiting to fully delineate Paul's thoughts in Galatians and Romans. As I show in Chapter 5, the phrase 'works of the law' does not merely specify 'identity markers' but also the broader remit of the Torah. Cf. James D. G. Dunn, 'The New Perspective on Paul', *BJRL* 65 (1983), pp. 5–122. I should also emphatically add that this does not mean Paul rejects 'Judaism' or the Law *tout court*.

[291] Fung, *Galatians*, p. 135.

[292] Heikki Räisänen, *Paul and the Law* (WUNT 29; Tübingen: Mohr Siebeck, 1983), p. 189.

[293] Abraham may arise in this context so suddenly and intensely because Paul's opponents used Abraham as a figure of scriptural interpretation in their own kerygma, but this is only speculative. Barclay, 'Mirror-Reading', p. 87; cf. G. Walter Hansen, *Abraham in Galatians: Epistolary and Rhetorical Contexts* (2nd edn (orig. 1989) London: Bloomsbury, 2015), p. 98. But in what sense was Abraham's 'faith' like the Gentiles' faith in Christ? Either Abraham had faith in Christ (cf. Justin Martyr's theology of the pre-existent Logos appearing to Abraham), or the 'faith of Christ' (πίστις Χριστοῦ: Gal. 2.16) should be read as the 'faithfulness of Christ' and compared retroactively with Abraham's faithfulness, or obedience to God. For a sampling of the vast literature on this topic, see, Longenecker, *Galatians*, pp. 112–15; Richard B. Hays, *The Faith of Jesus Christ: The Narrative Substructure of Galatians 3.1-4.11* (2nd edn; Grand Rapids: Eerdmans, 2002), and recently, Debbie Hunn, 'Galatians 3.6-9: Abraham's Fatherhood and Paul's Conclusions', *CBQ* 78 (2016), pp. 500–14. Hunn favours the idea that Abraham and the Gentiles are in a metaphorical father–son relationship, sharing a familial type of faith in God through exemplarity and imitation – and it is this familial relationship that brings 'justification' (idem, pp. 512, 514).

On the other hand, Paul reasons that 'all who are from the works of the law are under a curse' (ἐξ ἔργων νόμου εἰσίν; 3.10a). This verse alludes to the 'curse' found in Deuteronomy's long list of blessings and curses near the end of its book (Deut. 27.26): 'cursed be everyone who does not abide by all the things written in the book of the law, and *do them*' (ποιῆσαι αὐτά; 3.10). Paul then contrasts the 'sons of Abraham' who are akin to Abraham, that 'man of faith', with those who are under a 'curse' if they do not *do* all the things written in the law. This leads Paul to also contrast the (singular) 'work' (ἐξ ἔργων νόμου) of the law with the state of faith (cf. 3.10-12). Faith is not something that is 'done' – it is something that the 'righteous' will 'live by' (3.11, citing Hab. 2.4). But the Law (or the *laws*, the plural is implied in Paul's next citation from Lev. 18.5) is something that is *done*. Of course, the Law is also 'lived by' (cf. 3.11-12) – but Paul's emphasis is on the fact that the law is 'done', while faith is not 'done'. Hence, his concise formulation: 'but the law is not of faith' (3.12a). Paul described the 'sons' of Abraham as being 'of faith'; the Law does not share this category, nor does it partake of Abraham's 'blessing'. Indeed, the 'blessing of Abraham' came only to the Gentiles 'in Christ' (v. 14), because Christ, writes Paul, 'redeemed us from the curse of the law by becoming a curse for us' (3.13) – a reference to Christ's crucifixion, as Paul's final citation for this section indicates (Deut. 21.23).[294]

To support his point, Paul gives what he calls a 'human example' (3.15). It is at this stage that Paul refers to the 'seed' of Abraham four times in one verse (vv. 16a-d):

> Now the promises were made to Abraham and his seed (τῷ δὲ Ἀβραὰμ ἐρρέθησαν αἱ ἐπαγγελίαι καὶ τῷ σπέρματι αὐτοῦ).[295] It does not say, 'and to his seeds', referring to many, but referring to one, 'and to your seed', who is Christ (οὐ λέγει· καὶ τοῖς σπέρμασιν, ὡς ἐπὶ πολλῶν ἀλλ' ὡς ἐφ' ἑνός· καὶ τῷ σπέρματί σου, ὅς ἐστιν Χριστός). This is what I mean: the law, coming 430 years afterward, does not annul a covenant previously ratified by God, so as to make the promise void. For if the inheritance comes by law, it no longer comes by promise; but God gave it to Abraham as a promise. Why then the law? It was added because of transgressions (τῶν παραβάσεων), until the seed (τὸ σπέρμα) should come to whom the promise had been made, and it was put in place by an intermediary. (3.16-19)[296]

Just before making this point, Paul insists that 'human' covenants are never annulled after their ratification, nor altered by codicils (3.15), and so, *a fortiori*, God's covenant could never be annulled. God made a promise to Abraham in the form of a covenant (cf. Gen. 12.1-3), but the 'law, which came 430 years afterwards' cannot render the original promise void (3.17) – the promise made to Abraham had temporal (and

---

[294] For an excellent engagement with the literature around this citation, see O'Brien, 'The Curse of the Law', pp. 55–76.
[295] Recall that in the Torah, the promise was made *also* to Abraham's 'seed' in Gen. 13.15 and 17.8 – not to Abraham alone. In later passages, the promises were made to immediate descendants of Abraham (i.e. Isaac and Jacob) and these passages could also be part of Paul's emphasis.
[296] NRSV.

therefore moral) priority over Sinai.[297] It is striking that Paul never refers to the Mosaic Law as a 'covenant' but instead latches on to the covenantal overtones of the promises to Abraham, contrasting the (Mosaic) Law with the unbreakable covenant made with Abraham. What Paul means is not so much that the Mosaic Law could never annul the Abrahamic covenant/promise, but that the Law can never replace or override the inheritance the promise effected.[298] In that sense, Paul argues, the Abrahamic covenant was prior to the Law and therefore superior to it – the Law was simply 'added' to keep transgressions against the law (παράβασις) in check. Then Christ came (the singular 'seed' of Abraham) and realized the original promises made to Abraham (cf. 3.19). What is more, the Law was not the continuation of the original patriarchal 'promise' in the sense that it carried on the 'inheritance' promised to Abraham's seed; in Paul's view only 'faith' mediates this inheritance. Those of faith, therefore, are not only 'sons' of Abraham, but also *seed* of Abraham – those who inherit the blessing of Abraham (v. 29). 'Faith' and 'promise' are intrinsically related: the promise is 'inherited' through faith, and bypasses the Law, as it were (3.18). Because Paul contrasts 'faith' and 'law', the Abrahamic promise cannot come by the Law (3.18). Whereas many early Jewish texts understood 'belonging to the γενος of Abraham' as 'conditioned by observance of the Mosaic law',[299] Paul reads the scriptural blessings of the Gentiles through Abraham, as something conditioned on faith.[300]

In Paul's reading, 'Christ is not merely a descendant or a seed of Abraham, but *the* promised seed of Abraham. Since Christ is the seed of Abraham, gentile reception of Christ's *pneuma* results in them receiving the very stuff of Abraham's seed' (cf. Gal. 4.6).[301] While σπέρμα is a collective plural in the Genesis texts, Paul exploits the grammatical singularity of the word, adapting its referent to one person – Christ (3.16).[302] There is some evidence that the phrase 'seed of David' was used in the singular in a messianic sense, building upon the referent of the (singular) 'seed' to denote Solomon in 2 Sam. 7.12 (cf. Rom. 1.4).[303] Although the term 'seed of Abraham' did not hold messianic connotations in the biblical literature – we might count *Jub.* 16.20 in the parabiblical material – it remains to be asked why Paul would conflate, or associate, the messianic Davidic 'seed' with Christ, via a reading of Gen. 15.6 (LXX) on the 'seed of Abraham'.[304] The literal, biological sense of the noun σπέρμα possibly comes into play

---

[297] James G. D. Dunn, *The Epistle to the Galatians* (London: A&C Black, 1993), p. 186.
[298] Cf. Hansen, *Abraham in Galatians*, pp. 127–8.
[299] Birgit van der Lans, 'Belonging to Abraham's Kin: Genealogical Appeals to Abraham as a Possible Background for Paul's Abrahamic Argument', in *Abraham, the Nations, and the Hagarites*, pp. 307–18, at p. 312.
[300] Cf. Paula Fredriksen, 'Judaizing the Nations: The Ritual Demands of Paul's Gospel', *NTS* 56 (2010), pp. 232–52.
[301] Matthew Theissen, *Paul and the Gentile Problem* (New York: Oxford University Press, 2016), p. 122.
[302] Ibid. However, note that Paul uses the word in its collective sense again in ch. 3 v. 29, for Christians who are the 'seed of Abraham' through faith. Paul does not restrict the meaning of σπέρμα to its singular (Christocentric) connotations. Rather, Paul manipulates the language to fit his argument without concern for consistency.
[303] Ibid., pp. 123–6.
[304] Ibid., p. 126. Theissen tries to bring some texts together in Paul's mind that would have permitted such associations (Ps. 17.44-45 LXX and Isa. 11.14), but this is not entirely convincing. A stronger

in Paul's reading, coexisting with the metaphorical, as Theissen demonstrates. That is, the whole future person was thought to already exist in the semen ('seed') of the reproducing male. Christ was therefore already 'in the loins' of his ancestor Abraham; so, Gentiles 'become Abrahamic seed' and 'exist in Abraham' by partaking of Christ's spirit, that is being 'in Christ'.[305] The promised inheritance Gentiles receive in this state obviates the need for circumcision, or Torah observance, to belong to Abraham.[306] Becoming the 'seed of Abraham' was to acquire 'a distinctive and glorious identity'.[307] Paul finds a way to gift that ethnic Jewish identity to ex-pagan Christ-followers directly and all at once.

Nevertheless, Paul insists that the Law is not against the promises of God (3.21); the law does not remain a 'dead end track' at all.[308] But for Paul, 'righteousness' comes via a promise, as exemplified in the life of Abraham (cf. Gen. 12.3, 15.6). The Law was not given directly from God (Paul suggests that intermediaries were involved), but the promise to Abraham *was* direct.[309] The Law, for Paul, does not give life, and so righteousness does not come by the law (3.21). 'Scripture' has 'imprisoned everything under sin' (συνέκλεισεν ἡ γραφὴ τὰ πάντα ὑπὸ ἁμαρτίαν) until the 'promise' could be received by faith in Jesus (3.22), and so 'we' (Paul includes himself) were 'held captive under the Law' (3.23). Paul makes a direct association between the imprisoning function of the Law, and the imprisoning function of sin. He explains both as a temporary bondage, subject to the coming of Christ, and like the role of a 'guardian' (παιδαγωγός) in a child's education (3.24-25).[310] Faith in Christ released believers from the bondage of being under guardianship (the Law), enabling them to take their place as 'sons of God' – not merely 'sons of Abraham' (3.26). The very categories of 'slave/free', 'Jew/Greek', 'woman/man' no longer hold for those who are 'in Christ Jesus' (3.28).[311] To be 'in Christ' is to be Abraham's 'seed', God's 'son' and an heir to the Abraham promises (3.29).[312]

In the ensuing verses, Paul develops his metaphor of the Law as tutor or guardian. The child under a guardian is no different to a slave, even if he owns much. He

---

intertextual reference (not cited by Theissen) would be Jer. 33.23-25 which, although absent from the MT, provides a much clearer paralleling of David's 'seed' and Abraham's 'seed'.

[305] Ibid., p. 127.

[306] What is promised to Abraham in Paul's reading of Scripture? The Genesis promise of the land is never mentioned by Paul. It is likely that 'righteousness' itself is the inheritance and the promise, the status of being 'seed of Abraham', and the gift of the Spirit to the Gentiles. See Sam K. Williams, 'Promise in Galatians: A Reading of Paul's Reading of Scripture', *JBL* 107, no. 4 (1988), pp. 709–20, at p. 712.

[307] Philip F. Esler, 'Paul's Contestation of Israel's (Ethnic) Memory of Abraham in Galatians 3', *BTB* 36, no. 1 (2006), pp. 23–34, at p. 27.

[308] T. L. Donaldson, 'The "Curse of the Law" and the Inclusion of the Gentiles: Galatians 3.13-14', *NTS* 32 (1986), pp. 94–112, at p. 103.

[309] Cf. Esler, 'Paul's Contestation', p. 31.

[310] In life, this guardian/tutor figure was a domestic slave with an ambiguous status, who sometimes could not be trusted; cf. Catherine Hezser, *Jewish Slavery in Antiquity* (New York: Oxford University Press, 2004).

[311] Hansen, *Abraham in Galatians*, p. 138.

[312] Sonship and inheritance were intrinsically tied together in the ancient world – this included sonship via adoption as equally legitimate. See Michael Peppard, *The Son of God in the Roman World: Divine Sonship in Its Social and Political Context* (New York: Oxford University Press, 2011), p. 136; Erin M. Heim, *Adoption in Galatians and Romans* (BINS 153; Leiden: Brill, 2017).

cannot really own anything until his father releases him from his guardian (4.1).[313] Thus, writes Paul, 'God sent his Son, born under the law, to redeem those under the Law, so that we might be adopted sons' (ἵνα τοὺς ὑπὸ νόμον ἐξαγοράσῃ, ἵνα τὴν υἱοθεσίαν ἀπολάβωμεν; 4.5). The Spirit effects this adoption, as it is the living spirit of Jesus (4.6). When this happens, slaves become sons, and sons become heirs (4.7).[314] But Paul's audience are also described as being previously enslaved to 'those that by nature are not gods' (4.8). This group wants to 'turn back' to be enslaved once more to the 'elementary principles of the world' (4.9). They want to keep 'days and months and seasons and years' (4.10). For, they 'want to be under the Law' (4.21).

Paul develops a midrash on Genesis (Gen. 16.5, 21.2), with a renewed focus upon Abraham (Gal. 4.21-31), directed, it appears, at his (sub-)audience who wish to keep the Law. Yet, it is this law that testifies against them ('tell me, you who wish to keep the Law, do you listen to the Law?' 4.21).[315] Paul transposes his binary of slavery/freedom onto two female biblical figures intimately associated with Abraham, and the respective sons they bore him: Hagar the Egyptian bondswoman who bore Ishmael, and Sarah, Abraham's formerly 'barren' wife, who bore Isaac (cf. Gen. 16.5; 21.2). But Paul alters the structure of his argument slightly: Ishmael, 'the son of the slave' is associated with the 'flesh' (σάρξ) while Isaac is associated with the original promise made to Abraham (4.23-24).[316] Formerly in Paul's letter, the 'Law' was opposed to 'the promise' (cf. 3.19-29), but in this midrash 'the law' is paired with 'the flesh'. Both 'law' and 'flesh' are associated with the concept of 'slavery' and are structurally elucidated by it. The 'promise', as formerly (cf. ch. 3), is paired with 'freedom'. Paul adds another layer to this conceptual structure: Hagar and Sarah are 'allegories' (ἀλληγορούμενα) of *two* covenants (δύο διαθῆκαι; 2.24).[317] Hagar corresponds to 'Mount Sinai in Arabia' (or 'the present Jerusalem') and is 'in slavery with her children'; Sarah corresponds to the 'Jerusalem above', which is 'free' and is the mother of Paul and believers (4.24-26).[318]

Paul's thought gains in complexity as the passage develops. Applying the midrash to the Galatian situation, Paul notes that 'the brothers' (4.28) are 'like Isaac' and are 'children of the promise'. The Isaac/Ishmael binary (i.e. promise/flesh) now becomes another 'flesh/spirit' dichotomy, consonant with the structure of Paul's thought earlier

---

[313] Paul does not refer to manumission, for the *tutor* is the slave (household servant). The liberation and freedom experienced by the son is when he comes of age.

[314] Other than John 8, this might be the only text that positions the idea of *inheritance* together with the son/slave dichotomy, in the larger context of debate about being *sperma Abraam*.

[315] Susan Eastman, '"Cast Out the Slave Woman and her Son": The Dynamics of Exclusion and Inclusion in Galatians 4.30', *JSNT* 28, no. 3 (2006), pp. 309–36, at p. 313. Note that here, Scripture (the Torah from which Paul derives his midrash) is called 'the law' by Paul. Cf. Chapter 3 verse 22, where 'Scripture' confines everything under 'sin'.

[316] Dunn, *Galatians*, pp. 246-7, links 'the flesh' (Hagar/Ishmael) with Paul's opposition and their concern with a ritual of the flesh, that is circumcision.

[317] Martinus C. de Boer, 'Paul's Quotation of Isaiah 54.1 in Galatians 4.27', *NTS* 50 (2004), pp. 370–89, at p. 376: 'When Paul says "two covenants", he clearly means 'two *different* covenants," or even "two mutually exclusive covenants"'.

[318] Brendan Byrne, 'Jerusalems Above and Below: A Critique of J. L. Martyn's Interpretation of the Hagar-Sarah Allegory in Gal 4.21–5.1', *NTS* 60 (2014), pp. 215–31.

in the letter: Ishmael, who was born of the flesh *then* persecuted Isaac, who was born of the promise. And so *now*, Paul implies, the 'children of Ishmael' persecute the children of the spirit (the 'we', who are 'like Isaac', 4.29). Paul's earlier flesh–spirit polarization (3.3) illuminates the present verse, for there, the 'spirit' was likened to 'faith', while the 'flesh' was likened to 'works of the law', and Abraham was called 'the man of faith' (3.6). The Galatians were 'like Abraham' as much as they imitated the faith of Abraham; in Paul's midrash (4.28-29), the Galatians are 'like Isaac' and are born according to the spirit and according to the promise. The present-day children of Hagar correspond to the covenant of Sinai – a clear reference to 'Judaizers' (if not even Jews) who keep the Law and who want the Galatians to also keep the 'works of the law'.[319] The 'children of Hagar' are not only in slavery under the yoke of Rome (the cryptic reference to the sufferings of the 'present Jerusalem') but are also under the slavery of 'the law' because they do not profess faith in Christ, who has now come (as the 'seed of Abraham') to liberate them from the tutorship of the Law.[320]

The consequences of being 'born of Hagar' or 'born of Sarah' are stark and mutually exclusive. Citing Sarah's words to Abraham in Gen. 21.10, Paul continues: 'What does Scripture say? Cast out the slave woman and her son, for the son of the slave woman shall not inherit with the son of the free woman' (4.30). Paul concludes by reasserting that he and his audience ('we, brothers') are children of the 'free woman', not the 'slave woman' (4.31). Thus, the 'law' itself (in this sense, all of Scripture) indicates the consequences of continuing to uphold the Law in the face of Christ's coming (cf. 4.21). Christ is the one who has set Paul's audience 'free' for the sake of 'freedom', and so, Paul cautions them not to 'submit *again* to a yoke of slavery' (5.1). In Paul's midrash (4.21-31), 'slavery' is tied to the idea of 'birth/origins' via the status of the 'mother'; one is born into either slavery or freedom, and only the sons of the free mother can inherit from their father Abraham. The schema in ch. 4 vv. 1-7 depicts the son (who is like a slave) eventually 'redeemed' in time, leading to a natural change in status that differentiates him from the slave-born. In Gal. 4.21-31, Paul depicts the (free-born) son who will inherit *apart from* the slave-born son – the latter is ultimately destined to be 'cast out' of the household.

The following table represents Paul's thought in Gal. 4.21-31. The italicized sections show the structural oppositions that he develops from prior stages of his letter:

---

[319] Steven Di Mattei, 'Paul's Allegory of the Two Covenants (Gal. 4.21-31) in Light of First-Century Hellenistic Rhetoric and Jewish Hermeneutics', *NTS* 52 (2006), pp. 102-22, at p. 113.

[320] This reading highlights the consistency of Paul's thought in the letter. Although this is not a 'nice' reading (i.e. it does not reflect well on Paul's magnanimity towards Mosaic observance), it is, according to Byrne ('Jerusalems Above and Below', p. 216) more correct than J. Louis Martyn's reading ('The Covenants of Hagar and Sarah', in J. T. Carroll, C. H. Cosgrove and E. E. Johnson (eds), *Faith and History: Essays in Honor of Paul W. Meyer* (Atlanta; Scholars Press, 1990), pp. 160–92), which strained to make Paul's midrash amenable to a post-Shoah context by downplaying Paul's polemic against Judaism. Byrne wisely notes that although we might critique Martyn's thesis that Paul refers only to intra-Christian groups (e.g. Paul clearly refers to *two* covenants, not one split mission, *pace* Martyn), this does not mean we have to return to an anti-Jewish interpretation of the text.

Biblical type	Hagar	Sarah
Covenant	Sinai (Mount, in Arabia)	–
Which Jerusalem?	Present (earthly), associated with Ishmael	'Jerusalem above' (eschatological), associated with Isaac
Slave or free?	'in slavery' (*child as slave*)	'free' (*heir, grown son*)
Whose mother?	Children 'in slavery'; 'born according to flesh' (*law; doing works of the law*)	'she is our mother'; 'children of the promise'; born according to Spirit'; 'we, like Isaac' (*faith; righteousness that comes of faith*)
Consequences?	Cast out from the inheritance; the 'one who has a husband' will have fewer children than the 'barren one'	Sole heirs; inversion of barrenness: children of Sarah more numerous

Paul does not think that the giving of the Sinaitic Law could itself be a fulfilment of the promise made to Abraham; it is only a necessary implementation to keep 'transgressions' in check, but its 'works' do not effect 'righteousness' because everything has been 'imprisoned under sin' (4.19, 21-22). In that respect, the Law is in line with the 'promises of God' (note the plural in v. 19), but it is not the fulfilment of the promise made to Abraham – Christ, *the* 'seed' of Abraham is, for Paul, that fulfilment in person. The 'works of the law' for Paul are therefore intrinsically tied to sin, and to the condition of slavery, both of which Paul likens to the male child under a guardian, and to the 'children of Hagar' who are 'in slavery'. Abraham is the first recipient of the divine promise, and he exemplifies the kind of faith that comes with 'the spirit' and which liberates one from slavery. Paul's community can receive the same spirit ('by hearing by faith' and *not* by the observance of the 'works of the law'). The promises were made *to Christ* as the singular 'seed of Abraham' but the promise was also *of Christ and his spirit*. When believers 'put on Christ' in baptism (3.26) and thus belong to Christ, they become the (plural) 'seed of Abraham' and they inherit the promised 'spirit' of Christ. But with that, Paul 'excludes the law as the way to become Abraham's children and heirs, and threatens exclusion for all who rely on works of the law'.[321]

Romans 4.13, 16; 9.7-8

Paul's use of the concept of 'Abraham's seed' in his letter to the Romans (cf. 4.13, 16; 9.7-8) represents a later development in his thinking and, *prima facie*, expresses a more inclusive vision than that found in his letter to the Galatians. Paul is also less inventive inasmuch as he does not play with the grammatical form of the noun σπέρμα as at Gal. 3.16-19, but employs the noun in its plural sense to refer to Abraham's descendants, as in the Torah.

---

[321] Eastman, 'Cast Out the Slave Woman', p. 327.

Paul spends the opening section of his epistle discussing the universality of God's judgement upon sinners and the impartial reach of God's mercy towards those who repent (cf. 2.4; cf. 3.21-26). God rewards both Jew and Gentile alike for good works (2.6-11; cf. 3.29-30), and condemns both for their sinful behaviour (1.16-3.31; cf. 3.9).[322] Paul considers the Gospel as the salvation God intended 'to the Jew first and also to the Greek' (1.16b), depending entirely on faith (1.17). Paul ponders whether 'the Jew' (or 'circumcision') therefore has any distinct advantage (3.1-2). He affirms that the advantage lies in the fact that Jews first received God's 'oracles' (i.e. the Law and the prophets, the whole of Scripture, 3.2b), pointing out that human disobedience cannot nullify God's faithfulness anyway (3.3-8).[323]

For Paul, no one is inherently righteous (3.9-18), and no one can be 'justified' by 'deeds prescribed by the Law' (ἐξ ἔργων νόμου οὐ δικαιωθήσεται πᾶσα σάρξ), for the Law introduces awareness of sin (νόμου ἐπίγνωσις ἁμαρτίας; 3.20). Faith is effective to justify a person, whereas 'the works of the Law' fail (3.27a, 28).[324] Yet, the Law is not made redundant by faith – it is given its 'true footing' (ἀλλὰ νόμον ἱστάνομεν; 3.31), for faith perceives in the Law the message of the Law's insufficiency to 'justify'.[325] It is in this context that Paul turns to the figure of Abraham, and of Abraham's seed (4.1-25).[326] What about Abraham, who was most exemplary in his 'works' and was 'our forefather according to the flesh'? (προπάτορα ἡμῶν κατὰ σάρκα; 4.1-2). Even if Abraham 'was justified by works' (εἰ γὰρ Ἀβραὰμ ἐξ ἔργων ἐδικαιώθη) he could not boast before God (4.2), Paul concludes. Only Abraham's 'faith' guaranteed him righteousness (4.3).[327] If Abraham *had no works*, he could still trust in God and be reckoned righteous (4.4-5). And while 'works' are reckoned by God as deserving of 'wages' (μισθός), trust achieves something else – a gratuitous gift from God (4.5).[328] God will 'cover' and 'blot out' the sins of the person with faith (4.6-8).[329] God did as much to Abraham *before* he was

---

[322] For a full discussion of the opening rhetorical design of Paul's letter, its polemic and theological vision, see: Rafael Rodriguez and Matthew Thiessen (eds), *The So-Called Jew in Paul's Letter to the Romans* (Minneapolis: Fortress Press, 2016); Jonathan A. Linebaugh, 'Announcing the Human: Rethinking the Relationship Between Wisdom of Solomon 13-15 and Romans 1.18-2.11', *NTS* 57 (2011), pp. 21–40, at p. 37.

[323] Cf. David R. Hall, 'Romans 3.1-8 Reconsidered', *NTS* 29 (1983), pp. 183–97, at p. 185.

[324] Douglas J. Moo, *The Epistle to the Romans* (Grand Rapids: Eerdmans, 1996), p. 217: 'Works of the law are inadequate not because they are works of *the law* but, ultimately, because they are "works"'.

[325] Brendan Byrne, *Romans* (SP 5; 2nd edn; Collegeville: Liturgical Press, 2007).

[326] The text-critical problems of Rom. 4.1 have been well documented and need not detain us here. See, Michael Cranford, 'Abraham in Romans 4: The Father of All Who Believe', *NTS* 41 (1995), pp. 71–88, at pp. 73–6.

[327] Again, Paul is citing Gen. 15.6. For a thorough discussion on the relevance of Gen. 15.6 to Paul, and other Jewish writers of the Second Temple Period, see Benjamin Schliesser, *Abraham's Faith in Romans 4: Paul's Concept of Faith in Light of the History of Reception of Genesis 15.6* (WUNT 2/224; Tübingen: Mohr Siebeck, 2007), pp. 79–220.

[328] The economic overtones of this verse are important and will be raised in more detail in Chapter 5. For a solid background, see Simon J. Gathercole, *Where is Boasting? Early Jewish Soteriology and Paul's Response in Romans 1–5* (Grand Rapids: Eerdmans, 2002).

[329] Citing LXX Ps. 32.1; the crediting of 'justification' to a person entails the forgiveness of transgressions, the 'covering' of sin. When faith (rather than visible 'works') is credited as 'righteousness' this comes as a 'gift' from God. See Colin G. Kruse, *Paul's Letter to the Romans* (PNTC; Grand Rapids: Eerdmans, 2012), p. 208. Note also the connotations of idolatry inherent in ἀσεβής (4.5), a specific type of transgression linked with 'the nations'; see Edward Adams, 'Abraham's Faith and Gentile Disobedience: Textual Links Between Romans 1 and 4', *JSNT* 65 (1997), pp. 47–66, at p. 51.

circumcised, and can do so once more to all who are uncircumcised in the present (4.9-12). Indeed, for Paul, Abraham's circumcision was a sign of his faith, and as such, Abraham becomes the ancestor of 'all who believe without being circumcised' (4.11). Abraham is also the ancestor of the circumcised who demonstrate his faith (4.12).[330] Paul writes,

> For the promise that he would inherit the world did not come to Abraham or to his seed (τῷ Ἀβραὰμ ἢ τῷ σπέρματι αὐτοῦ) through the Law but through the righteousness of faith. If it is the adherents of the Law who are to be the heirs, faith is null and the promise is void. For the Law brings wrath; but where there is no Law, neither is there violation. (4.13-14)

The 'promise' given to Abraham or his 'seed' is phrased here as the 'inheritance of the world', which is rather curious, given that the patriarchal promises are never phrased in exactly this form in the Torah. What we do perhaps see, however, is a progressive expansion of the geographic territory of the Promised Land over time – thus, from texts such as Gen. 18.18; 22.17-18, to Ben Sira's reference to the 'inheritance' of Abraham's seed 'from sea to sea, from the Euphrates to the ends of the earth' (*Sir.* 44.21).[331] While Paul spiritualizes the 'promise' in his letter to the Galatians, here in Romans he gives it concrete formulation, but within an eschatological paradigm. Abraham is the father of 'many nations', not just one; anyone who exhibits Abraham's faith – never distrusting God's word despite the odds – can be Abraham's 'seed' (4.19-24).[332] The rewards of Abraham's faith pass directly to the person who believes in Jesus, who is the supreme agent of 'justification' (4.25).[333]

Paul's two references to Abraham's 'seed' in ch. 4 vv. 13-25 appear contradictory. On the one hand, the thematic refrain is a sense of *inclusiveness* – God is impartial and generous, rewarding Jews and Gentiles alike for righteous deeds and for faith. The 'seed of Abraham' are not only Jews who have the Law, but also Gentiles who live by faith (4.16). But on the other hand, Paul's claim that Jews have no intrinsic 'specialness' for obeying the Law morphs into his assertion that, actually, the Law is ineffective to 'justify' a person; only the kind of faith that Abraham demonstrated – focused now completely on Jesus' atoning death for sins – can justify a person. This leads Paul to reason that the promises made in the Torah to Abraham and his 'seed' did not come 'through the Law' but 'through the righteousness of faith' (4.13). Abraham's (or his descendant's) observance of the Law did not mediate or realize the divine promises.

---

[330] Cf. Tobin, 'What Shall We Say that Abraham Found?', p. 447.
[331] Frank J. Matera, *Romans* (Paideia Commentaries on the New Testament; Grand Rapids: Baker Academic, 2010), p. 114.
[332] Cranford, 'Abraham in Romans 4', p. 88.
[333] The quality of Abraham's faith in ch. 4 v. 20 has recently generated some discussion: was it the unflinching belief that his personal desolation (i.e. having no son and heir) would be turned around into a state of fulfilment? Or was it, perhaps, tied to early Jewish exegetical traditions about Abraham leaving idolatry and discovering monotheism? In a fascinating article, Benjamin Schliesser makes a strong case for the latter option, surprisingly via the text's reception by juggernauts of Christendom. See Schliesser, 'Abraham Did Not "Doubt" in Unbelief (Rom 4.20): Faith, Doubt, and Dispute in Paul's Letter to the Romans', *JTS* 63, no. 2 (2012), pp. 492–522, at p. 514.

Instead, those promises were realized only when, and because, Abraham had faith in God. Paul's apparent inclusiveness (e.g. 'all have sinned, and all are justified by faith') reveals itself to be a more particularistic ideology that implicitly defines Abraham's true 'seed' as those who display faith in Christ.

Paul confirms this perspective when he next refers to the 'seed' of Abraham (Rom. 9.7). In the beginning of a long digression on the fate of unbelieving Israel (9.1–11.36), Paul writes of his trouble over how his 'kindred according to the flesh ... [the] Israelites' (9.3b-4a)[334] seem to have rejected Jesus, although 'to them belong the adoption, the glory, the covenants, the giving of the Law, the worship and the promises', also 'the patriarchs' and 'the Messiah' (9.4-5).[335] Has 'the word of God failed'? (9.6a). Paul reasons against that assumption, explaining the conundrum thus: 'For not all Israelites truly belong to Israel, and not all of Abraham's children are his true seed' (οὐ γὰρ πάντες οἱ ἐξ Ἰσραὴλ οὗτοι Ἰσραήλ, ὐδ' ὅτι εἰσὶν σπέρμα Ἀβραὰμ πάντες τέκνα; 9.6b-7a); 'Israel' is not coterminous with 'Abraham's seed', because for Paul, the true seed of Abraham will be a remnant.[336] To back up his argument, Paul once again alludes to Gen. 21.9-13 (LXX), where Abraham expels Hagar because of Ishmael's affront to Isaac. God reassures Abraham that 'through Isaac shall your seed be named', but that Ishmael will nevertheless become 'a nation' because he too, is Abraham's 'seed' (Gen. 21.13). Paul cites God's promise to Abraham that the naming of his ('true') seed will occur through Isaac alone (Gen. 21.12; Rom. 9.7b).[337] Paul continues, 'this means that it is not the children of the flesh (ἃ τέκνα τῆς σαρκὸς) who are the children of God, but the children of the promise (τὰ τέκνα τῆς ἐπαγγελίας) are counted as seed' (λογίζεται εἰς σπέρμα; 9.8).[338]

Further reasoning through his puzzling theodicy, Paul writes that Israel tried to attain 'righteousness' through 'the Law' (διώκων νόμον) but failed to fulfil the Law; the Gentiles had no such striving but attained righteousness 'through faith' (9.30-31). For Paul, the Law represents a striving 'based on works' (9.32), a self-established righteousness (10.3) that fails to see Christ as 'the end of the Law' (10.4).[339] But Israel

---

[334] That is, 'empirical Israel': E. P. Sanders, *Paul, the Law, and the Jewish Peoples* (Minneapolis: Fortress Press, 1983), p. 175.

[335] A much-discussed text, Romans 9-11 still generates an enormous secondary literature because of its problematic focus on the 'destiny' of Israel (Torah-observant Jews who do not follow Paul's belief in Jesus as Messiah). For dedicated recent studies, see, Robert B. Foster, *Renaming Abraham's Children: Election, Ethnicity, and the Interpretation of Scripture in Romans 9* (WUNT 2/421; Tübingen: Mohr Siebeck, 2016); David R. Wallace, *Election of the Lesser Son: Paul's Lament-Midrash in Romans 9-11* (Minneapolis: Augsburg, 2014); Susan G. Eastman, 'Israel and the Mercy of God: A Re-reading of Galatians 6.16 and Romans 9-11', *NTS* 56, no. 3 (2010), pp. 367-95; Gert J. Steyn, 'Observations on the Text Form of the Minor Prophets Quotations in Romans 9-11', *JSNT* 38, no. 1 (2015), pp. 49-67; B. J. Oropeza, 'Paul and Theodicy: Intertextual Thoughts on God's Justice and Faithfulness to Israel in Romans 9-11', *NTS* 53, no. 1 (2007), pp. 57-80.

[336] Foster, *Renaming Abraham's Children*, p. 120.

[337] Cf. Oropeza, 'Paul and Theodicy', p. 61. Paul also creates a 'promise' and 'flesh' binary in these verses, which carries over into Rom. 8.1-17, where 'flesh' receives further pejorative connotative force.

[338] Contra Byrne, *Romans*, p. 293, Paul does seem to be aware of the honorific connotations of 'seed of Abraham' in ch. 9 v. 7, since he continues to refer to the 'promise'. Also, note that one would expect 'seed' to be the broader category, and 'children' to be the exclusive category, but Paul reverses this expectation: James D. G. Dunn, *Romans 9-16* (WBC 38b; Texas: Word Press, 1988), p. 541.

[339] Matera, *Romans*, p. 242.

is not rejected; Paul himself is 'an Israelite, a seed of Abraham, a member of the tribe of Benjamin' (ἐγὼ Ἰσραηλίτης εἰμί, ἐκ σπέρματος Ἀβραάμ, φυλῆς Βενιαμίν; 11.1).[340] God will save a 'remnant' of Israel 'chosen by grace' who will not rely on 'works' (11.4-6), and the rest will be 'hardened' (11.7). But Israel's election is still primary (11.20-21) and they will all 'be saved' in the end (11.26) by God's inscrutable wisdom (11.33-36).[341]

Whereas the object of the 'promise' in the Torah is most often the Land, in Romans and Galatians the object of the promise is either unstated or spiritualized to fit the eschatological phenomenon of salvation in Christ. At times, Paul's argument in Romans 9–11 does not appear completely cogent: for example, in ch. 9 vv. 6b-7a, Paul contrasts the 'children of Abraham' with the 'seed of Abraham' – the latter representing the 'truer' category (even though, contradictorily, it has earlier been associated with externality and 'the flesh'). In ch. 9 vv. 6-7, Paul implies that the 'seed of Abraham' is identical to the theological category of 'Israel'. But then in Rom. 9.8, Paul opposes the 'children of the flesh' to the 'children of the promise', arguing that it is not the former who constitute the 'children of God', but the latter who are the 'seed of Abraham'.

2 Cor. 11.22

The only other Pauline reference to the 'seed of Abraham' occurs in 2 Corinthians in the context of Paul's rhetorical dispute with certain 'false apostles' (2 Cor. 11.13) whose boasting threatens the stability of Paul's church (11.1-30). Paul pleads with his audience in an effort to undo the seductive spell his rival 'super-apostles' have cast on the church in Corinth, first by disproving the premise that his rivals' magnificent charisma and spiritual gifts indicate their apostolic superiority (11.1-15); and second, by asserting that Paul's weakness, supposed inferiority and sufferings constitute genuine grounds for 'boasting' because they reveal that Paul's strength comes from a divine source, therefore legitimating his ministry (11.16-33).[342]

Paul engages directly with the claims of his rivals, stating that he can match his rivals in their boasts: 'Are they Hebrews? So am I. Are they Israelites? So am I. Are they [the] seed of Abraham? (σπέρμα Ἀβραάμ εἰσιν?) So am I. Are they servants of

---

[340] The translation 'descendant of Abraham' (NRSV) reads better, because σπέρματος is in the singular, but I have opted for 'seed' to retain consistency with Paul's discussion of the 'seed' (σπέρμα) of Abraham in the wider context of this verse.

[341] The passage remains ultimately hopeful, as John P. Heil convincingly demonstrates through his intertextual reading of Isa. 10.22 (cited in Rom. 9.27). Isa. 10.22 subtly alludes to Abraham's 'seed' through language reminiscent of the patriarchal promises in the Torah: 'If the number of the sons of Israel be as the sands of the sea, at least a remnant will be saved'; Heil, 'From Remnant to Seed of Hope for Israel: Romans 9.27-29', *CBQ* 64 (2002), pp. 703–20, esp. pp. 704, 709.

[342] Paul's so-called 'fool's speech' (2 Cor. 11.21b-12.10) is recognized in the scholarship for its conformity with Greco-Roman rhetorical conventions on speeches of self-praise, although scholars are divided about whether Paul's litany of sufferings illustrate his honour or degradation. See Christopher Forbes, 'Comparison, Self-Praise, and Irony: Paul's Boasting and the Conventions of Hellenistic Rhetoric', *NTS* 32 (1986), pp. 1–30; Timothy B. Savage, *Power through Weakness: Paul's Understanding of the Christian Ministry in 2 Corinthians* (Cambridge: Cambridge University Press, 1996). Similarly, Paul's further autobiographical narrative about his escape yields conflicting interpretations, but is possibly intended to be paradoxical. Cf. L. L. Welborn, 'The Runaway Paul', *HTR* 92 (1999), pp. 115–63.

Christ (διάκονοι Χριστοῦ εἰσιν)? I am talking like a fool – I am a better one' (11.22-23a). Paul's greater physical sufferings – brought on by resistance to his preaching – qualify him as a better servant of Christ (11.23b-29). Paul implies that the claim to status as 'seed of Abraham' (or 'Hebrew' or 'Israelite': Ἑβραῖοί ... Ἰσραηλῖταί) that some Jewish preachers brought into Corinth functioned like a ticket of authenticity because it connected missionaries to Jesus of Nazareth.[343] Paul uses the collective plural σπέρμα Ἀβραάμ to refer to his opponents (as a plurality) and to himself (as an individual). The elasticity of the term is therefore evident; compare Rom. 11.1, where Paul uses the singular σπέρματος Ἀβραάμ to refer to himself and his credentials. It is likely that Paul has in mind both the covenantal overtones, and the 'ethnic' connotations, of the term σπέρμα Ἀβραάμ in 2 Cor. 11.22.[344]

So, Paul uses the traditional markers of his group identity as credentials in the same sense, reminding the Corinthian church that he is also the 'seed of Abraham', but a 'better one'. Ultimately, even if other apostles claimed to be 'seed of Abraham', Paul reasons that a scale of excellence still obtains: a person can be a *better* 'descendant of Abraham' or a *better* servant of Christ. Excellence is proved by behaviour (in Paul's case, submitting to suffering for the sake of the Gospel), not conferred by birth or status alone. Here is an example, therefore, of in-group comparisons: where being the 'seed of Abraham' still requires that one's 'deeds' align with one's reputation. 'Seed' and 'deed', we might say, are in tension, and one must be proved by the other.

Luke 1.55

Outside of the Pauline corpus, only a handful of other NT texts – apart from John 8 –use the term 'seed of Abraham' (Luke 1.55; Acts 3.25; Heb. 2.14-18; 11.18). What distinguishes them, however, and makes them worthy of analysis, is that they all use the concept of 'servanthood'/'slavery' in relation to being 'seed of Abraham'. Luke 1.46-55 constitutes Mary's song of praise for God's redemption of his people.[345] Mary's song is infused with themes from the Hebrew scriptures about the magnanimous mercy of God towards his creatures;[346] it thoroughly employs the Lukan *leitmotif* of God subverting human power structures, for example by demoting the proud and the rich

---

[343] The three terms, 'seed of Abraham', 'Israelite' and 'Hebrew' are, according to Harris, 'archaizing term[s]' with a nuance of 'special solemnity' (Murray J. Harris, *The Second Epistle to the Corinthians: A Commentary on the Greek Text* (NICNT; Grand Rapids: Eerdmans, 2005), p. 795).

[344] Dennis Duling, '2 Corinthians 11.22: Historical Context, Rhetoric, and Ethnicity', *HTS Theological Studies* 64, no. 2 (2008), pp. 819–43, at pp. 834, 838.

[345] Traditionally called the Magnificat, Mary's song is attributed to 'Elizabeth' in it as well as in some Latin MSS, but scholars now believe that the original Lukan reading was 'Mary'. See Joel B. Green, *The Gospel of Luke* (NICNT; Grand Rapids: Eerdmans, 1997), p. 97.

[346] In form and content, Mary's song recalls many biblical hymns of praise on behalf of the lowly individual, such as Exod. 15.1-18, 19-21; Judg. 5.1-31; 1 Chron. 16.8-36; and specifically, 1 Sam. 2.1-10. See Green, *Luke*, 101–2; R. Tannehill, 'The Magnificat as Poem', *JBL* 93 (1974), pp. 263–75; and recently, Hugo Méndez, 'Semitic Poetic Techniques in the Magnificat: Luke 1.46-47, 55', *JBL* 135, no. 3 (2016), pp. 557–47.

but exalting the humble and the poor (1.48, 50, 51-53).[347] Mary's song concludes with the following lines:

He [the Lord] has helped his servant (παιδὸς) Israel/mindful of his mercy/just as he spoke to our fathers (τοὺς πατέρας)/Abraham and his seed forever. (1.54-55)

At the beginning of her song, Mary identifies herself as the Lord's servant (δούλης; 1.48), thus personally identifying herself with God's mercy towards his 'servant' Israel in vv. 54-55.[348] Indeed, it is Mary's experience of pregnancy with the foretold 'son of the Most High' who will 'reign over the house of Jacob' (1.32-33) that leads her to view herself as the locus of God's saving work on behalf of all Israel. The reference to Abraham's 'seed' in Luke 1.55 is very different to the Pauline instances explored so far, as it appears to draw less on the iteration of the promises to the patriarchs found in the Torah and more on the post-exilic prophetic strain of the motif, wherein God comes to the aid of Abraham's 'seed' because of his boundless mercy.[349] In Luke's text, the promises spoken to the 'fathers' do not concern the inheritance of the Land, but God's *help* of Israel, his 'servant'. This divine help is due to God's unconditional mercy, but it is also defined by the fact that Israel is God's faithful 'servant' who 'fears' God, in the covenantal relationship (1.50a). Indeed, there is some evidence that 'mercy' was used as a metonym for 'covenant' in the psalms (cf. LXX Pss. 104.8; 110.5) and prophets – crucially, Mic. 7.20, where it is said of God, 'You will give truth to Jacob, mercy to Abraham, as you promised our fathers, from former days'.[350]

The thematic coherency of the song is impressive, suggesting that God has mercy upon Abraham's 'seed' in their lowliness (1.48), in their poor state of hunger and need (cf. vv. 53, 54). God's love for Abraham's 'seed' endures across the generations (1.50b, 55). Luke's text is thus an important witness to the continuation of what we have referred to as the 'prophetic' strain of the motif about the 'seed of Abraham'. Luke also frequently expresses the faithfulness of God in fulfilling his promises made to 'our father Abraham' without reference to the latter's 'seed' (cf. 1.73; 3.8; 19.9; Acts 7.2-17), in keeping with Lukan motifs of hope, promise/prophecy and fulfilment.[351]

---

[347] John T. Carroll, *Luke: A Commentary* (Louisville: Westminster John Knox, 2012), p. 48.
[348] The two different Greek terms used for 'servant' do not detract from the mirroring structure of the song and the way terminology functions within it. Both Mary and Israel are God's 'servant' – the one worshipping only God, the other held as God's beloved child. The closest intertext for Luke 1.55 is Isa. 41.8 (LXX) where the 'seed of Abraham' is positioned in close proximity to Israel as God's 'servant' (παῖς).
[349] Luke 1.46-55 is not in the least messianic, but exemplifies 'authentic Jewish piety' with its focus on God as the central agent in Israel's redemptive history; Carroll, *Luke*, p. 49. Yet, the reference to 'the son of the Most High' in the archangel's prediction (1.32) is ever in the background, so some Christocentric adaptation is occurring.
[350] See Méndez, 'Semitic Poetic Techniques', pp. 568–9.
[351] Cf. Luke Timothy Johnson, *Luke* (SP3; Collegeville: Liturgical Press, 1991), p. 42; Nils A. Dahl, 'The Story of Abraham in Luke-Acts', in Martyn and Keck (eds), *Studies in Luke-Acts*, pp. 139–58, at p. 147.

Acts 3.25

Unlike Luke 1.54-55, the reference to Abraham's 'seed' in Acts 3.25 takes the form of a free citation from Gen. 22.18. The context is Peter's address to the 'men of Israel' in the Temple, at the Portico of Solomon (3.11-12). Peter tells the men, 'You killed the author of life, whom God raised from the dead' (3.15). Peter concedes that they and their rulers 'acted in ignorance' (3.17), but their repentance will ensure that their 'sins' are 'wiped out' (ἐξαλειφθῆναι ὑμῶν τὰς ἁμαρτίας; 3.19).[352] All the prophets predicted the days that have now dawned (3.24); Peter's audience are 'the sons of the prophets and of the covenant that God gave to [their] fathers, saying to Abraham, "And in your seed shall all the families of the earth be blessed"' (καὶ ἐν τῷ σπέρματί σου [ἐν]ευλογηθήσονται πᾶσαι αἱ πατριαὶ τῆς γῆς; 3.25; cf. Gen. 22.18). Peter concludes by saying, 'When God raised up his servant (τὸν παῖδα αὐτοῦ), he sent him first to you, to bless you by turning each of you from your evil contrariness' (3.26).[353]

Acts 3.25-26 introduces fresh nuances into the NT's use of the motif of Abraham's 'seed'. Luke has Peter refer to the prophets three times (3.22-23, 24, 25), but does not cite a prophetic text from the HB. However, Peter does characterize Jesus as the mysterious prophet like Moses who demands to be heard at a fatal cost (Deut. 18.18); he tells his audience that *all* the prophets have pointed to the message that Peter is now announcing. Peter characterizes his audience as 'sons of the prophets', hinting that their status as sons ought to enable them to know the truth of his interpretation of events. Not only are the men of Israel 'the sons of the prophets' but they are also the sons of the *covenant* that God gave to the fathers, as a promise to Abraham's 'seed' (3.25). This combined designation ('sons of prophets'/'sons of the covenant') is unique within the NT.[354] Additionally, Luke twists the patriarchal promise in Gen. 22.18 to indicate that the 'blessing' for the 'seed of Abraham' now lies in the personal blessing (v. 26) that the risen Jesus will bring to Peter's audience.[355] As such, Luke conceives of Jesus as God's 'servant' (3.26) – using the same Greek term παῖς found in Luke 1.54-55 to describe Israel. But whereas in Luke 1.54-55, God's 'servant' Israel is the 'seed of Abraham', in Acts 3.25-26, God's 'servant' is Jesus, and the men of 'Israel' remain the 'seed of Abraham'.[356] The blessing they receive is fulfilled in, and realized by, the power of Jesus to return them to God from a state of sin.

---

[352] Peter's words 'you *and* your rulers' seem to indicate the whole Jewish people are in view here. On the topic of anti-Judaism in Acts, see Lawrence M. Wills, 'The Depiction of the Jews in Acts', *JBL* 110, no. 4 (1991), pp. 631–54.

[353] This translation is more specific than the NRSV's 'wicked ways'. In the NT, the noun πονηρία always designates a moral evil opposed to God (cf. Matt. 22.18; Mark 7.22; Luke 11.39; Rom. 1.29; 1 Cor. 5.8; Eph. 6.12). The noun adheres with the sense of intransigence in 'the Jews' reluctance to hear Peter's message: 'the priests, the captain of the Temple and the Sadducees' (NRSV) immediately arrest Peter and John (4.1-3).

[354] However, the pairing of 'sons of the covenant' with 'Abraham's seed' has a distinct parallel in the rabbinic literature.

[355] Darrell L. Bock, *Acts* (Grand Rapids: Baker Academic, 2007), p. 181.

[356] Another possible reading is that Abraham's 'seed' in Acts 3.25 is Jesus himself, following Paul's use of the singular nuance in Gal. 3.16 (thus, Bruce, *Acts*, p. 146; C. K. Barrett, *Acts: Volume 1, 1–14* (ICCNT; London: T&T Clark, 1994), p. 191), but I find this reading less plausible in light of ch. 3 v. 26, and the prospect of the men of Israel 'turning' from 'wickedness' to salvation: Jesus is

Hebrews 2.16; 11.18

A different reference to the 'seed of Abraham' is found in the letter to the Hebrews (2.16). The opening epistolary context sees the author discussing Jesus' superiority to the angels, inasmuch as Jesus, the Son, was appointed by God as 'heir of all things' and functioned as the agent of God's creation (1.2). Jesus, and no angel, now sits at the 'right hand' of God, having made 'purification' for sin (1.3-4; cf. 2.5-9). Because Jesus was able to 'taste death for everyone' (2.9b), he became the 'pioneer' of others' salvation (2.10). The purpose of Jesus' death was to destroy the devil, who held the 'power of death' over others (2.15), and to 'free those who all their lives were held in slavery (δουλείας) by the fear of death' (2.15). The author adds, 'For it is clear that he [Jesus] did not come to help angels, but the seed of Abraham' (2.16).[357] That is why Jesus had to be made like humanity 'in every respect' (2.17). The author cleverly uses the verb ἐπιλαμβάνομαι (2.16) to describe the way that Jesus comes to 'help' the 'seed of Abraham'. The middle indicative form of the verb can also mean 'to assume the nature of' something, or 'take hold' of something. Jesus takes on the 'nature' of humanity at the incarnation, and in that very act, exhibits his 'help' or concern for humanity.

This fascinating text appears to exploit the many traditions in the HB and Second Temple Judaism that saw the 'seed of Abraham' unconditionally helped and loved by God. However, in Heb. 2.14-17, it is *Jesus* who comes to help the 'seed of Abraham' by his empathetic suffering and death. Another unique element to Heb. 2.16 is that it does not at all allude to the patriarchal promises of the Torah; in other words, the 'seed of Abraham' are mentioned entirely without reference to Abraham's narrative, to the Land of Canaan or to the history of Israel. In fact, the 'seed of Abraham' refers to 'humanity' in general, rather than 'Israel' or 'the Jews'. And the honorific status of Abraham's seed lies in the fact that they enjoy a higher status than even the angels. What is more, Heb. 2.14-17 joins together the concepts of 'seed' and 'slavery' in a distinctive way. Jesus acts to deliver humans, who, by being 'greatly terrified' (ὅσοι φόβῳ θανάτου) of death, are subject to lifelong slavery (2.15). Slavery equates to the fear of death, that 'tyrannous instrument of coercion'.[358] Jesus is depicted as wresting the 'power of death' from the 'devil' by accepting his own suffering and death on behalf of humanity. Jesus 'sets free', 'releases' or 'cures' (ἀπαλλάσσω) them of their enslaved condition (ἔνοχοι ... δουλείας).

The Epistle mentions Abraham's 'seed' again in Heb. 11.18, in the context of a paean to Abraham and the other heroic patriarchs (11.8-19), although Abraham and his direct kin receive the lion's share of the honourable roster.[359] The author praises Abraham's exemplary 'faith' (11.8) which motivated Abraham to be obedient to God (11.8) and to produce 'as many as the stars of the heaven and as the innumerable

---

God's 'servant' but Israel are Abraham's 'seed', to whom God's servant was originally sent, in Luke's perspective.

[357] Although the author's point of contrast is that between angelic and human natures, the specificity of the 'seed of Abraham' as God's chosen people is not neglected; David M. Moffitt, *Atonement and the Logic of Resurrection in the Epistle to the Hebrews* (NovTSup 141; Leiden: Brill, 2011), p. 139.

[358] F. F. Bruce, *The Epistle to the Hebrews* (NICNT; rev. edn; Grand Rapids: Eerdmans, 1990), p. 86.

[359] Harold W. Attridge, 'God in Hebrews', in R. Bauckham et al. (eds), *The Epistle to the Hebrew and Christian Theology* (Grand Rapids: Eerdmans, 2009).

grains of sand by the seashore' (11.12, citing Gen. 22.17). Abraham 'died in faith' without seeing the reward of faith which God had promised to him, except from a 'great distance' (11.13). For Abraham, the promise was not the Land, for he could have returned to Canaan had he so wished (11.15) – instead, heroes like Abraham had a 'heavenly homeland' of promise (11.16). Abraham was the paradigmatic sojourner; his foreignness and strangeness are amplified by the author of the Epistle. Abraham is cast as a permanent 'resident alien' (παρεπίδημος; cf. LXX Gen. 17.8) in the Land, unwed to the Land on condition of the fulfilment of God's promise.[360] The promise to Abraham is ever deferred, his homeland and inheritance waiting for him in the world to come.[361] The three fathers, Abraham, Isaac and Jacob, are depicted as 'tent-dwellers', perennially anticipating their secure 'home' in heaven (11.9).[362]

Abraham's faith, according to the Epistle, was 'eschatological and transcendental' but at the same time, his faith found concrete expression in his obedience to the divine command.[363] Abraham's obedience was 'tested' at the *Akedah*, but 'through faith', Abraham was prepared to give up his son Isaac, even though he was promised: 'It is through Isaac that your seed shall be named for you' (11.17-18, citing Gen. 21.12; cf. Rom. 9.7).[364] Indeed, the author implies that Abraham typified the kind of faith that Christians have in Jesus: Abraham believed that if he had surrendered Isaac to his death at the *Akedah*, God would have been able to raise him from the dead (11.19).[365] The author makes it clear, through rhetorical parallelisms, that Abraham was willing to sacrifice God's promise by sacrificing his only son, and so the *Akedah* becomes for Abraham a great 'trial of faith' – and for the early Christian readers of the Epistle, an exemplary lesson to encourage their perseverance through suffering.[366]

In summary, the NT includes a wealth of material on being 'seed of Abraham', especially in relation to concepts of 'sin' and 'slavery', indicating that these collocated metaphors were circulating in the first-century environment. Paul speaks of the 'seed of Abraham' inheriting the 'promise' (through faith in Christ), or of *the* 'seed' of Abraham *being* Christ, drawing out complex schemata that position 'slavery' and 'freedom' in

---

[360] This is all the more curious given that other Jewish authors of the Second Temple Period were concerned to *downplay* Abraham's alien status, and instead, to emphasize that Abraham possessed the Land and left it to his descendants in his lifetime (cf. Josephus, *Ant.* 1.154-57). See the fine analysis in Benjamin Dunning, 'The Intersection of Alien Status and Cultic Discourse in the Epistle to the Hebrews', in Gabriella Gelardini (ed.), *Hebrews: Contemporary Methods, New Insights* (Leiden: Brill, 2005), pp. 177-98.

[361] Cf. Moffitt, *Atonement*, pp. 46-144.

[362] Ole Jakob Fillvedt, *The Identity of God's People and the Paradox of Hebrews* (WUNT 2/400; Tübingen: Mohr Siebeck, 2015), p. 212. Note the Sukkot resonances of the fathers dwelling in tents as sojourners.

[363] Markus Bockhmuehl, 'Abraham's Faith in Hebrews 11', in Bauckham et al. (eds), *The Epistle to the Hebrews and Christian Theology*, pp. 382-73, at p. 389.

[364] This hope, the 'Christian assurance' rests on God's solemn oath, sworn by God's own self, to Abraham (cf. Heb. 6.14-15): Barnabas Lindars, *The Theology of the Letter to the Hebrews* (Cambridge University Press, 1991), p. 71. Lindars sees the lack of a 'works' soteriology in this passage, but that interpretation might be an extraneous Paulinism.

[365] Matthew C. Easter, 'Faith in the God who Resurrects: The Theocentric Faith of Hebrews', *NTS* 63 (2017), pp. 76-91.

[366] Edward Kessler, *Bound by the Bible: Jews, Christians and the Sacrifice of Isaac* (Cambridge: Cambridge University Press, 2004), pp. 63-4.

relation to 'the law' and 'faith'. Other NT writers clearly develop prior traditions about the 'seed of Abraham' as beloved of God and helped by God. Paul bucks many trends, but this only goes to show that he was aware of them, with his focus on the nature of the promise to Abraham and how it can be (or cannot be) 'fulfilled' through the mediation of the Law. Writers like Luke and the author of the letter to the Hebrews also centralize their thinking on Christ, however. Although Luke draws on the celebratory promise of God's love for Abraham's seed being constant and unconditional, through mercy and hope in times of trouble (Luke 1.54-55), he nevertheless frames the realization of the promise as the birth of Jesus the Saviour, who will later 'turn Israel from sin' (Acts 3.25-26). The author of the letter to the Hebrews explicitly draws a connection between slavery and the 'fear of death' wielded by 'the devil' (Heb. 2.14-17). It is Jesus who sets humanity free from this terrifying slavery, because he made 'purification' for 'sin'. The motif of God 'helping' the 'seed of Abraham', so prominent in the late-biblical and post-biblical writings, is reconfigured in Hebrews to concern *Jesus* as he comes to the help of human beings, in preference to the angels. There is also, in Heb. 11.8-9, an allusion to Abraham as an observer of Sukkot, wandering in faith as he dwelt in tents. Abraham's exemplarity is boundless, as can be seen in his lifelong faith in God's promises, as he held out hope for the inheritance of a spiritual homeland.

Tannaitic rabbinic literature

Before returning to the Gospel of John, we will examine the early rabbinic literature – often called the Tannaitic literature – and its references to the 'seed' of Abraham. The Tannaitic literature is not naturally circumscribed; the designation is contrived in the scholarship for its convenience. When we use 'Tannaitic' as an adjective to denote a body of literature, we mean it in one of two senses: (1) chronological – meaning the earliest stratum of rabbinic writings composed in Mishnaic Hebrew, before 220 CE.[367] (The following rabbinic eras were the Amoraic (ca. 400–700 CE) and the Geonic (ca. 700–1100 CE).) (2) Characteristic – meaning specific collections that feature the personas (either in narrative form or through their spoken teachings) of the Tannai'im, the earliest Talmudic authorities who lived before the middle of the third century CE.[368] However, not all texts referring to the Tannai'im are 'Tannaitic' – some works deliberately copy the style and voice of the earlier texts for literary reasons, but they are dated much later than the third century CE.[369]

---

[367] For the best discussion of the complex interplay between orality and Tannaitic rabbinic scribal activity, see Martin S. Jaffee, *Torah in the Mouth: Writing and Oral Tradition in Palestinian Judaism 200 BCE-400 CE* (New York: Oxford University Press, 2001).

[368] Cf. Louis Finkelstein, 'The Sources of the Tannaitic Midrashim', *JQR* 31, no. 3 (1941), pp. 211–43.

[369] For example, the imputed 'Tannaitic' sections of the Babylonian Talmud (the Bavli), called *baraithot*, amoraic texts in the style of the tannai'im, such as *Midrash Tehillim* (Psalms) and *Pesikta de Rav Kahana*. The latter two texts are sometimes analysed as part of the variegated Tannaitic corpora – for example Steven D. Fraade, 'Rabbinic Polysemy and Pluralism Revisited: Between Praxis and Thematization', *AJS Review* 31, no. 1 (2007), pp. 1–40, at pp. 16–17, 25–6. Others dispute the authentically Tannaitic character of these texts – see Azzan Yadin-Israel, 'Rabbinic Polysemy: A Response to Steven Fraade', *AJS Review* 38, no. 1 (2014), pp. 129–41, at p. 130.

Generally, scholars accept the following rabbinic works as 'Tannaitic': the *Mishnah* – the code of Jewish Law (halakhah) composed in (Mishnaic) Hebrew; the *Tosefta* – the halakhic supplement to the Mishnah composed in Hebrew and partly in Aramaic;[370] and several exegetical midrashim on the final four books of the Torah (otherwise called the 'halakhic midrashim', distinct from the 'aggadic midrashim' of the Amoraic era).[371] The Tannaitic midrashim include: the *Mekhilta de Rabbi Ishmael* (on Exodus), the *Mekhilta de Rabbi Shimon bar Yochai* (also on Exodus), the *Sifra* (on Leviticus), the *Sifre on Numbers*, the *Sifre on Deuteronomy*, the *Sifre Zuta* (on Numbers) and the *Midrash Tannaim*.[372] This literature is typically divided into two 'schools': that of Rabbi Akiva and of Rabbi Ishmael.[373]

The seed of Abraham

Surprisingly, the Tannaim use the phrase 'seed of Abraham' (זרע אברהם) sparingly, preferring to use the 'children/sons of Abraham' except when citing biblical precedents. This is perhaps because there are no (extant) halakhic midrashim on Genesis, where the references to Abraham and his 'seed' are concentrated in the Torah. However, the rabbinic texts that *do* speak of the 'seed' of Abraham tend to focus on what we have been calling the post-exilic or prophetic stream of the motif in early Judaism – that is the notion that God loves his people unconditionally, on account of Abraham and the

---

[370] Scholars express diverse opinions on the dating of the Tosefta, some placing it as a Tannaitic companion piece beside the Mishnah, but others arguing that the Tosefta is an Amoriac work. See the review of scholarship in Judith Hauptman, *Rereading the Mishnah: A New Approach to Ancient Jewish Texts* (Tübingen: Mohr Siebeck, 2005), pp. 14–17.

[371] Again, these categories are insufficient, because the 'halakhic' midrashim still contain 'aggadic elements', and vice versa. Also, it is worth noting that biblical exegesis by the Sages took the form of halakhah or aggadah – the Torah was primary, but derived exegesis could pertain to legal matters or narrative exposition – and oftentimes, both together. See Michael S. Berger, *Rabbinic Authority* (New York: Oxford University Press, 2014), pp. 17–20. On 'midrash' as a *langue* of the rabbis, the seminal work of Daniel Boyarin (*Intertextuality and the Reading of Midrash* (Bloomington: Indiana University Press, 1990)) is still unsurpassed.

[372] I also include *Avot de Rabbi Natan* (*ARN*), others do not; Morton Smith, *Tannaitic Parallels to the Gospels* (SBLMS; Philadelphia: SBL, 1951; repr. 1968), p. xi includes the Amidah (Eighteen Benedictions), I do not. While *ARN*, which is collected in the back of the Bavli's Seder Nezikin (the minor tractates), many scholars agree that it significantly predates the Bavli. *ARN* is a midrash on *m. Avot* (or 'Pirkei Avot'), and may indeed 'preserve in some cases a different and earlier version of m. Avot'. See Tzvi Novick, 'Traditions and Truth: The Ethics of Lawmaking in the Tannaitic Literature', *JQR* 100, no. 2 (2010), pp. 223–43, at p. 230. I will return to *ARN* (mss. A and B) in more detail in Chapter 5.

[373] Cf. Azzan Yadin, *Scripture as Logos: Rabbi Ishmael and the Origins of Midrash* (Philadelphia: University of Pennsylvania Press, 2004); idem, *Scripture and Tradition: Rabbi Akiva and the Triumph of Midrash* (Philadelphia: University of Pennsylvania Press, 2015). Two outstanding pieces of scholarship dealing with the different thought-worlds of both schools are: Tzvi Novick, *What Is Good and What God Demands: Normative Structures in Tannaitic Literature* (JSJSup 144; Leiden: Brill, 2014), and Ishay Rosen-Zvi, *Demonic Desires: 'Yetzer Hara' and the Problem of Evil in Late Antiquity* (Philadelphia: University of Pennsylvania Press, 2011). Despite the little we know about the historical figures of the two major Tanna, recent scholarly biographies have emerged: cf. Barry W. Holtz, *Rabbi Akiva: Sage of the Talmud* (New Haven: Yale University Press, 2017); Ra'anan S. Abusch, 'Rabbi Ishmael's Miraculous Conception: Jewish Redemption History in Anti-Christian Polemic', in Adam H. Becker and Annette Yoshiko Reed (eds), *The Ways that Never Parted: Jews and Christians in Late Antiquity and the Early Middle Ages* (TSAJ 96; Tübingen: Mohr Siebeck, 2003), pp. 307–44.

fathers. Indeed, Isa. 41.8, where Abraham is cast as one who loves/is loved by God, is a source text for creative elaboration by the Sages as they reflect upon the Exodus event.

For example, in the *Mekhilta de Rabbi Ishmael*, the Tannaim discuss the verse of Exod. 22.20, 'And a stranger you shall not vex, and you shall not oppress him'. The Sages consider this verse as a reference to the convert (גר), the proscription of oppression meaning that one should not throw the new convert's idolatrous past back in his face. R. Eliezer offers a negative reading of the convert's nature, but the other Sages disagree: R. Shimon bar Yochai, asks, 'Now who is greater? One who loves the King or one whom the King loves? Certainly, one whom the King loves'. Citing Deut. 10.18, R. Shimon applies this maxim to the stranger/convert: 'And He [God] loves the stranger'. R. Shimon continues by saying that God in fact refers to *converts* as 'Israel'. Stringing together two passages from Scripture (*gezerah shawah*) that use the word 'servants' ('of Jacob') (עבדי יעקב), R. Shimon states, 'Israel is called "servants", as it is written: "For unto Me the children of Israel are servants" (Lev. 25.55)' – and the גרים are called 'servants', as it is written 'to love the name of the Lord and to be His servants' (Isa. 56.6). R. Shimon makes the same interpretive move to indicate that the גרים-as-Israelites are called 'ministers' of the Lord, and then he cites the text of Isa. 41.8 (and its reference to the 'seed of Abraham') to show that they are also called 'lovers' of God:

(ח:ישיעה מא)."ואתה ישראל עבדי יעקב אשר בחרתיך זרע אברהם אוהבי": שנאמר "אוהבים"נקראו ישראל
(ח:דברים י) "ואוהב גר": ונקראו הגרים אוהבים שנאמר

Israelites are called 'lovers', as it is written: 'But you Israel, the servants of Jacob whom I have chosen, the seed of Abraham, my lover'. And the strangers are called 'lovers', as it is written: 'And He loves the stranger'. (Deut. 10.18)

R. Shimon continues by saying that the גרים – as 'Israel' – are under 'covenant' with God, conflating Gen. 17.13 and Isa. 56.4. Finally, he turns to the lived example of Abraham himself: since the great patriarch was circumcised at the age of 'ninety-nine', all converts can come inside the covenant; had Abraham been circumcised at 'twenty or thirty', then only men younger than twenty could convert (*MRI* Nezikin, (ch. 18), Lauterbach II).[374] This fascinating text exploits the ambiguity of the Hebrew version of Isa. 41.8, which reads, 'the seed of Abraham, my beloved/who loves me', opting for the latter interpretive choice of 'the seed of Abraham' as the subject of the verb. Not only that, the Sages read the text as referring to *the seed* of Abraham as the collective 'lover' of God, not to Abraham in the singular. And even more – the Sages then apply this text to coverts, calling *them* 'Israel'![375]

The *Mekhilta* also alludes to Isa. 41.8 when commenting upon the song that Moses, Miriam and the freed Hebrews sang at the Red Sea. There, the Sages wonder if God

---

[374] Jacob Z. Lauterbach (ed. and trans.), *Mekhilta de-Rabbi Ishmael* (2 vols.; Nebraska: JPS and University of Nebraska Press, 2004).
[375] *MRI* perek 20.6.1 ...On Exod. 33: 'Remembering mercy to a thousand generations of those who love Me and keep my commandments': [R. Judah] 'For my lovers [those who love me] and for the keepers of my mitzvoth'; 'For my lovers, our father Abraham and the like'. R. Nathan: 'the Jews who dwell in Eretz Yisrael and give their lives for the mitzvoth'. Cf. *Sifrei Devarim* 352.5, 'the children of the Beloved (i.e. Abraham) enter the house of the Lord'.

had truly 'planted' his chosen people in their land, and the sanctuary established by God's hands (Exod. 15.18), now that the Temple has been destroyed (*MRI* Shira, perek 15.17.5). R. Yossi Haglili provides the final comment, alluding to biblical idioms, and specifically to Isa. 41.8:

> Had Israel at the sea said, 'The Lord reigns for ever and ever', no people or tongue could ever dominate them. But they said, 'The Lord will reign forever and ever – in time to come'. [You will reign] over your people, the flock of your grazing, the seed of Abraham your loved one, the children of Israel, your only one, the congregation of Jacob, your firstborn son, the vine that you have nurtured from Egypt, the plant which your right hand has planted.[376]

R. Yossi understands the destruction of God's Temple to be the result of a lack of faith, and he situates the crucial moment at the period of Israel's redemption from Egypt. According to R. Yossi, Israel did not voice their belief in God's reign forcefully enough; rather, they deferred their expectation of God's sovereignty to the age to come. Nevertheless, he suggests, God will reign over 'the seed of Abraham, your loved one', as shepherds watch over their flock, and as horticulturalists tend their plants. In *Sifrei Bamidbar* (42.1), commenting on Num. 6.26 ('The Lord lift his countenance upon you'): 'when you stand in prayer, as it is written in respect to the prayers of Abraham: "Behold, I have lifted your countenance" (Gen. 19.21). Now does this follow, *a fortiori* – "If I have lifted the countenance for Lot for the sake of Abraham, my beloved, shall I not do so for you, and for the sake of your fathers!"'[377] In *Sifrei Devarim* (32.19), in the context of an explication of the Shema, 'R. Meir says, "It is written: And you shall love the Lord your God with all your heart." Love Him with all your heart, as did Abraham our father, as it is written, "Abraham, my lover" (cf. Isa. 41.8) and – "and you found his heart faithful before you" (Neh. 9.8).'[378]

The Mishnah likewise refers to the 'seed of Abraham' by way of the Isaian citation depicting Abraham as loved by/lover of God (Isa. 41.8). The fifth tractate of *m. Avot* ('Pirkei Avot') is characterized by the discourse of enumeration: 'with ten words was the world created', 'ten miracles were performed for our fathers', 'seven things pertain to a *golam* and seven to a Sage', 'there are four character types in a person', 'there are four types of disciples' and so on.[379] In this vein, there are 'three attributes' (בידו שלושה) to 'the disciples of our father Abraham: a good eye, a humble spirit, and a lowly soul' (*m. Avot* 5.19). God loves Abraham and the disciples of Abraham so much that he grants them their fill in this world, with their 'inheritance' waiting for them in the world to come. The Sages allude to Isa. 41.8 by way of a direct citation of Prov. 8.21 to describe God's activity: 'I have much to bequeath to my lovers [in the world to come], and their stores I shall fill [in this world]'. In other words, Abraham and the 'disciples of Abraham'

---

[376] Compare *Mek Rabbi Sh. bar Yochai* (15.19); W. David Neslon (ed. and trans.), *Mekhilta de-Rabbi Shimon bar Yochai* (Nebraska: JPS, 2006).
[377] Jacob Neusner (ed. and trans.), *Sifre to Numbers* (2 vols.; Atlanta: Scholars Press, 1986).
[378] Reuven Hammer (ed. and trans.), *Sifre: A Tannaitic Commentary on the Book of Deuteronomy* (Yale Judaica Series; Yale: Yale University Press, 1987).
[379] Michael Danby (ed. and trans.), *The Mishnah* (Oxford: Oxford University Press, 1930).

are the 'lovers of God' who receive such largesse. Effectively, the Sages here read the reference to Abraham and his 'seed' in Isa. 41.8 as equivalent to 'Abraham and his disciples'. The implications are more significant than meet the eye: the Sages read 'lovers (of God)', or 'those who love Me'. Abraham is one who loves God, and this same attitude characterizes his 'disciples' in *m. Avot* 5.19 – both receive a full inheritance from God. But the 'disciples' of Abraham are not his natural 'sons' – they must imitate Abraham's attributes, learn (למד) Abraham's behaviour and qualities to receive Abraham's inheritance. The intertextual allusion to Isa. 41.8 (the 'seed of Abraham, who loves Me') is recast, through Prov. 8.21, to showcase Abraham's discernment, humility and lowliness as the prime marks of Abraham's 'disciples', and their promised inheritance shifts to the 'world to come'.

The Tannaitic midrashim do, nevertheless, mention the patriarchal promises in their own right, but the phrase 'seed of Abraham' is not necessarily foregrounded. For example, in *Sifrei Devarim* (8.1), the promise of the land and its inheritance is mentioned as the 'oath' that the Lord swore 'to your fathers, Abraham, Isaac and Jacob' (cf. Deut. 1.6-8). The Sages ask why it was necessary to mention each father individually, and the response – because each father was worthy of the promise in his own right (*Sifre Deut.* piska 8.1).[380] Slightly later, however, the Sages parse the clause 'to give them [i.e. the Land] and to their seed' (Deut. 1.8). The Sages simply explain that the clause 'and to their seed' means 'their children' (*Sifre Deut.* piska 8.2).[381]

Other references to the patriarchal promises in *Sifre Deut.* occur, for example, in a discussion about scriptural hyperbole, thus R. Shimon b. Gamliel spoke:

'When the Holy One, Blessed be He, says to our Father Abraham (Gen. 26.4): "And I will multiply your seed as the stars of heaven (Deut. 13.16)" and "I will make your seed as the dust of the earth, so that if a man can number the dust of the earth, so will your seed be numbered" – this is not hyperbole' (*Sifrei Devarim* piska 25.4).[382]

Otherwise, the Sages confront the issue of how the inheritance of the Land is merited. R. Shimon b. Yochai disagrees with R. Akiva on this topic, arguing that the inheritance of the Land doesn't come to those who, although belonging to Abraham, served idols and shed blood; the inheritance is not automatic, but dependent upon right behaviour (*Sifre Devarim* 31.3).[383]

Apart from the references to the beloved 'seed of Abraham' (as cited through Isa. 41.8) and the promises to Abraham and his seed (as expressed in the Torah), the Tannaitic literature also integrates another motif: that of 'slavery' in a positive sense. We find in *Sifre Numbers* (piska 115) a lengthy parable – delivered in the context of discussing

---

[380] Hammer, *Sifre to Deuteronomy*, pp. 32–3.
[381] Ibid., p. 33. This accords with my point that the preferable term for the rabbis is 'the children of Abraham', rather than 'seed of Abraham'.
[382] Ibid.
[383] In this piska, Akiva does not state his own view, but it is mediated (by negation) through the views of R. Shimon. However, as Hammer notes (p. 21), the wider concern of *Sifrei Deuteronomy* is to show God as one who grants favour to people out of his grace, and not because of their deeds. Another citation, citing the promise of multitudinous seed (*Sifre Deut.* piska 11; Hammer, *Sifre to Deuteronomy*, pp. 36–39).

tefillin – which illustrates how God redeemed the 'seed of Abraham' to himself. The parable from the *Sifrei* is one of many parables in rabbinic literature depicting Israel as part of a 'son–father' or 'slave–master' relationship with God.[384] The parable portrays God as a king, who has redeemed his beloved 'seed of Abraham' as slaves:

> To what may the matter be compared? To a king, the son of whose beloved [or 'friend'] was taken captive. But when he redeemed him, he did not redeem him as a free person but as a slave, so that if he issued a decree and he would not accept it, he would say to him: 'You are my slave'. When he entered a city, he said to him: 'Tie my sandals', and: 'Carry before me utensils for the bathhouse'. The son began to complain. He [the king] brought out against him the deed and said to him: 'You are my slave'. Likewise, when the Holy One, Blessed Be He redeemed the 'seed of Abraham' (זרע אברהם), his beloved, he did not redeem them as sons but as slaves. When he issues a decree and they do not accept, he says to them: 'You are my slaves'.[385]

This parable from *Sifrei Numbers* alludes to biblical texts such as Exod. 25.42 and Leviticus 26, where God declares that he has redeemed the Israelites from Egyptian bondage, thus acquiring them as his own 'slaves' – they are therefore not to give themselves over to the servitude of others.[386] In the *Sifrei* parable, God is depicted as a king who has the power to enforce a decree of ownership over the 'son' of his friend whom he has just redeemed from slavery. The king appears to redeem the son for the sake of his friend, but does not adopt the son as his own; rather he takes him as a slave. When the slave begins to complain about the labour, he is swiftly reminded of his status as the king's slave. The parable likens the 'friend' whose son was taken captive to 'Abraham', the 'son' of the friend to 'the seed of Abraham', and the 'king' to God. Although the Israelites are Abraham's progeny and are beloved by God for Abraham's sake, they are nevertheless also the 'slaves' of God: as such they *must* obey the divine decrees. The inference is that the 'king' can induce his slaves towards obedience like the (perhaps more lenient) father can towards his sons.[387] The parable conveys two notions: (1) the 'seed of Abraham' belong exclusively to God, the all-powerful 'king'; and (2) God redeemed them from (an oppressive) captivity in order to 'enslave' them to himself (in the positive sense of divine service).[388]

In the *Mekhilta* de-Rabbi Ishmael (Ba-Kodesh 5), when discussing the text of Exod. 20.2 ('I am the Lord your God, who brought you out of the Land of Egypt,

---

[384] Cf. Lev. R. 1.15; 12.1; Pes. R. 27 (28).3; *Sifrei Deut.* 38; 40; *Gen. R.* 2.2. 'In real life, the son's and slave's situation as dependents of the *paterfamilias* was similar in some regards and different in others' (Hezser, *Jewish Slavery in Antiquity*, p. 351).

[385] Neuser, *Sifre Numbers*, p. 115, 2.182. Notice that although the form is different from the other Tannaitic texts, we still see an allusion to Isaiah in that the seed of Abraham is God's 'beloved'.

[386] Another similar text is in the Bible: cf. Exod. 25.42: 'For they are my servants, whom I freed from the land of Egypt; they may not give themselves over into servitude'. God redeemed the Israelites from Egyptian bondage, thus acquiring them as 'slaves'. God has the ultimate claim on them.

[387] Cf. Hezser, *Jewish Slavery in Antiquity*, p. 352.

[388] Comparable texts on Israel's slavery as divine service developed in the Amoraim: *Gen. R.* 2.2; *Lev. R.* 12.1; (Hezser, *Jewish Slavery in Antiquity*, pp. 355–6).

out of the house of slavery'), the Sages proffer two distinct interpretations, triggered by the phrase 'house of slavery'. One interpretation is given: 'They [the Israelites] were servants/slaves to kings ... [then it is asked] were they servants to servants?' But 'another interpretation' (דבר אחר) counters this suggestion: 'Out of the house of slavery' (means) 'out of the house of worshippers, for they were worshippers of idols'. Azzan Yadin-Israel has convincingly demonstrated that the ubiquitous refrain דבר אחר ('another interpretation') in the Mekhilta signals not a dialogic, democratic openness in discussion, or the proffering of an alternative, but equally valid interpretation; rather, it is a textual marker of a 'juxtaposed' interpretation, demarcated as distinct, superior and closing off the conversation.[389] Adopting this reasoning draws attention to the association between idolatry and slavery in rabbinic thought. The play on words is evident in the Hebrew, where עבידם can mean 'servants' as well as 'worshippers'. The Israelites were redeemed from the (negative) 'slavery' of idolatry, into a new (positive) 'slavery' under covenant with God (*Sifrei Numbers* 115).

The Mishnah (*Nedarim* 3.11), in a complex passage concerning vows, gives us a final type of reference to the 'seed of Abraham'.[390] The text reads:

> [Someone who vows:] 'Konam, that I won't benefit from the sons of Noah' is permitted [to benefit from] Jews and forbidden [to benefit] from Gentiles. [One who vows] 'Konam that I won't benefit from the seed of Abraham' is forbidden [to benefit] from Jews and permitted [to benefit] from Gentiles. [One who vows] 'Konam that I won't benefit from the uncircumcised' is permitted to benefit from the uncircumcised of Israel but not from the uncircumcised of other nations. [One who vows] 'Konam that I won't benefit from the circumcised is prohibited [to benefit from] uncircumcised Jews and permitted [to benefit] from circumcised Gentiles'.

The core part of this passage, to which we should draw attention, is how the rabbis identify 'the seed of Abraham'. The Mishnah rules that the 'seed of Abraham' refers only to Jews and not to Gentiles.[391] Ishay Rosen-Zvi, commenting on this passage, wonders why the Mishnah goes to great lengths to make this association explicit – after all, in the Second Temple literature, the term 'seed of Abraham' denotes Jews or Israelites anyway, excluding Gentiles by definition.[392] Rosen-Zvi suggests that the Mishnah is implicitly responding to Pauline concessions to 'let the Gentiles in', so to speak, by including them as part of the 'seed of Abraham' even if they are not part of ethnic 'Israel' (cf. Gal. 3.7-9).[393]

Finally, as noted earlier, the rabbis frequently use other relational terms to designate the descendants of Abraham, which are briefly examined next.

---

[389] Cf. Yadin-Israel, 'Rabbinic Polysemy', p. 132.
[390] www.Sefaria.org.
[391] Cf. Ishay Rosen-Zvi, 'Pauline Traditions and the Rabbis: Three Case Studies', *HTR* 110, no. 2 (2017), pp. 169–94, at p. 185.
[392] Ibid.
[393] Ibid., pp. 186, 188.

Abraham's 'children', 'sons' and 'disciples'

The term 'sons' of Abraham (בני אברהם) – a more intimate appellation than the remote progenitor of a people that is conjured up by the term 'seed of Abraham' – correlates to the construal of Abraham as 'father'. In the Tannaitic literature, the rabbis use the term 'sons of Abraham' or 'sons of the fathers' much more frequently than the phrase 'seed of Abraham'. The idea of Abraham as 'father', and of certain groups who are defined as Abraham's 'children', finds distinct expression in contemporaneous and antecedent literatures (e.g. Matt. 3.9; Luke 1.55, 72; 3.8; Acts 7.2; John 8.39, 53; Rom. 4.12, 9.7a; Jas. 2.21; *4 Macc.* 16.20). In the rabbinic literature, the term 'our father Abraham' would become a standard honorific. Many references to 'our father Abraham' celebrate the patriarch's attributes and merits (cf. *m. Avot* 3.12; 5.2, 3, 19; *m. Nedarim* 3.11b; *m. Kidd* 4.14b; *Mekhlita Beschallach* II: 160-170; *b. Avodah Zarah* 9.2; *ARN, B*; cf. *Agg. Ber* 13a; or speak of the rewards Abraham received for his loyalty to God (cf. *Sifre Numbers*).[394]

By corollary, many rabbinic texts speak of 'Abraham's children' (or Abraham's 'sons'): The Mishnah states that 'all Israelites are sons of Abraham, Isaac, and Jacob' (*m. Bava Kamma* 8.6; cf. *m. Bava Metzia* 7.1; and see, in another context, *b. Betzah* 32a).[395] Other references include *Sifrei Deut.* 31.1; 352.5. In places where we would expect to see the term 'seed of Abraham' (זרע אברהם), we find instead 'the sons of Abraham' (בני אברהם). The Tosefta depicts God granting goodness to Abraham's descendants according to the direct measure of Abraham's good deeds. For example, in later times, kings bowed to Abraham's 'sons' because Abraham bowed down to the angelic men at the Oaks of Mamre (*t. Sotah* 4).[396] The water Abraham offered his guests at Mamre's place became the water that Abraham's 'sons' were given in the wilderness (*t. Sotah* 4 and so forth). Commenting upon Deut. 1.15 (which in its original context refers to Abraham's 'seed'), the Sages interpret the text as referring to the 'sons of Abraham, Isaac, and Jacob' (בני אברהם; *Sifre Deut.* piska 15.1).

Another, albeit unique, term of note is 'the disciples of Abraham [our father]', found in *m. Avot* 4. This Mishnaic text contrasts the 'disciples' of Abraham with the 'disciples of Balaam'; the former disciples have 'a kindly eye, a loyal spirit, and a lowly mind', whereas the latter have 'an evil eye, a proud spirit and a grasping soul'. In *Avot*, however, Abraham's disciples appear to learn from his exemplary character rather than from his instruction *per se*. Shaul Magid has claimed that the term תלמידי אברהם (*m. Avot* 4) is 'uncharacteristic of rabbinic teaching when discussing Abraham and his progeny'.[397] The reference to Abraham's 'disciples' may have had a particularly polemic purpose inasmuch as it presented a reaction to Christianity.[398]

---

[394] Lauterbach (ed.), *Mekhilta*, 2.133–4; Anthony Saldarini (ed. and trans.), *Avot de-Rabbi Natan B* (Leiden: Brill, 1975), pp. 81–2; p. 157; Danby (ed.), *Mishnah*; Neusner (ed.), *Sifre to Numbers*, 2.46. Cf. Lieve Tuegels (ed. and trans.), *Aggadat Bereishit* (JCPS 4; Leiden: Brill, 2001).

[395] Bavli at www. Sefaria.org.

[396] Jacob Neusner (ed. and trans.), *Tosefta, 2 Vols.* (Peabody: Hendrickson, 2002); cross-checked www. Sefaria.org.

[397] Shaul Magid, *From Metaphysics to Midrash: Myth, History and the Interpretation of Scripture in Lurianic Kabbala* (Bloomington: Indiana University Press, 2008), p. 152.

[398] Ibid. Magid relies on Urbach's speculative hypothesis that the rabbis were here presenting Abraham as an alternative teacher to Jesus. Cf. Ephraim Urbach, 'Rabbinic Homilies on Gentile Prophets

At this point, it is important to make some summative points. After a long journey through the dense tapestry of intertexts relating to the 'seed of Abraham' in Jewish antiquity and the early rabbinic era, we now draw the skeins of the argument together before returning to a close reading of John 8.31-37.

Part 2: The Johannine context

At this point, it is necessary to return to the context of the Gospel of John to explore the connotations around 'seed', 'slavery' and 'sin' (cf. 8.32-36) found throughout the rest of the Gospel. We can therefore determine if the reference to the 'seed of Abraham' in John 8.32 bears close parallels to the early Jewish (and early rabbinic) developments discussed in this chapter, or if the wider Johannine context, with its idiosyncratic uses of 'sin' and 'slavery', better informs our reading of John 8.32-36. While the noun σπέρμα occurs once elsewhere in the Gospel (7.42: 'the Christ comes from the seed of David'), there are a couple of references to slavery (in a positive sense), and a stronger number of references to sin.

Servanthood/slavery

The only other references to servanthood/slavery in the Gospel appear in the 'farewell discourse' (cf. 13.1-17.26), when Jesus takes leave of his disciples prior to his death.[399] After washing his disciples' feet in the Upper Room at Passover, Jesus tells them solemnly, 'no slave (οὐκ ἔστιν δοῦλος) is greater than their master, nor are messengers greater than the one who sent them'.[400] By washing his disciples' feet, Jesus set them an 'example' (ὑπόδειγμα) so that they should do the same for each other (cf. 13.15). Jesus' language in this passage ties into much of the Gospel's discourse about Jesus' identity as the 'Sent One'. God is depicted as the supreme Master, and Jesus as his envoy or slave/servant. This relational dynamic extends to Jesus and his disciples – just as he was 'sent into the world', so now, on the cusp of death, he 'sends' his disciples into the world, to testify on his behalf (15.27). Jesus speaks not on his own behalf, but on behalf of the Father (14.10b, 31; cf. 8.16-17). Jesus' disciples must 'abide' in Jesus in order to produce

---

and the Episode of Balaam', in Urbach, *Me-Olamam shel Hakhamim: Kovets mehkarim* (Jerusalem: Magnes, 1988), pp. 537–54 (in Hebrew).

[399] On the Johannine Farewell Discourse, see especially: Fernando F. Segovia, *The Farewell of the Word: The Johannine Call to Abide* (Minneapolis: Augsburg, Fortress Press, 1991); D. François Tolmie, *Jesus' Farewell to the Disciples: John 13.1-17.26 in Narratological Perspective* (Leiden: Brill, 1995); John C. Stube, *A Graeco-Roman Rhetorical Reading of the Farewell Discourse* (London: T&T Clark Continuum, 2006); George C. Parsenios, *Departure and Consolation: The Johannine Farewell Discourse in Light of Greco-Roman Literature* (NovTSup 117; Leiden: Brill, 2005); Ruth Sheridan, 'The Paraclete in the Johannine Farewell Discourse', *Pac* 20 (2007), pp. 125–41; idem, 'John's Gospel and Modern Genre Theory: The Farewell Discourse (John 13–17) as a Test Case', *ITQ* 75, no. 3 (2010), pp. 287–99.

[400] Most likely, this saying was a *logia* inherited by the Gospel's writer(s); see John Ashton, *Understanding the Fourth Gospel* (Blackwell: Oxford University Press, 2007), p. 218. The noun δοῦλος is used in its sociocultural context (the slavery system of the ancient world) to denote utter servility to the slave-master's domination.

'fruit' (μείνατε ἐν ἐμοί, κἀγὼ ἐν ὑμῖν: 15.4-7), and his 'words' must abide in them (15.7; cf. 8.31, 56-57). This is the mark of true discipleship (15.8; cf. 8.31). And because 'slaves are not greater than their master', the 'world' will persecute the disciples, because it persecuted Jesus first (15.20). The world's persecution of Jesus and his disciples/slaves is a manifestation of its 'sin' (ἁμαρτία; 15.22). Such sin is caused by deliberate, baseless 'hatred' and is not mitigated by ignorance (15.21-25; cf. 8.47-53). The intratextual web between these passages and John 8 is immediately evident, especially in the interplay between the terms 'slavery' and 'sin'. This connection will be explored shortly.

Sin

The secondary literature on the concept of *sin* in the Gospel of John is extensive.[401] One of the noticeable features of this scholarship is the tendency to reduce all uses of the term *hamartia* in John to a single, general meaning. Thus, Rainer Metzner argues that:

> The confrontation between God and the unbelieving world, which is implied in the prologue, constitutes the horizon for the unfolding of the idea of sin. The Fourth Gospel develops a pronounced understanding of manifestation, in which sin is dealt with not as a legal offence or a moral transgression but rather as a total contradiction of God's manifestation in Jesus Christ. The fact that Jesus Christ gave his life as atonement makes it obvious that the legal dispute between God and the unbelieving world was decided in favor of God, his manifestation and his community.[402]

The concept of 'sin' in John's Gospel is often interpreted in just such a systematic fashion. Craig Koester argues that for John, sin is 'first of all, a relational concept'.[403] It is directly opposed to faith, and signifies 'alienation from God'.[404] Sin is conceived of as 'blindness to one's own condition', the intimate truth about oneself. All other (plural) sins a person may commit flow from the fundamental 'sin' of unbelief. Sin can motivate the sinner to take Jesus' life, but it can also lead to the ultimate death of the sinner. Death is the 'final separation from God' for the sinner, begun in the life-choice to ignore Jesus' message of salvation.[405] Koester explains by example: 'The actions [of "the Jewish leaders"] show a consistent alienation from God, since they repeatedly reject the king who has come from above in order to embrace the powers of the world below, whether in the form of Barabbas or Caesar.'[406] Sin has the power to take away 'human freedom'. In ch. 8 vv. 31-32, Koester observes, 'If the truth gives people freedom, then

---

[401] This literature is engaged with throughout the following pages.
[402] Rainer Metzner, *Das Verständnis der Sünde im Johannesevangelium* (WUNT 1/122; Tübingen: Mohr Siebeck, 2000); cf. D. Moody Smith, *The Theology of the Gospel of John* (Cambridge: Cambridge University Press, 1995), pp. 81–2; Martin Hasitschka, *Befreiung von Sunde nach dem Johannesevangelium: eine bibeltheologische Untersuchung* (Innsbruck: Tyrolia, 1989); Craig R. Koester, *The Word of Life: A Theology of John's Gospel* (Grand Rapids: Eerdmans, 2008), pp. 65–73.
[403] Koester, *The Word of Life*, p. 65. Cf. Metzner, *Das Verständnis der Sünde*, p. 358.
[404] Koester, *The Word of Life*, p. 65.
[405] Ibid., p. 66.
[406] Ibid., p. 72.

falsehood holds them captive.' Historically, writes Koester, the 'children of Abraham' (*sic*) were not free – they were in bondage in Egypt, Babylon, then subjected to Roman dominion. The Jews of John 8.32-33 therefore 'cannot see the truth about their own history', and without this understanding, they cannot appreciate their 'slavery in a theological sense'.[407]

This scholarly preference to theologize the meaning of sin recalls the interpretive trends of the modern Gospel commentaries that we analysed at the very beginning of this chapter. What is not so helpful about the theologically reductive reading of existential 'sin' in the Gospel is its facile contrast with its putative opposite– the 'legalistic' category of sin. Metzner typifies this approach when he writes that John's Christological presentation of 'sin' (i.e. as the personal/relational rejection of the revealed Word in Jesus) differs starkly from the 'Pharisaic-rabbinic Judaism in the 1–2 centuries'.[408] That form of Judaism, according to Metzner, held a 'legalistic', 'forensic' notion of sin, where (plural) sins were seen as deeds infringing the Law. This so-called 'traditional' conception of sin has been subverted by the Evangelist, who shifts the idea of sin to the domain of confrontation between the Revealer and the World, claiming that the Law is now fulfilled in Jesus. The essence of the Johannine conceptualization of sin is found in the presentation of Jesus as revealing the salvation of God.[409] The Christological orientation of the concept means that 'sin' in John's Gospel transcends the 'moral', 'philosophical' and 'nomistic' connotations, into a cosmic 'revelation-theology'.[410] Plural 'sins' are simply manifestations of the fundamental sin of the 'world' in rejecting Jesus. Sin is only overcome by the judgement of the Cross, and in the resurrection, as well as the restoration of community that the post-Easter age heralds.[411] The Gospel's (apparently) superior understanding of sin is always contrasted – in Metzner's reading – with the limited historical 'legalism' of 'the Pharisees' and their 'nomism', as well as their prejudices that the *am-ha'aretz* are more sinful than they.[412] Reading Jesus' altercations with the Pharisees and the Jews of John 9, Metzner comments upon the 'Pharisaic' flavour of the debate as particular to 'early Jewish conceptualisations of sin' – sin is oriented to the Law, and constitutes individual violations against the Law.[413]

Problematically, Metzner characterizes 'early Jewish' understandings of sin on the basis of how John (pejoratively) portrays the Pharisees and the Jews in John 5.1-45 and 9.1-50, instead of independently sourcing out the primary texts of early Judaism in order to appreciate the variations and nuances in how sin was conceptualized. Furthermore, by reading every use of the word 'sin' in John's Gospel in light of the theological, relational conception that Metzner elucidates, he risks missing alternative understandings of sin that appear in the text, and which do not fit with the rest of the Gospel's 'fundamental' view of sin. One such example is in ch. 8 vv. 31-36, which

---

[407] Ibid., p. 73.
[408] Metzner, *Das Verständnis der Sünde*, p. 352; cf. p. 112.
[409] Ibid., p. 352.
[410] Ibid., p. 354.
[411] Ibid., pp. 354; 358.
[412] Ibid., p. 112.
[413] Ibid.

presents a different context for the discussion of sin. Here, as Meztner recognizes, sin is viewed as bondage.[414] The opposite of 'sin' is the 'freedom' that Jesus brings, a concept that Metzner squeezes into his theological reading of Johannine 'sin' by claiming that Jesus speaks of freedom from legalistic 'works' of the Law. The 'slave of sin' (8.33-34) is like a permanently dependent public servant (*Dienstverhaltnis*) having to toil to satisfy his master.[415] The freedom that Jesus speaks of is therefore the freedom of being Abraham's children, because Abraham's 'works' (8.39) were really his faith in God.[416] Metzner, rather spuriously, tries to fit the discussion of sin, slavery and Abraham's 'seed' in John 8.32-36 into the conception of sin as 'an expression of the revelation of God's truth in his son'.[417] While such a broad conception might be part of the context and is thus never wholly absent, I contend that the connotations of 'sin' in ch. 8 vv. 33 -34 stand apart from the characteristically Johannine concept of 'sin' as rejection of the incarnate Word.[418]

Of course, Metzner realizes that there is no monolithic vision of 'sin' in the Gospel – the ways in which Jesus' opponents perceive sin is, however, denied legitimacy in light of Jesus' claims.[419] But the issue is deeper than this: Metzner contrasts two conceptualizations of 'sin' and assigns the expression of each to two opposing groups in the Gospel. The Pharisees/the Jews are those who, on Metzner's reading, adhere to the deficient vision of sin, as the stereotypical 'legalism' (transgressions against the Law) of 'early Judaism'. Metzner does not attribute anything positive to the Jews' alternative perspective because he portrays it on the basis of how *John* characterizes the Jews.

None of this is to say that sin does not, on the whole, in John's Gospel, constitute the failure to believe in Jesus (cf. 8.21, 24, 26; 15.22-24; 16.8-9). But it is important to note the examples where 'sins' are not instantiations of the ontological refusal of Jesus' revelation and where they *do* seem to imply moral transgressions of community precepts (cf. 20.23; 5.14; cf. 8.7, 11 if *PA* is accounted for; and cf. 1 John 5.16-18). In fact, the text of ch. 5 v. 14 shows *Jesus* espousing the so-called 'nomistic' understanding of sin that Metzner disregards. Jesus tells the lame man, whom he has just healed, 'stop sinning, so that something worse does not come upon you' (5.14). Although the verse has caused commentators some angst, the implication that Jesus associates sin with illness in a causative sense cannot be avoided.[420] The idea is that if the man continues sinning, 'something worse' will befall him; remembering that the man had been lame for thirty-eight years, it is hard to think of any 'worse' ailment than death.[421] Given that Jesus otherwise speaks of 'dying in sin' (cf. 8.34; and cf. 1 John 5.16, the

---

[414] Ibid., p. 202.
[415] Ibid., p. 203.
[416] Ibid. See Chapter 5 for a discussion of texts that viewed Abraham's 'faith' as his 'works'.
[417] Ibid.
[418] The consensus was set before Metzner; cf. Brown, *John*, 1.56: 'sin' in the singular denotes a 'condition' rather than an 'act'.
[419] Metzner, *Das Verstandnis*, p. 352.
[420] John C. Thomas, 'The Man at the Pool in John 5', *JSNT* 59 (1995), pp. 3–20, at p. 15, and the commentary literature cited.
[421] Ibid., p. 17; cf. Rudolf Schnackenburg, *The Gospel According to St. John Volume 2* (trans. K. Smyth, London: Oliphants, 1982).

'sin unto death'), this reading is not wholly unfeasible. That such 'sin' might suggest a singular human condition or state, rather than a collection of acts (sins) infringing law/commandments is not wholly convincing.[422]

More anomalous still is John 1.29, where Jesus is described by the Baptist as the one who 'carries away' the 'sin of the world' (cf. 1 John 2.1; 3.5; 4.10).[423] The biblical precedents of 'bearing away' sin (Lev. 16.22) in the context of atonement rituals rely on the metaphor of sin as a burden to be borne – in this case, a burden vicariously carried away.[424] In Second Temple times, the metaphor of sin transformed to be figured as a debt to be repaid (or attenuated through the 'credit' of meritorious behaviour), and this metaphorical thinking is found throughout the Synoptic Gospels (e.g. Matt. 6.12). It is not commonly perceived to be present in John's Gospel, but passages such as ch. 1 v. 29 and ch. 8 vv. 31-36 indicate that this type of thinking did not elude John altogether. The cult and scapegoat associations that are metaphorically figured in John 1.29, both concerning the forgiveness of sin, enlarge the paschal resonance of Jesus described as the 'lamb of God'.[425] But the paschal imagery does not replace the underlying atonement concepts, which themselves depend upon transactional metaphors expressed in early Jewish literature concerning sin and its removal.

Therefore, while the Johannine (intratextual) context – the ways in which 'sin' and 'slavery' are otherwise expressed – is an important 'control' on our interpretation of 'sin' in John 8.32-36, it should by no means prevent the intertextual context of the early Jewish literature (and the ways in which 'seed of Abraham', 'sin' and 'slavery' coexist) from informing our understanding of the debate between Jesus and the Jews in John 8.[426]

Part 3: Reading John 8.31-36 intertextually

In this final section, I summarize the findings of the chapter, evaluating the key metaphors in John 8.31-16 ('seed of Abraham', 'slavery' and 'sin') for how they 'fit' with both the intertextual literature and the (Johannine) intratextual material. I also keep in mind the previous studies on John 8.31-36 (which were reviewed in the introduction) as well as the commentary tradition which, as we saw at the beginning of this chapter, presents a stereotyped recycling of anti-Jewish prejudices. As I show

---

[422] Contra Sandra Schneiders, 'The Lamb of God and the Forgiveness of Sin(s) in the Fourth Gospel', *CBQ* 73 (2011), pp. 1-30. It is precisely such a reading that views all occurrences of 'sin' in the singular as denotations of 'man's alienated condition' that lead to theological importations clashing with the sense of the Gospel, as the twentieth-century theological examples provided in Schneiders' article attest (sin is 'greed, lust pride', etc.). The ambiguity of Schneiders' title ('Sin(s)') is not carried forward into the article itself.

[423] For a variety of possible meanings for Jesus as the 'Lamb of God', see Brown, *John*, 1.58-63.

[424] Cf. Dorothy A. Lee, 'Paschal Imagery in the Gospel of John: A Narrative and Symbolic Reading', *Pac* 24 (2011), pp. 13-28, at p. 16. The metaphor here is 'not paschal', but symbolizes the Temple, which according to Lee is a 'manifestation of Torah'.

[425] Lee, 'Paschal Imagery', p. 17.

[426] The First Epistle of John has a number of key texts on 'sin' (e.g. 1 John 3.6-12). However, because those texts also intersect with the idea of 'works', I have decided to include their analysis in Chapter 5.

here, such imaginative excursions not only hold damaging pedagogical potential for students of the Gospel of John, but they also cannot be held as definitive in light of a comprehensive reading of the Abraham traditions.

This chapter was necessarily long and detailed. In many ways, the 'scripting' of the intertextual field that I undertook in this chapter functions as more than simply a 'background' reading to John 8.31-36. In many ways it can also be read as a mapping exercise in the development of the ideas of 'seed', 'slavery' and 'sin' as collocated concepts, where I have traced their connotations across a variety of texts and genres within early Judaism. Positioning John 8.31-36 in this network is akin to seeing the Gospel text as part of a broader conversation within Second Temple Judaism about Abraham's 'seed' and the role of Abraham's merits in relation to them. Often, John's Gospel is read in isolation from such broader literary-historical 'conversations' because of its presumed uniqueness; and certainly, John does control the conversation, so to speak, by reducing the topic to the Christocentric matter of 'abiding' in Jesus' 'word' – in short, of believing in Jesus. But it is important that we hear both 'sides' of this conversation, which is why this detailed scripting was important, because it results in a rich picture of what it means to be 'seed of Abraham', both theologically and soteriologically, a picture that has its roots in the HB and extends into a wide range of subsequent texts. The following, then, is a brief summary of the findings.

In relation to Abraham's seed, the HB associates:

- The *promise of the land of Canaan* to Abraham's 'seed', and the *promise of multitudinous descendants* to Abraham (or Isaac or Jacob).
- Abraham's *exemplarity* is also evident in the HB, where he is depicted as *obedient to all of God's laws* (e.g. Gen. 26.4) and for this reason, his 'seed' will benefit.
- The motif of *God 'remembering'* the *'fathers'* and 'remembering' Abraham is present in the Torah (cf. Exod. 33.32). This is typically within the context of a plea to God's mercy, forming the rudiments of later rabbinic notions of the 'merits of the fathers'.
- Abraham is remembered for his refusal to partake in the *idolatry* of his fathers; and Abraham's 'seed' is taken out of the *land of slavery for his sake* (Josh. 24.2-3).
- In the later biblical texts, there is a focus on the *return to the land*, and of Abraham's 'seed' keeping the land if they remain faithful to God's commandments (cf. Ps. 105).
- God establishes an *eternal covenant* to have *mercy* upon the seed of Abraham, Isaac and Jacob (Jer. 33.23-25).
- Post-exilic texts develop the motif of God's remembrance of Abraham and the promises to his 'seed' to focus on Abraham's 'seed' as *beloved of God for their own sake* **or** as *beloved of God for Abraham's sake* (2 Chron. 20.7, Isa. 41.8).
- *Sin* deeply affects the land and has consequences for its inhabitants. It must be 'requited' through suffering and punishment, construed as the repayment of 'debt' in order to be released from debt-bondage (exile; cf. Isa. 40.2). Abraham's seed is loved by God and will return from all corners of the earth (41.8).

We see the post-biblical literature expand upon these premises as follows:

- God *helps and loves Abraham's seed unconditionally* especially in the context of *'enslavement' to foreign* oppression (e.g. *Prayer of Azariah*; *3 Maccabees* 6; *Prayer of Manasseh*; *4 Ezra*).
- God's help comes to Abraham's seed either because *Abraham himself refused to sin* and thus was chosen by God (*4 Ezra* 3.12), or because Abraham's 'seed' are chosen by God.
- Abraham is an *exemplar to his 'seed'*, through the practise of exogamy (*Tob.* 4.12) or through the *observance of the law* (*Sirach* 44); or because he was a non-idolator (*Jubilees* 1–23; *LAB* 1–6); or believed in God (*LAB* 23), or had great piety (cf. *Maccabees* 4). One texts goes as far as to say the *fathers were sinless*, and their seed righteous (*Prayer of Manasseh*). Contrarily, Abraham is hospitable and kind, but needs to learn mercy for sinners (*Testament of Abraham*).
- Abraham, Isaac and Jacob are conceived as being *actively benevolent* on behalf of their 'seed' in the afterlife, interceding for their sake especially when they fall into sin (e.g. *Jubilees* 16; *T. Levi* 14.1).
- God will *never forsake* Abraham's 'seed' (*4 Ezra* 3).
- God cherishes the *'memory' of the fathers* (*Ant.* 2.169).

The NT has much material on the 'seed of Abraham', especially in relation to concepts of 'sin' and 'slavery'.

- Paul claims that the biblical 'promise' was made to *Abraham's 'seed'* (who is *Christ*, the recipient of the promise of inheritance). Those *'of faith'* are the 'seed of Abraham' inheriting the promise (Gal. 3.29). This process of 'adoption' comes by the Spirit of the Son (4.2-6) and with it comes *'redemption' from slavery* (immaturity).
- For Paul, *slavery* is tied to the idea of 'birth/origins' via the status of the 'mother'; one is *born into either slavery or freedom*, and only the sons of the free mother can inherit from their father Abraham (Gal. 4.1-7).
- The 'works of the law' for Paul are (I claim) tied intrinsically *to sin*, and to the *condition of slavery*, both of which Paul likens to the male child under a guardian, and to the 'children of Hagar' who are 'in slavery' (cf. Gal. 4.21-31).
- Paul implies that the concept 'seed of Abraham' is identical to the theological *category of 'Israel'* (Rom. 9.6-7). But then in Rom. 9.8, Paul opposes the 'children of the flesh' to the *'children of the promise'*, arguing that it is not the former who constitute the 'children of God', but the latter who are *the 'seed of Abraham'*.
- In 2. Cor. 11.22, Paul continues to specify how Abraham's 'seed' *prove their status through their 'deeds'*.
- The motif of God's *unconditional help and love for Abraham's seed* comes through in Luke 1.55 and the letter to the Hebrews (2.14). Luke expresses God's *love for Abraham's seed* as constant and unconditional, through *mercy and hope* in times of trouble, even as he centralizes this on the narrative of the birth of Jesus as 'Saviour' (cf. Acts 3.25-26 – the Saviour as one who *turns Israel from sin*).

- The *fear of death*, wielded by the devil, is equated to *slavery* and it is from this that Jesus came to *rescue the seed of Abraham* (Heb. 2.14-17).
- Abraham was exemplary in his unwavering faith, a sojourner who 'dwelt in tents' (cf. Sukkot) and inherited a spiritual homeland (Hebrews 11).

The rabbinic texts associate the 'seed of Abraham' with concepts in the following ways:

- Abraham's 'seed' *inherit not only the land, but the Torah*, which *protects from sin*.
- Abraham's 'seed' are *purchased as God's slaves*, meaning that they do not serve any other master (Sifrei). Although the Israelites are Abraham's progeny and are beloved by God for Abraham's sake, they are nevertheless also the *'slaves' of God*: as such they *must* obey the divine decrees.
- God loves Abraham and *Abraham's 'seed' unconditionally*, and indeed Abraham's 'seed' are collectively the 'lover of God' (reading Isa. 41.8).
- Abraham was *exemplary in his love for God*, and therefore so should be his 'seed'.
- The 'disciples' of Abraham are not his natural 'sons' – they must *imitate Abraham's attributes*, learn (למד) Abraham's behaviour and qualities to receive his inheritance.
- Idolatry is a form of bondage (slavery) characteristic of the exile into Egypt; monotheism and being yoked to the Torah is a form of permanent freedom by implication (*Mekhilta*).

What we also see is a building debate about the efficacy of merit/intercession for Abraham's seed across a variety of genres and periods. In the post-biblical literature, for example, texts start to speak of whether the fathers' virtues could vicariously benefit their posterity, or whether such virtues required imitation for the promises to the patriarchs to be fully realized. Even down to the specific, individual level, we see the question of whether or not a person can intercede for another in order to wipe out their sins (*4 Ezra* 7.102 says, 'No: everyone must bear their own righteousness or unrighteousness'. Abraham, however, was an exception in an age when the strong prayed for the weak).

In *LAB* we perceive the debate seeping into Pseudo-Philo's retelling of the story of the Judges. The debate about relying on the merits of the fathers vs. imitating the good works of the fathers is expressed in the retelling of Deborah's story: 'Do not hope in the fathers, you have to be like them if you wish to profit from them' (33.5b). Imitate the fathers in obedience to the Law (33.1-3). After death there is no chance to repent of sins. But by contrast, the same text implies that Israel's slavery is the result of their abandonment of the divine commandments (35.3). Nevertheless, the angel promises Gideon that God will have incomparable mercy upon Israel – but only on account of those who have died (35.3). Other post-biblical texts do not necessarily debate the issue so overtly within the frame of their own text – rather they will just assert a position one way or the other. Otherwise, the 'debate' is implied in the texts that position Abraham, Isaac and Jacob as able to affect their 'seed' in the afterlife. Meanwhile, once the Tannaitic period rolls to a close, the 'merits of the fathers' debate is in full swing, and it has largely gained acceptance across the board.

Now, let us return to John 8.31-36. The phrase 'seed of Abraham' (8.32), the notion of 'sin' (8.34) and the metaphor of slavery, are all used in the context of a debate between Jesus and the Jews. Jesus offers 'the Jews' freedom via the truth of his word (8.32), which they question on the basis that they are 'seed of Abraham' and have never been enslaved to anyone (8.33). Jesus replies that slavery to sin constitutes slavery as such (8.34); he then delivers a brief parable on the difference between the 'slave' and the 'son' in a 'household' – the son has a permanent inheritance, whereas the slave does not, and *the* son (i.e. Jesus) is the true liberator (8.36: οὖν ὁ υἱὸς ὑμᾶς ἐλευθερώσῃ). We will recall from Chapter 1 that a handful of studies on John 8.31-36 made the following observations and drew the following conclusions:

- The context for the dispute between Jesus and the Jews is 'remote from Paul's rabbinism'.[427] Whereas Paul is concerned that Christians, who like Christ are Abraham's 'seed' (Gal. 3.16-17), reproduce Abraham's faith, John is concerned that the Jews – who call themselves 'seed of Abraham' – reproduce Abraham's 'works' (8.39; C. H. Dodd).
- John's Abraham tradition related to the 'Judaizing' controversy in the early church, but John phrased his ideas out of the 'earliest strata of the gospel tradition' – specifically from the Synoptic material about 'true' Abrahamic paternity. John thus 'bypasses' Paul's theological agenda, reaching back to the 'primitive testimony' instead (C.H. Dodd).
- The term σπέρμα Ἀβραάμ in John 8.32 'is a technical term ... representing Christian Jews who advocate a law-observing mission'. The Johannine community 'advocate a Christology which demands freedom' – that is freedom from the Law. The Jews of John 8.32, self-styled as the 'seed of Abraham', see themselves continuing this Abrahamic mission to give the Law to the Gentiles (T. Dozemann).
- Chapter 8 verses 31-59 deals with the similar historical problem of a Jewish – Christian group (also coded as σπέρμα Ἀβραάμ) who were trying to foist a law-observant mission on everyone else (T. Dozemann).

The intertextual 'scripting' that I undertook in this chapter should by now bring these conclusions and assertions into question. Both scholars presume a similar (even equivalent) socio-historical scenario behind Paul's letter to the Galatians and John 8.31-59. Dodd eventually concludes that John took the topic in a different direction, tinging his language with Hellenisms ('truth' setting a person 'free' for example), while Paul remained wed to 'rabbinism' (presumably Dodd means a so-called 'legalistic' interpretation of sin, slavery and belonging to Abraham? Or does he use the noun with reference to Paul's style of biblical exegesis? It is not clear from his study). In any case, the argument of this chapter has shown the reverse to be true: the Jews' perspective in John 8.31-36 is deeply 'rabbinic' (or proto-rabbinic) in that it shows awareness of many traditions associating the 'seed of Abraham' with God's enduring love and covenant, with freedom from bondage (Egypt, idolatry) and with freedom from the debt of sin

---

[427] Dodd, 'Behind a Johannine Dialogue', p. 49.

through the merits of Abraham's 'works'. The parable from Sifrei, where the 'seed of Abraham' is bought by God as 'slaves' to one Master is also palpable. On the other hand, it is Paul who seems to be rejecting these traditions in favour of a more 'faith-based' reading of Abraham's 'works' (believing in God) and what this meant for his 'reckoning' before God and for his seed and their inheritance.

On a methodological level, we notice problems with comparing 'apples and oranges' here. There are, of course, incredible similarities between Galatians and John 8, but this does not make their every common expression a genuine 'parallel'. There are also key differences: *truth* and freedom are connected in John 8 and there is absence of the idea of 'slavery to the law'; for John, there is simply 'slavery' to sin; for John there is a focus on *doing*: 'Whoever commits sin is a slave' (v. 43). And quite plainly, *John 8.31-59 nowhere mentions the Law*. The debate across the whole of John 7–8 is not about belief in Christ *versus* observance to the Torah; indeed, on the one occasion that Jesus mentions the Law in this discourse (7.19-21) there is no question of an implied debate with a mission-oriented group of Jews, with Jesus advocating 'freedom from the law' – if anything, Jesus is concerned about *how to interpret the Law rightly*. On the other hand, Paul is concerned with the apparent redundancy of the Law and circumcision, and the righteousness of faith.

The Jews' reply to Jesus in ch. 8 v. 32 ('We are seed of Abraham, and have been slaves to no one, ever') opens out into a vast intertextual web that, when appreciated on its own terms, breaks John's monologic voice (or what Barthes called the proareitic and hermeneutic codes) to allow the polyvalence of the tradition to speak. What it reveals is that the Jews' claim to be Abraham's 'seed' reaches back into texts concerning God's faithful covenant promises; the 'inheritance' and observance of the Torah that is given to Abraham and his seed; God's unconditional love and help for Abraham's 'seed'; and the surplus 'merits' that Abraham accumulated that benefit his 'seed' in times of distress and sin. These traditions are premised on the fathers being alive to God, or alive to God's 'memory' as it were, and actively available to intercede for the sake of their seed.

This legitimately 'Jewish' voice comes through with a comprehensive scripting of the intertextual field and the connotations of Abraham's 'seed' in relation to ideas of sin and slavery. As we saw in Chapter 1, another study (this one by Adele Reinhartz) has focused on the 'Jewish voice in John 8.31-59' and how it can be recovered.[428] The intertextual background that Reinhartz produces focuses on the issue of the Jews' covenant fidelity, indicating that the central issue in John 8.31-59 may be that of monotheism. If the Jews viewed Jesus' claims for himself as an infringement of monotheism, then their own claims in ch. 8 v. 33 reassert their adherence to this fundamental Jewish belief. The current chapter adds to Reinhartz's focus on the post-biblical Jewish texts about 'slavery/servanthood' and idolatry/monotheism by also showing how the metaphor of being 'seed of Abraham' ties into these networks of texts about: idolatry as sin/slavery; positive slavery as serving only God through the commandments (Sifrei); freedom as removal from Egypt/Babylon; and debt-slavery as a form of sin now remitted.

---

[428] Reinhartz, 'John 8.31-59 from a Jewish Perspective', p. 795.

Detecting this grain of resistance in the speech of 'the Jews' counteracts the caricatures imputed to the Jews in the scholarly commentaries. To this day, Gospel commentators have been interpreting the Jews' words in ch. 8 v. 32 ('We are seed of Abraham, and have never been slaves of anyone') as indicative of their inordinate 'religious privilege', their 'national boast' and even their 'close affinity with the powers of evil'.[429] The Jews' self-asserted freedom was interpreted by commentators as 'empty pretensions' and unadulterated 'arrogance'.[430] The most common interpretation has been that the Jews' exhibit 'pride and complacency'.[431] Either that, or their sense of 'inherited privilege'.[432] These commentarial interpretations thankfully have had their challengers (especially the German commentaries in the last ten to fifteen years), but in the Anglophone world they are sadly still present. It should be clear from this extensive intertextual scripting that the Jews' response in John 8.32 is wholly in line with ideas about what it meant to be the 'seed of Abraham' in the Second Temple Period and beyond, that is that Abraham's seed rely upon the merits of their father Abraham, and his 'works' cover over their sins to release them from 'debt' (slavery).

This integrated interpretation has not been advanced in the Gospel scholarship to date. It is grounded, no doubt, in what Jonathan Smith would call my interpretation of 'articulate choice' in selecting the intertexts, but it is no less valid – and in fact, much less damaging – than interpretations that read the Jews' reply solely from the 'compliant' perspective of the Gospel's own cues. Such compliant readings end up in the commentaries and cannot in fact be substantiated by a comparison with the ancient literature at all.

This is not to say that one cannot or should not read John 8.31-36 in light of the Johannine context. Indeed, doing so makes eminent sense. As I showed in the final part of this chapter, John uses the noun 'servant/slave' elsewhere in the Gospel to denote the 'positive' slavery to one's Master. This is not only in the sense of service, but also in terms of the slave knowing one's subordinate place in relation to the Master (13.15; 15.20). This dynamic of servitude to the Master is modelled on Jesus' own relationship to the Father. This reinforces the sense in which the concept of slavery is used in John 8: Anyone who commits sin is a slave (v. 32), choosing to 'do the desires' of another master – the devil (v. 44). The Jews indicate that they have never served another Master other than God. The logic seems to be: Even Abraham was called God's faithful slave (cf. Isa. 41.8; *Testament of Abraham* 13), how then, if we are seed of Abraham, can we be slaves of anyone but God?

But for the Johannine Jesus, *sin* is construed as a refusal to believe in Jesus and to abide in him. With that being said, the argument is over: according to Jesus, the Jews are slaves to sin by virtue of the fact that they refuse to believe in his word, regardless of whether they are 'seed of Abraham'. Earlier, I argued that while this is the primary meaning of 'sin' in John's Gospel (i.e. a negative response to Jesus' revelation), there are also other instances in the Gospel where 'sin' implies the transgression of precepts that

---

[429] Westcott, *The Gospel*, p. 133.
[430] Hengstenberg, *Evangeliums St. Johannis*, pp. 453, 450.
[431] Schnackenburg, *The Gospel*, 2.207.
[432] Carson, *The Gospel*, pp. 348, 350.

draw down negative consequences for the sinner (illness, disease or retribution). If this notion of 'sin' were operative in the Jews' side of the debate in ch. 8 vv. 31-36 (which we wouldn't know because by now their voice has been silenced at ch. 8 v. 33), then their sense of confusion would still be present, and they would be speaking entirely at cross-purposes with Jesus. In fact, as the debate continues in ch. 8 vv. 37-59, the trenches are dug ever deeper, and the chasm widens between the two perspectives until it erupts in violence and escape (v. 59).

5

The works of Abraham (John 8.39-40 (37-48))

Introduction

This chapter explores the intertextual connotations of the phrase 'the works of Abraham' (John 8.39-40) within the literatures of early Judaism and Christianity. I depart from the text-by-text method of reading advanced in Chapter 4 in favour of a thematic approach; this is because the phrase 'the works of Abraham' – unlike references to the 'seed' of Abraham – is not nearly so prominent in the primary material. Thus, the textual analysis undertaken in this chapter relies on a broader understanding of how the term 'works' functions, grammatically and semantically, in the primary material, to gain a fuller picture of its various significations. Finally, I turn to examine the Johannine understanding of 'works', assessing the extent to which the intertextual field coheres with the Johannine framework.

As we saw in Chapter 4, critical Gospel commentaries routinely reproduced anti-Jewish interpretations of the Jews' claim to be 'seed of Abraham' in ch. 8 vv. 32-33. But when interpreting Jesus' injunction that the Jews' should 'do the works of Abraham' (8.39-40), these same commentaries are much milder in tone. One exception is the theological commentary of Brodie (1999). In John 8.37, Jesus concedes that the Jews are 'seed of Abraham', but they seek to kill Jesus because his 'word' finds no place in them. The Jews 'father' is not actually Abraham, according to Jesus, but a figure more diabolical (8.38, cf. v. 44). If, indeed Abraham were their father, Jesus tells the Jews, they would do (or ought to do) Abraham's 'works' (8.39-40).[1] Commenting on this exchange, Brodie writes, 'The scene opens with a Jewish assertion: "Our father is Abraham." It is a proud statement which is simple and clear'.[2] Rather than providing new information, Brodie's comment carries forward the prejudicial reading he expressed about the Jews' assertion to be 'seed of Abraham' in vv. 32-33. But for Brodie, the Jews need Jesus to 'explain the distortion' in their thinking.[3] In fact, Jesus becomes the master analyst, who has 'isolated [the Jews'] worst symptom – a death-bearing suppression of the truth' caused by an underlying refusal to acknowledge their real father.[4] Brodie reads

---

[1] Recall that the syntax and MSS readings here are complex. See Chapter 1 for fuller discussion.
[2] Brodie, *A Literary and Theological Commentary*, p. 330.
[3] Ibid., p. 331. The mimetic assessment of the Jews as characters amenable to psychological interpretation (or in this case, diagnosis), is deeply problematic. See further, Sheridan, 'Persuasion', pp. 205–24.
[4] Brodie, *A Literary and Theological Commentary*, p. 331.

Jesus' condemnation of the Jews in ch. 8 vv. 37-40 as evidence that 'their inspiration is evil, that there is something radically wrong with them'.[5]

Of course, interpretations such as this one – and thankfully, I could find no other quite like it – do nothing to reveal the meaning of the phrase 'the works of Abraham' (8.39, 40); instead, they only serve to damage contemporary Jewish–Christian relations, which have made such gains in recent decades.

How then, are we to understand 'the works of Abraham' in John 8.39-40? Grammatically speaking, how does the pronoun 'Abraham' modify the head noun 'works'? Is the term to be understood as a simple possessive genitive – thus, 'the works belonging to/possessed by Abraham'? Given the verbal action in the sentence ('do the works of Abraham'), we might read the phrase as a subjective genitive, as in the sense: 'Abraham [does] works'; do the works that Abraham does': 'the works of Abraham' would then be those actions that others are to imitate or reproduce. Or perhaps the 'works of Abraham' are those that Abraham commissioned or mandated. If we read the phrase as an objective genitive however, then the genitive substantive ('of Abraham') is read as the direct object of the verbal idea implicit in the head noun (do *the works*). The sense would thus be: 'Do the works for/in service of Abraham.' Although the latter option appears to make little sense, we could interpret it as meaning that the Jews do the 'works' in service of the Abrahamic covenant. The objective also coheres well with the possessive sense, that is that the Jews do the 'works' that Abraham did or owned. And, regardless of the grammatical points, the question remains: *what* are the works of Abraham? We could generally understand Abraham's 'works' to be a class of actions of some sort – but what kind of actions, and why would they be significant? Only intertextual interpretation can provide us with a broad enough canvas to begin answering that question in relation to John's context.

Part 1: Scripting the intertextual field

Unlike reference to Abraham's 'seed', we do not find 'works' predicated of Abraham at all, at least not in the Hebrew Bible (HB). There are various ways in which the word 'works' is used as a genitive, both in relation to a person and in relation to a thing in the biblical texts, and different words are used for the term 'works'. These words provide a range of different meanings; often a word does not match a single sense. For example, in the HB, different roots are employed to form the different nouns (e.g. מעבד מעשׂה מלאכה סחר). Most commonly, when the word 'works' is used in the Bible as a substantive in relation to a person, it denotes basic human activities, occupations, labours or behaviours (i.e. 'deeds') performed by the person, but it can also frequently denote the material handicraft of a person – the material product of his or her labour (used as a partitive genitive). Similarly, God's labour of creating the world is depicted as his 'work', and the various products of God's creation are also described as 'works'. God's 'works' can also

---

[5] Ibid.

denote his 'behaviour' or his 'ways' with his creation – or sometimes denote God's revealed 'commandments'.

In fact, the semantic scope of the term 'works' can be prohibitive. For that reason, it is important to be selective. Therefore, I do not examine the nuances of the term 'works' as it denotes human labour or occupation (e.g. Gen. 5.29; 46.33) – nor do I explore the idiomatic phrase 'the works of human hands' to refer to idol making (cf. Isa. 2.8, 41.29; Jer. 1.16, 48.7; Ezek. 6.6, etc.) or in other senses of human handicraft and skilled labour (cf. Deut. 4.28; 27.15; 2 Kgs 19.18; 2 Chron. 32.19, 25; Pss. 90.17, 115.4, 135.15; Jer. 10.3, 9; Lam. 3.64; Hos. 14.3; Hag. 2.14). Likewise, the expression 'works of your hands' when predicated of God's creation is also too numerously attested and beyond the scope of this analysis (cf. Pss. 8.6; 28.5b; 92.4b; 92.5a). The focus here is on 'works' as an indicator of human behaviour, especially in its moral dimensions.

Works as human behaviour in the Hebrew Bible

When used to describe a person's *behaviour*, the term 'works' in the HB carries moral connotations, whether good or bad. The Writings, particularly the Wisdom genres, contain several examples of this use of the term 'works'. Peoples actions ('works') are seen and judged by God: from his heavenly throne, God observes human beings and 'all their works' (Ps. 33.15: אֶל־כָּל־מַעֲשֵׂיהֶם/LXX 32.15: πάντα τὰ ἔργα αὐτῶν). God judges the behaviour of all people, leaving 'evildoers' (34.22b) no place to hide (Job 34.21-28). The 'mighty' of the earth are 'shattered', for God knows their 'works' (MT: מַעְבָּדֵיהֶם; LXX: αὐτῶν τὰ ἔργα; Job 34.25). The text of Job 34.26-28 concretely illustrates the nature of the evildoers' works: they turn aside from God's ways (v. 27b), they engage in wickedness (v. 26) and they oppress the poor (v. 28). Their works are deliberately godless (v. 30), and are a matter of choice, not chance (v. 33). And thus, God crushes them in the night (34.25).[6]

Another negative view of human 'works' is found in Ps. 106.35, where the disobedience of God's people in history is related: instead of 'destroying' the peoples when entering the land of Canaan, they 'mingled' with them, 'learning their works' (MT:/LXX: καὶ ἔμαθον τὰ ἔργα αὐτῶν).[7] These morally objectionable 'works' performed by Israel included idolatry (Ps. 106.36) and child sacrifice (106.37) to the point where they polluted the land with blood (106.38d), and 'defiled' themselves with their 'works' (v. 39: MT: וַיִּטְמְאוּ בְמַעֲשֵׂיהֶם וַיִּזְנוּ בְּמַעַלְלֵיהֶם/LXX 107.39: καὶ ἐμιάνθη ἐν τοῖς

---

[6] The scholarly path around the issue of 'acts and consequences' in the HB is well traversed. An early attempt at a theological synthesis was in the work of Klaus Koch, 'Gibt es ein Vergeltungsdogma im Alten Testament', *ZThK* 52 (1955), pp. 1–42. Klaus argued that the OT theme of divine retribution should not be read as the deity intervening in human affairs to punish evil deeds, but as the inherent destructiveness of sin itself 'recoiling' upon the sinner. Evil deeds contain the seeds of their comeuppance, which are borne out in violent consequences, according to Klaus' view. This view has since been challenged in German scholarship and beyond. See, H. Graf Reventlow, '"Sein Blut komme über sein Haupt"', *VT* 10 (1960), pp. 311–27; Peter Hatton, 'A Cautionary Tale: The Acts–Consequence "Construct"', *JSOT* 35, no. 3 (2011), pp. 375–84; John Barton, *Ethics in Ancient Israel* (Oxford: Oxford University Press, 2014), pp. 212–15. Passages such as Job 34.25 and Psalms 28 certainly envisage an 'interventionist' God reacting to humanity's evil works.

[7] The NRSV translates this clause as 'learning to do as they (i.e. the nations) did' – obscuring the fact that idolatry is depicted as 'their works'.

ἔργοις αὐτῶν).[8] A similarly pejorative use of the genitive is presented in Exod. 23.24, where the collective 'works' of humanity denotes their idolatry. Moses enjoins the people at Sinai to resist the idolatrous 'works' (MT: כמעשיהם ... תעבדם/LXX: τὰ ἔργα αὐτῶν) of the Canaanites in the Land that they are about to enter; Moses not only proscribes idolatry but also instructs the people to demolish all pillars and visible signs of idolatry in the Land (Exod. 23.23-24; cf. Lev. 18.3).[9]

The specific sense of human 'works' signifying idolatrous behaviour (cf. Ps. 106.35; Exod. 23.24) can also be found in Nehemiah. Ezra's prayer to God (Neh. 9.6-37) describes God as creator of the world (9.6), as one who chose Abraham for his 'faithful heart' (לבבו נאמן), and made a covenant with Abraham to give his 'seed' (לזרעו) the Land (9.7-8).[10] Ezra determines that God has fulfilled that promise to the returnees from exile.[11] God redeemed the ancestors in Egypt (9.9-12), established a covenant with them at Sinai and gave them 'right ordinances and true laws, good statutes and commandments' (משפטים ישרים ותורות אמת חקים ומצות טובים) specifically the Sabbath (9.13-14). God fed them with manna and water in the wilderness (9.15) but 'they and our ancestors' 'stiffened their necks' and did not obey the commandments (9.16). They returned to 'their slavery' (עבדותם) in Egypt – meaning that they practised idolatry at Mount Sinai (9.17). For Ezra, idolatry is a form of slavery: the real captivity of the Hebrews lay not in their political bondage but in their involvement with Egyptian idolatry.[12] Yet, in all of this, God's mercies did not forsake them (9.17b-22). God 'multiplied their seed like the stars of heaven' and brought them into the Land (9.23), which they duly captured and subjugated (9.24).

Ezra describes God as 'just' (צדיק) in all that has come upon them – for God has 'dealt faithfully and we have acted wickedly', and 'the works (מלכינו) of our rulers,

---

[8] Stefan C. Reif, 'On Some Connotations of the Word Ma'aseh', in Geoffrey Khan and Diana Lipton (eds), *Studies on the Text and Versions of the Hebrew Bible in Honour of Robert Gordon* (VTSupp 149; Leiden: Brill, 2012), pp. 337–52. Reif convincingly argues that עשׂי in these contexts does not generally refer to the Egyptian or Cannaanite 'ways of life' or ritual practices, but specifically to two types of evildoing: sexual immorality and idolatry.

[9] Here, עשׂי and מעלל used interchangeably; cf. Reif, 'On Some Connotations', p. 344. On the other hand, עשׂי is also used in the HB to designate the 'great, powerful' or 'impressive' acts of God redeeming his people; ibid., p. 348.

[10] Scholars view Nehemiah 9 as a typical penitential prayer of the Persian period; see Mark J. Boda, 'The Priceless Gain of Penitence: From Communal Lament to Penitential Prayer in the "Exilic" Liturgy of Israel', *HBT* 25, no. 1 (2003), pp. 51–75, and idem, *Praying the Tradition: The Origin and Use of Tradition in Nehemiah 9* (BZAW; Berlin: de Gruyter, 1999), pp. 21–73. A core feature of the genre is the 'admission of sins' and the acknowledgment that punishment (suffering, exile) is deserved; cf. Boda, 'The Priceless Gain', p. 54. Cf. Judith H. Newman, *Praying by the Book: The Scripturalization of Prayer in Second Temple Judaism* (Atlanta: SBL Press, 1999).

[11] 'The representation of Abraham as a journeyer – in later tradition, even as the first proselyte – will help to explain why the figure of Abraham became prominent, outside of Genesis, only in exilic and postexilic writings' (e.g. Isa. 51.2, 63.16). See Joseph Blenkinsopp, *Ezra-Nehemiah: A Commentary* (OTL; Philadelphia: Westminster Press, 1988), p. 303.

[12] Ibid., p. 304. Cf. Boda, *Praying the Tradition*, p. 153: the continuity of idolatrous practice is highlighted – a relationship of similar rebellion is drawn between the ancient Hebrews and the returned exiles. Gili Kugler goes against the grain to advance an earlier date – not the Second Temple Period, but the immediate period leading up to the Babylonian exile itself; if correct, the narrated continuity that Boda perceives needs to be rethought. See Gili Kugler, 'Present Affliction Affects the Representation of the Past: An Alternative Dating of the Levitical Prayer in Nehemiah 9', *VT* 63 (2013), pp. 605–26.

priests and fathers [was] not [to] keep your Law (תורתך) or pay heed to your commandments' (9.33-34). Despite the blessings of the Land that God gave to them, 'they did not serve' God 'and did not turn from their evil works' (9.35: ממעלליהם הרעים). Ezra connects this fact with the current situation facing the returnees: to this very day they are 'slaves in the land' (עבדים והארץ) that God gave to their ancestors (9.36). Instead of enjoying the rich yield of the land, the produce goes to the dominant kings, 'because of our sins' (9.37a). For this, Ezra and the priests and Levites, and all 'who have separated themselves from the peoples of the lands to adhere to the law of God' (10.28) made an oath to 'walk in God's law' as laid down by Moses (10.29).[13] In Neh. 9.6-37, we can perceive a complex interplay of ideas relating to God's 'righteousness', the promises made to Abraham's 'seed', the idolatrous sin of the ancestors now imputed to Ezra and the returnees, who are consequently 'slaves' in the land, and the idea of commendable behaviour as 'works' – specified as keeping the Torah.

The book of Isaiah provides us with two distinct usages of the concept of human 'works'. In line with most of the foregoing examples, the first Isaian usage integrates the ideas of 'works' as moral activity and 'works' as idolatry. For example, in Isa. 41.25-29, God promises that his chosen servant will triumph over rulers (41.25); God goes on to state that only he has declared that this will happen, and that when he looks around, no one responds to him (41.26-28). As such, the inhabitants of Jerusalem and Zion (41.27) 'are all a delusion; their works (מעשיהם) are nothing; their images (נסכיהם) are empty wind' (41.29).[14] In v. 29, the term 'their works' is paralleled to the term 'their images' (the word נסך meaning both 'image' and 'idol'), implying a correspondence between the two. Both are depicted as vain and useless – which provides us with the evaluative moral language – but in addition the 'images' produced by humans are 'works' in the sense of their material 'handicraft'. Another example is Isa. 66.18, where God judges the behaviour of those who depart from God's ways to follow the ways of other nations (66.17). God declares that he knows 'their works and their thoughts' (מעשיהם ומחשבתיהם/ LXX: τὰ ἔργα αὐτῶν καὶ τὸν λογισμὸν αὐτῶν; 66.18). In Isa. 59.6, God declares that 'their [Israel's] works are works of iniquity (מעשי־און/ἔργα ἀνομίας), and deeds of violence are in their hands'.[15]

The second type of Isaian usage employs the late-biblical Hebrew (LBH) word פעלה for 'works', with the LXX employing a variety of nouns in translation. It is preferable to translate these examples in the singular (i.e. 'work' instead of 'works'), as the possessive form of the genitive indicates the 'recompense' or 'result' of the work itself. One

---

[13] Michael Duggan, *The Covenant Renewal in Ezra-Nehmiah (Neh 7.72b–10.40): An Exegetical, Literary, and Theological Study* (Atlanta: Scholars Press, 2001).
[14] The double sense of מעשי as 'behaviour' and as 'property' (i.e. the *product* of behaviour) is used here to powerful effect. For lexicographic analysis, see Reif, 'On Some Connotations', p. 340; R. J. Clifford, 'The Function of Idol Passages in Second Isaiah', *CBQ* 42, no. 4 (1980), pp. 450–64. The Hebrew *rîb* pattern of forensic trial is used in Isa. 41.13-29, as has been extensively noted in the scholarship; cf. Westermann, *Isaiah 40–66*, p. 83.
[15] The prophet describes sins of the pre-exilic era in chs 57–59, but describes *the exilic community* as 'sons' of those who practised the evil deeds of idolatry, sorcery, child sacrifice, murder and violence; see Benjamin D. Sommer, *A Prophet Reads Scripture: Allusion in Isaiah 40–66* (Stanford: Stanford University Press, 1998), p. 90.

exception is Isa. 65.6-7, which reads well as a plural subjective genitive. God promises to 'repay' idolaters for their behaviour:

> I will indeed repay (ושלמתי שלמתי) into their laps their iniquities (עונתיכם) and their fathers' iniquities (ועונת אבותיכם) together, says the Lord; because they offered incense on the mountains and reviled me on the hills, I will measure full payment (ומדתי פעלתם ראשנה) into their laps. (Isa. 65.7 (MT vv. 6-7))[16]

The second half of this verse could be paraphrased as, 'I will measure the requisition of their works (i.e. their iniquities) into their laps'.[17] In this passage, there is no mention in the Masoretic Text (MT) of 'deeds' or 'actions' or 'works' being repaid/requited, but the LXX supplies this in translation, rephrasing the latter section as 'I will pay back their works into their laps' ('...ἀποδώσω τὰ ἔργα αὐτῶν εἰς τὸν κόλπον αὐτῶν'; v. 7b). In this phrase 'their works' signifies their (earlier stated) 'sin' (v. 7a) and the LXX translator changes the nominal form of פעלה ('payment'/'work') in the MT to the verbal ἀποδίδωμι – 'to give back' or 'pay back', supplying τὰ ἔργα αὐτῶν as the noun to ease the reading ('will measure full payment *for their works* into their laps). Other Isaian texts using פעלה for 'work' translate into the singular; for example, Isa. 40.10b prophesizes the coming of the Lord God, who carries with him his 'reward' and his 'recompense' (פעלה/τὸ ἔργον) for his 'flock'.[18]

The noun פעלה has a varied use in other 'late' biblical texts.[19] The noun can convey the sense of general human behaviour, or 'deeds'. For example, in Ps. 17.5 (MT) the psalmist promises God to be upright 'with regard to the works of man' (לפעלות אדם || LXX Ps. 16.4: τὰ ἔργα τῶν ἀνθρώπων), and to avoid the ways of the violent. In Jer. 31.16, פעלה is used to denote human toil and suffering that carries with it an eventual 'reward' – the human 'work' or 'toil' bears fruit in a 'reward' that grows organically from the 'work' itself (cf. Ps. 28.5; 2 Chron. 15.7). What makes פעלה such a rich word is that it can denote paradoxical concepts simultaneously. Thus, the noun can specify a 'good work', as in 2 Chron. 15.7, where Asa receives encouragement from Azariah in the latter's promise that Asa's 'work' (in countering idolatry) shall be rewarded (שכר לפעלתשם/LXX: μισθὸς τῇ ἐργασίᾳ ὑμῶν).[20] On the other hand, the noun

---

[16] On the warrior metaphors for God used in chs 63–65, see Marc Zvi Brettler, 'Incompatible Metaphors for Yhwh in Isaiah 40–66', *JSOT* 78 (1998), pp. 97–120, at pp. 105–6. The text is not wholly one-sided: Yhwh later promises that descendants (זרע 'seed') will come forth from the remnant, and these will be Yhwh's servants whom he will shepherd. See, Michael J. Chan, 'Isaiah 65-66 and the Genesis of Reorienting Speech', *CBQ* 72 (2010), pp. 445–63, at p. 462.

[17] On 'filling the measure' (of sin) and 'satisfying' debts, see the discussion in Anderson, *Sin*, pp. 48–54, 85–9 (Anderson does not look at Isa. 65.7). In this text, Yhwh is receiving 'payment', or 'satisfaction' of the (debt) of sin through punishment.

[18] Note that פעל covers two almost contradictory meanings: that of 'punishment' (Isa. 65.7) and that of 'reward' (Isa. 41.10b). Yet, this dual semantic feature of biblical Hebrew is not illogical but has comparable precedents; see the excellent discussion of other examples in Baruch Schwartz, 'Term or Metaphor: Biblical *nōśē 'āwōn/peša'/cheth*' (in Hebrew), *Tarbiz* 63 (1994), pp. 149–71.

[19] The scare quotes around the word 'late' indicate my awareness of the perils of dating HB texts as 'late' based on linguistic features alone. See, R. Rezetko and I. Young, *Historical Linguistics and Biblical Hebrew: Toward an Integrated Approach* (Atlanta: SBL Press, 2014).

[20] Literally, 'the reward of your recompense/work', which the LXX tries to render as 'the wage/reward of your work-as-gain' (i.e. profit). Thus, there is the 'work', which results in profit, and a further

can refer to evil deeds that bear fruit in punishment – as in Isa. 65.7, where idolaters themselves receive due 'payment' from God, and have their 'sins' 'worked into their laps'. Similarly, the text of Ps. 109.20 has the psalmist pray that his accusers receive 'recompense' (פעלת) from the Lord for their arrogance and oppression.

To further enrich the picture, in other texts of the HB another nuance – that of פעלה denoting the 'wages' earned by 'work' – is scaffolded upon the noun. One example is Prov. 11.18-19, which reads

> The wicked do deceitful works/but those who sow righteousness have a true reward.

> רשׁע עשׂה פעלת־שׁקר
>
> וזרע צדקה שׂכר אמת

> ἀσεβὴς ποιεῖ ἔργα ἄδικα/σπέρμα δὲ δικαίων μισθὸς ἀληθείας (LXX)

The first line of the proverb plays on the double meaning inherent in פעלה, signifying at once the 'work' itself and the 'wages' or result earned by the work.[21] One could translate the proverb more fluidly: 'the wicked receive the wage of deception, but the sowers of righteousness earn a faithful reward'. The economic overtones of this nuance are hard to miss. Human 'works' thus earn 'wages' to the point where the 'works' themselves equate to the 'wages' they produce. Righteous works earn a rewarding wage (e.g. 'life' in Prov. 11.19a), but wicked works produce the 'wage' of 'death' (e.g. Prov. 11.19b). Another proverb expresses this somewhat more explicitly:

> The wealth of the rich is their fortress/The poverty of the poor is their ruin
>
> The wages/works of the righteous leads to life/The yield of the wicked to sin.

> הון עשׁיר קרית עזו מחתת דלים רישׁם
>
> פעלת צדיק לחיים תבואת רשׁע לחתאת (MT Prov. 10.15-16)

> κτῆσις πλουσίων πόλις ὀχυρά συντριβὴ δὲ ἀσεβῶν πενία ἔργα δικαίων ζωὴν ποιεῖ καρποὶ δὲ ἀσεβῶν ἁμαρτίας (LXX Prov. 10.15-16)

These conceptualizations of 'work/works' approximate to the conceptualization of sin as debt, and of righteousness as credit, as analysed in Chapter 4. The 'yield' (תבואת) literally means 'product' or 'income' of the wicked bears fruit in 'sin', but the 'wage' or 'work' of the righteous is life.[22] The LXX translates פעלה as ἔργα ('works') in this case. Virtuous works produce a surplus ('wages') that stands in for the virtuous 'works' themselves. Likewise, the produce of wickedness is sin – the consequence and surplus

---

level of 'reward'/'wage' for the work and profit, almost like a commission. This rich metaphorization concerns Asa's behaviour, especially his obedience to the divinely mandated aniconistic purge.

[21] Richard J. Clifford, *Proverbs: A Commentary* (OTL; Louisville/London: WJK Press, 1999), p. 124.

[22] Cf. Michael V. Fox, *Proverbs 10-31: A New Translation with Introduction and Commentary* (AB 18b; New Haven: Yale University Press, 2009), p. 520.

of wickedness itself. This symbolic use of פעלה can be seen in two Isaian texts. For example, in Isa. 49.4, the voice of God's servant laments that his 'labour' has been in vain, but he consoles himself by asserting that his 'reward/wage' (פעלה) is with God. In Isa. 61.8, God promises to give 'recompense/payment' (פעלה) to his faithful and to make a covenant with them, so that their 'seed' shall be 'known among the nations' (61.9).[23]

Another way in which human behaviour is designated as 'works' in the HB is when the plural form of the noun צדקה is used to mean something like 'righteous deeds' or 'right doing'.[24] Of course, צדקות is predicated of God quite regularly in the biblical texts (1 Sam. 12.7; Ps. 103.6; Isa. 45.24; Mic. 6.5, 16; Dan. 9.16). The plural is not directly translatable into English (e.g. כל־צדקות would mean 'all of [God's] righteous acts/deeds' rather than 'all of God's righteousness'). When human acts are described as צדקות, the implication is that such acts are imitative of the divine. One example is found in Ps. 11.7 (MT) which states that 'the Lord is righteous; he loves righteous works' (כי־צדיק יהוה צדקות אהב/LXX Ps. 10.7: ὅτι δίκαιος κύριος καὶ δικαιοσύνας ἠγάπησεν). This psalm contrasts the way of the wicked – characterized by a penchant for violence (11.2, 5b) – with the way of the righteous. In Isa. 33.15 'walking [in] righteous deeds' (הלך צדקות/LXX: πορευόμενος ἐν δικαιοσύνῃ) is akin to living with integrity, shunning bribes and despising oppression, bloodshed and evil.

Another Isaian text contains a profound lament on human inadequacy before God, and the punishment that must be endured for sin (Isa. 64.1-12). Because of God's anger, his people sinned (64.5 (MT v. 4)), and consequently, they became 'like one who is unclean' (64.6a).[25] The people cry, 'All our righteous deeds (כל־צדקתינו/LXX: πᾶσα ἡ δικαιοσύνη ἡμῶν) are like a filthy cloth; we all fade like a leaf, and our sins, like the wind, take us away' (64.6b). Yet, they implore, 'O, Lord, you are our Father; we are the clay, and you are our potter; we are all the work of your hand (64.8)'.[26] A similar cry for mercy is repeated in Dan. 9.18, with Daniel pleading that God repair the sanctuary in

---

[23] The noun פעלה can also denote 'wages' in a non-metaphoric sense, as in Lev. 19.13, where God commands that the 'wages of the worker' not be held over by the employer until the next morning; (cf. Ezek. 29.19-20). This literal sense of the word probably pre-existed the secondary and metaphorical sense of the word as the 'reward/punishment' of works.

[24] I will address how this usage of the feminine plural eventually morphs into variations on the root זכי under my discussion of the rabbinic literature; cf. Rosen-Zvi, 'Pauline Traditions and the Rabbis', p. 179. The LXX δικαίωμα can mean 'justification' but also '[legal] cause' or 'case' (2 Chron. 6.35; Jer. 18.19), overlapping with the classical Greek usage (as per LSJ). The BAGD lexicon expands the semantic range of δικαίωμα to encompass two meanings that also find parallels in classical Greek literature, the Hellenistic Jewish writings, the LXX and in the Oxyrhinchus papyri: (1) 'regulation, requirement, commandment' (e.g. LXX Num. 30.17, 31.21; Philo; Josephus and P.Oxy 1119.5); (2) 'righteous deed' (Aristotle 1135a, Bar. 2.19; the NT, etc.). Another sense of the same noun is 'justice' (LXX) based on the forensic senses in classical Greek. See the brilliant discussion of Emanuel Tov, *The Greek & Hebrew Bible: Collected Essays on the Septuagint* (Leiden/Boston: Brill, 1999), p. 110. Building from this, the noun צדקה in the HB is usually rendered by the Greek noun δικαιοσύνη in the LXX, which more commonly translates to the concepts of 'righteousness' or 'justification' in the thought-world of Paul and other NT writers. Cf. 1QH 9[=1].26: מאשי התצדקה ('righteous deeds'/'works').

[25] On the connection in biblical thought between sin and filth, see Paul, *Isaiah 40–66*, p. 584.

[26] The preceding context of this powerful lament positions God as 'father', and 'redeemer' of Israel, drawing out rich evocations of the Exodus narrative: cf. Paul Niskanen, 'Yhwh as Father, Redeemer, and Potter in Isaiah 63.7–64.11', *CBQ* 68, no. 3 (2006), pp. 397–407.

Jerusalem 'not on the ground of our righteous deeds (MT: על־צדקתינו אנחנו/LXX: δικαιοσύναις ἡμῶν), but on the ground of your great mercies'. Indeed, it is in view of God's own 'righteous deeds' (ככל־צדקת) and even though his people have 'sinned' and 'done wickedly' – that Daniel implores the Lord to hear his prayer (9.15-16). These two texts (Isa. 64.5, Dan. 9.15-18) indicate that God' 'righteous deeds' far outweigh the merit that could obtain from humanity's 'righteous deeds'; there is simply no comparison, and all pleas for divine mercy must proceed from the basis of God's righteousness.

Yet coexisting with this perspective is another, almost contradictory, line of thought which advances the possibility that human sin *can* be 'redeemed' by righteous behaviour. The difference seems to be, in this latter case, that the behaviour pertains to an individual rather than to a collective. In Dan. 4.19-27, King Nebuchadnezzar is troubled by a second perplexing dream that he has had in the night. He asks Daniel to interpret his dream: the message is that the king has become so prosperous that he has neglected respect for the ultimate sovereignty of God. Daniel offers important counsel to the king: 'atone for your sins with righteousness and your iniquities with mercy to the oppressed (Greek Daniel: αὐτοῦ δεήθητι περὶ τῶν ἁμαρτιῶν σου καὶ πάσας τὰς ἀδικίας σου ἐν ἐλεημοσύναις λύτρωσαι, so that your prosperity may be prolonged' (ἵνα ἐπιείκεια δοθῇ σοι καὶ πολυήμερος γένη; 4.27). This text is one of the earliest examples of a specialized meaning for the noun צדקה at the dawn of the Second Temple Period: it comes to mean 'charity' or 'almsgiving' (especially in the rabbinic literature) when paired with the verb נתן rather than the more typically biblical (עשׂה), and the act of almsgiving is a meritorious means of alleviating the debt of sin accrued by a person (such as here, the king).[27]

There is also frequent mention of '*doing* righteousness' in the HB אשׂה צדקה. The participle can be glossed as 'doing righteous works'. In Isa. 56.1, 'doing righteousness' is voiced as an imperative עשׂו צסקה essential for the preparation for God's imminent salvation.[28] The 'doing of righteousness' in this context is highly concrete – caring for those in society who are oppressed; these constitute the 'works' that God desires.[29] God also condemns the 'sins' of 'the house of Jacob', who seek God on the pretence that they are 'a nation that did righteousness' but in fact they had forsaken God (Isa. 58.1-2).[30] The regular practice of 'doing righteousness' brings rewards to the doer, notably happiness (Ps. 106.3/LXX Ps. 105.3). Indeed, 'doing righteousness' is so powerful that it can lead sinners from death to life, completely overriding the effects of sin. In a well-known passage from Ezekiel, we see this concept polemically rejected, in the context of

---

[27] Cf. Seulgi L. Byun, *The Influence of Post-Biblical Hebrew and Aramaic on the Translator of Septuagint Isaiah* (LHB/OTS 635; London: T&T Clark/Bloomsbury, 2017), p. 50.
[28] Westermann, *Isaiah 40-66*, p. 309, notes the oddity of the admonition: 'Do righteousness ... for My righteousness (i.e. salvation, or deliverance) comes'.
[29] Cf. Brueggemann, *Isaiah 40–66*, p. 190.
[30] The address is to the whole people, and their rebellion and sin is conceived by means of bodily imagery: the finger (58.9), the fist (58.4), the hand (59.3, 6), the tongue (59.3) and the lips (59.3, cf. 58.9b) are engaged in sin. See Paul A. Smith, *Rhetoric and Redaction in Trito-Isaiah: The Structure, Growth, and Authorship of Isaiah 56–66* (VTSupp 62; Leiden: Brill, 1995), pp. 99–100.

a debate about the trans-generational effects of sin. Notably, in this passage 'doing righteousness' is equated with observing the commandments of God:[31]

> Yet you say, 'Why should not the son suffer for the iniquity of the father?' When the son has done what is lawful and right, and has been careful to observe all my statutes, he shall surely live. The person who sins shall die. A child shall not suffer for the iniquity of a parent, nor a parent suffer for the iniquity of a child; the righteousness of the righteous shall be his own, and the wickedness of the wicked shall be his own. But if the wicked turn away from all their sins that they have committed and keep all my statutes and do what is lawful and right, they shall surely live; they shall not die. None of the transgressions that they have committed shall be remembered against them; for the righteousness that they have done (בצדקתו אשר־עשה/LXX: ἐν τῇ δικαιοσύνῃ αὐτοῦ, ᾗ ἐποίησεν) they shall live. (NRSV Ezek. 18.20-22)

In Chapter 4, we saw how this debate gained traction within the Second Temple Period. As the question of the merits and virtues of the 'fathers' (Abraham, Isaac and Jacob) started to be expressed with greater clarity, the associated question of the intergenerational or vicarious benefits of those merits came to the fore. While some texts expressed scepticism about the possibility of the living to pray for the dead, or the dead to affect the living (e.g. *LAB* 18, 33–35), other texts asserted that the fathers' virtues could carry on benefitting their 'seed' on earth. Ezek. 18.20-22 provides one of the earliest biblical examples where the notion of intergenerational sin/virtue broadened beyond the schema of (Patriarchs → 'Seed') to that of (Fathers → Sons) in general. And, as Jurrien Mol shows, the text also expands past the 'Father–Son' schema to the 'righteous–guilty' schema.[32] Yet, this expansion is more than an emphasis on individualism over collectivism; it is a vibrant assertion of the power of Torah observance to wipe away one's 'iniquities' and 'transgressions' from God's memory because of the goodness (righteousness) inherent in performing God's statutes (את־כל־חקותי). This obtains *even if* one has formerly been a 'sinner' (cf. the reverse case in Ezek. 3.20; 18.24).[33] The variety of texts examined here illustrate how the concepts of 'righteousness'/'righteous works' and 'doing righteousness' were used as expressions of (good) works – either of justice or of the Torah – that humans were enjoined to undertake.[34]

---

[31] Cf. In Gen. 18.16-19, Abraham is presented as an exemplary figure, expected to teach his children to 'do righteousness' by 'keeping the way of the Lord'. It is for this very reason that God is described as having chosen Abraham (Gen. 18.19a).

[32] Jurrien Mol, *Collective and Individual Responsibility: A Description of Corporate Personality in Ezekiel 18 and 20* (Leiden: Brill, 2009), p. 219.

[33] Ezekiel's concept of guilt (עון) as something one 'bears' (נשא i.e. as punishment) accords with the 'scapegoat' metaphorical construction of 'sin' in the earlier biblical texts (Ezek. 16.58; 23.35; 36.15; 44.10, 12; cf. particularly Leviticus 16). But Ezekiel also mixes 'vocabulary of punishment due to guilt and sin with vocabulary of shame and disgrace'. Cf. Mark J. Boda, *Severe Mercy: Sin and Its Remedy in the Old Testament* (Winona Lake: Eisenbrauns, 2014), pp. 272, 278.

[34] A different example is found in Isa. 32.17, which reads, 'the works of righteousness will be peace, and the result of righteousness, quietness and trust forever' (Heb.: הצדקה השקט טבחת עד־עולם והיה מעשה הצדקה שלום ועבדת; LXX: καὶ ἔσται τὰ ἔργα τῆς δικαιοσύνης εἰρήνη καὶ κρατήσει ἡ

Certain exemplary individuals in the HB are praised for their moral behaviour. For example, Hezekiah is eulogized for his 'good deeds' for which he 'prospered in all his works' (2 Chron. 32.30-33). The anonymous, idealized wife of Proverbs 31 is deemed to deserve 'a share in the fruit of her hands' and to have 'her works (מעשיה) praise her in the city gates' (Prov. 31.30-31).[35] These uses of the subjective genitive of מעשיה signify the good works of the respective persons being lauded. These individuals both possess and perform their 'works', which have a highly praiseworthy quality. But there is one uncanny example wherein the term 'works' is predicated of a person in a negative sense, connoting not so much the unworthy sins of a person, but the whole behavioural habits and the destructive *statutes* of a person (Mic. 6.16). The text reads:

For you have kept the statutes of Omri (חקות עמרי/LXX: δικαιώματα Ζαμβρι) and all the works of the house of Ahab (מעשה בית־אחאב/LXX: τὰ ἔργα οἴκου Αχααβ) and you [pl.] have followed their counsels (ותלכו במעצותם/LXX: ἐπορεύθητε ἐν ταῖς βουλαῖς αὐτῶν)
Therefore, I will make you a desolation, and your inhabitants an object of hissing; so shall you bear the scorn of my people. (Mic. 6.16)

The text's preceding context suggests that commendable behaviour which atones for 'the sin of [the] soul' (6.7b) – is 'to do justice, and to love kindness, and to walk humbly' with God (6.8). But instead, God calls out the sins of the city (6.9) – greed, lack of integrity and abuse of justice (6.10-11), violence, lies and deceit (6.12). Because of this, God is depicted as striking down the population of the city for their sins (6.13-14), and the result of this devastation is constant frustration and lack (6.14-15). The sinful behaviour of the city's inhabitants, warranting such severe punishment, is characteristic of 'the works of the house of Ahab' (6.16), not the 'works' of God (cf. 6.7).[36] Mic. 6.16 uses the objective genitive, where the 'works' signify something done in the service of the person of whom they are predicated.

This explains why the term 'the works of ... Ahab' (v. 16b) is placed in synonymous parallelism with two other terms: 'the statutes of Omri' (v. 16a) and the 'commandments' (of Ahab and Omri) (v. 16c). As James Luther Mays puts it, 'This way of speaking assumes a tradition that the practices of policies of Omri and Ahab are so evil that the invocation of their names can serve as a final indictment'.[37] This use of the genitive of מעשיה invites us to read the phrase 'the works of Ahab' as equivalent to the 'statutes' and 'commandments' that Ahab/Omri commissioned (and, no doubt, were thought to

---

δικαιοσύνη ἀνάπαυσιν καὶ πεποιθότες ἕως τοῦ αἰῶνος). *Avodah* can also be translated as 'works' when used as a genitive in relation to a non-abstract noun (e.g. Num. 4.30, 35, 39, 43; Exod. 5.11; Ezra 4.24, 6.7) or in relation to human behaviour (Job 34.25).

[35] The LXX omits reference to the wife's 'works', noting only that the husband 'praises' his wife.
[36] Like those general texts about doing righteousness etc., antithetical to violence and injustice.
[37] James Luther Mays, *Micah: A Commentary* (OTL; Philadelphia: Westminster Press, 1976), p. 148; the sin of the Omrides was the apostasy to Baal (2 Kgs 10.18; 21.3).

perform themselves).[38] These statutes and commandments – glossed as 'works' in v. 16b – are the destructive ordinances of apostasy that the people of the city obeyed. Mic. 6.16 reveals the intriguing possibility that the 'works' of a person can be understood idiomatically as the counsels (or 'commandments') of a person. The 'works' of Ahab's house are not enumerated, but the context proves that they are sins of injustice and violence (cf. the 'works of Beliar' in the *T12P*). The only way to escape the divine punishment that these sins appear to warrant is to perform a set of alternate 'works' (although it is not phrased as such): namely, to undertake acts of kindness, justice and humility (6.8). These latter acts sum up the entire core of the commandments and statutes of God.

To summarize the examples analysed, the term 'works' in the HB, when referring to human behaviour, holds a variety of connotations. These include: 'works' which bear 'fruit' leading to reward or punishment, often metaphorically denoted as a wage or recompense (פעלה). This 'late' biblical Hebrew usage suggests that human 'works' (deeds, behaviour) earn 'credits' or 'debits' depending on whether the works are grounded in righteousness or sin. Virtuous 'works' produce a surplus ('wages') that stand in for the good works themselves (a notion that will develop significantly in Second Temple times). The book of Daniel shows how this concept was developing with the idea that works of charity (especially almsgiving) could atone for human sins, which took on the form of a 'debt' to be redeemed (Dan. 4.19-27). Other instances of 'works' in the HB use the constructs of the root צדק, usually in the imperative mood, to encourage righteous behaviour in line with what God demands specifically with a focus on social justice. Finally, we see 'works' predicated directly of named persons in the HB – similar to what we find in John 8.39-40 with the 'works' of Abraham. Examples include the (good) 'works' of Hezekiah, the personified 'works' of the woman of worth in Proverbs 30 and the evil 'works' of Ahab, structurally paralleled with the 'commandments' of the 'house of Omri' (Mic. 6.16).

Apocryphal and pseudepigraphical literature

There are several developments in the way the term 'works' is used in the post-biblical literature. The biblical precedents remain present – for example, the book of Sirach and the Wisdom of Solomon frequently emphasize the 'works' of God in creation (cf. *Wis.* 8.4; 9.9; 12.19-21; 14.5; *Sir.* 1.9; 16.26-27; 17.8-9; 18.4; 33.15; 38.68; 39.16; 42.15-17, 22; 43.28, 32), and the idea of 'works' describing human behaviour – whether positive or negative (cf. *Wis.* 1.11-12; 2.4; 3.11-13; 6.2; 9.12; 11.1; 12.4; *Sir.* 11.20; *Bar.* 3.15-18; cf. *2 Esd.* 16.64-67). But there are also new trajectories evident: for example, *4 Ezra* uses the term 'works' as the functional equivalent of human 'merit' – as the product of commendable behaviour that is 'stored' in a 'treasury' in heaven for future 'withdrawals'. In Chapter 4, we noted that the concepts of merit/sin functioned this way, that is in terms of economic metaphorization where behaviour was described

---

[38] Omri was the dynastic founder of the 'house of Ahab', although Ahab was his successor; the expression is always בית־אחאב in the Bible. See T. Ishida, 'The House of Ahab', *Israel Exploration Journal* 25, nos. 2/3 (1975), pp. 135–7.

as credit/debit. The concept of 'works' also fits into this metaphorical scheme within the thought-word of Second Temple Judaism. Other post-biblical developments are noteworthy: for example the 'works of the fathers' and their zeal for the law (the books of *Maccabees*); the notion of 'righteous works' as almsgiving that atone for sins (*Tob.* 4.5-7a; Dan. 9.27); and 'works' as God's commandments (cf. *Wis.* 6.2-5; *2 (Syriac) Baruch* 44). These developments continue within the NT and the Tannaitic literature. For the sake of brevity, we examine those texts in the apocryphal and pseudepigraphical literatures that use the concept of 'works' in conjunction with ideas of righteous deeds, obedience to the Torah, ancestral merit and correctives to sin.

In the apocryphal *Baruch* (end of first century CE), the term 'works' refers to the commandments of the Torah, in the context of the writer's reflection upon the theodicy of exile. In language reminiscent of Nehemiah 9, the speaker laments: [39]

> The Lord our God is in the right, but there is open shame on us and our ancestors this very day. All those calamities with which the Lord threatened us have come upon us. Yet we have not entreated the favour of the Lord by turning away, each of us, from the thoughts of our wicked hearts. And the Lord has kept the calamities ready, and the Lord has brought them upon us, for the Lord is just in *all the works that he has commanded us to do* (πάντα τὰ ἔργα αὐτοῦ, ἃ ἐνετείλατο ἡμῖν). Yet we have not obeyed his voice, to walk in the statutes of the Lord that he set before us. (2.6-10)[40]

Like the biblical text from Mic. 6.6 previously examined, this text parallels 'works' and 'statutes', but predicated of God (rather than Ahab/Omri). Baruch opines that the calamities of exile have been brought about as a consequence of the people's disobedience and refusal to follow the divine commandments – or the 'works' of the Lord. To do the 'works of the Lord' in this text, means to obey the commandments of the Torah. This theme finds lengthier expression later in the composition of *2 Bar.* 57.1-2.[41] Leading up to this reference are several key contextual cues. In ch. 48 vv. 1-24, the historicized character Baruch offers up a lengthy prayer to God, beseeching help:

> And do not take away the hope of our people, and do not make short the times of our help. For these are the people whom you have elected, and this is the nation of

---

[39] Cf. the similar insight, more fully developed, in Mark F. Whitters, 'Baruch as Ezra in *2 Baruch*', *JBL* 132, no. 3 (2013), pp. 569-84.

[40] Odil Hannes Steck, *Das apokryphe Baruchbuch: Studien zu Rezeption und Konzentration 'kanonischer' Überlieferung* (FRLANT 160; Göttingen: Vandenhoeck & Ruprecht, 1993), pp. 253-65 sees the introductory 'letter' as organic to the whole composition (Syriac) *2 Baruch* (which is only preserved in its entirety in the Ambrosian manuscript (Peshitta Institute siglum 7ᵃ¹)); cf. Lutz Doering, 'The Epistle of Baruch and Its Role in *2 Baruch*, in *Fourth Ezra and 2 Baruch*, pp. 151-74, at p. 157 (the letter is 'an original part of the composition').

[41] I will treat the epistolary frame and the body of *2 Baruch* here together, for the sake of convenience, without getting into the details of the composition history. While most scholars have dated *2 Baruch* independently of *Apoc. Baruch* after the calamity of 70 CE, Martin Goodman convincingly argues for an earlier date, putting it closer to the former text. See Goodman, 'The Date of 2 Baruch', in Christopher Rowland and John Ashton (eds), *Revealed Wisdom: Studies in Apocalyptic in Honour of Christopher Rowland* (AJEC 88; Leiden: Brill, 2014), pp. 116-21.

which you found no equal. But I shall speak to you now, and I shall say as my heart thinks. In you we have put our trust, because, behold, your Law is with us, and we know that we do not fall as long as we keep your statutes. (48.29)

Baruch's petition proceeds from the theological conviction that as God's elected people, the Jews of the diaspora possess a unique kind of hope and receive a particular form of help from God.[42] This conviction is not powered by a blindly wanton arrogance; rather, it is motivated by the acknowledgement that the Jews' trust in God is justified by the appointment of the Law over them – that the Torah 'is with us' – and that God's law provides the Jews with purpose and safety in the observance of God's 'statutes'. In other words, Baruch's sense of trust in God is based on the promise of the efficacy of the commandments to draw down the rewards, so to speak, inherent in their own observance: 'we do not fall as long as we keep your statutes'.[43] In Baruch's eschatological world view, the fate of the righteous and the wicked centre upon the 'works' of the Law: 'miracles, however, will appear at their own time to those who are saved because of their works and for whom the Law is now a hope, and intelligence, and expectation, and wisdom a trust' – but the wicked will not be spared because their deeds will bring upon them destruction (57.1-16).[44]

In the text, Baruch receives a complex vision from God: a great black cloud emerges from the sea, carrying lightning atop its girth, and moving across the whole world. The cloud pours its water down upon the earth, but the water alternates between being black and being very bright. Eventually, the cloud releases densely black-coloured water mixed with fire, causing large-scale destruction and devastation. Then, the lightning that was atop the cloud descends to the earth, healing the destruction (53.1-12). God then interprets the vision for Baruch (53.56-72); the black waters signify the transgressions of the first humans at creation and the consequent flood (cf. Genesis 6–11; *2 Bar.* 56.1-16). But the bright waters signify:

The fountain of Abraham and his generation, and the coming of his son, and the son of his son, and of those who are like them. For at the time the unwritten law was in force among them, and the *works of the commandments* were accomplished at that time, and the belief in the coming judgment was brought about, and the

---

[42] Cf. Chapter 4 on the 'seed of Abraham' and the motif of divine help from God given to Abraham's 'seed'.

[43] This does contrast with the more cynical world views expressed in Job and Qoheleth. The 'central aspect of [*2 Baruch*'s] apocalyptic world view', is, according to Matthias Henze, an appropriation of Deuteronomic theology, especially the call to heed the Torah and to 'choose life'. Henze, 'Torah and Eschatology in the *Syriac Apocalypse of Baruch*', in George J. Brooke, Hindy Najman and Loren T. Stuckenbruck (eds), *The Significance of Sinai: Traditions about Divine Revelation in Judaism and Christianity* (TBN; Leiden: Brill, 2008), pp. 201–16, at p. 204.

[44] The author 'resembles the early [rabbinic] Sages' in his emphasis on Torah, but he managed to merge this emphasis with an extraordinary eschatological outlook. Matthias Henze, 'Apocalypse and Torah in Ancient Judaism', in *The Oxford Handbook of Apocalyptic Literature*, pp. 312–25, at p. 321. The influence of Jeremiah's theme of the return from exile should also not be overlooked: see Kipp Davis, 'Prophets of Exile: 4QApocryphon of Jeremiah C, Apocryphal Baruch, and the Efficacy of the Second Temple', *JSJ* 44 (2013), pp. 497–529.

hope of the world which will be renewed was built at that time, and the promise of the life that will come later was planted. (57.1-2)

This is an important text because it uses the term 'works' to refer directly to the commandments of the Torah, indeed, to the performance of the commandment of the Torah. Additionally, the text associates the 'works of the commandments' with Abraham and his lineage – his 'seed' so to speak – in ways that suggest that Abraham and his sons were exemplary in their observance of the commandments. It is not simply Abraham's 'sons' who are idealized in their observance of the 'unwritten law' (i.e. the laws of the Torah before they were disclosed at Sinai), but 'those who are like them'. Resemblance to Abraham and his descendants is therefore achievable based on doing the 'works of the commandments'. Indeed, the text of *2 Bar.* 57.1-2 may well provide some important context for how later expressions could be understood – namely, that 'works of the law' (e.g. 4QMMT, Paul) specifies the commandments of the Torah in general, and that the shorthand term 'works' can signify the performance of the commandments as such.

In this text from *2 Baruch*, we begin to see the term 'works of' in this construct form moving from 'products' of righteous behaviour (cf. 'works of righteousness', Isa. 32.17) to 'acts inherently part of or belonging to' the commandments – that is, the term 'works' has moved from denoting the 'effect' (of righteousness) to 'the (implied righteous) commandments' themselves. Another notable feature in *2 Bar.* 57.1-2 is the way that the patriarchal promises from the Torah are reconfigured to refer to eternal life, not to the eternal inheritance of the land (cf. Genesis). This eschatological broadening of perspective is a common thematic feature of apocalyptic literature.[45] In *2 Bar.* 57.1-2, Abraham's exemplary performance of the 'works of the commandments' goes hand in glove with the hope of the renewal of the world in that generation; and due to Abraham's 'works' the 'promise of the life to come' was planted.

The text of *4 Ezra*, upon which *2 Baruch* is often thought to have depended, associates human 'works' with the Torah, but in the context of the people's disobedience and neglect (*4 Ezra* 7.22-25):

> They devised for themselves vain thoughts, and proposed to themselves wicked frauds; they even declared that the Most High does not exist, and they ignored his ways. They scorned his law, and denied his covenants; they have been unfaithful to his statutes, and have not performed his works. That is the reason, Ezra, that empty things are for the empty, and full things are for the full.[46]

As in the text from Baruch, but in more explicit detail, in God's disclosure to Ezra, the 'law', 'covenant' and 'statutes' are together correlated with God's 'works'. Importantly,

---

[45] Cf. Liv Ingebord Lied, *The Other Lands of Israel: Imaginations of the Land in 2 Baruch* (JSJSup 129; Leiden: Brill, 2008); Jörg Frey, 'Apocalyptic Dualism', in *Oxford Handbook of Apocalyptic Literature*, pp. 271–94; Collins, *The Apocalyptic Imagination*, pp. 251–4.

[46] *OTP* I, pp. 517–60. See the excellent article of David A. deSilva rebutting contemporary scholarly characterizations of *4 Ezra* as 'legalistic' and devoid of God's graciousness: idem, 'Grace, the Law and Justification in *4 Ezra* and the Pauline Letters: A Dialogue', *JSNT* 37, no. 1 (2014), pp. 25–49. The Tannaitic maxims that parallel this thought of 'empty things to the empty and full things to the full' will be developed in the final part of this section.

in the text from *4 Ezra*, God's 'works' are placed in the context of discussion about the punishment accruing to the ungodly. 'Empty things' go to 'the empty', and 'full things' go to 'the full'. The correlative implication is that those who 'perform' God's 'works' (his statutes, law) receive fullness from God. But this is not a 'legalistic' soteriology lacking in nuance; it should be noted that while repentance is possible (*4 Ezra* 9.12), the 'wicked' who 'scorned' God's law and did not 'perform his works' are those who suffer after death because in the afterlife there is no means for them to repent (7.82).[47]

The concept of 'works' as the commandments of God also finds expression in the *Testaments of the Twelve Patriarchs*. Recall that in the *Testament of Levi* (*T. Levi*), the sons of Levi will in the future choose to do 'every evil work', but they will be saved through the mercy of Abraham, Isaac and Jacob (15.4; cf. *T. Asher* 7.7). Earlier in his testamentary discourse, Levi encourages his sons to 'read the Law of God', to 'know the Law of God' and to walk according to God's law (13.1-3). If they do this, Levi's sons will be 'doing righteousness' on earth (13.4), thus allaying tribulation. The substantive noun 'doing righteousness' is collocated with studious attention to, and devout observance of, the Torah. While 'evil deeds' (15.1) are further defined as lawlessness and impiety (14.4-8), 'doing righteousness' is assumed to be the performance of 'works' aligned with the 'just ordinances' of God (14.4). This perspective is crystallized at the end of Levi's testament with his lapidary summary: 'And now, my children, you have heard everything. Choose for yourselves light or darkness, the Law of the Lord or the works of Beliar' (19.1). Levi's sons choose the Law of God (19.2) on solemn oath, confirming each other's witness to the promise (19.3-4a).[48] Levi is then buried in Hebron, with Abraham, Isaac and Jacob (19.5).[49]

In the *Testament of Levi*, the Torah ('the Law of the Lord') is diametrically opposed to 'the works of Beliar'. The suggestion is that one can choose to undertake either the 'works' of God (the commandments) or the 'works of Beliar' (impiety and sin). The Law of God produces righteousness, but the 'works of Beliar' signify a course of behaviour that is antithetical to moral integrity. Beliar is personified once in the *Testament of Levi*. Thus, in ch. 18 vv. 1-14, Levi prophesizes the coming of a new 'priest' following the wreckage of God's vengeance on the earth (18.1-2). The eschatological priest will know all the 'words of the Lord' and he will judge the earth, in peace, like a king (18.3-4); the whole earth will then rejoice abundantly (18.5).[50] During the reign of the priest, 'sin

---

[47] deSilva, 'Grace, the Law and Justification', p. 34.
[48] Note that the sons' responses are suddenly couched in the first-person plural, which has caused headaches for a number of interpreters of the T12P, as the shift in number implies that the author positioned himself as a descendant of Levi; cf. Dixon Slingerland, 'The Levitical Hallmark within the Testaments of the Twelve Patriarchs', *JBL* 103, no. 4 (1984), pp. 531-7; cf. de Jonge, 'The Testament of Levi and "Aramaic Levi"', p. 384.
[49] *OTP I*, pp. 775-828. The other testaments are not this specific in the concluding burial narrative – often the fathers are just buried at Hebron, or with 'their fathers' (thus *T. Ru* 7.1-2; *T. Sim.* 8.2; *T. Jud.* 26.4; *T. Issachar* 7.8-9; *T. Zeb.* 10.6; *T. Naph.* 9.1; *T. Gad.* 8.4b-5; *T. Asher* 8.1-2; *T. Joseph* 20.5; *T. Ben.* 12.1). Dan is another exception: he is buried specifically with Abraham, Isaac and Jacob (*T. Dan.* 7.2). Also, cf. Deut. 30.15-20 on the imperative of choosing between life and death.
[50] The following segment of the passage speaks about the uniqueness of this king – he will have no successor (18.8), and he will be spoken to by God as though he were Abraham or Isaac (18.6). He will illuminate the nations, but 'Israel will be diminished by her ignorance and darkened by her grief' (with regard to the priest) ch. 18 v. 9. Commentators agree that the passage is composed

shall cease and lawless men shall rest from their evil deeds, and righteous men shall find rest in him' ... 'And Beliar shall be bound by him' (18.9, 11-12). Consequently, 'Abraham, Isaac and Jacob will rejoice' (18.12).[51]

The (possibly inauthentic Pauline) text of 2 Cor. 6.14-16a provides a close parallel: 'Do not be mismatched with unbelievers. For what partnership is there between righteousness and lawlessness? Or what fellowship is there between light and darkness? What agreement does Christ have with Beliar? Or what does a believer share with an unbeliever? What agreement has the temple of God with idols?' 'Beliar' is here a corruption of 'Belial' ('the devil').[52] In the HB, adjectival cognates of the noun בליאל means 'wicked' (e.g. Deut. 15.9; Ps. 41.8; 101.3; Prov. 6.12).[53] The expression 'son' or 'man of Belial' connotes a worthless, lawless person (Judg. 19.22; 20.13; 1 Sam. 1.16; 2.12; 25.25).[54] But occasionally, the nominal construct can contain deeper connotations. For example, in Deut. 13.13, certain 'worthless ones' (בני בליאל) go out to entice the inhabitants of the city towards idolatry; in Deut. 15.9, the phrase 'wicked thought' (לבבך בליעל) refers to the selfish begrudging of alms as the Jubilee year approaches; other connotations include murder (1 Sam. 20.1), perjury (1 Kgs 21.13; Prov. 16.27), sodomy (Deut. 13.14) or rebellion (2 Chron. 13.7). The phrase 'works of Beliar' could encompass all of these nuances and shades. As a genitive phrase, 'the works of Beliar' (i.e. the devil) in *T. Levi* 18.12 constitutes a close parallel to John 8.44 and Jesus' reference to the Jews doing the devil's 'works'.

Because in the *Testament of Levi* the 'works of Beliar' are positioned appositely to 'the Law of the Lord', we can argue that their substance is 'lawless' or sinful behaviour in general. Looking at what makes up 'evil deeds' or unrighteousness in the *Testament of Levi* can also provide fruitful information. Levi prophesizes that just before vengeance comes upon the earth (18.1) there will arise other priests: these are 'idolaters, adulterers, money lovers, arrogant, lawless, voluptuaries, paedophiles, those who practice bestiality' (17.11). All of this generalized evil activity can be read as the 'works of Beliar'. Likewise, the future evil behaviour of Levi's sons is described as wandering astray, profaning the priesthood and defiling the sacrificial altars (16.1), setting aside the Law and the word of the prophets by their 'wicked perversity' (16.2), persecuting just men, hating the pious and regarding the word of the faithful with revulsion (16.2). The remaining *Testaments*, while not using the genitive term 'works

---

of Christian interpolations (there is a reference to the priest's baptism in the water, 18.6), but the (possibly anti-Jewish) reference to Israel as 'ignorant' and 'punished' goes unnoticed in the scholarship.

[51] Cf. Chapter 6 on Abraham 'seeing and rejoicing' for more detail on this text.
[52] Joseph A. Fitzmeyer, 'Qumran and the Interpolated Paragraph in 2 Cor 6.14-7.1', *CBQ* 23, no. 3 (1961), pp. 271–80; Stephen J. Hultgren, '2 Cor 6.14-7.1 and Rev 21.3-8: Evidence for the Ephesian Redaction of 2 Corinthians', *NTS* 49, no. 1 (2003), pp. 39–56. Jerome Murphy O'Connor prefers a Hellenistic Jewish influence, rather than an Essene thought-world, but this hypothesis is not completely convincing; idem, 'Philo and 2 Cor 6.14–7.1', *RevBib* 95, no. 1 (1988), pp. 55–69. Beliar/Belial (as the devil) is found in 1QS 1.18, 24; 11.5; CD 4.13, 15; *Jub.* 15.14. Otherwise, as we saw in Chapter 4, 'Mastema' is a favoured name for the devil. See Devorah Dimant, 'Between Qumran Sectarian and Non-Sectarian Texts: The Case of Belial and Mastema', in Devorah Dimant et al. (eds), *The Dead Sea Scrolls and Contemporary Culture* (Leiden: Brill, 2011), pp. 235–56.
[53] BDB., sv. בליאל
[54] Ibid.

of Beliar', also mention the evil figure in connection with such 'wicked deeds' as 'sexual promiscuity' (*T. Sim.* 5.3-4; *T. Judah* 18.1; *T. Dan* 5.6), or the 'temptations' of women, who are described in *T. Rueben* 6.3 as the very 'plague of Beliar'.

The dichotomy between the 'works' of Beliar and the 'works' of the Lord (i.e. the righteous commandments of the Torah) is drawn out in the *Testament of Benjamin* more explicitly. The wicked 'spirits of Beliar' are said to derange people, but Benjamin's sons are reassured that this will not be their fate (3.3). This is because the good man's plans cannot be overtaken by the 'deceitful spirit Beliar' (6.1). Benjamin warns his sons to flee from Beliar, as he leads to moral corruption, destruction, oppression, captivity, want, turmoil, desolation. Cain himself was handed over for punishment because he was subjected to Beliar. Abel condemned his brother for his 'evil deeds'; and those who are like Cain in corruption and hatred of their brother will be punished similarly (7.1-5). Benjamin enjoins his children instead to,

> Do the truth, each of you to his neighbour; keep the Law of the Lord and his commandments for I leave you these things instead of an inheritance. Give them, then, to your children for an eternal possession; this is what Abraham, Isaac and Jacob did. They gave us all these things as an inheritance, saying, 'Keep God's commandments until the Lord reveals his salvation to the nations.' (10.2-5)[55]

This text reconfigures the promise of inheritance (Land and covenant) made to the fathers (Abraham, Isaac and Jacob) in the Torah so that it becomes the intergenerational bestowal of the Torah itself (commandments, 'works of the Lord') as the inheritance. In the dualistic thought structure of the *T12P*, keeping the commandments of the Law is presented as the way of right living, and the alternative to doing the 'works of Beliar', which amount to sin, unrighteousness and consequent punishment.

In *Jubilees*, Abraham's righteous deeds, or 'works', receive mention in the context of his last testament. On his death bed, Abraham tells his grandson Jacob to 'do righteousness' and to do God's will. In this way, God will elect Jacob, and his 'seed' will become God's inheritance (22.10). Abraham enjoins Jacob to remember his 'words' and to 'keep the commandments of Abraham, your father' (22.16). Jacob is to separate himself from the Gentiles so that he does not perform 'deeds' like theirs (22.16). The 'deeds' of the Gentiles are 'defiled' and 'worthless' because they are rooted in idolatry (22.16b-18). The land, now called the 'house of Abraham', will be given to Jacob's 'seed' forever. Because Jacob is a 'son of Abraham', he will be saved from destruction and from 'the ways of error' leading to destruction, principally, idolatry (22.22-24).[56] What is unique about this text is its focus on the commandments *of Abraham* (not just the commandments of God) as objects of obedience and reverence. There is also a high level of consistency in *Jubilees*' presentation of Abraham's 'works' as exemplary because they betray no hint of idolatry. By contrast, the 'works' of the Gentiles are 'defiled' and

---

[55] *OTP I*, p. 828.
[56] Possibly a hint of favouritism here; cf. 'Abraham loved Jacob, but Isaac loved Esau' (*Jub.* 19.15). Pauline P. Buisch, 'The Absence and Influence of Genesis 48 (the Blessing of Ephraim and Manasseh) in the Book of Jubilees', *JSP* 24, no. 4 (2017), pp. 255–73, at p. 258; Segal, *The Book of Jubilees*, pp. 257–8.

are upheld as examples of idolatrous behaviour that Jacob and his seed must avoid if they are to be worthy of the house of Abraham.[57]

Human works are also spoken of in metaphorical language in the apocryphal and pseudepigraphical literatures. A well-known example is that of the virtuous person holding a 'treasury' of good works, a storehouse of credit with God. When misperceived, this 'economic' soteriology – if we could call it that – has looked to many critics of post-biblical Judaism like small-minded legalism.[58] While the caricatures of Strack and Billerbeck no longer hold hegemonic sway in the scholarship, it remains to be said that the dynamic, transactional way in which sin and merit were understood to function in antiquity are perhaps not fully appreciated.[59] The text of *4 Ezra* is a case in point. When Ezra asks God about the last judgement, he is told, 'I will show you that also, but do not include yourself with those who have shown scorn, or number yourself among those who are tormented. For you have *a treasure of works* stored up with the Most High' (7.[76]-[78]).[60] 'Scorning' the Law of God is the worst display of scorn possible, but Ezra observed the law, and so has a 'reward laid up' for 'trust[ing] the *covenant* of the Most High' (7.83). Yet, this does not mean Ezra presented as self-righteous or perfect (cf. 8.47-50); he trusted, and he persisted, but perfection was not required of him.[61]

Ezra's self-awareness leads him to intercede for sinners, for those 'who are deemed worse than wild animals', for 'we and our ancestors have passed our lives in ways that bring death'. Ezra calls upon God's reputation:

> For if you have desired to have pity on us, who have *no works of righteousness*, then you will be called merciful. For the righteous, who have many *works laid up* with you, shall receive their reward in consequence of *their own deeds*. But what are mortals, that you are angry with them; or what is a corruptible race, that you are so bitter against it? ... For in truth there is no one among those who have been born who has not acted wickedly; among those who have existed there is no one who has not done wrong. For in this, O Lord, your righteousness and goodness will be declared, when you are merciful to those *who have no store (repositus) of good works*. (8.30-36)

This text illustrates that the 'works' stored up in heavenly treasuries are 'works of righteousness' or 'deeds of righteousness', effective as a consequence of one's own behaviour. However, *4 Ezra* does not set 'faith' in opposition to 'works': there are those who 'stored up treasures of faith' too (6.5), and there are those who will be protected from peril because they will 'have works and faith before the Almighty' (9.7-8).[62] The

---

[57] Cf. van Ruiten, *Abraham in the Book of Jubilees*, p. 307.
[58] E. P. Sanders, *Comparing Judaism and Christianity: Common Judaism, Paul and the Inner and Outer in the Study of Religion* (Minneapolis: Fortress Press, 2016), p. 386.
[59] Bar the excellent work of Anderson, *Sin*, in the tradition of Sanders.
[60] *OTP I*, p. 539.
[61] deSilva, 'Grace, the Law and Justification', p. 36; similarly, Francis Watson, *Paul and the Hermeneutics of Faith* (2nd edn; London: T&T Clark/Bloomsbury, 2016), p. 456.
[62] deSilva, 'Grace, the Law and Justification', p. 39. Cf. a similar argument in Hogan, *Theologies in Conflict in 4 Ezra*, pp. 12–13. Stone, *Fourth Ezra*, p. 296, perceives a 'both/and' synthesis here, such that 'faith' is itself a 'work'.

'righteous' are those who have good deeds laid up with God; but sinners who have no such store of righteous works must rely on God's mercy. Ezra's point is that no one can claim to *not* have acted wickedly at some point, and that God's wonderful mercy is displayed by the fact that he has mercy on those who have not earned it.[63]

In other apocryphal texts, the 'heavenly treasury' plays upon the economic metaphor of 'crediting' good works to one's 'account' to hedge against the possibility of leaner times due to the 'debt' of sin. For Ezra, those who honoured and observed – and did not scorn – God's law, had their 'works' stored up in God's treasury (cf. also *Sir.* 35.1-2). For Tobit, however, one concrete commandment – that of giving alms to the poor – facilitates the accumulation of 'treasure in heaven'. Very much like the 'ten talents of silver Tobit has entrusted to a cousin, namely, to save one from future predicament or to secure oneself against the day of necessity', almsgiving wipes away all sin (*Tob.* 12.9; cf. 4.11) and 'helps in the accrual of merit and credit in this heavenly account'.[64] In the view of Tobit, almsgiving has the power to deliver a person from death (4.10; cf. Prov. 10.2); the recipient of alms functioned as a kind of 'direct conduit to heaven'.[65] Alms are a 'gift' made to God, much like the Temple offerings of old.[66] By placing 'a deposit in the hands of the needy', a person can 'balance one's ... account' so to speak, and atone for sins.[67] To reiterate: this 'economic' or 'transactional' mentality is not about self-interested legalism – it illustrates the ancient view of the nature of things. As Gary Anderson summarizes it, the concept of a 'treasury in heaven is about metaphysics more than morality'.[68]

Finally, the post-biblical Jewish literature uses the genitive of 'works' to refer to the behaviour or deeds of 'the fathers' – whether one's immediate genealogical ancestors, or more broadly, the three fathers Abraham, Isaac and Jacob. The Hebrew of *Sir.* 3.14 reads,

צדקת אב לא תמחה ... ביום צרה תזכר לך כחם על כפור להשבית עוניך

Kindness/righteousness to a father will not be blotted out;[69]
It will be as a sin offering (lit. substitute for sin), it will take root;
In a day of trouble, it will be remembered to you,
As warmth upon frost, it will melt away your sins.[70]

---

[63] Meira Z. Kensky, *Trying Man, Trying God: The Divine Courtroom in Early Jewish and Christian Literature* (WUNT 2/289; Tübingen: Mohr Siebeck, 2010), p. 154. Cf. Gathercole, *Where is Boasting?*, p. 137: 'The negativism of 4 Ezra has, in my opinion, been overplayed'.
[64] Macatangay, *The Wisdom Instructions in the Book of Tobit*, p. 249.
[65] Anderson, *Sin*, p. 149.
[66] Ibid.
[67] Ibid., p. 49.
[68] Anderson, *Charity*, p. 108.
[69] MS C reads, 'will not be forgotten' (על תשח, followed by Greek I and the Syriac versions). See Jeremy Corley, 'An Alternative Hebrew Form of Ben Sira: The Anthological Manuscript C', in Jean-Sébastien Rey and Jan Joosten (eds), *The Texts and Versions of the Book of Ben Sira: Transmission and Interpretation* (Leiden/Boston: Brill, 2011), pp. 3–22.
[70] MS A. Following in part, Ibolya Balla, *Ben Sira on Family, Gender, and Sexuality* (Berlin: Walter de Gruyter, 2011), p. 12.

In a highly perceptive article, Menahem Kister argues that this text should read: 'the righteousness *of your father* will not be wiped clean', and that righteousness here speaks of the merits accumulated by the father because of his good deeds.[71] Kister suggests that Ben Sira may be reversing Ps. 109.14: 'May the sin of his fathers be remembered before God and the iniquity of his mother not be wiped out'.[72] Kister comments that in the case of the psalm, 'the ancestors' iniquities are held against a person who is himself wicked', but that Ben Sira 'depicts the merits of ancestors as counteracting the iniquities of their descendants'.[73] This reading – certainly possible by the Hebrew grammar and syntax – would make the text of *Sir.* 3.14 one of the earliest explicit expressions of the (later rabbinic) doctrine of the זכות אבות, the 'merits of the fathers'.[74]

The Greek version of the text reads, 'For *alms* (ἐλεημοσύνη) towards a father will not be forgotten (οὐκ ἐπιλησθήσεται)', and 'instead of your sins, it will be credited (ἀντὶ ἁμαρτιῶν προσανοικοδομηθήσεταί σοι) in your favour; on a day of distress it will be remembered for you, as frost in good weather, your sins will be set free (ἀναλύω)'.[75] Although the Greek noun usually means 'mercy' or 'compassion', in the context of *Sirach* (3.14, 30; 7.10; 12.3; 16.14; 17.22; 29.8, 12; 31.11; 35.2) it acquires the specific meaning of 'almsgiving'.[76] Earlier in the Greek text (not preserved in Hebrew), Ben Sira speaks of 'atoning' for sins (ἐξιλάσκεται ἁμαρτίας) by honouring one's father (3.3-4), and of 'storing up treasures/riches' (ἀποθησαυρίζων) by glorifying one's mother (3.4).[77] Later in Sirach, keeping the Torah is likened to a 'peace-offering' in the Temple (*Sir.* 35.1). These contextual frames show how צדקת (works of righteousness) to one's father (or *of* one's father) – or, if you like, of 'almsgiving to one's father' – function like sin-offerings, wiping away the sin of the son, atoning for guilt and storing up treasure/credit with God to offset 'debt'.

These differences should not distract us from the fact that both the Hebrew and Greek manuscripts of *Sir.* 3.14-15 assume the reality and efficacy of intergenerational merit through good works. In the Greek (GI), the idea is that if a son performs works of kindness (almsgiving) towards his father in his old age, the son's works will be 'credited to him' against his own sins. In the Hebrew (MS. A), the idea is that the father's works of righteousness will be like a sin offering benefitting his son, which God will remember for the sake of his son. If we unpack the latter idea, we see that the father's righteousness (an attribute) stands for the thing it effects (merit); this metonymy was evident in the HB when צדקת was used in specific contexts, and also in *4 Ezra*. But

---

[71] Kister, 'Romans 5.12-21', pp. 391–424, at p. 394.
[72] Ibid.
[73] Ibid.
[74] Ibid., pp. 394–5. However, Kister's interpretation is hampered by the previous context: *Sir.* 3.12-13 speaks of the concrete acts of kindness a son can do towards his father (such as keeping him company in old age, and not despising him if his mind fails), not the enduring righteous works of the father himself.
[75] Greek I. Cf. the discussion in Kyoung-Shik Kim, *God Will Judge Each One According to Works: Judgement According to Works and Psalm 62 in Early Judaism and the New Testament* (Berlin: Walter de Gruyter, 2011), p. 87. The future passive is ἀναλυθήσονταί, but I have included the indicative active form to better draw attention to the λύω part of the verb, which carries the sense of loosening (of a bond), fitting in with the metaphor of sin being conceived as a 'debt-bondage'.
[76] Ibid., p. 87.
[77] Balla, *Ben Sira on Family*, p. 14.

whereas in the HB we saw 'righteousness' signify 'works', here we see 'righteousness' signifying 'works', and 'works' signifying 'merit'. This scaffolding of meaning is complexly mirrored in the Hebrew as well, as the roots צדק and זכר would overlap with זכי in Mishnaic Hebrew. That is, God's remembrance of the fathers' righteousness is a remembrance (or 'crediting') of the fathers' 'works' – and their 'works' are their 'merits', which wipe clean the sins of their descendants (their 'seed'). The texts analysed here are stepping stones in this development and are important to keep in mind for an intertextual reading of John 8.

Apart from the 'works' of one's biological father(s), there was also the idea of the 'works of the fathers' – that is Abraham, Isaac and Jacob – emerging in the Second Temple Period. In Mattathias' last testament (*1 Macc.* 2.50-52), he urges his children to

> Show zeal for the law (ζηλώσατε τῷ νόμῳ), and give your lives for the covenant of our fathers (διαθήκης πατέρων ἡμῶν) ... remember the *works of the fathers*, (τὰ ἔργα τῶν πατέρων) which they did in their generations; and you will receive great honour and an everlasting name. Was not Abraham found faithful when tested, and it was reckoned to him as righteousness? (ἐλογίσθη αὐτῷ εἰς δικαιοσύνην).[78]

This text draws together the 'testing' of Abraham at the Akedah (Genesis 22), and the imputation of righteousness to Abraham (Gen. 15.6). While the original text of Gen. 15.6 explains Abraham's *belief* in God as the reason for his imputed righteousness, in the speech of Mattathias, it is Abraham's fidelity when tested that is the underlying cause. Reconfigured in Mattathias' testament, the conflation of traditions bolsters the Maccabean cause in remaining faithful to the commandments of the covenant while tested to the point of death.[79] It is not only Abraham's example that is called upon as worthy of remembrance here, but *all* the 'deeds of the ancestors/the works of our fathers'. Moreover, 'zeal' for the Torah is presented as comparable to martyrdom for the sake of the covenant. Mattathias' concern that his sons 'remember' the works of the fathers is clearly meant to impress upon them the need to *do* the works of their fathers, to be like Abraham in faithfulness, when he faced the threat of the death of his son. In this way should they also be ready for martyrdom in the spirit of Abraham.[80]

---

[78] LXX (Rahlfs, rev. ed. Hanhart).
[79] For the growing literature on *1 Macc.* 2, see R. Egger-Wenzel, 'The Testament of Mattathias to His Sons in 1 Macc 2.49-70: A Keyword Composition with the Aim of Justification', in N. Calduch-Benages and J. Leisen (eds), *History and Identity: How Israel's Later Authors Viewed Its Earlier History* (Berlin: Walter de Gruyter, 2006), pp. 141-9; T. Hieke, 'The Role of "Scripture" in the Last Words of Mattathias (1 Macc 2.49-70)', in G. G. Xeravits and J. Zsengellér (eds), *The Books of Maccabees: History, Theology, Ideology* (JSJSup 118; Leiden: Brill, 2007), pp. 61-74; Christian M. M. Brady, 'What Shall We Remember, the Deeds of the Faith of Our Ancestors? A Comparison of 1 Maccabees 2 and Hebrews 11', in Alan J. Avery-Peck, Craig A. Evans and Jacob Neusner (eds), *Earliest Christianity within the Boundaries of Judaism* (Leiden/Boston: Brill, 2016), pp. 107-19.
[80] It is also worth noting that the twin phrases 'covenant of our fathers' and 'works of our fathers' are closely connected in the Tannaitic literature. To my knowledge, *1 Macc.* 2.49-52 is the only pre-rabbinic Jewish text using these concepts together.

Josephus and Philo

Much like the HB's range of referents for the term 'works', the use of 'works' (τὰ ἔργα) as a possessive genitive in Josephus spans various usages. When 'works' is predicated of God, the term typically means the wondrous miracles or favours that God produced on behalf of his people: the kindness of God to Jacob (*AJ* 2.7.1) or the miracles that God worked for the Israelites during their wandering in the desert (*AJ* 3.1.4).[81] God's 'works' exist to demonstrate proofs or legitimate claims; for example, Moses is presented as pleading with the people to hear him for the sake of God's works (*AJ* 3.5.3) and in refuting Gentile claims against the Jewish God, Josephus argues that God is manifest in all his 'works' (*C. Ap.* 2.23 [190, 192]).[82]

When predicated of human beings, the term 'works' is used by Josephus to signify corrupt or sinful behaviour especially as it tends towards violent ends. Discussing the factions in Jerusalem and their behaviour leading up to the destruction of the Temple, Josephus speaks of the 'barbarous' Sicarii who instigated transgressions in the city (*BJ* 7.8.1), becoming robbers and murderers among the festival crowds (*AJ* 20.8.6).[83] Josephus comments: 'These works, that were done by the robbers, filled the city with all sorts of impiety. And now these impostors and deceivers persuaded the multitude to follow them into the wilderness, and pretended that they would exhibit manifest wonders and signs, that should be performed by the providence of God' (*AJ* 20.8.6).

There is an idiosyncratic usage of 'works' in Josephus – a subjective genitive, signifying the behaviour of a biblical figure – whether good or bad. It is the commendable behaviour (the 'works') of the respective biblical figure that is described as being imitated by someone else. For example, Josephus expands upon the narrative of Kings Jehoshaphat and Asa to derive a lesson about how God loves 'good men' but destroys the wicked. In Josephus' view, Jehoshaphat imitated the 'works of David' who set an example for others by his piety and courage:

> Now by these events we may learn what concern God has for the affairs of mankind, and how he loves good men, and hates the wicked, and destroys them root and branch: for many of these kings of Israel, they and their families, were miserably destroyed, and taken away one by another, in a short time for their transgression and wickedness; but Asa, who was king of Jerusalem, and of the two tribes, attained, by God's blessing, a long and blessed old age, for his piety and righteousness, and died happily, when he had reigned forty and one years. And when he was dead, his son Jehoshaphat succeeded him in the government. He was born of Asa's wife Azubah. And all men allowed that *he followed the works of David his forefather*, and this both in courage and piety. (*AJ* 8.12.6)[84]

---

[81] Josephus, *Jewish Antiquities, Volume I: Books 1-3* (trans. Ralph Marcus; LCL 242; Cambridge: Harvard University Press, 1943).
[82] Josephus, *Against Apion* (trans. H. St. J. Thackeray; LCL 186; Cambridge: Harvard University Press, 1926), pp. 292–412.
[83] Josephus, *The Jewish War, Volume III: Books 5-7* (trans. H. St. J. Thackeray; LCL 210; Cambridge: Harvard University Press, 1928), pp. 306–436; Josephus, *Jewish Antiquities, Volume IX: Book 20* (LCL 365; 1943).
[84] Josephus, *Jewish Antiquities, Volume III: Books 7-8* (LCL 281; 1934).

In this text, the 'works of David' are his moral qualities, as well as the activities he undertook that made these qualities manifest: courage and piety. Josephus explains the exemplarity of David, Jehoshaphat and Asa as blessed, the latter for his 'piety and righteousness'.[85] Other wicked kings were not blessed, but rather, were 'destroyed root and branch'. Just prior to this text, Josephus provides an example of King Omri, who became wicked and turned others away from God; Omri's death, and the death of his family, is Josephus' evidence of God's hatred for the wicked (*Ant.* 8.12.16 [312-14]). Therefore, the (good) 'works of David' are to be understood in the same contextual frame as the 'righteousness' of Asa. Josephus' use of the phrase 'the works of David' can be read as a strong parallel to John's use of the phrase 'the works of Abraham' (John 8.39); both figures are described as ancestral in the respective texts and the exemplarity and goodness of their respective 'works' are strongly implied. In Josephus' text the 'works of David' are contrasted with the behaviour and fate of Omri. Thus, Josephus' reference to David's 'works' may allusively play on Mic. 6.16 which speaks of 'Omri's works' and the 'house of Ahab' in negative terms.[86]

We see a similar use of 'the works of ...' (a person), also in Josephus' discussion of King Amon of Judah (2 Kgs 21.19-24). The HB introduces Amon by summarizing his behaviour: 'He did evil in the eyes of the Lord, as his father Manasseh had done. He followed completely the ways of his father (MT: וילך בכל־הדרך אשר־הלך אביו ויעבד LXX v. 21: ἐπορεύθη ἐν πάσῃ ὁδῷ, ᾗ ἐπορεύθη ὁ πατὴρ αὐτοῦ), worshipping the idols his father had worshipped'. Josephus changes the language slightly to say that 'Amon *imitated those works of his father* which he insolently did when he was young: so he had a conspiracy made against him by his own servants, and was slain in his own house, when he had lived twenty-four years, and of them had reigned two' (*Ant.* 10.4.1 [47]).[87] Josephus envisages the 'works' of a person – whether good or evil – as the whole sum and tenor of one's habitual behaviour and life achievements. The phrase is not meant to denote one singular activity that was later emulated by another; the plural 'works' is a holistic signifier of the person's moral direction in life – in this case, whether the king followed the commandments of God or forsook the 'God of his ancestors' to worship idols (cf. 2 Kgs 21.22).

The texts of Philo demonstrate a range of meaning for the term 'works' (usually τὰ ἔργα). Like the biblical precedents, Philo uses 'works' to denote the product of human handicraft or artwork (*Op.* 2.10; 49.141; *Mos.* 1.7.38; *Spec. Leg.* 1.6.33; *Leg. All.* 2.8.26; 2.18.75; *Post.* 42.141).[88] Philo also talks about the commandment to refrain

---

[85] In Josephus' work, David is a non-messianic figure whose heroic virtues, as narrated in the biblical material, are generally greatly enhanced. Louis H. Feldman, 'Josephus' Portrait of David', *HUCA* 60 (1989), pp. 129–74. On David's bravery, see pp. 140–1.

[86] Note that Josephus' paralleling of 'righteousness' and 'works' in this passage further demonstrates the metonymic potential of these words.

[87] For the trope of imitation in Josephus' narration of the Kings and Chronistic history, see Christopher Begg, 'Jotham and Amon: Two Minor Kings of Judah According to Josephus', *BBR* 6 (1996), pp. 1–13, at p. 11.

[88] F. H. Colson and G. H. Whitaker, *Philo* (Greek and English text), (10 vols.; Cambridge: Harvard University Press, 1929–1962). Philo, *On the Account of the World's Creation* (Vol. 1, LCL 226; 1929), pp. 6–139; Philo, *On Moses (1 and 2)* (Vol. 6, LCL 289; 1935), pp. 276–596; Philo, *On the Special Laws* (4 vols. LCL 320 (Books 1–3), 341 (Book 4), 1937–1939); Philo, *Allegorical Interpretation of*

from 'works' on the Sabbath – those activities 'which are done in the seeking after and providing of the means of life' (*Op.* 43.128). He frequently uses the term 'works' to describe the creative activity of God (*Op.* 52.149; *Leg. All.* 1.6.16; 1.15.48; 3.2.4; *Quod. Deus.* 7.34; 17.78; 23.106; *Plant.* 30.128), the contemplation of which leads to knowledge of the Creator (*Praem.* 7.43; *Aet.* 8.41).[89] In this category, we would also place Philo's reference to the 'works of nature' (*Quod. Omn.* 11.74; *Aet.* 11.58).[90] As in the Bible, there is also the use of the term 'works' to describe God's miraculous and mighty activities in the world (*Post.* 48.167; *Mos.* 2.46.[257]), especially in the Israelites' redemption from Egypt (*Spec. Leg.* 2.35.218).

Like the biblical texts and the passages from Josephus, Philo uses 'works' in its genitive constructs to describe human behaviour. There are many 'works of wickedness' (*Leg. All.* 2.17.68) present in human society. Morally objectionable behaviours, such as corruption, bribery, rapine, premeditated murder, 'works of insolence' and acts of violence, are several such examples (*Spec. Leg.* 1.37.204). But wickedness begins with folly, or the absence of wisdom: in undertaking 'the works which are contrary to nature', a person enters the 'region of wickedness' (*Conf.* 15.68).[91] Philo equates 'works of wickedness' with 'transgression of the law', both of which were actively countered by Phinehas (*Mos.* 1.55.301).

Uniquely for Philo, wicked works are not confined to the sinful activities of humans as they transgress the commandments or the 'natural law' written in their conscience. Human labour upon the earth, the 'works of our hands' from which we desire rest, is an expression of injustice which the birth of the righteous Noah was to counteract (*Quaest in Gn.* 1.87).[92] According to Philo, God is not the cause of evils, but 'our own hands'; the 'figurative expression, the works of our hand' represents the human inclination to evil, which occurs when our minds turn towards baseness (*Det.* 32.119; 120; 121; 122). Just like the impious Cain, we then prefer wicked works over virtue. However, Noah signifies the participation of the mind in righteousness and virtue (*Quaest in Gn.* 1.87). Cain's example in fact illustrates the lesson that we ought to speedily pursue 'good works' and not delay (*Sac.* 13.52).[93] Cain's thoughts of impiety led ineluctably to his murderous 'works' (*Post.* 11.38). Conversely, human 'works of virtue' are like the 'works of God' (*Det.* 33.125).

Finally, as was common in ancient Greek literature, Philo contrasts 'works' with 'words'.[94] That is, 'works' possess a type of sincerity that empty promises cannot match:

Genesis 2 and 3 (Vol. 1, LCL 226; 1929), pp. 146–219, 224–94, 300–474; Philo, *On the Posterity of Cain and His Exile* (Vol. 2, LCL 227; 1929), pp. 328–442.

[89] Philo, *On the Unchangeableness of God* (Vol. 3, LCL 247; 1930), pp. 10–103; Philo, *Concerning Noah's Work as Planter* (Vol. 3, LCL 247; 1930), pp. 212–307; Philo, *On Rewards and Punishments* (Vol. 8, LCL 314; 1939), pp. 312–424; Philo, *On the Eternity of the World* (Vol. 9, LCL 363; 1941), pp. 184–294.

[90] Philo, *Every Good Man is Free* (Vol. 9, LCL 363; 1941), pp. 10–103.

[91] Philo, *On the Confusion of Tongues* (Vol. 4, LCL 261; 1932), pp. 8–122.

[92] Philo, *Questions on Genesis* (trans. Ralph Marcus; vol. 10; LCL 380; Cambridge: Harvard University Press, 1953).

[93] Philo, *That the Worse is Wont to Attack the Better* (Vol. 2; LCL 227; 1929), pp. 202–322; Philo, *On the Birth of Abel* (Vol. 2, LCL 227; 1929), pp. 94–197.

[94] See Bruce W. Winter, *Philo and Paul among the Sophists* (SNTSMS 96; Cambridge: Cambridge University Press, 1997); Jutta Leonhardt, *Jewish Worship in Philo of Alexandria* (TSAJ 84; Tübingen: Mohr Siebeck, 2001), pp. 27, 70, 176.

in the case of a thief desiring pardon, the measure of his repentance will become evident by his works of reparation (by returning what he has stolen) rather than by his words (*Leg. All.* 1.43.36). Demonstrating the truth of God's providence is likewise more convincing when done by 'works' than 'words' (*Praem.* 4.23). The ideal of perfection can be found in a soul when it attains virtue in both words and works, and when these perfectly align (*Quaest in Gn.* 3.32).[95]

The Dead Sea Scrolls

The Qumran document known as 4QMMT is one of only a few epistles discovered in the Judean desert.[96] It is also the only Jewish text from antiquity – apart from Paul's letters to the Galatians and Romans – to use the phrase [the] 'works of the law'.[97] Indeed, the proposed title of the document was derived from line C 26 (the epilogue) of the letter, *Miksat Ma-aseh ha-Torah* ('Some of the Works of the Law'). In 4QMMT, the author explains the *raison d'etre* of the Qumran community to his opponent, the 'Wicked Priest'.[98] To that end, he elaborates the halakhot grounding the community. But the tone of the halakhic content of the document is not as 'sectarian' as one might initially expect.[99] The laws enumerated in the letter appear to be addressed to Israel as a whole, which has inclined scholars to consider 4QMMT as pre-Qumranic and significantly earlier in date.[100]

---

[95] On the *topos* of 'speech and deeds' in Greco-Roman writings, see Alicia Myers, *Characterizing Jesus: A Rhetorical Analysis on the Fourth Gospel's Use of Scripture in Its Presentation of Jesus* (LNTS 458; London: T&T Clark, 2012), pp. 90–2; see also JoAnn Brant, *Dialogue and Drama: Elements of Greek Tragedy in the Fourth Gospel* (Peabody: Hendrickson, 2004), pp. 74–149.

[96] Elisha Qimron and John Strugnell et al., *Qumran Cave 4.V: Miqsat Ma'aseh Ha-Torah* (DJD 10; Oxford: Clarendon, 1994).

[97] This commonality explains why much of the bibliography on 4QMMT's phrase is discussed by way of Pauline theology. See Jacqueline C. R. De Roo, *Works of the Law at Qumran and in Paul* (Sheffield: Phoenix Press, 2007); Dunn, '4QMMT and Galatians', pp. 147–53; M. Abegg, 'Paul, Works of the Law, and the MMT', *BARev* 20, no. 6 (1994), pp. 52–5; idem, '4QMMT C 27, 31 and "Works Righteousness"', *DSS* 6, no. 2 (1999), pp. 139–47; N. T. Wright, '4QMMT and Paul: Justification, "Works" and Eschatology', in Aaron Son (ed.), *History and Exegesis: New Testament Essays in Honor of Dr. Earl Ellis for His 80th Birthday* (New York and London: T&T Clark, 2006), pp. 104–32; M. Bachmann, '4QMMT und Galaterbrief, מעשי התורה und ΕΡΓΑ ΝΟΜΟΥ', *ZNW* 89 (1998), pp. 91–113; Jean-Sébastien Rey (ed.), *The Dead Sea Scrolls and Pauline Literature* (Leiden: Brill, 2014).

[98] DJD 10, pp. 114, 119–20; cf. Hanne Von Weissenberg, *4QMMT: Reevaluating the Text, the Function, and the Meaning of the Epilogue* (STDJ 82; Leiden: Brill, 2009), p. 1. Yet, the content of the letter reads like a halakhic treatise, or a public letter from one group to another; idem, p. 10.

[99] Charlotte Hempel, 'The Laws of the Damascus Document and 4QMMT', in M. Baumgarten, E. G. Chazon and A. Pinnick (eds), *The Damascus Document: Centennial of the Discovery* (STDJ 34; Leiden: Brill, 2000), pp. 69–84, at pp. 70–1.

[100] Thus, Strugnell, 'MMT: Second Thoughts on A Forthcoming Edition', in E. Ulrich and J. C. VanderKam (eds), *The Community of the Renewed Covenant: The Notre Dame Symposium on the Dead Sea Scrolls* (Notre Dame: University of Notre Dame Press, 1994), pp. 57–73, at p. 68; Florentino Garcia Martinez, '4QMMT in a Qumran Context', in John Kampen and Moshe J. Bernstein (eds), *Reading 4QMMT: New Perspectives on Qumran Law and History* (Atlanta: Scholars Press, 1996), pp. 15–27, at p. 27. Cf. Weissenberg, *4QMMT*, p. 20. Yet this view is not uncontroverted: see recently Lutz Doering, *Ancient Jewish Letters and the Beginnings of Christian Epistolography* (WUNT 2.298; Tübingen: Mohr Siebeck, 2012), pp. 194–210.

The phrase 'works of the law' occurs in sections 4Q397 (MMT^d) and 398 (MMT^e) in the final section of the composite text.[101] The author writes,

> We have sent you some of the works of the Torah (מקסת מעשי התורה), according to our decision, for your welfare and the welfare of your people. For we have seen that you have wisdom and knowledge of the Torah. Consider all these things and ask Him that He strengthen your will and keep far from you the plans of the evil and the counsel of Belial, so that you may rejoice at the end of time, finding that some of our words are correct. And it will be reckoned to you as justice/righteousness (ונחשבה לך לצדקה) since you will be doing what is righteous and good in His eyes, for your own welfare and for the welfare of Israel. (C 25-32)[102]

Earlier in the document, the writer encourages his recipient to

> remember the kings of Israel and reflect on their works (מעשיך), how whoever of them who respected the Torah was freed from afflictions; and those were seekers of the Torah forgiven their sins. Remember David who was a man of the pious ones and he too was freed from many afflictions and was forgiven. (C 23-26)[103]

In MS B (1-2), the fragmentary text reads, 'These are some of our regulations/words (אלה מקסת דברינו) [...] which [...] [....] [the] works (המעשים) which we...'.[104] This fragment shows how the phrase 'works of the law' found shorthand expression in 'our words' and in '[our] works'. What were these regulations, these select 'works of the Law', that the Qumranites espoused?[105] The document contains more than eighty lines of halakhic rulings (דברינו) or the leaders (B 1-82), which are then taken up in the reference to the מעשי התורה in C 27.[106] The list of rulings deals with ritual purity concerns, such as how to properly dispose of animal foetuses, how to contain and handle streams of liquids and so forth; they relate also to the priesthood, and to sacrifices in the Temple. Wright argues that these 'rulings' are like halakhah in that they 'go beyond anything written in the Torah, and serve to define one group of Jews over against all others'.[107]

These 'rulings' are not called 'halakhot' הלכות but מעשים (B 2) and מעשי התורה (C 27). Qimron and Strugnell propose that the antecedent for this usage is found in the HB, where the singular מעשי is used 'to refer to the Law in general', as for example, in

---

[101] On the composite nature of the document based on the six discovered manuscripts, see von Weissenberg, *4QMMT*, pp. 25–6, 31–102. On the resumptive epilogue at C 25-32, see Lutz Doering, '4QMMT and the Letters of Paul: Selected Aspects of Mutual Illumination', in Rey (ed.), *The Dead Sea Scrolls and Pauline Literature*, pp. 69–88, at p. 80.
[102] DJD 10, p. 61; modified Qimron's translation slightly.
[103] DJD 10. Cf. John 8.32.
[104] DJD 10.
[105] The modifier מקסת can be translated as 'selected' or 'pertinent', as well as 'some'. Cf. Abegg, 'Paul, Works of the Law, and the MMT', pp. 141–2.
[106] DJD X, p. 187.
[107] Wright, '4QMMT and Paul', p. 18; cf. Dunn, '4QMMT and Galatians', p. 343. While I think the first part of Wright's assessment is accurate, I take issue with the second part of his sentence.

Exod. 18.20 ('teach them ... the law (מעשי) that they must perform').[108] They comment, 'It is only from the Second Temple period and onwards, however, that we find widespread use of the plural מעשים as a term specifically designating the laws of commandments of the Bible'.[109] Our foregoing analysis confirms this observation; however, the Qumranites use the plural construct form to denote additional laws – which are extensions and interpretations of the Mosaic Torah. And yet, like the rabbis, the Qumranites do not appear to distinguish – at an essentialist, authoritative level – between the written Mosaic Torah and the derived 'rulings'. In other words, these are self-reinforcing and coherent 'laws'.[110]

Another passage in part C (11-18) conveys a motif that should by this point be familiar to us from the pseudepigraphical writings – namely, the future predictions of Israel's waywardness and calamity, at the end of times:

> And in the book (of Moses) it is written ... that [you will stray] from the path (of the Torah) and that calamity will meet [you]. And it is written 'and it shall come to pass, when all these things [be]fall you', at the end of days, the blessings and the curses, ['then you will take] it to hea[rt] and you will return unto Him with all your heart and with all your soul', at the end [of time, so that you may live ... ...] [It is written in the book] of Moses [and in the books of the Prophets] that there will come [...] [the blessings have (already) befallen in ...] in the days of Solomon the son of David. And the curses [that] have (already) befallen from the days of Jeroboam the son of Nebat and up to when Jerusalem and Zedekiah King of Judah went into captivity.[111]

The scriptural and eschatological character of this text is also often acknowledged in the scholarship. Along with the Deuteronomic 'blessing' and 'curses' (cf. Deuteronomy 27), we also find an allusion to the Sh'ma (Deut. 6.10ff.: 'you shall love the Lord your God with all your heart, with all your soul'). In 4QMMT C 11-14, the Sh'ma is repurposed to fit the author's vision of the end times, when his audience will *return* to the Lord with all their heart and soul, and so fully 'live' (cf. also Deut. 30.30). Despite the author's articulation of the community's separateness, it is necessary to note that the language is not divisive. Indeed, the agreeable tone of the epilogue suggests that 'the ultimate purpose of 4QMMT is persuasion, not division, despite the articulation of ritual differences'.[112]

---

[108] DJD X, p. 139.
[109] Ibid.
[110] Cf. Michael Fishbane, 'Use, Authority and Interpretation of Mikra at Qumran', in Martin Jan Mulder (ed.), *Mikra: Text, Translation, Reading and Interpretation of the Hebrew Bible in Ancient Judaism and Early Christianity* (CRINT 1; Assen: Van Gorcum, 1988), pp. 339-77, at pp. 356-7.
[111] 4QMMT C 11-22, DJD 10, pp. 59-61.
[112] Bruce McComiskey, 'Laws, Works, and the End of Days: Rhetorics of Identification, Distinction, and Persuasion in Miqsat Ma'aseh ha-Torah (Dead Sea Scroll 4QMMT)', *Rhetoric Review* 29, no. 3 (2010), pp. 221-38, at p. 233. We should be cautious, therefore, in harmonizing 4QMMT with Galatians so that the former supports the interpretation of the latter. Contra, Dunn, '4QMMT and Galatians'.

Scholars have produced various translations and interpretations of the phrase מעשי התורה as Dunn has noted.[113] But what does the phrase mean? NT heavyweights like Dunn and Wright popularized the view that it means narrowly, Jewish rituals such as circumcision, *kashrut* and Sabbath (which helped to endorse their protective reading of Paul), but the scholarly tide is turning to interpret מעשי התורה as the observance of *all* of the Torah. Looking at 4Q174.1.7 where 'works of the law' equates to spiritual sacrifices, and CD 5.5b-6a where David's 'good works' are considered, De Roo argues that מעשי התורה in 4QMMT C 27 refers to the works/deeds of the pious kings (emulating David) rather than to the ritual laws in section B.[114] Abegg also thinks the referent is broader than what Dunn suggests: while the phrase מעשי התורה does embody 'the claim that the group's interpretation of the Torah at disputed points was the correct and only legitimate' one, and that the phrase מעשי התורה 'refers to the written Torah as well as the community's interpretation' of the Torah, it is also 'most certain' that, following this, the word התורה 'as used in 4QMMT is broader than the restricted issues of circumcision, Sabbath observance, and food laws'.[115]

Both of these points need to be underscored. The terms 'works', 'our words' and 'the works of the law' are distributed across MMT B and MMT C, and are, moreover, reinforced by similar references in CD 19-20 to the 'commandments' and the observance of 'virtuous works'. It is reductionist to interpret מעשי התורה in 4QMMT C 27 as referring only to the eighty-plus halakhot in MMT B. The 'works' of the pious kings, such as David, which were grounded in their reverence for the Torah, set them *free* from their afflictions, and brought them forgiveness of *sins* (MMT C 23-26). The general and most important point I would take away from this is that 4QMMT uses מעשים as a shorthand for the 'works' – or the commandments and precepts – of the Torah. Those 'works' are ascribed to key biblical figures such as David, as a means of obtaining 'freedom' (equated with wiping clean one's iniquities). 'Works' then, are like almsgiving in *Tob.* 4.12 – they accumulate credit with God to release one from the bondage of sin. The 'works of David', we could say, are exemplary in this regard, and are also reflected in the 'truth' of the specific halakhot laid down by the community. By such 'works' will the recipients of the epistle be 'reckoned righteous' (ונחשבה לך לצדקה) in God's sight for doing what is 'right' – for everyone's benefit. As we saw in previous text analysed, the phrase 'to be reckoned [to someone] for righteousness' was used of Abraham in Gen. 15.6, and in *1 Macc.* 2.52. It was not for three specific 'laws' (*pace* Dunn: circumcision, *kashrut* and Sabbath) that Abraham, for example, was 'reckoned as righteous', but for his generally pious behaviour: his trust in God (Gen. 15.6) and his fidelity when tested (*1 Macc.* 2.52).[116] This accords with the Qumranites view of the virtuous kings in 4QMMT C, who were pious seekers of the Torah. It is this

---

[113] Dunn, '4QMMT and Galatians', p. 342. E.g. 'the precepts of the Torah', the 'observances of the Law', the 'works of the law'. Dunn himself prefers 'deeds' or 'acts' of the Torah, but such hair-splitting is barely justified because the noun is naturally polyvalent. 'Deeds' of the Torah *are* 'precepts/commandments' of the Torah, cf. CD 19.33-20.12.
[114] De Roo, *Works of the Law*, p. 97.
[115] Abegg, '4QMMT C 27, 31', pp. 141–2.
[116] *Pace*, Dunn, '4QMMT and Galatians', p. 343.

wholeheartedly devoted behaviour that the author encourages his recipient to adopt as the end of days approach (4QMMT C, 11-22).

The New Testament

As in the HB and post-biblical literature, the New Testament (NT) uses the term 'works' to signify human behaviour, human activity or the product of human labour.[117] This section of the chapter examines several examples in detail: (1) instances where 'works' are directly predicated of a named biblical figure (e.g. Jezebel in Rev. 2.20; Abraham in Jas. 2.21 and Rom. 4.4-8; as well as Rahab in Jas. 2.25); and (2) the concept of 'good/beautiful works' which can be broken down into subcategories: (a) positive acts of benevolence towards others in the traditions of the Pastoral and Deutero-Pauline epistles; (b) public testimonies that are visible in God's sight and receive a reward from on high, and their opposite, sinful works that attract divine judgement; and (c) actions and activities that accumulate a metaphorical 'treasure in heaven' benefitting both the doer of the works and his posterity; then (3) antonymic terms such as 'works of the flesh', 'evil works', 'dead works' or 'works of darkness' which refer to highly specific vices in early Christian communities; (4) an excursus on the Pauline concepts of 'justification by works' (as well as 'judgement by works'), and how the figure of Abraham is connected to these; (5) other voices in the NT, such as the author of the epistle of James, that protest against the Pauline soteriology and insist that 'works' have the power to 'justify'; and finally, an excursus on Paul's unique, anarthous phrase 'works of the law', and how it relates to the concept of 'works' (as a stand-alone) and back again to the idea of 'justification'. All of these usages contain nuances that build upon the figuration of Abraham analysed earlier in the chapter from the HB and other post-biblical literature. In many ways, we also see embryonic debates emerging in the NT that would find further expression in the Tannaitic literature especially around the idea of 'works'/'righteousness' as productive of merit (or indeed as metonymic for 'merit'), which had a vicarious benefit beyond the lifetime of the doer of 'works'. Before turning to the final intertextual material in the rabbinic literature, this chapter presents another brief excursus on Jewish traditions on Abraham's Torah observance (the 'works' of the commandments) that would feed into Tannaitic discussions of the particular 'works' of Abraham that produced certain specific merits for Israel in biblical history and up to their own day.

In the NT, human 'works' can be either commendable or reprehensible, and are always visible to God. In the book of Revelation, for example, Jesus – through 'John' as his scribal medium – tells the Ephesians that he 'knows' their 'works', their 'toil' and their 'patient endurance' (οἶδα τὰ ἔργα σου καὶ τὸν κόπον καὶ τὴν ὑπομονήν σου: 2.1-2).[118] Jesus commends the church in Philadelphia for their 'works' of fidelity (3.8),

---

[117] We also find references to the 'works of the Lord' (cf. 1 Cor. 15.58; 16.10; Phil. 2.30); the 'work of God' (Heb. 1.10; 4.3, 4; 6.10) or of Jesus (Matt. 11.2; Acts 13.41; Rev. 15.3; 22.12). As in the previous analyses in this chapter, I will concentrate on human 'works' as expressive of behaviour and activities.

[118] On the book of Revelation as a 'scribal apocalypse', see Garrick Allen, *The Book of Revelation and Early Jewish Textual Culture* (SNTSMS 168; Cambridge: Cambridge University Press, 2017), pp. 1–37.

and warmly praises the church at Thyatira for their 'works' – their 'love, faith, service, and patient endurance' (2.19). On the other hand, Jesus urges the Thyatirans to repent of the 'works' of Jezebel upon pain of death (2.22).[119] 'Jezebel' – here referred to as a false prophet (2.20a) – has infiltrated Thyatira and enticed Jesus' 'servants' away from his teaching and towards 'idols' (2.20).[120] All Jezebel's 'children' will be struck dead if there is no repentance (2.23). While 'Jezebel's' fate is sealed, there is still time for her followers (her 'children') to allay their suffering. The biblical portrait of Jezebel is a damning one: an idolatress whose prophets ministered to Baal (1 Kgs 18.19), she killed the Lord's prophets (1 Kgs 18.13; cf. 1 Kgs 21.5-16) and practised forms of sorcery (2 Kgs 9.22). She is depicted as adorning herself with clothing and makeup before her violent death at the hands of Jehu, where she is thrown to the ground from her bedroom window and trampled upon by horses and eaten by dogs (2 Kgs 9.30-37). This graphic scene is alluded to in Rev. 2.21-23 wherein Jezebel is 'thrown' upon a bed and her followers are 'thrown' into 'great distress'.[121]

Human 'works' need not be disgraceful in order to be considered negative: people's 'works' may be middling or indifferent, and thus 'imperfect' (Rev. 3.1-3, 15-16). Everyone will be judged on the basis of his or her 'works' – God will 'give to each according to his works' (δώσω ὑμῖν ἑκάστῳ κατὰ ἔργα ὑμῶν; Rev. 2.23; cf. Rom. 9.20). At the same time, repentance is always an option, albeit not one which everyone chooses: later in Revelation we read of the woeful situation of the world following the global destruction of the plagues, where the only remaining human survivors did not repent of the 'works of their hands', their demon worship and material idols, nor did they repent of their other serious sins (9.20-21).

A subcategory of human 'works' in the NT is 'good works' or 'beautiful works'.[122] One usage identifies women as specifically capable of undertaking 'good works' as

---

[119] In a recent study, Martin Stowasser has argued that certain formal and stylistic features of the seven letters indicate their place in two distinct groups. The letter to Thyatira closes the first 'group' of letters, Sardis is the 'hinge' letter and Laodicea the opening letter of the second group. Stowasser shows that as the letters progress they become less localized and more universal in their message and outlook. Thus, the references to Jezebel serve as a warning to those inclined to follow her beyond Thyatira, where other churches may be infiltrated by her 'children'. Cf. Stowasser, 'Die Sendschreiben der Offenbarung des Johannes: Literarische Gestaltung – Buchkompositorische Funktion – Textpragmatik', NTS 61, no. 1 (2015), pp. 50–66, at pp. 60, 63–5.

[120] 'Jezebel' – whether the code for a real historical teacher in the community, or a local heresy – apparently encouraged the community to eat food sacrificed to idols and beguiled the community to practise 'fornication'. The latter charge is probably symbolic of the community's turn to idols (apostasy), given the biblical context in which Jezebel appears; cf. Matthew Streett, Here Comes the Judge: Violent Pacifism in the Book of Revelation (LNTS, London: T&T Clark, 2012), pp. 50, 51.

[121] Much ink has been spilled guessing the historical identity of the churches in Revelations 2: see the surveys of the literature in David E. Aune, Revelation 1–5 (WBC 52A; Dallas: Word, 1997), pp. 188ff. and George R. Beasley-Murray, The Book of Revelation (NBC; rev. edn; Grand Rapids: Eerdmans, 1981), pp. 85–6. It is less crucial here to discern what Jezebel's heresy may have been (or who Jezebel represented in the churches) than to highlight the rhetorical dimensions of the discourse. Like Abraham in John 8.39-42, Jezebel – a biblical figure – has 'works' that others presume to follow, and by doing so, they are called her 'children'. Likewise, the figure of 'Balaam' in Pergamum (Rev. 2.14) has 'teachings' (τὴν διδαχὴν Βαλαάμ) that others follow (to their detriment).

[122] The pastoral Epistles display a consistent concern with 'good' or 'noble' works, which most scholars and commentators understand as a sign that 'faith' was – in the later imperial context – coming to be seen as something proven only by the quality of Christian ethical behaviour. Cf. Pieter G. R. de

a form of reverence to God (1 Tim. 2.10).[123] The ideal Christian widow should be renowned for 'good works' (ἔργων ἀγαθῶν); she ought to have brought up children (ἐτεκνοτρόφησεν), be adept at showing hospitality (ἐξενοδόχησεν), have washed others' feet (ἁγίων πόδας ἔνιψεν) and be someone who is ready to help the afflicted (θλιβομένοις ἐπήρκεσεν; 1 Tim. 5.10). These 'good works' are a set of highly specific, practical ethical behaviours.[124] In Acts 9.36, Luke presents the example of Dorcas, who is described as 'full of good works and acts of almsgiving' (αὕτη ἦν πλήρης ἔργων ἀγαθῶν καὶ ἐλεημοσυνῶν ὧν ἐποίει).[125] But women are not exclusively encouraged to perform good works. Paul encourages Titus to be a model of good works for his community (Tit. 2.7), even, indeed to be a 'zealot for good works' (ζηλωτὴν καλῶν ἔργων; Tit. 2.14).[126] Likewise, all 'those who have come to believe in God' are meant to devote themselves to 'good works' that meet the urgent needs of the community (Tit. 3.8, 14). For 'good works' to flourish, it is imperative that Christians encourage one another, which is a sign of love (Heb. 10.24).[127]

'Good works' are also a form of testimony: they make a public statement to those who witness them. In Matt. 5.16, Jesus encourages his disciples to display their 'good works' (ὑμῶν τὰ καλὰ ἔργα) before others so that God may be glorified.[128] Likewise, the author of 1 Timothy states that 'good works' are always visible to others; he contrasts 'good works' to 'sins', the latter of which can be equally conspicuous, but which always

---

Villiers, 'Heroes at Home: Identity, Ethos, and Ethics in 1 Timothy within the Context of the Pastoral Epistles', in Jan G. van der Watt (ed.), *Identity, Ethics, and Ethos in the New Testament* (Berlin: Walter de Gruyter, 2006), pp. 357–86; Travis B. Williams, *Good Works in 1 Peter: Negotiating Social Conflict and Christian Identity in the Greco-Roman World* (WUNT 337; Tübingen: Mohr Siebeck, 2014), pp. 158–9; Philip H. Towner, *The Letters to Timothy and Titus* (NICNT; Grand Rapids: Eerdmans, 2006), p. 212.

[123] Raymond Collins, *1 & 2 Timothy and Titus: A Commentary* (NTL; Louisville: WJK, 2nd edn, 2012), pp. 66–8, places this injunction within the world view of Greco-Roman virtue, especially the idealized 'modesty' and simple attire of a woman.

[124] The specificity of the good works in 1 Tim. 5.10 might suggest that Christian praxis was developing away from civic benefaction (as a strategy to negotiate the power of the Roman Empire) towards faith-based codes of social responsibility; cf. Williams, *Good Works in 1 Peter*, p. 159. However, one should not overlook the early Jewish emphases on Abraham's hospitality, and help towards the afflicted (cf. *T. Abr.* Rec. A), which was itself grounded in the biblical portrait of Abraham as one who washed the feet of his guests (Genesis 18).

[125] Recall that almsgiving (cf. Dan. 9.34, Tob. 10.12) was thought to embody *the* commandment of the Torah and to uniquely 'redeem' one's sins.

[126] Benjamin J. Lappenga, 'Zealots for Good Works: The Polemical Repercussions of the Word ζηλωτής in Titus 2.14', *CBQ* 75, no. 4 (2013), pp. 704–18. Lappenga argues that the use of the adverb reflects both 'Jewish' and 'Greek' usage, by which he means the Maccabean type of Torah piety, and the concern for emulation of virtue, respectively (see esp. pp. 712–13 and 715–16).

[127] The case of Heb. 10.24 differs from the pastorals by its generality – the term 'good works' could denote any and every act of kindness and charity. Cf. Williams, *Good Works in 1 Peter*, n. 32, p. 146. Yet the specificity of 'good works' in Hebrews' perspective is alluded to in other parts of the paranesis, for example in the author's commendation of his readers' 'compassion' for those 'in prison' and their capacity to endure harsh treatment (10.32-34). Cf. James W. Thompson, *Hebrews* (Paideia; Grand Rapids: Baker Academic, 2008), pp. 205–6.

[128] See Roland Dienes, *Die Gerechtigkeit der Tora im Reich des Messias: Mt 5,13-20 als Schlüsseltext der matthäischen Theologie* (WUNT 177; Tübingen: Mohr Siebeck, 2004), esp. pp. 237–54. Matthew's use here is most likely equivalent to the later rabbinic concept of מעשים טובים (=good works), which are always associated with Torah observance; cf. *b. Ber.* 17a). Cf. Craig S. Keener, *A Commentary on the Gospel of Matthew* (Grand Rapids: Eerdmans, 1999), p. 175.

lead to judgement. On the other hand, even if one tries to do 'good works' covertly, the works 'cannot remain hidden' (1 Tim. 5.25).[129] This suggests that (good) 'works' and 'sins' are contradistinctive: just as sins inevitably lead to judgement, good works lead their doers to salvation. Related to this understanding is the idea that 'good works' will receive a reward from God, while wicked behaviour will receive judgement: those who persevere in 'good works' (ὑπομονὴν ἔργου ἀγαθοῦ) receive eternal life (Rom. 2.6-7). In this case, 'good works' are defined as 'seeking glory and honour and immortality' (Rom. 2.7).[130]

'Good works' can also hold a metaphorical currency in the afterlife or in the future life of the person who does them. In this sense, 'works' are understood not only as activities that benefit others, but also as acts that lay up 'treasure' for the person undertaking them, thereby benefitting the doer of the works as well. Thus, a person can be rich in 'good works' (πλουτεῖν ἐν ἔργοις καλοῖς) and thereby 'store up treasure' for himself (ἀποθησαυρίζοντας ἑαυτοῖς) in the future. Such 'good works' are defined as being generous and willing to share (1 Tim. 6.18), as well as keeping 'the commandment' (τὴν ἐντολὴν i.e. almsgiving; 1 Tim. 6.14). The 'treasure' accumulated by the performance of good works functions as a kind of insurance against trouble, laying a 'good foundation' for the 'future' (εμέλιον καλὸν εἰς τὸ μέλλον).[131] Also, the kind of works that 'store up treasure in heaven' (Matt. 6.20) are described as almsgiving, prayer and fasting (Matt. 6.1-18); otherwise almsgiving alone is depicted as the work that stores up an 'unfailing treasure in heaven' (Luke 12.33).

Finally, the NT describes 'bad' or 'evil' works in colourful language. The author of the letter to the Hebrews calls for repentance from 'dead works' (νεκρῶν ἔργων; Heb. 6.1); similarly, he states that the 'blood of Christ' is able to purify one's conscience from 'dead works' to worship God (Heb. 9.14).[132] Similarly, Paul describes 'the works of darkness' (τὰ ἔργα τοῦ σκότους) as 'drunkenness, debauchery licentiousness,

---

[129] This important text illustrates how 'works' and 'sins' are contrasting entities: sins lead to judgement, works apparently lead to the opposite, salvation. The text reads 'The sins of some people are conspicuous and precede them to judgment, while the sins of others follow them there'. (Cf. Dan. 12.3; Matt. 5.16; 13.43). Also, compare the text of the *Testament of Abraham* analysed in Chapter 4: there, Abraham saw an angel moving a soul's 'sins' and 'works' around at the final judgement so that he could be balanced in favour of good works before God; in rabbinic literature, God takes on this compassionate role himself, shifting the balance of a person's sins and good works so that the person does not perish (*ARN*).

[130] Naturally, these verses have stumped Pauline scholars as they appear to contradict the Apostle's trademark thought of 'justification by faith' (not 'works'): K. R. Snodgrass, 'Justification by Grace – To the Doers: An Analysis of the Place of Romans 2 in the Theology of Paul', *NTS* 32 (1986), pp. 72-93 Consequently, James D. G. Dunn conveniently splits Paul's audience in two: in Rom. 2.7, 10 and 2.26-29, Paul refers to Christian Gentiles, but in ch. 2 vv. 14-15, he refers to pagan Gentiles. Idem, *Romans* (2 vols.; WBC; Dallas: Word, 1988), 1.86, 106-7, 122-5. Otherwise a common scholarly position is that Paul is only arguing hypothetically in Romans 2 – cf. Kim, *God Will Judge Each One*, p. 183.

[131] Thus, Nathan Eubank, 'Almsgiving the "the Commandment": A Note on 1 Timothy 6.6-19', *NTS* 58, no. 1 (2012), pp. 144-50; cf. Anderson, *Sin*, p. 174.

[132] Perhaps too facilely, James Swetnam calls these 'dead works' (Heb. 6.1, 9.14) 'works of the Law' in the legalistic sense, contrasting them with the 'good works' the author advocates in Heb. 10.24. J. Swetnam, 'Form and Content in Hebrews 7-13', *Bib* 55, no. 3 (1974), pp. 333-48. Closer to the mark is the assessment of Colijn that the 'dead works' refer to works of sin – see B. B. Colijn, 'Let Us Approach: Soteriology in the Epistle to the Hebrews', *JETS* 39 (1996), pp. 571-86.

quarrelling and jealousy' which are to be put aside in favour of the 'armour of light', meaning honourable living (Rom. 13.12-13). The 'works of darkness' include any activities undertaken in shameful secret (Eph. 5.11-12), and which were related to the pagans' past state of 'darkness' (5.8). There are also the 'works of the flesh' which Paul directly opposes to the 'fruit of the Spirit' (Gal. 5.19-21a). The 'works of the flesh' include 'fornication, impurity, licentiousness, idolatry, sorcery, enmities, strife, jealousy, anger, quarrels, dissensions, factions, envy, drunkenness, carousing' and the like (Gal. 5.19-21a). These 'works' exclude a person from the 'kingdom of God' (5.21b).

'According to works': Judgement

The idea that humans will be judged by God 'according to their works' (κατὰ ἔργα) is prevalent in the NT, and follows a trajectory of thought present in prior sources (cf. *Sir.* 16.12; *4 Ezra* 7.3; *1 Enoch* 63.8, etc.). The author of 2 Peter counsels his readers to patiently wait for the final judgement, the 'day of the Lord', when all the 'works (τὰ ἐν αὐτῇ ἔργα) [done] on the earth' will be disclosed. Given this fact, Peter's readership ought to live in holiness (3.9-11).[133] A similar text is found in 1 Cor. 3.13-15. Paul encourages the Corinthian community to continue their 'work' in the knowledge that the 'day of judgment' will disclose the value of each person's work on behalf of the church – the coming 'fire' will test the material of the 'work', revealing the value of its foundational composition.[134] Paul's later letter to the Corinthian community assures them that the fate of the troublesome 'false apostles' in their midst will be unenviable: they pretend to be 'ministers of righteousness' but 'their end will match their works' (τὸ τέλος ἔσται κατὰ ἔργα αὐτῶν; 2 Cor. 11.13-15). And in Rom. 2.4-8, Paul chastises his readers for not recognizing God's forbearance for sinners, as he delays the final judgement to make room for repentance (v. 4). God's 'righteous judgement' will be made evident when he 'repays each according to works' (ὃς ἀποδώσει ἑκάστῳ κατὰ ἔργα αὐτοῦ; 2.6). To those who go about 'doing good' God will give eternal life; to those who 'obey wickedness' God will bestow wrath and fury (2.8). There is therefore no partiality in God's judgement (2.9) – a concept based on the HB's portrayal of God as righteous judge.[135] As troubling as Rom. 2.6 is to many Pauline interpreters, his view of the finality of judgement by works is not anomalous in his corpus (cf. Col. 3.23-25).[136]

'According to works': Justification

The prepositional phrase κατὰ τὰ ἔργα is also used in the NT to denote (implicitly commendable) behaviour in the sight of God. That is, people are not only *judged* by God 'according to works' but are also *justified* by God 'according to works'. The latter idea is present most notably in the writings of Paul, even though he subverts

---

[133] Terrance Callan, 'The Soteriology of the Second Letter of Peter', *Bib* 82 (2001), pp. 549–9.
[134] Cf. Daniel Frayer-Griggs, *Saved Through Fire: The Fiery Ordeal in New Testament Eschatology* (Eugene: Pickwick, 2016), pp. 199–219.
[135] Cf. Kent L. Yinger, *Paul, Judaism, and Judgment According to Deeds* (Cambridge: Cambridge University Press, 1999), p. 263.
[136] Gathercole, *Where is Boasting?*, p. 130.

it, contends with it and eventually overturns it. Interrogating what Paul means by 'justification by faith' (i.e. not by 'works') is no small feat: the Pauline concept has produced a near-infinite ream of scholarship – and with good reason. 'Justification by faith' has been, and in some scholarly circles, continues to be, a lodestone of ideological and theological interpretation, a concept coloured by the legacy of Lutheranism and beyond.[137] A recent tome by Douglas Campbell (at an incredible 1,248 pages), for instance, attempts to cut through the intricacies and inconsistencies of both Paul's reasoning on 'justification' as it is expressed in Romans 1–8 alone, and the paradigms of interpretation surrounding it; even Campbell acknowledges that the task is akin to running a footrace with tangled, knotted shoelaces.[138]

Given that I have no wish to trip over what is already a congested and convoluted debate, I restrict my analysis of Paul to three spaces, connected by the figure of Abraham: the idea of 'justification by works', the idea of 'works' as a stand-alone concept (cf. Rom. 4.2, 6) and the idiomatic anarthrous 'works of the law' (e.g. Rom. 3.2, 28). The latter two terms are both used in the context of Paul's debate about 'justification'; I contend that 'works' is not conceptually distinct from 'works of the law', but is a shorthand expression for it, that 'works of the law' may well suggest Torah observance, and that 'justification by works' signifies right living in community, according to the commandments.[139]

The New Perspective on Paul's (NPP) refutation of the denigrating characterization of rabbinic/later Pharisaic Judaism found in previous scholarship is, of course, commendable; yet, in an effort to overcorrect the former biases, the NPP risks producing something equally worrying: an inaccurately conciliatory portrait of Paul that meets the exigencies of contemporary interfaith relations, but which belie the negative or pejorative aspects of Paul's thought. Those aspects *are* distinct from other

---

[137] The paradigmatic studies, inaugurating the so-called 'New Perspective on Paul' are: E. P. Sanders, *Paul and Palestinian Judaism: A Comparison of Patterns of Religion* (Minneapolis: Fortress, 1977); James D. G. Dunn, 'The New Perspective on Paul', *BJRL* 65 (1983), pp. 95–122 (to whom the phrase is attributed); N. T. Wright, *Paul: Fresh Perspectives* (Minneapolis: Fortress, 2005); Thomas R. Schreiner, *The Law and Its Fulfillment: A Pauline Theology of Law* (Grand Rapids: Baker Books, 1993). Other surveys of the key studies and tradents exist: for example Mark A. Seifrid, *Justification by Faith: The Origin and Development of a Central Pauline Theme* (Leiden: Brill, 1992). The implied 'old perspective' on Paul hinged on an uncritical 'legalistic' reading of Paul's criticisms, which reinforced anti-Jewish interpretations of his assumed opponents. Cf. Rudolf Bultmann's existentialist, even individualistic, interpretation; Bultmann, 'Die Bedeutung der Eschatologie für der Religion des neuen Testaments', *ZThK* 27 (1917), pp. 85–6, and in response, Ernst Käsemann, 'Gottesgerechtigkeit bei Paulus', in *Exegetische Versuche und Besinnungen* (2nd edn; Vol. 2; Göttingen: Vandenhoeck & Ruprecht, 1965), p. 184. I find these labels ('new perspective', 'old perspective', and now 'new, new perspective' or 'radical perspective' on Paul) too factious, none of them doing justice to Paul's complex thought in its totality. Moreover, the labels often obscure the ideologies often lurking beneath: if a scholar were to claim that Paul's polemic against the law is broad-brush and *not* restricted to ritual observances (as per the NPP), she risks appearing like an adherent of the 'old perspective' and thus, a target for the accusation that her reading of Paul is anti-Jewish.

[138] Douglas Campbell, *The Deliverance of God: An Apocalyptic Rereading of Justification in Paul* (Grand Rapids: Eerdmans, 2009), pp. 931–4.

[139] I am aware that every one of these assertions is contentious in the secondary literature. The close reading that I undertake goes some way towards demonstrating these points; however, the fuller argument will be developed in a forthcoming article on the topic.

soteriologies in early Judaism that place a comparatively greater valuation on 'works' – and many examples of such texts have been detailed in this chapter up to this point.

Rom. 4.4-9

Paul first refers to 'works' when discussing Abraham, 'our forefather according to the flesh' (προπάτορα ἡμῶν κατὰ σάρκα; Rom. 4.1). Paul states that 'if Abraham was justified by works (εἰ γὰρ Ἀβραὰμ ἐξ ἔργων ἐδικαιώθη), he has grounds for boasting, but not before God' (4.2).[140] A proof text from Scripture provides Paul with the basis for this reasoning: 'Abraham believed God, and it was reckoned to him as righteousness' (ἐπίστευσεν δὲ Ἀβραὰμ τῷ θεῷ καὶ ἐλογίσθη αὐτῷ εἰς δικαιοσύνην: Gen. 15.6 LXX; Rom. 4.3).[141] Paul continues, 'Now to one who works (τῷ δὲ ἐργαζομένῳ), wages (ὁ μισθὸς) are not reckoned as a gift but as something due (κατὰ ὀφείλημα). But to one who, without works, (τῷ δὲ μὴ ἐργαζομένῳ) trusts him who justifies the ungodly, such faith is reckoned as righteousness' (εἰς δικαιοσύνην; Rom. 4.4-5). This rich passage deserves some unpacking.

First, the same verb (ἐργάζομαι) is used in vv. 4-5 to describe the activity of working or labouring. The New Revised Standard Version (NRSV) translates ἐργάζομαι in ch. 4 v. 4 as a present participle ('now, to one who works'), but in ch. 4 v. 5 as a (negated) noun ('but to one who, without works, trusts'). The literal rendition of the participle form in ch. 4 v. 4 makes Paul's analogy shine: he is making a theological point but drawing on the everyday metaphor of wage-earning labour. But when we get to ch. 4 v. 5 – where Paul balances his discourse by employing the same participle form of ἐργάζομαι – the complexity of the sentence might have led the NRSV translators to opt for the nominal form 'works'. For Paul introduces another verb in the participle form, 'to trust' (πιστεύω), giving this verb the weight of importance in his agenda. If we were to keep the participle form of ἐργάζομαι intact, we could render ch. 4 v. 5 more literally thus: 'But to the one who, [while] not working, *trusts* him who justifies the ungodly'. This option avoids the sense of a hypothetical person 'trusting' God who justifies the ungodly, although he *possesses* no 'works'.[142]

But the overall sense of Rom. 4.1-5 is still relevant: In ch. 4 v. 2, we see Abraham presented as a man who might be 'justified by [his] works' (presumably in human sight) – but 'not before God'. However, Paul states that Abraham found 'justification' by believing in God (4.3). The implication is that it was not because of the 'works'

---

[140] By far the best analysis of 'boasting' in Rom. 4.2 is Gathercole's, *Where is Boasting*, pp. 241–6, whose conclusions I support. Joshua Jipps argues that Paul debates with an assumed interlocutor who shares the commonly held view (in Second Temple Judaism) of Abraham as a man 'justified' by his 'works': his obedience and his fidelity; idem, 'Rereading the Story of Abraham, Isaac and "Us" in Romans 4', *JSNT* 32, no. 2 (2009), pp. 217–42, at p. 224.

[141] The vast literature on this verse need not be reiterated here. A fulsome summary can be found in Schliesser, *Abraham's Faith in Romans 4*, pp. 79–220, 404–16, and Gerhard H. Visscher, *Romans 4 and the New Perspective on Paul: Faith Embraces the Promise* (New York: Peter Lang, 2009); see also Wright, 'Paul and the Patriarch', pp. 207–41, and the response, Lambrecht, 'Romans 4', pp. 189–94. This sample alone not only contains widely divergent opinions about 'justification' and the 'works of the law' in Romans 4, but also highlights the spectrum of scholarship on the issues.

[142] While this idea of a person *having* no 'works' with which to come before God and be judged is common in the HB, as we have seen (e.g. Isaiah 26), it is imported into the NRSV translation of Rom. 4.5 here.

Abraham possessed (4.2) that he was 'justified' but because of his faith in God (4.3). It makes sense to read the hypothetical person who trusts in God to 'justify the ungodly' and has his faith 'reckoned as righteousness' (4.5), therefore, as Abraham himself (4.2-3).[143] Although Abraham possessed 'works', they could not justify him before God (4.2), yet he trusted God and this did justify him (4.3). How much more, then, could the hypothetical person who 'has no works' find justification with God if he has the same kind of faith in God? Paul claims that 'righteousness' is not due to 'works', as we might expect even in the case of an exemplary figure such as Abraham (4.2). In fact, 'righteousness' is *independent of* (χωρὶς) 'works' (4.6).

If we probe Paul's metaphor of wage-earning labour in Rom 4.4-5, we begin to see how he connects *doing* work to *having* works. The everyday reality of a person working for wages provides Paul with his starting point (4.4): the worker has 'wages' (ὁ μισθὸς) credited to his account (λογίζομαι) as a 'debt' or 'obligation' (κατὰ ὀφείλημα), not as a gratuity (κατὰ χάριν). The contract of hire stipulates that when the worker performs his designated labour, his employer is obligated to pay him wages. These wages are the worker's due; they are not a gift from the employer. There is a fine balance: the actual work undertaken by the employee places the employer in his debt (ὀφείλημα); it has to be repaid in the form of wages (ὁ μισθὸς). Wages constitute something owed to the worker – not a form of credit freely given in advance as it were – but something merited by the worker as a 'reward'. These are the basic terms for the contract of employment familiar to first-century readers.[144]

Concretely, ὁ μισθὸς can mean remunerated 'wages' but, metaphorically, it can also mean 'reward', 'gain' or 'recompense' in a more abstract sense.[145] In both senses – the literal and metaphorical – the connotation is positive: a given form of behaviour that is deemed either necessary or good (e.g. labour or virtue) generates a 'wage' or 'reward'. We have already noted instances of the metaphorical use of ὁ μισθὸς in the LXX; for example Prov. 11.18-19 stated that the 'wicked' do 'unjust works' (LXX: ἔργα ἄδικα), but that 'sowers of righteousness' gain a true 'reward' (μισθὸς ἀληθείας). In an even broader sense, ὁ μισθὸς can signify anything that is 'paid back', and this enables the noun to assume a paradoxical connotation – for it can refer to positive reward as much as the fruit of what is gained by unjust behaviour, hence 'retribution' or 'punishment' (cf. Rom. 6.23: 'the wage of sin is death': ἃ γὰρ ὀψώνια τῆς ἁμαρτίας θάνατος).[146]

Similarly, the verb λογίζομαι literally means 'to credit', 'to count' or 'to reckon' but can also mean 'to regard' or 'to consider'.[147] In Rom. 4.4, the verb is used to suggest that wages are 'reckoned' or 'credited' to the worker, and is thus infused with contractual and

---

[143] Lambrecht, 'Romans 4', p. 192.
[144] Gathercole, *Where is Boasting?*, p. 245, argues that the 'worker' of Rom. 4.4 is the same figure as the implied interlocutor in Rom. 2.1–3.20, and that both are evaluated negatively in Paul's view.
[145] Wright, ('Paul and the Patriarch') argues that the noun means 'promise', as in the Abrahamic promise in Gen. 15.1, but this reading is a stretch of the imagination. See Lambrecht, 'Romans 4', p. 193.
[146] Susan Eastman, 'Sin's Wages and God's Gift in the Divine Economy: Reflections on Romans 7 and the Cleansing of the Temple in John 2.13-17', *ExpTim* 121, no. 7 (2010), pp. 342–5: for Paul, sin 'dwells' in a person and operates like a 'household manager who repays humanity's service with death' (p. 343).
[147] BDAG, sv. λογίζομαι

economic connotations. Paul opposes the nouns 'debt' (ὀφείλημα) and 'gift' (χάριν), stating that a worker's wages are not 'credited' as a 'gift' but as 'something due'. The worker receives his wages as a 'debt' – this is hardly intuitive – but the sense is simply that the labourer's work puts his employer in arrears and makes him indebted to pay his labourer. What is intriguing is that the same word (ὀφείλημα) has the secondary meaning of 'sin', 'guilt' or 'wrong'. The nominal ὀφειλέτης denotes one who is obligated, a debtor – but also one who is guilty, that is a sinner. The verb ὀφείλω can mean 'to owe', but it can also mean 'to sin' or 'to wrong' a person (cf. Luke 11.4). In this sense, we are dealing with a 'Semitism' much like חוב/חייב which carries the dual sense of being obligated or indebted, and sinning.[148] Likewise, χάριν is contrasted with ὀφείλημα and means 'a gift', that is something not owed but kindly bestowed. This noun (χάριν) has a rich secondary sense in the early Christian theological lexicon, meaning the 'grace', 'kindness' or 'mercy' of God that comes upon believers.

Paul contrasts the 'one who works' for wages (4.4a, τῷ δὲ ἐργαζομένῳ) with the 'one who does not work' (4.5a, τῷ δὲ μὴ ἐργαζομένῳ), but trusts in God. In the first case, the worker's 'wages' are credited to his account (4.4a), in the case of the one who trusts in God to 'justify' the 'ungodly', it is this faith itself (ἡ πίστις) that is credited to him. It is this key verb (λογίζομαι) that permits the transfer of meaning from the literal to the metaphorical: as wages are counted and credited to a person to satisfy the 'indebtedness' of his employer, so faith can be 'credited' to a person's account to put them in clear standing – this time, with God.[149] 'Faith' is credited to a person who displays it 'as righteousness' (εἰς δικαιοσύνην). Faith is the 'reward' (or 'wage') of the person who has it, and its fruit is the concomitant imputation of righteousness by God. Paul therefore suggests that faith constitutes a kind of 'working' that receives a reward, but paradoxically implies that faith can effectively bypass 'working', sufficient as it is to enable the 'reckoning' of 'righteousness'. The gratuitousness of 'faith reckoned as righteousness' is what renders it 'blessed'. Paul continues:

> So also David speaks of the blessedness of those to whom God reckons righteousness apart from works: 'Blessed are those whose iniquities are forgiven, and whose sins are covered; blessed is the one against whom the Lord will not reckon sin'. (4.6-8)[150]

Here we begin to see the idea of 'working' – elaborated in ch. 4 v. 4 via the metaphor of a labourer – merge with the idea of 'works' as such. 'Working' in order to earn a wage morphs into possessing 'works' that might lead one to be reckoned as 'righteous' by God. Paul insists that such reckoning is possible independently of a person possessing

---

[148] Anderson, *Sin*, pp. 8, 9, 27–8, 96–7. Still, in Rom. 4.4, Paul employs ὀφείλημα in its literal sense of a 'debt' arising in a contractual setting.

[149] Whereas 'Sin' is the master who repays humanity with the wage of death, God is the abundantly kind 'household manager' who 'bestows overflowing life, not as a wage, but as a gift': Eastman, 'Sin's Wages and God's Gift in the Divine Economy', p. 344.

[150] Tobin, 'What Shall We Say Abraham Found?' p. 445, suggests that because David is the speaker of the psalm, Paul must 'refer to Jews' and that to them, the ideas were not radical: 'the forgiveness of sins, which takes place apart from works of the law, must already be part of the Jewish experience'.

'works', and he cites Ps. 31.1-2 LXX (MT 32.1-2) to this effect. The psalm citation adds a new dimension to the argument: Paul has so far spoken of God reckoning 'righteousness' to a person who displays trusting faith in God. The opening of Psalm 31 announces the possibility of God refraining from reckoning *sin* to a person. Paul equates God's *positive* imputation of righteousness to a person with God's *declining* to impute sin to a person.[151] This intertextual addition permits us to grasp more clearly why Paul referred to God's ability to 'justify the wicked' in ch. 4 v. 5: a person is 'reckoned righteous' and has his own wickedness wiped away, even if he has no 'works' to show, *because* he has faith in God's very ability to justify him. The psalm presents its reader with two different nouns for the concept of 'sin', and two different verbs to describe the way in which God chooses to forgive sin. Ps. 31.1 (LXX) declares the person blessed whose 'transgression' (ἀνομίαι) is 'forgiven' (ἀφέθησαν; MT Ps. 32.1: נְשׂוּי־פֶּשַׁע), and whose 'sin' (ἁμαρτίαι; MT: חטאה) is 'covered' (ἐπεκαλύφθησαν; MT: כסה). These are the people to whom God imputes 'no iniquity' (μὴ λογίσηται κύριος ἁμαρτίαν; MT: לא יחשׁב יהוה לו עון), for they have no 'deceit' (δόλος; MT: רמיה) in their spirits.[152]

These references to 'sin' in the psalm citation echo Paul's reference to 'debt' or 'obligation' (ὀφείλημα) in Rom. 4.4.[153] But for Paul, the remission of sins is shaped to fit the message of God 'crediting' righteousness to a person 'apart from works' (5.6). For Paul in Rom. 4.5-8, the imputation of righteousness as a result of faith is equivalent to the 'remission' of sins, of being 'acquitted' of 'debts'. This is quite different to 'working' for 'wages' as a 'debt' (4.4); it is the bestowal of a 'gift' without having 'worked' for it, and thus is received 'apart from works'. For Paul, ultimately then, 'works' cannot achieve the remission of the 'debt' of sin. The vexed question that remains, nevertheless, is What is meant by 'works' in Rom. 4.4-8? Paul repeats that Abraham's 'faith' was 'reckoned' to him as 'righteousness' (4.9) – and if God 'reckons righteousness apart from works' (4.6), we would presume that, in this immediate context, Abraham's circumcision constitutes a 'work' in this sense. For Paul states that the 'blessedness' received by faith comes to both the 'circumcised' and the 'uncircumcised' (4.9). God imputed righteousness to Abraham *prior* to his circumcision, when he demonstrated faith in God's promises (cf. Gen. 15.6). For Paul, circumcision itself becomes a 'seal' of that righteousness (4.11), not a 'work' in itself that produces righteousness.

This is not to say that 'works' (cf. 4.4-6) should be reduced to the commandment of circumcision every time Paul uses the word in the context of 'righteousness' or 'justification'.[154] Paul views circumcision as the visible sign and 'advantage' of 'the Jew' (Rom. 3.1), which signifies the entire 'law' (2.25). Indeed, *doing the law* is what leads one to be 'justified' (οἱ ποιηταὶ νόμου δικαιωθήσονται) and to be considered 'righteous

---

[151] Fitzmyer, *Romans*, pp. 369–77 thinks that this is an example of *gezarah shawah*, as we find λογίζομαι in Gen. 15.6 and in Ps. 31.2. Cf. Hays, *Echoes of Scripture*, p. 55.

[152] Because ἀφίημι does mean to acquit, to forgive and also to spare, to leave, to free and to remit a debt (e.g. Deut. 15.2 LXX). Here it is about specifically remitting 'lawlessness' – sins against the commandments.

[153] S. Westerholm, *Perspectives Old and New on Paul: The 'Lutheran Paul' and His Critics* (Grand Rapids: Eerdmans, 2004), p. 280.

[154] Contra Dunn, *Theology of Paul*, pp. 354–9.

in God's sight' as opposed to merely 'hearing the law' without observing it (2.13). Circumcision is 'of value' if one obeys the law, but if one does not, it 'has become uncircumcision' (ἀκροβυστία; 2.25). Those who keep the law's requirements (τοῦ νόμου φυλάσσῃ), although not sealed with the sign of circumcision, will be considered 'circumcised' by God (2.26). These statements suggest that Paul uses 'circumcision' as a code or signifier for the *whole* law, not for one isolated *mitzvoth*; as a seal of the covenant, circumcision stood for all the 'works' one could do in God's sight. If Abraham was 'justified' before his circumcision (before the 'works of the law'), he was justified as one of the 'ungodly'.[155] In Romans 4, 'works' constitute all the virtuous doings that a 'worker' would undertake for his Master – the mandates of the Torah vis-à-vis others.[156] 'Right doing', or δικαιοσύνη/צדקה, in Brendan Byrne's words, 'performance in a broader range of moral endeavour than the more "sociological" interpretations [of Dunn and the NPP] seems to allow'.[157] And yet, even if Abraham *had* all of these works to 'boast' about, before God (Paul argues), it would be as nothing; it was Abraham's *faith* that brought him gratuitous reward, remission from sin and made him 'blessed' (Ps. 32.1-2).[158]

Rom. 9.11-12, 30-32

As noted in Chapter 4, Romans 9–11 has been a contentious and controversial text for interpreters throughout the ages, dealing as it does with Paul's 'unceasing anguish' (9.2) that 'the Israelites' (9.3) have rejected 'the Messiah' (9.4). Paul ponders whether God's promises to Abraham were in vain (9.6), but he resolves this question by asserting that, 'Not all Israelites truly belong to Israel, and not all of Abraham's children are his true descendants' (9.6b-7a, NRSV). The 'children of the flesh' – the 'Israelites' – are therefore not necessarily 'children of God', but the 'children of the promise' do qualify as such (9.8). Paul elaborates with reference to two of Israel's matriarchs. The 'promise' of descendants to Abraham came through the word of an angel to Sarah, who believed up to that point that she was barren (Genesis 17–18). Likewise, Rebecca experienced 'something similar' when she conceived Jacob by Isaac (9.10). Through the stories of these two women, both of whom are told that they will bear a child who will carry on the original promise made to Abraham, Paul makes a point about God's elective purposes:

> Even before they had been born or had done anything good or bad (so that God's purpose of election might continue, not by works [οὐκ ἐξ ἔργων] but by his call) she was told, 'The elder shall serve the younger. As it is written, "I have loved Jacob, but I have hated Esau"'. (Rom 9.11-13, NRSV)

[155] Cf. Orrey McFarland, 'Whose Abraham, Which Promise? Genesis 15.6 in Philo's *De Virtutibus* and Romans 4', *JSNT* 35, no. 2 (2012), pp. 107–29, at p. 115.
[156] Fredrikson, 'Paul's Letter to the Romans', p. 808.
[157] Brendan Byrne, 'The Problem of ΝΟΜΟΣ and the Relationship with Judaism in Romans', *CBQ* 62 (2000), pp. 294–309, at pp. 299–300.
[158] The same movement now pertains to believers; Francis Watson, *Paul, Judaism, and the Gentiles: Beyond the New Perspective* (Grand Rapids: Eerdmans, 2007), p. 263; cf. Hays, *Echoes of Scripture*, pp. 55–6.

Paul continues by claiming that this is not mere whimsy on God's part (9.14). It is God's prerogative to have mercy or compassion upon whomever he pleases (9.15). In a similar way, God can 'harden' someone's 'heart' if it so pleases him (the case of Pharaoh furnishes Paul with the most pertinent example); ultimately, election is always grounded in the mercy of God and nothing else.[159] In fact, human behaviour – 'human will or exertion' (θέλω) – has no effect on God's purpose (9.16; cf. Rom. 11.30-32, where 'grace' is contrasted to 'works' in the same line of argument).[160] 'Works' represent a sort of human *striving* before God, but through the Gen. 25.23 citation, Paul also uses 'works' (9.12) to refer to 'merit'. A child in the womb cannot merit anything – he has no record of commendable behaviour that would earn God's favour, neither does he have demonstrably wicked deeds to his name that would earn him God's opprobrium. As Paul states, the child (i.e. Jacob) has not yet 'been born' and yet – against social convention – he is gifted with the promise of election (9.11a).[161]

Paul then makes a more provocative point: not only did God circumvent Esau's presumed prerogative by choosing Jacob – God in fact hated Esau as much as he loved Jacob (9.13). Paul has picked a late prophetic text (Mal. 1.2, 3) in which God reassures the tribe of Jacob (i.e. Israel) of his eternal love for them. God has loved the tribe of Jacob over and above the tribe of Esau; God has lain waste the dwellings of the latter out of hatred (Mal. 1.3), and for good measure, has frustrated the plans of the tribe of Edom to rebuild their cities in safety (Mal. 1.4-5).[162] God's love is relative, in this text, and Jacob holds pride of place in God's heart. Paul has retrofitted a text about God's constructed feelings of love and hatred towards the competing *tribes* of Jacob and Esau (Mal. 1.1-3) back onto the Genesis narratives dealing with God's choice of the *character* Jacob instead of Esau; yet Paul's focus is strictly on corporate, representative personalities rather than individuals.[163] Additionally, Paul's analogy in ch. 9 vv. 11-13 advances the confrontational proposition that 'Esau' the 'elder brother' (standing for the Jews) is meant to 'serve' Jacob, the 'younger brother' – standing not for the Jews, but for the newly formed Gentile church.[164]

---

[159] Susan Grove Eastman, 'Israel and the Mercy of God: A Re-reading of Galatians 6.16 and Romans 9–11', NTS 56 (2010), pp. 367–95, at p. 377.

[160] Ibid., p. 379.

[161] On the reception history of this Pauline motif, precisely in relation to a soteriology of desert, see John E. Curran Jr, 'Jacob and Esau in the Iconoclasm of Merit', SEL 49, no. 2 (2009), pp. 285–309.

[162] The tribe of Edom were perceived to be Esau's descendants; see the texts in B. J. Oropeza, 'Paul and Theodicy: Intertextual Thoughts on God's Justice and Faithfulness to Israel in Romans 9–11', NTS 53 (2007), pp. 57–80, at pp. 61–2.

[163] Brian J. Abasciano, *Paul's Use of the Old Testament in Romans 9.1-9: An Intertextual and Theological Exegesis* (London: T&T Clark, 2005), p. 222.

[164] Sigurd Grindheim accurately notes the conventional nature of this 'reversal' trope in the biblical literature, but his frame of interpretation is concerning, viz. that Paul's objective is to dethrone 'Jewish confidence' (excessive pride) in their election. Cf. idem, *The Crux of Election: Paul's Critique of the Jewish Confidence in the Election of Israel* (WUNT 2.202; Tübingen: Mohr Siebeck, 2005), pp. 136–57. For a more sensitive treatment of the topic that acknowledges the history of anti-Semitic interpretations of Paul's language of 'boasting' see Gathercole, *Where is Boasting?* pp. 2–8.

Paul's next reference to 'works' in Rom. 9.32 continues this theme, making the Jewish/Gentile distinction explicit:

> Gentiles, who did not press on toward righteousness, have seized upon it, that is, a righteousness that is by trust; but Israel, who did strive for a law of righteousness, did not attain toward that law. Why? Because not by trust, but as if upon the basis of works. They have stumbled over the stumbling stone. (9.30-32)
>
> ὅτι ἔθνη τὰ μὴ διώκοντα δικαιοσύνην κατέλαβεν δικαιοσύνην, δικαιοσύνην δὲ τὴν ἐκ πίστεως, Ἰσραὴλ δὲ διώκων νόμον δικαιοσύνης εἰς νόμον οὐκ ἔφθασεν. διὰ τί ; ὅτι οὐκ ἐκ πίστεως ἀλλ' ὡς ἐξ ἔργων · προσέκοψαν τῷ λίθῳ τοῦ προσκόμματος. (NA[28])

Paul understands righteousness (δικαιοσύνη) not only as something that can be attained or striven for, but also as something gifted to a person. But in Paul's view, the Gentiles (τὰ ἔθνη), through their faith (πίστις), arrived at righteousness without technically 'striving' for it. The verb Paul uses to denote 'striving' (διώκω) is a strong one, suggesting the intense pursuit of a goal – or in the more negative sense, the chasing down and persecution of a group of people (cf. in this latter sense, Rev. 12.13).[165] In the context of Romans as a whole, Paul views righteousness as something that can only be attained by 'trust' (cf. 4.1-11). Abraham trusted in God, and it was reckoned to him as 'righteousness' (4.3, 6). The Gentiles exhibited this same trust – and righteousness has virtually 'overtaken' them (κατέλαβεν δικαιοσύνην; 9.30), gratuitously and unexpectedly. On the other hand, claims Paul, 'Israel' *did* strive for righteousness – indeed, they did strive for *a law of righteousness* (νόμον δικαιοσύνης) but they did not arrive at that law (εἰς νόμον οὐκ ἔφθασεν). Notably, Paul does not argue that Israel did not attain 'righteousness' as such, but that they did not attain their *law of* righteousness. That Israel strove for a 'law of righteousness' implies that they strove for a law that produces righteousness – that they intensely practised a law that led them to holiness. For all that, they did not arrive at the righteousness produced by the law.[166]

Paul sums up his reasoning as to why this might have been so in the laconic formulation: ὅτι οὐκ ἐκ πίστεως ἀλλ' ὡς ἐξ ἔργων. In this verse, we see 'trust' (or 'faith') and 'works' mutually opposed, taking us back to Rom. 4.4-5. The reference to 'works' in Rom. 4.5, we determined, signified, in abbreviated and oblique fashion, the 'works' (duties, obligations, commandments, practices) of the law. This was so, even though the reference built upon the more general understanding of 'works' as indicative of human behaviour undertaken in order to achieve some result or reward (as in the metaphor of working for a wage in Rom. 4.4). Here, in Rom. 9.30-32, we see something similar. Paul's expression is idiosyncratic, meaning literally 'from out of works' (ἐξ ἔργων), and it is elsewhere commonly found in Galatians, where Paul speaks of those who are 'from

---

[165] BDAG, sv. Διώκω.

[166] Some interpreters qualify Paul's thought here: it is not 'the Law as such' but only 'the Law poisoned by the power of Sin that is the problem (7.7-12)'. Thus, John Paul Heil, 'Christ, the Termination of the Law (Romans 9.30–10.8)', *CBQ* 63, no. 3 (2001), pp. 484–98, at p. 487.

the works of the law'.¹⁶⁷ The spatial denotation is peculiar, to be sure, but balanced by the verb διώκω, used twice in Rom. 9.30-32 (vv. 30, 31) which also connotes spatiality, however, in the sense of movement *towards* something, or in pursuit of something. The idiomatic usage conveys a fluid, general sense of human activity based on something fundamental: (a law of) righteousness was pursued by Israel, but it was done so from the wrong basis – that of 'works'. Gentiles did not seek righteousness, but found it on the basis of faith (ἐκ πίστεως) in Christ.¹⁶⁸

Paul blends two conceptualizations of 'works' in ch. 9 vv. 30-32. He stays with the tenor of 'works' developed earlier in ch. 9 vv. 13-16 – as meritorious activity that exhibits a 'striving' quality – but he adds another dimension of 'works' as constitutive of a 'law' that was meant to lead to 'righteousness'. In this sense, Paul's phrase 'a law of righteousness' in ch. 9 v. 31 (νόμον δικαιοσύνης) could well be glossed 'works of righteousness', and given that Paul's formulation 'out of works' (ἐξ ἔργων) in ch. 9 v. 32 is so heavily resonant of 'out of works of the law' in Galatians (Gal. 2.15; 3.2, 5, 10; cf. also Rom. 3.2, 28), I surmise that the expression is being used in Rom. 9.32 as shorthand for the latter expression as well. Moreover, we find in Rom. 3.27 the curious and isolated expression 'a law of works', which, analogous to Rom. 9.30-32, is contrasted with 'the law of faith' (διὰ ποίου νόμου; τῶν ἔργων; οὐχί, ἀλλὰ διὰ νόμου πίστεως). What this suggests is that Paul uses the term 'works' in a general sense to refer to human behaviour, which might sway God's will one way or another – but which cannot do so (9.11-13), and on the other hand, that Paul develops this more general sense to delineate a specific connotation for the term 'works' which relates to *Israel's* behaviour in the pursuit of meritorious activity laid down and encapsulated within the 'law'. Importantly, *both* senses operate for Paul within the remit of his discussion about Israel's election, about God's call of the Gentiles and their role in the 'reconciliation' of Israel to God. Paul moves from 'works' as meritorious (or deleterious) behaviour (9.11-13) to 'works of the law' as meritorious behaviour that would lead Israel to righteousness, but which in Paul's view, did not, and cannot, do so.¹⁶⁹

James and Hebrews

In the letter of James, 'works' are not only something one does, but they are also something one *has* (ἔχω). In a passage that has drawn much commentary in the scholarship for its ostensible, implicit dispute with Pauline soteriology, James pronounces the inherent superiority of 'works' over 'faith' for the simple fact that the former demonstrably enliven the latter: 'What good is it, my brothers and sisters, if

---

[167] Thus, by 'works' in Rom. 9.32, Paul means 'the whole law apart from Christ', not ritual identity markers of Sabbath, kashrut and circumcision: Geoffrey Turner, 'The Righteousness of God in Psalms and Romans', *SJT* 73, no. 3 (2010), pp. 285–301, at p. 298; and Preston M. Sprinkle, *Paul and Judaism Revisited: A Study of Divine and Human Agency in Salvation* (Downers Grove: IVP Academic, 2013), p. 153.

[168] Westerholm, *Perspectives Old and New*, p. 399; cf. Ortlund, *Zeal Without Knowledge*, p. 122; C. E. B. Cranfield, 'Romans 9.30–10.4', *Int* 34, no. 1 (1980), pp. 70–4. The limitations of Cranfield's work are addressed by Preston M. Sprinkle, *Law and Life: The Interpretation of Leviticus 18.5 in Early Judaism and in Paul* (WUNT 2.2.41; Tübingen: Mohr Siebeck, 2008), pp. 173–5.

[169] See, similarly, 2 Tim. 1.8-9, and Eph. 2.8-10, both of which contrast 'grace' and 'works' directly and contain the notion of 'striving'.

you say you have faith but do not have works? Can faith save you?' (2.14, NRSV).[170] If a person, proclaiming to 'have faith', neglects to provide material assistance to a needy 'brother' who lacks food and clothing – and instead remarks to the brother 'go in peace' – there is no value in that person's faith (2.15-16). James concludes: 'So faith by itself, if it has no works, is dead' (οὕτως καὶ ἡ πίστις, ἐὰν μὴ ἔχῃ ἔργα, νεκρά ἐστιν καθ᾽ ἑαυτήν; 2.17; cf. 2.26). Faith itself, if it is to be genuine, must 'possess' works.[171] Equally, James dismisses the idea that faith is separable from works – as though one person can live by faith and another by works (2.18a). He writes, 'Show me your faith apart from your works, and I by my works will show you my faith' (2.18b, NRSV). Faith is only evident in the performance of 'works' – it is not sufficient in the absence of 'works'. Indeed, 'faith apart from works is useless' (ἡ πίστις χωρὶς τῶν ἔργων ἀργή ἐστιν; 2.20b).

James' use of the expression χωρὶς τῶν ἔργων ('apart from works') in ch. 2 v. 18b and ch. 2 v. 20b strongly suggests he is rebutting Paul's understanding 'that a person is justified by faith *apart from works of the law*' (χωρὶς ἔργων νόμου, Rom. 3.28), or that 'God reckons righteousness *apart from works*' (χωρὶς ἔργων, Rom. 4.6b). Even without drawing on Paul's expression, James can be validly interpreted as responding to Paul's insistence that 'faith' and 'works' are separable entities.[172] If so, then James' example of what the performance of 'works' entails (i.e. materially helping the needy, ch. 2 vv. 15-16) is telling indeed. The 'works' that James endorses – and which make faith real in the world – are works of 'charity' or almsgiving in the ancient Jewish tradition.[173] In fact, such 'works' are identical in kind to the '*good* works' cited in the examples enumerated in the previous section: showing hospitality and providing help to the downtrodden (1 Tim. 5.10); almsgiving (Acts 9.36; Matt. 6.1-18; Luke 12.33); meeting the urgent needs of the community (Tit. 3.14); and the giving of money to needy communities (2 Cor. 9.8b). For James, it seems, '*works*' *are the same as* '*good works*' – there is no distinction between them (cf. Jas. 3.13-14, and *contra* Eph. 2.8-10). These are the everyday 'good works' laid out in the Torah that were understood in early Judaism as having the potential to accumulate merit (cf. Matt. 6.1-20), 'righteousness' towards others.

James turns to the example of Abraham and the kind of 'works' by which Abraham was 'justified' (2.21). This text (2.21-24) provides us with our closest NT parallel to John 8.39, inasmuch as both texts refer to Abraham and his 'works'. However, James is thoroughly in conversation with Paul about the relevance of Abraham's 'faith', and not discernibly attuned to the Johannine text. James writes,

> Was not our father Abraham (Ἀβραὰμ ὁ πατὴρ ἡμῶν) justified by works (ἐξ ἔργων ἐδικαιώθη) when he offered his son Isaac on the altar? You see that faith was

---

[170] For the issue of the James–Paul debate (or the apparent debate between their respective communities), see Ralph P. Martin, *James* (WBC 48; Dallas: Word, 1988), pp. 82-4 and the bibliography cited therein; and earlier, T. Laato, 'Justification according to James: A Comparison with Paul', *TJ* 18 (1997), pp. 43-84; Luke Timothy Johnson, *The Letter of James* (AB 37a; New York: Doubleday, 1995), pp. 58-64, 111-16, 245-52, disputes James' reactiveness to Paul, but his argument is convincingly criticized by Matt A. Jackson-McCabe, *Logos and Law in the Letter of James: The Law of Nature, the Law of Moses, and the Law of Freedom* (Leiden: Brill, 2001), pp. 245-7.
[171] There may be a correlation between 'dead works' in Hebrews 6 and James' notion of 'dead faith' here.
[172] Cf. McCabe, *Logos and Law*, p. 246.
[173] See the previous discussion on the Apocrypha and Pseudepigrapha in the Second Temple Period.

working together with his works, and that by the works (ἐκ τῶν ἔργων) was faith completed. Thus, the scripture was fulfilled that says, 'Abraham believed God, and it was reckoned to him as righteousness,' and he was called the friend of God (καὶ φίλος θεοῦ ἐκλήθη). You see that a person is justified by works (ὁρᾶτε ὅτι ἐξ ἔργων δικαιοῦται ἄνθρωπος) and not by faith alone. (2.21-24)

In this text, James asserts that 'works' are capable of 'justifying' a person (2.21, 24). Like Paul, James adduces Abraham as an example (cf. Rom. 4.1-2; Galatians 3), but James utterly upturns Paul's claims by using the same scriptural proof text (Gen. 15.6 LXX). Whereas Paul argued that Abraham's act of belief in God at the scene of the 'covenant between the pieces' (Genesis 15) was itself the reason God 'reckoned' righteousness to Abraham, James states that it was at the *Akedah* that Abraham proved his 'belief' in God, and was therefore reckoned righteous (cf. Genesis 22).[174] Abraham's act of offering Isaac on the altar was a 'work' that justified him in God's sight because it evinced Abraham's core faith in God – Isaac was Abraham's only son, but Abraham trusted in God when he was asked to offer Isaac on the mountain. According to James, the *Akedah* constituted not only a 'work' producing 'justification', but also an act of faith that was brought to perfection by the performance of the sacrifice. James claims that it was also for this reason that Abraham was called 'friend of God' (cf. 2 Chron. 20.7; Isa. 41.8), because of his faithful 'work' of trusting obedience, while tested by God (cf. 2 Macc. 2.52).[175]

This raises a question, however. Abraham's sacrifice at Mount Moriah was a single 'work', yet James claims that Abraham was 'justified by *works*' (2:21), that his works operated together with his faith (2.2a) and that his faith was perfected by his works (2.22b).[176] What then, are the 'works of Abraham' in this passage? The ensuing context is of some importance in this regard. Immediately following the example of Abraham, James adduces one other biblical figure to serve as a comparison – 'the prostitute Rahab', who James claims, was 'also justified by works when she welcomed the messengers and sent them out by another road' (2.25; see Josh. 22.1-24; 6.17). At first glance, the example of Rahab welcoming – and sparing the lives of – the spies has nothing in common with the example of Abraham at the *Akedah*. Why does James single out Rahab alone of all biblical figures, and introduce her with the adverb ὁμοίως – 'in the same way' (2.25a)? A clue lies in the association of Abraham and Rahab in another NT text, Hebrew 11. There, Abraham is praised for being 'put to the test' when he 'offered up Isaac', ready as he was to 'offer up his only son' because of his faith (Heb. 11.17). The author of Hebrews tells his readers that Abraham 'considered the fact that God is able even to raise someone from the dead—and figuratively speaking, he did receive him [i.e. Isaac] back' (11.19). Abraham's faith leads him to reason about the power of God

---

[174] According to James, Abraham's 'faith' at Gen. 15.6 was only 'completed' or 'filled up' (τελειόω) in the *Akedah*. See Scot McKnight, *The Letter of James* (NICNT; Grand Rapids: Eerdmans, 2011), p. 254; Douglas J. Moo, *The Letter of James: An Introduction and Commentary* (Grand Rapids: Eerdmans, 1995), p. 113.

[175] Siker, *Disinheriting the Jews*, pp. 28–143, 163–84.

[176] Abraham is an exemplar of 'faithworks' according to Robert J. Foster, *The Significance of Exemplars for the Interpretation of the Letter of James* (WUNT 2.376; Tübingen: Mohr Siebeck, 2014), p. 103.

to raise the dead, and so he passes the test. Although the author of Hebrews advances many other examples of faithful biblical figures in ch. 11 (Isaac, Jacob, Joseph, Moses, Abel and Noah), he also refers to Rahab, writing: 'By faith Rahab the prostitute did not perish with those who were disobedient, because she had received the spies in peace' (11.31).[177] James could also be associating Abraham's 'works' at the Akedah and Rahab's 'works' of saving the spies through the interpretive thread of *pikuach nefesh* – the rabbinic imperative to save a life – meaning that both Isaac and the spies were saved from death through their actions. The positive commandment of *pikuach nefesh* is so strong that it overrides the observance of the Sabbath (cf. John 7.19-21; cf. 5.1-18).

Together, Jas. 2.25 and Heb. 11.31 represent two early Christian traditions about Rahab that emphasize her hospitality towards the spies, her kind treatment of them and the way she saved their lives, receiving in turn an oath that she and her family would be spared when Canaan was overrun by the invading army of Hebrews. Rahab was peaceable and hospitable. By saying that Rahab was 'justified' by her 'works', James may be alluding to the fact that her life was spared because of her kindness. In the perspective of Heb. 11.31, Rahab's life was spared because she lived by faith; she was singularly obedient.[178] And although there are plenty of traditions that attest to the *Akedah* as an opportunity for *Abraham* to successfully showcase his obedience before God, it is not clear if, and if so how, the same kind of hospitality was exemplified by Rahab (cf. Jas. 2.25).[179] Roy B. Ward suggests that the references to Abraham's 'works' in Jas. 2.21-22 do not merely refer to the *Akedah* as a single incident – they presuppose, but do not explicitly reference, whole traditions about Abraham as the paradigmatic hospitable man, thus setting up the comparison with Rahab in ch. 2 v. 25.[180] Abraham's 'works', argues Ward, were his acts of hospitality that 'justified' him in the sight of God.[181] Abraham's faith at the *Akedah* was but the prime instantiation of this hospitality (his 'works') and it 'acquitted' Abraham before God.[182]

Excursus 1: 'Works of the Law'

Few topics in NT studies have generated as much discussion as what Paul meant by the phrase 'works of the Law'. The secondary literature is prohibitively prolific, and the aim of this excursus is not to rehearse the intricacies of the scholarship, but only to integrate the most compelling findings of recent research with my interpretation

---

[177] Pamela Eisenbaum, 'Heroes and History in Hebrews 11', in Craig A. Evans and James A. Sanders (eds), *Early Christian Interpretation of the Scriptures of Israel: Investigations and Proposals* (JSNTSup 148; Sheffield: Sheffield Academic Press, 1997), pp. 380-96.

[178] Rahab was also, like the other heroes on Hebrews' list, a marginal character, a point well made by Eisenbaum, 'Heroes and History', p. 393.

[179] Ward, 'The Works of Abraham', pp. 283-90. The *Akedah* was an act of 'hospitality' inasmuch as Abraham 'offered' his son as a sacrifice to God (p. 285).

[180] Ward, 'The Works of Abraham', p. 286.

[181] Ibid., pp. 286, 288. Ward cites *Gen. R.* 54.5; 55.4, where Abraham had accrued merits because of his hospitality. The rabbis posited that because of these merits, Abraham was permitted to *not* carry out the sacrifice of Isaac. See Ward, 'The Works of Abraham', p. 287.

[182] Ward, 'The Works of Abraham', p. 288.

of how the term 'works' was operating in early Judaism and in the NT thus far.[183] The anarthous phrase ἔργα νόμου is used eight times in Paul's writings (Gal. 2.16 (×3); 3.2, 5, 10; Rom. 3.20, 28).[184] Paul uses the phrase ἔργα νόμου thrice when discussing the primacy of 'faith' in Christ for the achievement of 'justification' in his letter to the Galatians, which has received much comment in the scholarship (Gal. 2.16). Paul claims that a person is justified 'not by *works of the law* but through faith in Jesus Christ'.[185] So, Paul adds, have 'we come to put our trust in Christ Jesus, so that we might be made righteous by faith in Christ, and not by *works of the law*, because it is not by *works of the law*' that all flesh will be justified (all, Gal. 2.16). 'Justification' – what Paul Owen nicely summarizes as a soteriological 'acceptance' into the 'family of God' and the removal of divine condemnation due to the bondage of sin[186] – is the gospel and faith in a nutshell.

The prior context of this passage is important. Paul provides an autobiographical narrative supporting the validity of his apostolic authority (Gal. 1.11-24), and a reason for his conflict with the other apostles (2.1-10). Peter was central to this struggle, as he was compelling Gentile converts to 'live like Jews' despite the fact that Peter, although a Jew, used to eat with Gentiles until pressured by a certain group to refrain from doing so (2.11-14). Thus, 'justification' seems in Paul's view to be contrary to the practices driving this intra-apostolic conflict. Commonly, advocates of the NNP interpret 'works of the law' (2.16) as those specific commandments of the Torah that Peter upheld under duress: circumcision (the pagan Titus is described as 'compelled' to become circumcised upon conversion to faith in Jesus, Gal. 2.3), and *kashrut* (Peter, the 'apostle to the circumcised' (2.7b) abandoned *kashrut* until pressured to retain it by 'certain people from James' (τινας ἀπὸ Ἰακώβου), or those of 'the circumcision' (ἐκ περιτομῆς) – possibly a figurative expression for Jews in general; 2.12). There must be a means by which God 'justifies' 'all flesh' (πᾶσα σάρξ; 2.16c), Jew and Gentile

---

[183] Robert Keith Rapa, *The Meaning of 'Works of the Law' in Galatians and Romans* (New York: Peter Lang, 2001); James G. F. Dunn, *The New Perspective on Paul* (rev. edn; Grand Rapids: Eerdmans, 2005); idem, 'Works of the Law and the Curse of the Law (Galatians 3.10-14)', *NTS* (1985), pp. 523-43; and in dispute with Dunn, C. E. B. Cranfield, 'The "Works of the Law" in the Epistle to the Romans', *JSNT* 43 (1991), pp. 89-101; and T. R. Schreiner, '"Works of the Law" in Paul', *NovT* 33 (1991), pp. 217-44; Dunn responds to his critics in idem, 'Yet Once More – Works of the Law', by denying that ἔργα νόμου is in fact restricted to ritual observances designed to keep Jews apart from Gentiles. Rather, Dunn states that the term can denote general Jewish obedience to the Torah in Paul's writings; Dunn, 'Yet Once More', p. 109; idem, *The New Perspective*, p. 215: the phrase 'continues to denote what is required of the members of the covenant people, those to whom the law has been given to show them how to live as God's people, those who have been redeemed by him "from the house of bondage"'. But Dunn claims, this mandate to live as God's people took on a specific form of 'boundary' control after the Maccabean crisis (p. 215).

[184] The phrase appears as ἐξ ἔργων νόμου in all of these texts with the exception of Rom. 3.28, where the phrase is χωρὶς ἔργων νόμου. A closely related text is Rom. 2.15 (τὸ ἔργον τοῦ νόμου), where the singular ἔργον is used instead of the plural ἔργων, but there the phrase is not anarthrous, and contextually, does not adhere to the sense in which Paul uses the term in the other examples.

[185] The vast literature about whether Gal. 2.16 speaks of 'the faith of Christ' or the 'faith in Christ' need not be rehearsed here, as it is well known in the field. For a summary, see Richard B. Hays, *The Faith of Christ of Jesus Christ: The Narrative Substrucutre of Galatians 3.1–4.11* (Grand Rapids: Eerdmans, 2002), pp. 123-3.

[186] Paul L. Owen, 'The "Works of the Law" in Romans and Galatians: A New Defense of the Subjective Genitive', *JBL* 126, no. 3 (2007), pp. 553-77, at p. 555.

alike. So, the argument goes, Paul is disputing 'ethnic badges', ritual 'Jewish' identity markers that clearly policed boundaries between Jew and Gentile – he is not disputing the Torah *tout court*.[187] Rather, Paul takes aim at a Jewish 'nationalism' based in an assumed prerogative that typically excluded Gentiles.[188]

Yet the passage (2.15-16), when read in its ensuing context, throws up some difficulties that challenge this interpretation. Paul speaks of the *law*'s lack of ability to make a person righteous (εἰ γὰρ διὰ νόμου δικαιοσύνη: 2.21), suggesting that the entire Torah – and not specific *mitzvoth* contained in it – is in view when Paul dismisses 'works of the law' (2.16) for their incapacity to effect justification.[189] In addition is Paul's puzzling 'explanation' advanced in ch. 2 vv. 17-19. Paul writes that if, in attempting to be made righteous in Christ, 'we' eventually find ourselves to be 'sinners', does that therefore make Christ 'a servant of sin' (ἆρα Χριστὸς ἁμαρτίας διάκονος: 2.17)?[190] Not at all, counters Paul: for if a person rebuilds what he once tore down, he only proves himself to be a 'law-breaker' (παραβάτης: 2.18). Paul concludes: 'through the law I died to the law (ἐγὼ γὰρ διὰ νόμου νόμῳ ἀπέθανον), so that I might live to God' (2.19). In each case, the whole Torah is in view.[191]

Still, commentators try to squeeze Gal. 2.17-19 into the shape of the Jewish identity-marker argument. Frank Matera interprets Paul's explanation as follows: the path of 'faith in Christ' means that ethnic Jews must now turn to live like Gentiles – sinners who do not observe the laws of God. This would imply that Christ has thus been turned into Sin's agent, or servant.[192] And James Dunn considers Paul's reasoning in ch. 2 v. 17 to be a response to Peter: 'If we ourselves no less than the Gentiles turn out to be sinners', i.e. are thought of as sinners by other Jews for eating with Gentiles, then is Christ implicated?[193] Writes Dunn, 'this was the *reductio ad absurdum* of Peter's theology' – so that one could no longer categorize Gentiles as 'sinners'.[194]

However, Paul's reasoning in ch. 2 v. 17 could equally be expressed as follows: the path of faith in Christ is meant for Gentile converts to the church; the observance of the *mitzvoth* is not required for these converts, that is they do not need to become proselytes. But in the eyes of some (maybe of other Jews, cf. 2.12), this would still constitute an 'outer' sphere of sorts, open to sin because one has no means of remission of sin. This path of faith in Christ would inadvertently put Gentiles in the way of harm by Sin, that menacing, personified figure who enslaves humanity (cf. Gal. 1.4; 3.22). It would therefore put Christ in the way of – or under the dominion of – Sin. This imputed idea of Paul's opponents – who would therefore enforce the observance of the *mitzvoth* upon Paul's church – is then contended by Paul, repudiated in the form

---

[187] Dunn, 'The New Perspective on Paul', p. 107.
[188] Ibid., p. 118.
[189] Owens, 'The "Works of the Law" in Romans and Galatians', pp. 562–3. This text would provide the clearest instance for a subjective genitive, but Owens' other examples are sometimes strained.
[190] In most MSS ἆρα has a circumflex, indicating that ch. 2 v. 17 ought to be read as a question and not as a statement (although the following MSS do not show the circumflex). Paul asks the question rhetorically, followed by his typical, formulaic objection (μὴ γένοιτο).
[191] Cf. Heikki Räisänen, *Paul and the Law* (WUNT 29; 2nd edn; Tübingen: Mohr Siebeck, 1987), p. 177.
[192] Frank J. Matera, *Galatians* (Collegeville: Liturgical Press, 1992), p. 95.
[193] Dunn, *Galatians*, p. 141.
[194] Ibid., p. 142.

of a hypothetical situation: if Paul were to rebuild what he tore down, he would *then* be a 'sinner' in the sense of being a 'law-breaker' (παραβάτης: 2.18). In fact, if it were otherwise, Christ would have died 'without payment' (or, 'in vain'; δωρεάν; 2.21).

The next three references to 'works of the law' come in Gal. 3.2-5, 10, and can be taken together in the same sense. Paul berates his church for being 'bewitched' by the alternative gospel, asking them,

> Did you receive the Spirit by *works of the law* or by hearing with faith? Are you so foolish? Having begun with the Spirit, are you now finishing with the flesh? Did you endure so much for nothing (without payment: εἰκῇ) —if it really was for nothing. Does he who supports you with the Spirit and work miracles among you do so by *works of the law*, or by hearing with faith – just as Abraham 'believed God and it was reckoned to him as righteousness'? (Gal. 3.2-6)

Here, Paul creates an antithesis between the 'Spirit' and 'the flesh' (3.3), into which he draws his distinction between 'faith' and 'works of the law'. The latter works of the law – with which the community appear to be 'finishing' their path in Christ – are likened by Paul to 'the flesh'. On the other hand, 'faith' and the 'Spirit' coalesce as one reality. Paul counsels his readers that the Spirit was not bestowed as a reward for their observance of 'works of the law' but as a result of the fact that they believed the message they heard – just as Abraham once believed in what he heard and so was justified (cf. LXX Gen. 15.6). Paul therefore ultimately equates justification with the reception of the Spirit. He also connects the suffering of his Galatian community (3.4) with the suffering and death of Christ (2.21), both of which, in Paul's mind, must have some recompense, make some 'payment' to be worthwhile.

Further on, Paul contrasts those who are 'of faith' (ἐκ πίστεως; 3.9) with those who are 'of works of the law' (ἐξ ἔργων νόμου), using the same prepositional characterization. Scripture had foresight, and knew that the Gentiles would be 'blessed' in Abraham (3.8; citing Gen. 12.3). But were this order to change, and were Gentiles to be constituted as those who are 'of works of the law' like the Jews, then the blessing of the Gentiles would be forfeited – and in its place, would be a curse. Paul asserts,

> For those who are '*of works of the law*' are under a curse; for it is written, 'Cursed is anyone who does not continue in all the things written in the book of the law and do them [Deut. 27.26]'. Now it is evident that no one is justified before God by *the law*; for 'The one who is righteous will live by faith [Hab 2.4]'. (Gal. 3.10-11)

Paul conflates 'works of the law' (3.10a) with 'the law' in general (3.10b, 11), following the pattern observed in ch. 2 vv. 16, 19. There is no sense that the 'works of the law' refers exclusively to circumcision, *kashrut* or the observance of feast days.[195] To the contrary, Paul makes the astonishing claim that 'works of the law' entail the law as such. It is equally notable that Paul does not say that those who practise 'works of the law' are *cursed*, nor does he imply that the law is a source of curses; instead he says

---

[195] Schreiner, '"Works of Law" in Paul', p. 230.

that those who undertake to do 'works of the law' as a way of life are always liable to a 'curse' if they fail to observe the law that defines their life. In this sense, it is perhaps more accurate to understand the sense of Gal. 3.10 as 'those who live by works of the law' rather than those who 'rely on works of the law'.[196]

The supporting scriptural citation in Gal. 3.10 reads, 'Cursed is anyone who does not continue in all the things written in the book of the law and do them' (ἐπικατάρατος πᾶς ὃς οὐκ ἐμμένει πᾶσιν τοῖς γεγραμμένοις ἐν τῷ βιβλίῳ τοῦ νόμου τοῦ ποιῆσαι αὐτά). Paul has slightly changed LXX Deut. 27.26, which reads, 'Cursed is any man who does not continue in all the words of this law so as to do them' ('Επικατάρατος πᾶς ἄνθρωπος ὃς οὐκ ἐμμενεῖ ἐν πᾶσιν τοῖς λόγοις τοῦ νόμου τούτου τοῦ ποιῆσαι αὐτούς).[197] Deut. 27.26 concludes a long section of 'curses' pronounced upon any Israelite who transgresses key commandments of the law (Deut. 27.15-25). The commandments are framed as transgressions (e.g. idolatry (27.15); dishonouring parents (27.16); misleading the blind (27.18); depriving the neediest members of society (27.19; cf. v. 17); incest and bestiality (27.20-23); murder (27.24); and conspiracy to murder (27.25)), with a curse attached to their performance. That is, the performance of each of these transgressions carries a curse as its condition, thus the conditional formulation functions as a disincentive to commit the crimes listed. In ch. 27 v. 26, the final curse is pronounced upon all who *do not observe* 'the words of this law' – that is, all who do not positively refrain from the specific transgressions previously detailed. The text then moves on to state the *blessings* that come to anyone who observes all of God's commandments (28.1-14).

Paul's citation of Deut. 27.26 is curious; as Christopher Stanley has observed: 'Whereas the quotation pronounces a curse on the person who fails to abide by the requirements of Torah, Paul applies the curse to those who seek to *comply* with the laws of Torah'.[198] But to avoid the transgressions listed in ch. 27 vv. 14-25 *is*, from the perspective of the Deuteronomist, to 'continue in' the 'words of the law' – to comply with the law – or as Paul parses it, to be 'of the works of the law'. In Paul's view, it is the very condition of being subject to the law, of being enjoined to observe the law in its totality, that raises the ever-present spectre of a 'curse' befalling the person who fails to avoid transgression. Of course, the flipside is that observance of the Torah warrants a state of blessedness (cf. Deut. 28.1), but Paul does not follow the text of Deuteronomy that far. Instead, Paul concentrates upon how the Gentiles received the 'blessings' foretold to Abraham (cf. Gen. 12.3; 15.6) precisely because they are 'of faith' and *not* 'of works of the law' (Gal. 3.7-9). Paul denies that real blessing arises from the observance

---

[196] NRSV has 'rely on' as though Gentiles are included or could be included.

[197] 'The differences in wording between Paul's quotation of the verse and that which is found in the LXX may reflect the influence of some texts from later on in Deuteronomy that refer not simply to the Law or commandments, but to "this book" or "the book of the Law" (esp. 28.58, 61; 28.61; 29.20; 30.10)': Roy E. Ciampa, 'Deuteronomy in Galatians and Romans', in Steve Moyise and Maarten J. J. Menken (eds), *Deuteronomy in the New Testament* (London: T&T Clark, 2007), pp. 99–117, at p. 102. Francis Watson thinks that there is a shift form the law as oral proclamation ('the words of this law'), Deut. 27.26, to the specific idea of the 'law' being identified with the book of Deuteronomy itself (*Paul and the Hermeneutics of Faith*, London and New York: T&T Clark, 2004, p. 431).

[198] C. D. Stanley, *Arguing with Scripture: The Rhetoric of Quotations in the Letters of Paul* (London and New York: T&T Clark, 2004), pp. 123–4.

of 'works of the law' – 'no one is made righteous by the law' (ὅτι δὲ ἐν νόμῳ οὐδεὶς δικαιοῦται; 3.11a). Just as in ch. 3 vv. 2-6, where being 'made righteous' was equated with the reception of the Spirit, here it is associated only with the blessing of faith (3.11, cf. Hab. 2.4), which culminates in the 'promised Spirit' (3.14).[199] For Paul, this kind of blessing is entirely absent from 'the law' (3.12).

Paul's first reference to 'works of the law' in Romans appears in ch. 3 v. 20. It is worth situating this reference in the context of the opening chapters of Paul's letter, and its concern with the relationship between human behaviour and divine righteousness.[200] Paul concludes,

> Now we know that whatever the law says it speaks to those who are under the law (ὅσα ὁ νόμος λέγει τοῖς ἐν τῷ νόμῳ λαλεῖ) so that every mouth may be stopped, and the whole world may be held accountable to God. Therefore, it is not by works of the law that all flesh will be justified in his sight (διότι ἐξ ἔργων νόμου οὐ δικαιωθήσεται πᾶσα σὰρξ ἐνώπιον αὐτοῦ) since through the law (διὰ ... νόμου) comes knowledge of sin (ἁμαρτίας; 3.19-20).

Rom. 3.20 repeats Gal. 2.6, adding that the Law introduces awareness of sin (3.20).[201] Paul continues by stating that 'the righteousness of God' has now been revealed 'apart from the law' (χωρὶς νόμου; 3.21) – as attested by the law (ὑπὸ τοῦ νόμου) – through 'faith in Jesus Christ' (3.22), who justifies all sinners who turn to him in faith (3.23-24). Consider the various prepositions Paul uses to discuss 'the law' in these verses: the law pertains to those who are 'in the law' (or 'under the law': ἐν τῷ νόμῳ); no one who is 'of works of the law' will be justified (ἐξ ἔργων νόμου); knowledge of sin comes 'through the law' (διὰ ... νόμου); God's righteousness is revealed 'apart from the law' (χωρὶς νόμου); and this revelation is attested 'by the law' (ὑπὸ τοῦ νόμου). The law plays a contested role here; on the one hand Paul seems to state that the law is relevant only to those who are 'under' it (i.e. Jews; cf. Gal. 3.10), but on the other hand, Paul denies a legitimate place for the law to justify those who *are* 'under it' when he says that God's righteousness has been revealed 'apart from the law'. Yet, paradoxically, the law retains value because it testified to this very revelation.[202]

---

[199] Richard Hays writes: 'The "curse of the law" from which Christ redeems us (Gal 3.13) is not the law itself regarded as a curse, but the curse that the Law pronounces in Deuteronomy 27'. Hays, *Echoes of Scripture*, pp. 203–4, n. 24. Kelli O'Brien argues that the 'curse' is Paul's allusion to Deut. 21.23 ('For anyone hung on a tree is a curse'), in Gal. 3.13; O'Brien, 'The Curse of the Law', p. 59.

[200] 'The meaning of "works of law" here (i.e. in Rom 3.20) cannot be separated from what Paul says about the law in Romans 2, for Rom 3.19-20 function as the conclusion of all of Rom 1.18-3:18': Schreiner, 'Works of the Law in Paul', p. 226.

[201] A point that Paul develops further in Romans 7–8; taken in that context, Paul's point in ch. 3 v. 20 may be that without the vivifying Spirit of Christ, no one can 'fulfill Torah' (Gathercole, *Where is Boasting?*, p. 223). This is not to say that Paul thought no Jew could *observe* Torah – which would have been patently false – but he flips given theologies on their heads, arguing that now, under God's new order, Gentile believers in Christ could have the Torah fulfilled *in them* (cf. Phil. 3.3; so Gathercole, *Where is Boasting?*, p. 128).

[202] Paul is evidently using the 'law' in this latter case to refer to Scripture. Other contradictions abound: Paul asserts in ch. 3 v. 20 that knowledge of sin comes 'through the law', but in ch. 2 v. 12 he claims that there are those who have 'sinned apart from the law', and that these will also 'perish apart from the law'. And those who have sinned 'under the law' will be judged 'by the law'. Räisänen

Paul continues: if God's righteousness is showcased by his justifying anyone who has faith in Jesus (3.26) then 'boasting' becomes utterly irrelevant (3.27). The parallels to Rom. 4.2 are immediate ('If Abraham was justified by works, he has grounds for boasting, but not before God'). As Gathercole convincingly shows, within the context of early Judaism, this 'boasting' was neither ostentatious pretension nor inordinate pride based on national prerogatives – as commentators had assumed in the past – but a deep eschatological belief that God would vindicate the Jewish people over against the Gentiles on the basis of Israel's election and obedience.[203] Now, Paul argues that 'boasting' is excluded by a new kind of 'law' – not 'the law of works', but 'the law of faith' (3.27). Paul reiterates: 'For we hold that a person is justified by faith apart from works of the law' (Rom. 3.27-28). Both Jews and Gentiles – the circumcised and the uncircumcised – will be judged by the One God on the basis of faith, not on the basis of works (3.30). And just as Jews and Gentiles alike can engage in lawful behaviour and so be reckoned righteous (2.12-16), now both can display the same faith and be reckoned righteous. But the distinction is more than merely one between the particular and the universal: against Romans 9–11, 'Israel's error was to expect God's righteousness as a result of their obedience rather than to simply believe the promise'.[204]

Those who believe the promise, like Abraham (4.2), do not reproduce that error, according to Paul. I have already argued that 'works' in Rom. 4.2, 5-6 designates general human behaviour productive of merit. This would fit with Paul's pejorative emphasis on 'boasting' in ch. 3 vv. 27-28, and suggest that the expression 'works of the law' found in that context indicates the performance of commandments of the Torah, observed through faithfulness to the covenant, and as a means of attenuating individual and corporate sin.[205] But in Paul's view, the pervasiveness of sin means that 'works' (of the law) cannot make a person righteous; on the other hand, God is powerful to make the 'ungodly' righteous through faith and the forgiveness of sin (4.5-6). As we have seen, the 'works of the law' (cf. *2 Bar.* 47.2; 1QFlor; 4QMMT C26) could denote the gamut of *mitzvoth* in the Torah, which of themselves were 'works of righteousness' or 'merits'. Thus. *Tg. Onk.* to Gen. 15.6 glosses 'and it was reckoned to him [Abraham] as righteousness' as 'it was reckoned to him as *merit*'.[206] Abraham's faith *was* a meritorious 'work' in this (and related) traditions. Paul comes close to caricaturing such traditions when he splits a 'law of works' from a 'law of faith'. Even so, by his very response Paul indicates an awareness of the term 'works' as shorthand for 'works of the law', and the phrase 'works of the law' as suggestive of the Torah and its commandments.

Finally, the fuller picture shows us that we cannot reduce Paul's phrase to a single meaning in every context; his thoughts on the topic are often being worked out as he formulates them, and they betray considerable self-contradiction. 'Works of the law' can mean 'the Law' in general; it can mean 'works' (*mitzvoth*, requirements, deeds

---

(*Paul and the Law*) expertly draws out many of Paul's contradictions and paradoxes, never attempting to smooth them over.

[203] Gathercole, *Where is Boasting?*, p. 226.
[204] Ibid., p. 228.
[205] Even well within the same ideational context that saw God's mercy as effective in the absence of good works, as per *4 Ezra*.
[206] Targum Onkelos Genesis, at www.sefaria.org.

stipulated in the Torah, good works and deeds of righteousness that produce merit for the doer and his descendants). It is less likely that Paul's usage is determined solely by the sociological reality facing the Gentile converts, pressured to adopt selected *mitzvoth* of the Torah circumscribing Jewish 'identity'. But if the NPP reading is called into question – as I have tried to do here – there is good reason to look at the post-biblical traditions pertaining to Abraham's celebrated Torah observance, and to consider those traditions in light of our discussion of what is meant by Abraham's 'works'. If 'works of the law' can be understood as observances of the Torah that produce merit for the doer – and if we can pause and refrain from assuming that such a perspective necessitates the judgement of 'legalism' – we can examine afresh the traditions about Abraham's Torah observance as his meritorious undertaking of 'works of the law'.

Excursus 2: Abraham as Torah observant

Many post-biblical Jewish texts present Abraham as an exemplary figure who observed the Law – either in whole or in part – and discovered the One true God.[207] Two questions preoccupied the authors of these texts: Which commandments of the Torah did Abraham keep? How did Abraham come by his learning of what God required, long before the Torah was revealed at Sinai?

The book of *Jubilees* attempts to answer both of these questions. For example, Abraham revives the universal norms practised by Noah in the antediluvian era (12.25-27), and arrives at his understanding from his studious engagement with his father Terah's library. Indeed, Abraham even authors a code of law, from which Jacob reads when instructing his son Joseph (*Jub.* 39.6).[208] Philo considered Abraham to be so exemplary in his behaviour that he was 'a law and an unwritten statute' in his own right (*De Abr.* 275-276). Abraham 'did the divine law and the divine commandments', through 'unwritten nature' (*De Abr.* 275-276). Accordingly, Abraham was 'a veritable personification of the Torah' for Philo.[209] In Philo's understanding, the patriarchs were not scholars but philosophers who contemplated nature and arrived at what is right and just through reason.[210] In addition, Philo depicts Abraham – through the process of reasoning – as able to infer that God alone 'piloted' the world (*De Abr.* 70). Similar ideas about Abraham's 'discovery' of monotheism are found in the works of Josephus and various other post-biblical texts which depict Abraham as repudiating the idolatry of his Chaldean environment, as we saw in Chapter 4.[211]

Of course, certain biblical texts already displayed concern with this issue. Abraham, for example, is presented in Genesis as 'fully capable of offering sacrifices in the manner to be prescribed later in Leviticus and Numbers'.[212] Abraham is the first to

---

[207] Cf. Levinson, *Inheriting Abraham*, pp. 139–73; Siker, *Disinheriting the Jews*, pp. 20–3 Reed, 'The Construction and Subversion', p. 193; and especially on the Akedah, see Sybil Sheridan, 'Abraham From a Jewish Perspective', in Solomon, Harries and Winter (eds), *Abraham's Children*, pp. 9–17.
[208] Anderson, 'The Status of the Torah', p. 21, n. 38.
[209] Levenson, *Between Torah and Gospel*, p. 25.
[210] Ibid.
[211] Kugel, *The Bible As It Was*, pp. 134–5.
[212] Anderson, 'The Status of the Torah', p. 3; cf. Levenson, 'The Conversion of Abraham', p. 29.

practise circumcision (Genesis 17); despite the fact that the commandment is given at Sinai, it 'originates' with Abraham.[213] Gen. 18.17-19 presents Abraham as chosen by God to 'instruct his children and his seed to keep the way of the Lord by doing what is right and just'. And, as we also saw in Chapter 4, Gen. 26.2-5 relates God's promise that the nations shall bless themselves by Isaac's 'seed' for the sake of Abraham, who – God tells Isaac – 'obeyed me and kept my charge, my commandments, my laws and my teachings'.[214] Levinson argues that Abraham's obedience to God's charge is not a reference to minor incidents in the Genesis narrative, because 'the four terms used (charge, commandments, laws, teachings) are specialized', and that 'in the aggregate [the terms] suggest various categories of law rather than situational instructions given to a character in a story'.[215] The result is that, according to Levenson, 'Gen 26:5 has sought to present Abraham as one who is meticulously observant of Sinaitic revelation, even though Moses and the Torah given through him have yet to be'.[216]

One Tannaitic text depicts Abraham's observance of the Torah as producing a reward, developing the tradition present in Gen. 26.5. In *m. Kidd.* 4.14, R. Nehorai differentiates the study of the Torah from other wage-earning occupations, saying:

> I would lay aside all the occupations in the world and teach my son nothing but Torah, for a man enjoys its reward in this world, but its principle remains for the world to come. But all other occupations are not so. When a man falls into illness, old age, or adversity, and cannot engage in his work, what happens? He dies of hunger. But the Torah is not so. Rather, it protects him from all evil in his youth and grants him a future and a hope in his old age. Regarding his youth, what does it say? 'Those who wait for the Lord will have their strength renewed' (Isa 40.31). Regarding his old age what does it say? 'They shall still bear fruit in old age' (Ps 92.15). And thus it says about our father Abraham ... 'Abraham was now old ... and the Lord blessed Abraham in all things' (Gen 24.1). We find that our father Abraham practiced the whole Torah in its entirety before it had been given, as it is said, 'inasmuch as Abraham obeyed me and kept my charge: my commandments, my laws, and my teachings' (Gen 26.5).[217]

The notion that certain divine commandments produce 'fruit' for their adherents 'in this world' *and* accumulate a kind of secondary reward awaiting people in the 'world to come' is common in rabbinic literature (cf. *m. Peah* 1.1). Special works of the Torah are designated as providing 'interest' that the person collects in his lifetime, but the full 'principle' is yielded in the 'world to come'. Study of the Torah is thought to be the pinnacle of such works (cf. *m. Peah* 1.1). The idea in *m. Kidd.* 4.14 is that learning the commandments of the Torah (which entails also performing them) protects a person

---

[213] Levenson, *Between Torah and Gospel*, p. 29.
[214] Cf. Ibid., pp. 18–21. Cf. Megan Warner claims that the focus of Gen. 26.5 is less upon the Torah observance of Abraham's offspring, and more upon the ongoing significance of Abraham's merit across the generations for the upholding of covenant. Cf. idem, *Re-Imagining Abraham: A Re-Assessment of the Influence of Deuteronomism in Genesis* (Leiden: Brill, 2018), p. 73.
[215] Levenson, *Between Torah and Gospel*, p. 20.
[216] Ibid., p. 21.
[217] Herbert Danby (ed. and trans.), *The Mishnah*, p. 329. Also discussed in Levenson, *Between Torah and Gospel*, pp. 26–7. M. Kidd. 4 is often thought to be appended to the Mishnah at a later date.

from the ravages of life and makes him 'blessed in all things'. Other occupations, even though they earn a wage, cannot supply the kind of merit involved in keeping the Torah. So, Abraham, who became 'old' (Gen. 24.1) was not degraded by old age, but rather, became blessed in *all* things' (בכל). Nehorai reasons that this was because Abraham practised *all of* the Torah (את כל התורה) before it was given. The particular blessings that Nehorai conceives of Abraham receiving as a result of his Torah observance are twofold: in his youth, Abraham received renewed vigour due to his patient waiting upon God; and in his advanced age, Abraham received the ultimate 'fruit' of a life dedicated to God's commandments – the birth of his son Isaac (integrating two scriptural intertexts, Isa. 40.31 and Ps. 92.15). Thus, Abraham's Torah observance had intergenerational benefits as well.

Against the backdrop of *Jubilees*, Philo and the rabbis, Jon Levenson suggests – perhaps precipitously – that 'many of the evocations of Abraham in the early church have no resonance at all with this particular tradition of the Torah-observant patriarch'.[218] I have already examined Jas. 2.25-26, and concluded that Abraham's 'works' in this passage could well refer to his deeds of righteousness drawn from broad precepts in the Torah relating to mercy, hospitality, obedience and the imperative to save a life. And indeed, Levenson does concede that James appears to be rebutting Paul's exaggerated view on the same matter.[219] Levenson reads Paul as stating that Abraham *did not* carry out the works of the Law, rather, he had faith (and he was circumcised, but this is presented by Paul as secondary). Paul views the Abrahamic covenant as one of faith, and claims that those who exhibit a similar faith can enter into this covenant *without* having to observe the Torah.

Indeed, Levenson claims that Paul's characterization of Abraham – where the patriarch's 'faith' reigns supreme over his 'works' – is miles away from John's use of the term 'the works of Abraham' in John 8.39.[220] While Levenson does not clarify what John might mean by the phrase, by this statement he seems to indicate that it is somehow opposed to Pauline theology.[221] Levenson writes that the 'message' of John 8.39 is 'patent' – 'the Jews' of the text 'ought to be doing the same thing' as Abraham.[222] If Levenson perceives a contrast between Paul and John on this point, it would actually strengthen his case to argue that the traditions of Abraham as Torah observant are discernible in John's use of the term 'the works of Abraham' (8.39). The logic in this case would be that John viewed Abraham as carrying out the 'works' of the Law, and that on this basis, if Abrahamic paternity is to be claimed by any group, then that group must also imitate Abraham and faithfully keep the Law. Through Abraham's 'works' he garnered a treasury of merits that benefit his descendants vicariously, and which balance out the debt of 'sin' (cf. John 8.31-34). I would claim that John's Jesus asserts that Abraham's merits (his 'works') are only of value to the person who imitates them (John 8.39-40). If there is a contrast between John and Paul – as Levenson intuits, but does not develop – then at least one voice in the textual fabric of John 8 (namely, that of 'the Jews') disputes that faith in Jesus alone (cf. 8.31) leads to the soteriological 'freedom' of the Johannine perspective.

---

[218] Levenson, *Between Torah and Gospel*, pp. 32–3.
[219] Ibid., pp. 56–7.
[220] Ibid., p. 36.
[221] Ibid., p. 35.
[222] Ibid.

I will consider how such a view might actually align with John's Gospel overall, but for now – and as the final part of this section – I will turn to selected early rabbinic texts that deal with the 'works' of Abraham, expressed largely as Abraham's 'merits'. The Tannaitic material – like the other early Jewish material that came before – is not uniform in its perspective on the 'merits of the fathers' and the 'works' that produced these merits for their descendants. This is part of the rich tapestry of debate that informed early Judaism, nascent Christianity and the early rabbinic literature about the figure of Abraham (and the fathers more generally) and his role in protecting, interceding and benefitting his descendants. It is the contention of this book that such debates are incipiently present in John 8.31-59, and discernible only through an extensive intertextual analysis.

Tannaitic rabbinic literature

Abraham figures as an exemplar in the Tannaitic literature but not in the same senses found in the post-biblical texts or the Hellenistic Jewish writings of Josephus and Philo. Abraham – and like him, Isaac, Jacob and Moses – is presented by the rabbis as an ancestral figures of merit, either for his observances of the *mitzvoth*, or for his outstanding virtues in God's service. For example, in the context of discussing the narrative in Exodus where Moses' father-in-law Jethro was said to have heard of the Israelite's war with Amalek, the rabbis begin to talk about the biblical pattern of names being changed upon significant occasions: originally, Moses' father-in-law was merely called Jether (Exod. 4.18), but when he performed good works (מעשׂים טובים) they added a letter, changing his name to Jethro.[223] So with Abraham: initially, he was called 'Avram', but when he performed 'good works' his name gained another letter, and he was called 'Abraham'.[224] For Abraham, the 'good works' in question indubitably began with his circumcision, the first *mitzvah* of the Torah (cf. *m. Ned.* 3.11b).[225] Abraham's Torah observance – his 'works' – are not distinct from his 'good works' in this perspective.

In the *Avot de Rabbi Natan* (*ARN* A), Abraham is exalted far above any other biblical figure. In particular, the 'works' of Abraham are said to be greater than Job's. Despite the latter's works of hospitality and his feeding of the hungry, Job's 'works' did not even reach 'one half of the measure of Abraham'; the author of *ARN* then launches into a lengthy praise of Abraham's good works to show how the patriarch went above and beyond what the circumstances required.[226] This seemingly random one-upmanship between Job and Abraham makes sense in light of late Second Temple traditions praising Job for his exceeding virtues. Thus, in *T. Abr.* 15.14-15, the archangel Michael considers Abraham to be unlike any person on earth, 'not even Job, the wondrous man'.[227] The *Testament*

---

[223] Mekhilta, tractate Amalek 3.36-7, p. 272.
[224] Mekhilta, Amalek 3.41-51, p. 273. The same pattern follows for Sarah and Joshua, and others, all who performed good works and had their names changed.
[225] Danby, *Mishnah*, p. 268.
[226] Version A, par. 7, pp. 50–1.
[227] Other MSS read 'Jacob' instead of 'Job'; cf. Dale C. Allison, 'Job in the *Testament of Abraham*', JSP 12, no. 2 (2001), pp. 131–47, at p. 136. Other comparisons between Abraham and Job can be found in *b. Bava Barta* 15b, and *t. Sot.* 6.1.

of Job 9–12 considered Job's works to be superlatively good: Job was pious, generous, hospitable and excessively philanthropic (9.1-8; 10.1-7). He also gave away much of his wealth to charity (11.1-12), employed others in need and he would not keep his workers' wages overnight (12.1-4; cf. Lev. 19.13).[228] Furthermore, *ARN* favourably compares Abraham to the other fathers (Isaac and Jacob): 'our father Abraham' was worthier of his reward than the angels because he suffered ten trials but was found to be steadfast.[229] The other fathers were tested in ten trials but were not found to be perfect.[230] Abraham even outdoes King David in righteousness, for David was, according to *ARN*, an unjust judge.[231] Abraham was the first to walk in the ways of the Most High, and he received instruction in the divine laws at night.[232] In fact, in his works, Abraham was comparable only to the Holy One himself, for like God, he 'said little and did much'.[233]

More than a focus upon Abraham's exemplary goodness, however, the Tannaitic sources reflect a concern with Abraham's vicarious merits, the fruit of his good works. Earlier, I argued that in some post-biblical Jewish texts, such as *4 Ezra* and *2 Baruch*, the term 'works' was functioning as a precursor for the idea of 'merits', inasmuch as 'works' garnered a treasure in heaven for the doer, which aided them when their sins were weighed at the eschatological judgement. The noun 'righteousness' (צדקה) as we also noted earlier, could stand for 'righteous works', 'good works' or the 'commandments', such as almsgiving (*Tob.* 4.12), which paid back a store of 'credit' to the giver. The commandments, in their life-giving powers, could 'justify' a person (cf. *m. Makkot* 3.15-16).[234] Good deeds create merits that have vicarious effect across the generations in Tannaitic thought (cf. *m. Makkot* 3.15-16; *ARN* A, 77), but one logical step prior to this idea was the equation of 'works' with functional 'merits'. The overlapping uses of the terms צדק and זכות attest to the interconnection of these ideas: the rabbis in fact often translated the biblical Hebrew צדקה to the Mishnaic Hebrew זכות, which was based on the Aramaic.[235] The Targums commonly did the same, with *Tg. Onkelos* translating Abraham's 'righteousness' (צדקה : Gen. 15.6) as 'a meritorious deed' (זכות).

Tzvi Novick convincingly demonstrates that the *Mekhilta's* phrase 'the works/behaviour of the fathers' (מעשי אבות) functions as a 'contextual synonym' for זכות אבות 'the merits of the fathers' as, for example, in the rabbis' discussion of the manna in the wilderness (Exodus 16):

> 'And they turned to the wilderness' (Exod 16.10) ... R. Eliazar of Modi'in says: They turned only to *the works of the fathers*, as it says, 'the wilderness'; just as the wilderness has no trespass of sin, so the first fathers had no trespass or sin.[236]

---

[228] *OTP I*, p. 842ff.
[229] *ARN* B, p. 157.
[230] *ARN*, pp. 162–3.
[231] *ARN*, pp. 156–7.
[232] Ibid. *ARN*, pp. 156–7.
[233] *ARN*, pp. 81–2.
[234] Kister, 'Romans 5.12-21', p. 411; cf. Rosen-Zvi, 'Pauline Traditions', p. 178.
[235] Rosen-Zvi, 'Pauline Traditions', p. 179.
[236] Oxford MS Heb. D 22.5 (Kahana, *Genizah*, p. 71); Novick, *What is Good and What God Demands*, p. 186. The trope of sinlessness is rather extreme, and most rabbis admit the fallibility of the ancestors to some degree. The idea that מעשי prefigures the use of זכות and stands as its semantic

In Eliazar's view, Israel was about to face punishment for the sin of pestering God for food in the desert, and when all hope was lost, they turned to the merits of the fathers to save them (here glossed as the 'works of the fathers'). Earlier in the *Mekhilta*, the rabbis speak of 'turning' to the 'works of the fathers', which Novick takes to be idiomatic.[237] This idiom, and the substitutive phrase 'the works of the fathers' thus represent 'an idealized past that serves as a source of merit, but not of exempla, for later generations'.[238] Likewise, the phrase 'the craft of the fathers' (אבמנות אבות) plays into this same semantic field. In *Mehkilta R. Ish. Beshalach* 3 (27-65) on Exod. 14.9-14, the Israelites cry out to God at the Red Sea for deliverance from Pharaoh and his armies. At this point, they 'seized upon their father's craft' (היפשו לכם אבמנות אבותם), that is, they prayed fervently like Abraham, Isaac and Jacob.[239] This vision is indeed imitative: it is not the merits of the fathers to which the desperate Hebrews appeal, but the 'work' (craftwork) of the fathers – their example in prayer.[240] The merits of Abraham protect his descendants (his 'seed'), but the 'works' of Abraham (and the 'works of the fathers') serve as an example of the kind of behaviour that his descendants can 'turn towards' when they are in dire circumstances.

The early rabbinic concept of the זכות אבות is most likely not only an outgrowth of the idea of the 'works of the fathers', but also a result of the reconfiguration of the concept of 'sin' in the Persian period with the rise of Aramaic. Thus, when sin comes to be thought of as a 'debt', according to Anderson, 'human virtue assumes the role of merit or credit'.[241] This credit is often said to be housed in a metaphorical heavenly treasury that 'can be used to pay down the debt of one's sin' from which eventually comes the idea of the 'merits of the fathers', which construes the virtuous works of Israel's ancestors producing a fund of merit that their descendants can draw upon in times of trouble.[242] Forgiveness of sin comes by means of the remission of 'debt', which God brings about because of the merits of the fathers.

But this is not all: the rabbinic sources depict the wonders and marvels that God wrought on behalf of the Israelites as a result of the 'merits of the fathers'. That is, not only is the elimination of *bad* things (i.e. sins) explained by the countervailing concept of vicarious merits, but also the occurrence of *good* things is explained by the merits of the fathers. The rabbis therefore took the concept of merits in a holistic sense, as a means

---

equivalent is independently voiced by Arthur Marmorstein, *The Doctrine of Merits in Old Rabbinical Literature* (London: Oxford University Press, 1920), p. 10.

[237] Cf. Tractate Amalek 1 (180); Novick, *What is Good and What God Demands*, p. 186, n. 14.

[238] Novick, *What is Good and What God Demands*, p. 186.

[239] Lauterbach (ed.), *Mekhilta*, pp. 137–8, 'imitated their father's occupation'. Novick, *What is Good and What God Demands*, pp. 186–7, follows a different versification.

[240] Cf. *m. Kidd.* 4.14, cited in the previous section, where study of the Torah is presented as a 'craft' or 'occupation' that a father teaches to his son. Abraham was said to have been exemplary in that craft (cf. *m. Kidd.* 4.29a).

[241] Anderson, *Sin*, p. ix. Other precedents include texts such as *Sir.* 3.14-15, where the 'righteous deeds' ('works') of the father are 'remembered' (תזכור) on behalf of the son (cf. Kister, 'Romans 5.12-21', p. 394). Also, the biblical motif of God 'remembering' the fathers as a preventative stay upon his imminent judgement (cf. Exodus 33) probably plays a foundational role in the development of the concept of the merits of the fathers. I have already discussed the interpretive rabbinic overlap of צדק, with זכי which resonates with *Sir.* 3.14-15 and the idea that 'works' (here, righteous works) were a precursor to 'merits'.

[242] Ibid., p. ix.

of describing their total world view. Yet, the etymology of the Aramaic loan verb זכי is notoriously difficult to pin down, while the polysemy of the roots is generally acknowledged.[243] The verb can mean 'to acquire merit' or transitively, to lead someone to acquire merit;[244] it can also mean 'to benefit' or to be worthy;[245] in the pi'el the verb means 'to argue a case' or to plead for acquittal, while the form זכה can mean 'to be acquitted' (in a legal sense).[246] The noun זכות can mean 'acquittal' (cf. *m. San.* 4.1, where the noun displays this meaning sixteen times); it can also mean 'virtue' and 'merit' (as the fruit of virtue), with a specifically vicarious, or intergenerational, benefit.[247] Similarly, the antonym חוב can mean both 'sin'/'debt' and 'condemnation' (as the fruit of sin).

Compared to the vaster Amoraic material, the Tannaitic discussion of the merits of the fathers can appear rather meagre.[248] But this relative sparseness should not make us shy away from the richness of the contextual framework into which the concept is integrated. Notice, for example, the litany-like exposition of the Torah's commandments about Israel coming into the land of the promise in the *Mekhilta de Rabbi Simon bar Yochai* (on Exod. 13.5):

'When the Lord brought you (into the land) ...':

a. Do the commandment, for it is for its reward that you will enter the land
b. '... which He [God] swore to your fathers' (Exod. 13.5)
c. Everything is on account of the merit of your fathers
d. '... to give you' (Exod. 13.5)
e. So that it won't seem to you as if it is an inheritance of your fathers but as if it is now given to you as a gift
f. '...a land flowing with milk and honey' (Exod. 13.5)
g. R. Eliezer says, 'Milk refers to fruit and honey [to] the dates'.[249]

Similarly, in *Sifrei Deuteronomy* (Piskha 184), we find the following midrash (with the italicized texts functioning as the lemmata from Deuteronomy):

And if the Lord your God enlarges your borders – perform the commandment which is stated in this matter, and as a reward *the Lord your God will enlarge your border*; *As he has sworn to your fathers* – everything is due to the merit of your fathers – *and give you all the land* (which he promised to give to your fathers) – everything is due to the merit of your fathers.[250]

---

[243] Cf. Kister, 'Romans 5.12-21', p. 393.
[244] Ibid.
[245] Sanders, *Paul and Palestinian Judaism*, p. 187.
[246] Solomon Schechter, *Some Aspects of Rabbinic Theology* (New York: Macmillan, 1909), p. 171.
[247] Ibid.
[248] Both Schechter (*Aspects of Rabbinic Theology*) and Marmorstein (*The Doctrine of Merits in Old Rabbinic Judaism*) deal in greater depth with the Amoraic material in this regard.
[249] *Mekhilta de Rabbi Simon bar Yochai* Pisha 18.4.1-5A; Epstein-Melamed/Nelson, p. 68; cf. Pisha 19.1.4A-B; Epstein-Melamed/Nelson, p. 75; the version reproduced (MS Firkovich IIA 268).
[250] MS Vatican 32; Louis Finkelstein and H. S. Horovitz (eds), *Sifre al Sefer Devarim* (New York, 1939) [in Hebrew]; and Reuven Hammer (trans. and ed.), *Sifre: A Tannaitic Commentary on the Book of Deuteronomy* (New Haven: Yale University Press, 1986), p. 206.

According to these halakhic midrashim, the gift of the Land, promised to the fathers, comes to the Israelites because of the merits of the fathers. But this fact does not negate the requirement *to do the commandment*. The Land will then truly be their own 'gift' not only the seeming inheritance of their fathers. The version in the *Sifrei* (at least compared to the *Mekhilta bar-Yochai*) appears to be more emphatic of the fact that absolutely *everything* is due to the 'merits of the fathers' especially in relation to the promise of the Land and the enlargement of its borders.

Other Tannaitic texts impute the great wonders that God performed in the Exodus to the merits of the fathers. R. Eleazar of Modi'm interprets the gift of manna from heaven as a result of the 'merits of the fathers'. R. Joshua agrees: the words of God to Moses ('*Behold, I will cause to rain bread from heaven for you*') suggest that the manna came gratuitously; the words 'for you' mean 'surely it is not due to you' because it is the 'merits of Abraham, Isaac and Jacob' that bring the manna for their posterity (Deut. 28.12).[251] The *Mekhilta bar-Yochai* (Sanya 2.2.6A-C) interprets the entire goodness of God in the Exodus as the result of the merits of the fathers: 'In Egypt, Israel became worthy of destruction, but for the sake of the merits of the fathers [I refrained from such a punishment]. As it says, "God heard their moaning" (Exod. 2.24) ... and God remembered his covenant with Abraham, Isaac and Jacob' (Exod. 2.24b).[252]

Abraham is singled out for his good works acquiring merit for his descendants. Each specific deed garnered a corresponding and requisite merit. Speaking of the *Akedah*, R. Banaah says: 'Because of the merit of the deed which Abraham their father did I will divide the Sea for them. For it is said, "And he [Abraham] cleaved the wood for the burnt offering" (Gen. 22.3). And here it is written, "And the waters were cleft"'.[253] R. Simon of Teman claims that Abraham's meritorious deed was actually circumcision, which is why the Sea was divided ('cut'). R. Akiva disagrees, conveying God's words: 'That faith with which they [i.e. the Israelites] believed in Me merits that I should split the sea for them'. Finally, Shema'yah channels God's voice: 'The faith with which their father Abraham believed in me merits that I should divide the sea for them' (with reference to Gen. 15.6).[254]

These examples accept the idea that, in the words of the Mishnah, the fathers' merits and righteousness 'support' Israel forever (cf. *m. Avot* 2.2). But there are dissenting voices. For example, the *Sifre (Deut)* expresses a cynical perspective when commenting on Deut. 32.40 ('And there is none that can deliver out of my hand'):

> Fathers cannot save their children; Abraham cannot save Ishmael; nor can Isaac save Esau. This shows only that fathers cannot save sons. Where do we learn that brothers cannot save brothers? From the verse, *No man can by any means redeem his brother* (Ps 49.8); Isaac cannot save Ishmael, nor can Jacob save Esau. Even if one were to offer all the money in the world, he cannot be granted atonement, as it is said, *No man can by any means redeem his brother, for it is too costly the*

---

[251] *Mekh. De-R. Ishmael, Vayassa* 3.6 (1-5) (Lauterbach (ed.), *Mekhilta*, 2.233-4 MS Venice 1545).
[252] Epstein-Melamed/Nelson (ed.) p.7 (MS T-S Cambridge C 4a.4)*/(MhG).
[253] *Mekh. De-R. Ishmael, Beschallach*, 3.30; Lauterbach (ed.), *Mekhilta*, 2.137-8.
[254] *Mekh. De-R. Ishmael, Beschallach*, 3.30-64; Lauterbach (ed.), *Mekhilta*, 1.145-6 (MS Venice 1545).

redemption of their soul (Ps 49.8-9) – the soul is precious, and when one sins against it, there is no payment that would redeem it.[255]

The Tannaitic sources also express a questioning attitude towards the idea of ancestral merit by using a succinct maxim about merit accruing to meritorious behaviour. Its most basic formulation may be in the *Mekhilta (bar-Yochai), Nezikin* (61.2.4B): מגלגלין זכות על ידי זכאי וחובה על ידי חייב: 'One heaps merit upon the meritorious and culpability upon the culpable'.[256] In the *Tosefta*, we find the variation (attributed to R. Jose), 'merit flows to the days of merit and guilt to the days of guilt' (*t. Yoma* 4.12; *t. Taanit* 3.9).[257] In *Sifrei Deuteronomy* (Piska 229), this rather abstract maxim is given some flesh when contextualized in the case of a house-builder undertaking a positive commandment:

You shall make a parapet for your roof (Deut. 22.8): Rabbi (Judah Ha-Nasi) says: Make a parapet from the time that the house is new. What is the measurement of a parapet? Three handbreadths at the higher point, ten at the lower. *Then you shall make a parapet for you roof* – this is a positive commandment; *that you shall not bring blood (guilt) upon your house* – this is a negative commandment. *If he who falls from there* (22.8): It may be fitting that he should fall, nevertheless, merit is brought about by the meritorious and guilt by the guilty.[258]

In the same text, R. Hananiah ben Gamliel reflects: 'Merit is never replaced by guilt, nor guilt by merit, except in the cases of Reuben and David' (*Sifre Deut.* Piskha 347). R. Hananiah disagrees with the words of the Sages, who say: 'Merit is never replaced by guilt nor guilt by merit, but one receives a reward for the *mitzvoth* and punishment for transgressions' (*Sifre Deut.* Piskha 347).[259] These sayings appear to argue against the validity of the זכות אבות, by stating that wrongdoing (guilt) can never be attenuated by merit – whether that merit occurs in the future or did occur in the past – nor can a person's performance of the *mitzvoth*, or his works of virtue/merit, be affected by the

---

[255] *Sifre Deut.* Piskha 329 (Hammer (ed.), *Sifre: A Tannaitic Commentary on the Book of Deuteronomy*, p. 340 (Finkelstein and Horovitz (eds), *Sifre al Sefer Devarim*, BIR Online) *Sifrei Deut* asserts that descent from *Jacob* matters, not descent from Abraham (i.e. anyone can claim Abraham as their father). Abraham only obeyed one command, but Jacob observed the whole Torah (Piska 336, p. 345)! The progeny of Abraham included idolaters (Piska 31, pp. 55–6), but Jacob's progeny were pure (cf. p. 57). These are Hammer's notes on pp. 18–19. *Sifre Deut.* Piskha 31; Hammer (ed.) *Sifre: A Tannaitic Commentary on the Book of Deuteronomy*, pp. 55–7 has a positive view of Jacob's merits though. And Piska 146, p. 185).

[256] David Nelson, *Mekhilta De-Rabbi Shimon Bar Yochai: Translated into English with Critical Introduction and Annotation* (Philadelphia, PA: Jewish Publication Society, 2006); Epstein and Ezra Melamed, *Mehkhilta de-Rabbi Shimon ben Yochai* (Jerusalem: Mekize Nedarim, 1955) [in Hebrew], p. 278; MS Firkovich II A 268.

[257] For *t. Yoma* 4.12, accessed at BIR online.

[258] Finkelstein and Horovitz (eds), *Sifre al Sefer Devarim*, BIR online; (Hammer (ed.), *Sifre: A Tannaitic Commentary on the Book of Deuteronomy*, pp. 238–40) Other morals to the story in *Sifre*: What this shows is that merit flows to the meritorious and humiliation to those who are disgraceful (*Sifre Num.* 68, par. 5; Horowitz, p. 63/Neusner, pp. 28–9). Repeated par. 114, Horowitz, p. 123/Neusner, p. 175.

[259] Hammer (ed.), *Sifre: A Tannaitic Commentary on the Book of Deuteronomy*, pp. 359–60.

guilt and punishment of another person to whom he stands in some proximity of relationship.

Such contradictory opinions on the זכות אבות would continue to be worked out in the Amoraic period, where the aggadic midrashim would deal extensively with the topic (and one might argue, largely in a positive fashion). Abraham would also continue to figure as a source of merit for those near to him. For example, the pitcher of water that sustained Hagar in the wilderness remained full because of the merits of Abraham, until Hagar turned to idolatry (*PRE* 30).[260] The same can be said for those remote from Abraham: his merit provided a well for Hagar, which later sustained the seed of Abraham (*Yalk.Shim* 1, 764).[261] The Bavli viewed the success of Daniel's prayer (Dan. 9.4-19) as due to the merits of Abraham (*Berakot* 7b).[262] The Akedah was still seen as the greatest source of merit for Abraham's seed (*Gen. R.* 61; *Targum Pseudo-Jonathan* to Gen. 12.14).[263]

In sum, the Tannai'im were preserving and developing ideas found in the Second Temple literature, which included the NT (which is not to say that the rabbis were conversant with the NT, although this has been proposed in the scholarship before).[264] We can see the Tannaitic rabbis discuss the virtues of Abraham as causative of subsequent wonders and miracles experienced by Israel in history, as well as the presentation of Abraham as one lauded for his 'works' of hospitality and kindness. The 'works of the fathers' also merges to become the 'merits of the fathers' with the corollary that in times of need, these merits can be drawn upon by Abraham's descendants. Although dissenting voices emerge to protest that good works and merits cannot have a vicarious benefit, this is in line with what we have seen in the to and fro of the antecedent Jewish literature of antiquity.

Now that I have explored in considerable depth the intertextual fabric of Abraham's 'works' in early Judaism, it remains to examine the Johannine (intratextual) context to map out the meanings of 'works' and how that might inform the expression 'the works of Abraham' in John 8.39. What follows in the final part of the chapter is a brief reading of John 8.39-40 from a 'resistant' (or integrative) Jewish perspective in light of having 'scripted' this intertextual field.

Part 2: The Johannine context

There are several ways in which the terms 'works'/work (ἔργα/ἔργον) are used in John's Gospel and, similarly, in the First Epistle of John. A number of leading scholars have argued that in several places in the Gospel, these terms have a distinctively 'Johannine'

---

[260] www.sefaria.org.
[261] Cited in Sandmel, 'Philo's Place in Judaism: Part II', p. 330.
[262] www.sefaria.org.
[263] Ibid.
[264] Cf. Peter Schäfer, *Jesus in the Talmud* (Princeton and Oxford: Princeton University Press, 2007), especially the Gospel of John (pp. 72-3, 124-9) where Schäfer claims the Bavli is a 'powerful countergospel' to the Gospel of John.

presentation.²⁶⁵ Jesus' 'works' are said to designate the miraculous 'signs' of God, and ἔργα thus replaces σημεῖα (from John's ostensible source material).²⁶⁶ John's usage is also distinct from the Synoptic Gospels' in that the latter never have Jesus refer to his own activity by the words ἔργα/ἐργάζομαι.²⁶⁷ While the Gospel uses the term ἔργα to refer to miraculous 'signs' (e.g. 5.20-21; 7.3; 9.3-5; 10.25-26; 32-33; 14.10-14; 15.24),²⁶⁸ this usage is by no means the only one. It is important, therefore, to examine the uses ἔργα/ἐργάζομαι in John on a case-by-case basis, to avoid subsuming them under the rubric of John's idiosyncratic use of the term 'works'. In this way, we will be able to better address the question of whether the reference to 'Abraham's works' in John 8.39 aligns with the broader characteristic Johannine usage just identified, or whether it parallels certain other streams of tradition present within biblical and post-biblical Jewish literature.²⁶⁹

Works as signs and testimony

Jesus' 'works' are frequently presented as wondrous miracles of God, which simultaneously authenticate his mission and identity. As such, Jesus' 'works' often take place in the context of juridical debates with his opponents.²⁷⁰ Simultaneously, allusions to God's 'wondrous works' as 'signs' in the Exodus narrative coalesce with this forensic perspective.²⁷¹ We first encounter this usage in John 5. There, Jesus appears in Jerusalem at an unnamed 'feast of the Jews' (5.1) and heals a lame man at the pool of Bethsaida (5.2-9a). The narrator interjects to inform his readers that controversy subsequently arose between Jesus and the Jews because it was a Sabbath (5.9b).²⁷² After a short narrative interlude detailing the exchanges between the healed man and the Jews (5.10-12), between Jesus and the healed man (5.14) and between the healed man

---

[265] C. H. Dodd, *Historical Tradition in the Fourth Gospel* (Cambridge: Cambridge University Press, 1963), p. 185.
[266] Urban C. von Wahlde, *The Earliest Version of John's Gospel: Recovering the Gospel of Signs* (Wilmington: Michael Glazier, 1989), pp. 36–41. Cf. Robert T. Fortna, *The Gospel of Signs: A Reconstruction of the Narrative Source Underlying the Fourth Gospel* (SNTSMS 11; Cambridge: Cambridge University Press, 1970).
[267] Peter W. Ensor, *Jesus and His Works: The Johannine Sayings in Historical Perspective* (WUNT; Tübingen: Mohr Siebeck, 1996), p. 91.
[268] On the 'seven signs' in the Gospel, see, Jeannine K. Brown, 'Creation's Renewal in the Gospel of John', *CBQ* 72 (2010), pp. 275–90, at p. 287.
[269] Of course, John 8.39 could reflect both traditions, not simply one or the other.
[270] Some seminal monographs on this topic include: Andrew T. Lincoln, *Truth on Trial: The Lawsuit Motif in the Fourth Gospel* (Peabody: Hendrickson, 2000); Asiedu-Peprah, *Johannine Sabbath Conflicts as Juridical Controversy*; and Parsenios, *Rhetoric and Drama in the Johannine Lawsuit Motif*, WUNT 2.258.
[271] Cf. Jacob J. Enz, 'The Book of Exodus as a Literary Type for the Gospel of John', *JBL* 76 (1957), pp. 208–15; cf. Stan Harstine, *Moses as a Character in the Fourth Gospel: A Study of Ancient Reading Techniques* (London and New York: Sheffield Academic Press, 2002).
[272] The parenthetical nature of this remark has led some commentators to perceive it as incidental to the narrative, or a secondary redaction, for example Dodd, *Historical Tradition*, p. 178; Bultmann, *The Gospel of John*, p. 239, n. 2; Schnackenburg, *John* 2.96-8; Lindars, *The Gospel of John*, p. 215. However, as the Sabbath becomes the chief point of contention between Jesus and the Jews (5.12), the narrator's early explanation is critical, signifying an imminent and 'distinct turn' in the story (Thomas, 'The Man at the Pool', p. 12).

and the Jews once more (5.15), the narrator continues: 'Therefore the Jews started persecuting (διώκω) Jesus, because he was doing such things on the Sabbath' (5.16).[273] Without further comment, the text conveys Jesus' riposte to the Jews: 'My Father is still working, and I also am working' (ὁ πατήρ μου ἕως ἄρτι ἐργάζεται κἀγὼ ἐργάζομαι, 5.17), a response that illustrates Jesus' healing activity as wondrous 'works' performed in conjunction with, not just under the inspiration of, God.[274] The unity of Jesus and the Father has, in the Prologue, been emphasized (1.1-18), and the reader takes the reference to their conjoint 'working' to mean the ongoing work of creation.[275] The Jews do not respond, but the narrator explains that, beyond persecuting Jesus (cf. 5.16), the Jews wished 'all the more to kill' him, 'because he was not only breaking the Sabbath, but was also calling God his own Father, thereby making himself equal to God' (5.18).[276]

The text moves into a long monologue about the authority Jesus holds as only Son of the Father; in line with conventions found in both ancient Greco-Roman rhetorical handbooks and Jewish legal codes, Jesus adduces 'witnesses' to testify on his behalf (5.19-47).[277] Jesus tells the Jews that he has no power to do anything other than what he sees his father doing, because the Son does as the Father does (5.19). This is because the Father 'loves the Son' and willingly shows the Son his own activity (5.20a); in fact, the Father will show the Son 'greater works than these, so that you will be astonished' (καὶ μείζονα τούτων δείξει αὐτῷ ἔργα, ἵνα ὑμεῖς θαυμάζητε, 5.20b). One of these 'greater works' will be the Son's ability to give life to whomever he wishes, following his Father's ability to raise the dead (5.21). Jesus promises his audience that whoever 'hears' his word and thereby believes in God who sent him, receives eternal life without being brought to judgement (5.24a). This is how Jesus 'gives life' to whomever he pleases – for the absence of judgement entails the passage from 'death to life' (5.24b). God the Father has life in himself, and thus also the Son has life in himself (5.26), and also possesses the authority to judge humanity (5.27). The Son's judgement will be just: those who have 'done good' (οἱ τὰ ἀγαθὰ ποιήσαντες) will come to 'the resurrection of life' (ἀνάστασιν ζωῆς), and those who have 'practiced evil' (τὰ φαῦλα πράξαντες) will come to 'the resurrection of condemnation' (ἀνάστασιν κρίσεως, 5.29; cf. 3.19).

The discourse then shifts to the topic of Jesus' witnesses. Jesus tells the Jews that he only seeks to do the will of the One who sent him (5.30). If he were to testify about himself, his testimony would be invalid (5.31). The Father testifies as Jesus' first witness (5.32). John (the 'Baptist') also testified to Jesus, although Jesus refutes the need to rely upon human testimony (5.34). Jesus continues, 'I have a testimony greater than John's: the *works* that the Father has given me to complete (τὰ γὰρ ἔργα ἃ δέδωκέν μοι ὁ πατὴρ ἵνα τελειώσω αὐτά), the very works that I am doing (αὐτὰ τὰ ἔργα ἃ ποιῶ), testify on my behalf that the Father has sent me' (5.36). But, Jesus claims, the Jews

---

[273] Asiedu-Peprah observes that the imperfect ἐδίωκον is iterative (5.16), suggesting that Jesus' Sabbath-breaking' resulted in repeated accusations from the Jews – there were possibly other violations not known to the reader (*Johannine Sabbath Conflicts*, pp. 74-5).
[274] Asiedu-Peprah, *Johannine Sabbath Conflicts*, p. 76.
[275] Ibid.
[276] The μᾶλλον in this sentence (v. 18) reinforces the iterative ἐδίωκον above (v. 16), and the implicated, unstated narratives of other Sabbath violations.
[277] Alicia D. Myers, '"Jesus Said to Them...": The Adaptation of Juridical Rhetoric in John 5.19-47', *JBL* 132, no. 2 (2013), pp. 415-30.

have never 'heard' the Father's voice, neither have they 'seen' his 'shape' – and because they do not have the 'word' of the Father 'abiding' in them – they do not believe Jesus' words (5.38; cf. 8.31-32). In fact, Jesus tells them that they turn to the wrong source for 'eternal life': they 'search the scriptures' when they could easily come to Jesus to have life (5.39; cf. vv. 46-47). For Jesus, this amounts to the rejection of his person as the unique envoy of the Father (5.43). In a concluding word of judgement upon the Jews, Jesus tells them that they have 'no love of God' in them (5.42), and that they do not seek God's glory (5.44).

In the forensic reading, Jesus 'works' (τὰ ἔργα; 5.36) are pieces of evidence used to support his claim to be the Son of the Father, and which in turn, should lead the Jews to believe in him.[278] But to which 'works' does Jesus refer? The healing of the lame man is a 'work' that sets off the entire discourse about Jesus' authority and identity, and so it is obviously in view.[279] The healing of the lame man is referred to simply as a 'work' not as a 'sign'. Jesus expects his 'works' to produce belief, but paradoxically, he publicly regrets the fact that his '*signs*' produce belief (2.23-25; 6.27) – that is that there is an insufficient, 'signs-based' faith in him. Faith merely awakened on the basis of 'signs' seems too superficial, and Jesus is not satisfied with it. Yet, Jesus' 'signs' and his 'works' – at least here in Chapter 5 – seem to be of the same miraculous order, so why should the former pose a problem for belief, while the latter be required to elicit belief?

The answer seems to lie in the importance of the Sabbath (5.16). Not only does Jesus' violation of the Sabbath lead to his trial before the Jews in a narrative sense, but the concept of Jesus' 'works' is subtly defined by the prohibited activity of 'working'. Jesus' 'works' (τὰ ἔργα) point to his union with God *because* – as Creator God and 'Father' of Jesus – he is constantly 'working' (ἐργάζομαι, 5.17). Thus, Jesus is also permitted to 'work' at all times, even on the Sabbath. The healing of the lame man was therefore a necessary 'work' flowing from his source in God, the giver of life. And Jesus will continue to perform 'works' such as these – 'greater works' that also relate to the giving of life to those who believe. These are the 'works' that the Father has given Jesus to do, and the 'works' that Jesus faithfully does (5.37). As such, they testify to Jesus' origins in God and the fact that he is God's envoy, and so not subject to the prohibitions that restrict 'working' on the Sabbath.[280] It is notable that Jesus refers once again to the healing of the lame man in ch. 7 v. 21, in debate with the Jews at Sukkot, when he says, 'I performed one work (ἓν ἔργον ἐποίησα), and all of you are astonished'. Jesus wonders why the Jews accuse him for making a whole man well – as though Jesus had saved the man's life and not simply cured a chronic illness. Jesus compares his 'work' in ch. 5 vv. 2-9 to circumcision as an instance of making 'part' of a man well, and which also may be performed on the Sabbath (7.22-23). Jesus implies that the two are alike and that therefore he was engaging in *pikuach nefesh* – which justifies breaking the Sabbath. This is intriguing because it would mean that Jesus saw his 'works' (relating

---

[278] Cf. Haenchen, *John*, p. 293.
[279] The 'works' could refer to Jesus' entire ministry, or to the whole suite of his miracles thus far; cf. Ensor, *Jesus and His Works*, pp. 229–33.
[280] The prohibited 'works' included carrying objects (cf. the man carrying his mat) and any 'healing' of a person that is not immediately necessary. One may override the Sabbath to save a life (*pikuach nefesh*) but the lame man was ill for 38 years (i.e. he had a chronic condition and was not acutely ill).

to the giving of life; cf. 5.26) as his faithful performance of the *positive commandments* of the Torah, which override the 'negative' commandments (such as what one should not do on the Sabbath).

A similar scene unfolds in ch. 10. At Hanukkah, in the temple, the Jews confront Jesus again, demanding to know his identity: is he the Messiah or not? (10.22-24). Jesus replies in much the same manner as he did in ch. 5 vv. 36-37: 'The works that I do in my Father's name testify to me (τὰ ἔργα ἃ ἐγὼ ποιῶ ἐν τῷ ὀνόματι τοῦ πατρός μου ταῦτα μαρτυρεῖ περὶ ἐμοῦ); but you do not believe, because you do not belong to my sheep' (10.25-26). Jesus' 'sheep' hear his voice and follow him (10.27; cf. 10.15; 5.25), and Jesus gives them 'eternal life' (10.28; cf. 5.24). But it is when Jesus tells them 'The Father and I are one' (10.30) that events truly sour, and the Jews take up stones 'again' (πάλιν) to stone him (10.31; cf. 8.59). Seemingly perplexed by this turn of events, Jesus replies, 'I have shown you many good works (πολλὰ ἔργα καλὰ) from the Father. For which of these are you going to stone me?' (10.32).[281] The Jews reply, 'It is not for your good work (καλοῦ ἔργου) that we are going to stone you, but for blasphemy, because you, though only a human being, are making yourself God' (10.32-33; cf. 5.18). Jesus produces a convoluted argument on the basis of a scriptural proof text to show that he is indeed 'God's son' and not blaspheming (10.34-36). Then he adds, 'If I am not doing the works of my Father (τὰ ἔργα τοῦ πατρός μου), then do not believe me. But if I do them, even though you do not believe me, believe the works (τοῖς ἔργοις πιστεύετε), so that you may know and understand that the Father is in me and I am in the Father' (10.37-38).

There are a number of parallels between this text and ch. 5 vv. 19-47. Jesus does 'works' in his Father's 'name' (10.25a) – representing the Father's 'person'.[282] This appears not only to echo, but also to develop, the idea in ch. 5 v. 17 that Jesus 'works' in simultaneity with the Father. In ch. 10 v. 25b, Jesus states that the 'works' he does in his Father's name 'testify' to him, but that the Jews refuse to believe, an almost exact repetition of Jesus' statement in ch. 5 v. 36 that the 'works' the Father gave Jesus to do 'testify' on his behalf. The idea of the dead 'hearing' the voice of the Son in ch. 5 vv. 25, 28 is developed in ch. 10 v. 27 to convey the idea that the living can believe in Jesus, 'hear' his voice and belong to his sheepfold. In both cases, Jesus gives believers 'eternal life' (10.28; 5.24).[283] There is also a parallel scenario of the Jews confronting Jesus about the issue of his 'oneness' with God. In ch. 5 v. 18, the Jews are troubled by Jesus 'making himself equal to God' by calling God 'Father'. In ch. 10 vv. 32-33, the Jews charge Jesus with blasphemy for 'making himself God' although he is only a man. The narrator brings the murderous intentions and actions of the Jews to the fore in both texts. While the issue of Jesus' blasphemy occasions a lengthy, defensive discourse in ch. 5, in ch. 10 it warrants only a concluding statement by Jesus about the

---

[281] Possibly a reference to Jesus' wondrous healings (Ensor, *Jesus and His Works*, p. 233).
[282] D. Françoise Tolmie, 'The Characterization of God in the Fourth Gospel', *JSNT* 69 (1998), pp. 57–75, at pp. 66–7.
[283] Bruce, *The Gospel of John*, p. 233; John Painter, 'Tradition, History and Interpretation in John 10', in Johannes Beutler and Robert T. Forta (eds), *The Shepherd Discourse of John 10 and Its Context: Studies by Members of the Johannine Writings Seminar* (SNTSMS 67; Cambridge: Cambridge University Press, 1991), pp. 53–74, at p. 53.

evidence of Jesus' 'works'. And it is here that one of the differences between ch. 5 and ch. 10 emerges.

First, Jesus refers to the 'works' he performs as 'the works of my father' (τὰ ἔργα τοῦ πατρός μου, 10.37). The genitive indicates that the 'works' in question are not just the 'works' that Jesus does or has to do, but that in some sense they are his Father's 'works'.[284] The fact that they are also *Jesus'* works signals that he and the Father are 'one'. Second, Jesus hints that his visible 'works' might induce his interlocutors to believe that there is another source behind Jesus' works, that Jesus might be doing the 'works' of another figure who is *not* the Father of Jesus ('If I am not doing the works of my Father, then do not believe me. But if I do them', 10.37-38a).[285] If Jesus' 'works' are evidently destructive, they will be proven to be 'not of God'. Jesus speaks of the plain evidence of the works themselves as a reason for believing; there is no need to focus on Jesus' person (' even if you do not believe me', 10.38b), but there is an urgency to believe in the 'works' (10.38c). Thus, will the Jews come to see that the Father is 'in' Jesus and that Jesus is 'in' the Father (10.38d).

Another notable difference between ch. 5 vv. 19-47 and ch. 10 vv. 22-39 is that in ch. 10 vv. 32-33, Jesus refers to his 'works' as *good works* (ἔργα καλὰ). This calls into question the categorical distinction frequently made in NT scholarship between 'works' and 'good works'.[286] The two concepts are deliberately blended in ch. 10 vv. 22-39. The Jews acknowledge Jesus' 'good work' (καλοῦ ἔργου), perhaps as a positive *mitzvah* of the Torah, but they are riled by the fact that he is 'making himself equal to God' (10.33). The Jews in ch. 10 vv. 31-33 are clarifying their stance towards Jesus: his 'good works' are not contentious, but his rationale for performing those works is, and remains, highly problematic. The Jews want a direct answer about Jesus' identity (cf. 10.24), and in their view, Jesus' 'works' do not provide the requisite evidence to determine his identity. But Jesus' 'works' are, like his 'signs' (10.40-42), declarative testimonies to his identity, much like the miracles of Hanukkah – the feast contextualizing ch. 10 vv. 22-39 – are recalled in order to facilitate belief in God.[287]

Other texts in the Gospel speak more directly to the sense of Jesus' 'works' as testimony to his status as the 'sent one' of the Father. In the farewell discourse, Jesus questions the apparently doltish Philip, 'Do you not believe that I am in the Father and the Father is in me? The words that I say to you I do not speak on my own; but the Father who dwells in me does his works' (14.10). This statement moves a step further than ch. 5 v. 19, with Jesus acting on the basis of what he *sees* the Father doing; now he tells his disciples that all of his actions are really the product of the Father who indwells him, and they are the Father's 'works'. Jesus' prior statement in ch. 10 v. 38 about his 'works' as evidence of his mutual indwelling with the Father is also elaborated here. As in ch. 10 vv. 36-38, Jesus encourages Philip to believe in the mutual indwelling of the

---

[284] Ensor, *Jesus and His Works*, p. 234.
[285] Compare John 8.41 (44) to 1 John 3.
[286] Cf. Dunn, *The New Perspective*, p. 111; and, taking the Reformation polemics as his framework, N. T. Wright, *Justification: God's Plan and Paul's Vision* (Downers Grove: Intervarsity Press, 2009), p. 116.
[287] Brian C. Dennert, 'Hanukkah and the Testimony of Jesus' Works (John 10.22-39)', *JBL* 132, no. 2 (2013), pp. 431–51.

Father and the Son on the basis of 'the works themselves' (10.11). But in ch. 14 v. 10, Jesus' 'words' and his 'works' are aligned; even Jesus' speech is a reflection of his Father's 'works'.[288] Additionally, Jesus promises his disciples that they too will perform the very 'works' of Jesus – even greater works than Jesus – if they believe in him (14.12).[289] Jesus' departure to the Father will facilitate this (14.12); and when Jesus' disciples ask him for anything in his 'name', Jesus will do it so that the Father may be 'glorified' in the Son (14.13-14). Answer to prayer is intrinsically tied up with the disciples' performance of Jesus' 'works', suggesting that Jesus motivates his disciples' 'works' in the same way that his own 'works' were motivated by the Father. The new element in this part of the Gospel (cf. 13.1-17.26) is that the disciples' 'works' will lead to Jesus' 'glorification'.

A second reference to Jesus' 'works' in the farewell discourse is connected to the theme of the 'world's' sin (15.24), a new topic in the farewell discourse to this point.[290] The forensic connotations to Jesus' 'works' are brought to their logical conclusion at this point.[291] Jesus warns his disciples that the world 'hated' him, and that it will therefore also hate the disciples in his absence (15.18).[292] But, states Jesus, this is because the disciples do not 'belong' to the world (15.19). The world did not keep Jesus' word – instead, they persecuted him, and Jesus' disciples – as his servants – can expect the same treatment (15.20b). The world's persecution of the disciples will result from the fact that 'they' (the world) did not 'know' God (15.21).[293] Moreover, Jesus states that they ought to have known God because Jesus came and spoke to them; Jesus' words should have been enough to lead them to the knowledge of God. If Jesus had not come and spoken to them, 'they would not have sin; but now they have no excuse for their sin' (15.22). The 'sin' of the world is understood in this passage as a lack of knowledge for God resulting from an evident refusal to hear Jesus' words. And Jesus' 'words' leave the world with no excuse: once spoken, his words stands as irrefutable proof of his status as being 'sent' by God. The world's rejection of Jesus is configured as 'hatred' for both Jesus and God: 'Whoever hates me hates my Father also' (15.23; cf. 7.1-4b).

---

[288] Although not, as Bultmann would have, distinctly so – Jesus' 'works' encompass more than his words. (See Bultmann, *The Gospel of John*, p. 609.) On the trope of 'words' and 'works' aligning in Hellenistic Jewish literature, see the previous sections of this chapter. Raymond Brown (John 2.598) sees this motif of the alignment between words and works as evidence of the testamentary genre of John 13–17.

[289] Ashton, *Understanding*, p. 470, argues that these works are 'greater' insofar as the disciples will not be 'hampered by the restrictions of space and time' as Jesus was during his ministry. Jacobus Kok, *New Perspectives on Healing, Restoration, and Reconciliation in John's Gospel* (Leiden: Brill, 2017), p. 165, makes the case for an integrated reading of all the passages concerning the unity of the Father and Son, and Jesus' 'works' as healing actions.

[290] Troels Engberg-Pedersen, 'A Question of Genre: John 13–17 as *Paraklēsis*', in Kasper Bro Larsen (ed.), *The Gospel of John as Genre Mosaic* (SANt 3; Göttingen: Vandenhoeck & Ruprecht, 2015), pp. 283–302, at p. 288.

[291] Ensor, *Jesus and His Works*, p. 242, argues that the reference to Jesus' 'works' designates his entire ministry.

[292] They will not, like Jesus, be alone in their suffering; cf. Parsenios, *Departure and Consolation*, p. 94. Cf. Myers, *Characterizing Jesus*, p. 128.

[293] The plural is telling: the Jews are implied here – they alone are accused by Jesus throughout the Gospel as not knowing God (5.44; 8.53). On the places of overlap between 'the Jews' and 'the world' in John, see Lars Kierspel, *The Jews and the World in the Fourth Gospel: Parallelism, Function, and Context* (Tübingen: Mohr Siebeck, 2006).

Works and binary dualism

In John 3.19-21, the Gospel establishes a contrast between 'evil works' (ἔργα πονηρὰ) and 'works' done 'in God' (τὰ ἔργα ... ἐν θεῷ).[294] The narrator explains that those whose deeds are evil 'hate the light and avoid it' (3.20a) because the light exposes their evil activity (3.20b).[295] This, in turn, is the reason that people in general 'loved darkness rather than light, because their works were evil' (3.19). The narrator thus assigns the vast majority of people – who rejected the testimony of the community speaking in the narrator's name (3.11) – to the realm of evildoers. Those who choose not to believe in 'God's only son' are condemned already (3.18). Their judgement is the darkness in which they are enshrouded and which they 'love' (3.19). They are characterized as hiding from the light in order to undertake evil 'works' covertly. By contrast, those who do what is 'true' (ὁ δὲ ποιῶν τὴν ἀλήθειαν) come boldly into the light so that it may be evident to all that their 'works' are 'worked in God' (τὰ ἔργα ὅτι ἐν θεῷ ἐστιν εἰργασμένα, 3.21b). The revelation of their works of 'truth' also constitutes their judgement: they did not love darkness or evil, they are the ones who 'believed' and so 'are not condemned' (3.18a). Their belief in the 'son', and in God's love for the world (3.16) is identified with their propensity to 'do what is true', to come to the light, and to show that they 'works their works' in God.

Furthermore, in this text there is a play on the motif of openness and secrecy found later in the narrative (7.1-4). At the beginning of Sukkot, Jesus' brothers tell him that his (evidently *good*) 'works' must be made known to the world; people engaging in such wondrous works do not typically render themselves invisible. In ch. 3 vv. 19-21, the narrator explains that those who do evil works are the ones who typically hide from others' view, either out of shame or a desire not to be caught and held to account. The narrator explains that, nevertheless, the darkness into which evildoer's retreat is indicative of the judgement – which in John's realized eschatology occurs in the present – that they have chosen to bring upon themselves through their unbelief.[296] That judgement is clearly related to the wilful obtuseness of those who 'loved darkness' – evildoers are condemned because *although* the 'light' has 'come into the world', they still preferred to hide in darkness. Somewhat circularly, their preference for darkness is explained as a *result* of their 'evil works'. As in ch. 7 v. 6, where the world is described as 'hating' Jesus *because* he confronts it over the fact of its evil works, here in ch. 3 vv. 19-20 we read that the performance of 'evil works' creates a love of darkness and a shunning of 'the light'. Reading ch. 3 vv. 19-21 and ch. 7 vv. 1-6 in tandem, the 'love of darkness' (3.19) characteristic of evildoers is expressed as a hatred of the light (7.6): Jesus acts as a convicting 'light' revealing the evil works of the world, and he is hated for that reason (cf. 15.23-25).

---

[294] The expression is literally 'works worked in God'. For a discussion of the binary rhetoric of ch. 3 vv. 19-21, see Reinhartz, *Befriending the Beloved Disciple*, p. 25.

[295] There is much comment over whether ch. 3 vv. 11-21 represents the voice of Jesus, as he continues to speak to Nicodemus (3.1-10), or the voice of the narrator, who takes over Jesus' speech and delivers a discourse on the topic of revelation, addressing a plural audience.

[296] Keener, *The Gospel of John* 1.572.

This set of structured, dualistic binaries ('light' and 'darkness'; 'love' and 'hatred'; 'truth' and 'evil') which frame the concept of 'works', indicates another nuance to John's use of the term, which is taken up more complexly in the First Epistle of John. In 1 John, the plural ἔργα is used twice (3.8, 12; and once in the singular at 3.18), but its varied expression is inextricably bound up with a network of associated concepts, such as sin, righteousness, lawlessness and a person's predetermined origins, so that any discussion of what is meant by 'works' in 1 John is by no means straightforward. The first relevant text is 1 John 3.7-12:

> Little children, let no one deceive you. Everyone who does what is right is righteous, just as he is righteous. Everyone who commits sin is a child of the devil; for the devil has been sinning from the beginning. The Son of God was revealed for this purpose, to destroy *the works of the devil* (τὰ ἔργα τοῦ διαβόλου). Those who have been born of God do not sin, because God's seed abides in them; they cannot sin, because they have been born of God. The children of God and the children of the devil are revealed in this way: all who do not do what is right are not from God, nor are those who do not love their brothers and sisters. For this is the message you have heard from the beginning, that we should love one another. We must not be like Cain who was from the evil one and murdered his brother. And why did he murder him? Because his own works were evil (τὰ ἔργα αὐτοῦ πονηρὰ) and his brother's righteous.

The use of τὰ ἔργα in both 1 John 3.8 and 3.12 is immediately reminiscent of John 8.39, 41. The present participles ('doing sin' and 'doing righteousness') describe 'the characteristic way of being of a person' and not simply their singular acts.[297] Whoever 'does sin' is a 'child of the devil', but the Son came to destroy the devil's 'works', and by implication, to alter the fundamental characteristics of those who love to do evil (cf. John 3.19-21). The sinner is a 'child of the devil' (3.8a), because the devil 'has been sinning from the beginning' (3.8b). This ominous detail indicates that sin is not merely a 'contingent error, but something powerful and personified that can enslave a practitioner'.[298]

What is meant by 'the works of the devil' in 1 John 3.8? In the immediate context of this passage, the phrase appears to be explained by two things: the references to 'sin' in ch. 3 vv. 4-6, and the reference to the figure of Cain in ch. 3 v. 12.[299] As noted in Chapter 4, the author of 1 John conceives of 'sin' as 'lawlessness' (3.4), as something that occludes proper sight and knowledge of Jesus (3.6), and as the opposite of righteousness and right conduct (3.7). The allusions to the primeval figure of Cain, and the sin that crouched at his door, needing to be mastered (Gen. 4.7), are discernible.[300] The commonality with John 8.33-34 ('whoever commits sin is a slave') is also starkly evident.

---

[297] John Painter, *1, 2 and 3 John* (SP 18; Collegeville: Liturgical Press, 2002), p. 228.
[298] Lieu, *I, II & III John, A Commentary* (Louisville: Westminster/John Knox, 2008), p. 129.
[299] Lieu, *I, II & III John*, pp. 129, 139, suggests that the Cain narrative of Genesis 4 is also alluded to in 1 John 3.4 and 3.9.
[300] Lieu, *I, II & III John*, p. 129.

But however enslaving sin can be, the author of 1 John also perceives it as something that can be removed. The community is told, 'You know that he was revealed to take away sins (καὶ οἴδατε ὅτι ἐκεῖνος ἐφανερώθη, ἵνα τὰς ἁμαρτίας ἄρῃ), and in him there is no sin' (3.5). This statement is virtually repeated in ch. 3 v. 8b, 'The Son of God was revealed for this purpose (εἰς τοῦτο ἐφανερώθη ὁ υἱὸς τοῦ θεοῦ), to destroy the works of the devil' (ἵνα λύσῃ τὰ ἔργα τοῦ διαβόλου; cf. ἐκεῖνος in 2.6; 3.3). The 'taking away' (αἴρω) of 'sins' (ἁμαρτίας) in ch. 3 v. 5 (cf. John 1.29) corresponds with, and is to be interpreted by, the 'loosing' (λύω) of the devil's 'works' in ch. 3 v. 8. In that light, the 'works' of the devil (τὰ ἔργα τοῦ διαβόλου) must be understood as sin – and sin must be understood as 'lawlessness'. Lawlessness, by implication, is the opposite of righteousness (3.7), and thus to act rightly is to act lawfully. By taking away sin (3.5) and unbinding the devil's 'works' (3.8b), Jesus is positioned restoring something fundamental to the cosmic order – the ability of humans to reclaim righteous, lawful action.[301] The 'works' of the devil are therefore the very essence of 'sin', and the devil remains the instigator of all human sin (3.8a).

The author explains this connection by carefully explicating the biblical narrative of Cain and Abel, so that the 'works of the devil' (3.8b) – the sins he exhibits and instigates – are to be interpreted in light of Cain's own 'evil works' (3.12). First, allegiance to the devil is directly contrasted with allegiance to God (3.9), and the respective relationships are framed in metaphysical terms. The devil represents a personal force in a comparable manner to God. The 'belonging' to the devil that is hinted at here is essential and intrinsic. Just as there are those who are 'of God' (ἐκ τοῦ θεοῦ) and so cannot 'sin' (3.9), there are also those who, by sinning, reveal that they originate (ἐκ) in the devil (3.8a). This produces, or 'reveals' (φανερός), two distinct kinds of people: the 'children of God and the children of the devil' (τὰ τέκνα τοῦ θεοῦ καὶ τὰ τέκνα τοῦ διαβόλου; 3.10a). There is no middle ground between these two alternatives.[302] Moreover, a person is not 'of God' if he does not 'do righteousness' (ποιῶν δικαιοσύν ην), neither do those who do not 'love their brothers and sisters' belong to God (3.10b). Such people *ipso facto* are 'children of the devil'. The 'works' of the devil (3.8b) – the sins he personifies and prompts – are thus further explained as, specifically, a lack of righteous behaviour, and a lack of demonstrable love for siblings.

Second, the author furthers his case by explicitly introducing the biblical figure of Cain, as one who exhibited an egregious lack of concern for his brother. The author reminds his community of the message they received to 'love one another' (3.11). The author's καθὼς formulation that opens ch. 3 v. 12 is used to provide a warning to his readers: 'just so, *do not* be like Cain (οὐ καθὼς Κάϊν), who was from the evil one (ἐκ τοῦ πονηροῦ), and who slew his brother' (3.12). Cain is depicted as belonging to the 'evil one', as having his origins in the 'evil one'. This recalls ch. 3 v. 8b, where those who sin are said to be 'of the devil' (ἐκ τοῦ διαβόλου ἐστίν). The author segues into a statement about Cain's 'evil works' in ch. 3 v. 12b (ἔργα ... πονηρὰ): Cain's primary act was to murder his brother Abel. The text of Genesis 4 does not suggest that Cain killed

---

[301] Sin is lawlessness, and it is opposed to 'doing righteousness'. Lieu, *I, II & III John*, p. 130, thinks the concepts do not refer to the Torah.
[302] Painter, *1, 2, and 3 John*, p. 231.

his brother out of a lack of love; the author's use of the term σφάζω ('to slay', 'to murder', 3.12) suggests deliberate violence born of hostility, which infuses his interpretation of the biblical story.[303] Moreover, the author of the Epistle imputes a more specific reason for Cain's action by asking a didactic question and providing his own answer: 'And why did he murder him? Because his own deeds were evil and his brother's righteous', i.e. envy (καὶ χάριν τίνος ἔσφαξεν αὐτόν; ὅτι τὰ ἔργα αὐτοῦ πονηρὰ ἦν τὰ δὲ τοῦ ἀδελφοῦ αὐτοῦ δίκαια; 3.12b).

Many post-biblical texts would puzzle over Cain's motives for killing Abel, and some of these imputed to Cain a sense of jealousy over the fact that God preferred Abel's offering to his own. Yet, the question of whether Cain's murderous action was the result of his diabolic filiation, or whether his act established such filiation is a difficult one to answer.[304] He killed *because* he was 'of the devil' (cf. 3.8-10), but it could also be that the murder resulted in him abiding in the realm of evil, or the realm 'of death' (cf. 3.14b).[305] The author claims that whoever lacks love for their brother 'abides in death' (3.14b), that hatred of the brother is equivalent to murder, and that no murderer (ἀνθρωποκτόνος) can have eternal life (3.15). And lack of love is not abstract, but real, evident in the refusal to provide material needs to those who have no help (3.17; cf. James 2). This could be interpreted as metaphorical 'murder' inasmuch as it denies the needy brother a livelihood.[306]

The exegetically nuanced series of developments in 1 John 3.8-12 indicates that the author considers the 'works of the devil' (3.8b) to be of the same order as the 'evil works' of Cain (3.12b). Both are ultimately sinful and lawless, both are exemplified by hatred and murder. The reference to the 'devil' in ch. 3 v. 8 could itself be a reference to the figure of Cain.[307] In some extant post-biblical traditions, Cain was perceived to be fathered by the devil.[308] This implied that Cain, the first murderer, was motivated by his 'father', the devil, in the act of fratricide. 1 John 3.8, 12 would fit into this tradition well, for it would allude both to the fact that the devil was the primeval 'sinner' (who 'sinned from the beginning' in Genesis 1–3), as well as to the fact that murder is ultimately the product of devilish inspiration, since the relationship between a murderer and the devil is virtually determined ontologically. Such interpretive traditions may also lie behind John 8.41, 44, where Jesus accuses the Jews of having the devil as their 'father', describing the devil as a 'murderer from the beginning' who lies, and who has never stood in the 'truth'.[309]

---

[303] Cf. Lieu, *I, II & III John*, p. 144.
[304] Lieu, *I, II & III John*, p. 144.
[305] Painter, *1, 2, and 3 John*, p. 239.
[306] Similarly, by housing the spies, Rahab was effectively saving lives, and by drawing back the knife at the *Akedah*, Abraham was doing the same (Hebrews 11).
[307] Lieu, *I, II & III John*, p. 134.
[308] Jan Dochhorn, 'Mit Kain kam der Tod in die Welt: Zur Auslegung von SapSal 2,24 in 1 Clem 3,4; 4,1-7, mit einem Seitenblick auf Polykarp, Phil. 7,1 und Theophilus, Ad Autol. II, 29, 304', *ZNW* 98 (2007), pp. 150-9.
[309] Lieu, *I, II & III John*, p. 134. And the seminal work of Nils A. Dahl, 'Der Ersteborene Satans und der Vater des Teufels (Polyk. 7,1 und Joh 8,44)', in *Apophoreta* (FS Ernst Haenchen; BZNW 30; Berlin: Walter de Gruyter 1964), pp. 70-84.

These intertextual points of reference are strong, yet subtle. In 1 John 3, the devil is labelled a *sinner* 'from the beginning', and in John 8.44, he is labelled a *murderer* 'from the beginning'. In 1 John 3.12-15, Cain's crime is explicitly referred to as 'murder', and he is called a 'murderer'. Not only the act of fratricide itself, but the summation of Cain's 'works' are referred to as 'evil' in 1 John 3.12. Taking all of this together, the 'works' of the devil in 1John 3.8 connote sin, lawlessness, hatred, murder, lies, evil and hidden jealousy. These 'works' are opposed to truth, purity (3.3) and filiation in God. The 'works' of the devil, and of Cain, are opposed to 'righteous works' – which were ostensibly undertaken by Abel (3.12) – and which must now be urgently performed by the Johannine community in the form of service to those in need (3.11-18). The kinds of active expressions of love required by the community are those actions generally classified as *tzedakah* in the Jewish tradition: almsgiving and material care for those in need.

For the author of 1 John, the 'righteous works' exemplified by Abel constitute 'righteousness' in precisely this sense. It is not the respective *offerings* of the brothers that are contrasted here (Genesis 4), but their evil or good *works*. Abel's 'works' are not explicated in 1 John but they are clearly assumed with reference to the mandates that the community is to 'love, not in word or speech, but in truth and deed' (μὴ ἀγαπῶμεν λόγῳ μηδὲ τῇ γλώσσῃ ἀλλ' ἐν ἔργῳ καὶ ἀληθείᾳ; 3.18). Abel's implied 'works' are therefore advanced as worthy of imitation, and this subtle idea weaves an important intertextual thread into the fabric of John 8.31-59 and the concept of Abraham's 'works'. While 1 John 3.8 seems to suggest that 'offspring have no choice in their parentage and can take no credit or blame for it'[310] perhaps, thereby challenging the idea of imputed sin and merit within early Judaism, the 'works' of Abel are open to the community (who are protected from sin, 3.5) as the most exemplary behaviour, even if it incites the hostility of the world.

'Work the works of God'

The idiomatic expression 'to work the works' (of God; ἐργαζώμεθα τὰ ἔργα τοῦ θεοῦ) occurs twice in the Gospel of John (6.28-29; 9.3-5). Both texts display marked similarities. The wider contexts of both passages refer to Jesus as 'rabbi' (ῥαββί; 6.25; 9.2), suggesting that his remarks about 'working the works of God' relate to his capacity as teacher and learned Jewish man. Both texts introduce the performance of, or the discussion about, one of Jesus' miraculous 'signs': the multiplication of the loaves and fishes (6.1-13; 22-65), and the healing of the man born blind (9.1-41), respectively. Finally, both texts use the concept of God's 'works' in conjunction with the literal notion of subsistence labour, employment or otherwise general human 'working', creating a nuanced interplay between the noun (τὰ ἔργα) and the verb (ἐργάζομαι) and thus producing a classic Johannine double entendre. In John 3.21b those who 'do what is true' (ὁ δὲ ποιῶν τὴν ἀλήθειαν) are said to prove that their 'works' are 'worked in God' (τὰ ἔργα ὅτι ἐν θεῷ ἐστιν εἰργασμένα). This text does not refer to 'working

---

[310] Lieu, *I, II & III John*, p. 136.

God's works', but points to the fact that humans are capable of 'working' their own 'works' *in* God.

The first reference to 'working the works' of God is found in ch. 6 v. 28. The day following Jesus' multiplication of the loaves and fishes, 'the crowd' (ὁ ὄχλος) depart from the shores of Tiberias and cross over to Capernaum, looking for Jesus (6.22-24). When they find Jesus on the other side, they ask, 'Rabbi, when did you come here?' (6.25). Jesus does not give a direct answer, but tells them that they seek him not on the basis of the 'signs' (σημεῖα) that they saw, but because they had their fill of bread (6.26).[311] Assuming that they have come after more food, Jesus warns them, 'Do not work (ἐργάζεσθε μὴ) for the food that perishes, but for the food that endures for eternal life, which the Son of Man is giving you' (6.27a). Building on Jesus' reference to the activity of 'working' for sustenance, they ask Jesus, 'What must we do to work the works of God?' (τί ποιῶμεν ἵνα ἐργαζώμεθα τὰ ἔργα τοῦ θεοῦ).[312]

In this curious expression, the verb ποιέω seems redundant: after all, the crowd could have simply asked Jesus, 'How must we work God's works?' But the presence of the first verb (ποιέω) suggests that the complement clause 'to work the works of God' is idiomatic, and as a handful of commentators consider, Semitic in its duplicate phraseology. In support of this reading, the verb ἐργαζώμεθα is emphatic when used transitively, implying dedicated action in the pursuit of an accomplishment.[313] It is possible that the crowd's question (6.28), is a Johannine variation on the early Christian shorthand 'How shall we be saved?' (Luke 3.10, 12, 14; Acts 2.37).[314] But there is more at play than this; the crowd want to know something specific, namely, 'How are we to be pious? In what way should we be labouring in the Torah to find eternal life?' Early rabbinic texts appreciated the study of the Torah as 'work' (labour, occupation) which ought to occupy one's heart and soul, and from which one derived a 'sustenance' that was life-giving.[315] In early Jewish texts, the 'works of God' described not only God's wondrous miracles and acts of creation, but also his commandments in the Torah (cf. CD 2.14-15; *Bar.* 2.9-10; *T. Levi* 29.1; *4 Ezra* 7.24; cf. Jer. 31.10 LXX;).[316] It is surely in these senses that the crowd use the expression 'to work the works of God' (6.28), since ordinary humans could not 'do' God's wondrous miracles.[317]

---

[311] The only example in the Gospel where belief in Jesus on the basis of his 'signs' is preferred over another category (in this case, insatiable physical hunger; cf. 2.24).

[312] The crowd's response is often thought to be a typical Johannine 'misunderstanding' in the literature, cf. Keener, *The Gospel of John*, 1.677; Brown, *John*, 1.267.

[313] BGAD, sv.

[314] Keener, *The Gospel of John*, 1.678.

[315] Cf. *m. Kidd.* 4.14.

[316] Keener, *The Gospel of John*, 1.678.

[317] For the Fourth Evangelist, Jesus is the exception to this rule. Most interpreters and commentators read 'the works of God' in ch. 6 v. 28 as the objective genitive, that is the works that God requires of human beings. To read the phrase as a subjective genitive (the works God does in creation, his wonders) makes little sense in the context, but one recent study argues for this less common interpretation, albeit not very convincingly. The key point in that study is that God's gift of faith to humans is his 'work' that he performs on their behalf. See Sigurd Grindheim, 'The Work of God or of Human Beings: A Note on John 6.29', *JETS* 59, no. 1 (2016), pp. 63–6. An earlier attempt at this very argument was made by Johannes Beutler, 'The Structure of John 6', in R. Alan Culpepper (ed.), *Critical Readings of John 6* (Leiden: Brill, 1997), pp. 115–28, see p. 124.

Jesus responds to the crowd's question more directly: the 'work of God' is to believe in Jesus as the Sent One of the Father (τοῦτό ἐστιν τὸ ἔργον τοῦ θεοῦ, 6.29). Jesus is not concerned with the 'works of God' in the plural, but with *the* 'work of God' in the singular – in the fundamental attitude of belief towards Jesus that entails assenting to his identity as the one commissioned by God. This attitude of belief is equivalent to 'working for the food that endures'. However, this attitude of belief is not static, but dynamic, as indicated by the accusative preposition εἰς, which typically follows πιστεύω in the Gospel, and implies a movement into or towards the object, and in this case, illustrates faith as relational response to Jesus.[318] The 'work' of belief in Jesus is thus presented as an ongoing act characterizing a type of relationship between the believer and Jesus, summative of all the 'works' mandated by God in the Torah, effectively – in the eyes of the Evangelist – replacing them. It is important to recognize that the Johannine Jesus does not mouth the Pauline binary of 'faith' and 'works' here.[319] For John, faith *is* a 'work', indeed it is the supreme 'work' in the Gospel's world view. In this respect, 'working the works of God' in ch. 6 vv. 28-29 accords remarkably with Jewish tradition in antiquity, which did not categorically distinguish works from faith.[320] We have already noted some pertinent examples in this chapter regarding Abraham: his obedience and trust in God never wavered when he was tested (Genesis 22), and for this 'work' he was rewarded (cf. Jas. 2.24; Hebrews 11); and Abraham's faith in God (Gen. 15.6) was a meritorious deed (*Tg. Onkelos*) for which God was said to have split the Red Sea (*Mekhilta de Rabbi Ishmael*). In John 6.28-29, Jesus therefore supports the concept of faith (in him) as a divinely mandated 'work' of God.

Jesus and the crowd are therefore 'on the same page' in this discussion. The crowd do not 'misunderstand' Jesus' speech, neither does Jesus correct their apparent obtuseness by devaluing the concept of 'works'.[321] The shift from the plural (6.28) to the singular (6.29) indicates only a thematic alteration (faith in Jesus becomes the supreme 'work of God').[322] The conversation between Jesus and the crowd revolves around the resolution of how to labour for eternal life. According to Jesus, it is not necessary to labour in the Torah to attain eternal life, for such life is available in the present (Jesus is 'giving' it to them: 6.27b; cf. 5.44-47; cf. 1.16-18). The 'food that endures' is neither the physical bread multiplied the day before, nor the works of the Torah, but the gift of Jesus. But to

---

[318] Robert Kysar, 'The Dismantling of Decisional Faith: A Reading of John 6.25-71', in Culpepper (ed.), *Critical Readings of John 6*, pp. 161–82.

[319] As Urban C. von Wahlde has so expertly demonstrated: idem, 'Faith and Works in Jn VI 28-29', *NovT* 22, no. 4 (1980), pp. 304–15. Pace Brown, *John*, 1.264–5 and Barrett, *The Gospel*, p. 282.

[320] Also, Keener, *The Gospel of John*, 1.677.

[321] Von Wahlde, 'Faith and Works', p. 314. A different approach to the seeming contradictions between 'works' and faith in Jesus as the Bread of Life discourse progresses (cf. John 6.31-58), see Paul N. Anderson, *The Christology of the Fourth Gospel: Its Unity and Disunity in the Light of John 6* (WUNT 2.77; Tübingen: Mohr Siebeck, 1995).

[322] Von Wahlde, 'Faith and Works', p. 314, notes that the singular τί ποιῶμεν? from the crowd (6.28) expects a singular response from Jesus, which comes in v. 28. I disagree with von Wahlde on one point, namely his conclusion that 'the works of God' in vv. 28-29 means 'the will of God'. Such a view rests at least partially on his avoidance of a 'legalistic' reading. But why should we think that interpreting 'the works of God' as the commandments of the Torah requires us to adopt a pejorative 'legalistic' reading? It is perfectly sensible to read the Jewish and Christian texts of antiquity and their conceptualization of 'meritorious works' without the prejudicial connotations that have solidified over the centuries, as the scholarship of Gary Anderson so amply attests.

accept Jesus as the Sent One, the crowd ask him what 'sign' he will give them in order to validate their belief in him (6.30a). Their belief must rest on 'seeing' such a sign (ὁράω). They further associate such a 'sign' with a *work* that Jesus might perform for them, when they ask succinctly, τί ἐργάζῃ? (6.30b).[323] The 'work' of believing in the sent one, in the opinion of the crowd, must be based on the performance of a validating 'work' on the part of Jesus.[324]

Three uses of the term ἔργα and its cognates have thus coalesced in this passage: the idea of 'working' for food; the requirement of 'labouring' in God's 'works' (or commandments), clarified by Jesus as now encompassing the 'work' of belief; and the notion of Jesus' miraculous 'signs' as verificatory 'works' that substantiate his identity claims. The crowd tell Jesus that their 'fathers' ate manna in the desert – citing Ps. 78.24 – and that this was a gift of God's provision; can Jesus perform a like 'work' of such magnitude? (6.31). Jesus – assuming that the crowd understands the pronoun 'he' in the scriptural citation to denote Moses as the 'giver' (ἔδωκεν) – replies 'it was not Moses who gave you the bread from heaven, but my Father gives you the true bread from heaven' (6.32). Jesus implies that this same 'gift' is readily available to the crowd even today, suggested by the author's shift from the perfect tense δέδωκεν to the present δίδωσιν.[325] Jesus constitutes that gift in his person as the 'bread of life' (6.35).

The second reference to 'working the works of God' is found in ch. 9 v. 4. This text follows directly on from the conclusion of Jesus' debate with the Jews at Sukkot (8.31-59), and it continues some of the main themes of that text, notably those of 'sin' and 'works'. Jesus walks out of the Temple and happens upon a man who is congenitally blind (9.1). His disciples ask him, 'Rabbi, who sinned, this man or his parents, that he was born blind?' (9.2).[326] This text expresses two lines of thought debated in early Judaism – that sin could have a deleterious effect upon the perpetrator in the form of physical illness or disability (the correlative idea was that religiously dutiful action would lead to well-being and reward); and that sin and its effects could be imputed to the offspring of a sinner (the correlative idea was that the righteous behaviour of ancestors produced merit that vicariously benefited their descendants).[327] But here in ch. 9 of the Gospel, as in the preceding context of ch. 8, Jesus calls these theories into

---

[323] The question-and-answer structure of the Bread of Life discourse has been explored in a number of studies, for example Klaus Scholtissek, *In ihm sein und bleiben: Die Sprache der Immanenz in den johanneischen Schriften* (HBS 21; Freiburg: Herder, 2000), p. 196; Jean Zumstein, 'Die Schriftrezeption in der Brotrede (Joh 6)', in idem, *Kreative Erinnerung*, p. 136; and recently, Douglas Estes, *The Questions of Jesus in John: Logic, Rhetoric and Persuasive Discourse* (Leiden/Boston: Brill, 2013), p. 99.

[324] John Painter, 'Tradition and Interpretation in John 6', *NTS* 35 (1989), pp. 421–50, at p. 437.

[325] On the topic of the threefold negation in relation to Moses and the manna in ch. 6 vv. 32-33, see Menken, *Old Testament Quotations in the Fourth Gospel*, p. 54; Schuchard, *Scripture within Scripture*, pp. 42–3; Günter Reim, *Studien zum alttestamentlichen Hintergrund des Johannesevangeliums* (SNTSMS 22; Cambridge: Cambridge University Press, 1974), p. 15; and for a more extreme perspective on the imputed polemic, see Georg Richter, 'Zur Formgeschichte und literarischen Einheit von Joh 6,31-58', *ZNW* 60 (1969), pp. 21–55.

[326] The parallels between this text and the story of Tobit (esp. 11.10-14) have been noted by Ben Witherington III, *The Christology of Jesus* (Minneapolis: Augsburg/Fortress, 1990), pp. 170–1.

[327] See Keener, *The Gospel of John*, 1.777–8, for a range of ancient sources, both Greco-Roman and Jewish, on the connection between sin and illness/disability, and Sanders, *Paul and Palestinian Judaism*, p. 125ff. for a reading of the Jewish sources.

question. Just as Abraham's merits could not save the 'seed of Abraham' from sin (8.32), so the behaviour of the blind man's parents – sinful or not – had no causative impact upon the man's illness. Jesus replies:

> Neither this man nor his parents sinned so that he was born blind. But in order that the works of God (τὰ ἔργα τοῦ θεοῦ) might be revealed (φανερωθῇ) in him, we must work the works of him who sent me (ἐργάζεσθαι τὰ ἔργα τοῦ πέμψαντός με) while it is day; night is coming when no one can work (ἐργάζεσθαι). As long as I am in the world, I am the light of the world. (9.3-5)[328]

Jesus concedes that there is a reason this man was born blind. That reason is not explained, but the imperative to heal the man from his disability is described as the 'works of God' being 'revealed' in the man. Evidently, the phrase 'works of God' (τὰ ἔργα τοῦ θεοῦ) is being used differently here when compared to ch. 6 v. 28, where it implied, we argued, the commandments of the Torah. Here, the phrase relates to the miraculous healing work of Jesus, and to the fact that his 'works' are also the 'works' of God.[329] In that sense, the expression τὰ ἔργα τοῦ θεοῦ in ch. 9 v. 3 indicates that Jesus and the Father share the same 'works'. Of course, Jesus' healing 'works' too are presented as 'works' of the Torah, as we argued when reading John 5.19-47 in relation to ch. 7 vv. 1-6. In this text, as well as in those previous texts, the 'works' of God represents Jesus' healing activity as a unique revelation of the truth of his identity as the one sent by God. The connotations of the term 'works' in ch. 9 v. 3 are thus also forensic, indicating Jesus' singular prerogative, whereas in ch. 6 v. 28 the phrase τὰ ἔργα τοῦ θεοῦ spoke to the ability of anyone to faithfully and assiduously know and engage in the 'works of God'.

Although in ch. 9 it is Jesus alone who heals the man born blind, the possibility that others might undertake the same 'works of God' as Jesus is not wholly excluded. Jesus tells his disciples '*We* must work the works of the One who sent me' (9.4a).[330] The imperative, however, is that these 'works of God' must be 'worked' while it is day (ἕως ἡμέρα ἐστίν). The metaphor of day and night in ch. 9 vv. 4-5 works on a number of levels.[331] The verb ἐργάζομαι in ch. 9 v. 4a ('we must *work* the works') leads seamlessly

---

[328] I have followed John Poirier's alternative punctuation when translating vv. 3-4, which I find he has made a convincing argument for adopting. This alternative punctuation allows the ἵνα clause (but in order that) to justify the phrases that follow, rather than those that precede it, and consequently it avoids reading the man's blindness as caused by God for the purposes of Jesus' eventual miracle. See Poirier, 'Another Look at the "Man Born Blind" in John 9', *JRDH* 14, no. 1 (2010), pp. 60–5, at p. 61; and idem, '"Night and Day" and the Punctuation of John 9.3', *NTS* 42 (1996), pp. 288–94. This reading also accords with other references to 'works' in John's Gospel, where the works of Jesus are the works of God. Cf. Ensor, *Jesus and His Works*, p. 118.

[329] Ensor, *Jesus and His Works*, p. 118, 125.

[330] J. Louis Martyn (*History and Theology*, p. 28) considers the plural pronoun to be a cryptic reference to the Johannine community of 90 CE, but it is plausible that at the level of the narrative, the disciples are beginning to do works on par with Jesus as his 'hour' approaches (cf. 14.12-13). Oddly, Asiedu-Peprah reads the plural as something of a 'royal we', see idem, *Johannine Sabbath Conflicts*, p. 123.

[331] Cf. R. Alan Culpepper, *Anatomy of the Fourth Gospel: A Study in Literary Design* (Minneapolis: Fortress, 1983), p. 192.

into the metaphor of labouring in the daylight before nightfall, 'when no one is able to work' (ὅτε οὐδεὶς δύναται ἐργάζεσθαι, 9.4b). Night brings darkness, and with it the lack of ability to visually see and so to labour. Daylight endures for a limited period, and so human work must be accomplished in the window of temporal opportunity that it provides. This general, commonly understood reality serves as the basis for the Johannine metaphorical system around which the binary terms 'light' and 'darkness', 'sight' and 'blindness' are operating in John 9. Sight and light correspond: Jesus is 'the light of the world' for as long as he is in it (9.5), functioning in himself as the 'daylight' by which believers see (cf. 8.12). Darkness and blindness correspond: the man who is physically blind remains in a state of darkness, but this is not permanent, yet the Pharisees who proclaim to be able to 'see' in a moral sense – without 'believing' in Jesus – are condemned as being truly 'blind', indeed guilty of sin (9.38-41). On another level, the imminence of nightfall (9.4b) carries sinister connotations. It hints at Jesus' departure as the 'light', and his death at the hands of the 'world' in which he works. Jesus and his disciples must 'work the works of God' while he is still alive.[332]

The text of ch. 9 vv. 1-5 seems to contradict ch. 7 v. 3 where Jesus is accused of performing his 'works' not openly and for the world to see, but in secret, thus incurring the dislike of his brothers. As Jesus' public ministry progresses, his healing 'works' also increase in wonder and impact (cf. 9.1-7; 11.39-44). 'Daylight' is fading, and the imperative to work openly becomes more pressing. The idea that the 'works of God' are to be 'revealed' (φανερωθῇ) in the blind man through the restoration of sight, ties in with the theme of the disclosure of works before the world, expressed in ch. 7 v. 3. But there is also, in ch. 9 vv. 1-5, an intratextual allusion to ch. 3 vv. 19-21. That earlier text posited that while some people hide their 'evil works' for fear of being exposed (ἐλέγχω, 3.20), others who do 'true' works come into the light so that they may be revealed (φανερωθῇ, 3.21) as 'working their works in God'. In ch. 3 v. 21, 'light' and the revelation of 'works done in God' go together intrinsically;[333] so, in ch. 9 vv. 3-4, Jesus' healing of the man's blindness is a revelation of the 'works of God', and an action brought about by Jesus who *is* the 'light' (9.5).

Through the complex repetition of these interrelated themes across the Gospel, the reference to 'working the works of God' in ch. 9 v. 3 has accumulated several layers of significance: themes of 'sight', 'light', 'revelation' and 'works' done in truth (3.19-21) are reiterated in ch. 9 vv. 1-5 in the specific case of Jesus who 'works the works of God' by healing a blind man, restoring his light and bringing the 'light' into the world. The divine 'judgement' occasioned by various reactions to Jesus' 'work' in ch. 9 is expressed as Jesus making those who see become blind, and those who are blind gain sight (9.39). The prior state of blindness is connected to a state of innocence, but the *rendering* blind

---

[332] The reference to Jesus being the 'light of the world' and the need to 'work' in the daylight (9.5) also allude to God's work in creation (Genesis 3) which Jesus – and his disciples – now replicate. See Daniel Frayer-Griggs, 'Spittle, Clay, and Creation in John 9.6 and Some Dead Sea Scrolls', *JBL* 132, no. 3 (2013), pp. 659–70. NB, the disciples will still continue Jesus' 'works' after his departure and death (14.11-12).

[333] Although others argue that these terms are not naturally associated in John's binary thought-world as a whole; Poirier, 'The Punctuation', p. 293. For Poirier, John therefore uses a linking concept, φανερωθῇ, to associate them.

of those who see is construed as a judgement due to sin (9.41). Likewise, those who believe in Jesus will avoid condemnation (3.18), while those who prefer the darkness despite seeing the light come into the world (i.e. those who do not believe), will be condemned (3.19).

The Johannine context illustrates a variety of rich usages for the term 'works' and its many connotations. I have drawn out several categories to highlight the variety of nuances: Jesus 'works' as signs and testimony (where his miracles validate his identity and intend to lead to belief in the responses of those who see him); 'works' and the binary dualism of the Gospel's point of view (which places human beings into two realms, as it were, doing 'evil works' or good works, and as a consequence living in the darkness or the light); the idiomatic expression 'to work the works of God' (to labour in the Torah but reconfigured to mean faith in the Sent One); and some strong parallels between the First Epistle of John and John 8.31-59, especially around the Cain traditions that situated him as the bringer of death into the world (or as spawning the devil, i.e. literally being the devil's 'father'). The 'children of the devil' would then imitate the murderous 'works' of Cain (which are opposed to Abel's good works in the binary structure of 1 John). Cain's deliberate violence, arising from hostility and hatred towards his brother reveals the fact that he is not 'born of God'; these themes resonate clearly with John 8.44, where Jesus accuses the Jews of having the devil as their father and of not being 'born of God'.

Part 3: Reading John 8.39-41 intertextually

In this final section, I summarize the findings of the chapter, evaluating the key metaphor in John 8.37-47 (primarily the 'works of Abraham') against both the intertextual literature and the (Johannine) intratextual literature. I will return to the previous studies on John 8.39, 40 (which were reviewed in the introduction) as well as the commentary tradition which, as we saw at the beginning of this chapter, continues the anti-Jewish interpretations that we witnessed in ch. 8 vv. 32-33, although not as prevalently.

This chapter was extensive and detailed, but unlike Chapter 4, aimed to take a more thematic approach throughout the various corpora. The phrase 'works of Abraham' has no exact parallel in the literature of antiquity. However, there were many intertexts that use the 'works' in relation to a pronoun or noun, to signify forms of behaviour or activity, typically with moral connotations attached. Scripting the intertextual field for the possessive form of the term 'works' yielded many texts that had not previously been brought into conversation with John 8.

The HB was particularly nuanced in this regard, and we can map the following themes:

- One text (Neh. 9.6-37) included connotations highlighted in Chapter 4 ('seed of Abraham', 'slavery' and 'sin') directly in relation to the use of the term 'works' denoting human behaviour: idolatry is a form of slavery from which God redeemed Abraham's 'seed' out of love. The returnees from exile must keep *God's 'works'* (the Torah's commandments) in order to remain free. The 'works' of the commandments ensure that the returnees from exile don't fall into a state of slavery to the nations again ('because of our sins'); Abraham is specifically invoked as the one chosen by God for his 'faithful heart', the result of which was that God promised to give his seed the Land.

- The 'late' biblical word פעלה (Isa. 65.7; Ps. 17.5; Jer. 31.16) can denote paradoxical concepts: a *'good work'* (2 Chron. 15.7), bearing the 'fruit' of its own reward, or to *evil deeds* that bear fruit in punishment (Isa. 65.7). The word therefore signifies both the 'work' itself (of whatever nature) and the 'wage' or 'fruit' of the work. The economic metaphors are important: human 'works' thus earn 'wages' to the point where the 'works' themselves equate to the 'wages' they produce. This nuanced word is possibly a precursor to later ideas in the Second Temple Period that would see 'works' containing within themselves their own consequences, or indeed of creating a surplus-something that could vicariously affect others.
- Human behaviour is designated as 'works' under the plural form of the noun צדקה to mean 'righteous deeds' or 'right doing'. God also possesses 'righteous deeds' in a measure incomparable to human beings, which is why humans cannot rely on their 'merits' but only on God's mercy (Isa. 64.5; Dan. 9.15-18). But, contradictorily, human sin *can* be 'redeemed' by righteous behaviour (Dan. 4.19-27).
- The phrase 'doing righteousness' = doing 'righteous works' in context connotes highly specific acts of *tzedakah*, for example caring for the oppressed in society. This form of merciful action is so powerful that it can redeem sinners (Isa. 56.1; Ezek. 18.20-21).
- There were examples where a certain individual is praised for his or her exemplary 'works' (upright or pious behaviour). Good 'works' actively praise the doer before others, obtaining material or personified significance (Prov. 31.30-31). Negative examples are also evident: the whole behavioural habits and the destructive *statutes* of a person (Mic. 6.16): 'works' are not simply 'deeds' but synonymous with the 'commandments' of a person (!) – the *commandments of Omri* and the *works of Ahab* (namely apostasy, greed, lack of integrity and abuse of justice, violence, lies and deceit; 6.10-12). Others may choose to *do the 'works' of Ahab*, meaning sins *like* Ahab's (or possibly sins *in service to* Ahab, given the parallelism).

The post-biblical literature developed these usages. New trajectories included:

- The idea of *'works' as the functional equivalent of human 'merit'*, that is as the product of commendable behaviour that is 'stored' in a *'treasury'* in heaven for future withdrawals (e.g. *4 Ezra* 7). The 'heavenly treasury' plays upon the economic metaphor of 'crediting' good works to one's 'account' to hedge against the possibility of leaner times due to the 'debt' of sin (*Tob.* 4.11, 12.9).
- The idea of the *'works of the fathers'* and their *zeal for the Law* as imitable and exemplary behaviour; in this case, Abraham's 'works' align with the righteousness imputed to him by God (*1 Macc.* 2.50-52).

- The merging of the *'works'* and *'righteousness'* of one's (biological) 'father' as equivalent to the *'merits'* of one's father that effectively *wipe out the sins* of the son (*Sir.* 3.14).
- The notion of *'righteous works'* as specifically related to almsgiving that *atone for sins* (*Tob.* 4.5-7a; Dan. 9.27).
- The concept of 'works' as *God's commandments*, literally 'the works of the commandments' (cf. *Wis.* 6.2-5; *2 Bar.* 57.1-2; *T. Levi* 14.4). In the Dead Sea Scrolls (DSS), the much-studied phrase 'works of the Torah' connotes the imitation of virtue, the observance of the Torah's commandments, and its special rulings.
- The dichotomy between *the 'works' of Beliar* and the 'works' of the Lord (i.e. the righteous commandments of the Torah). This includes *the motif of Cain* as subject to the 'works of Beliar', which led to his evil works.
- As in the HB, there are examples where 'works' are predicated of a biblical figure in the genitive case, for example Josephus speaks of *the 'works of David'*, the 'father' of Jehoshaphat and *the 'works of [Amon's] father'*. The former 'works' were positive (courage and piety), and the latter were evil (apostasy and idolatry) – both were *imitable* and signified the totality and habituality *of one's moral direction in life*.
- The idea of Abraham himself as a keeper of the Torah (i.e. observing the *mitzvoth* of the Torah either in whole or in part) in a variety of texts (*4 Ezra* 3.16; Philo, Josephus, *Jubilees* and *m. Kidd.* 4.14).

The NT develops several categories under which we analysed human 'works':

- The 'works of' a person, that is a named biblical figure in the genitive: 'the works of Jezebel' (idolatry, metaphorically described as apostasy; Rev. 2.20).
- 'Good works': (1) charitable behaviours towards the needy (1 Tim. 2.10; Acts 9.36; Tit. 2.7, etc.); (2) works that testify to others and receive a reward from God (cf. Matt. 5.16, 1 Tim. 5.25, Rom. 2.7); (3) forms of 'credit', accumulating 'treasure in heaven': a metaphorical 'insurance' that generates currency in the afterlife or in the future life of the person who does them (1 Tim. 6.18; Matt. 6.20; Luke 12.33).
- Various instances of the attributive genitive: 'bad works', 'evil works', 'dead works' 'works of shame' (Eph. 5.11-12) and the 'works of darkness' as implied antonyms for 'good works'.
- The notion of 'justification by works'; the idea of 'works' as a stand-alone concept (cf. Rom. 4.2, 6); and the idiomatic anarthrous 'works of the law' (e.g. Rom. 3.2, 28). The latter two terms are both used in the context of Paul's debate about 'justification' by faith.
- Abraham's (implied) 'work' of faith (Rom. 4.4-5). For Paul, God remits the sin (i.e. does not account it as a debt) of a person who has faith (citing Psalms 32). 'Works' (i.e. *not* faith but meritorious activity striving for righteousness) cannot effect the remission of sin (Rom. 9.30-32). Other voices assert that 'works' *are* capable of 'justifying' a person (Jas. 2.23).

- Abraham's 'works' as acts of *pikuach nefesh* (e.g. at the Akedah) and hospitality, that together had the effect of justifying him before God (Jas. 2.23-25).

The rabbinic literature takes these ideas in the following directions:

- The three fathers are figures of merit, either because of their Torah observance or because of their fidelity to God. Abraham performed 'good works' which altered his status in God's sight and led to his change of name from Avram to Avraham (*Mekhilta*). Abraham is singled out for his good works acquiring merit for his descendants. Each specific deed garnered a corresponding and requisite merit – whether the Akedah, circumcision, his faith (*Mekhilta*).
- This perspective was also open to challenge: fathers cannot save their children; Abraham could not save Ishmael. Merit only accrues to the person performing the meritorious behaviour and it goes both ways: fathers cannot save their children and children cannot save their fathers (*Sifrei Deuteronomy*).
- Abraham's hospitality is lauded as going well beyond what the Torah demanded. Like 'Job', but superiorly so, Abraham had astonishing 'works' of kindness and hospitality (*ARN*).
- More than a focus upon Abraham's exemplary goodness, however, the Tannaitic sources reflect a concern with Abraham's vicarious merits, the fruit of his good works.
- Good deeds create merits that have vicarious effects across the generations (cf. *m. Makkot* 3.15-16; *ARN* A, 77), but one logical step prior to this idea was the equation of 'works' with 'merits' as seen in the overlapping uses of the terms צדקה and זכות – thus *Tg. Onkelos* translating Abraham's 'righteousness' (צדקה: Gen. 15.6) as 'a meritorious deed' (זכות).
- The phrase 'the works of the fathers' (מעשי אבות) functions in the *Mekhilta* as a contextual synonym for זכות אבות ('the merits of the fathers'). Instead of turning to the merits/works of the fathers to rely vicariously upon their store of credit, the sense is rather that one turns to the 'merits' (*works*) of the fathers as a source of imitation when in need, and *this* imitation covers over one's sins.
- The study and observance of the Torah accumulate 'fruit', that is is productive of a material surplus that benefits the learner and his children (e.g. Abraham; *m. Kidd.* 4.14).

These texts illustrate three key themes. First, we see a semantic development with the term 'works' functioning as a synonym for 'merits', which eventually fits in with the economic metaphorization of sin as 'debt', and virtue (or good works) as 'credit', with one attenuating the other. If we were to trace the roots of this development, we might find it in the LBH word פעלה (Isa. 65.7; Ps. 17.5; Jer. 31.16), which connotes both the deed and the 'fruit' of the deed performed. In the HB, the substantive 'doing righteousness' entailed doing righteous *works* (*tzedakot*) which would take on new life in the rabbinic era to mean 'works' productive of merit. But before then, we see an arc whereby the term 'works' was functioning as a precursor to the idea of 'merits', inasmuch as 'works' garnered a treasure in heaven for the doer, which aided them when their sins were weighed at the eschatological judgement (cf. *4 Ezra* 7).

Overlapping uses of the terms צדקה and זכות (e.g. *Tg. Onkelos* and *m. Makkot*) show how 'righteousness' was glossed as 'merit', while other post-biblical and rabbinic texts show how 'works' were explicitly paralleled with 'merits' (*Sir.* 3.14; *Mekhilta de-RI*). In those texts, we see 'the works of [one's] father' or 'the works of *the* fathers' (i.e. Abraham, Isaac and Jacob) used to 'wipe clean' or remit the sins of their posterity, but in two different senses: the first is a passive reception of the father's merits, while the second is an active imitation of the 'works' of the fathers for the merits of those works to be realized. The early rabbinic concept of the זכות אבות is most likely an outgrowth of the idea of the 'works of the fathers', and the theme of 'remembrance' of the fathers (or God acting 'for the sake of' the fathers) in the HB (see Chapter 4). This is an important point, because while the idea of the 'merit of the fathers' is reasonably well known in the scholarship on early Christianity, the precursor (and sometimes synonymous) idea of the 'works of the fathers' is not.

Neither were these traditions confined to the rabbis. The NT shows plenty of evidence that the incipient ideas were being debated. For Paul, 'works' cannot achieve the remission of the 'debt' of sin or produce a storehouse of credit in heaven. Paul seems to be parlaying the concepts found in *4 Ezra*, Tobit and other texts, but contesting them. Meanwhile, other texts of the period argued the opposite: the commandments, in their life-giving powers, could 'justify' a person (cf. *m. Makkot* 3.15-16), and 'works' had the power to justify believers as much as they justified great biblical figures such as Abraham and Rahab (Jas. 2.23-25). And lest we stereotypically assume that the 'Jewish' texts reflected only one side of this debate, while the 'Christian' texts reflected the other, we should be aware of the larger contexts: all have sinned; God shows his goodness in having mercy upon those who have no 'works of righteousness' or 'store of good works' (*4 Ezra* 7; cf. Rom. 2.28).

Second, 'works' as the *mitzvoth* of the Torah, were brought into the heart of this discussion in the ancient texts. Paul is aware of this by virtue of the fact that he rebuts the very idea, viz. Israel 'strove' for 'works' that *might have* justified them (i.e. been productive of surplus, soteriological merits), but did not do so (Rom. 9.32-35). Furthermore, in Rom. 4.4-8, the stand-alone term 'works' constitutes all the virtuous doings that a 'worker' would undertake for his Master, that is the mandates of the Torah vis-à-vis others. To condense my argument on Paul slightly, in the letters to the Romans and Galatians, 'works' is not conceptually distinct from 'works of the law', but is a shorthand expression for it. Also, the phrase 'works of the law' may well suggest Torah observance (akin to 4QMMT), and 'justification by works' touches upon the premise that 'works' may (or may not, in Paul's view) carry within themselves a surplus 'thingness' ('justification') that benefits the doer or works or his posterity.

'Works' *as* God's commandments (Torah), or 'the works *of* [God's] commandments' (cf. genitive in *2 Baruch* 57; 44) are by no means painted only in pejorative language. Thus, in *2 Bar.* 57.1-2, the Law is 'with' God's chosen people, and they do not 'fall away' as long as they keep 'the works of the commandments'. This text is framed in the context of God's love and help for his people in the diaspora (cf. the divine help motif to Abraham's seed that we noted in Chapter 4). Trust in God is based on the promise of the efficacy of the commandments to draw down the rewards, so to speak, inherent in their own observance. Saved because of 'works' – the Law (the 'works of the commandments') established at the time of Abraham (57.1-2) is 'wisdom, trust and hope' to the people Israel. Indeed, the text of *2 Bar.* 57.1-2 may well provide some important context for how later expressions could be understood – namely, that 'works of the law' (e.g. 4QMMT, Paul) specifies the commandments of the Torah in general, and that the shorthand term 'works' can signify the performance of the commandments as such (and cf. *T. Levi* 14.4).

Third, traditions about Abraham's Torah observance coexist with the thematic strands about merit and 'works of the commandments'. Whether Abraham was envisioned as obeying part of the Torah before it was given, or the whole thing, these various texts understand Abraham as undertaking what we could call the 'works of the Law'. If 'works of the law' can be understood as observances of the Torah that produce merit for the doer and his or her descendants, then Abraham's 'works' would fit in with this schema. Not only does Abraham observe the Torah in the ancient literature, but he possesses commandments of his own! Thus, in *Jubilees*, Abraham has both 'righteous deeds' and 'commandments' that must be kept. In his testament to Jacob, Abraham tells his grandson to 'do righteousness' and to 'keep the commandments of Abraham your father' (22.16). Abraham's works and commandments are diametrically opposed to the 'works of gentiles' (idolatry) and the inheritance of the land to Jacob's 'seed' is contingent upon their performance. Like the 'works of the commandments' that were 'established' in Abraham's time (*2 Bar.* 57), the text of *Jubilees* has Abraham initiating commandments (and festivals, cf. Sukkot). Finally, the *T12P* reconfigures the biblical promise of inheritance (Land and covenant) made to the fathers (Abraham, Isaac and Jacob) to become the intergenerational bestowal of the Torah itself (commandments, 'works of the Lord'; *T. Benj.*). The Torah *is* the promise, and the Torah was practised by the one to whom the promise was made – Abraham.

What does all of this mean for the figure of Abraham in John 8? Recall from Chapter 1 that the secondary literature on the 'works of Abraham' in ch. 8 vv. 39-40 was based on the idea of Abraham *doing* something singular and particular, with intertexts from the HB and the post-biblical literature scoured for clues. One popular reading is to connect Abraham's 'works' with Abraham's rejoicing at seeing Jesus' 'day' (v. 58). That is, Abraham's act of rejoicing (v. 58) is understood to be identical to Abraham's exemplary deed (8.39-40). In this reading, the Jews fail to do 'what Abraham did': whereas the patriarch *rejoiced* at seeing Jesus, the Jews *wish to kill* him instead (v. 40). Building on this, scholars posited the intertext of Genesis 18, where Abraham gladly served his three angelic visitors at the Oaks of Mamre as the allusion to Abraham's 'work' of joy. Furthermore, this was tied into the early Christian exegetical retellings of Genesis 18 that determined Abraham had seen the pre-incarnate Logos in the figures of the angels. This interpretation has the advantage of intertextual coherency across the pericope (one intertext explaining two Abraham references), but the drawback of signifying *one* 'work' of Abraham, rather than encompassing the plural 'works'. Moreover, it is important to see how the passage builds on the metaphors already advanced ('seed', 'slavery', 'sin', 8.31-36) and how Abraham's 'works' explain that preceding context.

The phrase τὰ ἔργα τοῦ Ἀβραάμ in ch. 8 v. 39 has no exact textual parallel, but as we see from this intertextual 'scripting' there are plenty of close approximations. Williams is correct to read the phrase as 'a form of metonymic referencing' typical of oral compositions, to recall for listeners a whole network of attributions relating to Abraham's 'works'.[334] Abraham's joy at seeing Jesus' day thus constitutes part of the 'works of Abraham' (8.39, cf. 40) that the Jews should be emulating, but it is not the whole picture. In keeping with the 'Jewish voice' for the Jews' claim to be 'seed of Abraham' that I scripted in Chapter 4, I suggest that the Jews express the position that, as Abraham's seed, they were redeemed freely out of love, and that they are metaphorically 'slaves' of God (vv. 32-33) who faithfully keep the 'works' of the commandments (cf. v. 39). Jesus then picks up on this line of thinking (paraphrased): 'I know that you are seed of Abraham' (v. 37), 'but you seek to kill me' (v. 38a) and 'you obey the commands of a [different] father' (v. 38b). When the Jews reassert their Abrahamic paternity (v. 39a), Jesus rejects this: 'if you were Abraham's children, you would do the works of Abraham' (v. 39b), 'but you seek to kill me, a man who has told you the truth as I heard it from God – this is not what Abraham did' (v. 40); 'you are doing the works of your [other] father]' (v. 41). In short, Jesus is attuned to the Jews' implicit perspective that being 'seed of Abraham' protects from the debt of sin (v. 34) by virtue of the merits of Abraham's works, and he immediately counters it by raising the matter of Abraham's 'works' as something amenable only to imitation, not to passive reception. This precisely coheres with the broader conversations about works and merits in early Judaism that I have scoped in this chapter. In John 8, this debate is concentrated on the figure of Abraham, and the exchanges between Jesus and the Jews.

I am therefore claiming that 'the works of Abraham' (John 8.39) refer implicitly to the Law observance of Abraham, which had the vicarious effect of lifting his descendants (his 'seed') out of the slavery of sin in the economy of merits. This is John's significantly different way of conceptualizing the Law in relation to sin (as say, compared to Paul in Galatians). It fits in with many traditions in early Judaism outside the NT, and with the early rabbinic literature as well. Secondly, Abraham's 'works' are the constellation of his righteous deeds that are exemplary for his posterity. This includes the spectrum of behaviours, deeds and habits that characterized the patriarch in antiquity, whether that was his 'zeal', his 'faith', his 'obedience', his 'hospitality', his *tzedakah* or any other number of traits attributed to Abraham as he was refigured to fit different narratives after the close of the biblical age.

There are other elements of the text (8.37-47) that require attention against the intertextual field scripted in the chapter thus far. Jesus tells the Jews that they are obeying the commands they hear from 'their father' (v. 38b), and that they do 'their father's works' (v. 40) in contrast to the works of Abraham. In v. 44, Jesus infamously clarifies that the Jews have 'the devil' as their father and that they 'choose to do his desires'. The desires, works and commands of the 'devil' are thus set against the 'works' of Abraham and the paternity of God ('if God were your father you would love me',

---

[334] Williams, 'First-Century Media Culture', p. 215.

v. 42; cf. 'if you were the children of Abraham, you would do the works of Abraham', v. 40). Other texts in the various traditions of early Judaism set the devil (or a devil-type figure) in opposition to Abraham, and indeed even the *works* of the devil in opposition to the 'works' of God. For example, the phrase 'the works of Beliar' (i.e. the devil) (*T. Levi* 18.12) constitutes a close parallel to John 8.44 and Jesus' reference to the Jews doing the devil's 'works'. The apocryphal *Testament of Abraham*, as we saw earlier in this chapter, contrasts the devil's 'works' with the purposes of Abraham. And in *m. Avot* 3, we saw that the 'disciples' of Abraham' are completely opposite to the 'disciples of Beliar' in their behaviour and dispositions. Of course, in 1 John 3.8-12 we saw the contrasts between Cain (who was 'born of the devil') and the children of God in the outcome of their respective 'works'. Cain, like the devil (8.44), was both a liar and a murderer, and his 'works were evil' while his brother Abel's 'works' were 'good'.

It is also important to notice how 'Abraham's works' in v. 39 are reiterated by negation in vv. 38a, 40. By suggesting that Abraham's 'works' do *not* include 'seeking to kill a man', we can infer that some action – or a group of positive, life-preserving actions, is entailed by ch. 8 vv. 39-40. In John 7.19-21, Jesus debates the overriding priority of the *mitzvah* of פיקוח נפש ('saving a life') in relation to the Sabbath, the latter of which is said to 'go back to the Patriarchs' (i.e. it is associated with Abraham). In the Epistle to the Hebrews and the Letter of James, we saw complex references to Abraham and Rahab, and their 'works' that had the effect of 'justifying' them. I argued that Abraham's 'works' (2.23-25) played upon the imperative to 'save a life'; by refraining from slaying his son Isaac at the Akedah, Abraham effectively saved a life and observed this commandment. Reading this in conversation with 1 John 3.8-12 and the texts immediately above, Abraham is the antithesis of the 'murderer', the one who takes a life. By telling the Jews that they 'seek to kill' him, Jesus emphasizes their difference from Abraham and their likeness to 'the devil'.

But resisting this negative characterization of the Jews is possible, even though John's harsh anti-Judaism displays its virulent impact in these verses. By recovering the legitimate 'voice' of the Jews through this intertextual scripting, I have tried to do just that. The Jews express a perspective about Abraham's 'works' creating a surplus of blessing (merit/credit) which his 'seed' could draw upon in times of need, especially if weighed down by the 'debt' of sin. Although the Jews' do not express the phrase 'the works of Abraham', the Johannine Jesus intuitively picks up on the Jews' line of reasoning by explicitly disputing this perspective; Jesus asserts that Abrahamic paternity must be proven by imitation of 'Abraham's works', that is that surplus merits will not avail his 'seed' if good works are absent. Whether such 'works' refer to the Torah's mandates to be hospitable (or to Abraham's own hospitable activities in the narratives of Genesis), or to the intratextual skeins in the NT that position Abraham as 'saving a life' (*pikuach nefesh*), the Johannine Jesus maintains that being 'seed' of Abraham must align with doing the 'deeds' of Abraham. In fact, the text of John 8.31-59 (and the wider context of the Sukkot discourse, especially 7.19-21) supports the idea that 'doing the law' requires the saving of a life (even if it overrides the Sabbath), and that to welcome Jesus (here conceived as refraining from killing him!, 8.40) is exactly what Abraham would have done.

Finally, we must consider how this interpretation fits with the Johannine context in terms of how 'works' are depicted and described (apart from 1 John 3). Abraham's 'works' are not in the category of Jesus' 'works' (construed as signs and testimony) because the former are clearly imitable, whereas the latter are unique in that they witness to Jesus' identity as the 'Sent One' of God (e.g. 5.20-21; 7.3; 9.3-5; 10.25-26; 32-33; 14.10-14; 15.24). Jesus' 'works' in these instances are often debated in the 'juridical' chapters of the Gospel (e.g. chs 5, 7–8 and 10), especially in terms of how his listeners respond to what they see. Abraham's 'works' on the other hand are supposedly meant to be copied from 'father-to-son' as proof of claims to identity. John's construction of the 'works of Abraham' and the 'works of the devil' (8.39-44) *does* fit with his overall binary dualism where the 'works' of a person reveal his or her origins and determine his or her fate (cf. 3.19-21; 7.1-4). And finally, Jesus' idiomatic expression 'to work the works of God' (which I argued meant to labour in the Torah but which John reconfigured to mean faith in the Sent One) in ch. 6 vv. 28-29 and ch. 9 vv. 3-5, reinforces (what I interpret to be) the Jews' understanding of 'works' as observance of the Torah (cf. *m. Kidd.* 4.14), accruing 'interest' for the doer in the afterlife. Thus, we have a marvellous synthesis of intertextual and intratextual meaning in this chapter in terms of our understanding of the 'works' of Abraham in John 8.39-40.

6

Abraham sees and rejoices: John 8.48-59

In this chapter, I examine John 8.48-59 and its intertextual field. Following the same method of procedure adopted thus far, I will begin by elaborating the text of ch. 8 vv. 48-59, drawing out its main thematic concerns relating to the figure of Abraham. Briefly stated here, the twin traits imputed to Abraham in this segment of text is that he *saw* Jesus' 'day' and *rejoiced* in it. Abraham is thus endowed with two characteristics: a preternatural vision of some kind, or an ability to 'see' Jesus in some way; and the quality of rejoicing in what he was able to see. I follow, therefore, with a detailed 'scripting' of the intertextual field for this text, as its references to Abraham's 'vision' and 'joy' have puzzled commentators for their apparent vagueness in relation to what we know about Abraham from the biblical material. Then, I examine the concepts of 'seeing' and 'rejoicing' in the Gospel itself, to provide the relevant intratextual background to John 8.47-59, before finally returning to that latter text in order to assess how both the intertextual and intratextual fields cohere with the presentation of Abraham found therein.

Introduction

In the final section of the debate between Jesus and the Jews, the subject shifts from the theme of contested origins to conceptions of honour, glory, obedience and Jesus' status in relation to Abraham. The Jews speak first, asking Jesus, 'Are we not right in saying that you are a Samaritan and have a demon?' (δαιμόνιον ἔχεις: 8.48).[1] Jesus negates

---

[1] According to Wayne Meeks, 'Samaritan' is a 'taunt' hurled at Jesus in this verse, as is the charge that he 'has a demon'. It is curious that the latter charge is refuted, whereas the former 'is passed over in silence (8.49)'. Meeks suggests that there may have been a Samaritan back-story to the Gospel where, historically, sympathizers to Jesus' mission came from Samaria (cf. 4.1-45) and Galilee. See idem, 'Galilee and Judea in the Fourth Gospel', *JBL* 85, no. 2 (1966), pp. 159–69, at p. 166. The charge about Jesus being a 'Samaritan' could result from the fact that this group was viewed as a threatening hybrid, neither fully Jewish nor wholly Gentile (cf. *m. Ned.* 3.10; *m. Kidd.* 43; *m. Git.* 1.5; cited in Johnson, 'Anti-Jewish Slander', p. 438). Being a 'Samaritan' and 'having a demon' may be a subtle jab at the infamous Simon Magus (Simon the Magician), who displayed preternatural powers like Jesus. Simon was a 'deceiver' assisted 'by demons' who tried to 'deify himself' according to Hippolytus (*Ref.* 6.2-18), and he was a 'sorcerer' who was 'deranged' according to Epiphanius (*Pan.* 21). Simon was a Samaritan who was considered a god by others, according to Justin Martyr (*Apol.* 1.26; *Dial.* 120), and according to Irenaeus, he led people astray and drove them mad (*Adv. Haer* 1, 23.1-4; cf. Acts 8.5-25). For more details, see Stephen Haar, *Simon Magus: The First Gnostic?* (BZNW 119;

the charge, telling the Jews that he 'honours' his father, whereas they 'dishonour' him (8.49).[2] Jesus insists that he does not seek his own glory – only God seeks it and is the judge of it (8.50). Jesus promises that 'if anyone' keeps his word, that person will 'never see death' (ἀμὴν ἀμὴν λέγω ὑμῖν, ἐάν τις τὸν ἐμὸν λόγον τηρήσῃ, θάνατον οὐ μὴ θεωρήσῃ εἰς τὸν αἰῶνα: 8.51). Keeping Jesus' word, and the attached promise that it will save a person from death (8.51) is thus an extension of Jesus' earlier promise that *abiding* in his word will set a person free (8.31-34). We begin to see here that, in Jesus' view, freedom is related to the release from 'eternal death', and that, by implication, slavery must have something to do with death – and be related intrinsically to the 'doing' of sin (cf. 8.34; cf. Heb. 2.14). But to the Jews, this promise confirms Jesus' state of demon possession (or possibly, his insanity), as they reply, 'Now we know you have a demon!' (νῦν ἐγνώκαμεν ὅτι δαιμόνιον ἔχεις: 8.52a).

At this point, Abraham is reintroduced. The Jews remark, 'Abraham died (Ἀβραὰμ ἀπέθανεν), as did the prophets, yet you say, "If anyone keeps my word he will never taste death"' (8.52).[3] The Jews then pose another question, one rooted in Jesus' presentation of his own status: 'Surely you are not greater than our father Abraham, who died?' (μὴ σὺ μείζων εἶ τοῦ πατρὸς ἡμῶν Ἀβραάμ, ὅστις ἀπέθανεν: 8.53a). The reference to Abraham as 'our father' is inclusive, with the Jews asserting the mortality they share together with Jesus, and their great ancestor. Of course, Jesus had claimed that anyone who kept his word would not see death; the Jews arrive at the conclusion that *a fortiori*, Jesus himself must be claiming to be beyond the realm of death. But even Abraham died: who is Jesus 'making himself out to be'? (τίνα σεαυτὸν ποιεῖς: 8.53c). Whenever Jesus is described as 'making himself' out to be something more than a mere man in the Gospel, implications of blasphemy are not far behind (5.16-18; 10.30-33).[4] Jesus seems to detect that hint when he replies that he does not seek his own glory (8.54, cf. v. 50).

Berlin: Walter de Gruyter, 2003), pp. 188–19. That Jesus is later accused of being 'mad' and having a 'demon' (10.20), and earlier alleged to have been leading the people astray (7.12), this intertextual association is strong.

[2] 'In a culture where the virtue of sons was linked with the command "honor your father," Jesus' exemplary respect for and loyalty to his Father stand out as an issue of great importance': Jerome H. Neyrey, *The Gospel of John in Cultural and Rhetorical Perspective* (Grand Rapids: Eerdmans, 2009), pp. 20–1.

[3] Jesus says 'never *see* death', and the Jews' relay his words, saying ' never *taste* death' which appears to be a re-expression of the same concept, simply using different sensory metaphors. It seems quibbling to make a point that the Jews 'misunderstand' Jesus at this point, as per Neyrey, *Cultural and Rhetorical Perspective*, p. 242. As Dorothy Lee ('The Gospel of John and the Five Senses', *JBL* 129, no. 1 (2010), pp. 115–27, at pp. 122-3) writes, 'the two [sensory verbs] are parallel: sight and taste, vision and gustation, both express, in their own ways, access to the deathless life that the Johannine Jesus bestows'.

[4] Von Wahlde perceives a repeated literary structure here, as the saying in ch. 8 v. 52 ('no one who keeps my word will ever see death') reiterates the statement in ch. 6 v. 37 ('all who the father gives to me will come to me, and I will not turn away any who come to me') and is echoed by the statement later made in ch. 10 v. 27 ('those who hear my voice know me and they come to me, and I will not lose them'). All three statements occur in the context of Jesus' debate with the Jews (although von Wahlde does not note that 'the Jews' are not yet mentioned in ch. 6 until v. 44, his argument is nevertheless compelling). Idem, 'Literary Structure and Theological Argument in Three Discourses with the Jews in the Fourth Gospel', *JBL* 103, no. 4 (1984), pp. 575–84, at pp. 576–77.

It is then Jesus' turn to report the speech of the Jews, and he tells them 'It is the Father who glorifies me, of whom you say "He is our God"' (8.54b). This is only for Jesus to deny that the Jews even know God, and to simultaneously assert that he knows God, because he keeps God's words; on the other hand, Jesus calls the Jews 'liars' (ψεύστης: 8.55, cf. v. 44). Then follows the climactic segment of the whole discourse (i.e. vv. 56-59), with Jesus forthrightly claiming his unique status relative to Abraham: 'Your father Abraham rejoiced that he would see my day; he saw it and was glad' (Ἀβραὰμ ὁ πατὴρ ὑμῶν ἠγαλλιάσατο ἵνα ἴδῃ τὴν ἡμέραν τὴν ἐμήν, καὶ εἶδεν καὶ ἐχάρη: 8.56). The inclusiveness of the phrase 'our father Abraham' (v. 53) gives way to an *ad hominem* riposte on Jesus' part, as the singular '*your* father Abraham' is hurled back at the Jews.[5] The aorist subjunctive ἴδῃ suggests that at some point, Abraham received a promise (from God?) about seeing Jesus' 'day'; this vision was at another point realized, and Abraham rejoiced both in the promise and the realization of the vision. It is a puzzling statement by any assessment, and the Jews' response admits as much. They probe Jesus' words, incredulous that, given Jesus' youth ('not yet fifty years old'), he could claim to have 'seen' Abraham (Ἀβραὰμ ἑώρακας: 8.57).

This is a proper example of the Jews' misquoting in reported speech; they misunderstand Jesus' claim *to have been seen by* Abraham and consider that Jesus is claiming *to have seen* Abraham. Their misunderstanding does not undermine the thematic centrality of 'seeing' in the text, but in fact reinforces it. Their misunderstanding also reveals the tension in this stage of the dialogue, as the climax nears, for the level of incorrectly related speech suggests 'high stakes' in the debate and a degree of emotiveness only inchoate at the beginning (8.32-32). Now, positions of difference solidify; it is as though Jesus accedes that the Jews 'belong' to Abraham (Ἀβραὰμ ὁ πατὴρ ὑμῶν) but that he simultaneously vacates that fact of genuine relevance by claiming to be the central point upon which Abraham's very life direction, yearning and purpose were built. Finally, Jesus is prompted to pronounce his third and final 'Amen, amen' statement in this discourse: 'Before Abraham was born, I am' (ἀμὴν λέγω ὑμῖν, πρὶν Ἀβραὰμ γενέσθαι ἐγὼ εἰμί: 8.58). To this, (οὖν) the Jews pick up stones to throw at Jesus, but he hides himself and leaves the Temple (8.59). The implication is that Jesus' statement is undoubtedly – to their ears – deserving of death by stoning, a claim to pre-existence (not merely primary importance), signalling the usurpation of the divine prerogative.[6]

What does the passage reveal about Abraham? The Jews again refer to Abraham as 'our father' (cf. 8.53a; cf. v. 39), and Jesus refers to Abraham as the Jews' 'father' (8.56; cf. vv. 37, 39). The Jews connect Abraham with 'the prophets' and state that both 'died' (8.52, 53). Jesus finally claims that Abraham 'saw' his 'day' and 'rejoiced' (8.56), and ultimately proclaims to have pre-existed Abraham (8.58). The unique focus of ch. 8 vv. 48-59 in relation to the rest of the pericope (8.31-47) is therefore the fact of Abraham's 'seeing' and 'rejoicing' – two active qualities that Jesus imputes to Abraham

---

[5] Lindars, *The Gospel of John*, p. 334.
[6] Cf. Freed, 'Who or What was before Abraham?' p. 55. The ἐγὼ εἰμί formula itself may be the Johannine Jesus' expression of the Divine Name; see D. Ball, *'I Am' in John's Gospel: Literary Function, Background and Theological Implications* (JSNTSupp 124; Sheffield: Sheffield Academic Press, 1996), pp. 215-24.

in relation to himself. Secondarily, the Jews' statements about Abraham's mortality, age and his connection to the prophets, are also intertextual features; all of these are explored in the chapter.

It is worth briefly mentioning that the modern commentary tradition pleasingly evinces less overtly anti-Semitic tropes when reflecting on ch. 8 vv. 48-59 (compared to, for example, 8.32-34). Still, some pejorative statements about the Jews as characters remain. Beasley-Murray inadvertently reproduces the Gospel's ideological stance against the Jews as unbelieving characters when he writes on ch. 8 vv. 56-58, 'He [Abraham] did not begrudge that Jesus was greater than he, but *exulted* in his work – the verb is expressive, "he was overjoyed." What a contrast, not to say a gulf, between Abraham and these descendants of his!'[7] George Beasley-Murray portrays the Jews as begrudging complainers who refuse to admit that Jesus is 'greater' than they are. Moreover, the exclamatory tone of Beasley-Murray's comment speaks to a level of emotive involvement in the text that inherently 'complies' with the Gospel's point of view. Our question is whether anything can be said from the perspective of a 'resistant reading' of John 8: does the early Jewish extant textual tradition resonate with the Jews' invocation of Abraham in ch. 8 vv. 48-59? It is important not only to include, but also to look beyond the references to 'seeing and rejoicing' if we want to explore the intertextual background of the Abraham references in ch. 8 vv. 56-58 from a 'resistant' point of view.

Part 1: Scripting the intertextual field

Reference to Abraham's visual capability (either literal or metaphorical) is sparsely attested in the biblical texts. Jesus' words about Abraham 'seeing' him (8.58) have no genuinely clear parallel in the Scriptures. Quite possibly, this ambiguity has led many such commentators to espouse the 'Mamre hypothesis', and to read the reference to Abraham's 'seeing' (John 8.58) as part of an early Christian interpretive tradition of Gen. 18.1-2 which contended that the biblical Abraham had a vision of the pre-existent Christ (*Logos*) in the guise of the three angelic figures visiting him at Mamre's Oaks. Although other parts of the Gospel have sometimes been drawn into this hypothesis in order to validate it as typically Johannine (cf. 1.12-13), the hypothesis remains essentially dependent on the later works of Justin Martyr and other early church apologists.[8] On the other hand, we do find an important biblical text narrating Abraham's revelatory dream about the future (Gen. 15.12), which fed into later post-biblical traditions about Abraham's intuitive 'visions'. This idea of Abraham as a visionary figure – in its cumulative force, articulated diachronically – is valuable as an allusive intertext for reading John 8.56-58, as we will demonstrate.

In like manner, the biblical texts are relatively silent about Abraham's emotions and in them we find no convincing parallel to Jesus' mention of Abraham 'rejoicing' (ἀγαλλιάω). The verb ἀγαλλιάω in John 8.56 is strong, denoting the state of being filled with great delight.[9] This does not generally cohere with the biblical portrait of

---

[7] Beasley-Murray, *John*, p. 138.
[8] See the discussion in Chapter 1 of this book.
[9] BDAG, sv. ἀγαλλιάω

Abraham, who, if not stoic, at least appears emotionless at critical junctures in his story. Even as Abraham leads his son Isaac to Mount Moriah to perform – so he thinks – an act of child sacrifice at God's behest, he is unquestioningly obedient and reserved (Gen. 22.1-10). Although, on occasion, Abraham appears distressed for the sake of Ishmael (Gen. 17.18; 21.11), we do not find indisputable evidence of strongly positive emotions on Abraham's part.[10] One possible exception is Abraham's 'laughter' in Gen. 17.17. It is worth keeping in mind that while the biblical texts do not provide explicit clues by which to understand John's reference to Abraham's 'seeing' and 'rejoicing' in ch. 8 vv. 56-58, they do form an important foundation for later interpretive developments in the Second Temple Period.

The Hebrew Bible

Abraham's dream (Gen. 15.12)

In Gen. 15.1-21, Abraham receives a promise from God that he will have a son and heir, that his 'seed' will be as numerous as the stars in the sky and the sand on the seashore, and that his descendants will possess the Land. Abraham believes in what God tells him, and this is accounted to him as 'righteousness' (15.6). When Abraham asks for assurance that the promise will be granted, God commands him to undertake a sacrificial ritual (15.9-11). At this point, as the sun is going down, Abraham falls into a 'deep sleep' (15.12a), and a 'terrifying darkness' overcomes him (15.12b). In this state, Abraham receives an answer from the Lord to his request for assurance. The Lord speaks to Abraham in his sleep, telling Abraham that his 'seed' will be foreigners and slaves in a land not theirs, that they shall be oppressed for 400 years, but that ultimately the nation oppressing them will be judged (15.13-14). Abraham himself will pass on to his ancestors in peace and buried in 'a good old age' (15.15). His 'seed' will only return to the Land of the promise 'in the fourth generation' when the 'sin of the Amorites' is complete (15.16). While the narrator does not recount Abraham waking from this dream, he does mention that the Lord 'made a covenant' with Abraham that day based on the promise of the Land to his seed (15.18-21). The reader assumes that Abraham is awake to witness the searing fire that passes between the 'pieces' of cut-up animal remains, which is the way in which God concludes his covenant with Abraham (15.17-18a).

In Chapter 4, we addressed this text for what it revealed about the motif of Abraham's 'seed'. Here, it is necessary to mention the narrative detail of Abraham's sleeping (15.12).[11] The narrative takes an unexpectedly dark turn when it depicts a

---

[10] The character of Abraham does possibly exhibit fear over losing Ishmael ('Oh that Ishmael might live in your sight!', Gen. 17.18). And we have reference to Abraham being very distressed (Sarah's words 'appeared very hard' to him: σκληρὸν δὲ ἐφάνη τὸ ῥῆμα σφόδρα, LXX) when his wife commanded him to cast out Hagar and Ishmael. In both cases, Abraham is concerned over the fate of his first-born son (21.11).

[11] On sleeping nightmares in the ANE and Hebrew Bible, see the excellent work of Jean-Marie Husser, *Dreams and Dream Narratives in the Biblical World* (London: Bloomsbury, 1999), esp. pp. 28, 159–60; and Scott Noegel, 'Dreams and Dream Interpreters in Mesopotamia and in the Hebrew Bible', in K. Bulkeley (ed.), *Dreams* (New York: Palgrave Macmillan, 2001), pp. 45–71. One of the earliest studies to which many scholars in this area are subsequently in debt is that of Ernst Ludwig Ehrlich, *Der Traum im Alten Testament* (BZAW 73; Berlin: Verlag Alfred Töpelmann, 1953). On the

'deep sleep' falling upon Abraham – as though, with sundown, a 'terrifying darkness' comes upon Abraham without warning and without his control.[12] In this state of deep sleep, Abraham receives a message from God in the form of spoken words. The prescient message that Abraham receives about his 'seed' occurs through the auditory senses, even though Abraham is asleep. It is not, as we might expect from a person in a dream state, a revelation of the future by means of the visual senses. The reader suspects that the revelation Abraham experiences is entirely internal; Abraham 'hears' the voice of the Lord from within his subconscious, in the form of a frightening message. Nevertheless, an earlier detail complicates this picture somewhat: earlier in the same narrative 'the word of the Lord' was said to come to Abraham 'in a vision' while he was awake (15.1). There, the ocular and auditory senses were combined, as Abraham was said to 'see' the 'word' of the Lord (not to 'hear' it). Indeed, the Lord speaks quite freely to Abraham, even leading him outside and showing him the stars of heaven (15.5). Abraham is told to 'look' towards the stars and count them (15.5). As Abraham hears the 'words' of God in this 'vision', he is also able to 'see' things in the material world. Just so, Abraham's 'dream' taking place in his sleeping state might be classed as a kind of 'vision' even though in it he hears the 'words' of the Lord.[13]

In both instances – the external 'vision' depicted in ch. 15 vv. 1-5 and the internal, dream revelation in ch. 15 vv. 12-13 – Abraham receives a message from God about his 'seed'. Abraham is given the ability to 'see' the future, but it is a future that specifically concerns him because of the fact that it concerns his descendants. On the one hand, Abraham sees that his seed shall be numerous (15.5), and on the other, he sees that they shall be enslaved for generations (15.13). The connection between the two 'visions' is not easy to establish. Could Abraham's question in ch. 15 v. 8 be the necessary linkage? Abraham, in this reading, demonstrates a lack of faith in God's promise (pronounced in 15.4-5) by asking for certainty, and the enslavement of his 'seed' in a foreign land is read as punishment for such audacity. This reading is difficult to sustain in light of the fact that Abraham was just declared 'righteous' for believing in God's promise (15.6). Yet, in Abraham's dream God does profess to offer Abraham certainty, when he says, 'Know this *for sure* (ידע תדע; γινώσκων γνώσῃ) that your seed shall be strangers in a land not theirs' (15.13). Abraham's 'seed' will suffer, but Abraham will not; instead he shall live to a ripe old age and be buried with his 'fathers' (there is no more honourable death than that). Thus, there is some traction to this interpretive tradition that considered the enslavement of Abraham's 'seed' to be a kind of vicarious suffering for Abraham's 'sin' of disbelief.[14] But the reading raises necessary questions, such as why the 400-year period is mandated, and why the Lord nevertheless concludes his covenant with Abraham without further ado (15.17-18).

---

patriarch's dreams, see especially Michael Oblath, '"To Sleep, Perchance to Dream...": What Jacob Saw at Bethel', *JSOT* 26, no. 1 (2001), pp. 117–26.

[12] For Job 33.15-16 as a comparator text, see Husser, *Dreams and Dream Narratives*, p. 159.

[13] Some scholars prefer to use the term 'vision theophany' to describe Abraham's experience, thus Dixon Sutherland, 'The Organization of the Abraham Promise Narratives', *ZNW* 95, no. 3 (1983), pp. 337–43.

[14] Cf. Levenson, *Inheriting Abraham*.

The point to draw attention to here, in relation to John 8.56-58, is that Abraham is portrayed as a recipient of divinely endowed dreams and 'visions' of future times. This text would establish traditions of interpretation in the post-biblical period that viewed Abraham capable of 'seeing' not only the future, but also the end times as God had ordained them. Even more pertinently, some texts portrayed Abraham as able to look down from heaven as it were and 'see' *the fate of his seed* on earth in 'real time'. Of course, such 'visions' – unlike the one narrated in Genesis 15 – postdate Abraham's actual lifetime and so are not thought of as proleptic visions. Yet, they do seem to have evolved organically from the Genesis 15 narrative inasmuch as they posit a direct concern on Abraham's part – even after he has died – with the future outcome facing his 'seed'. What the text of Genesis 15 establishes on its own, in this regard, is that Abraham is given the preternatural ability to 'see' events that are yet to take place long into the future.

Abraham's laughter (Gen. 17.17)

At the age of ninety-nine, God 'appears' to Abraham and reveals the covenant of circumcision (Gen. 17.1-14). All of Abraham's (male) 'seed' are henceforth to be circumcised (17.11-12), and even Abraham's household slaves are to be circumcised too (17.13). God's self-disclosure prefaces the communication of the covenant and its promise: 'I am El Shaddai, walk before me and become whole' (MT: לפני והיה תמים אני־אל שדי התהלך/LXX: Ἐγώ εἰμι ὁ θεός σου εὐαρέστει ἐναντίον ἐμοῦ καὶ γίνου ἄμεμπτος). God promises to 'make [Abraham] great' – that is, to multiply his descendants (17.2). Abraham's response to God's promise is to fall upon his face in evident reverence (17.3). God also promises that Abraham's wife Sarai – whose name is changed to Sarah (17.15) – will be blessed with a son; she shall give rise to nations and kings (17.16). At this, Abraham falls on his face a second time and laughs (MT: ויצחק/ἐγέλασεν LXX 17.17a). Abraham's ensuing monologue, however, suggests that this strong response is the product of incredulity: 'Can a child be born to a man who is a hundred years old? Can Sarah, who is ninety years old, bear a child?' (17.17b). Furthermore, Abraham takes God's promise to mean that his son by Sarah will replace Ishmael, as he cries out, 'O that Ishmael might live in your sight!' (17.18). God replies that Sarah will bear a son, whom Abraham will call Isaac (Hb lit. 'he laughs': יצחק), and that God's covenant will be established through him, not Ishmael (17.19). Nevertheless, Ishmael will also be blessed and made great (17.20).

It is not clear whether Abraham's 'laughter' in ch. 17 v. 17 indicates *faithless* incredulity. One can be stunned into disbelief by the prospect of unexpectedly good news, and laughter in these cases can be understood as a natural response demonstrating mixed feelings: happiness, but uncertainty over whether the good news would truly come to pass. That God 'names' Abraham's yet-to-be-born son in this text is curious: it is only after Abraham 'laughs' that God finds it appropriate to name Isaac after his father's reaction. This might suggest that God finds nothing inappropriate or condemnatory in Abraham's apparent incredulity.[15] Abraham's laughter could indeed be a sign of positive

---

[15] Ephraim A. Speiser, *Genesis* (AB 1; New York: Doubleday, 1964), p. 125 arrives at the same conclusion for a different reason, namely, that P never presents Abraham relating to God derisively. For a similar assessment of the priestly material, see Joseph Blenkinsopp, 'Abraham as Paradigm in the Priestly History in Genesis', *JBL* 128 no. 2 (2009), pp. 225–41., pp. 225–41. The Church Fathers

emotion. But this is complicated by the fact that Abraham's distress over Ishmael's fate follows so quickly on from his laughter over the coming birth of Isaac (17.18).

The issue is hardly clarified by subsequent references to Sarah's 'laughter' in the narrative. When the three messengers visit Abraham and Sarah at Mamre, and Sarah overhears their news that she will bear a son, she 'laughed to herself' (שׂרה בקרב ותצחק/ LXX: ἐγέλασεν δὲ Σαρρα ἐν ἑαυτῇ) saying, 'After I have grown old, and my husband is old, shall I have pleasure?' (Gen. 18.12). The narrator also explains that Abraham and Sarah are beyond the fertile years (18.11). This time, Yhwh interprets Sarah's laughter as faithless incredulity, asking Abraham why she laughed when 'nothing is too wonderful for the Lord' (18.13-14). Sarah is afraid (יראה; LXX: ἐφοβήθη) and denies that she laughed, but Yhwh replies ominously, 'Oh yes, you did laugh' (18.15). However, when Isaac is born, and Abraham is 100 years old (Gen. 21.1-5), Sarah responds by saying 'God has brought laughter for me; everyone who hears will laugh with me' (21.6). Sarah expresses her expectation that others will be astounded and incredulous by the birth: 'Who would ever have said to Abraham that Sarah would nurse children?' (21.7). But Sarah's speech, in this case, evidently associates laughter with joy, and she perceives her 'laughter' – like her son – as a gift from God. So, Genesis 21 contains positive connotations for Sarah's 'laughter', unlike Gen. 18.14-15. From a narrative-critical perspective though, this diversity does open the possibility that, globally speaking, Abraham and Sarah's 'laughter' over Isaac's conception and birth is not uniformly perceived as negative. This nuance could have been what led later interpreters of the texts to read Abraham's 'laughter' in Gen. 17.17 as an instance of great joy.

Abraham's visitors at the Oaks of Mamre (Gen. 18.1-15)

We have mentioned Abraham's 'vision' of the Lord in Gen. 15.1-2, mediated by the auditory senses, but including visual-spatial elements in the real world as well. Another text from the narrative of Abraham's life (Gen. 18.1-15) can be read in light of this theme of his visionary experiences. But there are notable differences, chief of which is that in Gen. 18.1, Abraham has a vision of the Lord in broad daylight, via his external ocular senses, in the guise of three men, who later turn out to be heavenly messengers (19.1). Gen. 18.1 reads, 'The Lord appeared to Abraham by the oaks of Mamre, as he sat at the entrance of his tent in the heat of the day'. The verb for 'appear' in Septuagint Greek is ὁράω, which denotes vision through the physical sense of sight; in the Hebrew Bible (HB), the verb is ראה. As if to emphasize this point as much as possible, the text continues, 'He [Abraham] lifted up his eyes (וישׂא עיניו; ἀναβλέψας δὲ τοῖς ὀφθαλμοῖς αὐτοῦ) and saw (וירא; εἶδεν) that – look! (והנה; ἰδοὺ) – there were three men standing near him' (18.2a). And 'seeing them' (וירא; καὶ ἰδὼν), Abraham ran to greet them (18.2b). After offering the three men generous hospitality (18.3-8), the men ask after Sarah's whereabouts (18.9) and one of the men promises to return to Abraham 'in due

---

sometimes thought differently. For example, Jerome interpreted Gen. 17.17 to refute the Pelagian ideas of human sinlessness – even a holy man such as Abraham could sin, and did so when he laughed at God (*Dialogue against the Pelagians* 3.2); cited in Elizabeth A. Clark, 'Interpretive Fate amid the Church Fathers', in Phyllis Trible and Letty M. Russell (eds), *Hagar, Sarah and Their Children: Jewish, Christian, and Muslim Perspectives* (Louisville: Westminster John Knox, 2006), pp. 127–48, at p. 144–5, n. 26.

season' at which time, he states, Sarah shall have a son (18.10).[16] Sarah's incredulous laughter then puts her in a precarious position when one of the men – now identified as 'the Lord' (18.13) – reproves them for their apparent disbelief.

Two features of this text stand out. First, the text goes to great lengths to point out that Abraham saw these men with his eyes in the clear light of day. This 'appearance' of the Lord to Abraham was therefore not a mystical encounter, but an actual, interpersonal one.[17] For all that, it was not any less a divine vision and a divine encounter. The *reader* knows that it is 'the Lord' who has appeared to Abraham in the guise of three men (18.1; or three angels, cf. 19.1), but *Abraham* only arrives at this knowledge incrementally (cf. 18.13, 17).[18] Second, and relatedly, is the didactic purpose that has been derived from this text in its history of reception. Abraham is exemplary in his hospitality towards these three 'men' (he washes their feet, lets them rest, brings them bread, has Sarah make them cakes, has a tender calf prepared for them and feeds them curds and milk, while keeping them company), and he later learns that he has been serving the Lord. This, no doubt, inspired one New Testament (NT) writer to encourage his community to show hospitality to strangers 'for by doing that, some have entertained angels without knowing it' (Heb. 13.2).[19] The idea is that one can encounter and 'serve' God by showing hospitality and kindness to those in need. The text of Genesis 18 also gave rise to the early Jewish traditions of Abraham as a paradigm of hospitality (cf. *Testament of Abraham*), whose example could be emulated.[20] Abraham's hospitality towards his visitors, while not described as arising out of 'joy' can still be read as actions that derive from a state of great excitement and generosity. Abraham's capacity as one who can 'see' the Lord is also underscored.

Abraham's intercession (Gen. 18.16-33)

Following the narrative of Abraham's visitors at Mamre (Gen. 18.1-15) is a connected narrative about the fate of Sodom (18.16-33).[21] Two of the angelic men move on from Mamre (18.16, cf. 22; 19.1) while Abraham remains with one, who is revealed to be 'the

---

[16] The text associates the divine promise of Isaac's improbably birth with the exceeding hospitality displayed by Abraham to the Lord, as if the former is contingent somehow upon the latter. See, Westermann, *Genesis 12–36*, p. 282.

[17] Early Christian interpretation begged to differ in many cases, particularly viewing Abraham's 'angels' as the Trinitarian God, or at least the pre-incarnate Logos. For an overview of the literature, see Helen Spurling and Emmanouela Grypeou, 'Abraham's Angels: Jewish and Christian Exegesis of Genesis 18-19', in idem, (eds), *The Exegetical Encounter*, pp. 181–203.

[18] In Gen. 19.1-3, the angels appear to Lot in a parallel story that has occasioned much commentary for its artistic narrative accomplishments. See Robert Ignatius Letellier, *Day in Mamre, Night in Sodom: Abraham and Lot in Genesis 18 and 19* (Leiden: Brill, 1995), pp. 39–42. For further inner-biblical allusions extending beyond Genesis 19, see Victor H. Matthews, 'Hospitality and Hostility in Genesis 19 and Judges 19', *BTB* 22 (1992), pp. 3–11; and the similarly titled essay by Nathan MacDonald, 'Hospitality and Hostility: Reading Genesis 19 in Light of 2 Samuel 10 (and Vice Versa)', in Diana Lipton (ed.), *Universalism and Particularism at Sodom and Gomorrah: Essays in Memory of Ron Pirson* (Atlanta: SBL Press, 2012), pp. 179–90.

[19] Cf. Jipp, *Divine Visitations and Hospitality to Strangers*, p. 133, n. 9.

[20] See the textual analysis provided in Chapter 5 on Abraham's 'works'.

[21] The story of Abraham's intercession at Sodom segues into the parallel story (Genesis 19) of Lot's contrasting inhospitality, as many scholars have noted; cf. Letellier, *Day in Mamre*, p. 51. See recently, Van Seeters, *Abraham in History and Tradition* (rev. edn), p. 216.

Lord' (18.17; cf. v. 13).²² In soliloquy, the Lord debates about whether to disclose to Abraham his plan to destroy the city of Sodom for its 'grave sin' (v. 20: רבה וחטאתם; ἁμαρτίαι αὐτῶν μεγάλαι σφόδρα), given that Abraham will 'become a great and mighty nation' (18.17-18).²³ Because God has chosen Abraham to be one who will teach his children to keep 'the way of the Lord' (18.19), God decides to let Abraham know his plans (18.22). Abraham immediately questions the Lord, 'Will you indeed sweep away the righteous with the wicked? Suppose there are fifty righteous within the city; will you then sweep away the place and not forgive it for the fifty righteous who are in it?' (18.23-24). The Lord replies, 'If I find at Sodom fifty righteous in the city, I will forgive the whole place for their sake' (18.26). Step by step, Abraham eventually takes the number of righteous men down to ten – will the Lord forgive the entire city for the sake of ten righteous men? (18.32a). The Lord replies, 'For the sake of ten I will not destroy it' (18.32b).

This text presents Abraham as so closely connected to Yhwh that he is able to influence the deity's actions, and to divert judgement from the wicked. Abraham not only receives communications from God, as would a prophet (cf. Gen. 15.1-2), but also enters into dialogue with God, much like Moses in his mediating role at Sinai (cf. Exod. 32.33).²⁴ Abraham argues that the 'Judge of the world' must show 'justice' and not slay the righteous with the wicked (18.25). If God were to slay the righteous, this would mean they receive the judgement due to the wicked, without warrant. But the text suggests more than the straightforward notion that the righteous do not deserve the judgement reserved for the wicked. The fact that there might be even ten righteous men in a city filled with depravity is enough to prevent the destruction of the whole city, or even part of the city – 'for the sake of' the ten righteous men (בעבורם). Indeed, the Lord will *forgive* (נשא) the whole city for the sake of the righteous (18.26). The righteousness of the few can neutralize the sinfulness of the many, and offset punishment, an idea that resonates with Ezekiel 18, and the debate about intergenerational sin and punishment.²⁵

What we find in this text then, is perhaps a basis for the later rabbinic idea of a person's זכוית ('merits') functioning to counter the sinfulness of others. We also see Abraham presented as a kind of mediator between God and humanity, able to arbitrate before God.²⁶ Several post-biblical Jewish writings drew on this motif of Abraham as

---

[22] Letellier, *Day in Mamre*, p. 57, suggests that the debate between Abraham and the remaining angel ('the Lord') is patterned on the Hebrew *rîb* narrative (court procedure). See also J. K. Bruckner, *Implied Law in the Abraham Narrative: A Literary and Theological Analysis* (JSOTSup335; Sheffield: Sheffield Academic Press, 2001). On the single angel who remains with Abraham, see Adele Reinhartz, *'Why Ask My Name?' Anonymity and Identity in Biblical Narrative* (New York: Oxford University Press, 1998), p. 172, who suggests that because the text identifies one angel as 'the Lord', the other men who visit Lot (19.1-3) do so only as angels, not as the deity.
[23] The 'grave sin' (cf. Gen. 4.9-11; Exod. 2.23; 3.7; Isa. 5.7) may well have been systematic forms of murder and oppression. See Weston W. Fields, *Sodom and Gomorrah: History and Motif in Biblical Narrative* (JSOTSup 231; Sheffield: Sheffield Academic Press, 1997), pp. 171–9.
[24] Diana Lipton, 'The Limits of Intercession: Abraham Reads Ezekiel at Sodom', in idem (ed.), *Universalism*, pp. 25–42, at p. 27.
[25] Lipton, 'The Limits of Intercession', p. 29.
[26] Ehud Ben Zvi, 'The Dialogue Between Abraham and YHWH in Gen. 18.23-32: A Historical Analysis', *JSOT* 53 (1992), pp. 27–46, surveys the scholarship on one of the key interpretive

peculiarly capable of influencing God's decrees with respect to sinners and righteous people alike. In the following section, I show how this text spawned certain traditions about Abraham that focused on his intercessory function, which of itself, I suggest, is closely linked to the apocryphal traditions about Abraham's divinely endowed prescience. Both traditions locate Abraham in a unique 'realm' where he alone can converse with God (either on earth in his lifetime, or in heaven after his death), and where God is able to reveal certain things to him.

Apocryphal and pseudepigraphical literature

In this section, I trace the traditions around Abraham's 'seeing' and 'rejoicing' as they exist in the post-biblical material of the Apocrypha and Pseudepigrapha. Most of these traditions build upon the biblical texts of Abraham's dream vision(s) and the promises God makes to him and his 'seed'. Some fascinating developments include the peculiar discernment that Abraham possesses that enables him to perceive the Oneness of God (e.g. through the 'stars', a play on Gen. 15.15, but positioning Abraham as an 'astronomer'). Others include the representation of Abraham as a visionary, and an interceder for his posterity on earth. These are considered here under the rubric of Abraham 'seeing' things beyond normal human ken. Under the category of 'joy and rejoicing', the post-biblical material adds some new developments as well, although the references are comparatively sparse: the testamentary literature have examples of Abraham, Isaac and Jacob rejoicing at the binding of Beliar (the devil) and the coming of the messiah; otherwise, there is the narrative of Abraham being commissioned to 'go forth' on his journey and to rejoice greatly for being chosen by God. Some of these themes tie into what we find in the NT, although in the latter corpus markedly polemical tones start to creep into the presentation of Abraham as 'all-seeing', as I show in the following section.

Abraham as visionary figure

Several post-biblical Jewish texts present Abraham as a visionary figure, one who perceives the future by means of dreams or through the interpretation of astral bodies. One example of Abraham's dream revelations comes from *Jub.* 14.1-16, which builds upon Gen. 15.1-17.[27] The passage begins by following Gen. 15.1, with some alteration: The word of the Lord came to Abraham *in a dream*, (בחלם) saying, 'Do not fear, Abraham, I am your defender, and your reward (will be) very great' (*Jub.* 14.1).[28] In Gen. 15.1, the word of the Lord is said to come to Abraham in a vision (בחזה), and only later does Abraham fall into a 'deep sleep' and experience his revelatory dream (Gen. 15.12-13).[29]

---

dimensions of this story through the ages, that is the 'vicarious preserving function' of the 'righteous' (הצדיקם) in this text.
[27] See *OTP I*, p. 84.
[28] *OTP I*, p. 84. I have modified 'Abram' to 'Abraham' in the citation for consistency.
[29] Van Ruiten, *Abraham in the Book of Jubilees*, p. 123.

Nevertheless, *Jub.* 14.1 follows Gen. 15.1 verbatim in terms of the substance of the Lord's speech/theophany. In comparison to the Torah text (Gen. 15.2-4), *Jubilees* slightly condenses Abraham's discussion with the Lord over his promised 'reward' of progeny (*Jub.* 14.2-3a). Then, the text moves quickly into the narrative of Abraham's vision of the stars: 'And he [the Lord] took him [Abraham] outside and he said to him: "Look into heaven and count the stars if you are able to count them". And he [Abraham] looked at the heaven and he saw the stars. And he [the Lord] said to him [Abraham], "Thus shall your seed be"' (*Jub.* 14.4-5). Once more, in this case *Jubilees* follows Gen. 15.5 closely.

The text diverges from the Genesis account slightly when Abraham makes the required animal sacrifice (cf. Gen. 15.9-13). In *Jub.* 14.9-13, Abraham takes the animals and slaughters them, and the author adds – as is elsewhere his custom with respect to time keeping – that this all took place 'in the middle of the month'. The place of the sacrifice is also specified (unlike Genesis 15), with Abraham dwelling at the Oaks of Mamre. Additionally, *Jubilees* presents Abraham's efforts to turn away the birds of prey from devouring the sacrifice in more insistent terms compared to Gen. 15.11. But Abraham, whom *Jubilees* presents as already in a dream state (*Jub.* 14.1), now experiences something else when the sun sets: we read that 'a terror fell upon Abraham. And behold, a great dark horror fell upon him' (*Jub.* 14.13). Unlike Gen. 15.12, Abraham is not described as falling into a 'deep sleep' before 'a terrifying darkness' descends upon him. Instead, Abraham is understood to have experienced the entire episode in a dream state (*Jub.* 14.1), and thus at this point his dream takes a dark turn, as he hears the words of the Lord again: 'Surely know that your seed will be strangers in an alien land' (*Jub.* 14.13). At this point, Abraham 'woke up from his sleep and stood up' (*Jub.* 14.17) – an incidental detail added to fill a gap in the Genesis text (Gen. 15.17).[30] The consequent covenant between Abraham and the Lord becomes, in the perspective of *Jubilees*, a renewable 'feast' and 'ordinance' that Abraham observes 'forever' (*Jub.* 14.20).[31]

Pseudo-Philo also retells the text of Gen. 15.1-17 (*LAB* 23.6). Curiously, *LAB* situates Abraham's dream and vision in the immediate context of the covenant renewal at Shiloh, under Joshua (cf. Josh 19.51; 23.2; the LXX locates the renewal at Shiloh, and the Masoretic Text (MT) at Shechem).[32] In Pseudo-Philo's intricate web of biblical texts, all mixed together at this point (*LAB* 23.1-14), it is actually Joshua who receives a 'dream vision' from God and is told to prophetically mouth the words of God to the people the next day (23.3). Thus, Joshua rises and speaks in the name of the Lord: 'There was one rock from which I quarried out your father ... Abraham and Nahor ... And Abraham took Sarah as a wife and Nahor took Melcha. And when all those

---

[30] Abraham also 'dreams' in other post-biblical literature, such as in 1QGen 19.14-21, where he experiences a revelation about the fate of his 'seed' in Egypt (Armin Lange, 'Divinatorische Träume und Apokalyptik im Jübiläenbuch', in Albani, Frey and Lange (eds), *Studies in the Book of Jubilees*, pp. 25–38, at p. 34), but the *Genesis Apocryphon* distinguishes between the types of dreams that biblical figures experience, for example Noah is given imminently eschatological dreams, whereas Abraham is not. Cf. Bennie H. Reynolds III, *Between Symbolism and Realism: The Use of Symbolic and Non-Symbolic Language in Ancient Jewish Apocalypses 333-63 BCE* (Göttingen: Vandenhoeck & Ruprecht, 2012), p. 207.

[31] Recall the concept of Abraham as Torah observant examined in Chapter 5.

[32] *OTP II*, p. 332.

inhabiting the land were being led astray after their own devices, Abraham believed in me and was not led astray with them' (23.4-5a). Pseudo-Philo presents Abraham as the pristine ancestral figure who *believed* in the Lord – a subtle play on Gen. 15.6 – but his belief is then described as the reason that the Lord spared Abraham from the fire (cf. ch. 6) and brought him into the land of Canaan (23.5b). Abraham was not an idolater like the men who surrounded him, evidenced in his capacity and willingness to have faith in the one God.

Pseudo-Philo then segues into a commentary on Abraham's dream vision in Gen. 15.1-17, perhaps picking up on the cue of Abraham's 'belief' expressed in that same text (cf. Gen. 15.6). When the Lord brought Abraham into Canaan, he spoke to him 'in a vision' with the words 'To your seed I will give this land' (23.5c). Joshua continues to relay the words of the Lord: 'And that man [Abraham] said to me, "Behold now you have given me a wife who is sterile. And how will I have offspring from that rock of mine that is closed up?"' (23.5d). The Lord narrates that, in response, he mandated an animal sacrifice from Abraham, and then: 'I sent upon him a deep sleep and encompassed him with fear and set before him the place of fire where the works of those doing wickedness against me will be expiated, and I showed him the torches of fire by which the just who have believed in me will be enlightened' (23.6). These twin visions of fire then become a 'witness' between the Lord and Abraham, proof that Sarah's 'closed up' womb will be opened (23.7a). The Lord then continues to promise Abraham that 'prophets' will proceed from his lineage, as well as wise men and multitudes of peoples – all of whom are symbolized by the various animals that Abraham has just sacrificed (23.7b). The Lord calls these promises 'prophecies' which – together with the events of that night – will forever stand as 'witnesses' between the Lord and Abraham, indicating that the Lord will be faithful to his words (23.7c).

There are some obvious divergences between Pseudo-Philo's account of Abraham's vision and the base text of Gen. 15.1-17. Notably, Abraham implicates his wife's sterility as the main reason for his lack of an heir, whereas in Gen. 15.2, Abraham simply states that he 'continues childless' with only Eliezar of Damascus to inherit his household. As Abraham was quarried from a 'rock' (*LAB* 23.4), just so should Sarah – who is Abraham's 'rock' – provide descendants for him (23.5d). Pseudo-Philo also makes God wholly responsible for the 'deep sleep' that comes upon Abraham. Whereas the Genesis text specifies no agent behind the 'terrifying darkness' that descends upon Abraham, Pseudo-Philo does not hide the fact that it was the Lord who made Abraham fall asleep and then surrounded him with 'fear'. The substance of Abraham's vision is also markedly different: there is no reference in Ps.-Philo 23.6-7 to the future slavery of Abraham's 'seed'; instead, God shows Abraham two 'fires' corresponding to two aspects of the divine judgement: one in which the wicked works of sinners will be expiated, and the other in which the just shall be enlightened. With regard to the latter aspect, Abraham has a vision of 'torches' that will enlighten the just, a detail that is derived from the 'flaming torches' that pass between the sacrificed animal pieces in the original Torah text (Gen. 15.17). This vision in itself stands as evidentiary proof that the Lord will keep his promise to give Abraham's 'seed' the land of Canaan. Pseudo-Philo omits altogether reference to the 'dark' vision of captivity found in Gen. 15.13, instead continuing to reward Abraham with prophets and wise men among his progeny.

Although not a lengthy narrative retelling of Gen. 15.1-17 in the manner of texts such as *Jubliees* and *Pseudo-Philo*, *4 Ezra* 3.14-15 nevertheless represents an allusive reference to the story of Abraham's dream vision found in Genesis. The trajectory spanning the antediluvian period up to the call of Abraham occupies the substance of Ezra's first apocalyptic revelation (*4 Ezra* 3.1-19). This primeval history is interpreted in such a way that Abraham represents the pinnacle of human goodness, as though the call of Abraham somehow repairs the damage inflicted upon the earth and human society by the 'ungodliness' of the earth's inhabitants (with the exception of Noah and his descendants; cf. 3.1-13). Abraham is presented as a worthy figure chosen by God to receive special revelations. Ezra speaks to God as follows: 'And when they were committing iniquity before you, you chose for yourself one of them, whose name was Abraham; and you loved him, and to him only you revealed the end of the times, secretly by night. You made with him an everlasting covenant, and promised him that you would never forsake his descendants' (3.14-15). The climax of Abraham's call and the covenant made with him takes place after the Exodus at Sinai, when God gives the Law to 'Jacob's descendants' (3.19).[33]

4 Ezra 3.12-19 alludes to several Torah texts, such as the call of Abraham (Gen. 12.1ff.), his vision by night and the covenant that ensues (Gen. 15.5-17), the Exodus from Egypt and the revelation at Sinai (Exod. 19.16-18). But the presentation of Abraham in *4 Ezra* 3.14-15 is also influenced by texts such as Isa. 48.1, Neh. 9 and 2 Chron. 20.7, which – as we saw in Chapter 4 of this book – depicted Abraham as especially loved by God. Those texts suggested that God's call of Abraham was motivated by love. *4 Ezra* 3.14 refers to Abraham as a 'worthy figure'. As such, Abraham's chosen status – and consequently, the Abrahamic covenant itself – is not thought of as fortuitous or random, but as guided by both divine 'grace' *and* merit on Abraham's part. Despite the ungodliness that surrounded him, Abraham alone was considered 'worthy'.[34] For this reason, the text of *4 Ezra* 3.15 suggests, God revealed secret things to Abraham by night. These secret revelations pertained to the 'end times' – Abraham, like Ezra, is depicted as an apocalyptic visionary![35] Yet specifically, the revelations conferred upon Abraham pertain to his 'seed', so that Abraham receives visions of the end times as they relate to the divine covenantal promise that God will never forsake his descendants. There are also parallels between this text and the rabbinic passages which presented Abraham as instructed in God's law by night, through the secret wisdom dispensed by his own 'kidneys'.[36]

---

[33] *OTP I*, pp. 528–9.

[34] For the author of *4 Ezra*, history develops by way of such elections; cf. Hindy Naijman, *Losing the Temple and Recovering the Future: An Analysis of 4 Ezra* (Cambridge: Cambridge University Press, 2014), p. 128.

[35] Jonathan A. Moo, *Creation, Nature and Hope in 4 Ezra* (Göttingen: Vandenhoeck & Ruprecht, 2011), p. 107.

[36] The kidneys were considered the most important internal organs, together with the heart, in ancient Israel. They were thought to contain secret thoughts, and to be the centre of a person's emotional life. Through the kidneys one could also discern moral directions and receive omens or inspiration. See G. Maio, 'The Metaphorical and Mythical Use of the Kidney in Antiquity', *The American Journal of Nephrology* 19, no. 2 (1999), pp. 101–6.

The text of Gen. 15.1-17 also gave rise to apocryphal traditions about Abraham as an astrologer in the Second Temple Period. The motif of Abraham's ability to see the future by the stars perhaps developed out of the Genesis accounts about Abraham 'counting the stars' at God's invitation, while receiving the promise that his future 'seed' would be multitudinous.[37] In *Pseudo-Eupolemus* 3, Abraham is depicted as superior in 'nobility and wisdom' and as one who sought out knowledge of astrology from his Chaldean environs. Abraham is, in this text, wholly eager to be pious, and his capabilities in the realm of astral divination do not at all detract from his piety.[38] Later in life, Abraham is described as living in Egypt and instructing the priests there in the craft of astrology and related 'sciences' (*Ps.-Eup.* 8). Additionally, Abraham is said to have attributed the discovery of astrology to Enoch, not the Egyptians or the Greeks, as the common knowledge would have it (*Ps.-Eup.* 9-10). The pseudonymous 'Orphica' describes a man 'of the Chaldeans' who was 'knowledgeable about the path of the Star' and the movements of the solar bodies (vv. 27-28), a probable reference to Abraham.[39] These texts, then, present a surprisingly positive valuation of Abraham's astrological abilities (at least in light of the post-biblical texts emphasizing Abraham's difference from his Chaldean environs). These texts appear to have 'embraced the view of astronomy/astrology as an emblem of extreme antiquity and as an integral part of humankind's scientific progress'.[40]

Yet other texts of the period portrayed Abraham's reputed facility in the astrological sciences as indicative of 'pagan' influence and thus as a negative characteristic. In *Jub.* 12.16, Abraham is depicted as seating himself before the stars at night in order to observe their path and thus determine what the future holds in store for agriculture. But it turns out to be a moment of revelation for Abraham: a 'word of the Lord' comes into his heart, convincing him that the Lord alone – who is the maker of the stars – sets the course of history (12.17). The text goes on to connect this momentous insight to the fate of Abraham's 'seed', thus alluding to the patriarchal promises of Genesis where Abraham's 'seed' are foretold to be as numerous as the stars of heaven. Abraham's insight becomes a vehicle for his discovery of monotheism, as he prays to the Lord that he might forever follow God's paths so that his 'seed' may be established forever (12.19-20). In the context of Abraham's recent repudiation of idolatry (*Jub.* 12.12-14), his renunciation of astrology (12.16-10) functions as an expression of his singular devotion to God and his immediate decision to abandon Chaldea (12.21).[41]

Josephus' views on Abraham's astrological abilities are more ambivalent.[42] On the one hand, Josephus is concerned to remove Abraham from the taint of Chaldean astrology (*Ant.* 1.155-157), but on the other hand, he remarks that Abraham was pleasingly renowned by Babylonian historians for his astrological skill (*Ant.* 1.158-159).

---

[37] Reed, 'Abraham as Chaldean Scientist', pp. 124–5.
[38] Enoch is described as first person to discover astrology (*Ps.-Eup.*). See Dozemann, '*Sperma Abraam*'.
[39] *OTP* 2, p. 799.
[40] Reed, 'Abraham as Chaldean Scientist', p. 127.
[41] It is possible that texts such as Deut. 4.19, 18.10 and Isa. 47.13, which ban celestial divination as contrary to monotheism, play a part in the negative valuation of astrology. In *LAB* 18.5, Abraham abandons astrology when he gets to Canaan. Subsequent rabbinic texts follow suit (*Gen. R.* 44.12, *b. Shabb.* 156a).
[42] Reed, 'Abraham as Chaldean Scientist', p. 129.

Indeed, Abraham is presented as a teacher of the Egyptians, instructing them in the science of astrology and mathematics, concluding that, 'Before the arrival of Abraham, the Egyptians were ignorant of these. For these matters reached Egypt from the Chaldeans, from whence they came also to the Greeks' (*Ant.* 1.166-168; cf. *Pseudo-Eupolemus*). In Josephus' view, Abraham's excellence in the celestial sciences, and his exemplarity as a teacher of the Egyptians, relates inextricably to his philosophical perceptiveness and cultivated sense of rational persuasion. It is through Abraham's insight into the workings of the natural world that he discovers the truth of monotheism (*Ant.* 1.55-156). Quite possibly, Josephus implies that Abraham intended to persuade the Egyptians of rational monotheism in the course of philosophical discussions.[43] Josephus' Abraham is 'visionary' then, not in the sense of being able to see by the stars, but in the sense of his possession of inner wisdom that leads him to infer the sovereignty of the one God.

It is another step from here to claim that Abraham could view the activities of humankind from a privileged vantage point in the heavens. Some apocryphal and pseudepigraphical texts took this step. In the *Testament of Abraham* 10-12, Abraham is figured as the recipient of a customized tour of the heavens and the earth at the hands of the archangel Michael. Using a cloud as a vehicle, Michael – together with an angelic entourage – takes Abraham on a soaring tour over the inhabited world (10.1). Accordingly, Abraham sees the whole host of humanity and the various activities with which they are occupied (10.2-3). Abraham sees everything 'good and evil' (10.3b).[44] He sees 'robbers' who desire to 'commit murder and rob and burn and destroy' (10.5). Abraham implores the Lord to command that 'wild beasts' emerge from the thicket and 'devour' the men (10.6). Immediately, Abraham's wish is granted (10.7). As he moves on, Abraham sees more immorality and violence, and he requests God to destroy these sinners; once more, Abraham's wishes are granted without hesitation (10.9b-11).[45] Eventually, God halts the carnage by ordering Michael to stop the tour, lest everyone on earth die by Abraham's will (10.12-13).[46]

God then commands Michael to conduct Abraham to the 'first gate of heaven' so that he may witness the 'judgements' and 'recompenses' of the sinners he destroyed, in the hope that he might change his mind about sinners (10.15).[47] Thence Abraham has a vision of the operations of the heavenly realms. The narrative proceeds to detail the way in which souls are judged at the 'first gate' of heaven (11.1-12). In a text heavy with NT interpolations (especially Matt. 7.13f), Abraham watches as the primordial Adam expresses excessive emotiveness: sometimes Adam rejoices and exults (11.9), while at other times he tears his hair, cries and wails (11.6). Michael explains that when souls

---

[43] Ibid., p. 134.
[44] Abraham's visions of the inhabited world are of activities taking place in the present, indeed, very much 'the world as it was that day' (10.2a, Rec A).
[45] Allison, *Testament of Abraham*, pp. 224-7, illustrates how these graphic punishments all have models in biblical stories.
[46] Abraham's excessive zeal is a parody of his righteousness in the Hebrew Bible; cf. Ludlow, *Abraham Meets Death*, p. 55.
[47] NB. That Rec B (12-13) omits the resuscitation of sinners at the end of the tour, perhaps out of sense of just deserts or a view that Abraham cannot intercede for the dead (Ludlow, *Abraham Meets Death*, p. 133).

enter through the 'strait gate' leading to 'life', they are saved, and consequently Adam rejoices (11.10); when souls enter through the 'broad gate' leading to 'destruction', they are eternally punished, and therefore Adam wails in grief (11.11). The text expresses a high degree of soteriological pessimism: 'for among seven thousand there is scarcely to be found one saved soul, righteous and undefiled' (11.12). Adam's empathetic role at the 'first gate' of heaven is cleverly juxtaposed with Abraham's impulsive sentencing of sinners to death as he toured the world (10.1-15).

At this point, the text shifts briefly to the first person, and Abraham recounts a vision he has while Michael speaks to him (12.1). Abraham sees two 'merciless' angels driving many souls and 'beating them with fiery lashes' (12.1). Abraham and Michael walk through the 'broad gate', and they see a 'wondrous man, bright as the sun' sitting on a 'terrifying throne' (12.3-4). A book lies upon a table before the throne (12.7), and on either side of the book stands an angel holding ink and pen (12.8). In front sits another angel with a 'balance in his hand', and nearby another 'merciless and relentless' angel with a 'trumpet in his hand', which has within it the 'fire' for 'testing sinners' (12.9-10). The 'wondrous' man seated on the throne is the one who sentences souls (12.11), and he is later revealed by Michael to be Abel, 'whom Cain the wicked killed' (13.3).[48] The two angels on either side of the throne record the deeds of souls in the book: one records 'righteous deeds'/'works', while the other records 'sins' (12.12). Then the judge Abel asks the angels to open the book and find the sins of a given soul (12.17). This soul's 'sins' and 'righteous deeds' are found to be 'equally balanced', and therefore it is 'set in the middle' rather than turned over either to destruction or salvation (12.18).

Related to the motif of Abraham's esoteric visions – or inner visionary propensities – is the notion of Abraham's intercessory function. We have already seen the conflation of these ideas in the *Testament of Abraham* 10, a text that ironically subverts the content of Gen. 18.22-33. Whereas the Genesis text positions Abraham as interceding with God to spare the sinners of Sodom for the sake of the righteous minority, the *Testament of Abraham* 10 has Abraham asking God to destroy sinners on a whim, until God cannot bear it any longer. This is certainly an atypical view in the literature of early Judaism. For example, in *Apoc. Zeph.* 11.1-4, the three fathers (Abraham, Isaac and Jacob) emerge at appointed times each day to pray for those souls in torment, and to avert their ultimate punishment – perhaps, conceptually, a precursor to later rabbinic notions of the זכות אבות. Similarly, in *T. Levi* 15.4, the mercy of the three fathers is said to give life to their descendants. And in *T. Asher* 7.7, God is compassionate towards his creatures on account of the three fathers. In *T. Jud.* 25.1, we read that in the end times, Abraham, Isaac and Jacob will be resurrected to life. Finally, in *3 Baruch*, the eponymous

---

[48] Abel does not appear in this role in any other text of antiquity. The reason for his selection might be his status as 'a proto-martyr': Laszlo Gallusz, *The Throne Motif in the Book of Revelation* (London: T&T Clark/Bloomsbury, 2014), p. 67. Yet, the only reason provided by the text is that Abel is Adam's successor (cf. John Byron, *Cain and Abel in Text and Tradition: Jewish and Christian Traditions of the First Sibling Rivalry* (Leiden: Brill, 2011), p. 188). The trope of the righteous judging the wicked in the afterlife was well known (Wis. 5.1; *1 En.* 38.5; 48.9; 95.3). Abel was the victim of a violent death at the hand of his brother Cain, and *1 Enoch* transforms Abel into 'a perpetual voice for the murdered righteous' (idem, *Cain and Abel*, p. 189). In *Testament of Abraham*, Abel takes this status to a higher level, acting as eschatological judge requiting injustice. Cf. Levenson, *The Death and Resurrection of the Beloved Son*, p. 77.

author writes a letter to Jeremiah enjoining the latter to rejoice, for God will not let them pass from earth grieving the desolation of Jerusalem: 'For this reason the Lord has taken pity on our tears and has remembered the covenant that he established with our fathers Abraham, Isaac and Jacob' (6.21). If the captives observe God's commandments once more, God will mercifully bring them out from Babylon (6.22-23).[49]

These texts suggest that the prayers, mercy and covenant of Abraham, Isaac and Jacob have power to benefit their descendants, even after their death. Implied in this perspective is the concept that the three fathers are somehow cognizant of the sufferings of others – those either left on earth or awaiting final judgement in an 'antechamber' of the heavenly realms. It is as though the three fathers, now living in God's presence, are able to see everything that unfolds in the various worlds. These understandings of the role of the three fathers constitute apocalyptic extensions of the more generally philosophical reasoning about the status of the three fathers in the afterlife, present pre-eminently in the text of *4 Maccabees*. The narrator of that text first states his claim in relation to the value of attending to 'religion' and controlling the body: 'But as many as attend to religion with a whole heart, these alone are able to control the passions of the flesh, since they believe that they, like our patriarchs Abraham and Isaac and Jacob, do not die to God, but live to God' (*4 Macc.* 7.18-19).[50]

Thus, the three fathers, although dead, are alive with God. Abraham, Isaac and Jacob attended to 'religion' with their 'whole heart' and their fate is not eternal death – and not mere remembrance by God – but vital ongoing life with God.[51] The body and its 'passions' should therefore be secondary to full religious devotion, since the latter is what will carry a person forward into the afterlife. Indeed, not only are the three fathers present with God after death, but they will also play an active role in welcoming others who die (and who, like them, are devout): 'For if we so die, Abraham and Isaac and Jacob will welcome us, and all the fathers will praise us' (*4 Macc.* 13.17). Martyrdom – dying 'for the sake of God' – bears fruit in 'living to God' after death, and this is what was exemplified in the lives of 'Abraham and Isaac and Jacob and all the patriarchs' (*4 Macc.* 16.25).[52]

Abraham's joy

There are not many references to Abraham's 'joy'/'rejoicing' in the literature of early Judaism. However, one conspicuous text has stood out, and consequently, has been the subject of analysis in several studies comparing John 8.58 to its perceptibly Jewish matrix. That text is *Jub.* 16.20-31. What makes *Jub.* 16.20-31 a particularly compelling intertext in light of the references to Sukkot in John 7.1-11, is its presentation of

---

[49] *OTP I*, p. 653.
[50] An influential idea as attested by the NT sources (cf. Luke 20.38 and par.). Cf. John W. Cooper, *Body, Soul, and Life Everlasting: Biblical Anthropology and the Monism-Dualism Debate* (Grand Rapids: Eerdmans, 1989), p. 122.
[51] For the author of *4 Macc.*, immortality was thought to be 'living with God *like Abraham, Isaac and Jacob*': Jonathan Klawans, *Josephus and the Theologies of Ancient Judaism* (New York: Oxford University Press, 2013), p. 97 (emphasis in the original).
[52] Cf. the prototypical Isaac in this regard: Huizenga, *The New Isaac*, pp. 118–19, n. 53.

Abraham as one who not only observes the festival of Sukkot but also actually initiates it. In the post-biblical literature prior to the NT, only *Jub.* 16.20-31 associates Abraham with Sukkot.[53]

The narrative frame of *Jub.* 16.20-31 is considerably significant in this regard. God has just appeared to Abraham and Sarah on the occasion of Sarah's pregnancy with Isaac (16.15-16). God promises more sons to the pair, telling them that they will have a 'holy seed' from one of the 'sons of Isaac' – one who would become a 'portion of the Most High', and give rise to a 'kingdom of priests' and a 'holy people' (16.17-19a–c). This news makes both Sarah and Abraham 'rejoice very greatly' (16.19d). Already, we sense a play on Gen. 17.17, with the author of *Jubilees* interpreting Abraham's 'laughter' at the news of Isaac's conception as his intense 'joy'.[54] The narrative continues with Abraham building an altar and celebrating the festival of Sukkot (16.20). Abraham is full of joy (16.20); he is the first person on earth to celebrate Sukkot (16.21) as 'a festival of rejoicing' for seven days. Abraham not only builds an altar to God, but he also 'builds booths for himself' (16.20-21). Subsequent celebrations of the festival are said to result from Abraham's personal experience of joy (cf. 16.30), not from God's narrated provision for the Israelites as they wandered in the wilderness, and their joy at being cared for by God as they sheltered in booths (cf. Lev. 23.40-42).

But Abraham's joy is not the sole reason he comes to observe the seven-day festival of Sukkot. Abraham continues to make 'offering every day, day by day' as an *intercessor*: he offers the animals to God 'on behalf of sins so that he [Abraham] might atone thereby on behalf of himself and his seed' (16.22).[55] Notably, Abraham is not presented as so exemplary that he is sinless; he needs to offer atonement sacrifices for his own sins. Nevertheless, consistent with other texts in the literature of early Judaism, Abraham is portrayed as able to behave in such ways that will vicariously benefit the well-being of his own posterity. This is the inverse of what we have seen in texts such as *4 Maccabees* and the testamentary literature, where Abraham's descendants, still on earth, benefit from his prayers or his mercy as he intercedes for them in the afterlife. In *Jubilees* 16, Abraham is narratively presented as, in his own lifetime, praying for his 'seed', acting to safeguard his descendants in the future. If they fall into sin, Abraham's atonements on their behalf will be efficacious.

Jub. 16.24-27 goes on to detail how Abraham, together with his household, rejoices 'with all his heart and all his soul' during the festival. The narrator adds that at this time no alien, nor any member of Abraham's household, was uncircumcised (16.25). The significance of this detail appears to be that as Abraham observed Sukkot, he also fully observed the covenant mandate of circumcision, and that his observance of the latter commandment somehow endowed his observance of Sukkot with genuine legitimacy. *Jubilees* 16 associates the origin of both the commandments of circumcision and the pilgrimage festival of Sukkot with Abraham – even though, in the Torah, both commandments are said to be delivered by God through Moses

---

[53] The notion of the *Ushpizin* is found in the Zohar, the medieval Kabbalisitic compendium (see Chapter 3).

[54] Thus, van Ruiten, *Abraham in the Book of Jubilees*, p. 188. In *Jub.* 16.15-19, however, both Abraham and Sarah rejoice together, and Sarah has evidently already conceived Isaac.

[55] Cf. Coloe, 'Like Father, Like Son', pp. 1–12.

at Sinai. Also, *Jub.* 16.25-26 characterizes God as the Creator: Abraham blesses God 'his Creator who created him' (16.25); God 'created' Abraham 'by his will' for God 'knew and perceived that from him there would be a righteous planting for eternal generations and a holy seed from him so that he might be like the one who made everything' (16.26). This announcement causes Abraham to bless God and rejoice once more, and to name Sukkot as 'the festival of the Lord, a joy acceptable to God Most High' (*Jub.* 16.27).

Elsewhere, *Jubilees* depicts Abraham as rejoicing at the news of Isaac's impending conception (15.17), in a retelling of Gen. 17.17.[56] After Abraham hears the news that Sarah will conceive Isaac, and that Isaac will become a 'people' (15.16), Abraham falls on his face and rejoices as he 'ponders in his heart whether a son would be born to one who was one hundred years old' (15.17). There is no indication in *Jub.* 15.17 that Abraham expresses incredulity at God's promises. Indeed, Abraham does not even 'laugh' in this text, but simply falls on his face and 'rejoices'.[57] The divine promise that an eternal covenant will be established with Isaac and his 'seed after him' (15.20) leads Abraham to immediately obey the commandment of circumcision (15.23-24). The root צחק occurs twice in MT Gen. 21.6, and the LXX translates its first occurrence as γέλως ('to laugh') but the second as συγχαίρω ('to rejoice'). It is possible that 'a parallel reading to the Septuagint might have had an influence on *Jubilees*' in the use of the Ethiopic root *tfs* to describe Abraham's responses to God's news.[58]

Outside of *Jubilees* there are other references to Abraham's joy/rejoicing, although none of them is as densely articulated as *Jub.* 16.20-31. The testamentary literature provides two examples. *T. Levi* 18.1-14 constitutes an extended meditation on the reign of God's eschatological priest, following a period of vengeance wrought upon the wicked. The text prophesizes that in this final era, the Levitical priesthood will lapse, but that the Lord will 'raise up a new priest' who will receive all the 'words of the Lord' (18.1-2a). This priest will 'effect judgment of truth' upon the earth (18.2b), removing 'darkness' and initiating peace (18.4). This will cause the heavens to 'rejoice greatly in his days', the earth to 'be glad' and the 'clouds' to be 'filled with joy' (18.5a).[59] Even the 'angels of the Lord' will be 'made glad' by the Lord's chosen priest (18.5b). Then the heavens will open and from the 'temple of glory', the Lord's priest will receive sanctification 'with a fatherly voice as from Abraham to Isaac' (18.6). At this point, 'the glory of the Most High shall burst forth upon' God's priest (18.7), and he shall pass on the divine majesty to those who are his 'sons in truth' (18.8a).[60] His priestly reign will

---

[56] Van Ruiten, *Abraham in the Book of Jubilees*, p. 188.
[57] Ibid.
[58] Thus Segal, *The Book of Jubilees*, p. 305, n. 84, cited in Van Ruiten, *Abraham in the Book of Jubilees*, p. 188.
[59] Allusions to the book of Daniel (12.3) have been noted; cf. Andrew Chester, *Messiah and Exaltation: Jewish Messianic and Visionary Traditions and New Testament Christology* (WUNT 207; Tübingen: Mohr Siebeck, 2007), pp. 167–8. The Christianization of *Testament of Levi* 18 has long been posited as a likely hypothesis. See Jürgen Becker, *Untersuchungen zur Entstehungsgeschichte der Testament der zwölf Patriarchen* (Leiden: Brill, 1970), pp. 257–306, 299–300.
[60] Apart from the Danielic allusions noted in n. 68, scholars also recognize the allusions to Isa. 11.1-9, and to characteristics assumed of the eschatological Davidic king. See George Nickelsburg, *Jewish Literature Between the Bible and the Mishnah* (Minneapolis: Fortress Press, 2011), p. 308.

be eternal; he shall have no successor (18.8b). But his 'children' will share in his holy powers (18.12a), and because of this 'the Lord will rejoice in his children' (18.12b), and be 'well-pleased' in them (18.13a). This will cause 'Abraham, Isaac, and Jacob' to 'rejoice' (18.13b), and Levi (the speaker) to 'be glad', while 'all the saints' are 'clothed in righteousness' (18.14). The *Testament of Levi* 18 thus contains a number of references to 'joy'/'rejoicing'. The advent of God's eschatological priest compels the whole created world to rejoice. God's priest will be like Isaac, receiving glory and sanctification as a son from a father (18.6). Similarly, Abraham's 'rejoicing' is paralleled to God's own rejoicing in the children of the priest (18.13-14).[61]

In *T. Ben.* 10.6, Abraham, Isaac and Jacob are depicted as rejoicing as the eschatological age dawns. As Benjamin lies dying, he exhorts his children to 'keep the Law of the Lord and his commandments' (10.4a), which Benjamin bequeaths in place of a material inheritance (10.4b). His children are to pass on the Law to their own children as 'an eternal possession' – just as 'Abraham, Isaac, and Jacob' did to their children (10.4c). The three patriarchs are said to have passed on the commandments to Benjamin and his children, enjoining them to observe the Law until God's salvation reaches the nations (10.5a). At that point in time, Benjamin's children 'will see Enoch and Seth and Abraham and Isaac and Jacob being raised up at the right hand in great joy' (10.6).[62] Simultaneously, Benjamin and his children 'will also be raised, each of us over his tribe' (10.7). The final judgement will be contingent upon their observance of the Law and their living in holiness – and in this way 'all Israel will be gathered to the Lord' (10.11). This text differs somewhat from other early Jewish articulations of Abraham, Isaac and Jacob's role in the afterlife inasmuch as the three fathers are not yet 'raised' to life and able to intercede on behalf of their 'children'. Instead, their own resurrection (being raised up to God's 'right hand' with joy) will have to await the end times when God's salvation reaches the nations, and at that point, all Israel will be raised with them.

Another reference to Abraham's 'rejoicing' can be found in the *Apocalypse of Abraham* 10.[63] In this text, Abraham experiences a strange encounter with the

---

[61] A different, although possibly antecedent tradition is found in 4Q541.9 (*Aramaic Levi*) with its focus on the role of the messianic priest. However, in the Qumran text the priest faces deep hostility from his enemies, whereas the Christianized priest in *Testament of Levi* 18 receives cosmic joy. Cf. Michael A. Knibb, 'Perspectives on the Apocrypha and Pseudepigrapha: The Levi Traditions', in F. G. Martínez and E. Noort (eds), *Perspectives in the Study of the Old Testament and Early Judaism* (Leiden: Brill, 1998), pp. 197–213, at p. 208.

[62] Note that the order of resurrection corresponds to the order in which the biblical figures are said to have lived. Lidija Novakovic, *Raised from the Dead According to Scripture: The Role of Israel's Scripture in the Early Christian Interpretations of Jesus' Resurrection* (JACT 12; London: Bloomsbury/ T&T Clark, 2012), p. 98.

[63] The *Apocalypse of Abraham* is a first- or second-century text preserved only in Slavonic, but which is thought to have existed in a previous Greek version, no longer extant. The Slavonic translation can be dated to the eleventh to twelfth century CE. A Hebrew or Aramaic *Vorlage* is also largely accepted in the scholarship. See Arie Rubenstein, 'Hebraisms in the Slavonic "Apocalypse of Abraham"', *JJS* 4 (1953), pp. 108–15, and idem, 'Hebraisms in the Slavonic "Apocalypse of Abraham"', *JJS* 5 (1954), pp. 132–5. On the Slavonic text and its presumed Greek predecessor, see Ryszard Rubinkiewicz, *L'Apocalypse d'Abraham en vieux slave: Introduction, texte critique, traduction et commentaire* (Towarzystwo Naukowe Katolickiego Uniwersytu Lubelskiego Źródła I monografie 129; Lublin: Société des Lettres et des Sciences de l'Université Catholique de Lublin, 1987). The Ezekelian

deity, and consequently falls face down upon the earth (10.1-3). From the ground, Abraham hears a voice calling upon an angel named Iaoel to go and consecrate him as he lies trembling (10.3). Iaoel then appears to Abraham in the likeness of a man and helps him to stand upright (10.4). The angel refers to Abraham as the 'friend of God who has loved you' (10.5, 6). Iaoel then reveals his identity and purpose to Abraham, informing him of all the aspects of the world over which he has charge (10.8-11). Surprisingly, Iaoel is the angel who was responsible for burning Terah's house to the ground, because Abraham's father 'honoured the dead' (10.12).[64] But Iaoel encourages Abraham to 'go boldly, be very joyful and rejoice' for God has prepared an honour for him (10.14). Abraham is tasked with carrying out the sacrifice that God has commanded (10.15).[65] The text then embarks on an unusual and protracted exegetical retelling of Abraham's dream vision in Gen. 15.1-17 with Abraham experiencing many visions and revelations that depart quite radically from the biblical narrative (11.1-32.6).

The scene of Abraham's dream/vision in Genesis 15 is reconfigured to become a 'trance' in which Abraham experiences a vivid pteromorphic revelation. One incident is worth exploring in some detail. As Abraham is driving away the birds of prey that come down to feed on the carcasses of the sacrifice, one of them starts speaking to Abraham (13.1-3; cf. Gen. 15.11). Confused, Abraham asks Iaoel who this bird truly is, and the angel reveals that it is 'Azazel' (13.7). Iaoel then commands Azazel to leave, for Abraham's 'portion is in heaven' while Azazel's is 'on earth' (13.6-8).[66] Iaoel calls Azazel the 'all-evil spirit' and a 'liar' whose wrath is evident in the generations of men who live impiously (13.9). While Azazel has a reputation for tempting the righteous, Iaoel commands him to leave Abraham alone, as he will have no chance of success in any case. This is because Abraham is beyond deception: he is 'the enemy of [Azazel] and those who follow [him]' and his desires (13.10-13). Azazel – the evil-spirit figure – is set in opposition to Abraham to the point where they inhabit mutually exclusive realms. When Azazel attempts to enter Abraham's world, he is immediately exposed

---

influence upon *Apocalypse of Abraham* is everywhere noted, so that the pseudepigraphon is known as the first text to combine apocalypticism and *erkabah* mysticism; Rubinkiewicz, *L'Apocalypse*, p. 87.

[64] Terah was an idolater and maker of idols, according to *Apocalypse of Abraham* 1–8, but this detail suggests that the author's anti-anthropomorphic theology extends even to Terah's 'honoring' of all corporeal forms – both anthropomorphic wooden and stone deities, whose 'corporeality' is available to the senses, and the dead, whose corporeality once existed but is now beyond the reach of the senses – extending the argument of Andrei A. Orlov, '"The Gods of My Father Terah": Abraham the Iconoclast and the Polemics with the Divine Body Traditions in the *Apocalypse of Abraham*', *JSP* 18, no. 1 (2008), pp. 33–53.

[65] Indeed, by the conclusion of the Apocalypse, Abraham is depicted as 'an archetypal sacerdotalist to whom God reveals "the idea of priesthood"', certainly a departure from the biblical traditions that, while they may show Abraham interceding with God (Genesis 18), or hearing God's prophecies (Genesis 15), never call Abraham a 'priest'. See Andrei A. Orlov, *Heavenly Priesthood in the Apocalypse of Abraham* (Cambridge: Cambridge University Press, 2013), p. 1.

[66] The spatial dualism is underscored by a moral, and perhaps ontological dualism. Iaoel and Azazel represent two opposing spirits, one good, the other evil. As Marc Phionenko astutely observes, their battle takes place indirectly, through the medium of Abraham. See Belkis Philonenko-Sayar and Marc Philonenko, *L'Apocalypse d'Abraham: Introduction, texte slave, traduction et notes* (Semitica 31; Paris: Adrien Maisonneuve, 1981), pp. 31–2.

and cast away by Iaoel. Interestingly, Azazel is depicted as a seductive liar with a body of followers who are eager to do his desires.[67]

In Philo's writings, we read of Abraham's 'joy' at one critical point in his life story: the account of Isaac's conception. God appears to Abraham and tells him that he and Sarah will conceive Isaac 'with extraordinary joy' and that, moreover, this will be an opportunity for Abraham to 'find virtue' (*Alleg.* 3.87.217). Sarah will bring forth all of her offspring 'with laughter and cheerfulness', and Isaac will 'be cheerfulness itself'. This is because the 'wise man' becomes a parent 'with joy and not with sorrow'. Philo then cites Gen. 17.17, explaining that this was why Abraham 'fell upon his face and laughed' (*Alleg.* 3.87.217). Philo comments that in this text Abraham 'appears ... to be in a state of joy, and to be laughing because he is about to become the father of happiness' and the father of virtue. For the same reason, Sarah laughs (*Alleg.* 3.87.218). Philo turns to the narrative of Genesis 21, when Sarah laughs after giving birth to Isaac, explaining that 'laughter is joy' (*Alleg.* 3.87.219). Indeed, whenever God begets virtue in the soul of a person, he also begets happiness (*Alleg.* 3.87.218). Philo evidently puts a very positive spin on Abraham and Sarah's 'laughter' in Genesis, refusing to read it as an expression of faithlessness, but rather, of great joy and cheerfulness, allegorically interpreted as the gift of virtue.

The New Testament

The first group of relevant references to the figure of Abraham in the Synoptic Gospels pertains to the presence of the three fathers at the eschatological banquet in the afterlife (Matt. 8.11; Luke 13.28). This theme closely parallels the concept of Abraham, Isaac and Jacob either welcoming the righteous dead into the afterlife with God (cf. *4 Macc.* 7.t, 18-19; 13.17), or being raised together with the law-observant at the end times (cf. *Testament of Benjamin* 10). In the two Synoptic texts, however, there is a detectably polemical strain that is absent from the comparative material. This polemical strain can be identified as one component of early Christian anti-Judaism, whereby 'Israel' – those reputedly 'belonging' to Abraham, Isaac and Jacob – are now 'cast out' of the eschatological banquet due to lack of faith in Jesus, while others who claim no intrinsic connection to the heritage of Israel but who exhibit such faith, are heralded into the 'kingdom'.[68]

Taking Matt. 8.5-13 as a starting point, we encounter Jesus in the early stages of his public ministry, healing the servant of a Roman centurion. As Jesus travels into Capernaum, a centurion approaches him, asking him to heal his paralyzed servant (8.5-6). Jesus readily agrees to come to the centurion's house, but the latter demurs,

---

[67] Azazel traditions have been explored by numerous scholars. See especially: William H. Shea, 'Azazel in the Pseudepigrapha', *JATS* 13 (2002), pp. 1-9; Dominic Rudman, 'A Note on the Azazel-goat Ritual', *ZAW* 116 (2004), pp. 396-401; Andrei Orlov, '"The Likeness of Heaven": The *Kavod* of Azazel in the *Apocalypse of Abraham*', in Daphna V. Arbel and Andrei A. Orlov (eds), *With Letters of Light: Studies in the Dead Sea Scrolls, Early Jewish Apocalypticism, Magic, and Mysticism in Honor of Rachel Elior* (Berlin/New York: De Gruyter, 2010), pp. 232-53.

[68] Cf. Tobias Hägerland, 'Jesus and the Rites of Repentance', *NTS* 52, no. 2 (2006), pp. 166-87, at p. 179. The reason for exclusion, however, does not appear to be a lack of repentance in Q 13.29, thus: L. Ann Jervis, 'Suffering for the Reign of God: The Persecution of Disciples in Q', *NovT* 44, no. 4 (2002), pp. 313-32, at p. 322.

stating that he is not worthy to have Jesus enter his home (8.8a). Rather, the centurion asks Jesus simply to give the order that his servant be healed; he has faith that such an order will be sufficient (8.8b). The centurion reasons on the basis of hierarchical authority: as a man who understands the function of orders and the value of obedience, he believes in their efficacy, extrapolating from this premise that Jesus' 'word' of healing will certainly be enough to heal his servant (8.9). Jesus is evidently astonished at the degree of faith displayed by the centurion, as he turns to his followers, saying:

> Truly I tell you, in no one in Israel have I found such faith. I tell you, many will come from east and west and will eat with Abraham and Isaac and Jacob in the kingdom of heaven, while the heirs of the kingdom will be thrown into the outer darkness, where there will be weeping and gnashing of teeth. (8.10b-12, NRSV)

Jesus then speaks to the centurion, with the words, 'Go; let it be done for you according to your faith', and the narrator informs his readers that the servant was indeed healed 'in that hour' (8.13). The impressive faith of the centurion in this passage leads Jesus to draw a contrast between the (unexpected and unnecessary) belief shown by one outside the covenant and those of 'Israel', to whom Jesus primarily ministers and hopes to elicit 'repentance' and belief (cf. 4.17). The contrast is stark because, we assume, those of 'Israel' have not shown this expected level of faith in Jesus' message or ministry (8.10b).[69] Yet, the early narrative chapters of Matthew's Gospel give no indication that Jesus' ministry was a source of contention or rejection on the part of his fellow Jews. Jesus begins his ministry in Galilee, drawing to himself a group of disciples and encountering no resistance to his teaching or his healing activities (4.12-25). On the contrary, multitudes are cured and great crowds follow him 'from Galilee, the Decapolis, Jerusalem, Judea, and from beyond the Jordan' (4.24-25; cf. 8.1-4).

It is only when Jesus delivers his 'sermon on the mount' (chs 5–7) that the reader senses a tension, a contrast even, between those who demonstrate a satisfactory level of righteousness according to the Law ('the Scribes and Pharisees'), and those who take righteousness to its logical extreme (and are thus commended):[70] those who not only refrain from murder, but also from anger (5.21-22); those who not only refrain from adultery, but also from lust (5.27-28); and those who not only refrain from perjury, but also from oaths of any sort (5.33-34). By extension, Jesus reproaches those who practise outward piety but perhaps not inward piety (6.1-4; 5–8; 16–18) and those who judge others without assessing their own conduct first (7.1-5). Jesus contrasts 'false prophets' with genuine ones on the basis of their 'fruits' (i.e. 'works' or behaviour; 7.15-

---

[69] One should note that Matthew does not sustain such a distinctive contrast across the scope of his Gospel. The Roman centurion in ch. 8 vv. 10-12 is an example of 'a good gentile', but there are also 'wicked gentiles' in Matthew's cast of characters. The same pertains to his variety of Jewish characters. See David C. Sim, *Apocalyptic Eschatology in the Gospel of Matthew* (SNTSMS 88; Cambridge: Cambridge University Press, 1996), p. 200.

[70] Élian Cuvillier, 'Torah Observance and Radicalization in the First Gospel. Matthew and First-Century Judaism: A Contribution to the Debate', *NTS* 55 (2009), pp. 144–59, at p. 154.

16), and he contrasts 'hearers' of the word with 'doers' of the word, saying that those who hear his words must act on them (7.24-27).[71]

It is in this light that the Roman centurion appears to warrant Jesus' explicit commendation. Not only does the centurion seek out Jesus and request healing for his servant, he goes a step further and believes in the sole efficacy of Jesus' word with respect to that healing. The centurion displays trusting faith in the logical extreme that Jesus otherwise delineates in ch. 5 v. 21 to ch. 6 v. 18 regarding the commandments of the Torah. The polemical tone of ch. 5 v. 1 to ch. 7 v. 29 thus provides a window into understanding the sudden viciousness of ch. 8 v. 10b-12, but does not fully explain it. Those descended from 'Abraham, Isaac, and Jacob' – here called the 'heirs of the kingdom' – are, in Jesus' words, to be disinherited *just as* non-Jews 'from the east and west' inherit the 'kingdom'. Not only will Israel be disinherited, they will be 'cast out into the outer darkness' – utterly rejected, and relegated to the Gehenna-like realm of 'weeping and gnashing of teeth' (10.12).

It is probable that the logion about Abraham, Isaac and Jacob found in Matt. 8.10b-12 represents a Q logion about the exclusion of disbelieving Israel from the covenant to which they profess to belong. The tradition is present in Luke's Gospel, but in a significantly different context compared to Matthew's version (Luke 13.28). The wider context of Luke's logion deals with Jesus' teaching and healing ministry, but Luke intersperses parables and prophecies found only in the latter sections of Matthew's Gospel. Moreover, Luke's Jesus is on the way to Jerusalem when he delivers the logion (13.22), teaching about the difficulty of attaining salvation (13.23-30). Still, Luke blends together two aspects of Matthew's 'sermon on the mount': the contrast between the wide and narrow paths (Matt. 7.13-14), and the hypocrisy of those professing to work miracles in Jesus' name, but who actually have no inner disposition of discipleship (Matt. 7.21-23). In Luke's text, someone approaches Jesus and asks, 'Lord, will only a few be saved?' (13.23). In reply, Jesus encourages him to strive to enter through the 'narrow door' (13.24); Jesus recounts a parable about the owner of a house shutting the door of his house with finality, while those outside knock on the door in vain crying, 'Lord, open to us' (13.25a). The householder says to them 'I do not know where you come from' (13.25b). Although those knocking on the door explain that they held company with the householder while dining and on the streets, the householder casts them out with the harsh words, 'I do not know where you come from; go away from me, all you workers of evil' (πάντες ἐργάται ἀδικίας; 13.27). Jesus then adds,

> There will be weeping and gnashing of teeth when you see Abraham and Isaac and Jacob and all the prophets in the kingdom of God, and you yourselves thrown out. Then people will come from east and west, from north and south, and will eat in the kingdom of God. (13.28-29 NRSV)

---

[71] Hans Dieter Betz, *The Sermon on the Mount: A Commentary on the Sermon on the Mount, including the Sermon on the Plain (Matthew 5.3–7.27 and Luke 6.20-49)* (Hermeneia; Minneapolis: Fortress Press, 1995).

The passage concludes with Jesus adding the characteristically Lukan 'subversion' principle as an explanatory cue: 'Indeed, some are last who will be first, and some are first who will be last' (13.30).[72] The 'last' are evidently the non-Jewish newcomers to the divine banquet who emerge from the ends of the earth ('east and west' *and* 'north and south'); the 'first' are the heirs of the covenant, who expect to feast with their ancestors, Abraham, Isaac and Jacob. Luke has Jesus address his *current audience* as those destined to be 'thrown out' from the 'kingdom of God' (ὑμᾶς δὲ ἐκβαλλομένους ἔξω), presumably because they have not sought entry through the 'narrow door', which Luke reframes as the same door belonging to the parabolic householder.[73] Luke provides no explanation as to why those knocking on the door and calling to be let into the house are deemed 'evildoers' in the parable. The reader assumes that even though they profess to have dined and taught with the householder (and thus expect a license for entry), they either lack sufficient self-discipline, or have exhibited an intolerable hypocrisy. A further detail added by Luke is that the *'prophets'* will dine with Abraham, Isaac and Jacob at the kingdom's banquet, an important association to keep in mind in respect of John 8.56-58.

These two Synoptic texts demonstrate the prevalence in early Judaism of the motif of the three 'fathers' (Abraham, Isaac and Jacob) 'welcoming' a select group of righteous individuals at the end of time. The Q logion presupposes an eschatological setting of joy and togetherness (signified by the 'feast' in the kingdom), but it is not specified whether the feast takes place in the afterlife, or during the 'end times' on earth. Moreover, the theme of joy is underplayed and rendered implicit by the strong focus on retribution in both passages. In fact, what is so striking about these Synoptic texts is that they appear to espouse the opposite view of Abraham 'rejoicing' in the fate of another person (i.e. Jesus in John 8.56-58) – together with Isaac and Jacob, Abraham seems to be complicit in the destruction of others.

Another Lukan text continues this theme in greater detail. The parable of the 'rich man and Lazarus' (Luke 16.19-30) plays upon the motif of Abraham seeing and

---

[72] Jesus enacts this principle in his own 'table-fellowship' with sinners in Luke's Gospel, bringing 'the kingdom of God' into the present. Michael S. Northcott, 'Eucharistic Eating, and Why many Early Christians Preferred Fish', in David Grumett and Rachel Muers (eds), *Eating and Believing: Interdisciplinary Perspectives on Vegetarianism and Theology* (London: T&T Clark/Bloomsbury, 2008), pp. 232–46, at p. 237. The 'paradigmatic link between the kingdom and fellowship at meals is widely accepted as an established feature of what Jesus taught' (cf. Matt. 22.1-14 || Luke 14.15-24; Matt. 20.21 || Mark 10.37). Thus, Bruce Chilton, *A Feast of Meanings: Eucharistic Theologies from Jesus Through Johannine Circles* (Leiden: Brill, 1994), p. 39.

[73] Leslie Baynes argues that Luke's version of the traditional source (i.e. eating with the patriarchs in the kingdom) is more exclusive than Matthew's; by contextualizing the tradition in the story of the Roman centurion, Matthew seeks to include (Gentiles), whereas by placing the tradition in a parable about Jesus-the-householder, Luke primarily excludes the people of Israel. See, idem, 'The Parables of Enoch and Luke's Parable of the Rich Man and Lazarus', in Loren T. Stuckenbruck and Gabriele Boccaccini (eds), *Enoch and the Synoptic Gospels: Reminiscences, Allusions, Intertextuality* (Atlanta: SBL Press, 2016), pp. 129–54, at p. 146. I would argue that the juxtaposition between Matthew and Luke is not as stark as Baynes suggests; the motif of exclusivism is present in both texts, and Luke's general picture of Abrahamic descent is a favourable one. Cf. Hägerland, 'Jesus and the Rites of Repentance', p. 178.

welcoming others into the afterlife.[74] But this parable also draws Abraham into the role of divine judge, rationalizing the rich man's fate in Hades and the poor man's bliss in a realm above. Jesus tells his audience of a certain 'rich man' who dressed in linen and feasted daily (16.19). At his gate was a poor man named Lazarus who was covered in sores (16.20). Lazarus longed even to eat the scraps from the rich man's table, but did not get the opportunity – he 'was carried away by the angels to Abraham's bosom' (16.22).[75] When the rich man also died, he found himself in Hades, looking up at Abraham from his torments below (16.23). When the rich man spies Lazarus by the side of Abraham, he calls out, 'Father Abraham, have mercy on me, and send Lazarus to dip the tip of his finger in water and cool my tongue' (16.24).[76] But Abraham replies, 'Child, remember that during your lifetime you received your good things, and Lazarus in like manner evil things; but now he is comforted here, and you are in agony' (16.25).[77] Even apart from this, Abraham tells the rich man, there is a great chasm between Abraham's bosom and Hades that cannot be crossed one way or the other (16.26).

The parable takes a fresh direction at this point, as the rich man asks Abraham to send Lazarus to his father's house to relay a message, for he has 'five brothers' who are presumably also living a life of indulgence; the rich man wants to warn them 'so that they will not also come into this place of torment' (16.27-28). But Abraham denies this request with the words: 'They have Moses and the prophets; they should listen to them' (16.29). The rich man disputes this as insufficient, saying: 'No, father Abraham; but if someone goes to them from the dead, they will repent' (16.30). Abraham concludes the parable with the definitive words, 'If they do not listen to Moses and the prophets, neither will they be convinced even if someone rises from the dead' (16.31).[78] Here, the parable morphs into an allegorical judgement upon those who refused to

[74] Rouven Genz reads the parable of the rich man and Lazarus as a continuation of the themes introduced in the parable of the householder (Luke 13.28-29). See, Genz, 'Reversal of Fate after Death?' in Beate Ego and Ulrike Mittmann (eds), *Evil and Death: Conceptions of the Human in Biblical, Early Jewish, Greco-Roman and Egyptian Literature* (Berlin: De Gruyter, 2015), pp. 221–58, at p. 238.

[75] 'Abraham's bosom' is a metaphor for 'paradise' or a 'representation of the blessed reality destined for the righteous'. See Alexey Somov, *Representations of the Afterlife in Luke-Acts* (London: T&T Clark/Bloomsbury, 2017), p. 100. See also Martin O'Kane, '"The Bosom of Abraham" (Luke 16.22): Father Abraham in the Visual Imagination', *BibInt* 15 (2007), pp. 485–518, for the text's reception history, and for the fullest current treatment, Outi Lehtipuu, *The Afterlife Imagery in Luke's Story of the Rich Man and Lazarus* (NovTSup 123; Leiden: Brill, 2007).

[76] Whether or not Lazarus and Abraham are enjoying a heavenly banquet is the subject of much debate. For a summation of the vast literature, see Baynes, 'The Parables', pp. 137–8.

[77] A reverse inequality consequently pertains in the afterlife, because 'Luke considers luxury alongside suffering to be flatly intolerable'. See, Christopher M. Hays, *Luke's Wealth Ethics: A Study in Their Coherence and Character* (WUNT 2.275; Tübingen: Mohr Siebeck, 2010), p. 156. The only rationale for the different fates of the two main characters appears to be their socioeconomic status in life. Cf. Matthew S. Rindge, 'Luke's Artistic Parables: Narratives of Subversion, Imagination, and Transformation', *Int* 68, no. 4 (2014), pp. 403–15, at p. 407. Taking into consideration the second half of the parable, however (if we regard it as integral, as we should) then Abraham's reasoning becomes clear: the rich man did not heed the Torah's injunctions to share his wealth with the poor and needy. Thus, Lehtipuu, *The Afterlife*, p. 165.

[78] This twist is frequently seen by scholars as 'out of place'; thus, Peter-Ben Smit, *Fellowship and Food in the Kingdom: Eschatological Meals and Scenes of Utopian Abundance in the New Testament* (WUNT 2.234; Tübingen: Mohr Siebeck, 2008), p. 167.

believe the 'proof' of their own scriptures ('Moses and the prophets'), since those scriptures putatively looked ahead to Jesus' coming ('someone rises from the dead').[79] The judgement upon the rich man (and his brothers and father) can thus be read as a judgement upon the Jews who refused to believe the Christian kerygma as Luke interprets it. The favour shown to Lazarus, on the other hand, can be read as the love and mercy shown to those who were in a position of relative lowliness in life, but who 'repented' (16.30b) and believed in the message.[80]

The figure of Abraham has a key role in this scene, effectively standing in for God as judge. The 'rich man' is surprised to find himself in Hades; but neither is there any indication that his negligent attitude towards Lazarus in his lifetime was deliberate or even culpable. Yet, the rich man recognizes Lazarus in Abraham's bosom, appearing even to know the poor man by name. Abraham does not disown the rich man – the rich man calls Abraham 'father' and Abraham in turn calls him 'child'. But there is an unbridgeable chasm between Hades and Abraham. The implication is that remedies cannot be made *after death*; there is only one chance in life to rectify injustice and so gain blessing in the afterlife, just as there is only one life in which to repent. In fact, the afterlife simply subverts the earthly reality: the poor receive good things in Abraham's bosom, and the rich, who had their enjoyment upon earth, experience torments.[81] The chasm between Hades and Abraham speaks of the impossibility of the dead influencing those still living: Lazarus cannot intercede from Abraham's bosom for others. On the level of Christian–Jewish polemic, the 'chasm' between Hades and Abraham signifies the finality of one's destiny with respect to belief: the writings of 'Moses and the prophets' ought to be enough to convince 'the Jews' of the Lukan kerygma, and there are no second chances if they fail in this regard.[82]

Finally, several other NT passages emphasize the notion that Abraham, Isaac and Jacob are, at the very least, 'alive to God' in some form, which implies their proximity to God and perhaps their capacity for a divine-like prescience, to 'see' what God sees on earth. In Matt. 22.32, Jesus defends the view of the 'resurrection of the dead' on the basis of Exod. 3.6, where God reveals himself to Moses at the burning bush. Jesus takes these words as spoken not only to Moses but also to his current audience: 'Have you not read what was said to you by God, "I am the God of Abraham, the God of Isaac, and the God of Jacob"? He is God not of the dead, but of the living.'[83] Luke's version of

---

[79] Lehtipuu, *The Afterlife*, pp. 166–8.
[80] On the centrality of repentance to the parable, in light of the preceding parable of the Prodigal Son, see Hanna Roose, 'Umkehr und Ausgleich bei Lukas: Die Gleichnisse vom verlorenen Sohn (Lk 15.11-32) und vom reichen Mann und armen Lazarus (Lk 16.19-31) als Schwestergeschichten', *NTS* 56, no. 1 (2010), pp. 1–21, esp. pp. 10–12, 15–17. Importantly, repentance (morally connoted) can bring about inversion and equalization – what Roose calls 'compensation' in the Lukan framework (ibid., p. 13).
[81] Recall Chapter 4 and the texts debating the possibility of the living interceding for the dead and vice versa (especially Ps.-Philo. 32-35). The parable of the rich man and Lazarus suggests a contribution to this debate as well, via the figure of Abraham, but Luke's implication is that there are no remedies to be had after death. Father Abraham himself in fact seems nonchalantly unconcerned about the fate of one of his 'children'.
[82] Jack T. Sanders, *The Jews in Luke-Acts* (Philadelphia: Fortress Press, 1987).
[83] R. T. France, *The Gospel of Matthew* (NICNT; Grand Rapids: Eerdmans, 2007), p. 837, notes the importance of Jesus grounding his argument in Scripture, particularly the book of Exodus, since

this text adds, 'For to him [God] all of them are alive' (Luke 20.37-38; cf. Acts 7.32). This line of thinking was elsewhere attested in early Jewish texts outside of the NT (cf. 4 *Macc.* 7.18-19; 13.17).

Tannaitic rabbinic literature

Abraham as seer

Several rabbinic texts extrapolate upon Abraham's ability to 'see' the future prospects of his descendants. The Aramaic Targums illustrate this tradition, notably when expanding upon two of the chief biblical texts presented earlier in this chapter: Gen. 15.12 (Abraham's dream vision and subsequent animal sacrifice) and Gen. 17.17 (Abraham's 'laughter' upon hearing of Isaac's conception).

In the Palestinian Targum to Genesis 15, when Abraham falls into sleep (which the Targum interprets as a 'dreaded darkness'), he is given a portentous vision of the long-suffering history of his descendants, and their final victory. Expanding upon the Hebrew of Gen. 15.12 (lit. 'dread darkness great falling upon him'), the Targumist parses the text as follows:

> And when the sun was about to set, a deep sleep was cast upon Abram, and behold four kingdoms were rising to enslave his children: *Dread* – that is, Babylon; *Darkness* – that is, Media; *Great* – that is, Greece; *Fell* – that is, Edom, which is to fall and shall never rise again, and from there the people of the house of Israel is to come forth.[84]

The Targum allusively gestures to the apocalyptic vision found in Dan. 7.1-14. In that text, Daniel experiences 'dreams and visions' while lying in bed (7.1). He arises, and writes down what he saw: 'the four winds of heaven, stirring up the great sea, and four great beasts' coming up out of the sea, 'different from one another' (7.2-3). Each hybrid beast is violent and destructive, the final beast more so than its predecessors (7.4-8). A great figure on a throne ('One like a son of man') arises to pass judgement upon the beasts; he kills the fourth beast, and takes away the dominion of the previous three (7.11-14).[85] Terrified and troubled, Daniel seeks out a dream interpreter, an angel who tells him that the four beasts represent four kingdoms of the earth (7.15-17). The angel tells Daniel that the fourth beast represents the most horrific kingdom to come,

---

his interlocutors (the Sadducees) disregarded the authoritative nature of the later books of Torah. Likewise, the Sadducees were apparently opposed to the doctrine of the resurrection in general (cf. Acts 23.6-8), and they engage Jesus in something of a trick question to illustrate the 'impossible dilemmas' the resurrection would entail. Thus, Keener, *A Commentary on the Gospel of Matthew*, p. 527.

[84] Cited in Martin McNamara, *Targum and Testament Revisited: Aramaic Paraphrases of the Hebrew Bible. A Light on the New Testament* (2nd edn; Grand Rapids: Eerdmans, 2010), p. 219. M. L. Klein, *The Fragment-Targums of the Pentateuch according to their Extant Sources*, vol. 1 (AB 76; Rome: Biblical Institute Press, 1980).

[85] Verse 13 must be 'the natural continuation' of v. 10, closely associating the roles of the 'son of man' and the 'Ancient of Days'; thus, Daniel Boyarin, 'Daniel 7, Intertextuality, and the History of Israel's Cult', *HTR* 105, no. 2 (2012), pp. 144–5.

that will 'devour the whole earth' (7.23b), persecute God's 'holy ones' and blaspheme against God and his Law (7.25).[86] But in time, 'the court shall sit in judgment' and the fourth kingdom's dominion will be taken away and destroyed (7.26). Then, 'the greatness of the kingdoms under the whole heaven shall be given to the people of the holy ones of the Most High' as an 'everlasting kingdom' (7.27).

That the Targum to Genesis 15 evokes the 'throne vision' in Daniel 7 is not surprising given the notable parallels between Daniel's vision and texts such as *1 Enoch*, as well as extant Canaanite mythologies.[87] If we grant Boyarin's reading of Dan. 7.2-14 that, if not 'messianic' in focus, then at least the text showcases 'the notion of a divinely appointed king over earth' – which 'has great potential for understanding the development of the messiah notion in later Judaism (including Christianity)'[88] – then, the Targum's creative substitution of Abraham as the apocalyptic visionary can be read in a new light. On Boyarin's reading, the 'one like a son of man' in Daniel 7 is a 'divine figure', an 'explicitly anthropomorphic divine figure as in Ezekiel'.[89] Therefore, there are 'two such divine figures in heaven, an old God, the Ancient of Days, and a young God, the One like a Son of Man'.[90] Boyarin finds this 'mythic pattern of second god as redeemer' 'crucial ... in interpreting the Gospels'.[91] If the Targumist subscribed to this ditheistic reading, then we would not be wrong to claim that Abraham is 'seeing' the emergence of 'the people of the house of Israel' in the future time of redemption, aided, implicitly, by the presence of the 'son of Man' figure. The Palestinian Targum to Gen. 15.17 expounds upon Abraham's visions of the fate of humankind, in a courtroom style of judgement also similar to Daniel 7. Much like the *Testament of Abraham*, and some of the *Testaments*, Abraham is able to see the fate awaiting the wicked (i.e. 'Gehenna').

Another intertextual strand shaping the Targum's presentation of Abraham in Genesis 15 can be drawn through *Targum Isaiah* (43.10-12).[92] This text expands upon MT Isa. 43.10, where the 'Servant' of the Lord becomes 'My servant *the messiah with whom I am well pleased*'. When the MT has the Lord speak: 'I declared and saved and proclaimed' (43.12), the Targum interpolates, somewhat randomly, 'I declared *to your father Abraham what was about to come... I saved you from Egypt just as I swore to him between the pieces*'.[93] The Isaian Targum shows familiarity with the Targumic

---

[86] The reference is to Antiochus Epiphanes IV and his persecution against Jews in Seleucid Judea. See Portier-Young, *Apocalypse against Empire*, pp. 179–80.

[87] Cf. Ryan E. Stokes, 'The Throne Visions of Daniel 7, 1 "Enoch" 14, and the Qumran "Book of Giants" (4Q530)', *DSS* 15, no. 3 (2008), pp. 340–58. For the possible antecedent ANE comparative traditions, see John J. Collins, 'Stirring Up the Great Sea: The Religio-Historical Background of Daniel 7', in A. S. van der Woude (ed.), *The Book of Daniel in the Light of New Findings* (Leuven: Leuven University Press, 1993), pp. 121–36, and Jürg Eggler, *Influences and Traditions Underlying the Vision of Daniel 7.2-14: The Research History from the End of the 19th Century to the Present* (Göttingen: Vandenhoeck & Ruprecht, 2000).

[88] Boyarin, 'Daniel 7', pp. 154–5.

[89] Ibid., pp. 148–9.

[90] Ibid., pp. 149.

[91] Ibid., pp. 160. Also, Dan. 7 is 'the best evidence we have for the continuation of a very ancient binitarian (or even ditheistic) Israelite theology deep into the Second Temple Period' (ibid., p. 161).

[92] Bruce Chilton, *The Isaiah Targum* (ed. Martin McNamara; Vol. 11; T&T Clark: Edinburgh, 1987). Cf. Coloe, 'Like Father, Like Son', pp. 8–10.

[93] The messianism of the Targum to Isaiah (especially ch. 53) has long been studied. Cf. K. Koch, 'Messias und Sündenvergebung in Jes 53-Targum', *JSJ* 3 (1972), pp. 117–48.

interpretation of Genesis 15, and the interpolation of God's 'servant' as 'messiah' in *Tg. Isa.* 43.10 brings an important element into the intertextual conversation, as it lends credence to the idea that Abraham's vision of the four kingdoms at the covenant 'between the pieces' resonates with Danielic ditheistic/messianic echoes. God's 'servant messiah' in *Tg. Isa.* 43.10 is, in the network of associations between Daniel 7, Genesis 15 and Isaiah 43, configured as a 'second god' persona, and brought into the future visions granted to Abraham as he slept.

Abraham's joy

Rabbinic traditions about Abraham's joy are also attested. In the Palestinian Targum to Genesis 22, at the *Akedah*, Abraham prays to God, after his hand was stayed as it neared Isaac's throat:

> I beseech, by the mercy from before you, O Lord! It is manifest before you that there was no deviousness in my heart, and that I sought to perform your decree with joy. Therefore, when the children of Isaac my son enter the hour of distress, remember them, and answer them and redeem them.[94]

This marvellous text from *Targum Pseudo-Jonathan* illustrates three things: Abraham's awareness of his pure intentions; his motivation to carry out God's decree with joy; and his intercession on behalf of his descendants, that when they enter 'the hour of distress' God may 'remember' them and 'redeem' them. The affinity of Abraham's prayer with the rabbinic conceptions of the זכות אבות (cf. ch. 4) are striking. The Targum to Genesis 22 enhances the *Akedah* narrative by depicting Isaac as a willing participant in the human sacrifice: he asks his father Abraham to bind his hands and body tightly so that he will neither move nor flinch.[95] This may be why Abraham calls upon God to have mercy upon *Isaac's* children, aware of the merit accruing to his son for such willingness. At the same time, Abraham is aware of the role that his honest, joyful obedience plays in the act itself, a fact he brings to God's attention when requesting mercy upon his descendants when they are in distress.

The *Targum Neofiti* offers a slightly verbose version of Abraham's prayer compared to Ps.-Jonathan:

> Please by the mercies from before you, O Lord, all is revealed and known before you, that my heart was not divided the first time when you said to me to offer Isaac my son, to make him dust and ashes before you, but immediately I got up in the morning, I rose up and did according to your command with joy, and I fulfilled your decree, and now when his sons stand in the hour of distress, remember the binding of Isaac their father and hear the voice of their prayers, and answer them and deliver them from all distress.[96]

---

[94] www.Sefaria.org.
[95] Ibid.
[96] Paul V. M. Fleischer and Bruce Chilton, *The Targums: A Critical Introduction* (Leiden/Boston: Brill, 2011), p. 466.

The *Targum Neofiti* to Genesis 22 offers a more repetitive version, perhaps for emphasis. Abraham 'did according to the command' of God with joy; he 'fulfilled' the divine 'decree'. There may be an allusion here to Gen. 26.5, where Abraham is depicted as fully obedient to God, observing all God's 'decrees', 'commandments' and 'laws'. The immediacy of Abraham's obedience is also reinforced in the *Targum Neofiti*, as the patriarch 'got up' straight away in the morning, 'rose up' and did as God commanded. Abraham pleads with God to remember the *Akedah* – 'the binding of Isaac' – not merely 'to remember them' (i.e. Isaac's sons), illustrating the importance of the event itself as an efficacious act before God.

The *Mekhilta de Rabbi Ishmael* (Beschallach 2, 160-70 (to Exod. 14.6)) also appears to acknowledge this interpretive tradition of Abraham rising with 'joy' to undertake the decree of God at the *Akedah*.[97] The Sages discuss the verse from Exod. 14.6, 'And he [Pharaoh] harnessed his chariot'. They notice that Pharaoh is described as harnessing his own chariot, which was uncommon for a king with a retinue of servants who would be ready to do the job for him. But Pharaoh's eagerness to equip his own horse indicates, according to the Sages, the extent of his wickedness. Contrarily, there were men in Israel's tradition who 'harnessed with joy':

> Abraham (Gen 22.3): 'And Abraham rose early in the morning [for the *Akedah*], and he saddled his ass'. Now, did he not have many servants? He did so, for the honour of the Lord.[98]

The text goes on to elucidate the other biblical characters who 'harnessed with joy' despite the fact that they had servants who might have assisted them: Joseph (Gen. 46.29), Balaam (Num. 22.21). The Sages suggest that the 'saddling' of Abraham will 'oppose the saddling of Balaam', who went to curse Israel; that the 'harnessing' of Joseph will in turn 'oppose' the 'harnessing of the wicked Pharaoh' who went to pursue Israel. Not only did Abraham rise in the morning and saddle his ass with 'joy' to do the will of God, but he did so without the help of his servants, for the honour of God. Moreover, the *Mekhilta* interprets Abraham's act of 'saddling with joy' as capable of undoing the wicked eagerness of Pharaoh to 'saddle' his chariot towards violent ends and against the will of God.

The other biblical source text commonly interpreted as indicative of Abraham's joy is Gen. 17.17, when Abraham 'laughed' at God's promise that Sarah would bear a son in their old age. The Targums avoid reference to Abraham's 'laughter', preferring to ascribe positive emotions to Abraham instead. Thus, *Targum Onkelos* (to Gen. 17.17) makes Abraham react with joy: 'And Abraham fell upon his face and rejoiced, and said in his heart, "Will the son of a hundred years have a child, and Sarah, the daughter of ninety years, bring forth?"'[99] Likewise, the Palestinian Targum (Gen. 17.17) reads: 'And Abraham fell on his face, and wondered and said in his heart, "Shall the son of a

---

[97] Lauterbach (ed.), *Mekhilta*, 2.133–4.
[98] Ibid.
[99] *Tg. Onk.*, www.Sefaria.org.

hundred years have progeny, and Sarah, the daughter of ninety years, bear a child?"'[100] Both Targum renderings of Gen. 17.17 soften Abraham's response so that it appears less like doubt and more like reverence for God's wondrous ways.

Finally, the Tannaitic midrashim give voice to another tradition about Abraham's 'happiness' that is not derived from a narrative source in Genesis. More a literary trope than a tradition, the expression 'Happy are you, father Abraham' is used to preface the commendation of one Sage by another, especially when a learned interpretation of a scriptural verse is professed. For example, in *Sifrei Numbers* (75.1), we find: 'Happy are you, father Abraham, from whose loins [Rabbi] Akiva came forth!' Similarly, in the *Mekhilta de RI* (13.2, par 3), R. Yehoshua cries out 'Happy are you, father Abraham, from whose loins Elazar b. Azariah emerged!'. Later in *b. Chag.* 14b, the same expression occurs: 'Happy are you, our father Abraham that Elazar ben Arakh came from your loins!'[101] This trope expresses a view of Abraham consonant with several of the other traditions we have surveyed in this chapter, namely, that the patriarch is knowledgeable of what his posterity are about on earth. According to the Rabbis, Abraham is especially pleased about their learning of the Torah, and rejoices in this knowledge.

Not yet fifty years old?

One rabbinic text from the Amoraic period – although considerably late for the purposes of comparisons with John's Gospel – provides a parallel with John 8.56-58 that, to my knowledge, is never addressed in relation to John 8. This rabbinic tale (*Gen. R.* 38.13) follows the tradition, already established within early Judaism, of Abraham's father Terah as a manufacturer of idols. As part of Abraham's awakening to monotheism, he is depicted as despising his father's idolatry and actively seeking to destroy Terah's idols. As in the *Apocalypse of Abraham* (1–8), the tale in *Gen. R.* 38.13 narrates how Abraham came to upset his father's system of idolatry by ironic subterfuge. Presumably because Abraham's words of reason fail to dissuade Terah from making and worshipping idols, Abraham resorts to trickery in order to demonstrate the futility of idolatry. One day, Abraham destroys Terah's idols while minding the family shop, and when questioned by Terah, explains that the idols themselves caused their own destruction. When Terah remarks upon the absurdity of such an event due to the idols' lack of sentience, Abraham convicts his father 'out of his own mouth', as it were. However, it is what the text adds to this tradition by way of preamble that is relevant here. A man enters the family shop to buy an idol, but Abraham asks him to divulge his age. The man replies that he is 'fifty years old'. Abraham turns him away in shame for being so advanced in age yet desirous of worshipping a newly crafted idol not yet 'one day old'. The text is worth citing at length:

> R. Hiyya said, 'Terah was an idolater. Once he went off somewhere and left Abraham to sell (idols) in his place. A certain man came wishing to buy. [Abraham] said to him, "How old are you?" He said, "Fifty". [Abraham] said, "Fifty years old and

[100] *Tg. Ps.-Jon.*, www.Sefaria.org.
[101] Bavli, www.Sefaria.org.

you are going to bow down to something only one day old!" [i.e. the idol]. The man went off in embarrassment. Later, a woman came bearing a container of flour. She said to him, "Here, offer this before [the idols]". [Abraham] took a stick and broke them [the idols] and then put the stick into the hand of the biggest of them. When his father came he said to him, "What happened to these?" He said to him, ... "One [idol] said, 'Let me be the first to eat', then the biggest one took a stick and broke them". [Terah said], "Why are you mocking me? – do these idols know anything?" [Abraham] said, "Cannot your ears hear the words coming from your own mouth?"' (*Gen. R.* 38.13)[102]

This text is important to evaluate in light of the post-biblical and rabbinic tradition of Abraham as the foremost rebutter of idolatry. Abraham rejected Terah's manufacture of idols (*Apoc. Abr.* 4.6 (cf. chs 1–8)), rejected idol worshippers (*Jub.* 21.3) and rejected idol worship itself (*Jub.* 11.16-17; 12.2-5; 13.8-9; *Ant.* 1.154-157). Abraham was considered to be the first monotheist, or the discoverer of the one true God (*Ant.* 1.155; cf. Philo, *De Opificio Mundo* 170). In *Gen. R.* 38.13, the specific age of a man wishing to buy idols ('fifty years old') is highlighted in relation to the newborn 'age' of the idol itself. In the rabbinic text, Abraham draws attention to the relevance of the man's age of fifty years – this round number, signifying the man's advanced age, ought to confer upon the man a solid understanding of the futility of idolatry, but it does not.

The final part of this chapter examines the concepts of 'seeing' and 'rejoicing' in the Johannine literature (both of which are dense and prevalent) before tying everything together and returning to look at John 8.48-59 in these combined contexts.

Part 2: The Johannine context

The intratextual threads in the Gospel of John that touch on 'seeing' and 'rejoicing' are highly relevant to the text of ch. 8 vv. 56-58. The category of 'sight' holds a prominent symbolic place in the Gospel's world view, and the theme of 'complete joy' is a recurrent one in the discourse segments of the Gospel. More than the reference to Abraham's 'seed' (8.32) or to Abraham's 'works' (8.39-40) the reference to Abraham 'seeing' and 'rejoicing' (8.56-58) is well-explained by the thematic context of the Gospel as a whole. This is not to say that the wider intertextual field that I have 'scripted' in this chapter has no explanatory relevance but only that we get a sense of a more complete *inter*textual and *intra*textual tapestry operating in this final segment of the pericope (8.48-59) than we do in the former two parts.

---

[102] J. Theodor and Ch. Albeck, *Midrash Bereshit Rabbah: Critical Edition with Notes and Commentary* (Hebrew, 3 vols.) (Jerusalem: Shalem Books, 1965 (orig. Berlin, 1912–36)), translated: H. Freedman and M. Simon (trans.), *Midrash Rabbah: Translated into English* (10 vols.; 3rd edn., London: Soncino, 1961); cited in Kugel, *The Bible As It Was*, p. 138.

'Joy' and 'rejoicing' in the Gospel of John

The themes of 'joy' and 'rejoicing' are prominent in the Johannine literature. One characteristically Johannine expression is that a person's joy is 'made complete'; here, the verb πληρόω ('complete', 'fulfill') is stated in the perfect passive (e.g. 3.29; 16.24; 17.13), or the aorist passive subjunctive (e.g. 15.11; 1 John 1.4, 12). The first instance of this expression occurs in ch. 3 v. 29, where John (the Baptist) discourses about his subordinate role in relation to 'the Messiah' (v. 28b). John refers to himself as 'the friend of the bridegroom' and to Jesus (v. 22) as 'the bridegroom' (v. 29a).[103] While the bridegroom is superior, for the fact that he 'has the bride' (v. 29a), 'the friend of the bridegroom, who stands and hears him (ὁ ἑστηκὼς καὶ ἀκούων αὐτοῦ), rejoices greatly (χαρᾷ χαίρει) at the bridegroom's voice' (v. 29b).[104]

Dorothy Lee explains that 'to hear means, for John, to recognize the Word (λόγος) in the words (λόγοι)'.[105] It is *hearing aright* that guarantees discipleship. Only by hearing can Jesus' disciples recognize who Jesus is, and follow him (cf. 10.10). 'To hear is to gain eternal life, since hearing is the sign that final judgement has taken place (5.24)'.[106] John the Baptizer 'hears' the words of the bridegroom from the side of the party, as it were, as the bridegroom's 'best man'. This is the experience of John, who concludes, 'for this reason my joy has been fulfilled' (αὕτη οὖν ἡ χαρὰ ἡ ἐμὴ πεπλήρωται; 29c).[107] John's *joy* therefore ties in with his arrival at true discipleship, and 'eternal life'. From now on, John's role – and his activity of baptizing – will diminish as Jesus' role 'increases' (v. 30).[108] It is as though the marriage metaphors in this passage suggest the consequent new 'birth' of Jesus' ministry, and of his 'offspring' (disciples), which now 'increase' (cf. 3.5).[109]

In fact, Calum Carmichael suggests that the motif of 'complete joy' in ch. 3 vv. 29-30 must be understood in the context of procreation as the completion of marriage.[110] The particular 'joy' that John the Baptist speaks of has deep roots in the HB. Carmichael considers Isa. 66.10 as a prime intertext in this regard: there, an eschatological Jerusalem (the bride) produces many citizens ('children') who are thriving, and everyone present

---

[103] Mary Coloe, 'John as Witness and Friend', in Paul N. Anderson, Felix Just and Tom Thatcher (eds), *John, Jesus, and History, Volume 2: Aspects of Historicity in the Fourth Gospel* (Atlanta: SBL Press, 2009), pp. 44–61, at p. 52. For a full study of the bridegroom metaphor in John, see Jocelyn McWhirter, *The Bridegroom Messiah and the People of God: Marriage in the Fourth Gospel* (Cambridge: Cambridge University Press, 2008).

[104] The Semitic nature of the phraseology has been established in the scholarship: cf. M. Black, *An Aramaic Approach to the Gospels and Acts* (3rd edn, Oxford: Oxford University Press, 1967), p. 7.

[105] Lee, 'The Gospel of John and the Five Senses', p. 121.

[106] Ibid.

[107] Sjef Van Tilborg, *Imaginative Love in John* (Leiden: Brill, 1993), pp. 75, 77.

[108] This detail may suggest that historically, John the Baptizer and Jesus worked two parallel ministries, where there was possibly some conflict between them over 'purity' matters (3.25). The Evangelist cheerily diminishes the Baptizer's role early in the Gospel narrative to enhance Jesus' standing. Cf. John W. Pryor, 'John the Baptist and Jesus: Tradition and Text in John 3.25', *JSNT* 66 (1997), pp. 15–26.

[109] Calum M. Carmichael, 'Marriage and the Samaritan Woman', *NTS* 26, no. 3 (1980), pp. 332–46, at p. 333. On the points of connection between John 3.5 and 16.21 (the parable of the birthing woman), see Ben Witherington, 'The Waters of Birth: John 3.5 and 1 John 5.6-8', *NTS* 35, no. 1 (1989), pp. 155–60, at p. 158.

[110] Carmichael, 'Marriage and the Samaritan Woman', p. 333.

participates in her joy.¹¹¹ The birth imagery introduced by Nicodemus in ch. 3 v. 5 sets the immediate context for the development of a metaphor ('joy' as the 'bridegroom') that implies its own *telos*: 'birth and new life are the final testimony to a complex social process that began with an initial approach by the bridegroom's friend [i.e. at betrothal] to the home of the intended bride'.¹¹² John the Baptizer's role as facilitator and witness to the 'marriage' of Jesus to his 'bride' (Israel) now shifts to the background, as Jesus' metaphorical progeny – his disciples – 'increase'.

The farewell discourse (13.1–17.26) is the only other section of the Gospel containing the characteristic expression of 'joy' being 'made complete'. The first example occurs in the context of Jesus encouraging his disciples to keep his commandments so that they will 'abide' in his 'love' (15.9-10). Jesus tells his disciples that he has spoken to them in this way 'so that my joy may be in you, and that your joy may be complete' (ἵνα ἡ χαρὰ ἡ ἐμὴ ἐν ὑμῖν ᾖ καὶ ἡ χαρὰ ὑμῶν πληρωθῇ; 15.11). Keeping the commandments of Jesus will lead to the fulfilment of the disciples' joy – a joy that is in fact Jesus' own, imparted to his disciples by virtue of their obedience. In like manner, Jesus' own joy derives from the fact that he keeps his 'Father's' commandments (15.12). There is a pattern of succession present in these verses, characteristic of ancient last testaments, wherein the disciples carry on Jesus' work, just as Jesus carried on his Father's work.¹¹³ 'Like father, like son', and so on to Jesus' disciples, this successive pattern of imitation and obedience aligns with the reading of ch. 3 vv. 29-30 provided in this chapter, namely, that John's 'complete joy' rested in witnessing the inception of Jesus' 'children' brought forth to life.¹¹⁴

The next example of this theme occurs in the 'parable' of the labouring woman, in ch. 16 vv. 20-22 (23-24). This short passage refers to 'joy' or 'rejoicing' five times (vv. 20, 21, 22, 24). Jesus' disciples wonder about Jesus' enigmatic announcement of his impending departure and return, expressed in a baffling statement about two 'little whiles' (μικρὸν καὶ οὐ θεωρεῖτέ με, καὶ πάλιν μικρὸν καὶ ὄψεσθέ με).¹¹⁵ Jesus explains to them:

> Very truly, I tell you, you will weep and mourn, but the world will *rejoice*; you will have pain, but your pain will turn into *joy*. When a woman is in labor, she has pain, because her hour has come. But when her child is born, she no longer remembers the anguish because of the *joy* of having brought a human being into the world. So, you have pain now; but I will see you again, and your hearts will *rejoice*, and no one will take your *joy* from you. On that day you will ask nothing of me ... ask and

---

¹¹¹ Ibid.
¹¹² Coloe, 'Witness and Friend', p. 60.
¹¹³ The 'succession motif' in John's farewell discourse is split between the ongoing role of the disciples, and the role of the Spirit-Paraclete. For more detail, see Ruth Sheridan, 'The Paraclete as Successor in the Johannine Farewell Discourse: A Comparative Literary Analysis', *AEJT* 18, no. 2 (2011), pp. 129–40.
¹¹⁴ Similarly, Carmichael, 'Marriage and the Samaritan Woman', p. 334.
¹¹⁵ Commentators devote significant attention to the statement because of what it might suggest about the eschatological chronology as John perceives it. Cf. Bultmann, *Gospel of John*, pp. 577–80; Barrett, *Gospel*, p. 492. Note that in this verse John uses both θεωρέω and ὁράω to refer to the disciples' 'seeing' of Jesus, without any ostensible semantic difference.

you will receive, so that your *joy* may be complete. (ἵνα ἡ χαρὰ ὑμῶν ᾖ πεπληρωμένη; 16.20-23a, 24b NRSV)

In this context, Jesus further tells his disciples that if they ask the Father anything in Jesus' name, they will receive it, so that their joy may be complete (ἵνα ἡ χαρὰ ὑμῶν ᾖ πεπληρωμένη; 16.24). In the foregoing parable, the disciples' joy will be contingent upon their 'seeing' of Jesus once again (16.22). This is one of only two other passages in the Gospel, including ch. 8 v. 58, where 'seeing' and 'rejoicing' are correlated (cf. 20.20). For the disciples, Jesus promises that their joy will be such that no one can take it from them – it will be permanent and enduring, as well as deeply felt (χαρήσεται ὑμῶν ἡ καρδία). Their great joy at seeing Jesus again will be inversely related to their 'sorrow' (λύπη) at Jesus' loss. Meanwhile, with hindsight the disciples will understand that the 'rejoicing' of the 'world' at Jesus' departure will be of no consequence in light of the joy – of a wholly different order – that they will experience upon Jesus' return. Jesus likens their temporary grief – and on another level, his own death and resurrection – to the 'sorrow' and physical pain that a woman experiences during labour, which, he claims, turns eventually to 'joy' at the birth of her baby. Her joy is such that it wipes away the very memory of her anticipated agony prior to labour.[116] In this sense, Jesus claims, his disciples will experience 'complete' joy (16.24), the kind that only emerges through extreme, unavoidable suffering.[117]

The third example of this expression occurs in Jesus' final prayer (17.13, cf. 17.1-26). Jesus tells his 'Father' of his impending 'homecoming', adding that he speaks 'these things in the world so that they [the disciples] may have *my joy* made complete in themselves' (ταῦτα λαλῶ ἐν τῷ κόσμῳ ἵνα ἔχωσιν τὴν χαρὰν τὴν ἐμὴν πεπληρωμένην ἐν ἑαυτοῖς).[118] Here, the reference is not to the disciples' *own* joy – which they are yet to experience upon Jesus' return (cf. 16.24) – but to Jesus' *imparted* joy that is 'made complete' *in them* (cf. 15.11). This imparted joy, described as Jesus' 'own', is connected to the words that Jesus speaks, as though through his speech alone Jesus is able to share his joy, and thus to realize it fully in his disciples. Jesus' joy is assumed to be permanent and constant, deriving from the fact that he obediently kept the will of his Father against all odds: 'I have given them your word, and the world has hated them because they do not belong to the world, just as I do not belong to the world' (17.14; cf. 15.24).[119]

Apart from the Johannine theme of 'complete joy', there are a number of other references to 'joy' and 'rejoicing' in the Gospel. Like the previous examples, these

---

[116] For a fuller development of this reading, see Ruth Sheridan, 'She Forgets Her Suffering in Her Joy: The Parable of the Laboring Woman (John 16.20-22)', in Beth M. Stovell (ed.), *Making Sense of Motherhood: Biblical and Theological Perspectives* (Eugene: Wipf & Stock, 2016), pp. 45–64.

[117] Moloney, *John*, p. 449. Cf. Paul A. Holloway, 'Left Behind: Jesus' Consolation of His Disciples in John 13,31—17,26', *ZNW* 96, nos. 1-2 (2005), pp. 1–34.

[118] Jesus' 'joy' is also connected to the central theme of the prayer, that is unity of believers. See Keener, *Gospel*, 2.1061-2.

[119] Cf. 1 John 1.3-4: the author explains that the very reason he writes his epistle is so that the joy of his readers 'may be complete' (1 John 1.4, but some MSS read 'our' joy). This text carries on the idea of communicating something in order to impart and realize complete joy in another person or group. Like Jesus' concern for unity in John 17.13, this First Epistle promotes a vision of inclusive communion with God, Jesus and each other, as the essence of 'joy'. Painter, *1, 2, and 3 John*, p. 138.

references are predominately located in the discourse segments of the text and are voiced by Jesus (4.36; 5.35; 14.28), although one reference occurs in a descriptive setting, voiced by the narrator (20.20). The first reference to 'rejoicing' is found in Jesus' speech to his disciples, following his encounter with the Samaritan woman (4.5-30). The disciples approach Jesus and urge him to eat some food (4.31b), presumably moved by Jesus' visible midday weariness (cf. 4.6). In reply, Jesus shifts immediately into a monologue about his 'real' source of nourishment – 'my food is to do the will of him who sent me and to finish his work' (καὶ τελειώσω αὐτοῦ τὸ ἔργον; 4.34).[120] Jesus then conjures the metaphor of harvesting in order to make a point about the labour in which the disciples are similarly engaged (4.35-38). In the case of God's 'work', the proverbial 'four months wait' for the harvest does not hold, for already the 'fields are ripe' (4.35-36). The reaper of the harvest is 'receiving wages and is gathering fruit for eternal life, so that sower and reaper may rejoice together' (ὁμοῦ χαίρῃ; 4.36). Although Jesus deems the disciples to be the metaphorical 'reapers', he insists that they were not the 'sowers' of the harvest: they are reaping what they did not sow – a sign of how quickly the harvest has yielded its produce – 'others have labored', and the disciples 'have entered into their labor' (4.37-38).[121] The 'sowers' in Jesus' metaphorical discourse are not identified, but they are depicted as 'rejoicing together' (ὁμοῦ χαίρῃ) with the 'reapers' over the wage/reward (μισθός) of their labour. Like each occurrence of the noun or verb 'joy'/'rejoice' that we have analysed in the Gospel so far, this example is also prospective, even if troublingly exploitative.

In the first 'Sabbath controversy' scene of the Gospel, and the discourse with the Jews that ensues (5.1-47), Jesus refers to the figure of John (the Baptist, 5.33), whom he describes as 'a burning and shining lamp' (5.35a). Jesus tells the Jews that they 'were willing to rejoice for an hour in [John's] light' (ἀγαλλιαθῆναι πρὸς ὥραν ἐν τῷ φωτὶ αὐτοῦ; 5.35), which is here construed as the 'light' of John's testimony to Jesus (cf. 5.32-33). The verb ἀγαλλιάω in ch. 5 v. 35 is emphatic, meaning 'to exceedingly delight in' something – and it is only otherwise used in John's Gospel in ch. 8 v. 56 to describe Abraham's joy in 'seeing' Jesus' day. The Jews are thus presented as exhibiting extreme joy for a *passing moment* of time; their joy in John's 'light' was neither moderate nor was it enduring.[122] As such, they appear fickle, and unwilling to be convinced by John's 'testimony'. Jesus therefore tells them that he has a 'greater testimony' than John's in the 'works' that the Father has given him to do (5.36).[123] The implication is that the Jews

---

[120] The singular 'work' of God as opposed to God's 'works' is rare in the Gospel. Doing the 'will' and 'work' of God in the context of John 4.1-42 means bringing others to recognize 'who Jesus is' and 'the new life he can offer them'. Thus, Ensor, *Jesus and His Works*, p. 151.

[121] Musa W. Dube provides a stimulating, decolonizing interpretation of these verses, emphasizing the exploitative, hidden intents masked by the Gospel's euphemisms, and the intense missionizing competition that may have driven Jesus and his disciples into Samaria (but which actually occurred in a later stage of the Johannine community's experience): Dube, 'Reading for Decolonization (John 4.1-42)', *Sem* 75 (1996), pp. 37–59, at p. 48.

[122] Yet John's own 'light' was temporary and derivative, in contrast to Jesus who is presented as the 'true light' (1.8-9). See Daniel S. Dapaah, *The Relationship Between John the Baptist and Jesus of Nazareth* (New York/Oxford: University Press of America, 2005), p. 133. The Elijan overtones are apparent in ch. 5 v. 35 to describe John's role; thus, Walter Wink, *John the Baptist in the Gospel Tradition* (SNTMS 7; Cambridge: Cambridge University Press, 1968), p. 92.

[123] See Chapter 5 for a more detailed discussion of this text.

ought to – at the very least – receive this greater testimony, even if they do not 'delight' in it.

In the farewell discourse, Jesus encourages his disciples not to be 'troubled' by the fact that he is soon due to leave them (14.27-28a). Although Jesus will leave his disciples, he will also return to them. Indeed, Jesus tells them that if they loved him, they would 'rejoice' (ἐχάρητε) that he is 'going to the Father' because 'the Father is greater' than Jesus (14.28).[124] Jesus' presence with the Father will enable the disciples to reap newly available gifts, such as the 'Spirit-Paraclete' (14.16-18) and immediately efficacious prayer (14.19-20). Thus, it is to the ultimate benefit of the disciples that Jesus departs to the Father (16.24). But it is not only for the accrued benefits arising from Jesus' departure that the disciples are told to 'rejoice' (14.28); rather, it is also because their rejoicing should demonstrate their active 'love' for Jesus that it is so strongly encouraged. *If* they loved Jesus, they *would* rejoice – this conditional phrasing is found elsewhere in the Gospel (notably, if 'the Jews' were children of Abraham they would do as Abraham did: 8.39-41).

The only narrative segment of the Gospel where characters are shown 'rejoicing' is found in ch. 20 v. 20. After his resurrection, Jesus appears to the disciples in the house where they routinely meet, shows them his hands and his side, and greets them with a benediction (20.19-20a). The narrator adds, 'Then the disciples rejoiced when they saw the Lord' (ἐχάρησαν οὖν οἱ μαθηταὶ ἰδόντες τὸν κύριον; 20.20b). Jesus proceeds to breathe the 'holy Spirit' upon the disciples and commissions them to continue his work in the world (20.21-22). Like John 8.56 and 16.20-22, this text correlates 'seeing' with 'rejoicing' – except that the verb used to denote the act of rejoicing in ch. 8 v. 56 (ἀγαλλιάω) is stronger than that found in ch. 16 vv. 20-22 and ch. 20 v. 20 (χαίρω). In the latter two texts, the disciples 'rejoice' (or will rejoice) as they behold the risen Jesus. But unlike ch. 16 vv. 20-22, the later narrative context of ch. 20 v. 20 concerns the relationship between 'seeing' and 'believing' (20.24-28), and it is the latter phenomenon that is given priority over the former in the Evangelist's perspective.

In light of the three texts that correlate 'seeing' with 'rejoicing' in the Gospel of John (8.56-58; 16.20-22; 20.20), some comments can be made about *what* Abraham could be said to have 'seen' when Jesus claims that Abraham 'rejoiced' when he 'saw' his 'day' (8.56). That the verb to denote 'seeing' is identical in all three texts – and that this verb touches upon the physical act of seeing something with the eyes – could lead us to claim that Abraham's vision of Jesus' 'day' pertains somehow to the resurrection, given that in ch. 16 vv. 20-22 and ch. 20 v. 20, the disciples' joy is associated with their 'seeing' of Jesus after his death. Jesus' 'day' (8.56) would not be his Parousia as such (cf.), but his post-Easter appearances to the disciples, and on this reading, Abraham could be configured as one of the disciples, indeed one of the 'witnesses' to Jesus in the post-resurrection period (cf. 15.25-26).

However, there are a couple of points to raise by way of caution: in ch. 8 v. 56, the verb ὁράω is rendered in the aorist (ἴδῃ), and as such, Abraham is presented as one

---

[124] Ruth Sheridan, 'The Paraclete and Jesus in the Johaninne Farewell Discourse', *Pac* 20, no. 2 (2007), pp. 125–41.

who *saw* – in the past, and perhaps in his lifetime – Jesus' 'day' before it occurred.[125] Thus, Jesus' 'day' could signify his incarnation on earth, his presence in Judea and his public ministry as John portrays it (but it is also possible that it signifies his 'vision' of the day of Jesus' resurrection into the future). More pertinently, it is worth noting that although these three Gospel texts (8.56-58; 16.2-22; 20.20) correlate 'seeing' with 'rejoicing', the latter verb is not identical in each case. Abraham's 'rejoicing' (ἀγαλλιάω) is of a higher order, we might say, as the verb is emphatic and describes a state of deep pleasure. The only other instance of the verb (ἀγαλλιάω) in the Gospel is ch. 5 v. 35, where the Jews are said to have rejoiced in John (the Baptist's) testimony to Jesus. While the Jews' rejoicing in John's 'light' is depicted as temporary (5.35), by contrast, Abraham's rejoicing in Jesus' 'day' (ἡμέρα) is assumed to be enduring (8.56-58). This contrast nevertheless upholds the forensic connotations of John 8.56 because both John (5.35) and Abraham (8.56) give rise to something (testimony, vision) in relation to Jesus that witnesses to him.

Seeing and sight in the Gospel of John

The theme of 'seeing' is central to the Gospel's theological and Christological agenda, and its overall importance for both the narrative and metaphorical shape of the text cannot be overstated. There have been a number of studies on the words relating to 'sight' and 'vision' in the Fourth Gospel.[126] Many of these studies, and other shorter examinations on the topic, have explored how sight is related to behaviour in the Gospel, and how different terms are used by the Evangelist to correspond to different degrees or types of 'sight': thus, some characters see Jesus and welcome him; some see with the eyes of faith; others see but do not respond; others again want to 'see' signs and wonders before they believe; some characters hate Jesus and his disciples despite having seen them; and some 'see' as a means of witnessing to the kerygma. We noted the studies of Phillips and Miller in Chapter 1 of this book; these authors argued that John uses the verb ὁράω to denote the ultimate type of 'seeing by faith' promoted by the Evangelist (cf. 1.18; 3.11; 4.45; 5.37; 8.38, 57; 9.37; 11.40; 14.7; 15.24; 16.16; 19.35; 20.18 and others). On the other hand, the verb θεωρέω denotes a less impressive category of seeing, but one that inches towards faith (cf. 2.23; 4.19; 7.3; 8.51; 9.8; 10.12; 12.19; 14.17; 16.10; 17.24; 20.6 and others). At the lowest rung of the ladder is the verb βλέπω which connotes mere oracular 'vision' with no faith content implied (cf. 1.29; 5.19; 9.7; 11.9; 13.22; 20.1; 21.9, 20 and others).[127]

This verbal schema has been influential in other studies on the topic, where the theological distinction between θεωρέω and ὁράω has attained a consensus. Thus, Jey

---

[125] This gives credence to the interpretations of the pre-existent Logos at Mamre (via Justin Martyr; see Chapter 5, and Chapter 1 of this book).
[126] F. Hahn, 'Sehen und Glauben im Johannesevangelium', in H. Bautensweiler and Bo Reike (eds), *Neue Testament und Geschichte: Historisches Geschehen und Deutung im Neuen Testament* (FS Oscar Cullman; Tübingen: Mohr Siebeck, 1972), pp. 125–41; Phillips, 'Faith and Vision in the Fourth Gospel', 83; Craig Koester, 'Hearing, Seeing and Believing in the Gospel of John', *Bib* 70 (1989), pp. 327–48; Miller, 'They Saw His Glory', pp. 127–51; Lee, 'The Gospel of John and the Five Senses', pp. 115–27.
[127] Miller, 'They Saw His Glory', pp. 135–6; Phillips, 'Faith and Vision in the Fourth Gospel', p. 83.

Kanagaraj writes of the 'two levels of perceiving Jesus: (1) ὁράω: to see at a superficial level, either by seeing signs or by hearing a testimony; and (2) θεωρέω: to perceive spiritually and intelligibly, which leads one to the commitment of faith to Christ and to testify about him'.[128] But there are subtleties within the way each verb is used. For example, the Johannine use of ὁράω itself has two dimensions: first, physical sight (e.g. of Jesus: 1.33, 39, 46; 4.45; 5.6; 6.22, 24; 7.52; 12.9, or alternately, of the 'signs' he performs: 2.23-25; 4.48; 6.14, 30). Physical sight alone is not sufficient for attaining the standard of Johannine faith in these texts. Second, physical sight working in conjunction with *insight*, or a deeper level of understanding Jesus' self-revelation (1.50-51; 3.3; 9.37-38; 11.40; 12.21, 41; 20.25, 27-29).[129]

Likewise, nuances exist in John's use of θεωρέω/θεάομαι. Physical seeing, especially eyewitness sighting which leads to testimony, can be referenced by the aorist ἐθεασάμεθα ('We saw his glory': 1.14).[130] The communal implications of genuine belief in *physically* 'seeing the glory' are evident (cf. 1 John 1.1-2). The indicative θεωρέω carries different connotations, that is of a 'seeing' that is rudimentary in terms of its faith insight – a type of 'theatrical beholding' without deeper understanding involved, or a 'seeing' that moves progressively to a higher-order perception (cf. 2.23; 6.2; 4.19; 20.6).[131] But the matter is not so cut and dried. John combines 'seeing' (θεωρέω) with 'tasting'/'knowing' (γεύομαι/γινώσκω) in ch. 8 vv. 51-52, a combination of sensory language that expresses 'access to the deathless life that the Johannine Jesus bestows'.[132] This type of 'seeing' therefore *does* connote a deeper experience of the divine than mere rudimentary knowledge allows (cf. 12.45).[133] The same can be said of how the verb θεωρέω is used of the disciples' future 'seeing' of Jesus again via the Paraclete (14.19), and of their 'seeing' the divine glory in Jesus' unity with the Father (17.24).[134]

Some of the problems with taxonomies and stratifications have been noted in Chapter 1. With categorical distinctions come hierarchical conclusions: if John always uses *x* verb to connote *y*, but uses *z* verb to connote *yy*, (and if *y* is superior to *yy*), then *x* verb must be the pinnacle of John's theology, linguistically construed. Aside from the issue that 'word' and 'concept' need not always align, this taxonomic logic can be not only incorrect, but also highly subjective. Where one scholar reads θεωρέω as the superior sight category in John, another might read ὁράω as the supreme sight category. Thus, as we saw in Chapter 1, Paul Miller argues that ὁράω connotes a type of seeing that always merges with 'belief' and is therefore superior to the observational type of seeing connoted by θεωρέω.[135] Yet, such is not always the case: ὁράω does not always

---

[128] Jey Kanagaraj, *Mysticism in the Gospel of John: An Inquiry into Its Background* (Sheffield: Sheffield Academic Press (repr. T&T Clark/Bloomsbury), 1998), p. 218.
[129] Ibid., p. 216.
[130] Ibid.
[131] Benny Thettayll, *In Spirit and Truth: An Exegetical Study of John 4.19-26 and a Theological Investigation of the Replacement Theme in the Fourth Gospel* (Leuven: Peeters, 2007), p. 52. Cf. Phillips, 'Faith and Vision in the Fourth Gospel', pp. 84–5.
[132] Lee, 'The Gospel of John and the Five Senses', pp. 122–3.
[133] Kanagaraj, *Mysticism in the Gospel of John*, p. 217.
[134] Ibid.
[135] Miller, 'They Saw His Glory', pp. 135–6.

imply 'belief' (cf. 6.36; 15.24), neither is 'seeing with belief' always the desirable mark of discipleship – in fact believing without seeing appears to be ultimately preferred (cf. 20.29).[136] It seems wise to avoid classifying John's sight verbs according to rigid schemata, since the crossover usages for 'sight' and 'seeing' in the Gospel suggest that he uses them synonymously. Thus, the 'specific linguistic context' of the verbs is still the best way to distinguish John's specific connotations.[137]

This is not to say that the concept of 'seeing' is void of theological – or 'Johannine' – meaning in the Gospel. To the contrary, John's employment of vision-related verbs and nouns is highly metaphorical and symbolic. It is also the case that John endorses a 'genuine' type of 'seeing' (inner perception, tending to belief and acceptance of Jesus as the Sent One) compared to a superficial assessment of who Jesus is based on what he can do ('signs', 2.23; 3.2).[138] Worse still is the 'spiritual blindness' of those who think that they can 'see' reality, but only in fact reveal their culpable short-sightedness (cf. 9.39-41). And although 'signs-based faith' gets a bad reputation in the secondary literature due to Jesus' scathing remarks in ch. 2 vv. 23-25 (where Jesus himself 'sees' inside the hidden motivations of others), there are other passages in the Gospel where Jesus evidently prefers a sign-based faith to a faith based on things even more mundane, such as an appetite for bread (cf. 6.26). Similarly, Jesus does not turn away his followers for having 'seen what he did' and believed (11.45; cf. 4.45). But just as 'seeing' does not guarantee 'believing' (cf. 'you see me, but do not believe': 6.36; 'they have seen and hated me': 15.24), so also believing may indeed be a prerequisite to truly 'seeing' ('If you believe, you will see the glory': cf. 11.40).

'Seeing the glory' (of Jesus and/or God) is no doubt a special kind of experience. It was given to Isaiah to see Jesus' 'glory' and to testify about it before Jesus came (12.42). And although 'no one has ever seen God' (1.18; 5.37; 6.46; cf. 1 John 4.12; 1 John 3.6; 3 John 1.11), the communal experience of the Johannine believers is grounded in having 'seen' Jesus' glory as the incarnate Logos (1.14; 1 John 1.1-2). Seeing Jesus' glory – seeing him 'lifted up' on the cross – inherently leads to the motivation to 'testify' [μαρτυρία]: 'he who saw it has testified' (19.35). Witnessing to what the community has 'seen' is a central element of the Johannine kerygma (cf. 1.34; 3.22; 20.18, 25; cf. 1 John 4.14), and it is tied up with intimate knowledge of Jesus and the Father (cf. 3.11; cf. 14.7). Jesus also 'bears witness' to what he has 'seen' at his Father's side: he speaks of what he sees (8.38) and does as he sees his Father doing (5.19). Sometimes, the Gospel gives the impression that 'seeing' Jesus in person is sufficient for the disciples to 'know' him and the Father (14.9; cf. 12.25; 9.37). 'Seeing' signs of Jesus' resurrection (20.5, 8) is, of course, causatively connected to belief, but belief can be motivated by 'hearing' the testimony of those who have already 'seen' (cf. 20.30-31; cf. 4.39). It is more sensible then, to understand the Johannine references to 'sight' and 'seeing' by way of close contextual analysis rather than lexical classification.

---

[136] Cf. Francis J. Moloney, *Johannine Studies: 1975–2017* (WUNT 372; Tübingen: Mohr Siebeck, 2017), p. 534.
[137] Thus Lee, 'The Gospel of John and the Five Senses', p. 117, n. 9.
[138] Koester, 'Hearing, Seeing and Believing', p. 335.

Another Johannine text links together the concepts of 'seeing' and 'rejoicing' (16.22), thus providing a close intratextual parallel to John 8.58 (where Abraham 'rejoiced' that he 'would see' Jesus' 'day'). In the parable of the woman in labour (16.20-22), the 'joy' of the metaphorical mother is projected into the future, following a necessary period of grief and tumultuous physical agony. This 'joy' is the mother's relief (she 'forgets her suffering') and thrill that a baby is born into the world. Like the mother 'seeing' her baby for the first time, the disciples will 'see' Jesus again, and their joy will be so great that no one will be able to dull it (16.21-22). Such 'seeing' has nothing to do with belief or testimony. It has to do with the heart's longing to be reunited with someone who has been taken away, with reconnection once again after a period of sorrow and grief. Jesus' 'return' to his disciples will occasion the type of 'joy' appropriate when celebrating the birth of a child (cf. the bridegroom metaphor in ch. 3 vv. 29-30). Seeing, in this case, is equated with relational experience, and with the creation of community against all odds, when all pain and sorrow have been removed. There is also, once again, the idea of rejoicing in the *prospect* of sight, of seeing something 'new' come into the world for the first time.

There is no one answer to the question, 'What is meant by seeing/sight in John's Gospel?' Seeing connotes the witnessing of physical realities, the cognitive dimension of knowing something deeply and the emotive aspect of committing to belief in something. When linked with the idea of 'joy', the concept of 'seeing' in John's Gospel touches on the realization of completion, of wholeness and of experiencing the risen Jesus in a way that overpowers all sorrow in the world. 'Seeing' is ultimately relational and leads to an outcome, whether to testify to what one has seen, or to rejoice, or to believe. To the figure of Abraham in ch. 8 vv. 56-58, Jesus appears to stand in a different relationship than the Jews; Jesus tells them 'your father Abraham *rejoiced* that he would see my Day' – Jesus is not so much Abraham's 'child' as someone to whom Abraham witnesses. He is 'before' and 'above' Abraham. And Abraham rejoices in the *prospect* of seeing Jesus' day, then rejoices again when he *has seen* it (8.57). Abraham's anticipation and response make him a characteristic 'witness' in the Gospel's Christology (like Moses in ch. 5 vv. 44-45 and Isaiah in ch. 12 v. 42), with a specific focus on rejoicing in Jesus' resurrection.

Part 3: Reading John 8.56-58 intertextually

In this final section, I summarize the findings of the chapter, focusing on the references to Abraham 'seeing' and 'rejoicing' in John 8.56-58, but also including other connotations, such as the association of Abraham with the prophets, and the age of Jesus relative to Abraham. As in Chapters 4 and 5, this summary will be concerned with 'scripting' the intertextual dimensions of the Jews' perspective, as their debate with Jesus heats up and reaches its conclusion in ch. 8 v. 59. Owing to the relative paucity of intertextuality relating to Abraham's 'joy' (or 'sight') within early Judaism, this chapter was shorter than the previous two, and structured rather differently, with the concepts of sight/vision and joy/rejoicing traced sequentially through the various literatures, ranging from the HB to the Tannaitic material.

The HB featured a few key narratives about Abraham that touched on these affective dimensions, that is his 'joy' and his inner/outer visions. These texts would spawn traditions that associated Abraham with direct revelations from God, and traditions about Abraham's enthusiasm and joy:

- Abraham's *dream vision* in Gen. 15.12 establishes the promise that he will bear a son and heir, that his *'seed' will go into slavery* in a foreign land but will return, and that Abraham will live a long life.
- Abraham *'sees'* (in the clear light of day) the three *angelic guests* at the Oaks of Mamre (Gen. 18.1-15) and *welcomes* them eagerly (implying a *response of joy*).
- Abraham the *mediator* speaks directly with God; he is able to *'see'* the peril in Sodom, so as to intercede for the city (Gen. 18.16-33). Abraham is *'prophet-like'* in his intercessory capacity and revelation-receptivity.
- Abraham responds to God's promise of a son with *laughter*. His response was interpreted in antiquity not as faithless incredulity but as *joy* (Gen. 17.17).

The post-biblical literature expanded upon these texts to include various new elements:

- Retellings of Genesis (*Jubilees* and *LAB*) added themes to the *dream vision* of Genesis 15, such as *Abraham's repudiation of idolatry* and his *fidelity to God's commandments*. Pseudo-Philo substituted the foretelling that Abraham's lineage would be enslaved in Egypt with the promise that Abraham's lineage would be populated by *prophets*.
- Abraham becomes the recipient of *secret nocturnal communications from God*, especially about the end times – Abraham is thus a *prophet* himself. God reveals himself as the eternal protector of Abraham's seed (*4 Ezra* 3.14-15).
- Abraham becomes an astrologer (cf. 'counting the stars', Gen. 15.21), with the *inner 'vision' to discern the mysteries* of the heavens, and ultimately, to come to the realization of the *One true God*.
- Abraham receives a customized tour of the heavens from the archangel Michael, *witnessing and judging* sinful human beings (*Testament of Abraham* 13–14).
- Abraham, Isaac and Jacob pray three times a day (cf. Jewish practice) interceding with mercy for their 'seed', with the gift of 'vision' to see the trouble of their seed from on high (T12P and *Apocalypse of Zephaniah*).
- Abraham *rejoices greatly* and initiates the festival of joy – *Sukkot*. Additionally, Abraham responds by praying for his future 'seed' that they not fall into 'sin' (*Jub.* 16.20-31).
- The three fathers can *see the future* fate of the demonic figure Beliar: the 'binding' of Beliar by the coming messianic figure leads *Abraham, Isaac and Jacob to 'rejoice'* (*T. Levi* 18.12)
- Abraham is commissioned by the angel Ioael and told to be *'filled with joy and courage'* because God has prepared an honour for him (*Apocalypse of Abraham* 10).
- Philo reads Abraham's 'laughter' in Gen. 17.17 as something very positive – a great *joy arising from his wisdom*.

The NT largely bypasses these mystical traditions about Abraham's ability to 'see' visions, instead refiguring the omniscient Abraham in the afterlife in rather more frightening terms:

- The 'bosom of Abraham' is a place of *repose* for the downtrodden and humble in the afterlife (Luke 16) and the eschatological 'banquet' is a place of *rejoicing* for those who are chosen; however, for those who do not believe, the alternative venue (towards which the three fathers have a directive role) is 'the outer darkness' (Matthew and Luke).
- These Synoptic parables with the three fathers are deeply polemical, warning unbelieving Jews that Abraham will be their *final judge* in the afterlife if they fail to believe even after Jesus' resurrection (Luke 16).
- Luke adds a detail missing in Matthew: the *prophets* will dine with the three fathers in the kingdom of heaven (13.28). Another striking feature of these texts is that they appear to espouse the *opposite* view of Abraham 'rejoicing' in the fate of another person (i.e. Jesus in John 8.56-58) – together with Isaac and Jacob, Abraham seems to be *complicit in the destruction of others* (cf. *Testament of Abraham* 13–14).

The rabbinic literature again takes the traditions in a unique direction:

- The Aramaic Targums develop Abraham's dream vision narrative (Gen. 15.12) to suggest that Abraham was '*seeing*' the emergence of Israel under the future *messianic redemption*.
- The Targum to Isaiah (on 43.10-12) introduces *God's disclosure of the future to Abraham* in the context of the Isaian Servant Song, to emphasize God's faithfulness in *redeeming Israel from slavery*.
- The *Targum Pseudo-Jonathan* depicts Abraham's awareness of his pure motivation to carry out God's decree (the Akedah) with *joy*; the same text includes his *intercession* on behalf of his *descendants*, that when they enter 'the hour of distress' God may '*remember*' them and '*redeem*' them.
- The *Mekhilta*'s take on this tradition emphasizes the *power of Abraham's joy* in fulfilling God's command: it undoes the wicked zeal of Pharaoh in violently chasing down the Hebrews at the sea. One 'harnessing [with joy]' undoes the wicked 'harnessing' (of Pharoah's chariot).
- The figure of speech, 'Happy are you, father Abraham [that this or that rabbi] descended from your loins!' indicates that Abraham is *aware of*, and *joyful about* his descendants' *Torah learning*.
- The Amoraic narrative of the man who is '*fifty years old*' and yet lacks the wisdom to refrain from purchasing an *idol from Terah*'s shop; Abraham rebukes him (*Gen. R.* 38.13).

We can observe a variety of traditions across a range of literatures and genres here. At first sight, there appears to be little consistency between these traditions. However, upon closer inspection, some common themes do emerge. For example, Abraham is frequently portrayed as an intercessor, especially for the well-being of his descendants. This motif, possibly expanding upon the narrative about Sodom in Gen. 18.16-33, can be found in the apocryphal and pseudepigraphical texts as well as the rabbinic texts. Likewise, the motif of God privileging Abraham with select revelations ('inner visions' we might call them) draws on the Genesis narratives about the promises to Abraham (15.12ff) as well as the Sodom narrative just mentioned. Sometimes, this motif is rather straightforwardly explained by God's love of Abraham and his fidelity to the covenant (as in *4 Ezra* 3.14), and other times the motif is expressed with fanciful, evocative elements, such as Abraham being 'tested' by God to prove whether he really is as perfect as he seems by riding a chariot in the heavens and 'seeing' how real human beings live (*Testament of Abraham* 1–14). Finally, the embellishments that some of these texts make to the Genesis texts is consistent in as much as they draw attention to Abraham's repudiation of idolatry, or his steadfast aniconism.

Another point worth noting is that Abraham's capacity to 'see' things (whether the future beyond his own lifetime, or the present world from his vantage point in the heavens) is commonly connected with the motif of Abraham as a *judge-type figure*. Of course, the *Testament of Abraham* provides us with a tongue-in-cheek version of this motif, with Abraham zapping sinners dead on the spot, only to be told by God that he has to learn the art of mercy. But other texts present a more sinister perspective. The Gospels of Matthew and Luke, for example, have Abraham, Isaac and Jacob rejoicing with believers in the afterlife, but casting out unbelievers to the netherworld where there is 'weeping and gnashing of teeth'. There is no comedic change of heart on Abraham's part in these parables. The *finality* of the judgement that Abraham oversees is also emphasized in the Gospel of Luke in his parable of Lazarus and the rich man (ch. 16). Even though the rich man pleads with Abraham, the latter of whom appears amenable enough, there is no chance for the dead rich man to repent and his fate cannot be changed (cf. Chapter 4 of this book, where we surveyed texts examining the question as to whether the dead could intercede for the living and vice versa). However, in the rabbinic literature, there is more of a focus on the future redemption that Abraham sees, whether in the messianic era, or the constancy of God's care in redeeming his people from slavery in Egypt. Also, Abraham's past actions (his pure joy in fulfilling the commandment of God at the Akedah) has permanent future benefits for his 'seed', for whom he intercedes *while* undertaking the divine command.

There are some texts in this selection that associate Abraham's 'seeing' with his 'joy', as we see in John 8.56-58. The narrative of Abraham 'seeing' the angelic/divine visitors at Mamre's Oaks contains allusions to joy, in as much as Abraham's eagerness to serve his visitors signifies a strong emotive response. *Jub.* 16.20-31 has Abraham 'rejoicing greatly' at the news of the conception of Isaac, which leads Abraham to initiate the festival of joy itself, namely Sukkot. And immediately following this, Abraham intercedes for his future 'seed' that they not fall into 'sin', as he continues to rejoice in the future emergence of a 'holy seed' from his loins. In *T. Levi* 18.12, the three fathers, from their place in heaven, can see the future fate of Beliar: the coming messianic figure will 'bind' Beliar, which, the text says, leads Abraham, Isaac and Jacob to 'rejoice' (a possible Christianization but nevertheless a parallel). The rabbinic motif of Abraham carrying out the command at the Akedah with 'pure joy' beautifully melds together several key concepts I have been analysing in this book – the efficacy of Abraham's 'works' (obedience to God's decree), Abraham's intercession on behalf of his 'seed' that they be redeemed from sin in times of distress and Abraham's capacity to 'see' the future troubles of his 'seed' (*Targum Pseudo-Jonathan* and *Mekhilta*). The affinity of Abraham's prayer with the rabbinic conceptions of the זכות אבות (cf. Chapter 4) is striking. Note that Abraham's *joy* is powerful enough to undo evil (not explicitly his works/merits, but his joy).

Returning now to John 8.56-58, we need to consider how these findings hold. Recall from the literature review in Chapter 1, a number of hypotheses were advanced about the 'background' texts to Abraham's 'seeing' and 'rejoicing', such as

- The Jewish traditions of the 'hidden messiah' as an explanatory cue for Jesus' ἐγώ εἰμί statement in John 8.24, 58 (E. D. Freed).
- The *Apocalypse of Abraham* as a 'close parallel' to John 8.56-58, with the angel Ioael functioning as a 'revealer-figure' after which John patterned his characterization of Jesus (J. Ashton).
- The book of *Jubilees* explaining the reference to Jesus being short of 'fifty years' in John 8.57, as the calendar of jubilees would measure the ages of the patriarchs (M. Edwards).
- A mixture of *Jub.* 16.26 (Abraham rejoicing and celebrating Sukkot, and seeing the future planting of a 'holy seed' that he will generate), and *Tg. Isa.* 43.10-12, where God (the text's speaker) 'interrupts' the prophecy of the 'Servant' to talk about giving Abraham revelations of the things to come (M. Coloe).
- Ps. 118.24 (MT; Ps. 117.24 LXX: 'this is the day the Lord has made, let us rejoice and be glad') as 'a partial background' to the reference of Abraham 'rejoicing' Jesus' 'day' in John 8.56 (A. Brunson).
- Gen. 15.1-17 is the most appropriate intertext, because the aorist of ὁράω in John 8.56 (ἴδῃ) points to a specific event during the narrated life of Abraham where Abraham has visions (C. Williams).

These suggestions have their strengths and weaknesses, as we noted in Chapter 1. None of them are 'incorrect' so to speak; in fact, all of them together make up the intertextual kaleidoscope of John 8.56-58. Often, the problem with previous scholarship is that it settles on one intertext to the exclusion of every other. Furthermore, in addition to the key verbs of 'seeing' and 'rejoicing', there are other connotations in John 8.56-58 that have resonances with the texts scripted in this chapter, such as Abraham's death (cf. *Testament of Abraham* 1–4 with Abraham belligerently refusing to die); the prophets' association with Abraham (cf. Luke 13.28, with the prophets dining with Abraham in the afterlife, or Pseudo-Philo recasting the patriarchal promise to mean Abraham will beget prophets); and Jesus' age in relation to Abraham (*Gen. R.* 38.13 with Abraham rebuking the man who was 'fifty years old' yet dense enough to purchase an idol). These intertexts weave with others that are not immediately related to them: thus, *Gen. R.* 38.13 teaches that 'fifty' should be an age of wisdom – idolatry is the greatest folly of all – and Abraham has the *nous* to discern the truth of the One God. This theme ties in with the post-biblical texts examined earlier in this chapter where Abraham discerns through his faculty of reason the truth of monotheism; and this is even further refracted through the connected motif of Abraham's joy, which arose from his great wisdom (Philo).

Many of the intertexts 'scripted' in this chapter have not yet been brought into conversation with John 8.56-58. The perspective of the Jews at this concluding stage of the discourse is increasingly cynical and embattled. Jesus' statements are becoming increasingly outlandish and provocative, thus the Jews remark, 'you are not yet fifty years old and yet you have seen Abraham? (8.57). The logic would be, 'You have not yet attained the age of wisdom' and yet you have seen (or been seen by) the wise patriarch? More pressingly, when considering the allusive undertones many of these intertexts have about Abraham's stringent rejection of idolatry, the Jews responses to Jesus' ἐγώ εἰμί statement in ch. 8 v. 58 makes sense from a Jewish perspective: Abraham and the prophets have died, yet Jesus claims that those who abide in his word will never 'see death' (8.52) – who then, does he claim to be, and why does he claim to pre-exist Abraham in such absolute terms? There is a sense of bitter irony: Jesus is making a claim to divine status somehow ('making himself a god', 10.32-33), invoking the figure of Abraham who fervently repudiated the idolatry of his father Terah, setting himself apart from his Chaldean environment. The two perspectives that Jesus and the Jews represent vis-à-vis Abraham are, by this point in the debate, intractably divided.

The 'voice' of the Jews in this final part of the pericope is often dismissed in the commentaries and scholarship as a 'misunderstanding' – Jesus says Abraham saw *him*, but the Jews think that Jesus said he saw *Abraham* (vv. 56-57). I think that is a little short-sighted. Many of the intertexts scripted in this chapter indicate that Abraham 'saw' the future prospects of his 'seed' or 'saw' future revelations of the end times, and that these visions were granted to him by God because of his unique status with God. For anyone else to 'see the great seer' as it were, would imply that person had a status exalted even above Abraham's own. The Jews ask how Jesus can claim to have 'seen' Abraham when, of all things, he is making what sound to be idolatrous claims about himself. The Johannine Jesus appropriates Jewish intertextual traditions about Abraham's joy and vision protecting his future seed from harm and distress, turning these intertexts around to position himself (or his 'day') as the object of Abraham's future vision and joy, in line with his assertions that he, not the Jews, is 'from God' (8.48-55). By the end of the pericope, Jesus' claim that the Jews wish to 'kill' him (vv. 38b, 40) becomes a self-fulfilling prophecy, as they take up stones to throw at him, but he hides and leaves the Temple (8.59). That is, by the end of the passage, the Jews' 'voice' has become totally obscured by the monologism of the Gospel's narrative design and point of view.

Finally – and perhaps consequently – the wider Johannine context was found in this case to resonate well with ch. 8 vv. 56-58, more so than the previous two sections ('seed of Abraham' and 'works of Abraham'). Themes of 'seeing' and 'rejoicing' are prominent in the Gospel and are often combined (16.22-24; 20.20 as well as 8.56-58), providing a strong intratext for the figure of Abraham in this passage. Both ch. 16 vv. 22-24 and ch. 20 v. 20 have the disciples rejoicing at the future (or realized) resurrected appearance of Jesus. The ideal 'joy' in the Gospel is a 'complete' joy, which is also a lasting joy, occasioned by the realization of something longed for and prospected.

All of these texts imply a physical seeing with the eyes *and* a 'seeing' of Jesus in his risen state, with the same verb used. From the analysis in the chapter, I concluded that Abraham 'saw' and 'rejoiced' in the risen Jesus, meaning that he is refigured as one of Jesus' witnesses and disciples, and ultimately subordinated to Jesus. Thus, the Gospel context explains John 8.56-58 well, but the intertexts also add depth and dimension to the tapestry. Importantly, the texts from within early Judaism that depict Abraham as an intermediary figure, 'seeing' and praying for the future of his descendants, or that position him as rejoicing in the Torah learning of his 'seed', or that remark upon the power of his joy to destabilize evil forces, all feed into the holistic, integrated tapestry I have been weaving throughout this book, recovering the legitimacy of the Jews' perspective about the efficacy of Abraham's 'works' in relation to what it means to be his 'seed'.

Conclusion

For the Jewish reader, John 8 is neither an easy nor a pleasant text to interpret. For many other readers, perhaps those who already subscribe to its Christology, the Gospel can indeed be a text of *plaisir*, but for those who do not, it can be a text of *jouissance* – an unsettling text, a text that mingles pleasure with pain (Barthes). John 8 is a text that demonstrates *doxa* in abundance, a monologic voice that overrides and 'others' the perspectives of the Jews. It is a text of *écrivance*: where the forceful ideology of 'the Author' speaks definitively, obscuring other voices with its violence, making it difficult for the 'birth of the reader' (Barthes) to come to pass. If *écrivance* is the language of power and 'truth', dictating only one path for the 'ideal' (compliant) reader to take, then the Gospel of John displays this clearly in ch. 8 vv. 31-59, with Jesus 'the Son' placed as the only means of 'freedom' from sin and to the inheritance of the 'household' (8.32-26), while those who do not 'abide' in his 'word' (vv. 31-32, 52) are slaves who do not belong (v. 36), and who will 'see death' (vv. 52-53). It is 'the Jews' of the text who fail to 'abide' in Jesus' word, and thus who bear the brunt of the text's violent *doxa*.

Even the most 'readerly' (*lisible*) texts – which Barthes theorizes, are filled with monologic 'doxa' – can have chinks in their armour, little gaps in the text that the reader can enter into to see which ways the text 'goes off' and disperses its meaning. The Gospel is strong in the proaretic (ACT) and hermeneutic (HER) codes that lock the reader into a contract of compliance ('This was written so that you may believe that Jesus is the Son of God', John 20.32-35). However, an 'intertextual' interpretation offers the reader the chance to 'reverse' the text, to open out the other 'codes' (SEM, SYM, REF) in conversation with a vast tapestry of other texts. This is the act of 'scripting' the text, turning the *lisible* 'work' into the *scriptable* ('writerly') text. From a Jewish perspective, this act has been called a 'resistant reading' (Reinhartz), with the purpose of recovering and reasserting the legitimacy of the Jews' voice in order to move them from Othered characters to empowered characters. Barthes would call this an assertion of the *para-doxa*: the act of challenging the *doxa* (which indeed, can already be in place within the text itself). This counter-approach need not be conceived of as a battle – for *para-doxa* challenges *doxa* all the time in the discursive development of culture. As we saw in Chapters 4 through 6, in the diachrony of intertextuality were constant debates challenging the status quo, whether that was by questioning the reality and validity of intergenerational intercession, the vicarious benefit of meritorious 'works' or the assumed superiority/exemplarity of Abraham.

Barthes reminds us that whether ideology is dominant (*doxa*) or resistant (*para-doxa*), as ideology it is always 'violent'. Because John's Gospel operates so heavily on binary dualisms, to take the 'opposite' pole (defending the voice of the Jews or undoing the 'othered' elements of his symbolic world) and to forcefully fight for its legitimacy is to do nothing more than to employ the same approach of monologism behind the implied author's drive for compliance. This is why nuanced heuristics are often supplied by scholars to address the complex dimensions of interpretation that take us beyond an either/or, 'us' and 'them' approach. Thus, Adele Reinhartz spoke also of a 'sympathetic reading' and an 'engaged reading' of the Fourth Gospel in addition to the face-value modes of 'compliance' or 'resistance' that the Gospel's dualism seems to invite.[1] Likewise, as we saw in Chapter 2, Barthes speaks of *jouissance* as a type of confrontation with the un-definitive, with our inability to fit things into neat categories, even with the loss of the subjective sense of self, a 'crisis' with language and identity. This crisis can arise from reading the text that dissolves and opens out into the 'intertextual', and which opens our minds in new directions.

By using the category of 'resistant reading' in this book, I am not attempting to counterpunch and de-legitimate the Gospel or its Christology. My own 'relationship' with the text of the Gospel is more complex than that, approximating to the *jouissance* that Barthes describes (pleasure and pain), otherwise I simply would not read it, much less write about it. Resistance is a creative dance; it ties in completely with my own subjectivity, with my own identity, as that is created and un-created over time – as Barthes says, '*I* read the text'. The intertext that I have 'scripted' is the 'text unbound'. It is an assertion of my own textuality (subjectivity) too. It is never neutral, but always personal and involved. From that standpoint, my identity as a Jewish reader and my commitment to Judaism are vital parts of what Smith called the 'articulate choice' of (intertextual) interpretation, the synchronic undertaking of reading John 8 together with other texts, and the choice of *which* particular texts I have examined.

Maybe I have a morbid fascination with vituperative language, discrimination and stereotypes. When I began to investigate John 8 many years ago, I imagined I would be probing the most notorious of its metaphors, that is the Jews as the children of 'the devil' (8.44), and that I would be looking forward through history for the *Wirkungsgeschichte* of this idea in Western Christendom. But when my initial research sent me to the Gospel commentaries I became acutely aware of a problem. There appeared to be more anti-Judaism (even classical tropes of anti-Semitism) reproduced in commentary on ch. 8 vv. 32-33 than on the infamous verse (8.44) about the Jews having the devil as their father. How could such a seemingly innocuous statement about the liberating power of 'truth' (8.31-32) and the counter-assertion of the Jews to be the 'seed of Abraham' (8.32) produce such negative reactions in the scholarship? What was going on here? Commentary is a strange genre: it carries a veneer of standardized authority as a supplemental source book to the Gospel. Yet, my analysis of the large volume of commentaries on John 8, from circa 1800 to 2012, led me to conclude that this genre is highly 'repetitive', that is, it recycles commentarial material from former commentators with an odd intertextuality of its own. Many of the anti-Jewish interpretations in the commentaries about the 'seed of Abraham' (e.g. Jewish nationalism, pride, prejudice, superiority, folly and evil) had roots in European Enlightenment thinking, especially in

---

[1] Reinhartz, *Befriending the Beloved Disciple*, pp. 99–159.

Germany's *Kaiserreich*, and these tropes continue to infiltrate modern commentaries even today, although the roots may be lost to contemporary commentators.[2]

At this point, I knew that it was important to understand the figure of Abraham in John 8.31-59, especially because the Jews' claim to be 'seed of Abraham' developed into discussions about Abraham's fatherhood and his 'works' (8.38-40), as well as his enigmatic vision of Jesus (8.56-58). My aim was to provide a holistic, intertextual reading of Abraham in John 8.31-59, from the Jews' perspective and in the context of the narrative setting of Sukkot. Too often, one of the metaphors associated with Abraham would be isolated from the rest in the secondary literature, and intertexts would be found to support that one metaphor without reference to the others. My purpose in this book was to argue for the coherency of the intertextual substructure about Abraham, especially to explain the Jews' claims to identity and their resistance to Jesus' claims in ways that would not pejoratively caricature them. This does not mean, of course, that there is a single *actual text* coherently linking the references to Abraham in John 8, as though John depended upon a definable 'source'. What it does mean is that, from my perspective as 'scriptor', we can postulate an integrative *texture* to what the Jews may be saying in John 8.31-59. To briefly summarize that here:

The Jews' express their collective identity as 'seed of Abraham' on the premise that they have never been slaves to anyone (8.32). Jesus replies that they are slaves because they commit sin (8.33-34). Intertextually, the Jews are not claiming 'nationalist' privileges (as the commentary traditions have it), but a covenant identity based on the promises made to Abraham in the Hebrew Bible (HB). Discursively, these biblical promises developed in different directions in the late-biblical and post-biblical era, emphasizing God's unconditional love and help for Abraham's 'seed' in times of oppression; portraying Abraham himself as cognizant of, and actively interceding for, his 'seed' in the future (or his 'seed' on earth in the afterlife); in the testamentary genres, showing Abraham as passing on the 'inheritance' of the Torah to his 'seed' which would protect them from sin; developing the idea that Abraham's 'seed' are remembered for Abraham's sake because of his merit with God; and in the rabbinic literature, parabolic illustrations of how Abraham's 'seed' are purchased as God's slaves, meaning that they do not serve any other master.

In the HB were other texts (such as *Nehemiah* 9) that spoke of the exilic returnees 'sinning' (i.e. not keeping the Torah) and therefore being 'enslaved' to foreign nations. But, these same texts say, Abraham was chosen and loved by God and so were his 'seed'. It is incumbent upon Abraham's 'seed' to keep the Torah. Simultaneously, many texts would draw on passages such as Gen. 26.5 to portray Abraham as an exemplary keeper of the Torah. There were thought to be 'works of the commandments' (Torah) that were established in 'Abraham's time' (*2 Baruch* 57). Abraham himself had specific commandments that he wanted his progeny to obey (*Jubilees* 20–22). In Chapter 5,

---

[2] See my essay, Sheridan, 'Seed of Abraham, Slavery and Sin', p. 330. I rely here on Anders Gerdmar, *Roots of Theological Antisemitism: German Biblical Interpretation and the Jews, from Herder and Semler to Kittel and Bultmann* (SJHHC 20; Leiden: Brill, 2009), p. 275. Note that my essay also explores contemporary German commentaries that 'correct' the course of these interpretations by reading the Jews' assertion to be 'seed of Abraham' as a rightful claim to their unbreakable covenant with God.

I argued that the intertextual field about Abraham's 'works' (cf. John 8.39-40) could include reference to his observance of 'the works of the Torah' (its commandments) and/or to the constellation of Abraham's 'righteous' deeds (his hospitality, his gentleness, his virtue and piety) found in the traditions. Many intertexts develop the idea of Abraham as a source of merit or remembrance for his 'seed'. This intertextual reading illustrated how Abraham's 'works' create righteousness (or merit). Metaphorically, 'merit' is conceptualized as a form of 'credit' that wipes away the sin imputed to a person. Abraham's 'seed' draw upon this meritorious fund in times of need to remit the 'debt' of their sin, which is depicted in the intertexts as 'debt-bondage' (or a form of slavery).

The melding of traditions provides a fascinating reading of the debate between Jesus and the Jews: while late-biblical sources viewed 'slavery' and 'sin' as the result of not keeping Torah, many contemporaneous texts started to view Abraham as a keeper of the Torah, and (in some rarer texts) even as beyond the taint of sin. The 'seed' of Abraham were to follow the example of their father and to do the Torah. Abraham was at once an *exemplar* but also a source of merit because of his 'works'. Jesus enjoins the Jews to 'do the works of Abraham' if they are his children (8.39-40); that is, relying on Abraham's merits effects nothing if one does not perform Abraham's 'works'. Although Moses 'gave' the Jews 'the law', according to Jesus, 'not one of [them] keeps the law' (7.19-21). Abraham is portrayed by Jesus as the type who would welcome him as a truth-teller from God, unlike the Jews who seek to kill him (8.37, 40, 52-53). And while Jesus 'saved a life' – which is the 'law' that 'goes back to the Patriarchs [Abraham]' that the Jews reputedly do not keep (7.19-21), Abraham also 'saved a life' (cf. the Akedah), which is why Jesus tells the Jews to 'do' his 'works': keep the law, save a life – in this case, refrain from taking Jesus' life (vv. 37-59). The Jews and Jesus thus speak at cross-purposes.

A few conceptual developments within early Judaism can be detected here. One is what I described in Chapter 5 as the diachronic development of the concept of 'works' to gradually mean 'merits'; another is the זכת אבות – the 'merits of the fathers' which of course, is a distinctly rabbinic concept but which has antecedents in so much of the literature examined in this book; a third is the influence of the Aramaic language that created new metaphors for the way 'sin' was conceived as debt (slavery) and merit (whether personal or vicarious) was conceived as 'credit' that balanced out and remitted the debt of sin. The rabbis would expound upon how God had given Israel a 'copious' Torah filled with *mitzvoth* in order to confer upon them 'merit' (*m. Makkot* 23b). What makes Abraham, as a keeper of the Law, an intermediary source of merit for his seed? Doing the Law accumulates merit, which can benefit Abraham's descendants vicariously. So, it is possible that the traditions about Abraham as Torah observant segued with the idea of the 'merits of the fathers'.

I therefore postulated that 'the Jews' reflect on their identity as the 'seed of Abraham' so that *if* they were caught in the 'debt' of sin, they could draw on Abraham's '*works*' and the vicarious merits these works produced. The Johannine Jesus refutes this by saying that the Jews must actively imitate the 'works' of their father, and the Torah that 'goes back to Abraham' (7.19) is actually welcoming Jesus as the truth-teller from God rather than seeking to kill him (8.37-52). This debate is analogous to the larger conversation within early Judaism about the primacy of '*doing*' the works of the fathers/one's father/

the Law over that of *depending upon* the surplus of merits produced by the fathers/one's father/the Law.

The traditions about Abraham 'seeing' and 'rejoicing' (John 8.56-58) were not as disparately related to the 'seed of Abraham' (8.32) or the 'works of Abraham' (8.39-40) as one might assume at first glance. That Abraham had the capacity for preternatural vision was an idea often connected to his status as intermediary between God and humanity, which in turn relates to the fundamental presuppositions behind the idea of the זכת אבות – that is that the fathers are actively aware of their descendants and have a ready fund of merits on hand to help them. Early Judaism appeals to Abraham as interceding on behalf of his 'seed', and judging sinners. Abraham is a 'seer', one who is peculiarly close to, and chosen by God, and therefore uniquely positioned to receive interior or exterior 'visions' of things to come. Indeed, God reveals himself through visions to Abraham as the protector of Abraham's seed in an unbreakable covenant (*4 Ezra* 3.15). In this light, the Jews of John 8.31-36 legitimately assert that, through their covenantal and physical connection with Abraham their 'father', they have never been abandoned by God.[3]

Abraham's capacities for discernment (his inner 'visions') also tie into the traditions examined in Chapter 5 of Abraham as the exemplary, first monotheist. There are also texts that connect the fathers' 'joy' with their capacity to 'see' the future. Some apocryphal material has Abraham 'seeing' his seed from heaven and interceding for his progeny thrice daily. The Targums and Tannaitic midrashim depict Abraham carrying out the commandments of God with 'pure joy' – especially the Akedah. Abraham's pure motives and his great joy were so powerful that they had redemptive consequences for Israel. Abraham is then given the capacity to foresee the fate of his 'seed' and he prays to God that they be 'redeemed in the hour of distress'. Likewise, at Sukkot, the festival of joy that Abraham initiates, his future 'holy seed' are protected by Abraham's prayers and offerings on their behalf that they be redeemed from their sin (*Jubilees* 16).

This integrative subtext makes sense of the three main parts of the pericope (8.31-37; 38-47; 48-59) as well as the eleven references to Abraham found therein. Of course, I am not simply claiming that the Jews of John 8 mouth the proto-rabbinic concept of the 'merits of the fathers' and that the Johannine Jesus disputes the idea by proffering the prevalent counterclaim of imitating one's 'father' instead. I am suggesting that the 'perspective' of the Jews in John 8.31-59 does fit within the broader conversation within early Judaism about Abraham as a figure of merit, but that this world view gets obscured by the Gospel's own Christocentric rhetoric.

Finally, the narrative context of Sukkot (John 7–8), and its intertextual resonances, provide context to ch. 8 vv. 31-59 as a thematically coherent textual unit. It is therefore important to read ch. 8 vv. 31-59 and the references to Abraham in light of this added intertextual layer. In Chapter 3 of this book, I showed how several key themes of the 'Sukkot intertext' that I 'scripted' were pertinent to my reading of John 8.31-59 (joy; repudiation of idolatry; sin, merit and mercy; the gift of water/rain; God's unconditional love for his people; and the learning of Torah).

---

[3] Siker, *Disinheriting the Jews*, p. 27.

The motif of joy at Sukkot (Lev. 23.33-43; Deut. 16.13-17; Neh. 8.14-18) is reworked in *Jubilees* with a focus on Abraham as the one who first celebrated Sukkot with profound joy. In *1 Esdras*, the motif of joy is centred upon observing the Torah at Sukkot, which can mitigate the divine punishment due to sin, irrespective of what one's ancestors may have done wrong. The motif of joy at Sukkot is critical to an appreciation of the reference to Abraham's 'joy' at seeing Jesus' day (8.58), because in the Johannine perspective whatever past reasons existed for celebrating Sukkot as a festival of joy are put aside as Abraham is now made to 'rejoice' in the prospect of Jesus' resurrection.

Monotheism and the repudiation of idolatry were significant motifs in the Sukkot intertext (cf. 1 Kgs 8.60 and in Zech. 14.16-19; *b. Sukk.* 51). Idolatry was a form of 'slavery' from which Israel was redeemed (see Chapter 4). At Sukkot, the Jews' assertion that they have never been slaves (John 8.32-33) can be read as their legitimate insistence upon fidelity to the Abrahamic covenant. The associated motifs of sin and divine judgement are also prevalent in the intertexts. The biblical texts already allude to this in the context of Sukkot (e.g. Zechariah 14 and the withholding of rain for disobedience), but in the rabbinic texts the rain is apportioned to the land to the degree in which the people have not strayed into sin – either that, or rain is provided as a blessing for the appropriate celebration of the Sukkot rituals. Either way, judgement takes place at Sukkot (*m. RH* 1.2). The medieval poetry of Eleazar ben Kalir develops this even further: rain is prayed for at Sukkot on the basis of the vicarious *merits of Abraham*, Isaac and Jacob, which rabbinic traditions described as being so powerful that they covered over the 'unpaid debts' (sins) of Israel and drew down the divine favour. God loved Abraham so much, according to this prayer, that he 'followed him like water'. In John 7.37-39, the water symbolism of Sukkot is centralized in Jesus' call for all who are 'thirsty' to 'drink' from the 'living water' that, the narrator tells us, will flow 'from his heart'. As such, the rain/water symbolism is not associated with Abraham in John 7–8. However, although Kalir's prayer is late, it speaks of Sukkot as an occasion to recall the merits of Abraham so that the sins of the penitents may be wiped clean – a motif I have drawn out in relation to the Jews' claim to be 'seed of Abraham' in ch. 8 v. 32. On the topic of judgement at Sukkot (cf. *m. RH* 1.2), it is important to note the juridical character of John's Sukkot discourse (7.1-8.59), especially how the Johannine Jesus appropriates the judgement motif so completely (cf. 8.23-25), centralizing divine judgement on belief in Jesus' origins and his destiny (see Chapter 3).

The provision of rain at Sukkot is also part of the third motif – that of God's protection and unconditional care for his people, which originated with the mandate to dwell in booths in order to commemorate God's protection in the wilderness (cf. Lev. 23.42-43; Zech. 14.16-19; *m. Sukk.* 4.10). God cares for Israel in this way *for the sake of* Abraham who sheltered his visitors at the Oaks of Mamre (Genesis 18; *Gen. R.* 48.10). Thus, Abraham is a welcome guest (the first of the Ushpizin) at every Sukkot festival. This motif coalesces with the trajectory of interpretation about Abraham's 'seed' that I traced in Chapter 4, originating in the post-exilic texts of the HB and continuing well into the post-biblical literature and the New Testament (NT), namely, God's unconditional love and help for Abraham's 'seed'. The idea of *welcoming* and sheltering guests at Sukkot (symbolized by the *sukka* itself) resonates with the debate in John 8.31-59, which unfolds along the lines of the Jews refusing to 'welcome' Jesus as a man sent from God (8.47-53). This is 'not what Abraham did' (8.40-41) according to Jesus, and thus the Jews are not imitating Abraham correctly as their 'father'.

Finally, the observance of Torah at Sukkot is an understudied theme that intersects with aspects of the argument presented in this book. For example, sin caused Israel to lose their land and go into exile, but renewed adherence to the Torah enabled a return to the land (1 Kgs 8). When Ezra reads the Torah at Sukkot, he counsels his listeners to *rejoice* in the words of the Torah and to not be sad, for they need fear no punishment if they are faithful to the Torah (Neh. 8.14-18). This deep intertexture provides context for my argument that the 'works' of Abraham (John 8.39-40) related to the traditions of his Torah observance, particularly given the Sukkot setting of the discourse. The Jews' claim to be 'free' as 'seed of Abraham' (8.32) reiterates the post-exilic understanding of fidelity to the Torah as intrinsically connected to the (re)inheritance of the Land, and the attenuation of sin. In ch. 8 vv. 34-36, Jesus upturns this allusive inference by telling that Jews that *because* they commit sin, they are 'slaves', due to receive nothing in the 'household' (inheritance), with their sin being the rejection of his person (8.32, 37, 52).

The figure of Abraham in John 8.31-59 has often perplexed scholars who find his sudden, concentrated appearance at this juncture of the Gospel curious, even difficult to explain. Abraham's association with the festival of Sukkot is not immediately apparent, but a deep intertextual engagement with the literature of antiquity has yielded rich insights into how Abraham is refigured in the Jewish traditions in ways that relate to the core themes explicated in my 'resistant' reading of John 8.31-59. In this book, I have drawn out the networked intertextuality of the concepts of 'seed', 'slavery' and 'sin' (John 8.32-33) in relation to Abraham and Jewish identity, and I have considered this network as part of a coherent structure of thought connecting the 'works' of Abraham (8.39-40), and Abraham's 'joy' and vision (8.56-58). In doing so, I have shown how nuanced and far-reaching are the connotations of these metaphors and concepts, which goes some way towards correcting the 'flat' and pejorative perspective on the Jews' words in ch. 8 vv. 31-59 that we still find, unfortunately, in many Gospel commentaries. The intertextual network that I 'scripted' hopefully undercuts the monologic *doxa* of John 8.31-59, breaking open the boundaries of the text, and legitimating the 'voice' of the Jews.

Bibliography

Primary sources

Colson, F. H. (ed. and trans.), *Philo, On the Special Laws II* (LCL 320; Cambridge, MA: Harvard University Press, 1937).
Colson, F. H. and G. H. Whitaker, *Philo* (Greek and English text) (10 vols; Cambridge, MA: Harvard University Press, 1929–62).
Danby, Michael (ed. and trans.), *The Mishnah* (New York: Oxford University Press, 1933).
Hammer, Reuven (ed. and trans.), *Sifre: A Tannaitic Commentary on the Book of Deuteronomy* (Yale Judaica Series; Yale: Yale University Press, 1987).
Josephus, *Against Apion* (trans. H. St. J. Thackeray; LCL 186; Cambridge, MA: Harvard University Press, 1926).
Josephus, *The Jewish War, Volume III: Books 5–7* (trans. H. St. J. Thackeray; LCL 210; Cambridge, MA: Harvard University Press, 1928).
Josephus, *Jewish Antiquities, Volume III: Books 7–8* (LCL 281; Cambridge, MA: Harvard University Press, 1934).
Josephus, *Jewish Antiquities, Volume I: Books 1–3* (trans. Ralph Marcus; LCL 242; Cambridge, MA: Harvard University Press, 1943).
Josephus, *Jewish Antiquities, Volume IX: Book 20* (LCL 365; Cambridge, MA: Harvard University Press, 1943).
Lauterbach, Jacob Z. (ed. and trans.), *Mekhilta de-Rabbi Ishmael* (2 vols; Nebraska: JPS and University of Nebraska Press, 2004).
Lust, John, Erik Eynikel and Katrin Hauspie (eds), *Greek-English Lexicon of Septuagint Greek* (rev. edn; Peabody, MA: Hendriksen, 2008; σπέρμα sv).
Marcus, Ralph, *Josephus, Jewish Antiquities Volume III: Books 7–8* (LCL 281; Harvard, MA: Harvard University Press, 1934).
Neslon, W. David (ed. and trans.), *Mekhilta de-Rabbi Shimon bar Yochai* (Nebraska: JPS, 2006).
Neusner, Jacob (ed. and trans.), *Sifre to Numbers* (2 vols; Atlanta, GA: Scholars Press, 1986).
Philo, *Allegorical Interpretation of Genesis 2 and 3* (Vol. 1; LCL 226; 1929).
Philo, *On the Account of the World's Creation* (Vol. 1; LCL 226; 1929).
Philo, *On the Birth of Abel* (Vol. 2; LCL 227; 1929).
Philo, *On the Posterity of Cain and His Exile* (Vol. 2; LCL 227; 1929).
Philo, *That the Worse Is Wont to Attack the Better* (Vol. 2; LCL 227; 1929).
Philo, *Concerning Noah's Work as Planter* (Vol. 3; LCL 247; 1930).
Philo, *On the Unchangeableness of God* (Vol. 3; LCL 247; 1930).
Philo, *On the Confusion of Tongues* (Vol. 4; LCL 261; 1932).
Philo, *On Moses (1 and 2)* (Vol. 6; LCL 289; 1935).
Philo, *On the Special Laws* (4 vols; LCL 320 [Books 1–3], 341 [Book 4]; 1937–1939).
Philo, *On Rewards and Punishments* (Vol. 8; LCL 314; 1939).
Philo, *Every Good Man Is Free* (Vol. 9; LCL 363; 1941).

Philo, *On the Eternity of the World* (Vol. 9; LCL 363; 1941).
Philo, *Questions on Genesis* (trans. Ralph Marcus; Vol. 10; LCL 380; Cambridge, MA: Harvard University Press, 1953).
Sacks, Jonathan, *The Koren Siddur, with Introduction, Translation and Commentary by Rabbi Sir Jonathan Sacks* (Jerusalem: Koren Publishers, 2009).
Thackeray, Henry St. John, *Josephus: The Jewish War, Volume I: Books 1-2* (LCL 203; Cambridge, MA: Harvard University Press, 1927).
Tuegels, Lieve (ed. and trans.), *Aggadat Bereishit* (JCPS 4; Leiden: Brill, 2001).

Commentaries

Barrett, Charles K., *The Gospel according to St John* (2nd edn; London: SPCK, 1978).
Beasley-Murray, George, *John* (2nd edn; WBC 36; Waco: Word Books, 1999).
Becker, Jürgen, *Das Evangelium nach Johannes* (ÖTKNT 4/1 and 4/2; 2 vols; Gütersloh-Würzburg: Mohn, 1985).
Bernard, John Henry, *A Critical and Exegetical Commentary on the Gospel according to St. John* (2 vols; ICC; Edinburgh: T&T Clark, 1928).
Betz, Hans Dieter, *Galatians* (Hermeneia; Minneapolis, MN: Fortress Press, 1989).
Blenkinsopp, Joseph, *Ezra-Nehemiah: A Commentary* (OTL; Philadelphia: Westminster Press, 1988).
Bright, John, *Jeremiah* (AB 21; New York: Doubleday, 1964).
Brodie, Thomas, *The Gospel according to John: A Literary and Theological Commentary* (New York: Oxford University Press, 1997).
Brown, Raymond E., *The Gospel according to John, I-XII* (AB 29; Garden City, NY: Doubleday, 1966).
Brueggemann, Walter, *A Commentary on Jeremiah: Exile and Homecoming* (Grand Rapids, MI: Eerdmans, 1998).
Brueggemann, Walter, *Isaiah 40-66* (Louisville, KY: Westminster/John Knox, 1998).
Bruner, Dale, *The Gospel of John: A Commentary* (Grand Rapids, MI: Eerdmans, 2012).
Bultmann, Rudolf, *Das Evangelium des Johannes* (KEK; Göttingen: Vandenhoeck & Ruprecht, 1941; English edition: *The Gospel of John: A Commentary*; trans. George Beasley-Murray et al.; Philadelphia: Westminster Press, 1971).
Bultmann, Rudolf, *The Gospel of John: A Commentary* (Louisville, KY: Westminster/John Knox, 1971).
Byrne, Brendan, *Romans* (SP 5; 2nd edn; Collegeville, MN: Liturgical Press, 2007).
Carroll, John T., *Luke: A Commentary* (Louisville, KY: Westminster John Knox Press, 2012).
Carson, Donald A., *The Gospel according to John* (Grand Rapids, MI: Eerdmans, 1991).
Clifford, Richard J., *Proverbs: A Commentary* (OTL; Louisville, KY/London: WJK Press, 1999).
Craigie, Peter C., *The Book of Deuteronomy* (NICOT; Grand Rapids, MI: Eerdmans, 1976).
Croy, N. Clayton, *3 Maccabees* (SCS; Boston, MA: Brill, 2006).
Dale Bruner, Frederick, *The Gospel of John: A Commentary* (Grand Rapids, MI: Eerdmans, 2012).
de Boer, Martinus C., *Galatians* (Louisville, KY: Westminster John Knox Press, 2011).

Dietzfelbinger, Christian, *Das Evangelium nach Johannes* (2 vols; ZBK, Zürich: Theologischer Verlag, 2001).
Dunn, James D. G., *The Epistle to the Galatians* (London: A&C Black, 1993).
Dunn, James D. G., *Romans 9-16* (WBC 38b; San Antonio, TX: Word Press, 1988).
Ellis, Peter F., *The Genius of John: A Composition-Critical Commentary on the Fourth Gospel* (Collegevile, MN: Liturgical Press, 1984).
Fox, Michael V., *Proverbs 10-31: A New Translation with Introduction and Commentary* (AB 18b; New Haven: Yale University Press, 2009).
France, Richard T., *The Gospel of Matthew* (NICNT; Grand Rapids, MI: Eerdmans, 2007).
Fung, Ronald Y. K., *The Epistle to the Galatians* (Grand Rapids, MI: Eerdmans, 1988).
Green, Joel B., *The Gospel of Luke* (NICNT; Grand Rapids, MI: Eerdmans, 1997).
Gunkel, Hermann, *Genesis* (trans. Mark E. Biddle, 3rd edn; Macon, GA: Mercer University Press, 1997).
Haenchen, Ernst, *John: A Commentary on the Gospel of John* (trans. and ed. Robert W. Funk; 2 vols; Hermeneia; Philadelphia, PA: Fortress Press, 1984).
Hamilton, Victor P., *Genesis 1-17* (NICOT; Grand Rapids, MI: Eerdmans, 2001).
Harris, Murray J., *The Second Epistle to the Corinthians: A Commentary on the Greek Text* (NICNT; Grand Rapids, MI: Eerdmans, 2005).
Hengstenberg, Ernst, *Über den Eingang des Evangeliums St. Johannis* (Berlin: Schlawitz, 1859).
Hoskyns, Edwyn C., *The Fourth Gospel* (ed. Francis N. Davey; London: Faber & Faber, 1947).
Johnson, Luke Timothy, *Luke* (SP3; Collegeville, MN: Liturgical Press, 1991).
Keener, Craig S., *A Commentary on the Gospel of Matthew* (Grand Rapids, MI: Eerdmans, 1999).
Keener, Craig S., *The Gospel of John: A Commentary* (Vol. 1; Grand Rapids, MI: Baker, 2003).
Lieu, Judith M., *I, II & III John, A Commentary* (Louisville, KY: Westminster/John Knox, 2008).
Lincoln, Andrew, *The Gospel according to John* (Black's New Testament Commentary 4; London: Continuum, 2005).
Lindars, Barnabas, *The Gospel of John* (NCBC; London: Oliphants, 1972).
Longenecker, Richard, *Galatians* (WBC 41; San Antonio, TX: Zondervan, 2015).
Malina, Bruce and Richard Rohrbaugh, *Social Science Commentary on the Gospel of John* (Minneapolis, MN: Fortress Press, 1998).
Martin, Ralph P., *James* (WBC 48; Dallas, TX: Word, 1988).
Martyn, J. Louis, *Galatians* (New York: Yale University Press, 2004).
Matera, Frank J., *Galatians* (Collegeville, MN: Liturgical Press, 1992).
Mays, James Luther, *Micah: A Commentary* (OTL; Philadelphia, PA: Westminster Press, 1976).
Meyers, Carol L. and Eric M. Meyers, *Zechariah 9-14* (AB 25C; New York: Doubleday, 1998).
Michaels, J. Ramsey, *The Gospel of John* (Grand Rapids, MI: Eerdmans, 2010).
Moloney, Francis J., *John* (SP 4; Collegeville, MN: Liturgical Press, 1998).
Moloney, Francis J., *Signs and Shadows: Reading John 5-12* (Minneapolis, MN: Fortress Press, 1996).
Moo, Douglas J., *The Epistle to the Romans* (Grand Rapids, MI: Eerdmans, 1996).
Morris, Leon, *The Gospel according to John* (Grand Rapids, MI: Eerdmans, 1971).
Painter, John, *1, 2 and 3 John* (SP 18; Collegeville, MN: Liturgical Press, 2002).

Paul, Shalom M., *Isaiah 40-66: A Commentary* (Grand Rapids, MI: Eerdmans, 2012).
Ridderbos, Herman. *The Gospel of John: A Theological Commentary* (Grand Rapids, MI: Eerdmans, 1997).
Schnackenburg, Rudolf, *The Gospel according to St. John* (trans. K. Smyth et al., Vol. 2; Herder's Theological Commentary on the New Testament; London: Burns & Oates, 1978).
Schnackenburg, Rudolf, *The Gospel according to St. John. Volume 2 – Commentary on Chapters 5-12* (London: Burns & Oates, 1980).
Theobald, Michael, *Das Evangelium nach Johannes: Kapitel 1-12* (RNT; Regensburg: Friedrich Pustet, 2009).
Thyen, Hartwig, *Das Johannesevangelium* (HNT 6; Tübingen: Mohr Siebeck, 2005).
Wenham, Gordon J., *Genesis 1-15* (Waco, TX: WBC, 1986).
Westcott, Brooke Foss, *The Gospel according to St. John* (London: John Murray, 1892).
Westermann, Claus, *Genesis 37-50* (Neukirchen-Vluyn: Neukirchener, 1981).
Westermann, Claus, *Isaiah 40-66* (trans. David M. G. Stalker; OTL 19; Philadelphia, PA: Westminster Press, 1969).
Williamson, Hugh G. M., *1 and 2 Chronicles* (NCBC; Eugene, OR: Wipf & Stock, 2010).

Secondary sources

Abasciano, Brian J., *Paul's Use of the Old Testament in Romans 9.1-9: An Intertextual and Theological Exegesis* (LNTS 317; London: T&T Clark, 2005).
Abegg, Martin, '4QMMT C 27, 31 and "Works Righteousness"', *DSS* 6, no. 2 (1999), pp. 139-47.
Abegg, Martin, 'Paul, Works of the Law, and the MMT', *BARev* 20, no. 6 (1994), pp. 52-5.
Abraham, Benjamin Schliesser, 'Did Not "Doubt" in Unbelief (Rom 4.20): Faith, Doubt, and Dispute in Paul's Letter to the Romans', *JTS* 63, no. 2 (2012), pp. 492-522.
Abusch, Ra'anan S., 'Rabbi Ishmael's Miraculous Conception: Jewish Redemption History in Anti-Christian Polemic', in Adam H. Becker and Annette Yoshiko Reed (eds), *The Ways That Never Parted: Jews and Christians in Late Antiquity and the Early Middle Ages* (TSAJ 96; Tübingen: Mohr Siebeck, 2003), pp. 307-44.
Adams, Edward, 'Abraham's Faith and Gentile Disobedience: Textual Links between Romans 1 and 4', *JSNT* 65 (1997), pp. 47-66.
Aichele, George, Peter Miscall and Richard Walsh, 'An Elephant in the Room: Historical-Critical and Postmodern Interpretations of the Bible', *JBL* 128, no. 2 (2008), pp. 383-404.
Alexander, Desmond, 'Genesis 22 and the Covenant of Circumcision', *JSOT* 25 (1983), pp. 17-22.
Allen, Garrick, *The Book of Revelation and Early Jewish Textual Culture* (SNTSMS 168; Cambridge: Cambridge University Press, 2017).
Allen, Graham, *Barthes* (Routledge Critical Thinkers; Abingdon: Routledge, 2003).
Allen, Graham, *Intertextuality* (London/New York: Routledge, 2000).
Allison, Dale C., 'Job in the *Testament of Abraham*', *JSP* 12, no. 2 (2001), pp. 131-47.
Allison, Dale C., *The Testament of Abraham* (Berlin: de Gruyter, 2003).
Alter, Robert, *The Book of Psalms: A Translation with Commentary* (New York: W. W. Norton & Company, 2007).

Anbar, Moshe, 'Genesis 15: A Conflation of Two Deuteronomic Narratives', *JBL* 101, no. 1 (1982), pp. 39-55.
Anderson, Bernard W., 'Exodus Typology in Second Isaiah', in B. Anderson and W. Harrelson (eds), *Israel's Prophetic Heritage: Essays in Honor of James Muilenberg* (New York: Harper & Brothers, 1962), pp. 177-95.
Anderson, Gary A., *Charity: The Place of the Poor in the Biblical Tradition* (New Haven, CT: Yale University Press, 2013).
Anderson, Gary A., *Sin: A History* (New Haven: Yale University Press, 2009).
Anderson, Gary A., 'The Status of the Torah before Sinai: The Retelling of the Bible in the Damascus Covenant and the Book of Jubilees', *DSD* 1 (1994), pp. 1-29.
Anderson, H., '3 Maccabees', in James H. Charlesworth (ed.), *The Old Testament Pseudepigrapha, Volume 2* (Peabody, MA: Hendrickson, 2010), p. 512.
Anderson, Paul N., *The Christology of the Fourth Gospel: Its Unity and Disunity in the Light of John 6* (WUNT 2.77; Tübingen: Mohr Siebeck, 1995).
Angermuller, Johannes, *Poststructuralist Discourse Analysis: Subjectivity in Enunciative Pragmatics* (London: Palgrave Macmillan, 2014).
Ashton, John, *Understanding the Fourth Gospel* (Oxford: Clarendon, 1991).
Ashton, John, 'Second Thoughts on the Fourth Gospel', in Tom Thatcher (ed.), *What We Have Heard From the Beginning: The Past, Present and Future of Johannine Studies* (Waco, TX: Baylor University Press, 2007), pp. 1-18.
Asiedu-Peprah, Martin, *Johannine Sabbath Conflicts as Juridical Controversy: An Exegetical Study of John 5 and 9.1-10.21* (WUNT 2.132; Tübingen: Mohr Siebeck, 2001).
Attridge, Harold W., 'Genre', in Douglas Estes and Ruth Sheridan (eds), *How John Works: Storytelling in the Fourth Gospel* (RBS 86; Atlanta, GA: SBL Press, 2016), pp. 7-22.
Attridge, Harold W., 'God in Hebrews', in Richard Bauckham et al. (eds), *The Epistle to the Hebrew and Christian Theology* (Grand Rapids, MI: Eerdmans, 2009), pp. 95-110.
Attridge, Harold W., *The Interpretation of Biblical History in the Antiquitates Judaicae of Flavius Josephus* (Missoula, MT: Scholars Press, 1976).
Attridge, Harold W., 'Thematic Development and Source Elaboration in John 7.1-36', *CBQ* 42 (1980), pp. 160-70.
Aune, David E., *Revelation 1-5* (WBC 52A; Dallas, TX: Word, 1997).
Avalos, Hector, *The End of Biblical Studies* (Buffalo, NY: Prometheus, 2007).
Avioz, Michael, 'Josephus's Portrayal of Lot and His Family', *JSP* 16, no. 1 (2006), pp. 3-13.
Bachmann, Michael, '4QMMT und Galaterbrief, התורה מעשי und ΕΡΓΑ ΝΟΜΟΥ', *ZNW* 89 (1998), pp. 91-113.
Baden, Joel, 'The Morpho-Syntax of Genesis 12.1-3: Translation and Interpretation', *CBQ* 72, no. 2 (2010), pp. 223-37.
Baden, Joel, *The Promise to the Patriarchs* (New York/Oxford: Oxford University Press, 2013).
Bakhtin, Mikhail, *Problems of Dostoyevsky's Poetics* (trans. and ed. C. Emerson; Minneapolis, MN: University of Minnesota Press, 1984).
Baldensperger, Wilhelm, *Der Prolog des vierten Evangeliums. Sein polemischapologetischer Zweck* (Tübingen: J.C.B. Mohr, 1898).
Ball, David, *'I Am' in John's Gospel: Literary Function, Background and Theological Implications* (JSNTSupp 124; Sheffield: Sheffield Academic Press, 1996).
Balla, Ibolya, *Ben Sira on Family, Gender, and Sexuality* (Berlin: Walter de Gruyter, 2011).
Bar-Asher Siegal, Michal, 'Shared Worlds: Rabbinic and Monastic Literature', *HTR* 105 (2012), pp. 423-56.

Barclay, John M. G., 'Mirror-Reading a Polemical Letter: Galatians as a Test Case', *JSNT* 31 (1987), pp. 73–93.
Barr, James, *The Semantics of Biblical Language* (New York: Oxford, 1961).
Barrett, K., *Acts: Volume 1, 1–14* (ICCNT; London: T&T Clark, 1994).
Barstad, Hans M., *A Way in the Wilderness: The 'Second Exodus' in the Message of Second Isaiah* (JJS 12; Manchester: University of Manchester Press, 1989).
Barthes, Roland, 'The Death of the Author', in *Image-Music-Text* (ed. and trans. Stephen Heath; New York: Hill and Wang, 1977), pp. 142–8.
Barthes, Roland, *Elements of Semiology* (trans. Annette Lavers and Colin Smith; New York: Hill and Wang, 1964).
Barthes, Roland, 'From Work to Text', in Roland Barthes (ed.), *The Rustle of Language* (trans. Richard Howard; Berkeley and Los Angeles, CA: California of University Press, 1989), pp. 56–64.
Barthes, Roland, *The Grain of the Voice: Interviews 1962–1980* (trans. Linda Coverdale; Evanston, IL: Northwestern University Press, 1981).
Barthes, Roland, *Mythologies* (trans. Annette Lavers; New York: Hill and Wang, 1972).
Barthes, Roland, 'On Reading', in Roland Barthes (ed.), *The Rustle of Language* (trans. Richard Howard; Berkeley and Los Angeles: University of California Press, 1986), pp. 32–43.
Barthes, Roland, *The Pleasure of the Text* (trans. Richard Miller; New York: Hill and Wang, 1975), p. 32.
Barthes, Roland, *Roland Barthes by Roland Barthes* (trans. Richard Howard; London: Macmillan, 1977).
Barthes, Roland, *S/Z* (trans. Richard Miller; New York: Hill and Wang, 1970).
Barthes, Roland, *The Semiotic Challenge* (trans. Richard Howard; Oxford: Blackwell, 1988).
Barthes, Roland, 'Theory of the Text', in Robert Young (ed.), *Untying the Text: A Poststructuralist Reader* (London: Routledge and Kegan Paul, 1981), pp. 31–47.
Barton, John, *Ethics in Ancient Israel* (Oxford: Oxford University Press, 2014).
Barton, John, *Reading the Old Testament: Method in Biblical Studies* (rev. edn; Louisville, KY: Westminster/John Knox, 1996).
Bassnet, Susan, 'Influence and Intertextuality: A Reappraisal', *Forum for Modern Language Studies* 43, no. 2 (2007), pp. 134–46.
Bauckham, Richard, 'The Apocalypses in the New Pseudepigrapha', *JSNT* 26 (1986), pp. 97–117.
Bauckham, Richard (ed.), *The Gospels for All Christians: Rethinking the Gospel Audiences* (Grand Rapids, MI: Eerdmans, 1998).
Bauckham, Richard, 'Is There Patristic Counter-Evidence? A Response to Margaret Mitchell', in Richard Bauckham (ed.), *The Christian World around the New Testament: Collected Essays II* (WUNT 2.386; Tübingen: Mohr Siebeck, 2017), pp. 41–80.
Baumgardt, David, 'Man's Morals and God's Will: The Meaning of Abraham's Sacrifice', *Commentary* 10 (1950), pp. 244–51.
Baynes, Leslie, 'The Parables of Enoch and Luke's Parable of the Rich Man and Lazarus', in Loren T. Stuckenbruck and Gabriele Boccaccini (eds), *Enoch and the Synoptic Gospels: Reminiscences, Allusions, Intertextuality* (Atlanta, GA: SBL Press, 2016), pp. 129–54.
Beach, Bradley and Matthew Powell (eds), *Interpreting Abraham: Journeys to Moriah* (Minneapolis, MN: Fortress Press, 2014).
Beal, Timothy K. 'Ideology and Intertextuality: Surplus of Meaning and Controlling the Means of Production', in Danna Nolan Fewell (ed.), *Reading between Texts:*

Intertextuality and the Hebrew Bible (Louisville, KY: Westminster/John Knox Press, 1992), pp. 27-40.

Beasley-Murray, George R., *The Book of Revelation* (NBC, rev. edn; Grand Rapids, MI: Eerdmans, 1981).

Becker, Adam H. and Annette Yoshiko Reed (eds), *The Ways That Never Parted: Jews and Christians in Late Antiquity and the Early Middle Ages* (Philadelphia, PA: Fortress Press, 2007).

Becker, Jürgen, *Untersuchungen zur Entstehungsgeschichte der Testament der zwölf Patriarchen* (Leiden: Brill, 1970).

Beentjes, Pancratius C., 'Tradition and Transformation Aspects of Innerbiblical Interpretation in 2 Chronicles 20', *Bib* 74, no. 2 (1993), pp. 258-68.

Beers, Bernhard, *Leben Abrahams* (Leipzig: Oskar Leiner, 1859).

Begg, Christopher, 'Jotham and Amon: Two Minor Kings of Judah according to Josephus', *BBR* 6 (1996), pp. 1-13.

Benjamin, Michael, '*Paulus als Yishmaelit?* The Personification of Scripture as Interpretive Authority in Paul and the School of Rabbi Ishamel', *JBL* 135, no. 3 (2016), pp. 617-37.

Bennema, Cornelis, *Encountering Jesus: Character Studies in the Gospel of John* (Colorado Springs, CO: Paternoster, 2009).

Ben Zvi, Ehud, 'The Dialogue between Abraham and YHWH in Gen 18.23-32: A Historical Analysis', *JSOT* 53 (1992), pp. 27-46.

Berger, Klaus, 'Abraham in den paulischen Hauptbriefen', *MTZ* 17 (1966), pp. 47-89.

Berger, Michael S., *Rabbinic Authority* (New York: Oxford University Press, 2014).

Berkley, Timothy, *From a Broken Covenant to Circumcision of the Heart: Intertextual Exegesis in Romans 2.17-29* (SBLDS 175; Atlanta, GA: SBL Press, 2000).

Betz, Hans-Dieter, *The Sermon on the Mount: A Commentary on the Sermon on the Mount, including the Sermon on the Plain (Matthew 5.3-7.27 and Luke 6.20-49* (Hermeneia; Minneapolis, MN: Fortress Press, 1995).

Beutler, Johannes, 'The Structure of John 6', in R. Alan Culpepper (ed.), *Critical Readings of John 6* (Leiden: Brill, 1997), pp. 115-28.

Biddle, Mark, 'The Literary Frame Surrounding Jeremiah 30.1-33.26', *ZAW* 100, no. 2 (1988), p. 409.

Bieringer, Reimund, Didier Pollefeyt and Frederique Vandecasteele-Vanneuville, 'Wrestling with Johannine Anti-Judaism: A Hermeneutical Framework for the Current Debate', in Reimund Bieringer, Didier Pollefeyt and Frederique Vandecasteele-Vanneuville (eds), *Anti-Judaism and the Fourth Gospel* (Louisville: Westminster/John Knox, 2001), pp. 3-37.

Bikerman, Elias J., 'Couper une alliance', *Archies d'Histoire du droit Oriental* 5 (1950/51), pp. 133-56.

Billerbeck, Paul, 'Abrahams Leben und Beduetung nach Auffassung der älteren Haggada', *Nathanael* 15 (1899), pp. 43-57, 118-28, 137-57, 161-79; *Nathanael* 16 (1900), pp. 33-57, 65-80.

Black, M., *An Aramaic Approach to the Gospels and Acts* (3rd edn; Oxford: Oxford University Press, 1967).

Boase, Elizabeth, 'Life in the Shadows: The Role and Function of Isaac in Genesis: Synchronic and Diachronic Readings', *VT* 51, no. 3 (2001), pp. 312-35.

Bock, Darrell L., *Acts* (Grand Rapids, MI: Baker Academic, 2007).

Bockhmuehl, Markus, 'Abraham's Faith in Hebrews 11', in Bauckham et al. (eds), *The Epistle to the Hebrews and Christian Theology* (Grand Rapids, MI: Eerdman, 2009), pp. 364-73.

Boda, Mark J., *Praying the Tradition: The Origin and Use of Tradition in Nehemiah 9* (BZAW; Berlin: de Gruyter, 1999).

Boda, Mark J., 'The Priceless Gain of Penitence: From Communal Lament to Penitential Prayer in the "Exilic" Liturgy of Israel', *HBT* 25, no. 1 (2003), pp. 51–75.

Boda, Mark J., *Severe Mercy: Sin and Its Remedy in the Old Testament* (Winona Lake, IN: Eisenbrauns, 2014).

Bogaert, Pierre Maurice, *Abraham dans la Bible et dans la tradition juive* (Brussels: Institutum Iudaicum, 1977).

Bogaert, Pierre Maurice, 'La figure d'Abraham dans les Antiquités Bibliques du Pseudo-Philon', in Pierre-Maurice Bogaert (ed.), *Abraham dans la Bible et dans la tradition juive* (Brussels: Institutum Iudaicum, 1977), pp. 40–55.

Boismard, Marie-Emile, 'De son ventre coulerant des fleuves d'eau (Jo. VII, 38)', *RB* 65 (1958), pp. 536–8.

Bowker, John, *The Targums and Rabbinic Literature* (Cambridge: Cambridge University Press, 1969).

Boyarin, Daniel, *Borderlines: The Partition of Judaeo-Christianity* (Philadelphia, PA: University of Pennsylvania Press, 2004).

Boyarin, Daniel, 'Daniel 7, Intertextuality, and the History of Israel's Cult', *HTR* 105, no. 2 (2012), pp. 144–5.

Boyarin, Daniel, *Intertextuality and the Reading of Midrash* (Bloomington, IN: Indiana University Press, 1990).

Boyarin, Daniel, 'Rethinking Jewish Christianity: An Argument for Dismantling a Dubious Category', *JQR* 99, no. 1 (2007), pp. 7–36.

Brady, Christian M. M., 'What Shall We Remember, the Deeds of the Faith of Our Ancestors? A Comparison of 1 Maccabees 2 and Hebrews 11', in Alan J. Avery-Peck, Craig A. Evans and Jacob Neusner (eds), *Earliest Christianity within the Boundaries of Judaism* (Leiden/Boston: Brill, 2016), pp. 107–19.

Brant, Jo-Ann, *Dialogue and Drama: Elements of Greek Tragedy in the Fourth Gospel* (Peabody, MA: Hendrickson, 2004).

Brettler, Marc Zvi, 'Incompatible Metaphors for Yhwh in Isaiah 40–66', *JSOT* 78 (1998), pp. 97–120.

Brettler, Marc Zvi, 'The Riddle of Psalm 111', in Deborah A. Green and Laura S. Lieber (eds), *Scriptural Exegesis: The Shapes of Culture and the Religious Imagination: Essays in Honour of Michael Fishbane* (New York/Oxford: Oxford University Press, 2009), pp. 62–73.

Brodie, Thomas L., *The Birthing of the New Testament: The Intertextual Development of the New Testament Writings* (Sheffield: Phoenix Press, 2004).

Brooke, George J., 'Commentary on Genesis C', in George J. Brooke et al. (eds), *Qumran Cave 4.XVII: Parabiblical Texts, Part 3* (DJD 22; Oxford: Oxford University Press, 1996).

Brooke, George J., 'Psalms 105–106 at Qumran', *RevQ* 14, no. 2 (1989), pp. 267–92.

Brown, Jeannine K., 'Creation's Renewal in the Gospel of John', *CBQ* 72 (2010), pp. 275–90.

Brown, Raymond E. *The Community of the Beloved Disciple* (New York: Paulist Press, 1977).

Bruce, Frederick F., *The Epistle to the Hebrews* (NICNT; rev. edn; Grand Rapids, MI: Eerdmans, 1990).

Bruce, Frederick F., *The Gospel of John: Introduction, Exposition, Notes* (Grand Rapid, MI: Eerdmans, 1994), p. 233.

Bruckner, James K., *Implied Law in the Abraham Narrative: A Literary and Theological Analysis* (JSOTSup335; Sheffield: Sheffield Academic Press, 2001).

Brunson, Andrew C., *Psalm 118 in the Gospel of John: An Intertextual Study on the New Exodus Pattern in the Theology of John* (WUNT 2.158; Tübingen: Mohr Siebeck, 2003).

Buisch, Pauline P., 'The Absence and Influence of Genesis 48 (the Blessing of Ephraim and Manasseh) in the *Book of Jubilees*', *JSP* 24, no. 4 (2017), pp. 255–73.

Bultmann, Rudolph, 'Die Bedeutung der Eschatologie für der Religion des neuen Testaments', *ZThK* 27 (1917), pp. 85–6.

Byrne, Brendan, 'Jerusalems Above and Below: A Critique of J. L. Martyn's Interpretation of the Hagar-Sarah Allegory in Gal 4.21–5.1', *NTS* 60 (2014), pp. 215–31.

Byrne, Brendan, 'The Problem of ΝΟΜΟΣ and the Relationship with Judaism in Romans', *CBQ* 62 (2000), pp. 294–309.

Byron, John, *Cain and Abel in Text and Tradition: Jewish and Christian Traditions of the First Sibling Rivalry* (Leiden: Brill, 2011).

Byun, Seulgi L., *The Influence of Post-Biblical Hebrew and Aramaic on the Translator of Septuagint Isaiah* (LHB/OTS 635; London: T&T Clark/Bloomsbury, 2017).

Callan, Terrance, 'The Soteriology of the Second Letter of Peter', *Bib* 82 (2001), pp. 549–59.

Calvert-Koyzis, Nancy, *Paul, Monotheism and the People of God: The Significance of Abraham Traditions for Early Judaism and Christianity* (JSNTSup 273; London: T&T Clark, 2004).

Campbell, Douglas, *The Deliverance of God: An Apocalyptic Rereading of Justification in Paul* (Grand Rapids, MI: Eerdmans, 2009).

Campbell, Lyle, 'The History of Linguistics', in Mark Aronoff and Janie Rees-Miller (eds), *The Handbook of Linguistics* (Oxford: Wiley-Blackwell, 2002), pp. 81–104.

Carmichael, Calum M., 'Forbidden Mixtures', *VT* 32 (1982), pp. 394–415.

Carmichael, Calum M., 'Marriage and the Samaritan Woman', *NTS* 26, no. 3 (1980), pp. 332–46.

Carroll, John T., Charles H. Cosgrove and E. Elizabeth Johnson (eds), *Faith and History: Essays in Honor of Paul W. Meyer* (Atlanta, GA: Scholars Press, 1990), pp. 160–92.

Cassuto, Umberto, *The Documentary Hypothesis and the Composition of the Pentateuch* (Jerusalem: Magnes, 1961).

Chan, Michael J., 'Isaiah 65-66 and the Genesis of Reorienting Speech', *CBQ* 72 (2010), pp. 445–63.

Charlier, Jean-Pierre, 'L'exégèse johannique d'un precepte legal: Jean VIII 17', *RB* 67 (1960), pp. 503–15.

Chester, Andrew, *Messiah and Exaltation: Jewish Messianic and Visionary Traditions and New Testament Christology* (WUNT 207; Tübingen: Mohr Siebeck, 2007).

Chilton, Bruce, *A Feast of Meanings: Eucharistic Theologies from Jesus through Johannine Circles* (Leiden: Brill, 1994).

Chilton, Bruce, *The Isaiah Targum* (ed. Martin McNamara, Vol. 11; T&T Clark: Edinburgh, 1987).

Chilton, Bruce, *Rabbi Paul: An Intellectual Biography* (New York: Penguin/Random House, 2005).

Chomsky, William, 'The Growth of Hebrew during the Middle Ages', *JQR* 57 (1967), pp. 121–36.

Ciampa, Roy E., 'Deuteronomy in Galatians and Romans', in Steve Moyise and Maarten J. J. Menken (eds), *Deuteronomy in the New Testament* (London: T&T Clark, 2007), pp. 99–117.
Clark, Elizabeth A., *History, Theory, Text: Historians and the Linguistic Turn* (Cambridge, MA: Harvard University Press, 2004).
Clark, Elizabeth A., 'Interpretive Fate amid the Church Fathers', in Phyllis Trible and Letty M. Russell (eds), *Hagar, Sarah and Their Children: Jewish, Christian, and Muslim Perspectives* (Louiseville, KY: Westminster John Knox Press, 2006), pp. 127–48.
Clarke, Ernest G. (ed.), *Targum Pseudo-Jonathan of the Pentateuch: Text and Concordance* (Hoboken, NJ: Ktav Publishing, 1984).
Clifford, Hywel, 'Deutero-Isaiah and Monotheism', in John Day (ed.), *Prophecy and Prophets in Ancient Israel: Proceedings of the Oxford Old Testament Seminar* (New York: T&T Clark, 2010), pp. 267–89.
Clifford, Richard J., 'The Function of Idol Passages in Second Isaiah', *CBQ* 42, no. 4 (1980), pp. 450–64.
Cohen, Shaye J. D., 'The Significance of Yavneh: Pharisees, Rabbis, and the End of Jewish Sectarianism', *HUCA* 55 (1984), pp. 27–53.
Colijn, B., 'Let Us Approach: Soteriology in the Epistle to the Hebrews', *JETS* 39 (1996), pp. 571–86.
Collins, John J., *The Apocalyptic Imagination: An Introduction to Jewish Apocalyptic Literature* (Grand Rapids, MI: Eerdmans, 1988).
Collins, John J., *Between Athens and Jerusalem: Jewish Identity in the Hellenistic Diaspora* (2nd edn; Grand Rapids, MI: Eerdmans, 2000).
Collins, John J., 'The Jewish Apocalypses', *Sem* 14 (1979), pp. 21–59.
Collins, John J., 'Stirring Up the Great Sea: The Religio-Historical Background of Daniel 7', in A. S. van der Woude (ed.), *The Book of Daniel in the Light of New Findings* (Leuven: Leuven University Press, 1993), pp. 121–36.
Collins, Raymond, *1 & 2 Timothy and Titus: A Commentary* (2nd edn; NTL; Louisville: WJK, 2012).
Coloe, Mary, 'John as Witness and Friend', in Paul N. Anderson, Felix Just and Tom Thatcher (eds), *John, Jesus, and History, Volume 2: Aspects of Historicity in the Fourth Gospel* (Atlanta, GA: SBL Press, 2009), pp. 44–61.
Coloe, Mary L., *God Dwells with Us: Temple Symbolism in the Fourth Gospel* (Collegeville, MN: Liturgical Press, 2001).
Coloe, Mary L., 'Like Father, Like Son: The Role of Abraham in Tabernacles (John 8.31-59)', *Pac* 12 (1999), pp. 1–11.
Conway, Colleen M., *Behold the Man: Jesus and Greco-Roman Masculinity* (New York: Oxford University Press, 2008).
Conway, Colleen M., 'Gender and Divine Relativity in Philo of Alexandria', *JSJ* 34, no. 4 (2003), pp. 471–91.
Coogan, Michael D. (ed.), *The New Oxford Annotated Apocrypha: New Revised Standard Version* (4th rev. edn; New York: Oxford University Press, 2010).
Cooper, John W., *Body, Soul, and Life Everlasting: Biblical Anthropology and the Monism-Dualism Debate* (Grand Rapids, MI: Eerdmans, 1989).
Corley, Jeremy, 'An Alternative Hebrew Form of Ben Sira: The Anthological Manuscript C', in Jean-Sébastien Rey and Jan Joosten (eds), *The Texts and Versions of the Book of Ben Sira: Transmission and Interpretation* (Leiden/Boston: Brill, 2011), pp. 3–22.
Cortés, Juan B., 'Yet Another Look at John 7,37-38', *CBQ* 29 (1967), pp. 75–86.

Cory, Catherine, 'Wisdom's Rescue: A New Reading of the Tabernacles Discourse (John 7.1-8.59)', *JBL* 116 (1997), pp. 95-116.
Cousland, Robert, 'Reversal, Recidivism, and Reward in 3 Maccabees: Structure and Purpose', *JSJ* 34, no. 1 (2003), pp. 39-51.
Cranfield, C. E. B., 'Romans 9.30-10.4', *Int* 34, no. 1 (1980), pp. 70-4.
Cranfield, C. E. B., 'The "Works of the Law" in the Epistle to the Romans', *JSNT* 43 (1991), pp. 89-101.
Cranford, Michael, 'Abraham in Romans 4: The Father of All Who Believe', *NTS* 41 (1995), pp. 71-88.
Cribbs, F. Lamar, 'St. Luke and the Johannine Tradition', *JBL* 90, no. 4 (1971), pp. 422-50.
Cronshaw, Darren, 'A Commission "Great" for Whom? Postcolonial Contrapuntal Readings of Matthew 28.18-20 and the Irony of William Carey', *Transformation: An International Journal of Holistic Mission Studies* 33, no. 2 (2016), pp. 110-23.
Culler, Jonathan, 'Presupposition and Intertextuality', *MLN* 91, no. 6 (1976), pp. 1380-96.
Culpepper, R. Alan, *Anatomy of the Fourth Gospel: A Study in Literary Design* (Minneapolis, MN: Fortress Press, 1983).
Culpepper, R. Alan, 'The Johannine Hypodeigma: A Reading of John 13', *Sem* 53 (1991), pp. 133-52.
Curran, John E. Jr, 'Jacob and Esau in the Iconoclasm of Merit', *SEL* 49, no. 2 (2009), pp. 285-309.
Curzer, Howard J., 'Abraham, the Faithless Moral Superhero', *Philosophy and Literature* 31 (2007), pp. 344-61.
Cuvillier, Élian, 'Torah Observance and Radicalization in the First Gospel. Matthew and First-Century Judaism: A Contribution to the Debate', *NTS* 55 (2009), pp. 144-59.
Dacy, Marianne, *The Separation of Early Christianity from Judaism* (Amherst, NY: Cambria Press, 2010).
Dahl, Nils A., 'Der Ersteborene Satans und der Vater des Teufels (Polyk. 7,1 und Joh 8,44)', in W. Eltester and F. H. Kettler (eds), *Apophoreta* (FS Ernst Haenchen; BZNW 30; Berlin: Walter de Gruyter, 1964), pp. 70-84.
Dahl, Nils A., 'The Story of Abraham in Luke-Acts', in J. Louis Martyn and Leander E. Keck (eds), *Studies in Luke-Acts: Essays Presented in Honor of Paul Schubert* (Nashville, TN: Abingdon, 1996), pp. 139-58.
Daise, Michael, '"If Anyone Thirsts, Let That One Come to Me and Drink": The Literary Texture of John 7.37b-38a', *JBL* 122, no. 4 (2003), pp. 688-9.
Daise, Michael, *Feasts in John: Jewish Festivals and Jesus' Hour in the Fourth Gospel* (WUNT 2.229; Tübingen: Mohr Siebeck, 2007).
Danker, Frederick W., Walter Bauer, William F. Arndt and F. Wilbur Gingrich (eds), *A Greek-English Lexicon of the New Testament and Other Early Christian Literature* (4th edn; Chicago: University of Chicago Press). OliveTree Biblical Software.
Dapaah, Daniel S., *The Relationship between John the Baptist and Jesus of Nazareth* (New York/Oxford: University Press of America, 2005).
Daschke, Dereck, *City of Ruins: Mourning the Destruction of Jerusalem through Jewish Apocalypse* (Leiden: Brill, 2010).
Davidson, Israel, 'The Study of Mediaeval Hebrew Poetry in the XIX Century', *PAAJR* 1 (1928-1930), pp. 33-48.
Davies, Margaret, *Rhetoric and Reference in the Fourth Gospel* (JSNTSup 69; Sheffield: Sheffield Academic Press, 1992).
Davis, Kipp, 'Prophets of Exile: 4Q*Apocryphon of Jeremiah C*, Apocryphal Baruch, and the Efficacy of the Second Temple', *JSJ* 44 (2013), pp. 497-529.

Davis, Stephen J., 'Crossed Text, Crossed Sex: Intertextuality and Gender in Early Christian Legends of Holy Women Disguised as Men', *JECS* 10, no. 1 (2002), pp. 1–36.

de Boer, Martinus C., 'Paul's Quotation of Isaiah 54.1 in Galatians 4.27', *NTS* 50 (2004), pp. 370–89.

de Jonge, Marinus, 'Jewish Expectations about the "Messiah" according to the Fourth Gospel', *NTS* 19, no. 3 (1973), pp. 246–70.

de Jonge, Marinus, 'The Testament of Levi and "Aramaic Levi"', *RevQ* 13, no. 1 (1988), pp. 367–85.

de Jonge, Marinus, 'The Two Great Commandments in the Testaments of the Twelve Patriarchs', *NovT* 44, no. 4 (2002), pp. 371–92.

de Lange, Tineke, *Abraham in John 8,31-59: His Significance in the Conflict between Johannine Christianity and Its Jewish Environment* (Amsterdam: Amphora Books, 2008).

Dennert, Brian C., 'Hanukkah and the Testimony of Jesus' Works (John 10.22-39)', *JBL* 132, no. 2 (2013), pp. 431–51.

De Roo, Jacqueline C. R., *Works of the Law at Qumran and in Paul* (Sheffield: Phoenix Press, 2007).

deSilva, David A., *4 Maccabees* (Sheffield: Sheffield Academic Press, 1998).

deSilva, David A., *4 Maccabees: Introduction and Commentary on the Greek Text in Codex Sinaiticus* (Leiden: Brill, 2006).

deSilva, David A., 'Grace, the Law and Justification in *4 Ezra* and the Pauline Letters: A Dialogue', *JSNT* 37, no. 1 (2014), pp. 25–49.

deSilva, David A., 'The Perfection of "Love for Offspring": Greek Representations of Maternal Affection and the Achievement of the Heroine of 4 Maccabees', *NTS* 52 (2006), pp. 251–68.

deSilva, David A., 'The Sinaiticus Text of 4 Maccabees', *CBQ* 68, no. 1 (2006), pp. 47–62.

de Villiers, Pieter G. R., 'Heroes at Home: Identity, Ethos, and Ethics in 1 Timothy within the context of the Pastoral Epistles', in Jan G. van der Watt (ed.), *Identity, Ethics, and Ethos in the New Testament* (Berlin: Walter de Gruyter, 2006), pp. 357–86.

Dienes, Roland, *Die Gerechtigkeit der Tora im Reich des Messias: Mt 5,13-20 als Schlüsseltext der matthäischen Theologie* (WUNT 177; Tübingen: Mohr Siebeck, 2004).

Dimant, Devorah, 'Between Qumran Sectarian and Non-Sectarian Texts: The Case of Belial and Mastema', in Devorah Dimant et al. (eds), *The Dead Sea Scrolls and Contemporary Culture* (Leiden: Brill, 2011), pp. 235–56.

Di Mattei, Steven, 'Paul's Allegory of the Two Covenants (Gal 4.21-31) in Light of First-Century Hellenistic Rhetoric and Jewish Hermeneutics', *NTS* 52 (2006), pp. 102–22.

Dochhorn, Jan, 'Mit Kain kam der Tod in die Welt: Zur Auslegung von SapSal 2,24 in 1 Clem 3,4; 4,1-7, mit einem Seitenblick auf Polykarp, Phil. 7,1 und Theophilus, Ad Autol. II, 29, 304', *ZNW* 98 (2007), pp. 150–9.

Dodd, Charles Harold, *According to the Scriptures: The Substructure of New Testament Theology* (London: Collins, 1952).

Dodd, Charles Harold, 'Behind a Johannine Dialogue', in Charles H. Dodd (ed.), *More New Testament Studies* (Manchester: Manchester University Press, 1968), pp. 41–57.

Dodd, Charles Harold, *Historical Tradition in the Fourth Gospel* (Cambridge: Cambridge University Press, 1963).

Doering, Lutz, '4QMMT and the Letters of Paul: Selected Aspects of Mutual Illumination', in Jean-Sébastien Rey (ed.), *The Dead Sea Scrolls and Pauline Literature* (Leiden: Brill, 2013), pp. 69–88.

Doering, Lutz, *Ancient Jewish Letters and the Beginnings of Christian Epistolography* (WUNT 2.298; Tübingen: Mohr Siebeck, 2012).

Doering, Lutz, 'The Epistle of Baruch and Its Role in *2 Baruch*', in Matthias Henze and Gabriele Boccaccini (eds), *Fourth Ezra and Second Baruch: Reconstruction after the Fall* (JSJSup 164; Leiden: Brill, 2013), pp. 151-74.

Doering, Lutz, 'Parallels without "Parallelomania": Methodological Reflections on Comparative Analysis of Halakhah in the Dead Sea Scrolls', in Steven D. Fraade, Aharon Shemesh and Ruth A. Clements (eds), *Rabbinic Perspectives: Rabbinic Literature and the Dead Sea Scrolls – Proceedings of the Eighth International Symposium of the Orion Center for the Study of the Dead Sea Scrolls and Associated Literature, 7–9 January 2003* (Leiden: Brill, 2006), pp. 13-42.

Donaldson, Terence L., 'The "Curse of the Law" and the Inclusion of the Gentiles: Galatians 3.13-14', *NTS* 32 (1986), pp. 94-112.

Dozeman, Thomas B., 'The Book of Joshua in Recent Research', *CBR* 15, no. 3 (2017), pp. 270-88.

Dozeman, Thomas B., '*Sperma Abraam* in John 8 and Related Literature: Cosmology and Judgment', *CBQ* 42 (1980), pp. 342-58.

Dozeman, Thomas B., 'The Wilderness and Salvation History in the Hagar Story', *JBL* 177, no. 1 (1998), pp. 23-43.

Drawnel, Henryk, *An Aramaic Wisdom Text from Qumran: A New Interpretation of the Levi Document* (JSJSup 86; Leiden: Brill, 2004).

Dube, Musa W., 'Reading for Decolonization (John 4.1-42)', *Sem* 75 (1996), pp. 37-59.

Duggan, Michael, *The Covenant Renewal in Ezra-Nehmiah (Neh 7.72b–10.40): An Exegetical, Literary, and Theological Study* (Atlanta, GA: Scholars Press, 2001).

Duling, Dennis, '2 Corinthians 11.22: Historical Context, Rhetoric, and Ethnicity', *HTS Theological Studies* 64, no. 2 (2008), pp. 819-43.

Dunn, James D. G., '4QMMT and Galatians', *NTS* 43 (1997), pp. 147-53.

Dunn, James D. G., 'The New Perspective on Paul', *BJRL* 65 (1983), pp. 95-122.

Dunn, James D. G., *Romans* (2 vols; WBC; Dallas, TX: Word, 1988).

Dunn, James G. F., *The New Perspective on Paul* (rev. edn; Grand Rapids, MI: Eerdmans, 2005).

Dunn, James G. F., 'Works of the Law and the Curse of the Law (Galatians 3.10-14)', *NTS* 31 (1985), pp. 523-43.

Dunning, Benjamin, 'The Intersection of Alien Status and Cultic Discourse in the Epistle to the Hebrews', in Gabriella Gelardini (ed.), *Hebrews: Contemporary Methods, New Insights* (Leiden: Brill, 2005), pp. 177-98.

Dupré, John, 'Materialism, Physicalism, and Scientism', *Philosophical Topics* 16, no. 1 (1998), pp. 31-56.

Easter, Matthew C., 'Faith in the God Who Resurrects: The Theocentric Faith of Hebrews', *NTS* 63 (2017), pp. 76-91.

Eastman, Susan G., 'Sin's Wages and God's Gift in the Divine Economy: Reflections on Romans 7 and the Cleansing of the Temple in John 2.13-17', *ExpTim* 121, no. 7 (2010), pp. 342-5.

Eastman, Susan G., '"Cast Out the Slave Woman and her Son": The Dynamics of Exclusion and Inclusion in Galatians 4.30', *JSNT* 28, no. 3 (2006), pp. 309-36.

Eastman, Susan G., 'Israel and the Mercy of God: A Re-reading of Galatians 6.16 and Romans 9-11', *NTS* 56, no. 3 (2010), pp. 367-95.

Edwards, Mark J., 'Justin's Logos and the Word of God', *JECS* 3, no. 3 (1995), 261-80.

Edwards, Mark J., '"Not Yet Fifty Years Old": John 8:57', *NTS* 40 (1994), pp. 449-54.

Egger-Wenzel, Renate, 'The Testament of Mattathias to His Sons in 1 Macc 2.49-70: A Keyword Composition with the Aim of Justification', in N. Calduch-Benages and J. Leisen (eds), *History and Identity: How Israel's Later Authors Viewed Its Earlier History* (Berlin: Walter de Gruyter, 2006), pp. 141-9.

Eggler, Jürg, *Influences and Traditions Underlying the Vision of Daniel 7.2-14: The Research History from the End of the 19th Century to the Present* (Göttingen: Vandenhoeck & Ruprecht, 2000).

Ego, Beate, 'Heilige Zeit – heiliger Raum – heiliger Mensch', in Matthias Albani, Jörg Frey and Armin Lange (eds), *Studies in the Book of Jubilees* (TSzAJ 65; Tübingen: Mohr Siebeck, 1997), pp. 207-20.

Ehrlich, Ernst Ludwig, *Der Traum im Alten Testament* (BZAW 73; Berlin: Verlag Alfred Töpelmann, 1953).

Eisenbaum, Pamela, 'Heroes and History in Hebrews 11', in Craig A. Evans and James A. Sanders (eds), *Early Christian Interpretation of the Scriptures of Israel: Investigations and Proposals* (JSNTSup 148; Sheffield: Sheffield Academic Press, 1997), pp. 380-96.

Eisenbaum, Pamela, 'Paul, Polemics, and the Problem of Essentialism', *BibInt* 13 (2005), pp. 224-38.

Eisenberg, Ronald, *Jewish Traditions* (Philadelphia, PA: Jewish Publication Society).

Elfenbein, Andrew, 'On the Discrimination of Influences', *MLQ* 69, no. 4 (2008), pp. 481-506.

Elliger, K. and W. Rudolph (eds), *Biblia Hebraica Stuttgartensia* (Stuttgart: Deutsche Bibelgesellschaft, 1983). OliveTree Software.

Engberg-Pedersen, Troels, 'A Question of Genre: John 13–17 as *Paraklēsis*', in Kasper Bro Larsen (ed.), *The Gospel of John as Genre Mosaic* (SANt 3; Göttingen: Vandenhoeck & Ruprecht, 2015), pp. 283-302.

Ensor, Peter W., *Jesus and His Works: The Johannine Sayings in Historical Perspective* (WUNT 2.85; Tübingen: Mohr Siebeck, 1996).

Enz, Jacob J., 'The Book of Exodus as a Literary Type for the Gospel of John', *JBL* 76 (1957), pp. 208-15.

Epstein, Jacob and Ezra Melamed, *Mekhilta de-Rabbi Shimon ben Yochai* (Jerusalem: Mekize Nedarim, 1955) [in Hebrew].

Esler, Philip F., 'Paul's Contestation of Israel's (Ethnic) Memory of Abraham in Galatians 3', *BTB* 36, no. 1 (2006), pp. 23-34.

Eslinger, Lyle, 'Prehistory in the Call to Abraham', *BibInt* 14 (2006), pp. 189-208.

Estes, Douglas, *The Questions of Jesus in John: Logic, Rhetoric and Persuasive Discourse* (Leiden/Boston: Brill, 2013).

Eubank, Nathan, 'Almsgiving the "the Commandment": A Note on 1 Timothy 6.6-19', *NTS* 58, no. 1 (2012), pp. 144-50.

Evans, Craig A., 'Abraham in the Dead Sea Scrolls: A Man of Faith and Failure', in Peter W. Flint (ed.), *The Bible at Qumran: Text, Shape and Interpretation* (Grand Rapids, MI: Eerdmans, 2001), pp. 149-58.

Evans, Craig A. and H. Daniel Zecharias (eds), *Early Christian Literature and Intertextuality* (2 vols; London: T&T Clark, 2009).

Faierstein, Morris M., 'Kabbalistic Customs and Rituals: An Introduction', *Conservative Judaism* 60, no. 3 (2008), pp. 90-8.

Feldman, Ari, 'The Bible in Neo-Hebraic Poetry', *JQR* 11, no. 4 (1899), pp. 569-84.

Feldman, Louis H., 'Abraham the Greek Philosopher in Josephus', *TPAPA* 99 (1968), pp. 143-56.

Feldman, Louis H., *Josephus' Interpretation of the Bible* (Berkeley, CA: University of California Press, 1998).
Feldman, Louis H., '"Josephus" Portrait of David', *HUCA* 60 (1989), pp. 129–74.
Ffrench, Patrick, 'Tel Quel 1967: Theory as Excess', *The Comparatist* 38, no. 1 (2014), pp. 97–109.
Ffrench, Patrick, *The Time of Theory: A History of Tel Quel* (New York/Oxford: Clarendon Press, 1995).
Fields, Weston W., *Sodom and Gomorrah: History and Motif in Biblical Narrative* (JSOTSup 231; Sheffield: Sheffield Academic Press, 1997).
Figueira, Dorothy M., 'Comparative Literature versus World Literature', *The Comparatist* 34 (2010), pp. 29–36.
Fillvedt, Ole Jakob, *The Identity of God's People and the Paradox of Hebrews* (WUNT 2/400; Tübingen: Mohr Siebeck, 2015).
Finkelstein, Louis, 'The Book of Jubilees and the Rabbinic Halaka', *HTR* 16 (1923), pp. 59–61.
Finkelstein, Louis, 'The Sources of the Tannaitic Midrashim', *JQR* 31, no. 3 (1941), pp. 211–43.
Finkelstein, Louis and H. S. Horovitz (eds), *Sifre al Sefer Devarim* (New York, 1939) [in Hebrew], p. 206.
Fishbane, Michael, 'Use, Authority and Interpretation of Mikra at Qumran', in Martin Jan Mulder (ed.), *Translation, Reading and Interpretation of the Hebrew Bible in Ancient Judaism and Early Christianity* (CRINT 1; Assen: Van Gorcum, 1988), pp. 339–77.
Fisk, Bruce N., *Do You Not Remember? Scripture, Story and Exegesis in the Rewritten Bible of Pseudo-Philo* (JSPSupp 37; Sheffield: Sheffield Academic Press, 2001).
Fisk, Bruce N., 'Offering Isaac Again and Again: Pseudo-Philo's Use of the Aqedah as Intertext', *CBQ* 62, no. 3 (2000), pp. 481–507.
Fitzmyer, Joseph A., 'Qumran and the Interpolated Paragraph in 2 Cor 6.14–7.1', *CBQ* 23, no. 3 (1961), pp. 271–80.
Fleischer, Paul V. M. and Bruce Chilton, *The Targums: A Critical Introduction* (Leiden/Boston: Brill, 2011).
Forbes, Christopher, 'Comparison, Self-Praise, and Irony: Paul's Boasting and the Conventions of Hellenistic Rhetoric', *NTS* 32 (1986), pp. 1–30.
Fortna, Robert T., *The Gospel of Signs: A Reconstruction of the Narrative Source Underlying the Fourth Gospel* (SNTSMS 11; Cambridge: Cambridge University Press, 1970).
Foster, Robert B., *Renaming Abraham's Children: Election, Ethnicity, and the Interpretation of Scripture in Romans 9* (WUNT 2/421; Tübingen: Mohr Siebeck, 2016).
Foster, Robert J., *The Significance of Exemplars for the Interpretation of the Letter of James* (WUNT 2.376; Tübingen: Mohr Siebeck, 2014).
Fraade, Steven D., *From Tradition to Commentary: Torah and Its Interpretation in the Midrash Sifre to Deuteronomy* (New York: Albany State University of New York Press, 1991).
Fraade, Steven D., 'Rabbinic Polysemy and Pluralism Revisited: Between Praxis and Thematization', *AJS Review* 31, no. 1 (2007), pp. 1–40.
Frayer-Griggs, Daniel, *Saved through Fire: The Fiery Ordeal in New Testament Eschatology* (Eugene, OR: Pickwick, 2016).
Frayer-Griggs, Daniel, 'Spittle, Clay, and Creation in John 9.6 and Some Dead Sea Scrolls', *JBL* 132, no. 3 (2013), pp. 659–70.
Fredriksen, Paula, 'Judaizing the Nations: The Ritual Demands of Paul's Gospel', *NTS* 56 (2010), pp. 232–52.

Freed, Edwin D., 'EGŌ EIMI in John VII.24 in the Light of Its Context and Jewish Messianic Belief', *JTS* 33, no. 1 (1982), pp. 163-7.
Freed, Edwin D., 'Who or What Was Before Abraham in John 8.58?' *JSNT* 17 (1983), pp. 52-9.
Fretheim, Terence E., *Abraham: Trials of Family and Faith* (Columbia, SC: University of South Carolina Press, 2007).
Frevel, Christian, '"Separate Yourself from the Gentiles" (*Jubilees* 22.16): Intermarriage in the Book of *Jubilees*', in Christian Frevel (ed.), *Mixed Marriages: Intermarriage and Group Identity in the Second Temple Period* (New York: T&T Clark, 2011), pp. 220-49.
Frey, Jörg, 'Apocalyptic Dualism', in John J. Collins (ed.), *The Oxford Handbook of Apocalyptic Literature* (New York/Oxford: Oxford University Press, 2014), pp. 271-94.
Frick, Heinrich, *Vergleichende Religionswissenschaft* (Berlin/Leipzig, 1928).
Frishman, Judith, '"And Abraham Had Faith": But in What? Ephrem and the Rabbis on Abraham and God's Blessing', in Helen Spurling and Emmanouela Grypeou (eds), *The Exegetical Encounter between Jews and Christians in Late Antiquity* (Leiden: Brill), pp. 163-79.
Frow, John, *Genre* (London/New York: Routledge, 2005).
Fujita, Shozo, 'The Metaphor of Plant in Jewish Literature of the Intertestamental Period', *JSJ* 7, no. 1 (1976), pp. 30-45.
Gadamer, Hans-Georg, *Truth and Method* (2nd edn; trans. Joel Weinsheimer and Donald G. Marshall; New York/London: Continuum, 2011).
Gager, John G., *The Origins of Anti-Semitism: Attitudes Toward Judaism in Pagan and Christian Antiquity* (New York: Oxford University Press, 1985).
Gallusz, Laszlo, *The Throne Motif in the Book of Revelation* (London: T&T Clark/Bloomsbury, 2014).
Garcia Martinez, Florentino, '4QMMT in a Qumran Context', in John Kampen and Moshe J. Bernstein (eds), *Reading 4QMMT: New Perspectives on Qumran Law and History* (Atlanta, GA: Scholars Press, 1996), pp. 15-27.
Garcia Marrtinez, Florentino, 'The Sacrifice of Isaac in 4Q225', in Ed Noort and Eibert Tigchelaar (eds), *The Sacrifice of Isaac: The Aqedah (Genesis 22) and Its Interpretations* (TBN 4; Leiden/Boston: Brill, 2002), pp. 44-57.
Gathercole, Simon J., *Where Is Boasting? Early Jewish Soteriology and Paul's Response in Romans 1-5* (Grand Rapids, MI: Eerdmans, 2002).
Genette, Gérard, *Palimpsests: Literature in the Second Degree* (trans. Channa Newman and Claude Doubinsky; Lincoln, NE: University of Nebraska Press, 1997).
Genette, Gérard, *Paratexts: Thresholds of Interpretation* (trans. Jane E. Lewin; Cambridge: Cambridge University Press, 1997).
Genz, Rouven, 'Reversal of Fate After Death?' in Beate Ego and Ulrike Mittmann (eds), *Evil and Death: Conceptions of the Human in Biblical, Early Jewish, Greco-Roman and Egyptian Literature* (Berlin: de Gruyter, 2015), pp. 221-58.
Ginzberg, Louis, *Legends of the Jews* (6 vols; Philadelphia, PA: Jewish Publication Society, 1909-1928).
Goodman, Lenn, *God of Abraham* (Oxford: Oxford University Press, 1996).
Goodman, Martin, 'The Date of 2 Baruch', in Christopher Rowland and John Ashton (eds), *Revealed Wisdom: Studies in Apocalyptic in Honour of Christopher Rowland* (AJEC 88; Leiden: Brill, 2014), pp. 116-21.
Goodman, Martin, 'Josephus on Abraham and the Nations', in Martin Goodman, George H. van Kooten and J. T. A. G. M. van Ruiten (eds), *Abraham, the Nations, and the*

Hagarites: Jewish, Christian, and Islamic Perspectives on Kinship with Abraham (TBN 13; Leiden: Brill, 2010), pp. 177-84.

Gosse, Bernard, 'Abraham père des exilés en Josué', in Ed Noort (ed.), *The Book of Joshua* (BETL 250; Leuven/Paris: Peeters, 2012), pp. 295-300.

Grabbe, Lester L., *Judaic Religion in the Second Temple Period: Belief and Practice from the Exile to Yavneh* (London: Routledge, 2000).

Gräßer, Erich, 'Die antijüdische Polemik im Johannesevangelium', NTS 11 (1964/5), pp. 74-90.

Green, William S., 'Doing the Text's Work for It: Richard Hays on Paul's Use of Scripture', in Craig A. Evans and J. A. Sanders (eds), *Paul and the Scriptures of Israel* (JSNTSup 83; Sheffield: Sheffield Academic Press, 1993), pp. 58-63.

Greenfield, Jonas, 'The Words of Levi Son of Jacob in Damascus Document IV,15-19', RevQ 13 (1998), pp. 319-22.

Gregory, Bradley C., 'Abraham as the Jewish Ideal: Exegetical Traditions in Sirach 44.19-21', CBQ 70 (2008), pp. 66-81.

Grélot, P. 'Jean 8,56 et Jubilés 16.16-29', Rev Q 13 (1988/9), pp. 621-8.

Griffiths, Terry, 'The Jews Who had Believed in Him' (John 8.31) and the Motif of Apostasy in the Gospel of John', in Richard Bauckham and Carl Mosser (eds), *The Gospel of John and Christian Theology* (Grand Rapids, MI: Eerdmans, 2008), pp. 183-92.

Grindheim, Sigurd, *The Crux of Election: Paul's Critique of the Jewish Confidence in the Election of Israel* (WUNT 2.202; Tübingen: Mohr Siebeck, 2005).

Grindheim, Sigurd, 'The Work of God or of Human Beings: A Note on John 6.29', JETS 59, no. 1 (2016), pp. 63-6.

Gruen, Erich, *Heritage and Hellenism: The Reinvention of Jewish Tradition* (Los Angeles, CA: University of California Press, 1998).

Grüneberg, Keith N., *Abraham, Blessing, and the Nations: A Philological and Exegetical Study of Genesis 12.3 in Its Narrative Context* (BZAW 332; Berlin/New York: de Gruyter, 2003), pp. 143-5.

Gupta, Nijay, 'Mirror-Reading Moral Issues in Paul's Letters', JSNT 34 (2012), pp. 361-81.

Gutman, Ariel and Wido van Peursen, *The Two Syriac Versions of The Prayer of Manasseh* (Piscataway, NJ: Gorgias Press, 2011).

Haar, Stephen, *Simon Magus: The First Gnostic?* (BZNW 119; Berlin: Walter de Gruyter, 2003).

Hacham, Noah, '3 Maccabees and Esther: Parallels, Intertextuality, and Diaspora Identity', JBL 126, no. 4 (2007), pp. 765-85.

Hadas, Moses, *The Third and Fourth Books of Maccabees* (New York: Harper & Row, 1953).

Hägerland, Tobias, 'Jesus and the Rites of Repentance', NTS 52, no. 2 (2006), pp. 166-87.

Hahn, F., 'Sehen und Glauben im Johannesevangelium', in H. Bautensweiler and Bo Reike (eds), *Neue Testament und Geschichte: Historisches Geschehen und Deutung im Neuen Testament* (FS Oscar Cullman; Tübingen: Mohr Siebeck, 1972), pp. 125-41.

Hahn, Scott W., *The Kingdom of God as Liturgical Empire: A Theological Commentary on 1-2 Chronicles* (Grand Rapids, MI: Baker Academic, 2012).

Hall, David R., 'Romans 3.1-8 Reconsidered', NTS 29 (1983), pp. 183-97.

Halpern-Amaru, Betsy, *The Empowerment of Women in the Book of Jubilees* (Leiden/Boston: Brill, 1999).

Halpern-Amaru, Betsy, 'Land Theology in Josephus' "Jewish Antiquities"', JQR 71, no. 4 (1981), pp. 201-29.

Halpern-Amaru, Betsy, *The Perspective from Mt Sinai: The Book of Jubilees and Exodus* (Göttingen: Vandenhoeck and Ruprecht, 2015).
Hansen, G. Walter, *Abraham in Galatians: Epistolary and Rhetorical Contexts* (Sheffield: JSOT Press, 1989).
Hansen, G. Walter, *Abraham in Galatians: Epistolary and Rhetorical Contexts* (2nd edn [orig. 1989]; London: Bloomsbury, 2015).
Harlan, David, 'Intellectual History and the Return of Literature', *AHR* 94, no. 3 (1989), pp. 581–609.
Harner, Phillip B., *The 'I Am' of the Fourth Gospel: A Study in Johannine Usage and Thought* (Facte Books; Philadelphia, PA: Fortress Press, 1970).
Harrington, Daniel J., 'Abraham Traditions in the *Testament of Abraham* and in the 'Rewritten Bible' of the Intertestamental Period', in George Nickelsburg (ed.), *Studies in the Testament of Abraham* (Atlanta, GA: Scholars Press, 1976), pp. 156–71.
Harrington, Daniel J., *Invitation to the Apocrypha* (Grand Rapids, MI: Eerdmans, 1999).
Harrington, Daniel J., 'The Original Language of Pseudo-Philo's "Liber Antiquitatum Biblicarum"', *HTR* 63, no. 4 (1970), pp. 503–14.
Harstine, Stan, *Moses as a Character in the Fourth Gospel: A Study of Ancient Reading Techniques* (London/New York: Sheffield Academic Press, 2002).
Harvey, E., *Jesus on Trial: A Study in the Fourth Gospel* (Atlanta, GA: John Knox, 1976).
Hasel, Gerhard F., 'The Meaning of the Animal Rite in Genesis 15', *JSOT* 19 (1981), pp. 61–78.
Hasitschka, Martin, *Befreiung von Sunde nach dem Johannesevangelium: eine bibeltheologische Untersuchung* (Innsbruck: Tyrolia, 1989).
Hatina, Thomas, 'Intertextuality and Historical Criticism in New Testament Studies: Is There a Relationship?' *BibInt* 7, no. 1 (1999), pp. 28–43.
Hatton, Peter, 'A Cautionary Tale: The Acts: Consequence "Construct"', *JSOT* 35, no. 3 (2011), pp. 375–84.
Hauptman, Judith, *Rereading the Mishnah: A New Approach to Ancient Jewish Texts* (Tübingen: Mohr Siebeck, 2005).
Hays, Christopher M., *Luke's Wealth Ethics: A Study in Their Coherence and Character* (WUNT 2.275; Tübingen: Mohr Siebeck, 2010).
Hays, Richard B., *Echoes of Scripture in the Letters of Paul* (New Haven, CT: Yale University Press, 1989).
Hays, Richard B., *The Faith of Jesus Christ: The Narrative Substructure of Galatians 3.1-4.11* (2nd edn; Grand Rapids, MI: Eerdmans, 2002).
Hayward, Robert, *Targums and the Transmission of Scripture into Judaism and Christianity* (Leiden: Brill, 2009).
Heike, Thomas, 'Atonement in the Prayer of Azariah (Dan 3.40)', in Géza G. Xeravits and Jósef Zsengellér (eds), *Deuterocanonical Additions of the Old Testament Books: Selected Studies* (Berlin: de Gruyter, 2010), pp. 43–59.
Heil, John Paul, 'Christ, the Termination of the Law (Romans 9.30–10.8)', *CBQ* 63, no. 3 (2001), pp. 484–98.
Heil, John Paul, 'From Remnant to Seed of Hope for Israel: Romans 9.27-29', *CBQ* 64 (2002), pp. 703–20.
Heim, Erin M., *Adoption in Galatians and Romans* (BINS 153; Leiden: Brill, 2017).
Hempel, Charlotte, 'The Laws of the Damascus Document and 4QMMT', in M. Baumgarten, Esther G. Chazon and Avital Pinnick (eds), *The Damascus Document: Centennial of the Discovery* (STDJ 34; Leiden: Brill, 2000), pp. 69–84.

Hendel, Ronald, *Remembering Abraham: Culture, Memory, and History in the Hebrew Bible* (New York/Oxford: Oxford University Press, 2005).
Henze, Matthias, 'Apocalypse and Torah in Ancient Judaism', in John J. Collins (ed.), *The Oxford Handbook of Apocalyptic Literature* (New York/Oxford: Oxford University Press, 2014), pp. 312-25.
Henze, Matthias, 'Torah and Eschatology in the *Syriac Apocalypse of Baruch*', in George J. Brooke, Hindy Najman and Loren T. Stuckenbruck (eds), *The Significance of Sinai: Traditions about Divine Revelation in Judaism and Christianity* (TBN; Leiden: Brill, 2008), pp. 201-16.
Hezser, Catherine, *Jewish Slavery in Antiquity* (New York: Oxford University Press, 2004).
Hieke, T., 'The Role of "Scripture" in the Last Words of Mattathias (1 Macc 2.49-70)', in Géza G. Xeravits and Jozsef Zsengellér (eds), *The Books of Maccabees: History, Theology, Ideology* (JSJSup 118; Leiden: Brill, 2007), pp. 61-74.
Hildebrandt, Ted, 'A Song of Our Father Abraham: Psalm 105', in Steven A. Hunt (ed.), *Perspectives on Our Father Abraham: Essays in Honor of Marvin R. Wilson* (Grand Rapids, MI: Eerdmans, 2010), pp. 44-67.
Hilhorst, A., 'The Bodmer Poem on the Sacrifice of Abraham', in Edward Noort and Eibert J. C. Tigchelaar (eds), *The Sacrifice of Isaac* (Leiden: Martinus Nijhoff/Brill, 2002), pp. 96-108.
Hodges, Zane C., 'Rivers of Living Water – John 7.37-39', *BSac* 136 (1979), pp. 239-48.
Höffken, Peter, 'Abraham und Gott, oder: wer liebt wen? Anmerkungen zu Jes 41.8', *BN* 103 (2000), pp. 17-22.
Hogan, Karina, *Theologies in Conflict in 4 Ezra: Wisdom, Debate, and Apocalyptic Solution* (JSJSupp 130; Leiden: Brill, 2008).
Hollander, John, *The Figure of an Echo: A Model of Allusion in Milton and After* (Berkeley, CA: University of California Press, 1981).
Holloway, Paul A., 'Left Behind: Jesus' Consolation of His Disciples in John 13,31–17,26', *ZNW* 96, nos. 1-2 (2005), pp. 1-34.
Holsinger, Bruce, '"Historical Context" in Historical Context: Surface, Depth, and the Making of the Text', *NLH* 42 (2011), pp. 593-614.
Holtz, Barry W., *Rabbi Akiva: Sage of the Talmud* (New Haven, CT: Yale University Press, 2017).
Hoskins, Paul M., 'Freedom from Slavery to Sin and the Devil: John 8.31-47 and the Passover Theme of the Gospel of John', *TrinJ* 31 (2010), pp. 47-63.
Hoskins, Paul M., 'The Use of Biblical and Extrabiblical Parallels in the Interpretation of First Corinthians 6.2-3', *CBQ* 63, no. 2 (2001), pp. 287-97.
Huizenga, Leroy, *The New Isaac: Tradition and Intertextuality in the Gospel of Matthew* (NovTSup 131; Leiden: Brill, 2009).
Hultgren, Stephen J., '2 Cor 6.14–7.1 and Rev 21.3-8: Evidence for the Ephesian Redaction of 2 Corinthians', *NTS* 49, no. 1 (2003), pp. 39-56.
Hunn, Debbie, 'Galatians 3.6-9: Abraham's Fatherhood and Paul's Conclusions', *CBQ* 78 (2016), pp. 500-14.
Hunn, Debbie, 'Who are "They" in John 8.33?' *CBQ* 66, no. 3 (2004), pp. 387-99.
Hunt, Steven A., 'And the Word Became Flesh – Again? Jesus and Abraham in John 8.31-59', in Steven A. Hunt (ed.), *Perspectives on Our Father Abraham: Essays in Honor of Marvin A. Wilson* (Grand Rapids, MI: Eerdmans, 2010), pp. 81-109.
Husser, Jean-Marie, *Dreams and Dream Narratives in the Biblical World* (London: Bloomsbury, 1999).
Irwin, William, 'Against Intertextuality', *PL* 28, no. 2 (2004), pp. 227-42.

Isaac, Erich, 'Circumcision as a Covenant Rite', *Anthropos* 59, nos. 3-4 (1964), pp. 444-56.
Ishida, T., 'The House of Ahab', *Israel Exploration Journal* 25, nos. 2-3 (1975), pp. 135-7.
Jackson-McCabe, Matt A., *Logos and Law in the Letter of James: The Law of Nature, the Law of Moses, and the Law of Freedom* (Leiden: Brill, 2001).
Jack Suggs, M., 'The Christian Two Ways Tradition: Its Antiquity, Form and Function', in David E. Aune (ed.), *Studies in New Testament and Early Christian Literature: Essays in Honor of Allen P. Wikgren* (Leiden: Brill, 1972), pp. 60-74.
Jaffee, Martin S., *Torah in the Mouth: Writing and Oral Tradition in Palestinian Judaism 200 BCE-400 CE* (New York: Oxford University Press, 2001).
Jansen, Nils, 'Comparative Law and Comparative Knowledge', in Mathias Reimann and Reinhard Zimmermann (eds), *The Oxford Handbook of Comparative Law* (New York: Oxford University Press, 2006), pp. 305-38.
Janzen, J. Gerald, '(Not) of My Own Accord: Listening for Scriptural Echoes in a Johannine Idiom', *Encounter* 67 (2006), pp. 138-60.
Japhet, Sara, *The Ideology of the Book of Chronicles and Its Place in Biblical Thought* (Leuven: Peeter Lang, 1997).
Jervis, L. Ann, 'Suffering for the Reign of God: The Persecution of Disciples in Q', *NovT* 44, no. 4 (2002), pp. 313-32.
Jipp, Joshua W., *Divine Visitations and Hospitality to Strangers in Luke-Acts: An Interpretation of the Malta Episode in Acts 28.1-10* (Leiden: Brill, 2013), p. 133.
Jipp, Joshua W., 'Rereading the Story of Abraham, Isaac and "Us" in Romans 4', *JSNT* 32, no. 2 (2009), pp. 217-42.
Johnson, Luke Timothy, *The Letter of James* (AB 37a; New York: Doubleday, 1995).
Kahl, Brigitte, *Galatians Re-Imagined: Reading with the Eyes of the Vanquished* (Minneapolis, MN: Fortress Press, 2010).
Kanagaraj, Jey, *Mysticism in the Gospel of John: An Inquiry into Its Background* (Sheffield: Sheffield Academic Press [repr. T&T Clark/Bloomsbury], 1998).
Käsemann, Ernst, 'Gottesgerechtigkeit bei Paulus', in Ernst Käsemann (ed.), *Exegetische Versuche und Besinnungen* (2nd edn; Vol. 2; Göttingen: Vandenhoeck & Ruprecht, 1965), p. 184.
Katz, Steven T., 'Issues in the Separation of Judaism and Christianity After 70 C.E.: A Reconsideration', *JBL* 103 (1984), pp. 43-76.
Kaufmann, Yehezkel, *Toledot Ha-Emunah Ha-yisre'elit (The History of the Religion of Israel from Antiquity until the End of Second Temple Times)* (4 vols; Tel Aviv: Dvir, 1937-56).
Kauppi, Niilo, *The Making of an Avant-Garde Tel Quel* (Berlin: de Gruyter, 1994).
Keener, Craig S., *A Commentary on the Gospel of Matthew* (Grand Rapids, MI: Eerdmans, 1999).
Kensky, Meira Z., *Trying Man, Trying God: The Divine Courtroom in Early Jewish and Christian Literature* (WUNT 2/289; Tübingen: Mohr Siebeck, 2010).
Kessler, Edward, *Bound by the Bible: Jews, Christians and the Sacrifice of Isaac* (Cambridge: Cambridge University Press, 2004).
Kierspel, Lars, *The Jews and the World in the Fourth Gospel: Parallelism, Function, and Context* (Tübingen: Mohr Siebeck, 2006).
Kim, Kyoung-Shik, *God Will Judge Each One according to Works: Judgement according to Works and Psalm 62 in Early Judaism and the New Testament* (Berlin: Walter de Gruyter, 2011).

Kippenberg, Hans G., 'Comparing Ancient Religions: A Discussion of J. Z. Smith's "Drudgery Divine"', *Numen* 39, no. 2 (1992), pp. 220-5.

Kister, Menahem, 'Romans 5.12-21 against the Background of Torah-Theology and Hebrew Usage', *HTR* 100, no. 4 (2007), pp. 391-424.

Klauck, H.-J., *Herrenmahl und hellenistischer Kult: Eine religionsgeschichtliche Untersuchung zum ersten Korintherbrief* (NTAbh n.s. 15; Münster: Aschendorff, 1982).

Klawans, Jonathan, *Josephus and the Theologies of Ancient Judaism* (New York: Oxford University Press, 2013).

Klein, Michel L., *The Fragment-Targums of the Pentateuch according to their Extant Sources* (Vol. 1; AB 76; Rome: Biblical Institute Press, 1980).

Knibb, Michael A., 'Apocalyptic and Wisdom in 4 Ezra', *JSJ* 13, nos. 1-2 (1982), pp. 56-74.

Knibb, Michael A., 'Perspectives on the Apocrypha and Pseudepigrapha: The Levi Traditions', in Florentino G. Martínez and Ed Noort (eds), *Perspectives in the Study of the Old Testament and Early Judaism* (Leiden: Brill, 1998), pp. 197-213.

Koch, Klaus, 'Gibt es ein Vergeltungsdogma im Alten Testament', *ZThK* 52 (1955), pp. 1-42.

Koch, Klaus, 'Messias und Sündenvergebung in Jes 53-Targum', *JSJ* 3 (1972), pp. 117-48.

Koch, Klaus, *Was ist Formgeschichte? Neue Wege der Bibelexegese* (Neukirchen-Vluyn: Neukirchener Verlag des Erziehungs-Vereins, 1964).

Koester, Craig R., 'Hearing, Seeing and Believing in the Gospel of John', *Bib* 70 (1989), pp. 327-48.

Koester, Craig R., *The Word of Life: A Theology of John's Gospel* (Grand Rapids, MI: Eerdmans, 2008).

Kok, Jacobus, *New Perspectives on Healing, Restoration, and Reconciliation in John's Gospel* (Leiden: Brill, 2017).

Kolenkow, Anitra Bingham, 'What Is the Role of Testament in the Testament of Abraham?' *HTR* 67, no. 2 (1974), pp. 182-4.

Koopmans, William T., *Joshua 24 as Poetic Narrative* (JSOT 93; Sheffield: Sheffield Academic Press, 1990).

Kratz, Reinhard G., 'Friend of God, Brother of Sarah, and Father of Isaac: Abraham in the Hebrew Bible and in Qumran', in Devorah Diamont and Reinhardt G. Kratz (eds), *The Dynamics of Language and Exegesis at Qumran* (Tübingen: Mohr Siebeck, 2009), pp. 80-7.

Kristeva, Julia, 'Intertextuality and Literary Interpretation' (interview), in Ross Guberman (ed.), *Julia Kristeva Interviews* (New York: Columbia University Press, 1996).

Kristeva, Julia, 'Interview with S. Clark and K. Hulley', in Ross M. Guberman (ed.), *Julia Kristeva Interviews* (New York: Columbia University Press, 1996), p. 53.

Kristeva, Julia, *Revolution in Poetic Language* (New York: Columbia University Press, 1984).

Kristeva, Julia, 'Word, Dialogue, Novel', in Julia Kristeva (ed.), *Desire in Language: A Semiotic Approach to Literature and Art* (trans. Thomas Gora, Alice Jardine and Leon S. Roudiez; ed. Leon S. Roudiez; New York: Columbia University Press, 1980), p. 66.

Kruse, Colin G., *Paul's Letter to the Romans* (PNTC; Grand Rapids, MI: Eerdmans, 2012).

Kugel, James L., *The Bible as It Was* (Cambridge, MA: Belknap/Harvard University Press, 1997).

Kugel, James L., *A Walk through Jubilees: Studies in the Book of Jubilees and the World of Its Creation* (SupJSJ 156; Leiden: Brill, 2012).

Kugler, Gili, 'Present Affliction Affects the Representation of the Past: An Alternative Dating of the Levitical Prayer in Nehemiah 9', *VT* 63 (2013), pp. 605-26.

Kuhn, Heinz-Wolfgang, 'The Impact of Selected Qumran Texts on the Understanding of Pauline Theology', in James H. Charlesworth (ed.), *The Bible and the Dead Sea*

Scrolls: Volume 3: The Scrolls and Christian Origins (Waco, TX: Baylor University Press, 2006), pp. 153–86.
Kundert, Lukas, Die Opferung/Bindung Isaaks, Vo. 1 (WMANT 78/79; Neukirchen-Vluyn: Neukirchener, 1998).
Kutsch, E., 'Der Begriff *bryt* in vordeuteronomidcher Zeit', in F. Maass (ed.), *Das Ferne und Nahe Wort* (FS L. Ost; BZAW; Berlin: de Gruyter, 1967).
Kynes, Will, 'Intertextuality: Method and Theory in Job and Psalm 119', in Katharine J. Dell and Paul M. Joyce (eds), *Biblical Interpretation and Method: Essays in Honour of John Barton* (New York: Oxford University Press, 2013), pp. 201–13.
Kysar, Robert, 'The Dismantling of Decisional Faith: A Reading of John 6.25-71', in R. Alan Culpepper (ed.), *Critical Readings of John 6* (Leiden: Brill, 1997), pp. 161–82.
Laato, Timo, 'Justification According to James: A Comparison with Paul', *TJ* 18 (1997), pp. 43–84.
Lambert, David, *How Repentance Became Biblical: Judaism, Christianity, and the Interpretation of Interpretation of Scripture* (New York: Oxford University Press, 2016).
Lambert, David, 'Last Testaments in the Book of Jubilees', *DSD* 11, no. 1 (2004), pp. 82–107.
Lambert, David, 'The Prayer of Manasseh', in Michael Coogan, Mark Zvi Brettler and Pheme Perkins (eds), *The New Oxford Annotated Bible* (New York: Oxford University Press, 2018), pp. 1656–8.
Lambrecht, Jan, 'Romans 4: A Critique of N.T. Wright', *JSNT* 36, no. 2 (2013), pp. 189–94.
Lange, Armin, 'Divinatorische Träume und Apokalyptik im Jübiläenbuch', in Matthias Albani, Jörg Frey and Armin Lange (eds), *Studies in the Book of Jubilees* (Tübingen: Mohr Siebeck, 1997), pp. 25–38.
Lange, Armin, 'In the Second Degree: Ancient Jewish Paratextual Literature in the Context of Graeco-Roman and Ancient Near Eastern Literature', in Philip Alexander, Armin Lange and Renate Pillinger (eds), *In the Second Degree: Paratextual Literature in Ancient Near Eastern and Ancient Mediterranean Culture and Its Reflections in Medieval Literature* (Leiden: Brill, 2010), pp. 3–40.
Langer, Ruth, *Cursing the Christians? A History of the Birkat HaMinim* (New York: Oxford University Press, 2011).
Lappenga, Benjamin J., 'Zealots for Good Works: The Polemical Repercussions of the Word ζηλωτής in Titus 2.14', *CBQ* 75, no. 4 (2013), pp. 704–18.
Lavers, Annette, *Roland Barthes: Structuralism and After* (London: Methuen, 1982).
Lee, Dorothy, 'The Gospel of John and the Five Senses', *JBL* 129, no. 1 (2010), pp. 115–27.
Lee, Jae Won, *Paul and the Politics of Difference: A Contextual Study of the Jewish-Gentile Difference in Galatians and Romans* (Cambridge: James Clarke & Co., 2015).
Lehtipuu, Outi, *The Afterlife Imagery in Luke's Story of the Rich Man and Lazarus* (NovTSup 123; Leiden: Brill, 2007).
Leonhardt, Jutta, *Jewish Worship in Philo of Alexandria* (TSAJ 84; Tübingen: Mohr Siebeck, 2001).
Letellier, Robert Ignatius, *Day in Mamre, Night in Sodom: Abraham and Lot in Genesis 18 and 19* (Leiden: Brill, 1995).
Leuenberger, Martin, *Ich bin Jhwh und Keiner Sonst: Der Exklusive Monotheismus des Kyros-Orakels Jes 45, 1–7* (Stuttgart: KBW Bibelwerk, 2010).
Levene, Nancy, 'Courses and Canons in the Study of Religion (With Continual Reference to Jonathan Z. Smith)', *JAAR* 80, no. 4 (2012), pp. 998–1024.

Levenson, Jon D., 'Abusing Abraham: Traditions, Religious Histories, and Modern Misinterpretations', *Judaism* 47 (1998), pp. 259–77.

Levenson, Jon D., 'The Conversion of Abraham to Judaism, Christianity and Islam', in Hindy Najman and Judith H. Newman (eds), *The Idea of Biblical Interpretation: Essays in Honor of James L. Kugel* (Leiden: Brill, 2004), pp. 3–40.

Levenson, Jon D., *The Death and Resurrection of the Beloved Son: The Transformation of Child Sacrifice in Judaism and Christianity* (New Haven, CT: Yale University Press, 1995).

Levenson, Jon D., *Inheriting Abraham: The Legacy of the Patriarch in Judaism, Christianity and Islam* (Princeton, NJ: Princeton University Press, 2012).

Levine, Amy-Jill, 'Diaspora as Metaphor: Bodies and Boundaries in the Book of Tobit', in J. Andrew Overman and Robert S. MacLennan (eds), *Diaspora Jews and Judaism* (Atlanta, GA: Scholars Press, 1992), pp. 105–18.

Levine, Amy-Jill, 'Tobit', in Michael Coogan (ed.), *The New Oxford Apocrypha* (3rd edn; Oxford: Oxford University Press, 2001), p. 11.

Lied, Liv Ingebord, *The Other Lands of Israel: Imaginations of the Land in 2 Baruch* (JSJSup 129; Leiden: Brill, 2008).

Lieu, Judith, 'Blindness in the Johannine Tradition', *NTS* 34 (1988), pp. 83–95.

Lieu, Judith, 'Temple and Synagogue in John', *NTS* 45 (1999), pp. 51–69.

Lieu, Judith, 'What was From the Beginning: Scripture and Tradition in the Johannine Epistles', *NTS* 39 (1993), pp. 458–77.

Lincoln, Andrew T., *Truth on Trial: The Lawsuit Motif in the Fourth Gospel* (Grand Rapids, MI: Baker Academic, 2000).

Lindars, Barnabas, 'Discourse and Tradition: The Use of the Sayings of Jesus in the Discourses of the Fourth Gospel', *JSNT* 13 (1981), pp. 89–97.

Lindars, Barnabas, 'Slave and Son in John 8.31-36', in William C. Weinrich (ed.), *The New Testament Age: Essays in Honor of Bo Reicke* (Macon, GA: Mercer University Press, 1984), pp. 270–86.

Lindars, Barnabas, *The Theology of the Letter to the Hebrews* (Cambridge: Cambridge University Press, 1991).

Linebaugh, Jonathan A., 'Announcing the Human: Rethinking the Relationship between Wisdom of Solomon 13-15 and Romans 1.18-2.11', *NTS* 57 (2011), pp. 21–40.

Lipton, Diana, 'The Limits of Intercession: Abraham Reads Ezekiel at Sodom', in Diana Lipton (ed.), *Universalism and Particularism at Sodom and Gomorrah: Essays in Memory of Ron Pirson* (Atlanta, GA: SBL Press, 2012), pp. 25–42.

Lipton, Diana, *Revisions of the Night: Politics and Promises in the Patriarchal Dreams of Genesis* (Sheffield: Sheffield Academic Press, 1999).

Littman, Robert J., *Tobit: The Book of Tobit in Codex Sinaiticus* (Leiden/Boston: Brill, 2008).

Litwak, Kenneth D., *Echoes of Scripture in Luke-Acts: Telling the Story of God's People Intertextually* (JSNTSup 282; London: T&T Clark, 2005).

Lohfink, N., *Die Landverheissung als Eid* (Stuttgart: Katholisches Bibelwerk, 1967).

Lona, Horatio E., *Abraham in Johannes 8. Ein Beitrag zur Methodenfrage* (EHS 23/65; Frankfurt/M.: Peter Lang, 1976).

Longenecker, Bruce W., *Eschatology and the Covenant: A Comparison of 4 Ezra and Romans 1–11* (JSNTSup 57; Sheffield: Sheffield Academic Press, 1991).

Longenecker, Bruce W., *Two Esdras* (Sheffield: Sheffield Academic Press, 1995).

Lowe, Malcom, 'Who Were the Ἰουδαῖοι?' *NovT* 18 (1976), pp. 101–30.

Ludlow, Jared W., *Abraham Meets Death: Narrative Humor in the Testament of Abraham* (JSPSup 41; Sheffield: Sheffield Academic Press, 2002).

Macatangay, Francis M., *The Wisdom Instructions in the Book of Tobit* (Deuterocanonical and Cognate Literature Studies 12; Berlin: de Gruyter, 2011).

MacDonald, Nathan, 'Hospitality and Hostility: Reading Genesis 19 in Light of 2 Samuel 10 (and Vice Versa)', in Diana Lipton (ed.), *Universalism and Particularism at Sodom and Gomorrah: Essays in Memory of Ron Pirson* (Atlanta, GA: SBL Press, 2012), pp. 179–90.

MacDonald, Nathan, 'Listening to Abraham – Listening to Yhwh: Divine Justice and Mercy in Genesis 18.16-33', *CBQ* 66, no. 1 (2004), pp. 25–43.

MacRae, George W., 'The Meaning and Evolution of the Feast of Tabernacles', *CBQ* 22, no. 3 (1960), pp. 251–76.

Magid, Shaul, *From Metaphysics to Midrash: Myth, History and the Interpretation of Scripture in Lurianic Kabbala* (Bloomington, IN: Indiana University Press, 2008).

Mahmoud, Jihan, 'Dialogic Interaction between the Historical Background and Events in the Novels of J. M. Coetzee and Jabra Ibrahim Jabra: A Contrapuntal Reading', *International Journal of Arts & Sciences* 7, no. 6 (2014), pp. 561–75.

Maio, G., 'The Metaphorical and Mythical Use of the Kidney in Antiquity', *American Journal of Nephrology* 19, no. 2 (1999), pp. 101–6.

Makiello, Phoebe, 'Abraham and the Nations in the Works of Philo of Alexandria', in Martin Goodman, George H. van Kooten and J. T. A. G. M. van Ruiten (eds), *Abraham, the Nations, and the Hagarites: Jewish, Christian, and Islamic Perspectives on Kinship with Abraham* (TBN 13; Leiden: Brill, 2010), pp. 139–62.

Marcus, Joel, '*Birkat ha-Minim* Revisited', *NTS* 55 (2009), pp. 523–51.

Marcus, Joel, 'Rivers of Living Water from Jesus' Belly (John 7.38)', *JBL* 117, no. 2 (1998), pp. 328–30.

Marcus, Joel, 'The *Testaments of the Twelve Patriarchs* and the *Didascalia Apostolorum*: A Common Jewish Christian Milieu?' *JTS* 61, no. 2 (2010), pp. 596–626.

Marmorstein, Arthur, *The Doctrine of Merits in Old Rabbinical Literature* (London: Oxford University Press, 1920).

Martin-Achard, R., *Actualité d'Abraham* (Neuchâtel: Delachaux and Niestle, 1969).

Martyn, J. Louis, *History and Theology in the Fourth Gospel* (3rd edn; Louisville, KY: Westminster/John Knox, 2003).

Marx, Alexander, 'A Survey of the Literature of Judaism', *JQR* 14, no. 2 (1923), pp. 275–80.

Matera, Frank J., *Romans* (Paideia Commentaries on the New Testament; Grand Rapids, MI: Baker Academic, 2010).

Matthews, Victor H., 'Hospitality and Hostility in Genesis 19 and Judges 19', *BTB* 22 (1992), pp. 3–11.

Mayer, G., 'Aspekte des Abrahambildes in der hellenistisch-jüdischen Literatur', *ET* 32 (1972), pp. 118–27.

McComiskey, Bruce, 'Laws, Works, and the End of Days: Rhetorics of Identification, Distinction, and Persuasion in Miqsat Ma'aseh ha-Torah (Dead Sea Scroll 4QMMT)', *Rhetoric Review* 29, no. 3 (2010), pp. 221–38.

McFarland, Orrey, 'Whose Abraham, Which Promise? Genesis 15.6 in Philo's *De Virtutibus* and Romans 4', *JSNT* 35, no. 2 (2012), pp. 107–29.

McKnight, Scot, *The Letter of James* (NICNT; Grand Rapids, MI: Eerdmans, 2011).

McNamara, Martin, *Targum and Testament Revisited: Aramaic Paraphrases of the Hebrew Bible. A Light on the New Testament* (2nd edn; Grand Rapids, MI: Eerdmans, 2010).

McWhirter, Jocelyn, *The Bridegroom Messiah and the People of God: Marriage in the Fourth Gospel* (Cambridge: Cambridge University Press, 2008).
Meeks, Wayne A., 'Galilee and Judea in the Fourth Gospel', *JBL* 85, no. 2 (1966), pp. 159-69.
Meeks, Wayne A., *The Prophet-King: Moses Traditions and the Johannine Christology* (Leiden: Brill, 1967).
Méndez, Hugo, 'Semitic Poetic Techniques in the Magnificat: Luke 1.46-47, 55', *JBL* 135, no. 3 (2016), pp. 557-47.
Menken, Maarten J. J., *Old Testament Quotations in the Fourth Gospel: Studies in Textual Form* (CBET 15; Kampen: Kok Pharos, 1996).
Metzner, Rainer, *Das Verständnis der Sünde im Johannesevangelium* (WUNT 1/122; Tübingen: Mohr Siebeck, 2000).
Miller, Geoffrey David, *Marriage in the Book of Tobit* (Berlin: Walter de Gruyter, 2011).
Miller, Patrick D., *They Cried to the Lord: The Form and Theology of Biblical Prayer* (Minneapolis, MN: Fortress Press, 1994).
Miller, Paul, '"They Saw His Glory and Spoke of Him": The Gospel of John and the Old Testament', in Stanley E. Porter (ed.), *Hearing the Old Testament in the New Testament* (Grand Rapids, MI: Eerdmans, 2006), pp. 127-51.
Mimouni, Simon, *Comptes rendus de l'Académie des inscriptions & belles lettres* (Janvier – Mars, 2015).
Mirguet, Françoise, 'Attachment to the Body in the Greek *Testament of Abraham*: A Reappraisal of the Short Recension', *JSP* 19, no. 4 (2010), pp. 251-75.
Mitchell, Margaret, 'Patristic Counterevidence to the Claim that the Gospels Were Written for All Christians', *NTS* 51 (2005), pp. 36-79.
Moberly, R. Walter L., 'The Earliest Commentary on the Akedah', *VT* 38, no. 3 (1988), pp. 302-23.
Moffitt, David M., *Atonement and the Logic of Resurrection in the Epistle to the Hebrews* (NovTSup 141; Leiden: Brill, 2011).
Mol, Jurrien, *Collective and Individual Responsibility: A Description of Corporate Personality in Ezekiel 18 and 20* (Leiden: Brill, 2009).
Moloney, Francis J., *Johannine Studies: 1975-2017* (WUNT 372; Tübingen: Mohr Siebeck, 2017).
Moo, Douglas J., *The Letter of James: An Introduction and Commentary* (Grand Rapids, MI: Eerdmans, 1995).
Moo, Jonathan A., *Creation, Nature and Hope in 4 Ezra* (Göttingen: Vandenhoeck & Ruprecht, 2011).
Moody Smith, D., *The Theology of the Gospel of John* (Cambridge: Cambridge University Press, 1995).
Moore, Stephen D., *Literary Criticism and the Gospels: The Theoretical Challenge* (New Haven, CT and London: Yale University Press, 1989).
Moore, Stephen D., *Poststructuralism and the New Testament: Derrida and Foucault at the Foot of the Cross* (Minneapolis, MN: Fortress Press, 1994).
Moore, Stephen D. and Yvonne Sherwood, *The Invention of the Biblical Scholar: A Critical Manifesto* (Minneapolis, MN: Fortress Press, 2011).
Morgan, Robert, '*Sachkritik* in Reception History', *JSNT* 32, no. 3 (2010), pp. 175-90.
Morgan, Thais E., 'Is There an Intertext in This Text?: Literary and Interdisciplinary Approaches to Intertextuality', *American Journal of Semiotics* 3, no. 4 (1985), pp. 1-40.
Morgenstern, Julian, 'The Calendar of the Book of Jubilees', *VT* 5 (1955), pp. 74-6.
Moriarty, Michael, *Roland Barthes* (Oxford: Polity Press, 1991).

Moscicke, Hans, 'The Concept of Evil in 4 Maccabees: Stoic Absorption and Adaptation', *JJTP* 25 (2017), pp. 163–95.

Moss, Candida, 'Polycarp', *VC* 67, no. 2 (2013), pp. 117–36.

Motyer, Stephen, *Your Father the Devil? A New Approach to John and the Jews* (PBN; Carlisle: Paternoster, 1997).

Motyer, Steve, 'Method in Fourth Gospel Studies: A Way Out of the Impasse?' *JSNT* 66 (1997), pp. 27–44.

Moyise, Steve, 'Intertextuality and Biblical Studies: A Review', *Verbum et Ecclesia* 23, no. 2 (2002), pp. 418–31.

Moyise, Steve, 'Intertextuality and Historical Approaches to the Use of Scripture in the New Testament', in Richard B. Hays, Stefan Alkier and Leroy A. Huizenga (eds), *Reading the Bible Intertextually* (Waco, TX: Baylor University Press, 2009), pp. 23–32.

Müller, F. Max, *Introduction to the Science of Religion: Four Lectures Delivered at the Royal Institution with Two Essays on False Analogies and the Philosophy of Mythology* (London: Longmans, Green and Co., 1878).

Müller, Hans-Peter, 'Die weisheitliche Lehrerzählung im Alten Testament und in seiner Umwelt', *Die Welt des Orients* 9, no. 1 (1977), pp. 77–98.

Murphy, Frederick J., 'The Eternal Covenant in Pseudo-Philo', *JSP* 3 (1988), pp. 43–57.

Murphy, Frederick J., *Pseudo-Philo: Rewriting the Bible* (New York: Oxford University Press, 1993).

Murphy, Frederick J., 'Retelling the Bible: Idolatry in Pseudo-Philo', *JBL* 107, no. 2 (1988), pp. 275–87.

Myers, Alicia D., *Characterizing Jesus: A Rhetorical Analysis on the Fourth Gospel's Use of Scripture in Its Presentation of Jesus* (LNTS 458; London: T&T Clark, 2012).

Myers, Alicia D., '"Jesus Said to Them…": The Adaptation of Juridical Rhetoric in John 5.19-47', *JBL* 132, no. 2 (2013), pp. 415–30.

Nader, Laura, 'Comparative Consciousness', in Robert Borofsky (ed.), *Assessing Cultural Anthropology* (4th edn; New York: McGraw Hill, 1993), pp. 84–96.

Naiweld, Ron, 'The Father of Man: Abraham as the Rabbinic Jesus', in Jörg Rüpke and Wolfgang Spikermann (eds), *Reflections on Religious Individuality: Greco-Roman and Judaeo-Christian Texts and Practices* (Berlin: Walter de Gruyter, 2012), pp. 145–71.

Najman, Hindy, 'Interpretation as Primordial Writing: Jubilees and Its Authority Conferring Strategies', *JSJ* 30, no. 4 (1999), pp. 379–410.

Najman, Hindy, 'The Law of Nature and the Authority of the Mosaic Law', *StPhAnnual* 11 (1999), pp. 55–73.

Najman, Hindy, *Losing the Temple and Recovering the Future: An Analysis of 4 Ezra* (Cambridge: Cambridge University Press, 2014).

Najman, Hindy, 'Reconsidering Jubilees: Prophecy and Exemplarity', in Gabriele Boccaccini and Giovanni Ibba (eds), *Enoch and the Mosaic Torah: The Evidence of Jubilees* (Grand Rapids, MI: Eerdmans, 2009), pp. 229–43.

Nanos, Mark D., 'How Inter-Christian Approaches to Paul's Rhetoric Can Perpetuate Negative Valuations of Jewishness – Although Proposing to Avoid That Outcome', *BibInt* 13, no. 3 (2005), pp. 254–69.

Nanos, Mark D., *The Irony of Galatians: Paul's Letter in First-Century Context* (Minneapolis, MN: Fortress Press, 2002).

Nelson, David, *Mekhilta De-Rabbi Shimon Bar Yochai: Translated into English with Critical Introduction and Annotation* (Philadelphia, PA: Jewish Publication Society, 2006).

Nestle, Eberhard, Erwin Nestle, Barbara Aland, Kurt Aland, Iōan D. Karavidopoulos, Carlo Maria Martini, Bruce M. Metzger and Holger Strutwolf, *Nestle-Aland, Novum Testamentum Graece* (28th edn; Stuttgart: Deutsche Bibelgesellschaft, 2012). OliveTree Software.
Neusner, Jacob (ed. and trans.), *Tosefta* (2 vols; Peabody, MA: Hendrickson, 2002).
Newman, Judith H., 'The Form and Settings of the Prayer of Manasseh', in Mark J. Boda, Daniel K. Falk and Rodney A. Werline (eds), *Seeking the Favor of God, Volume 2: The Development of Penitential Prayer in Second Temple Judaism* (Atlanta, GA: SBL Press, 2007), pp. 105–25.
Newman, Judith H., 'God Condemns the Arrogance of Power: The Prayer in 3 Maccabees 6.2-15', in M. Kiley et al. (ed.), *The Prayer from Alexander to Constantine* (London: Routledge, 1997), pp. 48–52.
Newman, Judith H., *Praying by the Book: The Scripturalization of Prayer in Second Temple Judaism* (Atlanta, GA: SBL Press, 1999).
Newman, Judith H., 'Three Contexts of Manasseh's Prayer in the *Didascalia*', *JCSSyrSt* 7 (2007), pp. 3–15.
Neyrey, Jerome H., *The Gospel of John in Cultural and Rhetorical Perspective* (Grand Rapids, MI: Eerdmans, 2009).
Neyrey, Jerome H., 'Jesus the Judge: Forensic Processes in John 8.21-59', *Bib* (1987), 509–42.
Nickelsburg, George W. E., 'Prayer of Manasseh', in Michael Coogan (ed.), *The New Oxford Apocrypha* (3rd edn; Oxford: Oxford University Press, 2001), pp. 322–6.
Nickelsburg, George W. E., 'Stories of Biblical and Early Post-Biblical Times', in Michael E. Stone (ed.), *Jewish Writings of the Second Temple Period* (Philadelphia, PA: Fortress Press, 1984), pp. 33–81.
Niehoff, Maren, 'Mother and Maiden, Sister and Spouse: Sarah in Philonic Midrash', *HTR* 97, no. 4 (2004), pp. 413–44.
Niskanen, Paul, 'Yhwh as Father, Redeemer, and Potter in Isaiah 63.7–64.11', *CBQ* 68, no. 3 (2006), pp. 397–407.
Noegel, Scott, 'Dreams and Dream Interpreters in Mesopotamia and in the Hebrew Bible', in K. Bulkeley (ed.), *Dreams* (New York: Palgrave Macmillan, 2001), pp. 45–71.
Noort, Ed and Eibert Tigchelaar (eds), *The Sacrifice of Isaac: The Aqedah (Genesis 22) and Its Interpretations* (TBN 4; Leiden/Boston: Brill, 2002).
Northcott, Michael S., 'Eucharistic Eating, and Why many Early Christians Preferred Fish', in David Grumett and Rachel Muers (eds), *Eating and Believing: Interdisciplinary Perspectives on Vegetarianism and Theology* (London: T&T Clark/Bloomsbury, 2008), pp. 232–46.
Novakovic, Lidija, *Raised from the Dead according to Scripture: The Role of Israel's Scripture in the Early Christian Interpretations of Jesus' Resurrection* (JACT 12; London: Bloomsbury/T&T Clark, 2012).
Novick, Tzvi, 'Test and Temptation in *4 Ezra*', *JSP* 22, no. 3 (2013), pp. 238–44.
Novick, Tzvi, 'Traditions and Truth: The Ethics of Lawmaking in the Tannaitic Literature', *JQR* 100, no. 2 (2010), pp. 223–43.
Novick, Tzvi, *What Is Good and What God Demands: Normative Structures in Tannaitic Literature* (JSJSup 144; Leiden: Brill, 2014).
Obermann, Andreas, *Die christologische Erfüllung der Schrift im Johannesevangelium: Eine Untersuchung zur johanneischen Hermeneutik anhand der Schriftzitate* (WUNT 2.83; Tübingen: Mohr Siebeck, 1996).
Oblath, Michael, '"To Sleep, Perchance to Dream…": What Jacob Saw at Bethel', *JSOT* 26, no. 1 (2001), pp. 117–26.

O'Brien, Kelli S., 'The Curse of the Law (Galatians 3.13): Crucifixion, Persecution, and Deuteronomy 21.22-23', *JSNT* 29, no. 1 (2006), pp. 55-76.
Och, Bernard, 'Abraham and Moriah: A Journey to Fulfillment', *Judaism* 38 (1989), pp. 293-309.
O'Connor, Jerome Murphy, 'Philo and 2 Cor 6.14-7.1', *RevBib* 95, no. 1 (1988), pp. 55-69.
O'Day, Gail R., 'Jeremiah 9.22-23 and 1 Corinthians 1.26-31: A Study in Intertextuality', *JBL* 109 (1990), pp. 259-67.
Oeming, Manfred, 'Ist Genesis 15,6 ein Beleg für die Anrechnung des Glaubens zur Gerechtigkeit?' *ZAW* 95, no. 2 (1983), pp. 182-97.
O'Kane, Martin, '"The Bosom of Abraham" (Luke 16.22): Father Abraham in the Visual Imagination', *BibInt* 15 (2007), pp. 485-518.
Ong, Walter, *Orality and Literacy: The Technologizing of the World* (London/New York: Methuen, 1982).
Orlov, Andrei A., '"The Gods of My Father Terah": Abraham the Iconoclast and the Polemics with the Divine Body Traditions in the *Apocalypse of Abraham*', *JSP* 18, no. 1 (2008), pp. 33-53.
Orlov, Andrei A., *Heavenly Priesthood in the Apocalypse of Abraham* (Cambridge: Cambridge University Press, 2013).
Orlov, Andrei A., '"The Likeness of Heaven": The *Kavod* of Azazel in the *Apocalypse of Abraham*', in Daphna V. Arbel and Andrei A. Orlov (eds), *With Letters of Light: Studies in the Dead Sea Scrolls, Early Jewish Apocalypticism, Magic, and Mysticism in Honor of Rachel Elior* (Berlin/New York: de Gruyter, 2010), pp. 232-53.
Oropeza, B. J., 'Paul and Theodicy: Intertextual Thoughts on God's Justice and Faithfulness to Israel in Romans 9-11', *NTS* 53, no. 1 (2007), pp. 57-80.
Orr, Mary, *Intertextuality* (Cambridge: Polity Press, 2003).
Owen, Paul L., 'The "Works of the Law" in Romans and Galatians: A New Defense of the Subjective Genitive', *JBL* 126, no. 3 (2007), pp. 553-77.
Painter, John, 'Tradition, History and Interpretation in John 10', in Johannes Beutler and Robert T. Forta (eds), *The Shepherd Discourse of John 10 and Its Context: Studies by Members of the Johannine Writings Seminar* (SNTSMS 67; Cambridge: Cambridge University Press, 1991), pp. 53-74.
Painter, John, 'Tradition and Interpretation in John 6', *NTS* 35 (1989), pp. 421-50.
Parsenios, George C., *Departure and Consolation: The Johannine Farewell Discourse in Light of Greco-Roman Literature* (NovTSup 117; Leiden: Brill, 2005).
Parsenios, George L., *Rhetoric and Drama in the Johannine Lawsuit Motif* (WUNT 2.258; Tübingen: Mohr Siebeck, 2010).
Parsons, Mikeal C., 'Son and High Priest: A Study in the Christology of Hebrews', *EvQ* 60 (1988), pp. 198-216.
Patai, Raphael, 'The Control of Rain in Ancient Palestine', *HUCA* 14 (1930), p. 275.
Pearce, Sarah, '3 Maccabees', in Martin Goodman, John Barton and John Muddiman (eds), *Apocrypha* (Oxford: Oxford University Press, 2012), pp. 328-31.
Peleg, Yitzhak, *Going Up and Going Down: A Key to Interpreting Jacob's Dream (Gen 28.10-22)* (trans. Betty Rozen; London: Bloomsbury T&T Clark, 2015).
Peppard, Michael, *The Son of God in the Roman World: Divine Sonship in its Social and Political Context* (New York: Oxford University Press, 2011).
Perrot, Charles and Pierre-Maurice Bogaert, *Pseudo-Philon: Les Antiquités Bibliques* (SC, 229/30; Paris: Les Éditions du Cerf, 1976).
Phillips, G. L., 'Faith and Vision in the Fourth Gospel', in F. L. Cross (ed.), *Studies in the Fourth Gospel* (London: Mowbray, 1957), pp. 83-96.

Philonenko-Sayar, Belkis and Marc Philonenko, *L'Apocalypse d'Abraham: Introduction, texte slave, traduction et notes* (Semitica 31; Paris: Adrien Maisonneuve, 1981).
Pohlmann, Karl-Friedrich, '3. Esra-Buch', in *Historische und legendarische Erzählungen* (Gütersloh: Gerd Mohn, 1980), pp. 375-425.
Poirier, John C., 'Another Look at the "Man Born Blind" in John 9', *JRDH* 14, no. 1 (2010), pp. 60-5.
Poirier, John C., 'Hanukkah in the Narrative Chronology of the Fourth Gospel', *NTS* 54, no. 4 (2008), pp. 465-78.
Poirier, John C., '"Night and Day" and the Punctuation of John 9.3', *NTS* 42 (1996), pp. 288-94.
Polanski, Donald C., 'On Taming Tamar: Amram's Rhetoric and Women's Roles in Pseudo-Philo's *Liber Antiquitatum Biblicarum* 9', *JSP* 13 (1995), pp. 79-99.
Popović, Mladen, 'Abraham and the Nations in the Dead Sea Scrolls: Exclusivism and Inclusivism in the Texts from Qumran and the Absence of a Reception History for Gen 12.3', in Martin Goodman, George H. van Kooten and J. T. A. G. M. van Ruiten (eds), *Abraham, the Nations, and the Hagarites: Jewish, Christian, and Islamic Perspectives on Kinship with Abraham* (TBN 13; Leiden: Brill, 2010), pp. 77-103.
Portier-Young, Anathea, 'Alleviation of Suffering in the Book of Tobit: Comedy, Community, and Happy Endings', *CBQ* 63 (2001), pp. 35-54.
Portier-Young, Anathea, *Apocalypse Against Empire: Theologies of Resistance in Early Judaism* (Grand Rapids, MI: Eerdmans, 2011).
Portier-Young, Anathea, 'Jewish Apocalyptic Literature as Resistance Literature', in John J. Collins (ed.), *The Oxford Handbook of Apocalyptic Literature* (New York/Oxford: Oxford University Press, 2014), pp. 145-62.
Portier-Young, Anathea, 'Three Books of Daniel: Plurality and Fluidity among the Ancient Versions', *Int* 7, no. 2 (2017), pp. 143-53.
Pryor, John W., 'John the Baptist and Jesus: Tradition and Text in John 3.25', *JSNT* 66 (1997), pp. 15-26.
Qimron, Elisha and John Strugnell, *Qumran Cave 4.V: Miqsat Ma'aseh Ha-Torah* (DJD 10; Oxford: Clarendon, 1994).
Räisänen, Heikki, *Paul and the Law* (WUNT 29; Tübingen: Mohr Siebeck, 1983).
Räisänen, Heikki, *Paul and the Law* (2nd edn; WUNT 29; Tübingen: Mohr Siebeck, 1987).
Ramsey, George W., 'Is Name-Giving an Act of Domination in Genesis 2.23 and Elsewhere?' *CBQ* 50, no. 1 (1988), pp. 24-35.
Rapa, Robert Keith, *The Meaning of 'Works of the Law' in Galatians and Romans* (New York: Peter Lang, 2001).
Rata, Tiberius, *The Covenant Motif in Jeremiah's Book of Comfort: Textual and Intertextual Studies of Jeremiah 30-33* (StudBibLit 105; New York: Peter Lang, 2007).
Reed, Annette Yoshiko, 'Abraham as Chaldean Scientist and Father of the Jews: Josephus, *Ant.* 1.154-168, and the Greco-Roman Discourse about Astronomy/Astrology', *JSJ* 35 (2004), pp. 119-58.
Reed, Annette Yoshiko, 'The Construction and Subversion of Patriarchal Perfection: Abraham and Exemplarity in Philo, Josephus, and the *Testament of Abraham*', *JSJ* 40 (2009), pp. 185-212.
Reed, Annette Yoshiko, '"Jewish-Christian" Apocrypha and the History of Jewish/ Christian Relations', in P. Piovanelli (ed.), *Christian Apocryphal Texts for the New Millennium: Achievements, Prospects, and Challenges* (Texts and Studies in Ancient Judaism 171; Tübingen: Mohr Siebeck, 2018), pp. 85-110.

Reed, Annette Yoshiko, 'Old Testament Pseudepigrapha and Post-70 Judaism', in Simon Claude Mimouni, Bernard Pouderon and Claire Clivas (eds), *Les Judaïsmes dans tous leurs etats aux Ier-IIIe siecles* (Paris: Cerf, forthcoming).

Reed, Annette Yoshiko, 'Textuality between Death and Memory: The Prehistory and Formation of the Parabiblical Testament', *JQR* 104, no. 3 (2014), pp. 381-412.

Reif, Stefan C., 'On Some Connotations of the Word *Ma'aseh*', in Geoffrey Khan and Diana Lipton (eds), *Studies on the Text and Versions of the Hebrew Bible in Honour of Robert Gordon* (VTSupp 149; Leiden: Brill, 2012), pp. 337-52.

Reim, Günter, *Studien zum alttestamentlichen Hintergrund des Johannesevangeliums* (SNTSMS 22; Cambridge: Cambridge University Press, 1974).

Reinhartz, Adele, 'And the Word Was Begotten: Divine Epigenesis in the Gospel of John', *Sem* 85 (1999), pp. 83-103.

Reinhartz, Adele, *Befriending the Beloved Disciple: A Jewish Reading of the Gospel of John* (New York: Continuum, 2001).

Reinhartz, Adele, *Jesus of Hollywood* (New York: Oxford University Press, 2009).

Reinhartz, Adele, 'John 8.31-59 from a Jewish Perspective', in John K. Roth and Elisabeth Maxwell (eds), *Remembering for the Future: The Holocaust in an Age of Genocide, vol. 2: Ethics and Religion* (Palgrave: Macmillan, 2001), pp. 787-97.

Reinhartz, Adele, *"Why Ask My Name?" Anonymity and Identity in Biblical Narrative* (New York: Oxford University Press, 1998).

Reinink, G. J., 'The Lamb on the Tree: Syriac Exegesis and Anti-Islamic Apologetics', in Ed Noort and Eibert Tigchelaar (eds), *The Sacrifice of Isaac: The Aqedah (Gen 22) and Its Interpretations* (TBN 4; Leiden: Brill, 2001), pp. 109-24.

Reventlow, H. Graf., '"Sein Blut komme über sein Haupt,"' *VT* 10 (1960), pp. 311-27.

Rey, Jean-Sébastien (ed.), *The Dead Sea Scrolls and Pauline Literature* (Leiden: Brill, 2014).

Reymond, Eric D., 'Prelude to the Praise of the Ancestors, Sirach 44.1-15', *HUCA* 72 (2001), pp. 1-14.

Reynolds, Bennie H. III, *Between Symbolism and Realism: The Use of Symbolic and Non-Symbolic Language in Ancient Jewish Apocalypses 333-63 BCE* (Göttingen: Vandenhoeck & Ruprecht, 2012).

Reynolds, Kent Aaron, *Torah as Teacher: The Exemplary Torah Student in Psalm 119* (Leiden: Brill, 2010).

Rezetko, Robert and Ian Young, *Historical Linguistics and Biblical Hebrew: Toward an Integrated Approach* (Atlanta, GA: SBL Press, 2014).

Richardson, Ken and David S. Wester, 'Analogical Reasoning and the Nature of Context: A Research Note', *British Journal of Educational Psychology* 66 (1996), pp. 23-32.

Richter, Georg, 'Zur Formgeschichte und literarischen Einheit von Joh 6,31-58', *ZNW* 60 (1969), pp. 21-55.

Richter, Wolfgang, *Exegese als Literaturwissenschaft: Entwurf einer atl. Literaturtheorie und Methodologie* (Göttingen: Vandenhoeck & Ruprecht, 1971).

Rickett, Dan, 'Rethinking the Place and Purpose of Genesis 13', *JSOT* 36, no. 1 (2011), pp. 31-53.

Riesenfeld, H., *Jésus Transfiguré* (Copenhagen: Munksgaard, 1947).

Riffaterre, Michael, 'Compulsory Reader-Response: The Intertextual Drive', in Michael Worton and Judith Still (eds), *Intertextuality: Theories and Practices* (Manchester/New York: Manchester University Press, 1990), pp. 56-78.

Riffaterre, Michael, 'Intertextual Representation: On Mimesis as Interpretive Discourse', *CI* 11, no. 1 (1984), pp. 141-62.

Riffaterre, Michael, 'Interpretation and Undecidability', *NLH* 12, no. 2 (1980), pp. 227–42.
Riffaterre, Michael, *Semiotics of Poetry* (Bloomington, IN: Indiana University Press, 1978).
Rindge, Matthew S., 'Luke's Artistic Parables: Narratives of Subversion, Imagination, and Transformation', *Int* 68, no. 4 (2014), pp. 403–15.
Robbins, Vernon K., 'Rhetography as a New Way of Seeing the Familiar Text', in C. Clifton Black and Duane F. Watson (eds), *Words Well Spoken: George Kennedy's Rhetoric of the New Testament* (Waco, TX: Baylor University Press, 2008), pp. 81–106.
Robertson Smith, W., *The Religion of the Semites* (3rd edn; London: A&C Black, 1927).
Rodriguez, Rafael and Matthew Thiessen (eds), *The So-Called Jew in Paul's Letter to the Romans* (Minneapolis, MN: Fortress Press, 2016).
Roitman, Adolfo D., 'The Traditions about Abraham's Early Life in the Book of Judith (5.6-9)', in Esther G. Chazon et al. (eds), *Things Revealed: Studies in Early Jewish and Christian Literature in Honor of Michael E. Stone* (JSJS 89; Leiden: Brill, 2004), pp. 73–87.
Roose, Hanna, 'Umkehr und Ausgleich bei Lukas: Die Gleichnisse vom verlorenen Sohn (Lk 15.11-32) und vom reichen Mann und armen Lazarus (Lk 16.19-31) als Schwestergeschichten', *NTS* 56, no. 1 (2010), pp. 1–21.
Rosen-Zvi, Ishay, *Demonic Desires: 'Yetzer Hara' and the Problem of Evil in Late Antiquity* (Philadelphia, PA: University of Pennsylvania Press, 2011).
Rosen-Zvi, Ishay, 'Pauline Traditions and the Rabbis: Three Case Studies', *HTR* 110, no. 2 (2017), pp. 169–94.
Rubenstein, Arie, 'Hebraisms in the Slavonic "Apocalypse of Abraham"', *JJS* 4 (1953), pp. 108–15.
Rubenstein, Arie, 'Hebraisms in the Slavonic "Apocalypse of Abraham"', *JJS* 5 (1954), pp. 132–35.
Rubenstein, Jeffrey L., *The History of Sukkot in the Second Temple and Rabbinic Periods* (Atlanta, GA: Scholars Press, 1995).
Rubenstein, Jeffrey L., 'Sukkot, Eschatology and Zechariah 14', *RB* 103 (1996), pp. 161–95.
Rubinkiewicz, Ryszard, *L'Apocalypse d'Abraham en vieux slave: Introduction, texte critique, traduction et commentaire* (Towarzystwo Naukowe Katolickiego Uniwersytu Lubelskiego Źródła I monografie 129; Lublin: Société des Lettres et des Sciences de l'Université Catholique de Lublin, 1987).
Rudman, Dominic, 'A Note on the Azazel-goat Ritual', *ZAW* 116 (2004), pp. 396–401.
Said, Edward W., *Culture and Imperialism* (London: Vintage [reprint], 1994).
Sailhamer, John H., *Introduction to Old Testament Theology: A Canonical Approach* (Grand Rapids, MI: Eerdmans, 1995).
Salkin, Rabbi Jeffrey, *The Gods Are Broken! The Hidden Legacy of Abraham* (Lincoln: University of Nebraska Press/JPS, 2013).
Sandelin, Karl-Gustav, 'Philo as a Jew', in Torrey Seland (ed.), *Reading Philo: A Handbook to Philo of Alexandria* (Grand Rapids, MI: Eerdmans, 2014), pp. 19–46.
Sanders, E. P., *Comparing Judaism and Christianity: Common Judaism, Paul and the Inner and Outer in the Study of Religion* (Minneapolis, MN: Fortress Press, 2016).
Sanders, E. P., *Paul, the Law, and the Jewish Peoples* (Minneapolis, MN: Fortress Press, 1983).
Sanders, E. P., *Paul and Palestinian Judaism: A Comparison of Patterns of Religion* (Minneapolis, MN: Fortress Press, 1977).
Sanders, Jack T., *The Jews in Luke-Acts* (Philadelphia, PA: Fortress Press, 1987).
Sanders, Jack T., 'Paul's "Autobiographical" Statements in Galatians 1-2', *JBL* 85, no. 3 (1966), pp. 335–43.

Sandmel, Samuel, 'Parallelomania', *JBL* 81, no. 1 (1962), pp. 1–13.
Sandmel, Samuel, 'Philo's Place in Judaism: A Study of Conceptions of Abraham in Jewish Literature, Part II', *HUCA* 26 (1955), pp. 151–332.
Sandmel, Samuel, *Philo's Place in Judaism: A Study of Conceptions of Abraham in Jewish Literature* (Cincinnati, OH: Hebrew Union College Press, 1956).
Satlow, Michael L., *Jewish Marriage in Antiquity* (Oxford and Princeton, NJ: Princeton University Press, 2001).
Satlow, Michael L., 'Philo on Human Perfection', *JTS* 59, no. 2 (2008), pp. 500–19.
Satterfield, Bruce, 'John 7-9 in Light of the Feast of Tabernacles', in Who (ed.), *The Testimony of John the Beloved: The 1998 Sperry Symposium on the New Testament* (Salt Lake City, UT: Deseret Books, 1998), pp. 249–65. Accessed online: https://emp.byui.edu/SatterfieldB/Papers/John7-9.5.html 28 September 2018.
Saussy, Haun, 'Comparative Literature?' *PMLA* 118, no. 2 (2003), pp. 336–41.
Savage, Timothy B., *Power through Weakness: Paul's Understanding of the Christian Ministry in 2 Corinthians* (Cambridge: Cambridge University Press, 1996).
Sawyer, John F. A., 'Combating Prejudices about the Bible and Judaism', *Theology* 94, no. 760 (1991), pp. 269–78.
Schäfer, Peter, *Jesus in the Talmud* (Princeton, NJ and Oxford: Princeton University Press, 2007).
Schauer, Frederick, 'Why Precedent in Law (and Elsewhere) Is Not Totally (or Even Substantially) about Analogy', *Perspectives on Psychological Science* 5, no. 6 (1998), pp. 454–60.
Schechter, Solomon, *Some Aspects of Rabbinic Theology* (New York: Macmillan, 1909).
Scheuer, Blaženka, *The Return of YHWH: The Tension between Deliverance and Repentance in Isaiah 40-55* (Berlin: de Gruyter, 2008).
Schliesser, Benjamin, *Abraham's Faith in Romans 4: Paul's Concept of Faith in Light of the History of Reception of Genesis 15.6* (WUNT 2/224; Tübingen: Mohr Siebeck, 2007).
Schmitz, Thomas, *Modern Literary Theory and Ancient Texts: An Introduction (Moderne Literaturtheorie und antike Texte)* (Oxford: Blackwell, 2007).
Schmutzer, Andrew J., 'Did the Gods Cause Abraham's Wandering? An Examination of התעו אתי אלהים in Genesis 20.13', *JSOT* 35 (2010), pp. 149–66.
Schniedewind, William M., 'A Qumran Fragment of the Ancient "Prayer of Manasseh"?' *ZAW* 108, no. 1 (1996), pp. 105–7.
Scholtissek, Klaus, *In ihm sein und bleiben: Die Sprache der Immanenz in den johanneischen Schriften* (HBS 21; Freiburg: Herder, 2000).
Schreiner, Thomas R., *The Law and Its Fulfillment: A Pauline Theology of Law* (Grand Rapids, MI: Baker Books, 1993).
Schreiner, Thomas R., '"Works of Law" in Paul', *NovT* 33 (1991), pp. 217–44.
Schuchard, Bruce G., *Scripture within Scripture: The Interrelationship of Form and Function in the Explicit Old Testament Citations in the Gospel of John* (SBLDS 133; Atlanta, GA: Scholars Press, 1992).
Schwartz, Baruch, 'Term or Metaphor: Biblical *nōśē' 'āwōn/peša'/cheth*' [in Hebrew], *Tarbiz* 63 (1994), pp. 149–71.
Seebas, H., 'Gen 15,2b', *ZAW* 75 (1963), pp. 317–19.
Segal, Michael, *The Book of Jubilees: Rewritten Bible, Redaction, Ideology and Theology* (SupJSJ 117; Leiden: Brill, 2007).
Segovia, Fernando F., *The Farewell of the Word: The Johannine Call to Abide* (Minneapolis, MN: Augsburg, Fortress Press, 1991).

Seifrid, Mark A., *Justification by Faith: The Origin and Development of a Central Pauline Theme* (Leiden: Brill, 1992).
Seim, Turid Karlsen, 'Abraham, Ancestor or Archetype? A Comparison of Abraham-Language in 4 Maccabees and Luke-Acts', in Adela Yarbro Collins and Margaret M. Mitchell (eds), *Antiquity and Humanity: Essays on Ancient Religions and Philosophy Presented to Hans Dieter Betz on His 70th Birthday* (Tübingen: Mohr Siebeck, 2001), pp. 27–42.
Seim, Turid Karlsen, 'Descent and Divine Paternity in the Gospel of John', in Stephen P. Ahearne-Kroll, Paul A. Holloway and James A. Kelhoffer (eds), *Women and Gender in Ancient Religions: Interdisciplinary Approaches* (WUNT 263; Tübingen: Mohr Siebeck, 2010), pp. 99–123.
Shäfer, Peter, *The Jewish Jesus: How Judaism and Christianity Shaped Each Other* (Princeton, NJ: Princeton University Press, 2012).
Shea, William H., 'Azazel in the Pseudepigrapha', *JATS* 13 (2002), pp. 1–9.
Sheridan, Ruth, 'Jewish Readings of the Fourth Gospel: Beyond the Pale?' in Jione Havea, David Neville and Elaine Wainwright (eds), *Bible, Borders, Belongings: Engaging Readings from Oceania* (Atlanta, GA: SBL Press, 2014), pp. 93–108.
Sheridan, Ruth, 'Johannine Sectarianism: A Category Now Defunct?' in Hughson Ong and Stanley E. Porter (eds), *The Origins of John's Gospel* (JoSt 2; Leiden: Brill, 2015), pp. 142–66.
Sheridan, Ruth, 'John's Gospel and Modern Genre Theory: The Farewell Discourse (John 13–17) as a Test Case', *ITQ* 75, no. 3 (2010), pp. 287–99.
Sheridan, Ruth, 'Identity, Alterity and the Gospel of John', *BibInt* 22, no. 2 (2014), pp. 188–209.
Sheridan, Ruth, 'Issues in the Translation of οἱ Ἰουδαῖοι in the Fourth Gospel', *JBL* 132, no. 3 (2013), pp. 671–96.
Sheridan, Ruth, 'The Paraclete in the Johannine Farewell Discourse', *Pac* 20 (2007), pp. 125–41.
Sheridan, Ruth, 'The Paraclete as Successor in the Johannine Farewell Discourse: A Comparative Literary Analysis', *AEJT* 18, no. 2 (2011), pp. 129–40.
Sheridan, Ruth, 'Persuasion', in Douglas Estes and Ruth Sheridan (eds), *How John Works: Storytelling in the Fourth Gospel* (Atlanta, GA: SBL Press, 2016), pp. 205–24.
Sheridan, Ruth, *Retelling Scripture: The Jews and the Scriptural Citations in John 1:19-12:15* (Leiden/Boston, MA: Brill, 2012).
Sheridan, Ruth, 'Seed of Abraham, Slavery, and Sin: Reproducing Johannine Anti-Judaism in the Modern Commentaries on John 8.31-34', in R. Alan Culpepper and Paul N. Anderson (eds), *John and Judaism: A Contested Relationship in Context* (Atlanta, GA: SBL Press, 2017), pp. 313–32.
Sheridan, Ruth, 'She Forgets Her Suffering in Her Joy: The Parable of the Laboring Woman (John 16.20-22)', in Beth M. Stovell (ed.), *Making Sense of Motherhood: Biblical and Theological Perspectives* (Eugene, OR: Wipf & Stock, 2016), pp. 45–64.
Sheridan, Ruth, 'The Testimony of Two Witnesses: John 8.17', in Alicia D. Myers and Bruce G. Schuchard (eds), *Abiding Words: The Use of Scripture in the Gospel of John* (RBS 81; Atlanta, GA: SBL Press, 2015), pp. 161–84.
Sheridan, Sybil, 'Abraham from a Jewish Perspective', in Normal Solomon, Richard Harries and Tim Winter (eds), *Abraham's Children: Jews, Christians and Muslims in Conversation* (London: T&T Clark Continuum, 2006), pp. 9–17.
Sherwood, Yvonne, *A Biblical Text and Its Afterlives: The Survival of Jonah in Western Culture* (Cambridge: Cambridge University Press, 2001).

Siker, Jeffrey, 'Abraham in Graeco-Roman Paganism', *JSJ* 18 (1988), pp. 188–208.
Siker, Jeffrey, *Disinheriting the Jews: Abraham in Early Christian Controversy* (Louisville, KY: Westminster/John Knox, 1991).
Sim, David C., *Apocalyptic Eschatology in the Gospel of Matthew* (SNTSMS 88; Cambridge: Cambridge University Press, 1996).
Sim, David C., 'The Gospels for All Christians? A Response to Richard Bauckham', *JSNT* 84 (2001), pp. 3–27.
Slingerland, Dixon, 'The Levitical Hallmark within the Testaments of the Twelve Patriarchs', *JBL* 103, no. 4 (1984), pp. 531–37.
Smit, Peter-Ben, *Fellowship and Food in the Kingdom: Eschatological Meals and Scenes of Utopian Abundance in the New Testament* (WUNT 2.234; Tübingen: Mohr Siebeck, 2008).
Smith, Charles W. F., 'No Time for Figs', *JBL* 79, no. 4 (1960), pp. 315–27.
Smith, D. Moody, *John among the Gospels* (2nd edn; Columbia, SC: University of South Carolina Press, 2015).
Smith, Jonathan Z., 'Acknowledgements: Morphology and History in Mircea Eliade's "Patterns in Comparative Religion" (1949–1999), Part 2: The Texture of the Work', *History of Religions* 39, no. 4 (2000), pp. 332–51.
Smith, Jonathan Z., *Drudgery Divine: On the Comparison of Early Christianities and the Religions of Late Antiquity* (Chicago, IL: University of Chicago Press, 1990).
Smith, Jonathan Z., *Relating Religion: Essays in the Study of Religion* (Chicago, IL and London: University of Chicago Press, 2004).
Smith, Jonathan Z., 'When the Bough Breaks', *History of Religions* 12, no. 4 (1973), pp. 342–71.
Smith, Morton, *Tannaitic Parallels to the Gospels* (SBLMS; Philadelphia, PA: SBL Press, 1951, repr. 1968).
Smith, Paul A., *Rhetoric and Redacton in Trito-Isaiah: The Structure, Growth, and Authorship of Isaiah 56–66* (VTSupp 62; Leiden: Brill, 1995).
Snodgrass, Klyne R., 'Justification by Grace – To the Doers: An Analysis of the Place of Romans 2 in the Theology of Paul', *NTS* 32 (1986), pp. 72–93.
Solomon, Norman, Richard Harries and Tim Winter (eds), *Abraham's Children: Jews, Christians and Muslims in Conversation* (London: T&T Clark, 2006).
Sommer, Benjamin D., *A Prophet Reads Scripture: Allusion in Isaiah 40–66* (Stanford, CA: Stanford University Press, 1998).
Somov, Alexey, *Representations of the Afterlife in Luke-Acts* (London: T&T Clark/Bloomsbury, 2017).
Spaulding, Mary B., *Commemorative Identities: Jewish Social Memory and the Johannine Feast of Booths* (London: Continuum International, 2009).
Speiser, Ephraim A., *Genesis* (AB 1; New York: Doubleday, 1964).
Spilsbury, Paul, *The Image of the Jew in Flavius Josephus' Paraphrase of the Bible* (TSzAJ 69; Tübingen: Mohr Siebeck, 1998).
Spivak, Gayatri Chakravorty, 'Rethinking Comparativism', *NLH* 40, no. 3 (2009), pp. 609–26.
Sprinkle, Preston M., *Law and Life: The Interpretation of Leviticus 18.5 in Early Judaism and in Paul* (WUNT 2.2.41; Tübingen: Mohr Siebeck, 2008).
Sprinkle, Preston M., *Paul and Judaism Revisited: A Study of Divine and Human Agency in Salvation* (Downers Grove: IVP Academic, 2013).
Spurling, Helen and Emmanouela Grypeou, 'Abraham's Angels: Jewish and Christian Exegesis of Genesis 18–19', in Helen Spurling and Emmanouela Grypeou (eds), *The*

Exegetical Encounter between Jews and Christians in Late Antiquity (Leiden: Brill, 2009), pp. 181–203.

Stanley, Christopher D., *Arguing with Scripture: The Rhetoric of Quotations in the Letters of Paul* (London/New York: T&T Clark, 2004).

Steck, Odil Hannes, *Das apokryphe Baruchbuch: Studien zu Rezeption und Konzentration 'kanonischer' Überlieferung* (FRLANT 160; Göttingen: Vandenhoeck & Ruprecht, 1993).

Stemberger, Guenter, 'Genesis 15 in Rabbinic and Patristic Interpretation', in Emmanouela Grypeou and Helen Spurling (eds), *The Exegetical Encounter between Jews and Christians in Late Antiquity* (JCP 18; Leiden: Brill, 2009), pp. 143–62.

Stewart, Alexander E., 'Narrative World, Rhetorical Logic, and the Voice of the Author in 4 Ezra', *JBL* 132, no. 2 (2013), pp. 373–91.

Steyn, Gert J., 'Observations on the Text Form of the Minor Prophets Quotations in Romans 9–11', *JSNT* 38, no. 1 (2015), pp. 49–67.

Stokes, Ryan E., 'The Throne Visions of Daniel 7, 1 "Enoch" 14, and the Qumran "Book of Giants" (4Q530)', *DSS* 15, no. 3 (2008), pp. 340–58.

Stone, Michael E., 'Coherence and Inconsistency in the Apocalypses: The Case of "The End" in 4 Ezra', *JBL* 102, no. 2 (1983), pp. 229–43.

Stone, Michael E., *Fourth Ezra: A Commentary on the Book of Fourth Ezra* (Hermeneia; Minneapolis, MN: Fortress Press, 1990).

Stone, Michael E. and Matthias Henze (eds), *4 Ezra and 2 Baruch: Translations, Introductions, and Notes* (Minneapolis, MN: Fortress Press, 2013).

Stowasser, Martin, 'Die Sendschreiben der Offenbarung des Johannes: Literarische Gestaltung – Buchkompositorische Funktion – Textpragmatik', *NTS* 61, no. 1 (2015), pp. 50–66.

Streett, Matthew, *Here Comes the Judge: Violent Pacifism in the Book of Revelation* (LNTS, London: T&T Clark, 2012).

Strugnell, John, 'MMT: Second Thoughts on A Forthcoming Edition', in Eugene Ulrich and James C. VanderKam (eds), *The Community of the Renewed Covenant: The Notre Dame Symposium on the Dead Sea Scrolls* (Notre Dame: University of Notre Dame Press, 1994), pp. 57–73.

Stube, John C., *A Graeco-Roman Rhetorical Reading of the Farewell Discourse* (London: T&T Clark Continuum, 2006).

Sutherland, Dixon, 'The Organization of the Abraham Promise Narratives', *ZNW* 95, no. 3 (1983), pp. 337–43.

Swetnam, James, 'Form and Content in Hebrews 7–13', *Bib* 55, no. 3 (1974), pp. 333–48.

Swetnam, James, 'The Meaning of πεπιστευκότας in John 8.31', *Bib* 61 (1980), pp. 106–9.

Tannehill, Robert, 'The Magnificat as Poem', *JBL* 93 (1974), pp. 263–75.

Taylor Gench, Frances, 'John 7.53–8.11', *Interpretation* (2009), pp. 398–400.

Teeter, D. Andrew, 'On "Exegetical Function" in Rewritten Scripture: Inner-Biblical Exegesis and Abram/Ravens Narrative in *Jubilees*', *HTR* 106, no. 4 (2013), pp. 373–402.

Theissen, Matthew, *Paul and the Gentile Problem* (New York: Oxford University Press, 2016).

Theodor, Jehuda and Hanokh Albeck, *Midrash Bereshit Rabbah: Critical Edition with Notes and Commentary* [Hebrew, 3 vols] (Jerusalem: Shalem Books, 1965 [orig. Berlin, 1912–36]; H. Freedman and M. Simon (trans.), *Midrash Rabbah: Translated into English* (10 vols; 3rd edn; London: Soncino, 1961)).

Thettayll, Benny, *In Spirit and Truth: An Exegetical Study of John 4.19–26 and a Theological Investigation of the Replacement Theme in the Fourth Gospel* (Leuven: Peeters, 2007).

Thomas, Chantal, *Pour Roland Barthes* (Paris: Éditions du Seuil, 2015).
Thompson, Alden, *Responsibility for Evil in the Theodicy of IV Ezra: A Study Illustrating the Significance of Form and Structure for the Meaning of the Book* (SBLDS 29; Missoula: Scholars Press, 1977).
Thompson, James W., *Hebrews* (Paideia; Grand Rapids, MI: Baker Academic, 2008).
Tobin, Thomas H., 'What Shall We Say That Abraham Found? The Controversy behind Romans 4', *HTR* 88, no. 4 (1995), pp. 437–52.
Todorov, Tzvetan, 'Comment lire?' in Tzvetan Todorov (ed.), *Poétique de la prose* (Paris: Seuil, 1974), pp. 241–53.
Tolmie, D. Françoise, 'The Characterization of God in the Fourth Gospel', *JSNT* 69 (1998), pp. 57–75.
Tolmie, D. François, *Jesus' Farewell to the Disciples: John 13.1–17.26 in Narratological Perspective* (Leiden: Brill, 1995).
Tolonen, Anna-Lüsa and Elisa Uusimäki, 'Managing the Ancestral Way of Lide in the Roman Diaspora: The Mélange of Philosophical and Scriptural Practice in 4 Maccabees', *JSJ* 48 (2017), pp. 113–41.
Torrey, Charles C., 'Isaiah 41', *HTR* 44, no. 3 (1951), pp. 121–36.
Tov, Emanuel, *The Greek & Hebrew Bible: Collected Essays on the Septuagint* (Leiden/Boston, MA: Brill, 1999).
Towner, Philip H., *The Letters to Timothy and Titus* (NICNT; Grand Rapids, MI: Eerdmans, 2006).
Trachtenberg, Joshua, *The Devil and the Jews: The Medieval Conception of the Jew and Its Relation to Modern Anti-Semitism* (2nd edn; Philadelphia, PA: JPS, 2002).
Trotter, Jonathan R., 'The Developing Narrative of the Life of Job: The Implications of Some Shared Elements of the Book of Tobit and the *Testament of Job*', *CBQ* 77, no. 3 (2015), pp. 449–66.
Turner, Geoffrey, 'The Righteousness of God in Pslams and Romans', *SJT* 73, no. 3 (2010), pp. 285–301.
Tyrrell-Hanson, Anthony, *The Prophetic Gospel: A Study of John and the Old Testament* (London: Continuum, 1991).
Ulfgard, Håkan, *The Story of Sukkot: The Setting, Shaping, and Sequel of the Biblical Feast of Tabernacles* (Tübingen: Mohr Siebeck, 1998).
Underwood, Grant, 'Attempting to Situate Joseph Smith', *Brigham Young University Studies* 44, no. 4 (2005), pp. 41–52.
Urbach, Ephraim, 'Rabbinic Homilies on Gentile Prophets and the Episode of Balaam' [in Hebrew], in Ephraim Urbach, *Me-Olamam shel Hakhamim: Kovets mehkarim* (Jerusalem: Magnes, 1988), pp. 537–54.
Utzschneider, Helmut, 'Text–Reader–Author. Towards a Theory of Exegesis: Some European Viewpoints', in Ehud Ben Zvi (ed.), *Perspectives on Biblical Hebrew: Comprising the Contents of Journal of Hebrew Scriptures volumes 1–4* (Piscataway, NJ: Gorgias Press, 2006), pp. 1–22.
van Bekkum, Wout J., 'The Aqedah and Its Interpretations in Midrash and Piyyut', in Ed Noort and Eibert Tigchelaar (eds), *The Sacrifice of Isaac: The Aqedah (Gen 22) and Its Interpretations* (TBN 4; Leiden: Brill, 2001), pp. 86–95.
van der Horst, Pieter W., 'Portraits of Women in Pseudo-Philo's *Liber Antiquitatum Biblicarum*', *JSP* 5 (1989), pp. 29–46.
VanderKam, James C., *Textual and Historical Studies in the Book of Jubilees* (Missoula, MT: Scholars Press, 1977).

van der Lans, Birgit, 'Belonging to Abraham's Kin: Genealogical Appeals to Abraham as a Possible Background for Paul's Abrahamic Argument', in Martin Goodman, George H. van Kooten and J. T. A. G. M. van Ruiten (eds), *Abraham, the Nations, and the Hagarites: Jewish, Christian, and Islamic Perspectives on Kinship with Abraham* (TBN 13; Leiden: Brill, 2010), pp. 307–18.

Van Os, Bas, 'The Jewish Recipients of Galatians', in Stanley E. Porter (ed.), *Paul: Jew, Greek, and Roman* (PSP 5; Leiden: Brill, 2008), pp. 51–64.

van Ruiten, J. T. A. G. M, *Abraham in the Book of Jubilees: The Rewriting of Genesis 11.26–25.10 in the Book of Jubilees 11.14–23.8* (JSJS 161; Leiden: Brill, 2012).

van Ruiten, J. T. A. G. M, 'Abraham, Job and the *Book of Jubilees*: The Intertextual Relationship of Genesis 22.1-19, Job 1.1-2:13, and *Jubilees* 17.15–18:19', in Ed Noort and Eibert Tigchelaar (eds), *The Sacrifice of Isaac: The Aqedah (Gen 22) and Its Interpretations* (TBN 4; Leiden: Brill, 2001), pp. 58–85.

van Seters, John, *Abraham in History and Tradition* (New Haven/London: Yale University Press, 1975).

van Seters, John, *The Life of Moses: The Yahwist as Historian in Exodus-Numbers* (CBET 10; Kampen: Kok Pharos, 1994).

van Seters, John, 'A Response to G. Aichelle [sic], P. Miscall an R. Walsh, "An Elephant in the Room: Historical-Critical and the [sic] Postmodern Interpretations of the Bible"', *JHS* 9 (2009), pp. 1–13.

Van Tilborg, Sjef, *Imaginative Love in John* (Leiden: Brill, 1993).

van Wolde, Ellen, *A Semiotic Analysis of Genesis 2-3. A Semiotic Theory and Method of Analysis Applied to the Story of the Garden of Eden* (Assen: Van Gorcum, 1989).

van Wolde, Ellen, 'Texten lessen we allemaal', *Schrift* 91 (1984), pp. 3–7.

Vermes, Geza, *Scripture and Tradition in Judaism: Haggadic Studies* (SPB 4; 2nd edn; Leiden: Brill, 1973).

Visscher, Gerhard H., *Romans 4 and the New Perspective on Paul: Faith Embraces the Promise* (New York: Peter Lang, 2009).

von Wahlde, Urban C., *The Earliest Version of John's Gospel: Recovering the Gospel of Signs* (Wilmington, NC: Michael Glazier, 1989).

von Wahlde, Urban C., 'Faith and Works in Jn VI 28-29', *NovT* 22, no. 4 (1980), pp. 304–15.

von Wahlde, Urban C., 'Literary Structure and Theological Argument in Three Discourses with the Jews in the Fourth Gospel', *JBL* 103, no. 4 (1984), pp. 575–84.

von Wahlde, Urban C., '"You are of Your Father the Devil" in Its Context: Stereotyped Apocalyptic Polemic in Jn 8:38-47', in Reimund Bieringer, Didier Pollefeyt and Frederique Vandecasteele-Vanneuville (eds), *Anti-Judasim and the Fourth Gospel: Papers from the Leuven Colloqium* (Assen: Van Gorcum, 2001), pp. 437–48.

Von Weissenberg, Hanne, *4QMMT: Reevaluating the Text, the Function, and the Meaning of the Epilogue* (STDJ 82; Leiden: Brill, 2009).

Wallace, David R., *Election of the Lesser Son: Paul's Lament-Midrash in Romans 9-11* (Minneapolis, MN: Augsburg, 2014).

Ward, Roy Bowen, 'The Works of Abraham: James 2.14-26', *HTR* 61 (1968), pp. 283–90.

Warner, Megan, *Re-Imagining Abraham: A Re-Assessment of the Influence of Deuteronomism in Genesis* (Leiden: Brill, 2018).

Watson, Francis, *Paul and the Hermeneutics of Faith* (2nd edn; London: T&T Clark/Bloomsbury, 2016).

Watson, Francis, *Paul, Judaism, and the Gentiles: Beyond the New Perspective* (Grand Rapids, MI: Eerdmans, 2007).

Weissenrieder, Annette, 'Spirit and Rebirth in the Gospel of John', *Religion and Theology* 21 (2014), pp. 58–85.
Welborn, Laurence L., 'The Runaway Paul', *HTR* 92 (1999), pp. 115–63.
Wellhausen, Julius, *Prolegomena to the History of Ancient Israel* (trans. J. Sutherland Black and Allan Menzies; Edinburgh: Adam & Black, 1885).
Wenham, Gordon J., 'The Deuteronomic Theology of the Book of Joshua', *JBL* 90, no. 2 (1971), pp. 140–8.
Werman, Cana, 'Levi and Levites in the Second Temple Period', *DSD* 4, no. 2 (1997), pp. 211–25.
Werrett, Ian C., *Ritual Purity and the Dead Sea Scrolls* (STDJ 72; Leiden: Brill, 2007).
Westerholm, Stephen, *Perspectives Old and New on Paul: The 'Lutheran Paul' and His Critics* (Grand Rapids, MI: Eerdmans, 2004).
Weyde, Karl William, *The Appointed Festivals of YHWH: The Festival Calendar in Leviticus 23 and the Sukkôt Festival in Other Biblical Texts* (FAT 2/4; Tübingen: Mohr Siebeck, 2004).
Whitters, Mark F., 'Baruch as Ezra in *2 Baruch*', *JBL* 132, no. 3 (2013), pp. 569–84.
Widmer, Michael, *Moses God, and the Dynamics of Intercessory Prayer: A Study of Exodus 32-34 and Numbers 13-14* (FAT 2/8; Tübingen: Mohr Siebeck, 2004), pp. 113–18.
Wieser, Friedrich E., *Die Abrahamvorstellungen im Neuen Testament* (Bern: Peter Lang, 1987).
Wilkins, George, 'The Prayer of Manasseh', *Hermathena* 16, no. 36 (1910), pp. 167–78.
Williams, Catrin, 'First-Century Media Culture and Abraham as a Figure of Memory in John 8.31-59', in Tom Thatcher and Anthony le Donne (eds), *The Fourth Gospel in First-Century Media Culture* (London: T&T Clark, 2011), pp. 205–22.
Williams, Sam K., 'Promise in Galatians: A Reading of Paul's Reading of Scripture', *JBL* 107, no. 4 (1988), pp. 709–20.
Williams, Travis B., *Good Works in 1 Peter: Negotiating Social Conflict and Christian Identity in the Greco-Roman World* (WUNT 337; Tübingen: Mohr Siebeck, 2014).
Williamson, Paul R., *Abraham, Israel and the Nations: The Patriarchal Promise and Its Covenantal Development in Genesis* (JSOTSup 315; Sheffield: Sheffield Academic Press, 2000).
Wills, Lawrence M., 'The Depiction of the Jews in Acts', *JBL* 110, no. 4 (1991), pp. 631–54.
Wills, Lawrence M., *The Jewish Novel in the Ancient World* (Ithaca/London: Cornell University Press, 1995).
Wills, Lawrence M., 'Prayer of Azariah and the Song of the Three Young Men', in Gale A. Yee, Hugh R. Page Jr and Matthew J. M. Coomber (eds), *The Apocrypha: Fortress Commentary on the Bible Study Edition* (Minneapolis, MN: Fortress Press, 2016), pp. 1043–6.
Wilson, Marvin R., *Our Father Abraham: Jewish Roots of the Christian Faith* (Grand Rapids, MI: Eerdmans, 1989).
Wilson, Walter T., '4 Maccabees', in Michael D. Coogan (ed.), *The New Oxford Annotated Apocrypha: Augmented Third Edition* (New York/Oxford: Oxford University Press, 2007), pp. 362–3.
Wink, Walter, *John the Baptist in the Gospel Tradition* (SNTMS 7; Cambridge: Cambridge University Press, 1968).
Winter, Bruce W., *Philo and Paul among the Sophists* (SNTSMS 96; Cambridge: Cambridge University Press, 1997).
Witherington, Ben III, *The Christology of Jesus* (Minneapolis, MN: Augsburg/Fortress, 1990).

Witherington, Ben III, 'The Waters of Birth: John 3.5 and 1 John 5.6-8', *NTS* 35, no. 1 (1989), pp. 155-60.
Wright, Benjamin G., 'Biblical Interpretation in the Book of Ben Sira', in Matthias Henze (ed.), *A Companion to Biblical Interpretation in Early Judaism* (Grand Rapids, MI: Eerdmans, 2011), pp. 361-86.
Wright, Benjamin G., 'Torah and Sapiential Pedagogy in the Book of Ben Sira', in Bernd U. Schipper and D. Andrew Teeter (eds), *Wisdom and Torah: The Reception of 'Torah' in the Wisdom Literature of the Second Temple Period* (Leiden: Brill, 2013), pp. 157-86.
Wright, N. T., '4QMMT and Paul: Justification, "Works" and Eschatology', in Aaron Son (ed.), *History and Exegesis: New Testament Essays in Honor of Dr. Earl Ellis for His 80th Birthday* (New York and London: T&T Clark, 2006), pp. 104-32.
Wright, N. T., *Justification: God's Plan and Paul's Vision* (Downers Grove, IL: Intervarsity Press, 2009).
Wright, N. T., *Paul: Fresh Perspectives* (Minneapolis, MN: Fortress Press, 2005).
Wright, N. T., 'Paul and the Patriarch: The Role of Abraham in Romans 4', *JSNT* 35 (2013), pp. 207-41.
Yadin, Azzan, *Scripture as Logos: Rabbi Ishmael and the Origins of Midrash* (Philadelphia, PA: University of Pennsylvania Press, 2004).
Yadin, Azzan, *Scripture and Tradition: Rabbi Akiva and the Triumph of Midrash* (Philadelphia, PA: University of Pennsylvania Press, 2015).
Yadin, Yigal, *The Temple Scroll* (Vol. 1; Jerusalem: Israel Exploration Society and Shrine of the Book, 1983).
Yadin-Israel, Azzan, 'Rabbinic Polysemy: A Response to Steven Fraade', *AJS Review* 38, no. 1 (2014), pp. 129-41.
Yee, Gail A., *Jewish Feasts in the Gospel of John* (Eugene, OR: Wipf & Stock; repr. 2007).
Yinger, Kent L., *Paul, Judaism, and Judgment According to Deeds* (Cambridge: Cambridge University Press, 1999).
Yoon, David I., 'The Ideological Inception of Intertextuality and its Dissonance in Current Biblical Studies', *CBR* 12, no. 1 (2012), pp. 58-76.
Zeitlin, Solomon, 'The Book of Jubilees: Its Character and Its Significance', *JQR* 30 (1939-40), pp. 1-31.
Zumstein, Jean, 'Die Schriftrezeption in der Brotrede (Joh 6)', in Jean Zumstein (ed.), *Kreative Erinnerung: Relecture und Auslegung im Johannesevangelium* (ATANT 84; Zürich: Theologischer Verlag, 2004).
Zumstein, Jean, *Kreative Erinnerung: Relecture und Auslegung im Johannesevangelium* (Abhandlungen zur Theologie des Alten und Neuen Testaments 84; Zürich: TVZ, 2004).
Zurawski, Jason M., 'The Two Worlds and Adam's Sin: The Problem of *4 Ezra* 7.10-14', in Gabriele Boccaccini and Jason M. Zurawski (eds), *Interpreting 4 Ezra and 2 Baruch: International Studies* (LSTS 87; London: T&T Clark, 2014), pp. 97-106.

Author index

Abasciano, B. J.   61, 267
Abegg, M.   252, 253, 255
Abraham, B. S.   199
Abusch, R. S.   208
Adams, E.   198
Aichele, G.   48, 61, 65, 71, 77, 80, 81
Albeck, H.   348
Alexander, D.   137
Allen, G.   62, 63, 68, 70, 71, 74–8, 83, 256
Allison, D. C.   180, 282, 330
Alter, R.   151
Anbar, M.   137
Anderson, B. W.   149
Anderson, G. A.   5, 44, 147, 169, 170, 177, 179, 232, 245, 246, 259, 264, 279, 284, 301
Anderson, H.   158
Anderson, P. N.   3, 301, 349
Angermuller, J.   47
Ashton, J.   35, 60, 215, 239, 294, 361
Asiedu-Peprah, M.   105, 110, 289, 290, 303
Attridge, H. W.   24, 102, 186, 205
Aune, D. E.   160, 257
Avalos, H.   48
Avioz, M.   186

Bachmann, M.   252
Baden, J.   134, 135
Bakhtin, M.   61, 62, 76, 132
Baldensperger, W.   30
Ball, D.   317
Balla, I.   246, 247
Bar-Asher Siegal, M.   56, 58
Barclay, J. M. G.   191
Barr, J.   9, 131
Barrett, C. K.   93, 99, 105, 108, 204, 301, 350
Barstad, H. M.   149
Barthes, R.   42, 47, 50, 60, 62, 68–87, 365, 366

Barton, J.   10, 159, 229
Bassnet, S.   47
Bauckham, R.   79, 97, 165, 205
Baumgardt, D.   138
Baynes, L.   340, 341
Beach, B.   138
Beal, T. K.   67
Beasley-Murray, G.   132, 257, 318
Becker, A. H.   2, 208
Becker, J.   1, 334
Beentjes, P. C.   153
Beers, B.   5
Begg, C.   250
Ben Zvi, E.   9, 324
Benjamin, M.   49, 115
Bennema, C.   82
Berger, K.   8
Berger, M. S.   208
Berkley, T.   64
Bernard, J. H.   132
Betz, H. D.   166, 189, 339
Beutler, J.   292, 300
Biddle, M.   150
Bieringer, R.   1
Bikerman, E. J.   137
Billerbeck, P.   5
Black, M.   349
Blenkinsopp, J.   230, 321
Boase, E.   140, 141
Bock, D. L.   204
Bockhmuehl, M.   206
Boda, M. J.   161, 230, 236
Bogaert, P. M.   5, 171, 173
Boismard, M.-E.   104
Bowen Ward, R.   7
Bowker, J.   139
Boyarin, D.   55, 155, 208, 343, 344
Brady, C. M. M.   248
Brant, J.-A.   252
Brettler, M. Z.   153, 160, 232
Bright, J.   149
Brodie, T.   29, 133, 227

Brodie, T. L.   61, 90
Brooke, G. J.   151, 153, 182, 183, 240
Brown, J. K.   289
Brown, R. E.   34, 91, 92, 99, 108, 132, 218, 219, 294, 300, 301
Bruce, F. F.   205
Bruckner, J. K.   324
Brueggemann, W.   146, 235
Bruner, D.   90
Brunson, A. C.   38, 48, 61, 361
Buisch, P. P.   244
Bultmann, R.   34, 94, 101, 132, 261, 289, 294, 350, 367
Byrne, B.   195, 196, 198, 200, 266
Byron, J.   331
Byun, S. L.   235

Callan, T.   260
Calvert-Koyzis, N.   8
Campbell, D.   261
Campbell, L.   53
Carmichael, C. M.   169, 349, 350
Carroll, J. T.   196, 203
Carson, D. A.   29, 38, 91, 92, 94, 132, 133, 225
Cassuto, U.   113
Chan, M. J.   232
Charlier, J.-P.   34
Chester, A.   334
Chilton, B.   49, 340, 344, 345
Chomsky, W.   128
Ciampa, R. E.   276
Clark, E. A.   2, 79, 80, 322
Clarke, E. G.   139
Clifford, H.   149
Clifford, R. J.   231, 233
Cohen, S. J. D.   6
Colijn, B.   259
Collins, J. J.   156, 158, 180, 241, 344
Collins, R.   258
Coloe, M. L.   37, 82, 333, 344, 349, 350, 361
Colson, F. H.   124, 250
Conway, C. M.   187
Coogan, M. D.   157, 165, 167, 168
Cooper, J. W.   332
Corley, J.   246
Cortes, J. B.   104
Cory, C.   105

Cousland, R.   158
Craigie, P. C.   144
Cranfield, C. E. B.   269, 273
Cranford, M.   198, 199
Cribbs, F. L.   49
Cronshaw, D.   58
Croy, N. C.   158, 374
Culler, J.   74
Culpepper, R. A.   3, 104, 300, 301, 303
Curran, J. E. Jr.   267
Curzer, H. J.   4, 134
Cuvillier, É.   338

Dacy, M.   125, 127
Dahl, N. A.   7, 203, 298
Daise, M.   104, 111
Dale Bruner, F.   90
Danby, M.   127, 210, 214
Dapaah, D. S.   352
Daschke, D.   162
Davidson, I.   128
Davies, M.   39
Davis, K.   240
Davis, S. J.   67
de Boer, M. C.   189, 195
de Jonge, M.   102, 160, 183, 242
de Lange, T.   2, 3, 8, 12–15
De Roo, J. C. R.   252, 255
de Villiers, P. G. R.   257
Dennert, B. C.   293
deSilva, D. A.   165–7, 241, 242, 245
Di Mattei, S.   196
Dienes, R.   258
Dietzfelbinger, C.   133
Dimant, D.   243
Dochhorn, J.   298
Dodd, C. H.   22–4, 28, 63, 90, 92, 98, 101, 223, 289
Doering, L.   56, 57, 239, 252, 253
Donaldson, T. L.   194
Dozeman, T. B.   22, 25, 26, 101, 138, 145, 189, 223, 329
Drawnel, H.   183
Dube, M. W.   352
Duggan, M.   231
Duling, D.   202
Dunn, J. D. G.   8, 191, 193, 195, 200, 252–5, 259, 261, 265, 266, 274, 293
Dunn, J. G. F.   273, 274, 293

Dunning, B. 206
Dupré, J. 79

Easter, M. C. 206
Eastman, S. G. 195, 197, 200, 263, 264, 267
Edwards, M. J. 30, 36, 37, 361
Egger-Wenzel, R. 248
Eggler, J. 344
Ego, B. 178, 341
Ehrlich, E. L. 319
Eisenbaum, P. 8, 272
Eisenberg, R. 127, 129
Elfenbein, A. 63
Ellis, P. F. 101
Engberg-Pedersen, T. 294
Ensor, P. W. 289, 291–4, 303, 352
Enz, J. J. 289
Epstein, J. 287
Esler, P. F. 194
Eslinger, L. 4, 134
Estes, D. 24, 83, 302
Eubank, N. 259
Evans, C. A. 5, 61, 64, 182, 248, 272
Eynikel, E. 135

Faierstein, M. M. 129
Feldman, A. 128
Feldman, L. H. 4, 184, 185, 250
Ffrench, P. 47
Fields, W. W. 324
Figueira, D. M. 53
Fillvedt, O. J. 206
Finkelstein, L. 5, 207, 285, 287
Fishbane, M. 153, 254
Fisk, B. N. 173, 174
Fitzmeyer, J. A. 243
Fleischer, P. V. M. 345
Forbes, C. 201
Fortna, R. T. 289
Foster, R. B. 200
Foster, R. J. 271
Fox, M. V. 233
Fraade, S. D. 55, 56, 59, 207
France, R. T. 342
Frayer-Griggs, D. 260, 304
Fredriksen, P. 193
Freed, E. D. 33–5, 317, 361
Fretheim, T. E. 144, 166

Frevel, C. 179
Frey, J. 178, 241, 326
Frick, H. 54
Frishman, J. 5
Frow, J. 63
Fujita, S. 178, 179
Fung, R. Y. K. 189, 191

Gadamer, H.-G. 69
Gager, J. G. 185
Gallusz, L. 331
Garcia Marrtinez, F. 139, 252
Gathercole, S. J. 198, 246, 260, 262, 263, 267, 277, 278
Genette, G. 62, 63, 172
Genz, R. 341
Ginzberg, L. 5
Goodman, L. 4
Goodman, M. 5, 159, 185, 239
Gosse, B. 146
Grabbe, L. L. 113
Gräßer, E. 1
Green, J. B. 202
Green, W. S. 64
Greenfield, J. 183
Gregory, B. C. 5, 170, 171
Grélot, P. 36
Griffiths, T. 97
Grindheim, S. 267, 300
Gruen, E. 158
Grüneberg, K. N. 134
Grypeou, E. 5, 323
Gunkel, H. 136
Gupta, N. 8
Gutman, A. 160

Haar, S. 315
Hacham, N. 159
Hadas, M. 158
Haenchen, E. 90, 132, 291, 298
Hägerland, T. 337, 340
Hahn, F. 354
Hahn, S. W. 154
Hall, D. R. 198
Halpern-Amaru, B. 178, 179, 184–6
Hamilton, V. P. 135
Hammer, R. 210, 211, 285, 287
Hansen, G. W. 8, 191, 193, 194
Harlan, D. 60, 61, 69, 71

Harner, P. B.   34
Harries, R.   4, 279
Harrington, D. J.   5, 156, 170, 172
Harris, M. J.   202
Harstine, S.   289
Harvey, E.   104
Hasel, G. F.   137
Hasitschka, M.   216
Hatina, T.   48, 61, 64
Hatton, P.   229
Hauptman, J.   208
Hauspie, K.   135
Hays, C. M.   341
Hays, R. B.   61, 63, 64, 191, 265, 266, 273, 277
Hayward, R.   173
Heike, T.   156
Heil, J. P.   201, 268
Heim, E. M.   194
Hempel, C.   252
Hendel, R.   145
Hengstenberg, E.   132, 225
Henze, M.   162, 170, 240
Hezser, C.   194, 212
Hieke, T.   156, 157, 248
Hildebrandt, T.   151, 152
Hodges, Z. C.   104
Höffken, P.   149
Hogan, K.   163, 164, 245
Hollander, J.   63
Holloway, P. A.   103, 351
Holsinger, B.   3
Holtz, B. W.   208
Holtzmann, H. J.   30–1
Horovitz, H. S.   285, 287
Hoskins, P. M.   49, 104
Hoskyns, E. C.   30
Huizenga, L.   61, 64, 65, 332
Hultgren, S. J.   243
Hunn, D.   91–6, 191
Hunt, S. A.   30–2, 38, 39, 151
Husser, J.-M.   319, 320

Irwin, W.   61, 66
Isaac, E.   137
Ishida, T.   238

Jack Suggs, M.   159–60
Jackson-McCabe, M. A.   270

Jaffee, M. S.   207
Jansen, N.   51, 52
Janzen, J. G.   103
Japhet, S.   149, 154
Jervis, L. A.   337
Jipp, J. W.   323
Jipps, J.   262
Johnson, L. T.   203, 270, 315

Kahl, B.   190
Kanagaraj, J.   354–5
Käsemann, E.   261
Katz, S. T.   6
Kaufmann, Y.   113
Kauppi, N.   47
Keener, C. S.   101, 258, 295, 300–2, 343, 351
Kensky, M. Z.   246
Kessler, E.   206
Kierspel, L.   294
Kim, K.-S.   67, 247, 259
Kippenberg, H. G.   56
Kister, M.   49, 247, 283–5
Klauck, H.-J.   56
Klawans, J.   332
Klein, M. L.   343
Knibb, M. A.   163, 335
Koch, K.   10, 229, 344
Koester, C. R.   216, 217, 354, 356
Kok, J.   294
Kolenkow, A. B.   180
Koopmans, W. T.   146
Kratz, R. G.   154
Kristeva, J.   11, 47, 61–3, 65–7, 85
Kruse, C. G.   198
Kugel, J. L.   4, 178, 279, 348
Kugler, G.   230
Kuhn, H.-W.   49
Kundert, L.   166
Kutsch, E.   145
Kynes, W.   47
Kysar, R.   301

Laato, T.   270
Lambert, D.   160, 161, 179
Lambrecht, J.   8, 262, 263
Lange, A.   172, 178, 326
Langer, R.   6
Lappenga, B. J.   258
Lauterbach, J. Z.   209, 214, 284, 286, 346

Lavers, A. 74-6, 83
Lee, D. 316, 349, 354-6
Lee, J. W. 191
Lehtipuu, O. 341, 342
Leonhardt, J. 251
Letellier, R. I. 323, 324
Leuenberger, M. 149
Levene, N. 55
Levenson, J. D. 4, 137, 138, 140, 171, 186, 279-81, 320, 331
Levine, A.-J. 167-9
Lied, L. I. 241
Lieu, J. M. 103, 105, 106, 296-9
Lincoln, A. T. 30, 104, 289
Lindars, B. 22, 89, 92, 101, 189, 206, 289, 317
Linebaugh, J. A. 198
Lipton, D. 137, 142, 230, 323, 324
Littman, R. J. 167
Litwak, K. D. 61
Lohfink, N. 136
Lona, H. E. 8-12, 39
Longenecker, B. W. 162, 164
Longenecker, R. 189, 191
Lowe, M. 37
Ludlow, J. W. 180-2
Lust, J. 135

Macatangay, F. M. 168, 246
MacDonald, N. 141, 323
MacRae, G. W. 113, 114
Magid, S. 214
Mahmoud, J. 59
Maio, G. 328
Makiello, P. 187
Malina, B. 101, 105
Marcus, J. 6, 117, 159
Marcus, R. 125, 249, 251
Marmorstein, A. 284, 285
Martin, R. P. 270
Martin-Achard, R. 5
Martyn, J. L. 13, 25, 78, 91, 189, 196, 203
Marx, A. 128
Matera, F. J. 199, 200, 274
Matthews, V. H. 323
Mayer, G. 4
Mays, J. L. 237
McComiskey, B. 254
McFarland, O. 266

McKnight, S. 271
McNamara, M. 343, 344
McWhirter, J. 349
Meeks, W. A. 4, 315
Melamed, E. 287
Mendez, H. 202, 203
Menken, M. J. J. 48, 104, 276, 302
Metzner, R. 216-18
Meyers, C. L. 116
Meyers, E. M. 116
Michaels, J. R. 32, 33
Miller, G. D. 169
Miller, P. D. 16, 17, 142, 354, 355
Mimouni, S. 160
Mirguet, F. 180
Miscall, P. 48, 60, 61
Mitchell, M. 79
Moberly, R. W. L. 139
Moffitt, D. M. 205, 206
Mol, J. 236
Moloney, F. J. 90, 94, 97, 98, 101, 105, 351, 356
Moo, D. J. 198, 271
Moo, J. A. 328
Moody Smith, D. 24, 216
Moore, S. D. 48, 67
Morgan, R. 60
Morgan, T. E. 67
Morgenstern, J. 36
Moriarty, M. 70
Morris, L. 39, 94
Moscicke, H. 166
Moss, C. 65, 66
Motyer, S. 1, 30, 61
Muller, F. M. 53
Muller, H.-P. 168
Murphy, F. J. 172, 175, 176
Myers, A. 252, 294
Myers, A. D. 106, 290

Nader, L. 52
Naijman, H. 188, 328
Naiweld, R. 5
Najman, H. 4, 172, 179, 240
Nanos, M. D. 8, 190
Nelson, D. 287
Neslon, W. D. 210
Neusner, J. 210, 214, 248, 287
Newman, J. H. 158, 160, 161, 230

Neyrey, J. H.   30, 104, 316
Nickelsburg, G. W. E.   161, 180, 334
Niehoff, M.   187
Niskanen, P.   234
Noegel, S.   319
Noort, E.   5, 138, 139, 146, 335
Northcott, M. S.   340
Novakovic, L.   335
Novick, T.   163, 208, 283, 284

Obermann, A.   83
Oblath, M.   320
O'Brien, K. S.   8, 192, 277
Och, B.   4
O'Connor, J. M.   243
O'Day, G. R.   61
Oeming, M.   136
O'Kane, M.   341
Ong, W.   17
Orlov, A. A.   336, 337
Oropeza, B. J.   200, 267
Orr, M.   63
Owen, P. L.   273

Painter, J.   292, 296–8, 302, 351
Parsenios, G. C.   104, 215, 289, 294
Parsons, M. C.   49
Patai, R.   127
Paul, S. M.   146, 147, 149
Pearce, S.   159
Peleg, Y.   142
Peppard, M.   194
Perrot, C.   171
Phillips, G. L.   16, 354, 355
Philonenko, M.   336
Philonenko-Sayar, B.   336
Pohlmann, K.-F.   120
Poirier, J. C.   98, 109–11, 123, 303, 304
Polanski, D. C.   175
Pollefeyt, D.   1
Popović, M.   5
Portier-Young, A.   156, 168, 344
Powell, M.   138
Pryor, J. W.   349

Qimron, E.   252, 253

Räisänen, H.   191, 274, 277
Ramsey, G. W.   138

Rapa, R. K.   273
Rata, T.   150
Reed, A. Y.   2, 5, 7, 180, 182–4, 208, 279, 329
Reif, S. C.   230, 231
Reim, G.   2, 302
Reinhartz, A.   1, 3, 22, 27, 28, 82–4, 86, 93, 102, 224, 295, 324, 365, 366
Reventlow, H. G.   229
Rey, J.-S.   246, 252, 253
Reymond, E. D.   171
Reynolds, K. A.   153
Reynolds III, B. H.   326
Rezetko, R.   232
Richardson, K.   51
Richter, G.   302
Richter, W.   9, 11
Rickett, D.   135
Ridderbos, H.   38, 133
Riesenfeld, H.   116
Riffaterre, M.   62
Rindge, M. S.   341
Robbins, V. K.   82
Robertson Smith, W.   137
Rodriguez, R.   198
Rohrbaugh, R.   101, 105
Roitman, A. D.   5
Roose, H.   342
Rosen-Zvi, I.   208, 213, 234, 283
Rubenstein, A.   335
Rubenstein, J. L.   116–19, 120, 121–7
Rubinkiewicz, R.   335, 336
Rudman, D.   337

Sacks, J.   128
Said, E. W.   58
Sailhamer, J. H.   10
Salkin, R. J.   5
Sandelin, K.-G.   188
Sanders, E. P.   200, 245, 261, 285, 302
Sanders, J. T.   190, 342
Sandmel, S.   2, 4, 41, 49, 50, 54, 59, 166, 185–8, 288
Satlow, M. L.   169, 187, 188
Satterfield, B.   108
Saussy, H.   53, 59
Savage, T. B.   201
Sawyer, J. F. A.   154
Schäfer, P.   288

Schauer, F.   51
Schechter, S.   285
Scheuer, B.   147
Schliesser, B.   262
Schmitz, T.   60, 68
Schmutzer, A. J.   4
Schnackenburg, R.   29, 89, 104, 105, 132, 218, 225, 289
Schniedewind, W. M.   160
Scholtissek, K.   302
Schreiner, T. R.   8, 261, 273, 275, 277
Schuchard, B. G.   26, 48, 106, 302
Schwartz, B.   232
Seebas, H.   136
Segal, M.   177, 244, 334
Segovia, F. F.   215
Seifrid, M. A.   261
Seim, T. K.   103, 166
Shäfer, P.   55
Shea, W. H.   337
Sheridan, R.   2, 3, 24, 29, 41, 78, 82-4, 86, 106, 132, 215, 227, 350, 351, 353, 367
Sheridan, S.   279
Sherwood, Y.   4, 48
Siker, J.   2, 5-7, 271, 279, 369
Sim, D. C.   79, 338
Slingerland, D.   242
Smit, P.-B.   341
Smith, C. W. F.   115
Smith, D. M.   24, 216
Smith, J. Z.   53-6, 58, 59, 86, 225
Smith, M.   208
Smith, P. A.   235
Snodgrass, K. R.   259
Solomon, N.   4, 110, 115, 117, 118, 120, 121, 123, 193, 204, 254, 279
Sommer, B. D.   231
Somov, A.   341
Spaulding, M. B.   119, 122
Speiser, E. A.   321
Spilsbury, P.   184
Spivak, G. C.   52
Sprinkle, P. M.   269
Spurling, H.   5, 323
Stanley, C. D.   276
Steck, O. H.   239
Stemberger, G.   5
Stewart, A. E.   164

Steyn, G. J.   200
Stokes, R. E.   344
Stone, M. E.   5, 162-4, 180, 245
Stowasser, M.   257
Streett, M.   257
Strugnell, J.   252, 253
Stube, J. C.   215
Sutherland, D.   320
Swetnam, J.   93, 259

Tannehill, R.   202
Taylor Gench, F.   90
Teeter, D. A.   153, 179
Thackeray, H. St. J.   125, 249
Theissen, M.   193, 194
Theobald, M.   133
Theodor, J.   348
Thettayll, B.   355
Thiessen, M.   198
Thomas, C.   68
Thompson, A.   164
Thompson, J. W.   258
Thyen, H.   133
Tigchelaar, E.   5, 138, 139
Tobin, T. H.   8, 199, 264
Todorov, T.   10
Tolmie, D. F.   215, 292
Tolonen, A.-L.   165
Torrey, C. C.   148
Tov, E.   234
Towner, P. H.   258
Trachtenberg, J.   1
Trotter, J. R.   168
Tuegels, L.   214
Turner, G.   269
Tyrrell-Hanson, A.   31

Ulfgard, H.   112, 114, 119, 120, 123
Underwood, G.   49
Urbach, E.   214, 215
Utzschneider, H.   9
Uusimäki, E.   165

van der Horst, P. W.   175
van der Lans, B.   193
Van Os, B.   190
van Peursen, W.   160
van Ruiten, J. T. A. G. M.   5, 139, 176, 178, 245, 325, 333, 334

van Seters, J. 60, 137
Van Tilborg, S. 349
van Wolde, E. 67
Vandecasteele-Vanneuville, F. 1
VanderKam, J. C. 176, 252
Vermes, G. 5, 173
Visscher, G. H. 262
von Wahlde, U. C. 1, 289, 301, 316
Von Weissenberg, H. 252, 253

Wallace, D. R. 200
Walsh, R. 61
Ward, R. B. 7, 272
Warner, M. 280
Watson, F. 245, 266, 276
Weissenrieder, A. 103
Welborn, L. L. 201
Wellhausen, J. 113
Wenham, G. J. 135, 145
Werman, C. 183
Werrett, I. C. 183
Westcott, B. F. 132, 225
Wester, D. S. 51
Westerholm, S. 265, 269
Westermann, C. 136, 148, 149, 231, 235, 323
Weyde, K. W. 113
Whitaker, G. H. 250
Whitters, M. F. 239
Widmer, M. 143

Wieser, F. E. 4
Wilkins, G. 161
Williams, C. 17–20, 32, 39, 311, 361
Williams, S. K. 194
Williams, T. B. 258
Williamson, H. G. M. 154
Williamson, P. R. 135
Wills, L. M. 158, 168, 169, 204
Wilson, M. R. 4, 30
Wilson, W. T. 165
Wink, W. 352
Winter, B. W. 251
Winter, T. 4, 279
Witherington, B. 349
Witherington III, B. 302
Wright, B. G. 153, 170
Wright, N. T. 8, 190, 252, 253, 255, 261–3, 293

Yadin, A. 208
Yadin, Y. 123, 124
Yadin-Israel, A. 207, 213
Yee, G. A. 112
Yinger, K. L. 260
Yoon, D. I. 63, 67
Young, I. 232

Zecharias, H. D. 61
Zeitlin, S. 5
Zumstein, J. 89, 302
Zurawski, J. M. 164

Subject index

Note: Page numbers followed by "n" refer to notes.

Abraham
   dream   319–21
   as exemplar to his seed   167–82
   as figure of memory   17–18
   in Gospel of John   8–39
   intercession   323–5
   and intertextuality   20–1
   joy   332–7, 345–7
   laughter   321–2
   in narrative and communal worlds   15–20
   post-biblical 'afterlives,' range of   4–8
   as rhetorical figure of Christian discursivity   6
   seed of (*see* 'seed of Abraham')
   seeing and rejoicing   33–9
   as seer   343–5
   as Torah observant   279–82
   as visionary figure   325–32
Abraham Cycle   134–9
   texts outside the   139–42
Abraham in Johannes 8: Ein Beitrag zur Methodenfrage (Lona)   8
Abraham in John 8,31–59: His Significance in the Conflict between Johannine Christianity and Its Jewish Environment (de Lange)   8
Abrahamology   12, 14
Acts 3.25, 'seed of Abraham' in   204
afterlives
   range of   4–8
age of Abraham   347–8
Aichele, George   65, 71, 77–8, 80, 81
Akedah   138, 139, 171, 173, 185, 206, 271, 272, 345
Allen, Graham   62, 63
anachronism   56
analogical reasoning   51
analogy   54–6

Anderson, Gary   246
anti-Judaism   1, 3 n.10, 6, 12, 86
   Johannine   3
Antiquities, 'seed of Abraham' in   184
Apocalypse of Abraham   347
Apocalypse of Zephaniah, 'seed of Abraham' in   165
apocryphal literature
   John 8.48-59 (Abraham sees and rejoices)
      Abraham as visionary figure   325–32
      Abraham's joy   332–7
      'works of Abraham' in   238–48
Aramaic Levi, 'seed of Abraham' in   183–4
Arnold, Matthew   47
Ashton, John   35, 60
Assmann, Jan   18
authorial filiation   69–70, 71
authorial intention   48

Bakhtin, Mikhail   132
Baldensperger, W.   30, 31
Balzac, H. de   72, 76, 84
Bar-Asher Siegal, Michal   56
Barr, James   9
Barthes, Roland   42, 60, 66, 365, 366
   theorization of intertextuality   68–87
Bassnett, Susan   67–8
belief   103–4
biblical semantics   9
Billerbeck, P.   50
binary dualism, works and   295–9
binary nomenclature of 'the work'/'the text'   71
Birkat Ha-Minim   79
Brown, Raymond   91, 132
Bruner, Frederick   133

Subject Index

Brunson, Andrew 38
Bultmann, Rudolf 132

calendrical reforms 36
Carson, Donald 91
characterization theory 82
'childrens' of Abraham 214–15
classic philological criticism 10
code of semes (SEM) 73, 74, 82–6, 365
Codex Alexandrinus 167 n.162
Codex Sinaiticus 167 n.162
Codex Vaticanus 167 n.162
Codex Venetus 167 n.162
collective memory 17
Coloe, Mary 37–8
communicative memory 18
comparative anatomy 53
comparative ethnology 53
comparative law 53
comparative literature 53
Comparative Literature (*Weltliteratur*) 53
comparative philology 53
comparative reasoning in textual analysis 51–60
comparative religion 53
comparativism 58
compliant reading 83, 86
contrapuntal interpretation 58
copyright 70
Crypto-Christians 91
cultural code (REF) 73, 74, 82–4, 86, 365
  Sukkot as 112–30
cultural memory 18

Dead Sea Scrolls (DSS) 5, 20, 112
  'seed of Abraham' in 182–4
  'works of Abraham' in 252–6
'dead works' 259–60
'The Death of the Author' (Barthes) 50, 69, 80, 81
degeneracy 54
degrees of similarity 51–2, 54
de Lange, Tineke 2, 8–15
Derrida, Jacques 57
description and interpretation, distinction between 10–11
Dialogue with Trypho (Martyr) 25, 26
Dietzfelbinger, Christian 133

'disciples' of Abraham 214–15
Disinheriting the Jews (Siker) 6–7
diversity 7
Dodd, C. H. 22–4, 92
Doering, Lutz 56–7
doxa 76–8, 84, 365
Dozeman, Thomas 25–6
dream of Abraham 319–21
DSS, *see* Dead Sea Scrolls
Dupré, John 79

Echoes of Scripture in the Letters of Paul (Hays) 63
écrivance 77, 84, 365
Edwards, M. J. 36–7
Elfenbein, Andrew 64
Eliade, Mircea 55
endogamy 169, 170, 185
Endoxa 76
engaged reading 84 n.233
ethnocentrism 52
Eurocentrism 52
exegesis 3, 9, 26, 91

'The Facts in the Case of M. Valdemar' (Poe) 76
false believers 90
fatherhood 23, 171, 187, 367
favouritism 145
festival setting, determination of 108–12
focused studies 21–39
Forester, E. 82
4 Ezra
  'seed of Abraham' in 162–4, 172
  'works of Abraham' in 241–2, 245–6
4 Maccabees, 'seed of Abraham' in 165–7
4QMMT 252–6, 309, 310
Fraade, Steven 55 n.43
Freed, Edwin 33–5
freedom 110
Frow, John 63
full-length studies 8–15

Galatians 22–5
  'seed of Abraham' in 189–97
Gathercole, Simon J. 278
genealogy 54
Gennette, Gerard 62, 172
Gentile Christians 6, 26

Gentile inclusion in the Jewish
    covenant 6, 6 n.24
'good works' 257–9, 306
The Gospels for All Christians 79
Griffiths, T. 97

Haenchen, Ernst 132
Halbwachs, Maurice 18
Halpern-Amaru, Betsy 184
hamartia 216
Hays, Richard B. 63, 64
Hebrew Bible (HB)
    Abraham Cycle 134–9
    Isa. 41.8, 146–9
    John 8.48-59 (Abraham sees and
        rejoices)
        Abraham's dream 319–21
        Abraham's intercession
            323–5
        Abraham's laughter 321–2
        Abraham's visitors at the *Oaks of
            Mamre* 322–3
    Jos. 33.26, 149–51
    Josephus 184–6
    Josh. 24.2-3, 145–6
    Philo 186–8
    post-Biblical apocrypha and
        pseudepigrapha 154–82
    Psalm 105.6-12 (MT)/104.6-12
        (LXX) 151–3
    texts from Torah 142–5
    texts outside the Abraham
        Cycle 142–5
    2 Chron. 20.7, 153–4
    works as human behaviour in
        229–38
Hebrews, 'works of Abraham' in
    269–72
Hebrews 2.16; 11.18, 'seed of Abraham'
    in 205–7
Hellenism 53
Hellenistic Judaism 4
hermeneutic code (HER) 73, 74, 81–3,
    365
Hezekiah 237, 238
historical criticism 9–11
Hollander, John 63
homology 54
homology/analogy distinction 56

Hunn, Debbie 93–5
Hunt, Steven A. 31–2, 39

iniquity 163, 236
intentionality 48
intercession 323–5
interpretation and description, distinction
    between 10–11
intertextual field, scripting 134
    John 8.48-59 (Abraham sees and
        rejoices)
        Hebrew Bible 319–25
    'seed of Abraham'
        Abraham Cycle 134–9
        Isa. 41.8, 146–9
        Jos. 33.26, 149–51
        Josephus 184–6
        Josh. 24.2-3, 145–6
        Philo 186–8
        post-Biblical apocrypha and
            pseudepigrapha 154–82
        Psalm 105.6-12 (MT)/104.6-12
            (LXX) 151–3
        texts from Torah 142–5
        texts outside the Abraham
            Cycle 139–42
        2 Chron. 20.7, 153–4
    'works of Abraham' 228–88
        Abraham, as Torah
            observant 279–82
        apocryphal pseudepigraphical
            literature 238–48
        Dead Sea Scrolls 252–6
        Josephus and Philo 249–52
        New Testament 256–72
        Tannaitic rabbinic literature
            282–8
        works as human behaviour in
            Hebrew Bible 229–38
    'works of the law' 272–9
intertextuality 42
    Abraham and 20–1
    application to Gospel of John 78–87
    Barthes' theorization of 68–87
    comparative reasoning in textual
        analysis 51–60
    metaleptic 63, 64
    postmodern 60
    poststructuralist 58, 64–6, 85

poststructuralist theories of   11, 86–7
Sukkot   112–30
textual analysis   72–4
theoretical foundations of   47–87
writerly and readerly texts   74–8
Isa. 41.8, 'seed of Abraham' in   146–9
Isaac, helping to 'seed of Abraham'   155–67

Jacob, helping to 'seed of Abraham'   155–67
James, 'works of Abraham' and   269–72
Jauß, H. R.   57
Jer. 33.26, 'seed of Abraham' in   149–51
Jewish Christians   6, 22, 24
Jews and Christians, conflict between   12–14
Johannine anti-Judaism   3
Johannine community   2, 78, 79, 91
Johannine context
    John 8.48-59, 348–57
        joy and rejoicing   349–54
        seeing and sight   354–7
    'seed of Abraham' in   215–19
        servanthood/slavery   215–16
        sin   216–19
    'works of Abraham'   288–305, 310
        works and binary dualism   295–9
        works and signs and testimony   289–94
    'work the works of God'   299–305
John 8.31-36 intertextually, reading   219–26
John 8.39-41 intertextually, reading   305–13
John 8.48-59 (Abraham sees and rejoices)   315–63
    intertextual field, scripting   318–48
        apocryphal and pseudepigraphical literature   325–37
        Hebrew Bible   319–25
        New Testament   337–43
        Tannaitic rabbinic literature   343–8
    intertextually, reading   357–63
    Johannine context   348–57
Josephus   124–5
    'seed of Abraham' and   184–6
    'works of Abraham' and   249–52

Josh. 24.2-3, 'seed of Abraham' in   145–6
jouissance   78, 85, 366
joy of Abraham
    in apocryphal and pseudepigraphical literature   332–7
    in Johannine context   349–54
    in Tannaitic rabbinic literature   345–7
Jubilees   28, 36–8, 112, 121, 130
    'seed of Abraham' in   171, 172, 176–9, 185
    'works of Abraham' in   244–5
Judaism   2–4, 7, 44, 53, 64, 86, 91, 154
    Hellenistic   4
    normative   13
    rabbinic   5
    Second Temple Judaism   13 n.59, 14, 25, 32, 189, 205, 220, 239, 262 n.141
judgement   104–6, 260
justice   140, 141 n.52
justification   260–2, 273

Kalir, Eleazar ben   128–30
Kister, Menahem   247
Kittel, Gerhard   9
knowledge   103–4
Koester, Craig   216–17
Kommentar zum Neuen Testament aus Talmud und Midrasch (Strack and Billerbeck)   50
Kristeva, Julia   47 n.3, 61–2, 65–7, 85

laughter   321–2
Lavers, Annette   76
Law of Moses   185
Levene, Nancy   55
Levine, Amy-Jill   167
lexias   72, 73
literary criticism   9, 10, 12
literary semiotics   9
Lona, Horatio E.   8–15, 40
Lowe, Malcolm   37
Luke 1.55, 'seed of Abraham' in   202–3

Mansfield Park   58
Martyn, J. Louis   13, 25, 78
Martyr, Justing   6, 25, 30
'maximalist' approach to allusions   50
Mays, James Luther   237

Mekhilta de Rabbi Ishmael 209-10, 212-13, 346, 347
memory
 collective 17
 communicative 18
 cultural 18
 social 18
memory-based oral composition 17
metaleptic intertextuality 63, 64
methodological pluralism 9
Metzner, Rainer 216-19
Michaels, J. Ramsey 32-3
Midrashim 5
Miller, Geoffrey 169
Miller, Paul 16-17
Mishnah 5
Mishnaic Hebrew 207
Mol, Jurrien 236
Moloney, Francis J. 94, 97
monotheism 27, 370
Moriarty, Michael 70-1
Mosaic Law 23, 188
Moses
 as figure of memory in ancient Egyptian texts 18
Moss, Candida R. 65-6
Müller, Friedrich Max 53

'Nailing Down and Tying Up: Lessons in Intertextual Impossibility from the *Martyrdom of Polycarp*' (Moss) 65-6
Najman, Hindy 172
neologism 41, 49
New Comparativism 87
New Perspective on Paul (NPP) 261, 279
New Revised Standard Version (NRSV) 29, 166, 262
New Testament (NT)
 'dead works' 259-60
 'good works' 257-9
 John 8.48-59 (Abraham sees and rejoices) 337-43
 'seed of Abraham' in
  Acts 3.25, 204
  Galatians 189-97
  Hebrews 2.16; 11.18, 205-7
  Luke 1.55, 202-3
  Romans 4.13, 16; 9.7-8, 197-201
 2 Cor. 11.22, 201-2
 'works of Abraham' in 256-72
  James and Hebrews 269-72
  judgement 260
  justification 260-2
  Rom. 4.4-9, 262-6
  Rom. 9.11-12, 30-32, 266-9
nihilism 75
NPP, *see* New Perspective on Paul
NRSV, *see* New Revised Standard Version

Oath of Mamre, Abraham's visitors at 322-3
origins 102-3
ownership 70, 85

para-doxa 77, 84, 86, 365
parallelism 35, 35 n.197, 52
parallelomania 41, 49, 52, 86
Phillips, G. L. 16
Philo 124-5
 and 'seed of Abraham' 186-8
 'works of Abraham' and 249-52
plaisir 85
pluralism 7
 methodological 9
poetics of literary criticism 10
Pohlman, K. F. 120
Poirier, John 109-12
post-biblical apocrypha 154-82
poststructuralism 41, 72
poststructuralist intertextuality 58, 64-6, 85
poststructuralist theories of intertextuality 11, 86-7
Prayer of Azariah (PrA), 'seed of Abraham' in 155-8, 162
Prayer of Manasseh (Pr. Man.), 'seed of Abraham' in 160-2
privy council 83
proairetic code (ACT) 73, 74, 81, 83, 365
The Prophetic Gospel (Tyrell-Hanson) 31
the Prophets 115-17
Psalm 104.6-12 (LXX), 'seed of Abraham' in 151-3
Psalm 105.6-12 (MT), 'seed of Abraham' in 151-3
pseudepigraphaical literature 121-4, 154-82

John 8.48-59 (Abraham sees and
    rejoices)
  Abraham as visionary figure
    325-32
  Abraham's joy 332-7
  'works of Abraham' in 238-48
Pseudo-Philo's *Biblical Antiquities*
    (LAB) 171-7, 222

rabbinic Judaism 5
rabbinic literature 125-30
rabbinism 23, 86, 223
reader, as consumer 70
readerly (*scriptable*) texts 74-8, 84, 365
Reinhartz, Adele 27-9, 40, 83, 84 n.233, 224, 365, 366
rejoicing 30, 32-9, 44-5, 130, 315-63, 369
  in Johannine context 349-54
Religionswissenschaft 53
rereading 70-1
resistant reading 365, 366
reversibility 74, 75, 83
Richter, Georg 10, 11
Riffaterre, Michael 62
Robbins, Vernon K. 82
Rom. 4.4-9, 'works of Abraham' in 262-6
Rom. 4.13, 16; 9.7-8, 'seed of Abraham' in 197-201
Rom. 9.11-12, 'works of Abraham' in 266-9
Rom. 9.30-32, 'works of Abraham' in 266-9
Rosen-Zvi, Ishay 213

Sacks, Jonathan 128
Said, Edward 58
Sandmel, Samuel 2, 41, 49, 50, 52, 56, 185, 187
Sarrasine (Balzac) 72-4, 76, 84
Satlow, Michael 169, 187
Saussy, Haun 53, 59, 87
Schmitz, Thomas 68
Schnackenburg, Rudolf 132
scientism 79-80
scripting 60, 72, 85, 87, 220, 223
  intertextual field (*see* intertextual field, scripting)
  Sukkot intertext 108-30

scriptural hermeneutic 16
Second Temple Judaism 13 n.59, 14, 25, 32, 189, 205, 220, 239, 262 n.141
'seed of Abraham' 2, 12, 13, 21-9, 41-4, 99, 129, 131, 366-8
  Dead Sea Scrolls 182-4
  Hebrew Bible
    Abraham Cycle 134-9
    Isa. 41.8, 146-9
    Jos. 33.26, 149-51
    Josephus 184-6
    Josh. 24.2-3, 145-6
    Philo 186-8
    post-biblical apocrypha and pseudepigrapha 154-82
    Psalm 105.6-12 (MT)/104.6-12 (LXX) 151-3
    texts from Torah 142-5
    texts outside the Abraham Cycle 139-42
    2 Chron. 20.7, 153-4
  Johannine context 215-19
    servanthood/slavery 215-16
    sin 216-19
    John 8.31-36 intertextually, reading 219-26
  New Testament
    Acts 3.25, 204
    Galatians 189-97
    Hebrews 2.16; 11.18, 205-7
    Luke 1.55, 202-3
    Romans 4.13, 16; 9.7-8, 197-201
    2 Cor. 11.22, 201-2
  Tannaitic rabbinic literature 207-15
    Abraham's 'children,' 'sons' and 'disciples' 214-15
seeing/sight 33-9, 44-5, 315-63, 369
seer, Abraham as 343-5
semantic analysis 10
semiotics 10-11
servanthood 215-16
shorter studies 15-21
Sifrei Devarim 211, 212
Sifre Numbers 212-13, 347
signification 72
signified 79
Siker, Jeffrey 6-7
Simchat Beit ha-Sho'evah ('rejoicing of the house of water-drawing') 125-6

similarity, degrees of 51–2, 54
sin 21, 29, 42–4, 86, 99, 120, 129, 131, 136 n.33, 155, 163, 168, 216–19, 225–6, 232
Sirach 170–1
Sitz-im-Leben 22, 28, 126
slavery 86, 99, 131, 155, 215–16
Smith, Jonathan 53–4, 59, 86, 225
social memory 18
sonship 23, 131
'sons' of Abraham 214–15
soteriology 269
source-critical approach 22
'*Sperma Abraam* in John 8 and Related Literature' (Dozeman) 25
Stanley, Christopher 276
Strack, H. L. 50
structuralism 10, 11, 69, 72
structuralist literary criticism 10
Sukkot 1, 3, 101, 106, 369–71
    as cultural code and intertext 37, 38, 42, 112–30
    festival setting, determination of 108–12
    intertext, scripting 108–30
    Josephus 124–5
    Philo 124–5
    the Prophets 115–17
    pseudepigrapha 121–4
    rabbinic literature 125–30
    the Torah 112–15
    writings 117–21
Swetnam, James 93–4
symbolic code (SYM) 73, 74, 82–5, 365
sympathetic reading 84 n.233

Tanakh 6, 81
Tannaitic rabbinic literature 207–15
    Abraham's joy 345–7
    John 8.48-59 (Abraham sees and rejoices)
        Abraham as seer 343–5
        age of Abraham 347–8
    'seed of Abraham' in 208–13
    'works of Abraham' in 282–8
Targum Neofiti 345–6
Targum Onkelos 346–7
Targum Pseudo-Jonathan 139, 345
Tel Quel 77

tertium comparationis 86
Testament of Abraham (*T. Abr.*)
    'seed of Abraham' in 171, 172, 177–82
    'works of Abraham' in 312
Testament of Asher (*T. Ash.*), 'seed of Abraham' in 159–60
Testament of Benjamin
    'works of Abraham' in 244
Testament of Levi (*T. Levi*)
    'seed of Abraham' in 160
    'works of Abraham' in 242–4
Testaments of the Twelve Patriarchs
    'works of Abraham' in 242
testimony 106–8
text, as communication 11
textual addressees, problem of 90–8
textual analysis 3, 42, 72–4
    comparative reasoning in 51–60
textual referentiality 62
thematic coherence 101–8
Theobald, Michael 133
theurgic ritual for rain 126–9
3 Maccabees, 'seed of Abraham' in 158–9, 162
Thyen, Hartwig 133
Todorov, Tzvetan 10
the Torah 112–15
    texts 142–5
tripartite structure 98–101
2 Baruch
    'works of Abraham' in 241
2 Chron. 20.7, 'seed of Abraham' in 153–4
2 Cor. 11.22, 'seed of Abraham' in 201–2
'two-level drama' hypothesis 13
Tyrell-Hanson, Anthony 31

unity 101–8

virtue 44
visionary figure, Abraham as 325–32

water-drawing ceremony 125–6
Williams, Catrin 17–20, 32, 39
willow procession 126
Wirkungsgeschichte 366
works, and binary dualism 295–9
works, as signs and testimony 289–94

works as human behaviour, in Hebrew Bible   229–38
'works of Abraham'   29–33, 43–4, 227
   intertextual field, scripting   228–88
      Abraham, as Torah observant   279–82
      apocryphal and pseudepigraphical literature   238–48
      Dead Sea Scrolls   252–6
      Josephus and Philo   249–52
      New Testament   256–72
      Tannaitic rabbinic literature   282–8
      works as human behaviour in Hebrew Bible   229–38

'works of the law'   272–9
   Johannine context   288–305
      works and binary dualism   295–9
      works as signs and testimony   289–94
      'work the works of God'   299–305
   John 8.39-41 intertextually, reading   305–13
'works of the law'   272–9, 310
'work the works of God'   299–305
writerly (*lisible*) texts   74–8, 84
writings   117–21

Yossi Haglili, R.   211

Reference index

OLD TESTAMENT
Genesis (Gen) 208
1-3   298
1.3   110 n.82
1.11   135 n.24
4   135 n.27,
             296 n.300,
             297–8
4.7   296
4.9-11   324 n.23
5.9-9.17   122
5.29   229
6-11   240
9.15-16   151 n.98
11   172
11.31   134
12-22   157
12.1-9   134, 169
12.1-3   118, 134 n.22,
             163, 184, 192
12.1   134
12.1ff   328
12.2a   134
12.2b   134
12.3   25, 134, 194,
             275, 276
12.3 LXX   191
12.4-5   134
12.6   135
12.7   134, 135 n.28
12.7 LXX   134
12.7 MT   134
12.7b   135
12.14   288
13   186
13.5-7   135
13.8-9   135
13.14-16   134, 135, 169
13.14a   135 n.28
13.14b   135 n.28
13.15   192 n.295

15   39, 137, 138,
             186, 271, 321,
             326, 336, 343,
             344–5, 358
15.1-26   163
15.1-21   319
15.1-20   134, 137, 169
15.1-17   39, 325, 326,
             327, 328,
             329, 361
15.1-6   136
15.1-2   136, 324
15.1-2a   135
15.1, 12, 17 19 n.112
15.1   135, 263
             n.146, 320,
             325–6
15.2-4   326
15.2   327
15.2b-3   135
15.4-5   320
15.4 LXX   135
15.4 MT   135
15.4, 6, LXX 31
15.5-17   328
15.5   136, 320, 326
15.5 LXX   136
15.5 MT   136
15.6   174, 194, 248,
             255, 265, 276,
             278, 283, 286,
             301, 308, 319,
             320
15.6 LXX   136, 191,
             193, 262, 275
15.6 MT   136
15.8   136, 320
15.9-13   326
15.9-11   319
15.9   136
15.10-11   136

15.11   326, 336
15.12-20   136
15.12-13   320, 325
15.12   318, 319–21,
             326, 343,
             358, 359
15.12 LXX   136
15.12 MT   136
15.12a   319
15.12b   319
15.12ff   360
15.13-14   319
15.13   136, 320, 327
15.15   136, 177,
             319, 325
15.16   319
15.16b   136
15.17-18   320
15.17-18a   319
15.17   326, 327, 344
15.18-21   319
15.18b-20   137
15.21   358
16.5   195
17-18   266
17   138, 140,
             185, 279–80
17.1-30   163
17.1-27   134, 137, 169
17.1-14   321
17.2   321
17.2b   137
17.3   321
17.4, 5   137
17.6a   137
17.6b   137
17.6c   137
17.7, 8, 9, 14 137
17.7a, b, c,
   8a, 9, 10a,
   19   138

17.8	192 n.295	18.17	323–4	22.18	204
17.8 LXX	206	18.18	141, 199	24.1	280, 281
17.11-12	321	18.19	141, 179, 324	24.14	148 n.86
17.12b	137	18.19a	236 n.31	25.23	267
17.13	209, 321	18.20	324	26.1-33	139–40
17.15-21	137	18.22-33	331	26.1-5	139, 141
17.15	321	18.22	324	26.2-5	280
17.16	137, 321	18.23-32	142 n.58,	26.2a	140
17.17	19 n.112,		324 n.26	26.2b-5	139–40
	38–9, 137,	18.23-24	324	26.3-5	153
	319, 321–2,	18.25	324	26.3	140
	333, 334,	18.26	324	26.3b	140
	337, 343,	18.32b	324	26.4	140, 141,
	346–7, 358	19	323 n.21		211, 220
17.17a LXX	321	19.1-3	323 n.18	26.5	118 n.102,
17.17a MT	321	19.1	322, 323		140, 153,
17.17b	321	19.21	210		171 n.185,
17.18	319, 321, 322	20.1-21.16	138		280, 346,
17.19	138, 321	20.1-21.7	178		367
17.19, 21	137–8	20.13 LXX	138	26.6-22	141
17.20	138, 321	20.13 MT	138	26.23-24b	139, 141
17.22-27	137	20.14a	138	26.23	141
18–19	181 n.234	21	39, 322, 337	26.24	135 n.29,
18	30, 31–2, 140,	21.1-5	322		141, 148 n.86
	141 n.52,	21.2	195	26.24b	141
	142, 179	21.6	322	26.24b	
	n.218, 310,	21.6 LXX	334	LXX	141
	323, 370	21.6 MT	334	26.24b MT	141
18.1-15	322–3, 358	21.7	322	26.25b	141
18.1-2	318	21.8-14	134, 169	27.1-40	141
18.1	322	21.9-13		27.41-45	141
18.2-5	129	LXX	200	27.46-28.2	141
18.2a	322	21.10	196	28	141
18.2b	322	21.11	319	28.3-4	141–2
18.3-8	322	21.12	200, 206	28.4-5,	
18.10	322–3	21.17	135 n.29	13–15	139
18.11	322	22	39, 139, 185,	28.4	141
18.12	322		248, 271, 301,	28.10-11	142
18.13-14	322		323, 345, 346	28.12-23	142
18.13	323, 324	22.1-19	138	28.13	141
18.13, 17	323	22.1-10	319	28.14	142
18.14-15	322	22.1	139	30.27	142 n.56
18.15	322	22.3	286, 346	35.9	142
18.16-33	323–5, 358,	22.14	139 n.47	35.11-12	139, 142
	360	22.15-19	134, 169	35.17	135 n.29
18.16-19	236 n.31	22.15-18	171	43.23	135 n.29
18.16	323	22.16-18	138	46.29	346
18.17-19	280	22.17-18	199	46.33	229
18.17-18	324	22.17	206	50.19, 21	135 n.29

Reference Index

Exodus (Exod)
2.23	324 n.23
2.24	151 n.98, 286
2.24b	286
3.6	342
3.7	324 n.23
4.18	282
4.22	133
5.11	237 n.34
13.3	149
13.5	1285
14.6	346
14.9-14	284
14.31	148 n.86
15.1-18, 19-21	202 n.346
15.18	210
16	283
16.10	283
18.20	254
20.2	212–13
22.20	209
23.13b-19	112, 113
23.14-17	113
23.14	113
23.15	113
23.16	112, 113, 114
23.23-24	230
23.24	230
25.42	212
32	142 n.58, 143
32.1-6	142
32.1	142
32.9-10	142
32.11	142
32.12-14	185
32.13-14	143
32.13	142, 143, 144
32.14	143
33	209 n.375, 284 n.242
33.1	143 n.61
33.32	220
34.6	169

Leviticus (Lev)
16	236 n.33
16.22	219
18.3	230
18.21	135 n.24

19.13	234 n.23, 283
19.18	179
23	113 n.92, 117, 121, 125
23.1-44	113
23.33-43	112, 113–14, 130, 370
23.34 LXX	113
23.35-41	114
23.35	114
23.36	108 n.73
23.36, 37	114
23.36d	114
23.37b, 39b	114
23.39	114
23.40-42	178, 333
23.40	121, 122
23.40a	114
23.42-43	370
23.42	113
23.43	113–14, 124
25.42	149
25.55	149, 209
26	147, 212
26.13	149
26.41	147

Numbers (Num/Nu)
4.30, 35, 39, 43	237 n.34
6.26	210
12.7, 8	148 n.86
21–22	173
22–24	173 n.197
22.21	346
28.1-29.40	114
29.12-39	123
29.12-38	112, 114
29.35-38	114
30.17 LXX	234 n.24
31.21 LXX	234 n.24

Deuteronomy (Deut)
1.1-5	144
1.6-8	211
1.8	142, 144, 211
1.9	144
1.10-11	144
1.15	214
4.19	329 n.41
4.28	229
4.37	144, 161
5.3	144 n.66, 145
5.6-10	149
5.10	154
6.4	116
6.12-15a	149
7.3-4	169
7.8-10a	149
7.10	154
8.7	114
9.5	136 n.32
9.18-29	144 n.62
9.27	143, 144
9.28	143–4
9.29	143
10.10-15	144–5
10.12	145
10.13	145
10.15-20	145
10.15	144
10.16-17	145
10.18-20	145
10.18	209
13.13	243
13.14	243
13.16	211
15.9	243
16.1-17	114
16.1	114
16.2, 7, 15	115
16.3	114
16.11-12	115
16.11	114
16.13-17	130, 370
16.13-15	112, 114–15
16.13	115
16.14	115, 121
16.14a	115
16.14b	115
16.15	121
16.15a	115
16.15b	115
16.16-17	115
18.10	329 n.41
21.23	192
22.8	287
27	254
27.14-25	276
27.15-25	276

Reference Index

27.15	229, 276	12.3	34	**2 Chronicles**	
27.16	276	12.7	234	(2 Chr)	120, 122,
27.17	276	20.1	243		160 n.133
27.18	276	25.25	243	5–7	112, 117
27.19	276			5.1-7.10	117
27.20-23	276	**2 Samuel (2 Sam)**		5.1-3	117
27.24	276	7.12	193	5.2-14	117
27.25	276	21	167	5.10	118
27.26	275, 276			5.12	117
27.26 LXX	276	**1 Kings (1 Kgs)**	120, 122	5.14	117
28.1-14	276	8	121, 1236,	6	120
28.1	276		371	6.1-11	118
28.12	286	8.1-13	117	6.1-2	118
30.15-20	242 n.49	8.1-2	117	6.5	118
34.1-3	144	8.2-66	117	6.12-20	118
34.4	142, 144	8.2	112, 115	6.22-42	118
34.4a	144	8.10	117	6.22, 24,	
34.4b	144	8.11	115	26 (x2),	
34.5	148 n.86	8.13	118	27, 36 (x2),	
		8.14-21	118	37, 39	118
Joshua (Josh)		8.22-29	118	6.25, 27	118
19.51	326	8.30-51	118	6.35	234 n.24
22.1-24	271	8.33-50	130	7.6	117
23.2	326	8.33, 34,		7.10	118
23.12-13	169	35 (x2), 36,		13.7	243
24.1-28	145	46 (x2),		15.7	232, 306
24.2-6	145–6	47, 50	118	19.1-20.37	153
24.2-3	145–6, 220	8.59-61	118	20.1	153
24.5-7	136 n22	8.60	115, 130, 370	20.4	153
24.5	146	8.66	118	20.6-7	153, 154
24.14-24	145	16.1	153	20.7	153–4, 155,
24.16-18	149	18.13	257		157, 161, 163,
24.25-28	145	18.19	257		182, 186, 220,
		21.5-16	257		271, 328
Judges (Judg)		21.13	243	20.7 LXX	154
4–5	175			20.20-23	153
5.1-31	202 n.346	**2 Kings (2 Kgs)**		32.19, 25	229
5.31	154	9.22	257	32.30-33	237
6.1-10	175	9.30-37	257	36.20-21	136 n.33
19.22	243	10.18	237 n.37		
20.13	243	19.18	229	**Ezra**	122
21	115	21.3	237 n.37	3	119
21.19	112, 115	21.19-24	250	3.1-6	117, 119
21.22	115	21.21 LXX	250	3.1	119
		21.22	250	3.3-6	119
1 Samuel (1 Sam)				3.3-4	119
1.16	243	**1 Chronicles (1 Chr)**		4.24	237 n.34
2.1-10	202 n.346	6.22-39	130	6.7	237 n.34
2.12	243	16.8-36	202 n.346	9.1-10.6	157
7.3	27	20.6	167	9.1-5	160 n.134

432   Reference Index

9.2	169, 179 n.216, 183	34.21	229	104.6-12 LXX	151–3
10.10-12	169	34.25	229, 237 n.34	104.6 LXX	151
		34.25 LXX	229	104.8 LXX	203
		34.25 MT	229	105	153, 220
Nehemiah (Neh)		34.26-28	229	105.1	151
1.1-11	157	34.26	229	105.2	151
1.4-11	160 n.134	34.27b	229	105.3	151
1.5	154	34.28	229	105.3 LXX	235
2.17	185	34.30	229	105.4	151
3.15	108 n.73	34.33	229	105.5	151
8.1-2	118			105.6	18 n.103, 151, 152
8.8	118	**Psalms (Pss/Ps)**			
8.9	119	7.3, 6c	118		
8.9d, 11	118	8.6	229	105.6-12	161
8.13	119	10.7 LXX	234	105.6-12 MT	151–3
8.14-18	112, 117, 118–19, 130, 370, 371	11.2, 5b	234	105.6 MT	151
		11.7 MT	234	105.7b-8	151
		16.4 LXX	232	105.8-15	151
8.14	119	17.5	306, 308	105.9	151
8.15	119	17.5 MT	232	105.10	151
8.16	119	17.44-45 LXX	193 n.304	105.11	151, 152
8.17	119			105.16-23	152
8.18	119	18.11	118	105.24-27	152
9	230 n.1, 239, 328	22.26-27	147	105.28-36	152
		27.1	110 n.82	105.36	27
9.1-10.40	157	28.5	232	105.37-43	152
9.6-37	160 n.134, 230, 231, 305–6	28.5b	229	105.42-45	152, 153
		31	265	105.42	153
		31.1 LXX	265	105.44-45	151, 152, 153
9.6	230	31.1-2 LXX	265	106.3	141 n.52, 235
9.7-8	230	32	307	106.35	229, 230
9.8	210	32.1-2 MT	265	106.36	229
9.9-12	230	32.1 LXX	198 n.329	106.37	229
9.13-14	230	32.1 MT	265	106.38d	229
9.15	230	32.15 LXX	229	106.39 MT	229
9.16	230	33.15	229	107.39 LXX	229–30
9.17	230	34.22b	229	109.14	247
9.17b-22	230	36.9	110 n.82	109.20	233
9.24	230	41.8	243	110.5	203
9.33-34	231	49.8-9	286–7	115.4	229
9.35	231	51	160 n.134	117	38
9.36	231	90.17	229	117.24 LXX	38, 361
9.37a	231	92.4b	229	118	38, 118
10.28	231	92.5a	229	118.24	38, 361
10.29	231	92.15	280, 281	118.25	126
		97.2	118	119	153
Job		97.10	154	119.105	110 n.82
7.1	147	101.3	243	132.13-14	118
30.26	110 n.82	103.6	141 n.52, 234	135.15	229

Reference Index

Proverbs (Prov)
4.18-19	110 n.82
6.12	243
8.21	210, 211
10.2	246
10.15-16 LXX	233
10.15-16 MT	233
11.18-19	233, 263
11.19a	233
11.19b	233
16.27	243
31	237
31.30-31	237, 306

Qohelet/Ecclesiastes (Qo/Eccl)
2.13	110 n.82

Isaiah (Isa)
1-39	146
2.5	110 n.82
2.8	229
5.7	324 n.23
8.6	108 n.73
10.22	201 n.341
11.1-9	334 n.60
11.14	193 n.304
12.3	117 n.100, 126
12.41	16
32.17	236 n.34, 241
33.15	234
40-55	146
40.1-15	136 n.33
40.1-2	146, 147, 148 n.86
40.2	220
40.6-31	147
40.10b	232
40.27	149
40.31	148, 280, 281
41.1-8a	147-8
41.1	148
41.1-20, 21-29	147
41.2, 25	148 n.86
41.4 LXX	34, 37
41.7-8	155
41.8	18 n.103, 146-9, 153, 154, 155, 157, 163, 182, 186, 209-11, 220, 222, 225, 271
41.8 LXX	154, 203 n.348
41.8-9	161
41.8-9c	148, 149
41.8-9c LXX	148
41.8-9c MT	148
41.9d	148
41.10	148
41.10b	232 n.18
41.13-29	231 n.14
41.25-29	231
41.25	231
41.26-28	231
41.27	231
41.29	229, 231
43.10-13	149
43.10-12 LXX	37, 38
43.10 LXX	34, 37
44.1, 5	149
45.1-4 LXX	34 n.187
45.4-6	149
45.24	234
47.13	329 n.41
48.1	328
49.4	234
50.1	147
51.2	230 n.11
54.7	110 n.82
56.1	141 n.52, 306
56.4	209
56.6	209
57-59	231 n.5
58.1-2	235
58.2	141 n.52
58.4	235 n.30
58.9	235 n.30
58.9b	235 n.30
59.3	235 n.30
59.3, 6	235 n.30
59.6	231
61.8	234
61.9	234
63-65	232 n.16
63.16	230 n.11
64.1-12	234
64.4 MT	234
64.5	234, 235, 306
64.6a	234
64.6b	234
64.8	234
65.6-7	231-2
65.6-7 MT	232
65.7	232, 233, 306, 308
65.7a LXX	232
65.7b LXX	232
66.10	349-50
66.17	231
66.18	231
66.18 LXX	231

Jeremiah (Jer)
1.16	229
5.19	27
10.3, 9	229
18.19	234 n.24
22.3, 15-16	141 n.52
27.7	136 n.33
29.10	136 n.33
31.10 LXX	300
31.16	306, 308
33	183 n.249
33.1-6	150
33.14-26	150
33.17-18	150
33.22	150
33.23-25	161, 194 n.304, 220
33.23	150
33.25-26	150
33.25	150
33.26	149-51
48.7	229

Lamentations (Lam)
3.64	229

Ezekiel (Ezek)
3.20	236
6.6	229

16.58	236 n.33	**Hosea (Hos)**		14.20	116
18.20-22		11.1	133	14.21	116
NRSV	236	14.3	229		
18.20-21	306			**Malachi (Mal)**	
18.22	141 n.52	**Amos (Am)**		1.1-3	267
18.24	236	4.13	34 n.187	1.2, 3	267
23.35	236 n.33			1.3	267
29.19-20	234 n.23	**Micah (Mic)**		1.4-5	267
36.15	236 n.33	5.1	34 n.187		
44.10, 21	236 n.33	6.5, 16	234	**APOCRYPHA**	
45.9	141 n.52	6.7	237		
45.25	112, 115	6.7b	237	**Baruch (Bar)**	
		6.8	237, 238	1.15-3.8	160 n.134
Daniel (Dan)		6.9	237	2.6-10	239
1–3	156	6.10-12	306	2.9-10	300
3	156	6.10-11	237	2.19	234 n.24
3.1-2	156	6.12	237	3.15-18	238
3.3-20	156	6.13-14	237		
3.23	155–6	6.14-15	237	**1 Esdras (1 Esd)**	120,
3.24	155–6	6.16	237, 238,	130, 370	
3.28	156–7		239, 250, 306		
3.28 LXX	157–8	6.16a	237	**2 Esdras (2 Esd)**	
4.19-27	235, 238, 306	6.16b	237, 238	3–14	162
4.27	235	6.16c	237	12.32, 13.37	34
7	344, 345	7.20	203	13.26, 52	34
7.1-14	343			14.9	34
7.1	343	**Habakkuk (Hab)**		16.64-67	238
7.2-14	344	2.4	192, 275		
7.4-8	343	3.13	34 n.187	**1 Maccabees (1 Macc)**	
7.10	343 n.85			1.10	122
7.11-14	343	**Haggai (Hag)**		2.49-52	248 n.80
7.13	343 n.85	2.14	229	2.50-52	248, 306
7.15-17				2.52	255
7.23b	344	**Zechariah (Zech)**		4.59	123
7.25	344	14	115–16, 122,	10.21	112, 122
7.26	344		127, 370	10.21b	122
7.27	344	14.1-2	116		
9	147	14.4-5	116	**2 Maccabees (2 Macc)**	
9.1-27	157	14.5b	116	110, 124, 165	
9.4-19	160 n.134,	14.6	116	2.52	271
	288	14.8	116, 117	5–7	123
9.15-18	235, 306	14.9	116	10	123
9.15-16	235	14.11-12	117	10.1-8	123
9.16	234	14.12, 15	116	10.1	122
9.18	234–5	14.13	116	10.3-8	112
9.27	239, 307	14.14	116	10.3	122
9.34	258 n.126	14.16-19	112, 115,	10.4	123
12.2	175 n.203		130, 370	10.5	123
12.3	259 n.130,	14.16	116	10.6	122
	334 n.59	14.17	116	10.6a	123

Reference Index

10.6b	123	39.16	238	4.19	169
10.7	123	42.15-17, 22	238	10.12	258 n.126
		43.28, 32	238	12.9	169, 246, 306
Prayer of Azariah (PrA)		44–50	170	14.10	170
155–7, 162, 167, 221		44	221		
1.3	156	44.16-18	170	**Wisdom of Solomon**	
1.4-9	156	44.19-21	170, 171	**(Wis)**	
1.4	156	44.19-20	171	1.11-12	238
1.10-22	157	44.19	34, 171	2–5	158
1.11-13	157	44.19 LXX	171	2.4	238
1.12-20	157	44.20	171	3.11-13	238
1.13	157	44.21	199	5.1	331 n.48
		44.21a LXX	171 n.185	6.2-5	239, 307
Prayer of Manasseh		44.22	171	6.2	238
(Pr. Man.)	160–2,	45.1-2	4	8.4	238
167, 221				9.9	238
v. 1-2	161	**Tobit (Tob)**	**167–8**	9.12	238
v. 1	162	1.3	168	11.1	238
v. 3	162	1.5-7	168	12.4	238
v. 7c-8	161	1.8-9	168	12.19-21	238
1.8	162	1.10-12	168	14.5	238
1.9	162	1.16	168		
		1.17	168	**NEW TESTAMENT**	
Sirach/Ecclesiasticus		2.7-9	168		
(Sir)		2.11-12	168	**Matthew (Mt)**	
1.9	238	2.13	168	3.9	214
3.3-4	247	2.14	168	4.12-25	338
3.4	247	3.2-6	161 n.134	4.17	338
3.12-13	247 n.74	3.3	168	4.24-25	338
3.14-15	247, 284	3.5a	168	5–7	338
	n.242	3.16	168	5.1-7.29	339
3.14	246, 247,	4	168 n.167	5.16	258, 259
	307, 309	4.1-19	168		n.130, 307
3.14, 30	247	4.5-7a	239, 307	5.21-22	338
7.10	247	4.5-6	169	5.21-6.18	339
11.20	238	4.6-11, 14,		5.27-28	338
12.3	247	16-17	169	5.33-34	338
16.12	260	4.7-19	167 n.162,	6.1-20	270
16.14	247		168 n.168	6.1-18	270
16.26-27	238	4.7-8	169	6.1-4, 5-8,	
17.8-9	238	4.9-11	169	16-18	338
17.22	247	4.10	246	6.12	219
18.4	238	4.11	246, 306	6.20	259, 307
29.8, 12	247	4.12	168, 169,	7.1-5	338
31.11	247		183, 221,	7.3	4
33.15	238		255, 283	7.13-14	339
35.1-2	246	4.14-17	170	7.13ff	330
35.1	247	4.14a	169	7.15-16	338–9
35.2	247	4.14b	169	7.21-23	339
38.68	238	4.16	169	7.24-27	339

8.1-4	338	1.54-55	203, 207	1.19-12.1	81
8.5-13	337	1.55	202–3, 221	1.23	83
8.5-6	337	1.55, 72	214	1.29	16, 219, 354
8.8a	338	1.73	203	1.33, 39, 46	355
8.8b	338	2.22	4	1.34	356
8.9	338	3.8	24, 203, 214	1.45	5
8.10b-12	339	3.10, 12, 14	300	1.49	82
8.10b-12		11.4	264	1.50-55	355
NRSV	338	11.39	204 n.353	2.3	95
8.10b	338	12.33	259, 270, 307	2.4	111
8.11-12	24	13.28-29	341 n.74	2.13	111
8.11	337	13.28	337, 339,	2.17	83
8.13	338		359, 361	2.21	39
10.12	339	16	359	2.23-25	91, 94, 291,
11.2	256 n.117	16.19-30	340–1		312, 355, 356
13.22	339	16.19	341	2.23	16, 354, 355,
13.23-30	339	16.20	341		356
13.23	339	16.22	341	2.24	92, 104
13.24	339	16.23	341	3.2	356
13.25a	339	16.24	341	3.3	355
13.25b	339	16.25	341	3.5	349
13.27	339	16.26	341	3.9-10	81
13.28-29		16.27-28	341	3.11	95, 354, 356
NRSV	339	16.29-31	4	3.11, 32, 36	16
13.30	340	16.29	341	3.14	4
13.43	259 n.130	16.30b	342	3.16	295
19.7-8	4	16.31	341	3.18	81, 94, 295,
22.18	204 n.353	16.74-75	24		305
22.24	4	19.9	203	3.18a	295
22.32	342	20.37-38	343	3.19-21	295, 304, 313
23.2	4	20.38	332 n.50	3.19-20	295
23.9	24	24.27	4	3.19	290, 295, 305
				3.20	304
Mark (Mk)		**John (Jn)**	48, 78–87	3.20a	295
1.44	4	1.1-18	81, 290	3.20b	295
5.15	93	1.1-8	82	3.21	304
7.10	4	1.1-3	30, 82	3.21b	295, 299–300
7.22	204 n.353	1.10-11	105 n.69	3.22	349, 356
12.26	4	1.11	31	3.23	95
		1.12-13	19, 318	3.28b	349
Luke (Lk)		1.12	31, 105 n.69,	3.29-30	349, 350
1.32-33	203		110	3.29	349
1.46-55	202,	1.14	355, 356	3.29a	349
	203 n.349	1.16-18	301	3.29b	349
1.48	203	1.17	4	3.32	105 n.69
1.48, 50,		1.18	354, 356	3.33	105 n.69
51-53	202–3	1.18, 34, 39,		4.1-38	82
1.50a	203	50, 51	16	4.5-30	352
1.50b, 55	203	1.19-12.50	109	4.6	352

Reference Index

4.19	16, 354	5.32-33	352	6.37	316 n.4	
4.29	82, 104	5.32	290	6.41	37 n.206	
4.31b	352	5.33	352	6.41, 66	82	
4.34	352	5.34	290	6.42, 69	81	
4.35-38	352	5.35	352, 354	6.44	93, 316 n.4	
4.35-36	352	5.35a	352	6.60-71	97	
4.36	352	5.36-37	292	6.68	82	
4.37-38	352	5.36	290, 291, 292, 353	6.69	94	
4.39	356			7–9	111, 112	
4.45	16, 354, 355, 356	5.37	16, 291, 354, 356	7–8	3, 26, 36, 83, 89, 90, 93, 95, 96, 98, 101–2, 103, 104, 105–7, 108–30, 313
4.48	95, 355	5.38	291		
5	104, 110 n.81, 289, 292–3, 313	5.39	291		
		5.42	291		
		5.43	291		
5.1-47	352	5.44-47	301	7	108
5.1-45	217	5.44-45	357	7.1-39	109
5.1	289	5.44	39, 291, 294 n.294	7.1-11	332
5.2-9	291			7.1-8.59	1, 3, 7 n.26, 42, 89, 101–8, 130, 370
5.2-9a	289	5.45	4		
5.6	355	5.46-47	291		
5.9b	289	5.46	16, 17		
5.10-12	289	6–7	109	7.1-8.30	107
5.14	218, 289	6.1-13, 22-65	299	7.1-7	106
5.15	290			7.1-6	295, 303
5.16-45	92	6.2	355	7.1-4	295, 313
5.16-18	316	6.2, 19, 40, 62	16	7.1-4b	294
5.16	290, 291	6.4	111	7.1-2	101 n.53, 102
5.17	290, 291	6.14, 30	355	7.1	34, 101
5.18	82, 292	6.22-24	300	7.1, 10	101
5.19-47	290, 292, 293, 303	6.22, 24	355	7.1, 11	37
5.19-20, 27	106	6.25	299, 300	7.1, 11, 14, 37	112
5.19	16, 290, 293, 354	6.26	300, 356	7.1, 20	82
		6.27	291	7.2	89, 108, 112, 124, 289
5.20-21	289, 313	6.27a	300		
5.20a	290	6.27b	301	7.3	16, 106–7, 108, 313, 354
5.20b	290	6.28-29	299, 301, 313		
5.21	290	6.28	31, 300, 301, 303	7.3, 10	102
5.22, 27	105			7.4	104, 107
5.24	292, 349	6.29	31, 301	7.6-7	107
5.24a	290	6.30a	302	7.10-12a	108
5.24b	290	6.30b	302	7.10	108
5.25, 28	292	6.31	302	7.11	96, 102
5.26	290, 292	6.31, 45	83	7.12-13, 14-15, 16-19, 26, 32, 35	95, 96
5.27	290	6.32	4, 302		
5.29	290	6.35	109, 302		
5.30	290	6.36	17, 355–6		
5.31	290	6.36, 46	16		

7.12	316 n.1	7.38	104,	8.21, 22, 25,	
7.12, 31, 43	102		117 n.100	27, 31,	
7.13	102	7.41b-42	102	33, 39,	
7.14-23	105	7.42	215	41, 48,	
7.14	108	7.45	102	52, 57	102
7.15-36	108	7.50	102	8.21, 22, 51,	
7.15	96, 102,	7.51	105	52, 53	110
	104 n.62	7.52-10.40	109	8.21, 24	34
7.16	96	7.52	102, 111, 355	8.21, 24, 26	218
7.18	103, 106	7.53-8.11	108, 111	8.21, 25,	
7.19-42	92	7.53	90	27, 33,	
7.19-22	4	8–10	123 n.124	39, 41	102 n.55
7.19-21	26, 33, 224,	8–9	109	8.21, 34, 46	110
	312, 368	8	9, 10, 11–12,	8.22	96
7.19-20	96, 189		13–14,	8.23-25	370
7.19	368		15–20, 25, 26,	8.23	103
7.20, 40-41	102		39, 40–1, 44,	8.24	34, 81, 103,
7.21-26	102		45, 108–9,		104, 106–7
7.21	291		110, 132,	8.24, 28	37
7.22-23	291		195 n.314,	8.24, 28, 58	34
7.24	105		365, 366	8.24, 58	361
7.24, 51	34	8.3	35	8.26	105, 106,
7.25-28	96	8.3, 13, 19	102		107
7.25	95	8.5	4	8.26, 28,	
7.25, 30	102	8.7, 11	218	38, 40	106
7.26	81, 95	8.11	90	8.27	103
7.26, 48	102	8.12-20	106	8.28	104, 110
7.27	102	8.12-13	95	8.30-59	23–4, 90
7.28-29	102–3	8.12	93, 102, 108,	8.30-37	23
7.28	103, 106		109, 111,	8.30-32	94–5
7.30	95, 96, 111		126, 304	8.30-31	22, 24, 90–1,
7.31	104	8.12, 24, 58	112	92–3,	
7.32	95, 96, 104	8.13-14	106	95, 97	
7.32, 45, 46	102	8.14	103	8.30	82, 90–8
7.32, 45,		8.14, 16	105	8.30, 31	89, 104
48 (x2)	102	8.15	106	8.31-59	1–3, 6–7,
7.32b	104 n.63	8.15, 16,			8, 9, 12, 13,
7.33-34, 36	103	26, 50	34, 105		17–18,
7.33	95	8.16-17	215		19–20, 21,
7.34-44	96	8.16	105, 107		25, 26, 27, 28,
7.34	107	8.17-18	106		31, 33, 40, 41,
7.35	95, 96	8.17	105, 107		42, 45, 50, 85,
7.37-39	83, 104, 108,	8.17, 18	34		86, 89–90,
	109, 110,	8.18, 38, 42	103		98, 100–1,
	117 n.100,	8.19	103		102, 107–8,
	127, 370	8.20	95, 96, 109,		282, 299, 302,
7.37	108–9, 112,		111		305, 365, 367,
	126	8.21	103		369, 370, 371

8.31-58	22	8.32	14, 18, 21, 22,	8.37-48	44
8.31-47	14, 19, 33,		24, 26, 27, 41,	8.37-47	17, 18, 19,
	317		43, 94, 96, 97,		305, 311–12
8.31-40	130		121, 131, 215,	8.37-42	21
8.31-38	32		223, 224, 225,	8.37-40	228
8.31-37	24, 98, 189,		348, 366, 367,	8.37	2, 99, 103,
	215, 369		369, 370, 371		227, 311, 317
8.31-37,		8.32, 33-34,		8.37, 40	82
38-47,		39-40	129	8.37, 40,
48-59	369	8.32, 37, 52	371	52-53	368
8.31-36	15, 17, 18, 19,	8.32, 39	40	8.38-47	99, 369
	21, 28, 29,	8.32, 40,		8.38-40	120
	40, 43, 131,	44d, 45,		8.38	99, 107, 227,
	217–18,	46, 55	100		354, 356
	219–20,	8.32, 45	107	8.38, 41, 44	103
	223–6,	8.32, 52	104	8.38, 47	28
	310–11	8.33-59	95, 96	8.38, 57	16
8.31-34	13, 21–9, 32,	8.33-47	22	8.38a	311, 312
	42, 112, 281,	8.33-34	43, 91, 218,	8.39-59	30–1
	316		296, 367	8.39-47	29–33
8.31-33	1–2, 27,	8.33	21, 25, 27,	8.39-44	313
	150–1		28, 29, 94,	8.39-42	257 n.121
8.31-32	95, 98, 107,		96, 98, 99,	8.39-41	140 n.51,
	110, 216–17,		103, 132,		305–13, 353
	365, 366		223, 224, 226	8.39-40	2, 24, 29–30,
8.31	14, 22, 24,				32, 41, 42,
	25, 28, 89,	8.33, 37,			105 n.67,
	90–8, 99,	39 (x3),			112, 189, 227,
	104, 107,	40, 52,			228, 238, 288,
	110, 281	53, 56,			310, 312, 313,
		57, 58	1, 18, 20		348, 3686,
8.31, 43,		8.33, 37,			371
47, 51,		39a, 39b,			
53	100	40, 52, 53,		8.39	19, 20, 23,
8.31, 56-57	216	57, 58	100		29–30, 31,
8.32-59	89, 91, 92	8.33, 56	21		32, 33, 40,
8.32-42	317	8.34-36	1, 236, 371		43–4, 99,
8.32-36	215, 218,	8.34	15, 21–2, 98,		103, 107–8,
	219, 365		100, 107, 110,		218, 250,
8.32-34	15, 22, 33,		120, 131, 218,		281, 288,
	318		223, 311, 316		289 n.270,
8.32-33	15, 27–8, 29,	8.34, 46	107		311, 317
	33, 38 n.219,	8.35-58	15	8.39, 40	18, 228,
	41, 120, 121,	8.35-36	39, 98, 131	305	
	130, 133, 149,	8.35	23	8.39, 41	296
	217, 227, 305,	8.36	21, 22, 98,	8.39, 53	214
	311, 366, 370,		110, 223	8.39a	21, 99, 311
	371	8.37-59	368	8.39b	21, 311
8.32-33, 38	33	8.37-52	368	8.40-41	371

8.40	20, 21, 29, 32–3, 107, 310, 311, 312	8.52-53	365			107, 226, 292, 317, 357, 362
		8.52	100, 316, 362, 365			
8.40a	99	8.52, 53	317	8.59a	33, 98	
8.40b	99	8.52a	108, 316	8.59b	33, 98	
8.41-44	107	8.52b	108	9	101 n.53,	
8.41	92, 99 n.49, 311	8.53	19, 21, 294 n.294,		108 n.73, 110–11,	
8.41, 44	298		317		302–3	
8.41a	99	8.53a	100, 316, 317	9.1-50	217	
8.41b	99	8.53c	316	9.1-41	107, 299	
8.42-43	110	8.54	100, 103, 108, 316	9.1-10.21	110 n.81	
8.42	97, 99, 103, 106, 108, 311–12	8.54b	100, 317	9.1-7	106, 304	
		8.55	99, 100, 107, 317	9.1-5	304	
8.42, 47, 53	103			9.1	98, 302	
8.43	99, 24	8.55a	103	9.2	98, 299, 302	
8.43a	103	8.55b	103	9.3-5	289, 299, 303, 313	
8.43b	103	8.55c	103	9.3-4	303 n.329, 304	
8.44-46	92	8.56-59	33, 38, 100, 105, 317	9.3	303, 304	
8.44	1, 28, 90, 92, 97, 107, 110, 225, 227, 243, 305, 311, 312, 317, 366	8.56-58	12, 19, 21, 33–9, 40, 41, 42, 44–5, 112, 120–1, 130, 318, 319, 321, 340, 348, 353, 354, 357–63, 367, 3696, 371	9.4-5	111, 303	
				9.4	302	
				9.4a	303–4	
				9.4b	304	
8.44a	99, 100			9.5	109, 111, 304	
8.44b	99			9.7	108 n.73, 126, 354	
8.44c	99					
8.45	99–100			9.7, 15, 19, 21, 25, 39, 41	16	
8.45, 46	104, 107					
8.46	100, 107	8.56-57	362			
8.47-59	315	8.56	16–17, 20, 21, 33, 37, 38, 39, 40, 100, 318, 352–3, 354, 361	9.8	16, 354	
8.47-53	216, 371			9–10	109	
8.47	19, 103, 106, 110			9.13-34	106	
				9.22	78	
8.47a, b	100			9.28-29	4	
8.48-59	17, 19, 33, 100, 315, 317, 318, 348, 369	8.57	21, 36, 100, 317, 357, 361, 362	9.37-38	355	
				9.37	16, 354, 356	
				9.38-41	304	
		8.58	2, 19, 21, 30, 31, 32, 33–5, 36, 37, 38, 41, 98, 100, 106, 310, 317, 318, 332, 351, 370	9.39-41	356	
8.48-55	362			9.39	106, 304	
8.48	100, 315			9.41	98, 106, 305	
8.49-50	103			10	101 n.53, 104, 110, 111, 292–3, 313	
8.49	100, 316					
8.50	100, 107, 316					
8.50, 54	106	8.59	2, 31, 34, 35, 90, 97, 98, 100, 101 n.53,			
8.51-52	355			10.1	110	
8.51	16, 19, 100, 316, 354			10.10	110, 349	
				10.11	294	

Reference Index

10.12	16, 354	12.25	356	15.23	294
10.20	316 n.1	12.36	34	15.24	16, 17, 289, 294, 313, 351, 354, 355–6
10.21	98, 109	12.37	95		
10.22-39	107, 293	12.38	83		
10.22-24	292	12.40	106		
10.22	109, 110, 112	12.41	16–17	15.25-26	353
10.24	81, 293	12.42	39, 78, 91, 356, 357	15.25	83
10.25-26	292			15.27	215
10.25-26, 32-33	289, 313	12.45	355	16.2-22	354
		13-18	83	16.2	78
10.25a	292	13-17	294 n.289	16.8-9	218
10.25b	292	13.1-17.26	81, 89, 215, 294, 350	16.10	354
10.27	292, 316 n.4			16.10, 16, 17, 19	16
10.28	292	13.1	111		
10.30-33	316	13.15	215, 225	16.16	354
10.31-33	293	13.18	83	16.16, 17, 19, 22	16
10.31	292	13.22	16, 354		
10.32-33	292, 362	14.7	354, 356	16.20-23a, 24b NRSV	350–1
10.32	292	14.7, 9	16		
10.33	293	14.9	356		
10.34	83	14.10-14	289, 313	16.20-22 (23-24)	350, 353
10.36-38	293	14.10	293, 294		
10.37-38	292	14.10b, 31	215	16.20, 21, 22, 24	350
10.37-38a	293	14.12-13	303 n.331		
10.37	293	14.12	294	16.22-24	45, 362
10.38	293	14.13-14	294	16.22	351
10.38b	293	14.16-18	353	16.24	349, 351, 353
10.38c	293	14.17	354	16.27	94
10.38d	293	14.17, 19	16	17.1-26	351
10.39	107	14.19-20	353	17.1	111
10.40-42	293	14.19	355	17.13	349, 351
11.9	16, 354	14.27-28a	353	17.14	351
11.27	82, 94, 104	14.28	352, 353	17.24	16, 354, 355
11.39-44	304	15.1-6	97	18–19	83
11.39b	94	15.4-7	215–16	18.28-32	82
11.40	16, 354, 355, 356	15.6	95	18.33-38	81
		15.7	216	19-20	105
11.45	93, 356	15.9-10	350	19.4	95
11.53	82	15.11	349, 350, 351	19.7-12	82
12	104	15.12	350	19.16	95
12.1-50	81	15.18, 27	107, 294	19.24, 36	83
12.1	111	15.19	294	19.25-27	81
12.9	355	15.20	216, 225	19.29	95
12.11	93	15.20b	294	19.35	354, 356
12.13-14	83	15.21-25	216	19.35, 37	16
12.19	354	15.21	294	20–21	81
12.19, 45	16	15.22-24	218	20.1	354
12.21, 41	355	15.22	216, 294	20.1, 5	16
12.23, 27	111	15.23-25	295	20.5, 8	356

20.6	354	1.16b	198	4.2, 5-6	278		
20.6, 12, 14	16	1.17	198	4.2, 6	261, 307		
20.8, 16	82	1.29	204 n.353	4.3	198, 262, 263		
20.13	95	2.1–3.20	263 n.145	4.3, 6	268		
20.18	354	2.4-8	260	4.3, 13, 16	37		
20.18, 25, 29	16, 356	2.4	198, 260	4.4-9	262–6		
20.19-20a	353	2.6-7	259	4.4-8	256, 265, 309		
20.20	45, 352, 353, 354, 362	2.6	260	4.4-6	265		
		2.7	259, 307	4.4-5	198, 262, 263, 268, 307		
20.20b	353	2.7, 10	259 n.131				
20.21-22	353	2.8	260	4.4	262, 263–5, 268		
20.23	218	2.9	260				
20.24-28	353	2.12-16	278	4.4a	264		
20.25, 27-29	355	2.13	266	4.5-6	278		
20.29	17, 94, 356	2.15	273 n.185	4.5	198		
20.30-31	356	2.25	265, 266	4.5a	264		
20.32-35	365	2.26-29	259 n.131	4.6-8	198		
21.9, 20	16, 354	2.26	266	4.6	263		
21.24	95	2.28	309	4.6b	270		
		3.1-2	198	4.9-12	199		
Acts		3.1	265	4.9	265		
2.37	300	3.2, 28	261, 269, 307	4.11	199, 265		
3.1-12	204	3.2b	198	4.12	199, 214		
3.15	204	3.3-8	198	4.13-25	199		
3.17	204	3.9-18	198	4.13-14	199		
3.19	204	3.9	198	4.13	199		
3.22-23, 24, 25	204	3.19-20	277	4.13, 16	197–201		
		3.20	198, 277	4.16	199		
3.22	4	3.20, 28	273	4.19-24	199		
3.24	204	3.21-26	198	4.20	199 n.333		
3.25-26	204, 207, 221	3.21	277	4.25	199		
3.25	202, 204	3.22	277	6.23	263		
6.11, 14	4	3.23-24	277	7.7-12	268 n.167		
7.2-17	203	3.26	278	8.1-17	200 n.337		
7.2	214	3.27-28	278	9–11	200 n.335, 201, 266		
7.22	4	3.27	269, 278				
7.32	343	3.27a, 28	198	9.1-11.36	200		
7.35	4	3.28	270, 273 n.185	9.2	266		
9.36	258, 270, 307			9.3	266		
11.2	22	3.30	278	9.4	266		
13.39	4	3.31	198	9.4-5	200		
13.41	256 n.117	4	25, 266	9.6-7	201, 221		
15.5	22	4.1-25	8, 198	9.6	25		
21.20	22	4.1-11	268	9.6a	200		
25.45	22	4.1-5	262	9.6b-7a	200, 201		
		4.1-2	198, 271	9.6b-7a NRSV	266		
Romans (Rom)		4.1	262				
1.4	193	4.2	198, 262–3, 278	9.7-8	197–201		
1.16–3.31	198			9.7	200, 206		

9.7a	214	11.21b-12.10	201 n.342	3.4a	191
9.7b	200	11.22-23a	202	3.6	37
9.8	200, 201, 221	11.22	25, 201–2,	3.7-9	213, 276
9.10	266		221	3.7a	191
9.11-13	267, 269	11.23b-29	202	3.7b	191
9.11-13				3.8	275
NRSV	266	**Galatians (Gal)**	**26–7**	3.8b	191
9.11-12,		1–2	190 n.287	3.8c	191
30-32	266–9	1.4	274	3.9	25, 191
9.11a	267	1.6, 7	190–1	3.10-11	275
9.13-16	269	1.11-24	273	3.10	192, 276, 277
9.13	267	2–4	7 n.26, 8	3.10-12	192
9.14	267	2	189	3.10a	192, 275
9.15	4, 267	2.1-10	273	3.10b, 11	275
9.16	267	2.3	190, 273	3.11-12	192
9.20	257	2.4-5a	189	3.11	192, 277
9.27	201 n.341	2.6	190, 277	3.11a	277
9.30-32	268–9, 307	2.7b	273	3.12	277
9.30-31	200	2.11-14	190, 273	3.12a	192
9.30	268	2.12	22, 273, 274	3.13	192, 277
9.31	269	2.15-16	191, 274		n.200
9.32-35	309	2.15-16a	190	3.14	192, 277
9.32	200, 268, 269	2.15	269	3.15	192
10.4	200	2.16	190,	3.16-19	192, 197
10.19	4		191 n.293,	3.16-17	23, 223
11.1	201, 202		273, 274	3.16	204 n.356
11.4-6	201	2.16, 19	275	3.16, 29	189
11.7	201	2.16 (x3)	273	3.16 (x3),	
11.20-21	201	2.16c	273	29	189
11.26	201	2.17-19	274	3.16a-d	192
11.30-32	267	2.17	274	3.17	192–3
11.33-36	201	2.17a	190	3.18	193
13.12-13	260	2.17b	190	3.19-29	195
		2.18	274, 275	3.19	193
1 Corinthians (1 Cor)		2.19-20a	190	3.21	194
3.13-15	260	2.19	274	3.22	194, 274
5.8	204 n.353	2.21	190, 191,	3.23	194
10.2	4		274, 275	3.24-25	194
15.58	256 n.117	2.24	195	3.26	194, 197
16.10	256 n.117	3–4	189	3.28	194
		3	25, 195, 271	3.29	193, 194, 221
2 Corinthians (2 Cor)		3.1	190	4.1-7	196, 221
6.14-16a	243	3.2-6	275, 277	4.1	195
9.8b	270	3.2-5, 10	275	4.2-6	221
11.1-30	201	3.2, 5, 10	269, 273	4.3-7	23
11.1-15	201	3.2a	191	4.5	195
11.13-15	260	3.2b	191	4.6	193, 195
11.13	201	3.3	191, 275	4.7	195
11.16-33	201	3.4	275	4.9	195

4.10	195	2.10	205	2.25-26	281
4.19	197	2.14-18	202	2.25	256, 271, 272
4.19, 21-22	197	2.14-17	205, 207, 222	2.25a	271
4.21-31	195, 196–7, 221	2.14	221, 316	2.26	270
		2.15	205	3.13-14	270
4.21	195, 196	2.16	205		
4.23-24	195	2.17	205	**2 Peter (2 Pet)**	
4.24-26	195	3.2	4	3.9-11	260
4.28-29	196	4.3, 4	256 n.117		
4.28	195	6.1	259 n.133	**1 John (1 Jn) 305**	
4.29	196	6.10	256 n.117	1.1-2	355, 356
4.30	196	6.14-15	206 n.364	1.3-4	351 n.119
5.1	196	9.14	259	1.4, 12	349, 351 n.119
5.19-21a	260	11	222, 272, 298 n.307, 301		
5.21b	260			2.1	219
8.31, 36	189	11.8-19	205	3	299, 313
		11.8-9	207	3.3	299
Ephesians (Eph)		11.8	205	3.4	296
5.8	260	11.8, 17	37	3.4-6	296
5.11-12	260, 307	11.9	206	3.5	219, 297, 299
6.12	204 n.353	11.12	205–6	3.6-12	219 n.426
		11.13	206	3.6	296, 356
Philippians (Phil)		11.15	206	3.7-12	296
2.30	256 n.117	11.16	206	3.7	296
		11.17-18	206	3.8-12	298, 312
Colossians (Col)		11.17	271	3.8-10	298
3.23-25	260	11.18	202, 205–6	3.8	296
		11.19	206, 271	3.8, 12	296, 298
1 Timothy (1 Tim)		11.31	272	3.8a	296
2.10	257–8, 307	13.2	323	3.8b	296, 297
5.10	258, 270			3.10a	297
5.25	259, 307	**James (Jas)**		3.10b	297
6.14	259	2.14 NRSV	270	3.11-18	299
6.18	259, 307	2.15-16	270	3.11	297
		2.17	270	3.12-15	299
2 Timothy (2 Tim)		2.18a	270	3.12	296, 297, 298, 299
1.8-9	269 n.170	2.18b NRSV	270		
		2.20b	270	3.12b	297, 298
Titus (Tit)		2.21-24	270–1	3.14b	298
2.7	258, 307	2.21-22	272	3.15	298
2.14	258	2.21	214, 256, 270, 271	3.17	298
3.8, 14	258			3.18	296, 299
		2.21, 24	271	4.10	219
Hebrews (Heb)		2.22a	271	4.14	356
1.2 205		2.22b	271	5.16-18	218
1.3-4	205	2.23-25	308, 309	5.16	218–19
1.10	256 n.117	2.23	37, 307		
2.5-9	205	2.24-25	8	**3 John (3 Jn)**	
2.9b	205	2.24	301	1.11	356

Jude (Jud)
5.6   167

Revelation (Rev)
2.1-2	256
2.14	257 n.121
2.19	257
2.20	256, 307
2.20a	257
2.21-23	257
2.22	257
2.23	257
3.1-3, 15-16	257
3.8	256
9.20-21	257
12.13	268
15.3	256 n.117
22.12	256 n.117

JEWISH SOURCES

QUMRAN/DEAD SEA SCROLLS (DSS)
5, 56, 307

Aramaic Levi Document
16-17   183-4

CD (Damascus Document)
2.14-15	300
4	183
5.5b-6a	255
19-20	255

1QFlor
278

1QGen
19.14-21   326 n.30

4Q174.17
255

4Q216
176 n.207

4Q252
182

II (5-8)   182

4Q347
4

4Q397
253

4Q398
253

4Q541.9
335 n.61

4QMMT
	241, 309, 310
B 1-2	253
B 2	253
C 11-22	255-6
C 11-18	254
C 11-14	254
C 23-26	253, 255
C 25-32	253
C 26	252, 278
C 27	252, 255

4QpIsa
34

11QT
11.13	123
27.10-29.6	123
29	123-4
42.10-17	124
44.6	124

JOSEPHUS

Antiquitates judaicae (Ant./AJ)
1.7, 1 155	25
1.57	184
1.154-157	206 n.360, 348
1.155-157	329
1.155-156	330
1.155	28, 348
1.158-159	329
1.166-168	330
1.183	186
1.184-85	186
1.185	185
1.191	185
1.235	185
2.7.1	249
2.8-10	269 n.170, 270
2.169	221
3.1.4	249
3.5.3	249
3.244-247	125
3.244	125
3.320	4
4.8, 2	26
8.12.6	249
8.12.16 [312-14]	250
10.4.1 [47]	250
11.154-158	120
20.8.6	249
II,169	185

Bellum Judaicum (J.W./BJ)
1.73	125
2.515	125
4.483	186
7.8.1	249

Contra Apionem (C. Ap./Ag. Ap.)
2.23 [190, 192]   249

PHILO OF ALEXANDRIA

Abr. (De Abrahamo)
52-54	187
62-65	187
66	187
69-71	28
70	279
71	186
88-89	187
99	186
248-50	187
262	187
273-275	187
275-276	279

Aet. (De Aeternitate Mundi)
8.41	251
11.58	251

Cher. (De Cherubim)
1-10	187
10	187

Conf. (De Confusione Linguarum)
15.68   251

Cong. (De Congressu Eruditionis Gratia)		*Op. (De Opificio Mundi)*		2.35.218	251
		2.10	250	2.204-214	124–5
69	187	43.128	251	2.204-206	124
		49.141	250	2.207	124
Det. (Quod Deterius Potiori Insidiari Soleat)		52.149	251	2.208-10	124
		170	348	2.211	124–5
16	188	*Plant. (De Plantatione)*		*Virt. (De Virtutibus)*	
32.119	251	30.128	251	39 217-19	25
33.125	251				
120	251	*Post. (De Posteritate Caini)*		**PSEUDEPIGRAPHA**	
121	251	11.38	251		
122	251	42.141	250	***Apocalypse of Abraham***	
		48.167	251	***(Apoc. Ab.)***	**361**
Her. (Quis Rerum Divinarum Heres Sit)				1–8	336 n.64, 347, 348
		Praem. (De Praemiis et Poenis)		1.1-8.6	28
277-79	188	4.23	252	4.6	348
		7.43	251	9–10	35
Leg. All. (Legum Allegoriae)				9.2-3	35
		Quaest in Gn./QG (Quaestiones et Solutiones in Genesim)		9.6	35
1.6.16	251			9.10	19 n.112, 39
1.15.48	251			10	35, 335–6, 358
1.43.36	252	1.87	251		
2.8.26	250	3.32	252	10.1-3	336
2.17.68	251	4.60	186-7	10.3	336
2.18.75	250			10.4	336
3.2.4	251	*Quod Deus./Deus. (Quod Deus Sit Immutabilis)*		10.5, 6	336
3.87.217	337			10.8-11	336
3.87.218	337	7.34	251	10.12	336
3.87.219	337	17.78	251	10.14	336
3.244	187	23.106	251	10.15	19 n.112, 336
				11.1-32.6	336
Migr. (De Migratione Abrahami)		*Quod. Omn./Prob. (Quod Omnis Probus Liber Sit)*		13.1-3	336
				13.6-8	336
28	187	11.74	251	13.7	336
113-14	188			13.10-13	336
		Sac. (De Sacrificiis Abelis et Caini)		24.2	19 n.112, 39
Mos. (De Vita Mosis)				29.2	19 n.112, 39
1.1.158	4	1-10	187	31.1-3	16 n.90
1.7.38	250	13.52	251	31.1-2	19 n.112, 39
1.55.301	251				
2.12-14	188	*Somn. (De Somniis)*		***Apocalypse of Zephaniah***	
2.46 [257]	251	1.160	187	***(Apoc. Zeph.)***	
				10.1-14	165
Mut. (De Mutatione Nominum)		*Spec. Leg. (De Specialibus Legibus)*		11.1-4	331
				11.1-3	165
84	185	1.6.33	250	11.5-6	165
154-69	19 n.112	1.37.204	251	11.5	165

Reference Index

2 Baruch (2 Bar.)		6.5	245	12.22b	177 n.209
239 n.41, 283		7	306, 309	12.23	177–8
44	16 n.90, 239, 309	7.3	260	12.24	178
		7.22-25	241	12.25-27	279
47.2	278	7.24	300	13.4, 20 (x3),	
48.1-24	239–40	7.[76]-[78]	245	21	177
48.29	240	7.83	245	13.8-9	348
53.1-12	240	7.102-115		14.1-16	325
53.56-72	240	(36-45)	164	14.1	325, 326
56.1-16	240	7.102-15	182 n.236	14.2-3a	326
57	309, 310, 367	7.102	164, 222	14.2, 5, 7,	
57.1-16	240	7.102ff	164	13, 21,	
57.1-2	239, 240–1, 307, 309–10	7.112-13	164 n.147	22	177
		8.30-36	245	14.4-5	326
		8.47-50	245	14.9-13	326
3 Baruch (3 Bar.)		9.7-8	245	14.13	326
6.21	332	9.12	242	14.17	326
6.22-23	332			14.20	326
		Jubilees (Jub.)	36,	14.21	19 n.112
1 Enoch (1 En.)	34–5	171–2, 176 n.207, 307,		15.9 (X2),	
10.16	179 n.217	328, 370		10, 12,	
38.5	331 n.48	1–23	221	20	177
39.6, 7	34	4.33	169 n.169	15.16	334
48.2, 3, 6	34	10.1-13	177 n.209	15.17	19 n.112, 334
48.9	331 n.48	11.11-13	177 n.209	15.20	334
51.3	34 n.187	11.14-17	176	15.23-24	334
63.8	260	11.16-17	348	16	112, 221, 369
93.5, 10	179 n.217	11.16	176	16.9 (x2),	
95.3	331 n.48	12	178	16, 17 (x2),	
104.2, 6	175 n.203	12.1-7	178	18, 22,	
		12.1-4	176	26, 28	177
2 Enoch (2 En.)		12.2-5	348	16.15-19	333 n.54
53.1	182 n.236	12.2	176 n.208	16.15-16	178, 333
		12.3-5	176 n.208	16.17-19	19 n.112
4 Ezra	162, 167, 172, 238, 283	12.3b, 5b	176 n.208	16.17-19a-c	178, 333
		12.9-11	177	16.19d	178, 333
3	221	12.12-14	28, 329	16.20-31	121, 178, 322–3, 334, 358, 360
3.1-19	328	12.12	177		
3.1-13	328	12.13-14	177		
3.12-19	328	12.14	177	16.20-30	38
3.12-15	163	12.16-10	329	16.20-27	37
3.12	221	12.16	177, 329	16.20-21	333
3.14-15	328, 358	12.17-18	177	16.20	178, 193, 333
3.14	16 n.90, 19 n.112, 39, 328, 360	12.17	329	16.20, 25, 27, 28,	
		12.19-20	329	29, 31	121
		12.20, 24	177	16.21	178, 183
3.15	163, 328, 369	12.20a	177	16.22	178, 333
3.16	307	12.21	177, 329	16.24-27	178, 333–4
3.19	328	12.22	177		

16.25-26	334	6.18-19	173	**3 Maccabees (3 Macc.)**	
16.25	333, 334	7.5	173	162, 167	
16.26	36, 37, 38,	8.3	176	2.25-7.23	158
	179 n.217,	11.5	176	3.11-30	158
	334, 361	13.10	174, 175	4.1-21	158
16.27	334	18	174, 236	5.1-51	158
16.30	333	18.1-14	173	6	221
17.3, 7 (x2)	177	18.5	329 n.41	6.1-15	158
17.25-7	19 n.112	18.5a	173	6.1-3	158, 159
18.15, 16, 19	177	18.5b	173	6.3	18 n.103
18.18-19	177 n.209	18.6b	173	6.16-29	158
18.18	178 n.214	18.7a	173	7	159
19	28	23	221	9.16-29	158
19.15	244 n.56	23.1-14	326		
19.28	177 n.209	23.3	326	**4 Maccabees (4 Macc.)**	
19.29	28	23.4-5a	327	221	
20–22	367	23.4	327	6.17	165
20	179 n.218	23.5	174	6.27b-29	166
20.2	179	23.5b	327	7.18-20	166
20.4	179	23.5c	327	7.18-19	332, 337, 343
20.20b	177	23.5d	327	9.21	166
21.3	348	23.6-7	327	9.21 NSRV	166
22	179	23.6	326, 327	9.22-24	166
22.10	244	23.7a	327	13.17	332, 337, 343
22.16	179, 244,	23.7b	327	14.20	166
	310	23.7c	327	15.6	166 n.159
22.16b-18	244	23.10-13	174	15.27-28	166
22.22-24	244	23.12	174	15.28	166
23.10-11	36	23.13	174	16.20	166 n.158,
25.5	179	23.14	174		214
30	179	25.9-13	172	16.24-25	166
32.1-9	121	32–35	343 n.81	16.25	332
32	124	32	175 n.202	17.5-6	166
32.4-6	121	33–35	236	18.1-2	167
32.16-22	121	33	175	18.1	135 n.24,
39.6	279	33.1-6	176		165
49.2	177 n.209	33.1-3	175, 222	18.20	166
		33.2	175	18.20, 23	166
Pseudo-Philo		33.3	175	18.23	166
LAB (Liber antiquitatum		33.5	182 n.236		
biblicarum)	122,	33.5a	175	**Psalms of Solomon**	
171–2		33.5b	175, 222	**(Pss. Sol.)**	
1–6	221	35.1-5	175	9.9	18 n.103
4.5	176	35.2	175	17.25	34
6–7	174, 177	35.3	175, 176,	17.32-34	34 n.187
6.1-18	172		222	19.7 LXX	34 n.187
6.2-3	172	35.4	176		
6.3	172–3	36.3	172	**Pseudo-Eupolemus**	
6.4	173	44.1-5	172	**(Ps.-Eup.)**	
6.13-18	173	44.10	176	3	329

8	329	11.9	330	7.7	242, 331
9–10	329	11.10	331	8.1-2	242 n.49
		11.11	331		

Testament of Abraham
(T. Abr.) 171, 172, 180, 221, 312, 323

		11.12	181, 331	*Testament of Benjamin*	
		12.1-2	181	*(T. Benj.)*	310
		12.1	331	3.3	244
1–14	360	12.3-4	181, 331	7.1-5	244
1–4	361	12.7	181, 331	10	337
1.1-2	180	12.8-9	181	10.2-5	244
1.1	181	12.8	331	10.4a	335
1.3	181	12.9-10	331	10.4b	335
1.4	180	12.11	181, 331	10.4c	335
1.5	180, 181	12.12	181, 331	10.5a	335
1.6-7	181	12.13-14	181	10.6	335
1.7	180	12.17	181, 331	10.7	335
2.5-12	180	12.18	181, 331	10.11	335
4.1-5	180	13–14	358, 359	12.1	242 n.49
4.6	180	13	225		
4.12	182	13.3	181, 331	*Testament of Dan*	
7.2-7	180	14.1	181–2	*(T. Dan)*	
7.8-9	180	14.2c	182	5.6	244
7.10	180	14.3-4	182	7.2	242 n.49
7.11	180	14.5	182		
8.1-4	180	14.7-8	182	*Testament of Gad*	
8.7	180–1	14.9	182	*(T. Gad)*	
8.9	181	14.10	182	8.4b-5	242 n.49
8.12b	181	14.11	182		
9.2a	181	14.14	182	*Testament of Isaachar*	
9.3-6	181	15.14-15	282	*(T. Iss.)*	
9.4	181			7.8-9	242 n.49
9.5	181	*Testament of Job (T. Job)*			
9.6	181	9–12	282–3	*Testament of Joseph*	
10–12	330	9.1-8	283	*(T. Jos.)*	
10	182, 331	10.1-7	283	20.5	242 n.49
10.1-15	331	11.1-12	283		
10.1	181, 330	12.1-4	283	*Testament of Judah*	
10.2-3	330			*(T. Jud.)*	
10.3b	181, 330	*Testament of Moses*		18.1	244
10.4-5	181	*(T. Mos./Asc. Mos)*		25.1	331
10.5	330	109	175 n.203	26.4	242 n.49
10.6	181, 330				
10.7	181	**TESTAMENT**		*Testament of Levi*	
10.8-11	181	**OF TWELVE**		*(T. Levi)* 167	
10.12-13	330	**PATRIARCHS (T12P)**		13.1-3	242
10.12-13a	181	159–60, 238, 242 n.48,		13.4	242
10.13b	181	310, 358		14.1	160, 221
10.14	181			14.4-8	242
10.15	330	*Testament of Asher*		14.4	242, 307, 310
11.1-12	330	*(T. Ash.)* 159–60, 167			
11.6	330	7.2, 5, 6a, 7	159	15.4	160, 242, 331

16.1	243	**RABBINIC**		*Ta'anit (Tan.)*	
16.2	243	**LITERATURE**		1.1	127
17.11	243				
18.1-14	242, 334	*Mishnah (=m.)*		*Yoma*	
18.1-2	242	125 n.139, 208		2.5	112
18.1-2a	334	*Bava Kamma*			
18.1	243	8.6	214	*Tosefta (=t.)* 208	
18.3-4	242			*Rosh Hashanah (RoshHa)*	
18.4	334	*Bava Metzia*		1.12	127
18.5	242	7.1	214	1.13	127
18.6	242 n.50, 334, 335	*Kiddushin (Kidd)*		*Sotah (Sot.)*	
18.7	334	4.14	280-1, 307, 308, 313	4	214
18.8	242 n.50			6.1	282 n.228
18.8a	334	4.14b	214		
18.8b	334-5			*Sukkah (Suk.)*	
18.9, 11-12	243	*Makkot*		3.1ff	112
18.12	243, 358, 360	3.15-16	283, 308, 309	3.18	127, 130
		23b	368		
18.12a	335			*Ta'anit (Tan.)*	
18.12b	335	*Nedarim (Ned.)*		3.9	287
18.13-14	335	3.11	213		
18.13b	335	3.11b	214, 282	*Yoma*	
18.14	16 n.90, 335			4.12	287
		Peah			
19.1	242	1.1 280		**Halakhic Midrash**	
19.2	242			*Sifra (on Leviticus)* 208	
19.3-4a	242	*Pirkei Avot (Avot)*			
19.5	242	2.2	286	*Sifrei Bamidbar*	
25.47-55	36	3	312	42.1	210
29.1	300	3.5	26		
		3.12	214	*Sifrei Devarim*	
Testament of Naphtali		4	214	8.1	211
(T. Naph.)		5.2, 3, 19	214	31.3	211
9.1	242 n.49	5.19	210, 211	32.19	210
				Piska 25.4	211
Testament of Reuben		*Rosh Hashanah (RoshHa)*			
(T. Reu.)		1.2	127, 130	*Sifre Deuteronomy* 208, 308	
6.3	244	1.13	130		
7.1-2	242 n.49			31.1	214
		Sanhedrin (San.)		32.40	286
Testament of Simeon		4.1	285	38	212 n.384
(T. Sim.)				40	212 n.384
5.3-4	244	*Sukkah (Suk.)*	112	352.5	214
8.2	242 n.49	4.3	126	Piska 8.1	211
		4.5	126	Piska 8.2	211
Testament of Zebulon		4.6	126	Piska 15.1	214
(T. Zeb.)		4.9-10	111	Piska 184	285-6
10.6	242 n.49	4.10	126, 370	Piska 347	287

Sifrei Numbers	208, 214	*Zevahim (Zev.)*		44.21, 22	19 n.112, 39
75.1	347	62a	158	44.22, 28	16 n.90
115	213			48.10	129, 370
Piska 115	211–12	***Jerusalem Talmud (=y.)***		54.5	272 n.182
		Sukkah (Sukk.)		55.4	272 n.182
Sifre Zuta (on Numbers)		5.1	117 n.100	61	288
208		48, 54d	112		

Leviticus Rabbah (Lev. R.)
1.15   212 n.384
12.1   212 n.388

LATER RABBINIC SOURCES

Ta'anit (Tan.)
1.1   127
2.1   158

Pesikta Rabbati (Pes. R.)
27 (28).3   212 n.384

Avot de Rabbi Natan (ARN)   208 n.372, 214
A   282, 283
A, 77   283, 308

Mekhilta de Rabbi Ishmael (MRI) 208, 209–10, 301, 309
13.2, par 3   347

OTHER LATER RABBINIC SOURCES

Ba-Kodesh
5   212–13

Targumim
Targum Isaiah (Tg. Isa.)
43.10-12   344, 359, 361
43.10   344, 345
43.12   344

Babylonian Talmud (=b.)
56, 207 n.369
Avodah Zarah (Av. Zar.)
9.2   214

Beschallach
2, 160-170   214, 346
3 (27-65)   284

Bava Barta
15b   282 n.228

Nezikin
18   209
61.2.4B   287

Targum Neofiti   345–6

Betzah
32a   214

Targum Onkelos

Shira
15.17.5   210

Genesis   283, 301, 308, 309, 346

Shabbat (Shabb.)
156a   329 n.41

Mekhilta de Rabbi Shimon bar Yochai
208, 285, 287
4   173 n.196

Targum Pseudo-Jonathan (Tq. Ps.-J.)   139, 288, 359, 361
4   345

Sukkah (Sukk.)
4.9-10   125
45b   126
48b   112
51   130, 370
51a-b   125, 126
51b   126

Sanya
2.2.6A-C   286

Yalk.Shim.
1, 764   288

Midrash Rabbah
Genesis Rabbah (Gen. Rab./Gen. R)
112
2.2 212 nn.384, 388
38.13   347–8, 359, 361
44.12   329 n.41

EARLY CHRISTIAN AND GNOSTIC SOURCES

Ta'anit (Tan.)
2b   127

Didascalia Apostolorum
6   160 n.133
7   160 n.133

Yoma
5a   173 n.196

Eusebius
Praeparatio evangelica (Praep. Ev.)
9.17, 102 25

OTHER GRECO-ROMAN SOURCES

Epictetus
Discourses II (Diss. II)
1.23 23 n.127

Justin Martyr
Dialogue with Trypho 28
23–24,
 44, 47 25–6
47 26

First Apologia (1 Apol.)
30

OSTRACA, MANUSCRIPTS & PAPYRI

P.Oxy. (Oxyrhynchus Papyri)
1119.5 234 n.24

Lightning Source UK Ltd.
Milton Keynes UK
UKHW022055300123
416216UK00017B/204